DARKER LEGACIES OF LAW IN EUROPE

The legal scholarship of the National Socialist and Fascist period of the twentieth century and its subsequent reverberation throughout European law and legal tradition has recently become the focus of intense scholarly discussion. This volume presents theoretical, historical and legal inquiries into the legacy of National Socialism and Fascism written by a group of the leading scholars in this field. Their essays are wide-ranging, covering the reception of National Socialist and Fascist ideologies into legal scholarship; contemporary perceptions of Nazi Law in the Anglo-American world; parallels and differences among authoritarian regimes in the Third Reich, Austria, Italy, Spain, and Vichy-France; how formerly authoritarian countries have dealt with their legal antecedents; continuities and discontinuities in legal thought in private law, public law, labour law, international and European law; and the legal profession's endogenous obedience and the pains of Vergangenheitsbewältigung. The majority of the contributions were first presented at a conference at the EUI in the autumn of 2000, the others in subsequent series of seminars.

Darker Legacies of Law
in Europe

*The Shadow of National Socialism and
Fascism over Europe and its Legal Traditions*

EDITED BY

Christian Joerges

and

Navraj Singh Ghaleigh

WITH A PROLOGUE BY MICHAEL STOLLEIS
AND AN EPILOGUE BY JHH WEILER

·H A R T·
PUBLISHING

HART PUBLISHING
OXFORD AND PORTLAND, OREGON
2003

Published in North America (US and Canada) by
Hart Publishing
c/o International Specialized Book Services
5804 NE Hassalo Street
Portland, Oregon
97213–3644
USA

Hart Publishing is a specialist legal publisher based in Oxford, England.
To order further copies of this book or to request a list of other publications
please write to:

Hart Publishing, Salters Boatyard, Folly Bridge,
Abingdon Rd, Oxford, OX1 4LB
Telephone: +44 (0)1865 245533 Fax: +44 (0) 1865 794882
email: mail@hartpub.co.uk
WEBSITE: http//:www.hartpub.co.uk

British Library Cataloguing in Publication Data
Data Available
ISBN 1–84113–310–8 (hardback)

Typeset by J & L Composition, Filey, North Yorks
Printed and bound in Great Britain by
Biddles Ltd, http://www.biddles.co.uk

In memoriam, Eugen Rothenberg
- CJ

To my parents and brother, with love
- NSG

CONTENTS

PREFACE AND ACKNOWLEDGEMENTS

Why explore the era of National Socialism and Fascism while Europe undertakes such efforts to get ahead with its integration project? An answer to this question cannot content itself by pointing to the recent successes of the new populist movements in so many European countries. These movements do indeed renew and surf upon nationalist and xenophobic sentiments which belong to Europe's darker heritage. But our links with the past are deeper, more complex and more troubling. As Jürgen Habermas argued in his contribution to the *Historikerstreit* on the uniqueness of Auschwitz, 'Our form of life is connected with that of our parents and grandparents through a web of familial, local, political, and intellectual traditions that is difficult to disentangle—that is, through a historical milieu that made us what and who we are today.'[1] We have to face our past in order to understand our present and we do so in the interests of our future.

It was not by chance that the first step in the project from which this book originates was undertaken by a German (Christian Joerges) and an Italian (Massimo La Torre). It seemed simply obvious to us, that National Socialism and Fascism must be remembered, if and because they form such an essential part of our contemporary history. And it seemed equally obvious to us that we should take the intellectual background to these political movements seriously, that we should not treat it as an aberrant remnant of the past but as a challenge to our own theoretical and normative orientations. When we offered our first seminar series in the spring term of 1999, we were to experience the complexity of our agenda more fully. Not only do the German and the Italian perceptions of the past differ more fundamentally than we had expected; in seminar discussion we became aware of even deeper cultural *and* generational differences. Germany's problems with its past are unique. Germany's *Vergangenheitsbewältigung* is a German problem. But more unexpectedly, the problematics took on a pan-European dimension. To insinuate that there are European dimensions to these dark pages of Germany's history easily, and understandably so, provokes anxieties. The project of European integration is an *answer* to Germany's aggressive nationalism, which must not be suspected to have inherited elements of that past.

Such concerns were raised by members of the Research Council of the European University Institute. They indicated how difficult and sensitive this project really was. It is one thing to argue, that Germany's National Socialism

---

[1] J Habermas, 'On the Public Use of History,', *The New Conservatism* (Cambridge: MIT Press, 1990), 233.

was not an isolated phenomenon. It is another to argue that Italian Fascism and other anti-democratic movements and authoritarian regimes need to be understood as a European problem. It was at this point that a Briton joined the project—Navraj Singh Ghaleigh. The fact of Fascism in France and Spain, its uncritical acceptance by British and American scholars, and the remnants of these traditions in extant legal regimes cannot simply be ignored on grounds of distaste, inconvenience or embarrassment. And it is as difficult as it is essential to avoid the instrumentalisation of historical facts, guilt, and shame. It is as difficult as it is essential to disentangle theoretical issues from their historical context and it is equally important to remain aware of the context which generates theoretical issues and determines their meaning. 'Was Nazi law Law?' 'Did its proponents believe what they wrote?' 'How is their thinking linked to real-world atrocities?' 'Who can, after the breakdown of the regime, be held legally accountable or at least be morally blamed?' Questions of this sort relate to Germany's history but are not merely historical. They force us to address very general issues but their discussion will not provide us with easy recipes: it is easier to agree about the failures of the past than on the lessons we should draw.

The majority of the contributions to this volume were first presented on a conference at the EUI on 'Perceptions of Europe and Perspectives on a European Order in Legal Scholarship During the Era of Fascism and National Socialism' in September 2000. Others were presented in a year long seminar series at the EUI from spring 2001. Discussions at the conference and in the seminars were intense. They inspired the revision of texts and the exploration of new themes. And far from being a research project undertaken by Germanists, for their sectional interests alone, the variety of scholars engaged points to the range of more profound matters—both substantive and methodological—that this project unearthed. This volume now covers a broad spectrum of interdependent topics. These include the contents of legal debates in international, public, labour and private law, constitutional theory and legal methods in the era of National Socialism and Fascism, explore their perception in the Anglo-American world and reflect upon the adequacy of the term 'law' for the destructive efforts of the Nazi ideology. They explore the continuities and discontinuities in legal thought from the 1920s to the post-War reconstruction of the constitutional state and the legal design of the European integration project. They reach out into the history of (some of) Germany's allies and victims.

The widening and deepening of our inquiries into our intellectual heritage has opened our eyes for the complexity of the European project. We have become aware of so many differences in our perception of the European past and of the impact of these perceptions on our constructions of the European future. Europeans must not content themselves with delineating illegal impediments to free trade from mere selling arrangements, with supervising the implementation of Community measures against mad cows, with commenting upon the moves of the Convention process. All this is important. However, 'Europeansiation' presupposes much more. The Europeans cannot change or get rid of their past. What they can do is to engage in discussions about their histories, to insist that the past is remembered, to question the validity of national memories. The participants of our project have experienced that this is indeed possible. This, then, is the message this volume seeks to transmit. It is a message which confirms and renews what the Germans call *Vergangenheitsbewältigung*—the effort to cope with one's past. The term cannot be translated literally but captures an important dimension of Europe's integration project.

Numerous debts were accumulated during the course of this project and unfortunately space does not permit us to acknowledge all those many colleagues who were so generous with their time and expertise. Nonetheless, a few people deserve a special mention. During the seminar series we were fortunate to have received first class presentations from a number of scholars, many of which are included in this volume. Of those which are not, we thank in particular Arthur J Jacobson (New York City), Martti Koskenniemi (Helsinki), Bernard Schlink (Berlin), Ilse Staff (Frankfurt aM) and JHH Weiler (New York City)—all of whom contributed greatly to the intellectual wellbeing of our collaborative effort. Bardo Fassbinder (Berlin) gave valuable perspectives on many of our concerns, as did Gopal Balakrishnan (Chicago) who was often our most insightful interlocutor and a generous source.

We are grateful to the Georg-Kolbe-Foundation in Berlin for their permission to reproduce Georg Kolbe's 1945 sculpture 'Liberated Man' (*Befreiter*), likewise to Iain Fraser without whose invaluable translations many of our contributors would not have had access to an English speaking audience. Lastly and most importantly, Marlies Becker provided her characteristically superb support throughout and without her, our work would have been less successful and much less enjoyable.

Christian Joerges and Navraj Singh Ghaleigh
Florence
August 2002

LIST OF CONTRIBUTORS

J. PETER BURGESS is Research Professor at the International Peace Research Institute, Oslo and editor of *Security Dialogue*. His most recent publication is *Culture and Rationality: European Frameworks of Norwegian Identity* (Norwegian Academic Press). He has published on Hegelian philosophy, political theory, cultural history, European and Norwegian identity, feminist philosophy and literary studies. His most recent work deals with the evolution of the concept of value in European construction.

GIACINTO DELLA CANANEA is Professor of Administrative Law at the Faculty of Political Sciences, University of Urbino (Italy). His current research regards the constitutional and administrative foundations of the European Union on which he is going to publish a book in 2003. Recent publications include: 'Beyond the State: the Europeanisation and Globalisation of Administrative Procedures', in *European Public Law*, 2003, forthcoming, and a monograph on administrative rule-making (*Gli atti amministrativi generali* Padua, Cedam, 2000).

VIVIAN GROSSWALD CURRAN is Professor of Law at the University of Pittsburgh. Her other writings dealing with National Socialism and Vichy France have appeared in Boston College Law Review, Hastings Law Journal, Fordham Journal of International Law and Cornell International Law Journal.

DAVID FRASER is Professor of Law at Brunel University. His articles on legal aspects of the Shoah have appeared in *The International Journal of the Semiotics of Law* and *Holocaust and Genocide Studies*. He is the author of 'The Jews of the Channel Islands and the Rule of Law, 1940–1945', (Sussex Academic Press, 2000) and 'Law After Auschwitz: Towards a Jurisprudence of the Holocaust, (Carolina Academic Press, 2003).

NAVRAJ SINGH GHALEIGH is Lecturer in Public Law at Edinburgh Law School, University of Edinburgh. His primary research interests are in comparative constitutional law and theory. All of the work for this volume was completed whilst he was a Researcher at the Department of Law, European University Institute and an EU-US Fulbright Research Fellow, at Boalt Hall School of Law, University of California at Berkeley. He was previously a Lecturer-in-Laws at King's College, University of London and has practised as a Barrister in London.

INGO HUECK has been a Permanent Research Fellow at the Max Planck Institute for Legal History, Frankfurt a.M., Germany (on leave) and Senior Lecturer of Law at Humboldt University Berlin. He was Visiting Fellow and

Scholar at several Universities, including Hebrew University Jerusalem (1992), University of California at Berkeley (1995–96), Harvard Law School (2000–1), European University Institute at Florence (2001). His current projects dealing with a case book on the European Convention of Human Rights and a new project on global governance in co-operation with the ZEIT Foundation. Recent publications include articles and essays on German and European constitutional law, international law and human rights, international politics, and the history of international law (www.ingohueck.com).

CHRISTIAN JOERGES has been a full-time Professor at the European University Institute since 1998, and was formerly co-director of the Centre for European Law and Politics at the University of Bremen. His writings (edited volumes, monographs and journal articles) are concerned with private and economic law, the Europeanisation of private law and comparative law as well as legal and political theory.

MASSIMO LA TORRE is Professor of Law, Catanzo, and since September 2000 has been Professor of Legal Theory at the Law School of the University of Hull. His publications include *Karl Larenz e la dottrina giuridica nazionalsocialista* (Giuffrè, Milano, 1988), *Disavventure del diritto soggettivo. Una vicenda teorica* (Giuffrè, Milano, 1996), and *European Citizenship. An Institutional Challenge* (Kluwer, Dordrecht,1998). He is an Associate Editor of *Ratio Juris*.

OLIVER LEPSIUS is Professor of Public Law, Foreign Public Law and Philosophy of Law at the University of Bayreuth. His books include *Die gegensatzaufhebende Begriffsbildung. Methodenentwicklungen in der Weimarer Republik und ihr Verhältnis zur Ideologisierung der Rechtswissenschaft im Nationalsozialismus* (1994), *Verwaltungsrecht unter dem Common Law* (1997), *Steuerungsdiskussion, Systemtheorie und Parlamentarismuskritik* (1999) and *Besitz und Sachherrschaft im öffentlichen Recht* (2002).

LAURENCE LUSTGARTEN is Professor of Public Law at the University of Southampton, specialising in issues of national security, policing, criminal justice, European human rights and comparative constitutional law. This is his first foray into the territory covered by his essay. He is presently working on legal and political issues relating to 'terrorism'. His publications include *In From the Cold: National Security and Parliamentary Democracy* (with Ian Leigh), *Libel and the Media: The Chilling Effect* (with Eric Barendt et al)—both Oxford University Press, *The Governance of Police* (Sweet & Maxwell) and *Legal Control of Racial Discrimination* (Macmillan).

MATTHIAS MAHLMANN is an Assistant Professor at the Law Faculty of the Free University of Berlin. His current research is concerned with German and European public law, legal sociology and legal philosophy. Recent publications include *Rationalismus in der praktischen Theorie*, (Baden-Baden, Nomos,

1999), M Mahlmann & GP Calliess, *Der Staat der Zukunft* (Steiner 2002). Law and Force—20th Century radical legal philosophy, post-modernism and the foundation of law, res publica (2003), The liberalism of freedom in the history of moral philosophy (with J Mikhail) *Archives for Philosophy of Law and Social Philosophy* (2003).

JOHN P. MCCORMICK is Associate Professor of Political Science, Yale University. His articles have appeared in scholarly journals such as the *American Political Science Review* (1992, 1999, 2001), and *Political Theory* (1994, 1998, 2001); he is the author of *Carl Schmitt's Critique of Liberalism: Against Politics as Technology* (Cambridge University Press, 1997), and the editor of *Confronting Mass Democracy and Industrial Technology: German Political and Social Thought from Nietzsche to Habermas* (Duke, 2002). Prof. McCormick is presently working on two monographs: *Weber, Habermas and Transformations of the European State: Constitutional, Social and Supranational Democracy* (Cambridge University Press, forthcoming) and *Machiavellian Democracy*.

AGUSTÍN JOSÉ MENÉNDEZ is senior researcher at ARENA, University of Oslo. His current research is concerned with Tax Law, Legal Theory and the Constitutional Law of the European Union. Recent publications include 'Constituting Deliberative Democracy' (2000) *Ratio Juris*; *Justifying Taxes* (Dordrecht, Kluwer,2001) and 'Chartering Europe', *Journal of Common Market Studies* (2002).

PIER GIUSEPPE MONATERI is Professor at the University of Turin and at the Faculté Internationale de Droit Comparé (Strasbourg). He is an Associate Member of The International Academy of Comparative Law. Recent publications include *La responsabilità civile*, in *Trattato di Diritto civile* (Torino, Utet, 1998), R Sacco (ed); *The Law of Contract—Italy* (with A. Musy e F.A. Chiaves) in R Blanpain, *International Encyclopaedia of Laws* (London, Kluwer, 1999).

GERALD L. NEUMAN is the Herbert Wechsler Professor of Federal Jurisprudence at Columbia Law School. His publications include *Strangers to the Constitution: Immigrants, Borders and Fundamental Law* (1996), *Human Rights* (1999) (with Louis Henkin, David Leebron, and Diane Orentlicher), and articles in the fields of US constitutional law, immigration and nationality law, comparative constitutional law, and human rights law.

LUCA NOGLER is a Professor of Comparative Labour Law at the University of Trento (Italy). His interests also cover the history of labour law, particularly Hugo Sinzheimer and his influence on European labour law, the enforcement of collective agreements and other topics of labour law in the Weimar Republic. Recent publications include *Labor Law*, in JS Lena, U Mattei (eds), *Introduction to Italian Law* (Kluwer, London, 2002); *Lavoro a domicilio*, (Giuffrè, Milano,

2000); *Saggio sull'efficacia regolativa del contratto collettivo* (Cedam, Padova, 1997).

ALEXANDER SOMEK is an Associate Professor in the Law Faculty of the University of Vienna. His current research focuses on supranationality as a distinct type of human association and on the conception of social solidarity in European Union law. Recent publications include *Rationalität und Diskriminierung. Zur Bindung der Gesetzgebung an das Gleichheitsrecht* (Vienna—New York, Springer, 2001) and *Soziale Demokratie* (Vienna, Verlag Austria, 2001).

ALESSANDRO SOMMA has been Researcher at the Max Planck Institut für Europäische Rechtsgeschichte since 2002 and is now Professor at the University of Ferrara. Recent publications include *Autonomia privata e struttura del consenso contrattuale. Aspetti storico-comparativi di una vicenda concettuale,* (Milano, Giuffré, 2000); *L'uso giurisprudenziale della comparazione nel diritto interno e comunitario,* (Milano, Giuffré, 2001) and Temi e problemi di diritto comparato, vol 4, *Diritto comunitario vs. diritto comune europeo,* (Torino, Giappichelli, 2003).

MICHAEL STOLLEIS is Professor of Public Law and History of Modern Law at the University of Frankfurt a.M., and since 1991 he has been Director of the Max-Planck-Institut for European Legal History. His publications include, *Gemeinwohlformeln im nationalsozialistischen Recht,* (Berlin, 1974); *History of Public Law in Germany, 3 vols.* (1988, 1992, 1999) (vol.1 translated into French, vol. 2 translated into English, vol. 3 English translation in preparation); *Law under the Swastika* (Chicago University Press, 1998).

NEIL WALKER is Professor of European Law at the European University Institute and Professor of Legal and Constitutional Theory at the University of Aberdeen. He is the author of various publications on the theory and practice of European constitutionalism, and also on the emergence of the European Union as an internal security community.

J.H.H. WEILER is University Professor at NYU and holder of the European Union Jean Monnet Chair. He is Director of the Global Law School Program at NYU Law School. Among his most recent books are *The Constitution of Europe—Do the New Clothes Need an Emperor?* (Cambridge, Cambridge UP, 1998) and *Der Fall Steinmann* (München, Piper Verlag, 2000) (trans. Michael Cochu).

JAMES Q. WHITMAN is Ford Foundation Professor of Comparative and Foreign Law at Yale University. He publishes widely on problems in legal history and comparative law.

PROLOGUE

RELUCTANCE TO GLANCE IN THE MIRROR: THE CHANGING FACE OF GERMAN JURISPRUDENCE AFTER 1933 AND POST-1945

*Michael Stolleis**

I

As long as there have been lawyers in any significant number in Central Europe—that is to say since about the fourteenth century—there has been criticism of them. There is a German saying first recorded around 1300 'Juristen böse Christen' (Lawyers are wicked Christians).[1] Ever since, attitudes towards this new administrative elite has oscillated between respect and disdain, trust and distaste. There is a sense of dependence, of needing them when disagreements turn into lawsuits, and of having to pay dearly for their services. The clergy, the nobility, peasants and bourgeoisie alike all had their own problems with this new administrative elite, with the increasing importance of legislation and the emphasis this placed on the written word and professional training.

I have briefly alluded to this historical background because it goes some way towards explaining the ambivalence with which lawyers and jurists were treated under National Socialism. In the Third Reich, too, lawyers were regarded as hybrid creatures. The NSDAP saw the traditional civil service system, dominated as it was by lawyers, as a reactionary force that was an impediment to the Nazi movement. At the same time, the Party was dependent on these structures at every level, from the highest offices in the Reich to the regional and municipal authorities. The many conflicts between the 'state' and the 'movement' were, however, conflicts between lawyers and non-lawyers. This is reflected in the gradual removal of 'jurists' (Hans Frank, Wilhelm Frick, Franz Gürtner) while anti-judicial, power-hungry individuals asserted themselves (Himmler, Heydrich,

---

* Professor of Public Law and Legal History, University of Frankfurt a.M.; Director, Max-Planck-Institute for European Legal History.

[1] M Stolleis, *Juristenbeschimpfung, oder: Juristen böse Christen* in T Stammen, H Oberreuter, & P Mikat (eds), *Politik—Bildung—Religion. Hans Maier zum 65. Geburtstag,* (Paderborn, Schöningh, 1996), 163–70.

Goebbels, Freisler, Thierack).[2] Hitler, in his 'Table-talk' conversations with his henchmen at the Fuehrer's Headquarters, was dismissive and aggressive in his remarks about lawyers. In the Reichstag in 1942, in a fit of rage, he made brutal threats against judges whose rulings he considered too lenient. Thierack's commentaries on rulings, the so-called '*Richterbriefe*' or Judges' Letters, followed—intended as both guidance and intimidation.[3]

The generally antagonistic attitude towards the judiciary that prevailed among the leading figures of the Nazi regime, the suppression of regular justice and administrative jurisdiction from the political arena, and, in particular, the infamous Reichstag speech of 1942, fitted well with the lawyers' own self-image. Indeed, it seemed heaven-sent, for it underpinned their notion of a 'suffering judiciary' and lent credence to the idea of lawyers as the 'most hated profession' in the Third Reich, not to mention the violation of justice by a criminal legislator. [4]

This self-image took hold and remained dominant for two decades. It formed the basis of the Federal German legal system—a basis that was apparently necessary for re-stabilisation. The conclusions drawn from it were the following.

After Germany's 'Catastrophe' and 'Zero Hour', a return to Western values of idealism and natural law was seen as the only possible path to take. Natural law alone seemed 'to provide law with a backup against the pressure of political power and naked violence.'[5] This was favoured by the fact that in 1945, the churches, especially the less compromised Catholic Church, were virtually the only major organisations in a position to restore Germany's place in the civilised world. 'Legal positivism'—little more than a phantom of legal theory—was regarded as outmoded.[6] This meant that the polemical criticism of legal positivism that had prevailed throughout the Weimar period and the Nazi period continued unabated. Only the anti-Jewish aspect of the arguments, such as the attacks against Hans Kelsen, disappeared. It also meant that general or blanket clauses found favour as points where the new political order could revert to older law, precisely repeating the patterns of 1933—though this time around it seemed excusable because the 'contents' were now right. And after all, the restitution of a neo-

[2] L Gruchmann, *Justiz im Dritten Reich 1933–1940: Anpassung und Unterwerfung in der Ära Gürtner* (München, Oldenbourg, 1987).

[3] H Boberach (ed), *Richterbriefe: Dokumente zur Beeinflussung der deutschen Rechtsprechung 1942–1944*, (Boppard, Bundesarchiv, 1975).

[4] H Schorn, *Der Richter im Dritten Reich*, (Frankfurt, Klostermann, 1959); H Weinkauff & Albrecht Wagner, *Die deutsche Justiz und der Nationalsozialismus*, (Stuttgart, Deutsche Verlags Anstalt, 1968), vol 1.

[5] H Coing, *Die obersten Grundsätze des Rechts: Ein Versuch zur Neubegründung des Naturrechts*, (Heidelberg, Lambert Schneider, 1947), 7.

[6] A well-balanced defender of legal positivism is W Clever, 'Zur Nachkriegskritik des Rechtspositivismus,' (1949) *Deutsche Richter-Zeitung*, 348.

idealistic methodology was part and parcel of this internal reconstruction of jurisprudence.[7]

In terms of constitutional theory, this approach was equivalent to establishing a 'scale of values' that could be worn as a protective shield in the Cold War, both at home and abroad. It was developed from the text of the constitution and other authoritative sources, almost as a kind of spiritual and intellectual substratum. In terms of method, this was undeniably the heritage of the 1930s when not only Carl Schmitt propagated the distinction between (actual) constitution and (mere) constitutional text, but when Rudolf Smend had also transcended positive constitutional law by emphasizing the spiritual and intellectual process of 'integration'. The 'scale of values' was the constitutional and methodological counterpart to the 'liberal democratic basic order' (*fdGO*) that was imposed on the legal system. So much for the intellectual climate.[8] Very soon, the 'scale of values' became a disciplinary tool.[9] Consider, for example, the Communist Party ban pursued from 1951 onwards and finalised in 1956 with the so-called KPD ruling that declared the party unconstitutional (*BVerfGE* 5,85); or the political justice meted out to communists;[10] or the fundamental difficulties in defining 'constitutional enemies' during the inner political unrest after 1968; or the '*Berufsverbot*' debate about banning individuals with certain political affiliations from occupations such as teaching or civil service posts; or finally the debate about limitations on freedom to demonstrate and the limitations of civil disobedience.

In retrospect, we can recognise in the founding of the Federal Republic a distinct pattern of defensive 'common values' in which the 'others' were excluded by these values. For German lawyers after 1945, who formed an even more specific professional community of shared values, this meant having to band together in order to gain a foothold and dispel the criticism leveled, for example, at their involvement in National Socialism. Through tacit coalition and active association, virtually all the lawyers who had practiced in the Third Reich were reinstated in public office and private law firms. There were hardly any abrupt breaks or dismissals. Like the rest of the nation, they were reluctant to look back into the abyss.[11] Only those considered to have gone beyond the pale were

[7] C Joerges, *Die Wissenschaft vom Privatrecht und der Nationalstaat*, in D Simon (ed), *Rechtswissenschaft in der Bonner Republik: Studien zur Wissenschaftsgeschichte der Jurisprudenz*, (Frankfurt, Suhrkamp, 1994), 311–63.

[8] E Denninger (ed), *Freiheitliche demokratische Grundordnung*, (Frankfurt, Suhrkamp, 1977).

[9] Carl Schmitt also saw this. See his contribution, *Die Tyrannei der Werte: Überlegungen eines Juristen zur Wertphilosophie*, in *Säkularisation und Utopie: Ebracher Studien. Ernst Forsthoff zum 65. Geburtstag*, (Stuttgart, Kohlhammer, 1967), 37–62.

[10] A von Brünneck, *Politische Justiz gegen Kommunisten in der Bundesrepublik Deutschland 1949–1968* (Frankfurt, Suhrkamp, 1978), 117.

[11] N Frei, *Vergangenheitspolitik: Die Anfänge der Bundesrepublik und die NS-Vergangenheit*, (München, CH Beck, 1996).

excluded, but even that was not public knowledge.[12] In an essay published anonymously in November 1949, Carl Schmitt invoked a theme that typifies the spirit of the time: 'amnesty, the power of forgetting'.

What this new departure meant was that Germany's recent history under National Socialism could be disregarded or, at most, remembered only as a time marred by a regrettable perversion of justice. The legal authors of those years kept silent about their earlier publications. Their pupils adjusted the bibliographies. Librarians were instructed to sift out the writings from the relevant period and stash it away in the vaults. In fact, the Allies did the same in the immediate post-war period, and had lists drawn up by 'untainted' specialists. So the process of 'denazification', in this very broad sense, not only meant demotion or professional exclusion, but was actually undertaken by the individuals themselves in a bid to make their past disappear. In other words, it was a self-imposed *damnatio memoriae*. As such, it seemed only logical that there were very few studies in legal history to address the period before 1965 and that 'contemporary legal history' did not take shape as a discipline until much later.[13] Younger scholars were taught that the time was not yet ripe and, in addition, that nobody without first hand experience of those days had any right to comment.

This broad consensus was rarely disturbed by dissonant voices crying that it was not 'legal positivism' that had been the main problem—but a dearth of courage and a general compliance on the part of the lawyers. Nor was the world of lawyers caught up in National Socialism the non-political, unsuspecting victim it was made out to be, but rather, it was a politically conscious group whose nationalistic tendencies were often perfectly in keeping with National Socialist thought. After all, what was needed was not a return to natural law (which provided no practically feasible directives anyway) but a move towards the 'unfinished project of the Enlightenment'—in other words, western constitutional and legal ideas.

A glance at the Soviet zone of occupation and the emerging East German state of the GDR indicates that very similar processes were at work there, although with a quite different political content. A new world view was being established, a kind of Socialist natural law, albeit under another name.[14] The same tendency towards polemical criticism of consistent legal positivism (especially in the form given by Hans Kelsen) could be found there, for this expressly politically neutral legal theory could not be applied for their own purposes. It served as the bogeyman of a bourgeois academic discipline feigning

---

[12] M Stolleis, 'Die Vereinigung der Deutschen Staatsrechtslehrer: Bemerkungen zu ihrer Geschichte,' (1997) *Kritische Vierteljahresschrift für Gesetzgebung und Rechtswissenschaft*, 339–58, concerning the inner debates around the acceptance of former members of the NSDAP.

[13] M Stolleis (ed.), *Juristische Zeitgeschichte—ein neues Fach?*, (Baden-Baden, Nomos, 1993).

[14] R Alexy, *Der Rechtsbegriff Walter Ulbrichts*, in *Enquête-Kommission Aufarbeitung von Geschichte und Folgen der SED-Diktatur in Deutschland*, (Baden-Baden, Nomos, 1995), vol 4, 19.

objectivity as a mantle beneath which to pursue its own class interests.[15] West and East, then, for all their political differences, were both 'anti-positivist'.

Admittedly, beyond this common denominator, there were more differences than similarities. Under the rule of the Soviet military administration, the new regime systematically destroyed the bourgeois state based on the rule of law. The situation in Thuringia was to set the scene.[16] Staffing policies were aimed at ousting conventional lawyers as quickly as possible and replacing them with Party members who had trained in special courses as People's Judges.[17] This program was gradually extended from public prosecutors to judges, lawyers and university teaching staff, so that by 1955 it was more or less fully in place. However, the most important aim was the general elimination, or weakening, of the rule of law as a means of control. It was one of the most painful long-term experiences of East German lawyers that they were never able to accept fully that the GDR government believed it could dispense with 'law' in the sense of a structured system of checks and balances and that it could do without publicly debated textual criticism or commentaries—an attitude it had clearly held since the Babelsberg Conference of 1958.[18] It was only in the final decade of the GDR that there appeared to be signs of a return towards independent control of the administration, albeit with little success.

II

There is no simple way of summing up the shape of jurisprudence after 1945. Almost all the colleagues driven into exile by National Socialism were missing. Many others had died or been murdered. With so few qualifying as professors during the Nazi era, there was no broad-based, politically untainted younger generation to take over the task of teaching and training. The core of the faculties that now began to regroup was still formed by the same professors who had taught at the universities from 1933 to 1945. A few of the older generation who had gone into retirement in 1933 were reinstated. And a few younger ones who had had no opportunity to advance under National Socialism, were added. Almost all the 'bourgeois' professors from the universities in the Soviet zone came to the west. The 'denazification' of professors was conducted along the same lines as happened with any other administrative elites. Colleagues without a Nazi past wrote dozens of certificates, known in Germany as 'Persil notes', attesting the recipient's conscience to be

[15] H Klenner, *Rechtsleere: Verurteilung der Reinen Rechtslehre*, (Frankfurt, Verlag Marxistische Blätter, 1972).

[16] T Heil, *Die Verwaltungsgerichtsbarkeit in Thüringen 1945–1952*, (Tübingen, Mohr, 1996).

[17] J Pfannkuch, *Volksrichterausbildung in Sachsen 1945–1950*, (Frankfurt, Lang, 1993).

[18] J Eckert (ed), *Die Babelsberger Konferenz vom 2./3. April 1958*, (Baden-Baden, Nomos, 1993).

'whiter-than-white'.[19] Lengthy correspondences were conducted, old contacts revived, a helping hand was given to colleagues in the 'eastern zone', and by 1950, almost all of them were back at their old desks.

Some of the more famous exceptions to this rule in the field of public law should be mentioned. Carl Schmitt was barred from holding any position of public importance, and few doubted the justice of that. Yet the fact that he nevertheless went on to exert a far-reaching influence on society in the Federal Republic of Germany is part and parcel of the country's social and intellectual history.[20] His less able counterpart in the Third Reich, Otto Koellreutter,[21] seemed to have forgotten his former enthusiasm for Nazi ideals. Embittered and unrepentant, he fought in vain to reinstated. Though he was barred from the Association of German Teachers of Public Law, he did become Honorary President of the Federation of Victims of Denazification. Reinhard Höhn, at one time an influential SS lawyer, but an outsider on the Berlin faculty, kept a low profile after 1945 and later founded a successful 'Führungsakademie' in Bad Harzburg. Ernst Rudolf Huber, probably the most important scholar in the group apart from Carl Schmitt, was regarded as particularly problematic because of his 1939 book on constitutional law in Greater Germany (*Verfassungsrecht des Grossdeutschen Reiches*). He returned to university much later, and then only gradually.[22] His monumental study of constitutional history since 1789, seven volumes covering the period up to 1933, also contains the message: No more politics.

There were others who went on to enjoy careers with a meteoric success impressive enough to parallel the economic miracle itself. Hermann von Mangoldt became involved in regional constitutional law and served as a member of the Parliamentary Council; Hans-Peter Ipsen drew up early commentaries on the new Basic Law; Hans-Carl Nipperdey[23] became President of the Labor's Supreme Court and Theodor Maunz[24] even became Minister of Science and Culture. The associations of teachers of civil and penal law, public law teachers and legal historians regrouped. They could greet one another with an enigmatic smile, united in silence about the past. Today, now that we have the opportunity of examining the post-war correspondence of such figures as Carl Schmitt, Rudolf Smend, Walter Jellinek, Erich Kaufmann, Friedrich Giese and others, we find that they did indeed express their opinions quite clearly in

---

[19] Collections of those 'Persil-Notes' for example are to be found in the Archives of the Federal Republic of Germany, Koblenz, in the papers of Walter Jellinek and Friedrich Giese.

[20] D van Laak, *Gespräche in der Sicherheit des Schweigens: Carl Schmitt in der politischen Geistesgeschichte der frühen Bundesrepublik*, (Berlin, Akademie Verlag, 1993).

[21] M Stolleis, *Geschichte des öffentlichen Rechts in Deutschland 1914–1945*, Munich 1999, vol 3, *passim*.

[22] R Walkenhaus, *Konservatives Staatsdenken: Eine wissenssoziologische Studie zu Ernst Rudolf Huber*, (Berlin, Akademie Verlag, 1997).

[23] J Rückert, *H.C.Nipperdey*, in *Neue Deutsche Biographie* (1999), vol 19, 280–82.

[24] M Stolleis, *Law under the Swastika*, (Chicago, Chicago University Press, 1998), 185–92.

private. Gerhard Leibholz, who returned from exile, spoke disparagingly in 1950 of what he called the 'National Socialist shadow faculty'. Jellinek wrote at the time that 'there are more Nazis among our colleagues than we in our harmlessness might suspect'.[25] Hans Peters, the only public law specialist in the resistance, who taught initially in Berlin and later in Cologne, was president of the Görres Society. He wrote a letter threatening to resign if any more 'old Nazis' were admitted to the association.

Yet those who really did have nothing to hide did not join forces in order to make a new start. They had far too little in common. There were people of all age groups and personality types, some who tried to equate their professional insignificance with political integrity, others who felt they had escaped a living hell they could not bear to talk about. Still others took an opportunistic attitude towards the more powerful and more active colleagues who so breezily maintained that they had written some things in the past that they would not write in the present, explaining that it had been, as Max Frisch put it, 'a time of excitement', that they had only been commenting on prevailing law (Maunz), that they had sprinkled their reservations and subtle warnings between the lines, and that they had often expressed their misgivings about the regime off the record. In short, the members of the new faculties gradually reached a mutual accommodation and took the pragmatic approach of letting sleeping dogs lie,[26] especially since many colleagues kept their distance from the more sensitive issues and may even have made it clear in private that they had put their past behind them. Johannes Heckel in Munich turned to canon law. Theodor Maunz in Freiburg was allowed to work only in the field of administrative law at first. Ernst Rudolf Huber turned his attention to constitutional history. Karl Larenz abandoned legal philosophy to make his name instead in the least political aspect of civil law (BGB; German Civil Code, law of obligations).[27] Georg Dahm, an outstanding educator, shifted from penal law to international law. Many new teaching books and fundamental outlines proved to be little more than superficially revised re-editions of works published in the 1930s. As Joachim Rückert pointed out in his major survey, this was particularly true of the core areas of civil law, penal law, legal philosophy and legal history, whereas constitutional law, administrative law and labour law presented rather more serious problems in terms of continuity.[28]

---

[25] Above note 12, 348.

[26] J Rückert, 'Abbau und Aufbau der Rechtswissenschaft nach 1945,' (1995) *Neue Juristische Wochenschrift*, 1251–9.

[27] W Wolf, 'Zivilrechtswissenschaft ohne Larenz: Die Positionierung des Privatrechts zwischen 1945 und 1953,' (1997) *Kritische Vierteljahresschrift für Gesetzgebung und Rechtswissenschaft*, 400–25.

[28] Above note 26.

III

If we go back to 1933, defying the seemingly linear course of history, to examine the situation of German jurisprudence, we find it difficult enough to obtain statements of any substance relating to individual aspects of legal disciplines, let alone generalise about a body of several hundred active individuals, a plethora of institutions and countless publications. Add to that all the problems of self-image and retrospective self-description. The deeper the waters plumbed by research, however, the more clearly the picture emerges. On the whole, it is possible to trace a typical development in attitudes to the regime. First of all, what we find is an administrative elite, half-willing, without really knowing what it wants, half-fearful without really knowing how justified its fears will prove, being drawn into a political avalanche and torn into the abyss along with it. Whether the confusion of voices was the sound of triumphal whooping or anguished screaming, is unclear. This confused, exhilarated yet inhibited early stage lasted until about mid–1934. After that, it became obvious that the regime would gain stability. This, depending on one's point of view, was either a threatening or a reassuring prospect. The November pogrom of 1938 and the outbreak of war the following year marked, for many, the beginning of a sense of detachment from the regime, though that sense of detachment would soon be tested by the pressures of war. This ambivalence held sway until the final days of the regime.

In the summer semester of 1933, jurisprudence regrouped in a new political climate in which colleagues were dismissed and NS students given power. Yet the new pattern that was clearly emerging cannot be described in purely political terms. Most professors of jurisprudence teaching in 1933 were critics of the republic without being actively anti-constitutional. They envisaged an outwardly and inwardly strong state in which a politically neutral civil service (*Berufsbeamtentum*)would have no party links. This majority was, for the most part, affiliated to what might be termed the centre field, but also embracing the *Deutsche Staatspartei* and even the *Deutschnationale* Party. Most of them were bourgeois and conservative, and were willing to co-operate with the new regime as long as it was able to produce further achievements and success, willing to temper its persecution of dissenters, and otherwise refrain from upsetting the apple cart. It was on this sandy soil that the symbiotic relationship between government and traditional elites, so typical of National Socialism, was built.

An occupational pattern based, for example, on disciplines or specific areas of jurisprudence, cannot be discerned. All fields of law were involved to more or less the same degree, with the exception of those areas in which there was a particularly high proportion of Jewish scholars, as was the case in international law, comparative law, international private law and the history of civil law. Indeed, the last if these had some difficulty in developing any kind of identification, given that it was explicitly targeted for disparagement by the NSDAP party program. Nonetheless, even in that area, there were also specialist representatives who strove to be historians of roman law and National Socialists (E. Schönbauer).

Age proves a more revealing factor, based on the assumption that the older generation did not waver as readily as the enthusiastic and ambitious 'young wolves' who replaced them as professors in 1933 (Georg Dahm, Karl Larenz, Franz Wieacker, Friedrich Schaffstein, Ernst Forsthoff, Theodor Maunz, Ernst Rudolf Huber *et al.*). Yet there are exceptions to this rule in both camps. Some older academics (Conrad Bornhak, Philipp Heck, Justus W. Hedemann) did try to jump on the bandwagon, while some younger colleagues (Ernst Friesenhahn, Hermann Mosler, Wolfgang Kunkel, Ludwig Raiser) resisted the temptation. Their resistance may have been based on religious faith, social background or personal character. Whatever their reasons, the sectors typically regarded as less conducive to National Socialism (working class, Catholic communities, landed gentry, *Wehrmacht* officers) do not apply here. At the time, the educated protestant bourgeoisie (*Kulturprotestantismus*) dominated university life.

This brings us to the fairly unremarkable conclusion that professors of jurisprudence were average individuals with average reactions, and that their connivance with the regime only casts a dark shadow where ideal and reality met. As the publications indicate, the first wave of enthusiasm, like the first wave of silence, came in 1933–35, and was followed by a period of stabilisation in 1935–38, when power groups formed within the system. After that came a period of publishing shaped by the war, including a 'war effort' in the field of arts and social science activities organised by Paul Ritterbusch, rector of Kiel University.[29] Throughout this period, publishing in the field of jurisprudence typically produced innumerable publications that typically give little indication of the political climate in which they were written. These were practice-related specialist publications that concentrated on conveying and commentating upon standard legislation without actually having to take any political stance. Indeed, leafing through the legal periodicals of those years is likely to give the impression that this dry, specialist approach was prevalent. Of course, this does not apply to the periodicals founded during the Third Reich with the specific aim of providing ideological training for lawyers in *Deutsches Recht, Deutsche Verwaltung, Reich—Volksordnung—Lebensraum*. Yet it is interesting to note that the mood of enthusiasm that emerged between 1933 and 1935 did not swell still further with the outbreak of war. On the contrary, from 1939 onwards, debates started to become more objective, occasionally even cautious, accommodating a broad spectrum of opinion.[30]

If we are to do justice, as it were, to jurisprudence as a field so closely linked to court and administrative practice that its scientific character has always been questioned, then only jurisprudence itself can provide the appropriate yardstick.

---

[29] F-R Hausmann, *'Deutsche Geisteswissenschaft' im Zweiten Weltkrieg: Die 'Aktion Ritterbusch' (1940–1945)*, (Dresden, Dresden University Press, 1998).

[30] Above note 21, vol 3, 299–311.

We must look both to its actively involved apologists and to those who seek to apply today's standards to its evaluation. The history of the subject must first of all reflect upon the functions that jurisprudence as a subject, with all its sub-divisions, has had to fulfill. Only a small minority of its protagonists pursue the maxims of basic research. Legal theoreticians and legal historians—when they are not delving into utterly esoteric issues—also have a tendency to attribute contemporary references to their findings. They, too, are dependent upon the political context in the creation of research hypotheses and in the selection of sources and references as well as in the presentation of findings.

Essentially, the parallel tasks of research and teaching in the field of jurisprudence are as follows: (1) introducing the next generation to the system of prevailing law, in other words, conveying legislation in the broadest sense; (2) drawing political givens, new legislation and jurisdiction into a coherent system of dogma. This coherence and clarity help, on the one hand, to convey standards of legislation for teaching purposes, while, on the other hand, they play an important role in ensuring that legislation is accepted as reliable and predictable by those to whom it is addressed; (3) adapting the system to changes, real or perceived, in the political situation. This involves defining and interpreting changes in state, law and society, as a means of prognosis and as mediation between political and legislative systems. In the case of National Socialism, jurisprudence specifically served the political system by the conventional means of molding what the political system wanted into authoritative legal doctrine. Legislation, jurisdiction and even academia transformed such violent acts as annulment of citizenship, arrest, murder and pogroms into 'lawful acts'. Consider, by way of example, the law passed following the Röhm murders of June 1934. In a move unparalleled in legal history, this law, consisting of a single sentence, declared the 'measures' to be lawful acts of self-defense on the part of the state. When a respected leading authority in the field of jurisprudence justified this law with such conviction as to make it sound inevitable, he was appealing to his readers to accept the unacceptable.[31] The Nazi state, which was able to clothe its acts of violence in the formal standards of the bourgeois state that were based on the rule of law, had every reason to assume that many citizens who should have known better would accept the form as content and thereby be persuaded to go along with it. Thus, the technique of legally seizing power became a legal assertion and implementation of power. The legal form in which injustice was clothed made it seem as though a limit had been set.

Jurisprudence in the years 1933 to 1945 fulfilled the functions described here in various ways. There was a drop in the number of new lawyers being trained. Whereas there were some 22,000 students of law registered in the summer

---

[31] See the famous article by C Schmitt, 'Der Führer schützt das Recht,' (1934) *Deutsche Juristen-Zeitung*, 945–50.

semester of 1930, that figure had fallen to 4,555 by the summer semester of 1939. During the war, the numbers declined still further, reaching barely 3,000 in the winter semester of 1941. The number of women studying law fell even more dramatically (from 1175 in the summer semester of 1930 to just 42 in the summer semester of 1938). This trend went so far that there was talk of closing down some of the smaller faculties (such as Frankfurt am Main, Marburg and Halle). Whether the quality of legal training also declined is difficult to say, but there is little affirmative indication of its decay. Admittedly, there were certain distractions, in the form of student 'camps' and various obligations connected with the institutional procedures of the Nazi state, but, on the whole, the university teaching staff that remained was as highly qualified as it had been in the days of the Weimar Republic. The faculties were fairly successful in warding off infiltration of the staff by party loyalists.

Given the increasingly hectic and uncoordinated lawmaking of the Nazi state, let alone its sheer volume, it was hardly possible to shape the new legislative material into a coherent system. As there was no longer any parliamentary discussion of new legislation, and since new laws were soon being passed by the ministries, any control at all was now in the hands of a ministerial bureaucracy that frequently found its aims thwarted by orders from the various power centers of the NSDAP. The new legislation took both the public and the academic world alike by surprise. There could no longer be any talk of jurisprudence as a shaping force. Even Ernst Rudolf Huber's enormous endeavour to systematise public law was clearly an artificial construct that was no longer seen as in any way binding.[32] The many legislative proposals drawn up in the Academy of German Law suffered the same fate. Even if a few of them did find their way into social law, penal law, civil procedure or other legal fields, it was not because of the authority of the academic body, but, at most, because of their acceptance by the ministerial bureaucracy.

Things look different if we ask what jurisprudence did in terms of adapting to the new situation created by the Nazi state. Here, we find a number of effective contributions, such as the 'specific-general concept' (coined by Larenz), the acceptance of a graduated concept of property and ownership and the abolition of the general section of the Civil Code (BGB) (Wieacker), the implementation of a new vocabulary relating to the '*Gemeinschaft*' or 'community' and the corresponding exclusion of those deemed 'alien to the community' in labour law (the corporate community), landlord and tenant law (the household community) and other areas. Carl Schmitt's remarkable formula 'thinking in terms of concrete order' proved highly successful. It was Carl Schmitt, too, who, just before Germany launched its campaign of aggressive expansion, introduced the notion of the *Grossraum* (Greater Space Theory with prohibition of

---

[32] ER Huber, *Verfassungsrecht des Großdeutschen Reiches*, (Hamburg, Hanseatische Verlaganstalt, 1939).

intervention by foreign powers). In administrative law, Ernst Forsthoff described local state benefits as '*Daseinsvorsorge*' or 'existence assurance'—a well-chosen term borrowed from Jaspers that was not to be fully accepted until the Federal Republic. In penal law, the definition of criminal types, '*Tätertypenlehre*' (Edmund Mezger), the inclusion of 'characteristics of will' in the facts of the case (Hans Welzel), and the shift of focus from the 'crime' itself to the 'criminal will', helped to bring traditional penal law closer in line with the new political will, placing it more fully in its service. In a similar spirit, jurisprudence addressed such issues as easier divorce proceedings in the case of childless marriages, forced sterilisation, the killing of the mentally ill, the dismissal of legal protection in 'political' cases as a '*justizloser Hoheitsakt*' ('act of sovereignty bar justice') and many other specific political issues related to National Socialism. In this respect, it must unfortunately be said that jurisprudence fulfilled its core function very well indeed—fundamentally reflecting the spirit of the times and implementing such reflection in a wealth of proposals, small and large. In this, it remained a creative force, with prolific publication occurring until well into the war years.

IV

The reluctance to glance in the mirror after 1945, of which I have already spoken, is hardly surprising, given what we know about the psychology of memory. Every author writes 'in his time', and every writer feels that his own work is more coherent and free from influence than it really is. No-one wants to have his life's work declared worthless. These are understandable attitudes. As Friedrich Nietzsche put it so succinctly: "This I have done," says my memory. "This I cannot have done," says my pride and remains intractable. In the end, memory gives in.'[33]

The resulting reluctance of academics to look into their own academic history after 1945 has been noted and criticised many times. Explanations have been offered, many of them plausible enough, such as the lack of impartial detachment or an unwillingness to indulge in self historicising. There was probably also a sense of shame, for the most part suppressed but nevertheless subconsciously present, at having succumbed so readily to the spirit of the times. This sense of shame easily co-exists with an aversion towards those who were born late enough to feel righteous and who so often took the moral high ground in expressing their surprise at the behaviour of their elders. It was a gesture of accusation that not only sealed the lips of the older generation, but proved academically unproductive, for the oft-repeated talk of the older generation's alleged failure was a moralist stance that obscured more than it enlight-

---

[33] F Nietzsche, *Jenseits von Gut und Böse, Viertes Hauptstück*, (Leipzig, A. Kröner, 1930), 68.

ened. It defined the problem primarily as a moral one, linking it to a single 'misled' generation, and thereby not only avoiding an actual historical explanation, but also distorting the view of their own conformity and capacity to adapt. That is something the older generation was only too happy to point out to the revolutionary generation of 1968 at every opportunity.

In fact, the history of jurisprudence in the Federal Republic has barely been tackled to date. A joint project undertaken by Dieter Simon, and a broad survey by Joachim Rückert clearly did not set anything in motion.[34] This may have something to do with the continued emphasis on treating the National Socialism complex, together with a reluctance to explore one's own personal lines of continuity. There may also be a special kind of irritation that tends to be triggered by any historicising of those subjects in which dogmatic truths are involved.

As a number of new findings have shown, the first decades of the Federal Republic, at least, have now become history. Norbert Frei has systematically examined the way the young Republic dealt with its Nazi past, albeit without going into the history of jurisprudence. Nevertheless, he does touch upon the subject indirectly, in talking of the reconstruction of the legislative content of Article 131 of the Basic Law regarding the legal relations of persons formerly employed in public service.[35] University staff, too, were persons who had been 'in public service on 8 May 1945' and who now sought reinstatement at the universities. This process had been concluded by 1950, bar a few exceptions.

The three years between capitulation and currency reform saw a heated and almost anarchic debate flare up in periodicals and conferences, after which silence ruled. The annual meetings of the individual specialist disciplines did not take place again until about 1949. When they did, they did not discuss their own past. Those who had believed in genuine moral renewal were disappointed to see the public sector filling up again with former NSDAP members. Those who really did have a guilty past refused to confront the matter. All this was overshadowed by the *Wirtschaftwunder*—the economic miracle—by integration into Western Europe, by the euphoria of winning the 1954 World Cup and the status that victory conferred, along with a new-found affluence reflected in holidays abroad and a general mood of 'eat, drink and be merry'. The furies, it seemed, had been silenced.

Yet a new sense of unrest had been fomenting after 1960. Eichmann's trial in Jerusalem in 1961, the anti-nuclear movement, an increasingly strong GDR that sought to prove the continuity of fascist tendencies in the West, Western publications (such as Seeliger's *Die Braune Universität*), the Auschwitz trial in 1965, and the first series of lectures at Munich, Tübingen and Berlin on the Nazi past of the universities created a climate in which any accusation of a Nazi past had

---

[34] D Simon (ed), *Rechtswissenschaft in der Bonner Republik: Studien zur Wissenschaftsgeschichte der Jurisprudenz*, (Frankfurt, Suhrkamp, 1994); J Rückert at note 26 above.
[35] Above n 11, 69.

a good chance of being believed. With new cases emerging all the time, the younger generation's suspicions were fuelled. All this, together with the first critical voices raised against America and emotions fuelled by an underlying generation conflict, created the volatile mixture that exploded in 1967–1969.

The lawyers, on the whole, responded by withdrawing into their own closed world. Anyone who admitted their own 'involvement' was likely to be shunned. Such an admission was *infra dignitatem*. Those who criticised too strongly or expressed solidarity with the students were marginalised. For this reason, many who were eager to establish their careers avoided the subject of the Nazi past rather than risk clashing with the leading figures of the faculties. The wheels of legal history moved slowly. In those days, there was no such thing as 'contemporary legal history'. Irrespective of such internal hindrances, 1968 saw the start of a new direction in scholarly writing in that field. It was Herbert Jäger in 1967 and Bernd Rüthers in 1968 who first began to explore the subject in any real depth with their post-doctoral theses. In 1968, the Institute for Contemporary History also began its major, albeit flawed, project on the German judiciary and National Socialism.[36] From then on there was a steady stream of publications, dealing at first with the judiciary, then with the legislation and administration of National Socialism, and finally with jurisprudence itself.

At first, the question of criminal wrong, that is to say the question of guilt, took the fore. It was often linked with calls for the punishment of Nazi crimes to be pursued more energetically.[37] At the end of the 1970s, there followed a phase of greater emphasis on analysing the political system as a whole. By the 1980s, when it came to writing an encyclopaedia article on Nazi law, I had the impression that interest had already waned.[38] But this was only a temporary phenomenon, for interest has increased again enormously since then, and has, as it were, taken off in two directions. On the one hand there is a continued tendency towards historicising that goes hand in hand with a sober analysis of functions and a willingness to compare systems. On the other hand, there is a new collective sense of shock when contemplating the Holocaust. There is also an awareness of a change of generation, international interest in Steven Spielberg's film *Schindler's List*, the debate about compensation for slave laborers, an international neo-Nazi scene and many other factors, possibly including a newly awakened fear of German unity. Finally, there was and still is a considerable financial interest in the marketing of publications concerning the terror of this era.

---

[36] J Rückert, *Justiz und Nationalsozialismus: Bilanz einer Bilanz*, in *50 Jahre Institut für Zeitgeschichte: Eine Bilanz*, (Munich, Oldenbourg, 1999), 181.

[37] B Diestelkamp, 'Die strafrechtliche Ahndung von NS-Unrecht: Ein Forschungsbericht,' (1999) 21 *Zeitschrift für Neuere Rechtsgeschichte*, 417–35.

[38] M Stolleis, *Nationalsozialistisches Recht*, in Erler et al. (eds), *Handwörterbuch zur Deutschen Rechtsgeschichte*, (Berlin, E.Schmidt, 1984) vol III, 873–92.

An interesting example of delayed self awareness is the way in which the Association of German Public Law Teachers has so far painstakingly avoided undertaking any form of analysis of its past. Having reconstituted their association in 1949 with considerable inner conflict and a certain amount of defiance, they have consistently avoided glancing in the mirror. Only once, on 17 December 1953, when the Federal Constitutional Court (*BVerfG*) determined the end of public employee status on 8 May 1945, sending a cry of dismay through their ranks, did they turn to the theme of 'professional public service and state crises'.[39] Needless to say, the predominant view was that professional public service had re-emerged from the state crisis of 1945 and that civil servants had been greatly wronged by the Federal Constitutional Court. It was fifty years after the re-founding of the Association of Public Law Teachers that it was decided that the subject of their Nazi past should be examined.[40]

The question I put now, by way of conclusion, is aimed at a theoretical gain. Allow me to outline briefly wherein this might lie. It all began with the trivial assertion that jurisprudence is a science based on specific responsibilities, actions, transactions or punishments. Jurisprudence makes statements of a preparatory, commentating, correcting and systematising nature in respect of political, economic and social issues. Its scientific character is often questioned. It is 'involved' in politics in every sense. Only in marginal areas of jurisprudence (legal history, legal sociology, comparative law, philosophy of law) is its active role diluted and its scope for 'free' scientific or academic reflection increased— in so far as it is possible at all to achieve a 'disinterested' meta-level through the contemplation of social contexts.

Praxis-oriented jurisprudence, embedded within the system of co-ordinates of politics and contemporary values, is part and parcel of social communication and interaction. It seems unrealistic to demand of it more reflection and unbiased observation of its own past than we expect from society as a whole. Administrative elites, by definition, have to adapt to changing circumstances, because otherwise they would not be able to function.

The processes of adaptation, however, take place at different speeds. The years after 1933 and the period after 1945 differ fundamentally in this respect. After 1933, there were enormous inner tensions, because the traditional image of the legal profession and the scale of values that prevailed in a state based on the rule of law came into conflict with a political sea change, one that many bourgeois lawyers, in particular, had welcomed. Bonds between colleagues were torn apart, and at the same time jobs became available for the next generation. The type of 'moderate' anti-Semitism acceptable in bourgeois circles was

---

[39] R Naumann & H Spanner, 'Das Berufsbeamtentum und die Staatskrisen,' (1955) 13 *Veröffentlichungen der Vereinigung der Deutschen Staatsrechtslehrer*.

[40] H Dreier & W Pauly, 'Die deutsche Staatsrechtslehre in der Zeit des Nationalsozialismus,' (2001) 60 *Veröffentlichungen der Vereinigung der Deutschen Staatsrechtslehrer*, 9–147—the best survey currently available.

pandered to, albeit at the price of professional ethics. Political satisfaction and moral shame continued to coexist. It was only when the final phase of the war increased their own suffering that the shame was suppressed and forgotten.

After 1945, it was the memory of personal suffering and, with that, the instinct for survival, that dominated. The legal profession as a whole, including most of the university faculties, focused on short term goals: physical survival and keeping their families together, 'denazification', getting back their old job or securing a new professorship, building up the curriculum, drawing up new textbooks, re-founding professional organisations. Psychologically, they concentrated on defending themselves against accusations, sometimes perhaps even shutting out the feelings of guilt they sensed on renewing contacts with colleagues who had emigrated. Politically, they had no problems in detaching themselves from National Socialism after its collapse; there was a tendency to claim that one had never really been a part of it, that one had always resisted mentally, and sometimes even in word and deed. This may have not been entirely mistaken, but as a general description of the group, neither was it entirely correct.

The reluctance to glance in the mirror may be morally reprehensible, but in retrospect, there is a certain rationality about it. It served, and still does, as the cement that bonds groups who are threatened or who feel threatened and who seek to climb back up the ladder. Too much retrospective or introspective thinking would appear to be detrimental to an outward assertiveness. And so, as the saying so aptly goes, the skeletons were left in the closet, in the hope that the problematic memories would disappear into thin air all by themselves—that time would take care of them (the so-called biological solution), though participants tended to forget that their own biological solution was nearing and that they would not be able to tell the following generation what to think, let alone to seal their lips.

What I find surprising is not so much what the philosopher Hermann Lübbe called the 'communicative silence',[41] but the fact that it worked so well for so long. However, there is an explanation for that, too. Small groups, such as the clergy, business managers or academics have a tendency to co-opt younger colleagues. In other words, they push their own disciples through the eye of a needle to make them part of the system. This makes the up and coming generation extremely dependent on the patronage and good will of the older generation. In such a situation, breaking the taboo of mentioning the past can be a risky business. The cartel of silence does not collapse until public pressure on the older generation increases or until the job market expands and diversifies to the extent that the profession can no longer respond homogeneously.

This can be observed in retrospect at the threshold already mentioned: the period from 1964 to around 1970. Since then, we have seen that it is indeed

---

[41] H Lübbe, 'Der Nationalsozialismus im deutschen Nachkriegsbewußtsein,' (1983) *Historische Zeitschrift*, 579–99.

possible to ask questions about the Nazi past of the legal profession, but at the same time, we find the answers given superficial and uninteresting as long as the only aim is to show up the 'brown spots' in the spirit of a denazification process. Today, there are many monographic studies examining individual representatives of jurisprudence during the National Socialist era (Carl Schmitt, Ernst Rudolf Huber, Karl August Eckhardt, Erwin Bumke, Franz Gürtner, Karl Larenz, Theodor Maunz, Otto Koellreutter, Heinrich Lange, Hermann von Mangoldt, etc.). Needless to say, these studies do not have all the answers. They are, without exception, doctoral theses, whose 'life and work' structure tends to be too much for the average doctoral candidate to handle. Yet, no matter how methodical the approach, and no matter which issues are confronted, the fact is that studies on the history of jurisprudence did start moving, although they began later (which seems to be fairly typical) than the studies of the matter itself, such as research focusing on penal law, analysis of jurisdiction in other fields, or histories of specific institutions (regional courts, Reich Administrative Court, Reich Ministry of Justice etc.).

Today, there is no succinct and comprehensive history of science linking the history of mentalities, ideas and institutions. For this reason, we have to form our image from the histories of private law, constitutional and administrative law and penal law. One particular area that requires greater scholarly attention is the history of penal law and philosophy of law.[42] A history of the history of law would also be a fascinating subject. And in fact there are already two volumes of individual studies on that.[43]

The idea of drawing up a comparative history of twentieth century European jurisprudence would appear to verge on the impossible, for the project seems to be dogged by insurmountable obstacles. As far as I am aware, there is no country that has undertaken a study of the internal development of this profession in the course of the last fifty years—a study highlighting the key experiences of the generation in question and linking the immanent changes in academic debate with shifts within the academy and society. These studies would have to focus microscopically on individual figures while at the same time drawing macroscopic structural outlines. What is more, they would have to be written with moral courage, without fear of the reactions of colleagues or their students, especially when the insignificant is to be deemed insignificant. In France, this would mean pointing to the collaboration with the Vichy regime and, above all, the many years of (post-Stalinist) Communist involvement by French intellectuals. Italians would have to confront the ease with which former Fascists were rehabilitated and take a closer look at the Italian left, including

---

[42] S Hürstel, *Néo-Hégélianisme et Philosophie du Droit de la République de Weimar au Troisième Reich*, (Paris, Presses Universitaires du Septentrion, 1998).

[43] M Stolleis and D Simon (eds), *Rechtsgeschichte im Nationalsozialismus*, (Tübingen, Mohr, 1989); J Rückert and D Willoweit (eds), *Die deutsche Rechtsgeschichte in der NS-Zeit, ihre Vorgeschichte und Nachwirkungen*, (Tübingen, Mohr, 1995).

the *Brigate Rosse*. The same applies to other countries that were victims of National Socialism (Netherlands, Denmark, Norway) or Stalinism (Poland, Hungary, Bulgaria, Romania, the Baltic states) or those which operated profitably on the margins (Sweden, Switzerland). That is something that has not happened yet and is likely to be some time in coming. Just how deep the wounds are and how profound the self-deception, is evident, for example, in Detlev Tamm's major study of Danish collaboration,[44] a work which caused a sensation. The same is true of the Papon trial in France and the beginning of Swiss and Swedish studies of their countries' collaboration with the Nazi state. Yet we are still a long way from an analysis of jurisprudence, which is not the focal point of such studies. This is particularly true of states that have only recently freed themselves from their own forms of Fascism, such as Spain and Portugal, where the 'phase of silence' continues. In the case of Russia, the difficulties are further compounded by the fact that there was no sudden changing of the guard in the faculties of jurisprudence during the transition to the post-Soviet era. Instead, it would seem that the current blend of old and new is a guarantee that no unbiased history of twentieth century jurisprudence is likely to be forthcoming in the foreseeable future.

[44] D Tamm, *Retsopgöret efter Besaettelsen*, 2nd edn, (Copenhagen, Jurist-og Økonomforbundets Forlag, 1985).

PART I

Continuity and Rupture

1

THE PROBLEM OF PERCEPTIONS OF NATIONAL SOCIALIST LAW OR: WAS THERE A CONSTITUTIONAL THEORY OF NATIONAL SOCIALISM?

*Oliver Lepsius**

Introduction

National Socialism is a drastic fact of German, but also European, history that continues to make itself felt into the present. It is associated with the collapse of the first German republic, the first parliamentary democracy.[1] The constitutional order of the Federal Republic of Germany, but also its political culture, rest upon a basic antifascist consensus.[2] Nonetheless, the years of National Socialism cannot be isolated like some sort of industrial accident. Why were so many lawyers around 1933 prepared voluntarily to abandon the values of democracy, fundamental rights and the rule of law in favour of a comparatively open, unspecified ideology? Why did many not adequately recognise the National Socialist ideology's specific effect of destroying law, thereby becoming involved in the self-destruction of legal science too? Politically, the years 1930–1933 and 1945–1949 unquestionably constituted breaks. But were they also intellectual breaks? Today's perceptions of National Socialist law depend upon this question. If 1933 symbolises a break in law and legal thinking, the consequence would be the literature and ideas of those times stand suspect of

* Professor for Public Law, University of Bayreuth, Dr.jur. (University of Munich), LL.M. (University of Chicago). Translated by Iain L Fraser.

[1] See generally JJ Linz, Crisis, 'Breakdown, and Reequilibration', in JJ Linz (ed) *The Breakdown of Democratic Regimes* (Baltimore, Johns Hopkins, 1978) part I 3–86. Specifically on Germany, MR Lepsius, 'From Fragmented Party Government to Government by Emergency Decree and National Socialist Takeover: Germany', op. cit., part II, 34–79; KD Bracher, *Die Auflösung der Weimarer Republik*, 5th rev edn (Villingen, Ring Verlag, 1971); KD Bracher, *The German Dictatorship* (New York, Praeger, 1970).

[2] MR Lepsius, 'Das Erbe des Nationalsozialismus und die politische Kultur der Nachfolgestaaten des 'Großdeutschen Reiches', in MR Lepsius, *Demokratie in Deutschland* (Göttingen, Vandenhoek & Rupprecht, 1993), 229–48.

being influenced or stamped by National Socialism. But is the political breakdown of 1933 really followed by a turnover in legal thinking as well? Or is
there a continuity in legal thinking from the Weimar Republic to National
Socialism, with the consequence that particular lines of tradition from the
1920s that do not as such have anything to do with National Socialism
appear in a questionable light?

Defining continuities and breaks in the development of law presupposes that
National Socialist law itself can be classified and assessed. Even this is not an
easy task. This essay will enquire whether there were definite special features of
National Socialist law making it possible to attribute positions and concepts to
National Socialism, and correspondingly also to show continuities and breaks
in the development of legal thinking.

Assessing legal literature from the period of National Socialism raises a classification problem.[3] What distinguishes specifically National Socialist legal
thinking? Is it particular contents or particular methodical positions? Ought
one to trace the subjective views and motives of individual authors, or attempt to
dissect out objective features of National Socialist legal thinking over and above
individual perceptions? Both 'subjective' and 'objective' approaches display difficulties. A subjective procedure would have to reconstruct the individual
motives and intentions. Are they the point, however, or is it not more the range
of recipients that is decisive? But even focusing on objective criteria, one
encounters problems: did there really exist a specific idea of National Socialism
in an objective sense, so that comparability of individual texts and National
Socialist ideas can be brought about? Was National Socialism not very much a
syncretistic ideology, so that attempts to make objective demarcations are
doomed to failure? Finally, one could focus on criteria centred on neither the
author's subjective notions nor objective levels of comparison, but on particular methodological approaches and patterns of justification. I wish to show
below that the assessment of legal literature and ideas under Nazi rule can be
grasped with neither the subjective nor the objective approach, since both
require a substantive level of comparison, which however can hardly be found
in view of the syncretistic nature of the National Socialist ideology. Instead, the
perception and assessment of methodological criteria should be to the fore. It
is only with these, according to the position put forward here, that the specific
features of National Socialist law and legal writing can be demarcated and

---

[3] See O Lepsius, 'Personengebundene oder strukturorientierte Bewertungskriterien für juristis-
ches Verhalten im Nationalsozialismus', in H Nehlsen/G Brun (ed) *Münchener rechtshistorische
Studien zum Nationalsozialismus* (Frankfurt/Main, Peter Lang, 1996) 63–102; M Stolleis/D Simon,
Vorurteile und Werturteile der rechtshistorischen Forschung zum Nationalsozialismus, *NS-Recht in
historischer Perspektive* (München, Oldenbourg, 1981) 13–51; M Stolleis, *Recht im Unrecht*
(Frankfurt/Main, Suhrkamp, 1994) 57–93, translated *Law under the Swastika* (Chicago, University
of Chicago Press, 1998).

analysed.[4] Neither the quest for individual political preferences nor for an objective comparison of individual texts with an 'authentic' National Socialist ideology furnishes this goal: the first approach requires psychological investigations which cannot reveal generalisable results, the second approach is thwarted by the indefinable and syncretistic nature of the Nazi ideology. Instead, we have to look for methodological patterns for comparison and assessment.

This approach can here of course be studied only on examples from one partial area of National Socialist legal thinking. One object of study that suggests itself is constitutional law and constitutional theory, a topic which was recently debated at the 2000 annual meeting of the association of German scholars of constitutional law.[5] I shall confine myself below to the aspects of constitutional law and theory and shall not take into account the administrative law of National Socialism.[6]

The development of law in National Socialism: destruction and reconstruction

A sketch of the whole legal development in National Socialism cannot be given here even for constitutional law alone. I must confine myself to essential points of the development. Two opposite processes seem to me worth emphasising. One can distinguish, firstly, a process of the decline and destruction of the Weimar constitutional order. Though the Weimar constitution formally remained in force, substantively is was suspended. The material destruction of the Weimar constitutional order is an essential feature of National Socialist constitutional theory. Alongside that, secondly, came a process of building up new National Socialist legal principles. We are accordingly confronted with an ambivalent development: destruction and construction, decline and progress.

---

[4] For a detailed treatment see O Lepsius, *Die gegensatzaufhebende Begriffsbildung. Methodenentwicklungen in der Weimarer Republik und ihr Verhältnis zur Ideologisierung der Rechtswissenschaft im Nationalsozialismus* (München, Beck, 1994). For a different treatment of methodological explanations see VG Curran, 'Fear of Formalism: Indications from the Fascist Period in France and Germany of Judicial Methodology's Impact on Substantive Law', (2001) 35 *Cornell International Law Journal* 101. According to her, methodology did not have a significant impact on substantive outcome.

[5] H Dreier, 'Die deutsche Staatsrechtslehre in der Zeit des Nationalsozialismus', *Veröffentlichungen der Vereinigung der Deutschen Staatsrechtslehrer Heft 60* (Berlin, de Gruyter, 2001) 9–72; W Pauly, 'Die deutsche Staatsrechtslehre in der Zeit des Nationalsozialismus', 73–105. See also the comment by O Lepsius, 'Die Tagung der Vereinigung der Deutschen Staatsrechtslehrer 2000 in Leipzig', (2001) 126 *Archiv des öffentlichen Rechts* 441–69 at 447–48.

[6] See on this M Stolleis, *Geschichte des Öffentlichen Rechts in Deutschland, Dritter Band 1914–1945* (München, Beck, 1999), 351–79; M Stolleis, 'Verwaltungsrechtswissenschaft und Verwaltungslehre im Nationalsozialismus', in G Jeserich et al. (eds) *Deutsche Verwaltungsgeschichte Band 4* (Stuttgart, DVA, 1985) 705.

The development of National Socialist constitutional law can be understood only through the interaction of destruction and construction.

1 De-legalisation

The essential stages in legal development towards establishing and consolidating National Socialist rule while simultaneously suspending the Weimar constitutional order are fairly well known.[7] I wish here to recall them only briefly, breaking them down into three stages:

a) Suspension of the constitutional principles

The first step was suspension of civil rights and definitive departure from the parliamentary system of government, which had admittedly already, with the presidential cabinets, become the exception. The essential legal bases were the decree of 27 February 1933 on the 'protection of people and State', the so-called 'Reichstag Fire Decree', and the *Ermächtigungsgesetz* (Enabling Act) of 23 March 1933. In the upshot, the Weimar constitution of the Reich nominally remained in force, but shrunken to a formal shell: the binding of State power by the constitution was suspended, the fundamental rights deprived of force, parliamentary control removed, and lawmaking transferred to the executive, even for statutes amending the constitution.

b) Suspension of social pluralism

The second stage removed social pluralism, with the so-called *Gleichschaltung* (enforced conformity) of the political parties and intermediate associations. The most important laws here were the act of 'Restoration of the Professional Civil Service' of 7 April 1933, the *Gleichschaltung* of the trade unions on 2 May 1933, the law against formation of new parties of 14 July 1933 (after there had already been party bans in June), and finally on 1 December 1933 the law on 'Safeguarding the Unity of Party and State'. The ending of intermediary associations meant removal of social pluralism, and the one-party system in practice suspended the separation of State and society.

c) Suspension of Federalism

The third strand was the gradual *Gleichschaltung* of the *Länder*, ending with the law of 30 January 1934 on the new structure of the Reich.

The 1933/4 volume of the *Reichsgesetzblatt* witnesses the process of destroying the democratic, pluralist constitutional order. The seizure and consolida-

---

[7] R Echterhölter, 'Das öffentliche Recht im nationalsozialistischen Staat', *Die deutsche Justiz und der Nationalsozialismus Band 2* (Stuttgart, DVA, 1970) 13–84.

tion of power consistently pursued the suspension of the constitutional order and the oblivion of constitutional categories. This process of suspension can be described in three directions: the National Socialist State dissolves the difference with the constitution, with society and with the *Länder*. Conversely, the concept of the State was redefined: in relation to the constitution, to its territorial parts and to society. This is expressed in terms of positive law in the dissolution of all the pillar principles of the constitution: fundamental rights and parliamentarianism, rule of law and binding by statute, federalism and separation of powers. We thus see a comprehensive process of delegalisation, in other words the destruction of constitutional law. But what replaced it in positive terms?

2 Dynamics and Movement

The decline, suspension and destruction were accompanied by an opposite process of establishing new legal principles and substantive promises. From the outset National Socialism did not just engage in a work of destruction, but had a constructive view directed at quite different principles and legal devices than was the tradition of the democratic constitutional State. Three core principles of National Socialist law embodied the new substantive promises that Nazi law was supposed to follow:[8] the concept of the *Volksgemeinschaft* (national community), the *Führerprinzip* (leader principle) and a dynamic mode of proceeding, symbolised by the unity of party and State, of people and movement (*Bewegung*).

a) The concept of the Volksgemeinschaft

Of the substantive principles of National Socialist constitutional law, the *Volksgemeinschaft* deserves mention in first position. The term *Volksgemeinschaft*, or also *völkisches Recht*, was used in inflationary fashion in various connotations.[9] In content, it was characterised negatively by rejection of the individualistic, normative concept of the people (the people [Volk] as the sum

---

[8] On these three constitutional principles of the National Socialist State see the commented document collection: M Hirsch, D Majer, J Meinck (eds) *Recht, Verwaltung und Justiz im Nationalsozialismus* (Köln, Bund Verlag, 1984) 139–294; D Majer, *Grundlagen des nationalsozialistischen Rechtssystems* (Stuttgart, Kohlhammer, 1987); Bundesminister der Justiz (ed) *Im Namen des Deutschen Volkes. Justiz und Nationalsozialismus*, (Köln, Verlag Wissenschaft und Politik, 1989), 104–9. On the renovation of law see also B Rüthers, *Entartetes Recht. Rechtslehren und Kronjuristen im Dritten Reich* (München, Beck, 1992) 23–40.

[9] See M Stolleis, 'Gemeinschaft und Volksgemeinschaft. Zur juristischen Terminologie im Nationalsozialismus', (1972) *Vierteljahreshefte für Zeitgeschichte* 16, English translation of this article in: *Law under the Swastika*, n 3; U Kalbhen, *Die NS-Rechtstheorie als Herrschaftsideologie* (Heidelberg, Dissertation, 1969) 98–105; J Gernhuber, 'Das völkische Recht. Ein Beitrag zur Rechtstheorie des Nationalsozialismus', *Tübinger Festschrift für Eduard Kern* (Tübingen, Mohr Siebeck, 1968) 167–200.

of nationals of the State), as presented in the Weimar Republic. In positive terms, the term *Volksgemeinschaft* promised a collective unity defined in value terms by, for instance, features of *Blut und Boden* (blood and soil), community experiences, and thus also inner ideas and feelings of belonging together.[10] Conceptual definitions of the *Volksgemeinschaft* typically use a dual reference to conceptual features, contradictory as such, of both factual and normative origin: for instance nature and spirit, body and soul, history and future, value and reality.[11] The interesting feature of the term *Volksgemeinschaft* is that on the one hand it cannot be exactly defined, but on the other hand nonetheless embodied the National Socialist legal idea that was perceived as obligatory. The idea of *Volksgemeinschaft* was both compulsory and vague. Additionally, racist, anti-Semitic elements kept recurring. However, that supplemented the concept of the *Volk* only in negative respects. Most definitions of and appeals to the *Volksgemeinschaft* did without anti-Semitism.

The concept of the *Volksgemeinschaft* had the function of supplying a substantive National Socialist idea of law. Thus, Helmut Nicolai, a prominent National Socialist party lawyer who became ministerial director in the Reich Ministry of the Interior after 1933, says 'that the ultimate and supreme source of law is the National Socialist idea of law, which finds its expression in the legal sense of the *Volk*.'[12] The idea of the *Volksgemeinschaft* postulated the identity of political rule with the convictions of the *Volk*. It served on the one hand to heighten the value of National Socialist reality, to glorify its essence, and on the other acted as a legal idea of commitment to the National Socialist ideology, glorifying what ought to be. The concept of the *Volksgemeinschaft* was accordingly central to National Socialist law. It was used to assert the legitimacy of the ruling order, discredit fundamental rights, and collectivise and delegalise the position of the individual.

[10] For a more detailed study of the concept of the Volk [people] and Gemeinschaft [community] in National Socialism and their substantive and methodological definition see Lepsius, n 4 32–49, 62–69. On the origin of these and other terms from the repertoire of the so-called 'conservative revolution' cf S Breuer, *Ordnungen der Ungleichheit—die deutsche Rechte im Widerstreit ihrer Ideen 1871–1945* (Darmstadt, Wissenschaftliche Buchgesellschaft, 2001); S Breuer, *Anatomie der konservativen Revolution* (Darmstadt, Wissenschaftliche Buchgesellschaft, 1993).

[11] For more on this see Lepsius, n 4, at 46–8, 67–70, 145–55.

[12] See H Nicolai, *Grundlagen der kommenden Verfassung* (Berlin, Carl Heymanns, 1933) at 20; H Nicolai, *Der Neuaufbau des Reiches nach dem Reichsreformgesetz vom 30. Januar 1934* (Berlin, Carl Heymanns, 1934). Nicolai had written a book claiming to be a fundamental work already in 1932: H Nicolai, *Die rassengesetzliche Rechtslehre. Grundzüge einer nationalsozialistischen Rechtsphilosophie* (München, Eher, 1932). On this book see Lepsius, n 4 at 73–4; E Bristler (= J Herz), *Die Völkerrechtslehre des Nationalsozialismus* (Zürich, Europa Verlag, 1938) at 25–8, 68–71. On Nicolai generally see M Schmoeckel, 'Helmut Nicolai. Ein Anfang nationalsozialistischen Rechtsdenkens', in Verein Junger RechtshistorikerInnen Zürich (ed) *¿Rechtsgeschichte(n)?* (Frankfurt/Main, Peter Lang, 2000) 325–50; M Schmoeckel, 'Helmut Nicolai', (1999) 19 *Neue Deutsche Biographie* 204; M Housden, *Helmut Nicolai and Nazi Ideology* (New York, St. Martin's Press, 1992).

b) The Führerprinzip

Leadership was treated as an innovative core concept of National Socialist constitutional law.[13] The idea was of some higher unity between leadership and followers. The Führer (leader) was supposed to articulate the true knowledge and will of the community and bring it to its expression through action. The function of the *Führerprinzip* lies in a formal tie to the National Socialist ideology as executed by the Führer. As a 'formal principle' it supplemented the 'substantive legal principle' of the concept of the *Volksgemeinschaft*. Both principles are accordingly connected, and cover the form and content of National Socialist law.

The formal function of the *Führerprinzip* can be explained also from the needs of the National Socialist ideology of rule. The *Führerprinzip* acted as a trans-personal system of representation.[14] Ernst Rudolf Huber, then a prominent young professor of constitutional and administrative law at the University of Kiel, describes the Führer principle in his treatise on National Socialist constitutional law as follows:

> in the Führer the essential principles of the Volk come into manifestation; it is he who lets them become the guiding thread of all the work of the *Volk* . . . He embodies the overall will of the *Volk* as an objective quantity[15]

The Führer as an 'Übermensch' was supposed to possess the objective consciousness of the *Volk* and have a spiritual identity with it. The substantive principle of the *Volksgemeinschaft* was thereby constitutively linked with the subject of the Führer. As the executant of the people's will, he had to enforce himself in organisational terms. Führer orders thus had primacy over all other sources of law. Ernst Forsthoff, also a prominent young professor of public law then at the University of Frankfurt, put things in 1935 laconically by saying that creation of the Führer State had ended the constitutional question.[16]

At first sight, *Volksgemeinschaft* and *Führerprinzip* seem incompatible: 'Gemeinschaft [community]' appeals to a collective subject, the *Führerprinzip* by contrast to monocratic rule. In reality they complemented each other: in the *Volksgemeinschaft* individual subjects could no longer have any legal value. There was only one materialised subject of the community-related *Volk* left. Subject and object were blended together. It was only the Führer principle that made it possible to attribute the value decision, but only to the actual person of the Führer. Values over and above his will could no longer exist. We discover a

---

[13] See C Schmitt, *Staat, Bewegung, Volk* (Hamburg, Hanseatische Verlagsanstalt, 1933) at 36.

[14] On the substantive and methodological use of the term 'Führer' see Lepsius, n 4 at 85.

[15] ER Huber, *Verfassungsrecht des Großdeutschen Reiches* (Hamburg, Hanseatische Verlagsanstalt, 2d ed. 1939) at 197.

[16] E Forsthoff, 'Das neue Gesicht der Verwaltung und die Verwaltungsrechtswissenschaft', (1935) *Deutsches Recht* 331. On Forsthoff see U Storost, *Staat und Verfassung bei Ernst Forsthoff* (Frankfurt/Main, Peter Lang, 1979).

process where categories contradictory in themselves were arranged in comple-
mentary fashion: with the *Volksgemeinschaft* the law becomes substantively
open, with the Führer principle it is formally closed. Neither the substantive
principle of the *Volksgemeinschaft* nor the formal one of the *Führerprinzip* can,
however, be defined precisely in detail. *Volksgemeinschaft* contains a hodge-
podge of substantive features, and the Führer principle as a formal principle is
not bound to forms at all. The Führer's will is enforced irrespective of whether
it is proclaimed as a statute of the Reich, a regulation or a mere decree. Form
and content seem to be guaranteed and newly defined, but have in reality been
destroyed and brought to absurdity.

The formlessness of the formal principle can, moreover, be seen also in the
loss of meaning by the Reichstag and Reich government. Between 23 March
1933 and its last session in April 1942 the Reichstag passed only seven more
formal statutes.[17] Legislation was replaced by a process of circular approval in
the Reich government. Horst Dreier calls this process 'a development from
indifference to form into loss of form.'[18] The hierarchy of norms was removed.
Führer decrees could supplement, break down or substitute for statutes.
Eventually, Führer orders were not even published any longer. That was when
loss of form had come in. This development can also be termed a renewed
process of delegalisation. A delegalisation of values and of forms came about.
This delegalisation through idealisation by the National Socialist ideology
('Weltanschauung') was accompanied by that other form of delegalisation, the
destruction of the Weimar constitutional order.

c) The principle of the movement

The third new element in National Socialist law was the principle of the movement, expressed above all in the postulated unity of party and State. It can also
be called a dynamic principle. The dynamic resolved the 'in itself' contrary relationship between *Volksgemeinschaft* and *Führerprinzip*; it linked the subject of
the Führer and the object of the *Volksgemeinschaft*, it linked form and value.
The dynamic principle transposed the breakdown of the clear ordering of functions and competences for tasks. Conversely, it justified the continuing state of
emergency and the National Socialist polyocracy of rule. Using the dynamic
principle, formal and substantive fixations could be avoided. While *Volksgemeinschaft* and *Führerprinzip* delegalised content and form, the principle of
the movement prevented them from ever again becoming legalised or even only
limited, defined or canonised. Any closer definition of the weltanschauung

---

[17] n 5, Dreier, above at 50. These included the 1934 Reconstruction Act, the 1935 Nuremberg
Acts, the two extensions of the Enabling Act in 1937 and 1941, and the law incorporating Danzig
in 1939. On the decay of the concept of statute see also D Kirschenmann, *'Gesetz' im Staatsrecht
und in der Staatsrechtslehre des NS* (Berlin, Duncker & Humblot, 1970) 29–36; W Pauly, n 5, at 92.

[18] n 5, Dreier, above at 53–7.

would have to have led to its fixation and would have enabled it to be tied down. There occurred, however, neither a canonisation of the National Socialist ideology nor a fixation of particular binding forms or sources of law apart from the Führer's orders.[19] The effect was the maintenance of permanent substantive openness with simultaneous direct occasional commitment to this openness. This outcome suited Hitler personally. Hitler retained the right of final decision on all questions. He himself avoided all fixation and decided on a one-off basis, so that there could not be any prejudicial tying by Führer orders either. Moreover, he hated lawyers and legal rules in general,[20] something that can also be explained by his disinclination for any formal or substantive fixations.[21]

Dynamics and movement on the one hand guaranteed the processes of deformalisation and dematerialisation, but on the other turned it around into something positive.[22] The dynamic aspects of the movement promised a synthesis and a new unity. The National Socialist weltanschauung made propaganda for the overcoming of traditional quantities and categories like individualism, pluralism and separation of powers. Even dichotomies like content and form, subject and object, is and ought, can be counted in here. On the other hand, it promised new conglomerates, for instance the unity of order and freedom, of *Volk* and State, party and State. The Nazi ideology contained a metaphor of building unity by transcending contradictions. This thought pattern of unity and transcendence was applied equally to contents and forms, and used a dynamic of heightening. This dynamic, movement or transcendence combined elements that in themselves were opposite. In this way it made possible delegalisation and prevented the emergence of any new binding by law. With a dynamic principle there could be neither any consensus on values nor on legal forms; it was compatible with a dynamic development only point by point, in relation to individual places, but not in principle, in any generalisable way.

---

[19] See M Broszat, *Der Nationalsozialismus. Weltanschauung, Programm und Wirklichkeit* (Stuttgart, DVA, 1960) 21–46; M Broszat, *Der Staat Hitlers* (München, Oldenbourg, 1969) 33–49; K Anderbrügge, *Völkisches Rechtsdenken—Zur Rechtslehre in der Zeit des Nationalsozialismus* (Berlin, Duncker & Humblot, 1978); W Altgeld, 'Die Ideologie des Nationalsozialismus und ihre Vorläufer', in KD Bracher/L Valiani (ed) *Faschismus und Nationalsozialismus* (Berlin, Duncker & Humblot, 1991) 107–36; E Jäckel, *Hitlers Weltanschauung* (Stuttgart, DVA, 2d ed. 1981); Lepsius, n 4, at 102–16, 124–25.

[20] See M Broszat, *Der Nationalsozialismus*, n 19, at 34; H Mommsen, 'Hitlers Stellung im nationalsozialistischen Herrschaftssystem', in G Hirschfeld/L Kettenacker (ed) *Der 'Führerstaat': Mythos und Realität* (Stuttgart, DVA, 1981) 43–70 at 44, 50.

[21] On Hitler's hate for law and lawyers see H Weinkauff, 'Die deutsche Justiz und der Nationalsozialismus. Ein Überblick', in H Weinkauff/A Wagner (ed) *Die deutsche Justiz und der Nationalsozialismus* (Stuttgart, DVA, 1968) 19–188 at 40–55.

[22] Just as the sacrificing of formal legal principles brought loss of legal values, at maintaining which sacrificing the forms was often aimed, has been discussed, not just for National Socialist law, by: I Maus, *Rechtstheorie und politische Theorie im Industriekapitalismus* (München, Wilhelm Fink, 1986).

3 Assessment

What picture of National Socialist constitutional law can one draw at this point?

a) Delegalisation

On the one hand we can see three new features of the new construction of National Socialist law (*Volksgemeinschaft*, *Führerprinzip* and principle of dynamic movement); on the other hand there is a three-stage process of breaking down the old constitutional order. National Socialism all in all led to delegalisation: delegalisation of the substance of law through the idea of the *Volksgemeinschaft*, delegalisation of legal forms through the *Führerprinzip* and of course an annihilation of law through the destruction of the Weimar constitutional order. The non-law nature of National Socialist law is to be seen not merely from its results, but already from its mode of procedure and its development. It was a development oriented towards destroying legal categories and values. If one then asks what was new about National Socialist constitutional law, one has to refer to categories that can no longer be grasped as legal principles (*Volksgemeinschaft–Führerprinzip–*'dynamics'), because they aimed at destroying these. The specifically new feature of National Socialist law can accordingly no longer be described by categories belonging to the recognised legal repertoire. Since National Socialism was directed at overcoming traditional categories of constitutional law, it can be grasped by them only in negative terms, namely to delimit it, but not in positive terms, that is, in its objectives.

b) Destatalisation

A similar picture comes from the counter-test of what remained of the object of constitutional law. German constitutional theory traditionally has a twofold object: it is concerned primarily with a theory of State (*Staatsrecht*) as well as constitutional law (*Verfassungsrecht*). Hence a decay only of constitutional law would not automatically deprive constitutional theory of its object or categories. *Staatsrecht* could survive *Verfassungsrecht*. But what could a theory of the State under Nazi rule be directed at? The constitution as an object had from the outset to be excluded from National Socialism. Since in National Socialism there was no longer any constitution, and its ruling order could not be grasped by legal categories, all that was left as an object was the State. In the German tradition the State customarily has an emphatically special position in categorical terms.[23] It typically has attributed to it an additional formal and material

---

[23] This special German tradition is comprehensively analysed and criticised in relation to any additional legal value by C Möllers, *Staat als Argument* (München, Beck, 2000).

value vis-à-vis the constitution. This may explain why many constitutional theorists were not yet alarmed by the breakdown of constitutional categories alone, as long as the additional value of the State not just remained conserved but even seemed to be refounded by National Socialism. But regarding the object of the State too, an interesting phenomenon of dissolution is discernible. For if we ask how the three generally recognised features of the concept of the State since Georg Jellinek (State people, State territory, State power) have developed in the 1930s,[24] we similarly obtain a picture of dissolution and transcendence. The State people as first element of the concept of the State was dissolved by the idea of the *Volksgemeinschaft*, which first of all excluded German citizens and second included extra-territorials. *Volksgemeinschaft* and the idea of race replaced the people as conceptual element of the State. Power as a second feature of the concept of the State was eroded by the Führer principle, particularly by the transcendence of the hierarchy of norms, the emergence of a polycratic system of rule with occasionalism, and the Führer's right of ultimate decision. The third feature of the State, territory, can no longer be defined either. The ideology from the outset used the formula from the Twenties of a 'Volk ohne Raum' (people without space)[25], and at latest with the aggressive war, conquests and the *Grossraum* theory[26] the concept of a definable territory became obsolete. Here too, then, on the whole accrued was a process of dissolution: constitutional theory (*Staatsrecht*) lost its object. There was neither a constitution nor a State in the traditional legal sense.[27] Constitutional theory, however, lost not just its object but also, and this is the more important insight, its categories. The traditional categories of constitutional law, legitimation, binding by law, fundamental rights, the rule of law, separation of powers, federal statehood, and finally even the concept of statute, had all become useless. The new order could no longer be grasped through them; they had degraded into constitutional historical reminiscences.

The summary of this review of the objective development of constitutional law in National Socialism seems as clear as crystal: in National Socialism there

[24] G Jellinek, *Allgemeine Staatslehre* (Berlin, Julius Springer, 3d ed. 1914) at 394–434. On Jellinek's constitutional theory see J Kersten, *Georg Jellinek und die klassische Staatslehre* (Tübingen, Mohr Siebeck, 2000); *Georg Jellinek—Beiträge zu Leben und Werk* ed. SL Paulson/M Schulte (Tübingen, Mohr Siebeck 2000).

[25] The expression 'people without space' comes from H Grimm's novel, *Volk ohne Raum* (München, Langen, 1926), set in an Afrikaner settler environment and without any direct reference to Germany.

[26] See Dreier, n 5, at 62–6; M Schmoeckel, *Die Großraumtheorie. Ein Beitrag zur Geschichte der Völkerrechtswissenschaft im Dritten Reich, insbesondere der Kriegszeit* (Berlin, Duncker & Humblot, 1994), at 152; L Gruchmann, *Nationalsozialistische Großraumordnung. Die Konstruktion einer 'deutschen Monroe-Doktrin'* (Stuttgart, DVA, 1962).

[27] On the loss of the State as object see also Dreier, n 5, at 59–62; W Pauly, n 5, at 79; H Wilms, 'Die Staatsrechtslehre im Nationalsozialismus', (2000) *Deutsches Verwaltungsblatt* 1237–49 at 1249.

was objectively no constitutional law nor theory. There was no longer any area of law deserving the name. The National Socialist weltanschauung wanted, even in what it itself claimed, to set up something new, at any rate not to modify some order based on a constitution. After the seizure of power National Socialism needed law neither to establish nor to delimit rule.

c) Paradoxes of perception

This finding contrasts, however, with contemporary perceptions. Constitutional law and theory (*Verfassungsrecht* and *Staatsrecht*) were taught at German universities. Engagement with the constitutional law of National Socialism in the literature too by no means ceased in the first years after the seizure of power. In 1937, with a second edition in 1939, Ernst Rudolf Huber published his voluminous work on the 'Constitutional Law of the "Grossdeutsches Reich"'.[28] In this book Huber analysed the legal development clearly, dividing National Socialist constitutional law into the sections 'the Volk', 'the Führer', 'the movement'. The bases of the specific National Socialist notion of constitutional law were correctly analysed in categorical terms.[29] Other works too firmly grasped the development and the legal changes. As early as 1933 Carl Schmitt clearly recognised the basic nature of the new order in the triplet of State, Movement, and *Volk*.[30] And Otto Koellreutter, an early supporter of National Socialism before the seizure of power, in 1935 wrote a book with the title 'German Constitutional Law'.[31]

Thus, today's perception that there was no constitutional law *of* National Socialism diverges from the verdict of contemporaries. They did not just want law of the State or constitutional law in National Socialism, but indeed wanted to *write* the constitutional law of National Socialism. We must accordingly below deal with the problem of whether and how the real legal development was perceived at the time.

---

[28] Cf R Walkenhaus, *Konservatives Staatsdenken. Eine wissenssoziologische Studie zu Ernst Rudolf Huber* (Berlin, Akademie Verlag, 1997); M-E Geis, *Kulturstaat und kulturelle Freiheit: eine Untersuchung des Kulturstaatskonzepts von Ernst Rudolf Huber aus verfassungsrechtlicher Sicht* (Baden-Baden, Nomos, 1990).

[29] There follow sections on 'The Structure of the Reich', 'The Legal Position of the Volk-comrades', 'The Public Service', 'Self-administration of the estates', 'Reich and Church'.

[30] See Schmitt n 13.

[31] O Koellreutter, *Deutsches Verfassungsrecht* (Berlin, Junker & Dünnhaupt, 1935). On Koellreutter cf J Schmidt, *Otto Koellreutter: 1883–1972* (Frankfurt/Main, Peter Lang, 1995); J Schmidt, 'Theodor Otto Koellreutter', in *Münchener rechtshistorische Studien zum National-sozialismus*, n 3, 331–46; Lepsius, n 4, at 36, 47, 59.

Contemporary perceptions of the National Socialist theory of State and constitution

In investigating the subjective perception of National Socialist theory of State and constitution, a separation should be made. Faithful to the findings described above, a distinction should be drawn between the decline of the Weimar constitution, the new structure of the National Socialist law with *völkisches Recht* and the Führer principle, and the element of movement, along with dynamics and justificatory methods.

1 Perceptions of the decline of the Weimar constitution

The destruction of the Weimar constitutional order was naturally perceived variously. One should distinguish three groups of persons: the group of those who overwhelmingly welcomed the decline and very consciously perceived it, the group that remained silent and fled into so-called 'internal emigration', and finally the group that had to emigrate.[32]

A quantitatively large group of lawyers welcomed and consciously perceived the fall of the Weimar constitutional order. The legal development of 1933–34 described above met with support and in part enthusiasm. Directly, this response had nothing to do with the question of specific National Socialist law. It belongs in the context of the decline of the Weimar Republic. Once the destruction of the Weimar constitution had come about, by 1934 or at latest 1935, this literature came to its end.

Next comes the group of those who remained silent and took refuge in so-called 'internal emigration'. The two editors of the standard work on Weimar constitutional law,[33] Richard Thoma and Gerhard Anschütz, could be mentioned here.[34] Anschütz gave up his chair at Heidelberg in 1933 for political reasons, the sole case among lawyers.

---

[32] For a general overview see B Limperg, 'Personelle Veränderungen in der Staatsrechtslehre und ihre neue Situation nach der Machtergreifung', in E-W Böckenförde (ed) *Staatsrecht und Staatsrechtslehre im Dritten Reich*, (Heidelberg, Müller, 1985) 44–67; on expulsions and new appointments at individual universities see: Stolleis, *Geschichte* n 6, 254–99.

[33] G Anschütz/R Thoma (eds), *Handbuch des Deutschen Staatsrechts* 2 vol. (Tübingen, Mohr Siebeck, 1930, 1932).

[34] On Richard Thomas see H Döring, *Der Weimarer Kreis. Studien zum Bewußtsein verfassungstreuer Hochschullehrer in der Weimarer Republik,*(Meisenheim, Hain, 1975); HD Rath, *Positivismus und Demokratie. Richard Thoma 1874–1957* (Berlin, Duncker & Humblot, 1981); C Schönberger, 'Elitenherrschaft für den sozialen Ausgleich: Richard Thomas 'realistische Demokratietheorie' im Kontext der Weimarer Diskussion', in C Gusy (ed) *Demokratisches Denken in der Weimarer Republik* (Baden-Baden, Nomos, 2000) 156–90. On Anschütz see H Dreier, 'Ein Staatsrechtslehrer in Zeiten des Umbruchs: Gerhard Anschütz (1867–1948)', (1998) 20 *Zeitschrift für Neuere Rechtsgeschichte* 28; W Pauly, 'Zu Leben und Werk von Gerhard Anschütz', in W Pauly (ed) *Gerhard Anschütz, Aus meinem Leben* (Frankfurt/Main, Klostermann, 1993); H Döring, above at 161.

And there was the group of those that had to emigrate.[35] Here the picture is multi-layered in content and cannot be gone into any more closely here.[36] Among constitutionalists one might mention the great constitutional lawyer of parliamentary democracy and defender of the Weimar Republic, Hans Kelsen, who went first to Geneva and then to the US; Erich Kaufmann, who went to ground in the Netherlands; Hermann Heller, who died in Madrid in late 1933; Gerhard Leibholz, who in 1938 fled to Oxford; and of course the names of Ernst Fraenkel and Franz Neumann, who wrote the two famous contemporary analyses of National Socialist law, should also be mentioned.[37] Fraenkel and Neumann were able to do so, because they still used the categories of constitutional law, whereas those thinkers who wanted to presumably correctly grasp the specific notion of Nazi rule were unable to draw upon these categories.

2 Perception of the new construction of a National Socialist law

This leads us to the perceptions of those who wanted to decipher the notion of the National Socialist State and to exercise an influence on its substance. In their eyes, the categories of constitutional law had to be overcome deliberately. There is a widely shared understanding to give up the traditional categories of constitutional law. As far as the new parts of National Socialist law are concerned, the position is more complicated. Here I should like to distinguish between the criteria of *Volksgemeinschaft* and *Führerprinzip* on the one hand, and the element of the dynamic movement on the other.

---

[35] On this in general see: W Röder/H A Strauss (ed) *Biographisches Handbuch der deutschsprachigen Emigration*, 2 vols. (München, Saur, 1980, 1983); EC Stiefel/F Mecklenburg, *Deutsche Juristen im amerikanischen Exil (1933–1950)* (Tübingen, Mohr Siebeck, 1991); MR Lepsius, 'Juristen in der sozialwissenschaftlichen Emigration', in M Lutter et al. (ed) *Der Einfluß deutscher Emigranten auf die Rechtsentwicklung in den USA und in Deutschland* (Tübingen, Mohr Siebeck, 1993) 19–31.

[36] On those named below cf H Dreier, 'Rechtslehre, Staatssoziologie und Demokratietheorie bei Hans Kelsen' (Baden-Baden, Nomos, 2d ed 1990); E Castrucci, *Tra Organicismo e „Rechtsidee". Il pensiero giuridico di Erich Kaufmann* (Milano, Giuffré, 1984); W Schluchter, *Entscheidung für den sozialen Rechtsstaat. Hermann Heller und die staatstheoretische Diskussion in der Weimarer Republik* (Baden-Baden, Nomos, 2d ed 1983); A Dehnhard, *Dimensionen staatlichen Handelns. Staatstheorie in der Tradition Hermann Hellers* (Tübingen, Mohr Siebeck, 1996); MH Wiegandt, *Norm und Wirklichkeit. Gerhard Leibholz (1901–1982)* (Baden-Baden, Nomos, 1995).

[37] E Fraenkel, *The Dual State* (New York, Oxford University Press, 1941); Franz Neumann, *Behemoth* (Frankfurt/Main, Fischer, 1977) orig. 1942. Also to be added is the study of National Socialist international law by E Bristler (i.e. J Herz), n 12. On Fraenkel see H Buchstein/R Kühn, Vorwort, in H Buchstein/R Kühne (eds) *Gesammelte Schriften von Ernst Fraenkel Band 4* (Baden-Baden, Nomos, 2000) 7–48, and the prefaces to the other volumes; on Neumann see: J Rückert, Franz L. Neumann—ein Jurist mit Prinzipien, in M Lutter et al. (eds) *Der Einfluß deutscher Emigranten auf die Rechtsentwicklung in den USA und in Deutschland* (Tübingen, Mohr Siebeck, 1993) 437–74.

a) Volksgemeinschaft and Führer principle

On the substantial criterion of the *Volksgemeinschaft* and *Volk* law and the formal criterion of the Führer principle, there are numerous contemporary attempts at interpretation. Since the new substantive and formal content of National Socialist law lay in these features, it is not surprising that these two principles in particular led to intensive literary efforts. On the official side, admittedly, the two principles were neither defined in detail nor canonised, so that there was no binding interpretation.

A closer study of how legal science understood the two National Socialist principles reveals a noteworthy phenomenon:[38] the attempts at legal definition are highly varied, and we see a picture of great openness in content. The attempts at defining the terms *Volksgemeinschaft* and *Führerprinzip* can be generalised only in negative terms. Here they mean anti-liberalism, anti-parliamentarianism, anti-federalism, and in part also anti-Semitism. In positive respects, however, a substantive correspondence is hard to see. One further phenomenon deserves attention: despite the great range of content, almost every interpreter regards his interpretation as correct and binding. We thus see a picture homogeneous only on the negative side but very heterogeneous on the positive. That on the whole, however, did not irritate interpreters at the time. This is surprising since as such the discrepancy of content ought to have been striking, so that each author ought no longer to have been convinced of the accuracy of precisely his interpretation. The situation is ambivalent: on the one hand a far-reaching substantive openness and indefiniteness, and on the other the general notion of substantive bindingness and correctness. We cannot here investigate in detail why the authors on the one hand were convinced of the correctness of their various subjective interpretations and why on the other they were apparently not struck by the subjective differences. We would here note one feature that played a key part in contemporary conceptual definitions. One is struck by a specific procedure of concept formation by the transcendence of dichotomies and contradictory conceptual elements. Here are some examples of this commonly used method of concept formation in the 1930s taken from standard works of National Socialist constitutional law:

Ernst Rudolf Huber finds the specific feature of the concept of the *Volksgemeinschaft* and thus the basis of the *völkische Verfassung* not in an 'abstract concept of the State people', but in the 'concrete concept of the living "Volk"'. This, he claims, is always a politicised concept, that is, it embraces the people in its specific political nature.[39] Huber particularly stresses the dynamics, the peculiarity of the concept of the *Volksgemeinschaft*, a 'political concept', a 'concrete concept of the living people'. The definition of the term *Volksgemeinschaft* is thus arrived at with the help of dynamic elements, so that a static, abstract definition hardly seems possible.

[38] On this and below, see for more detail and numerous examples Lepsius, n 4, 33–49, 62–9.
[39] n 15 Huber, above at 151.

We find a similar procedure in Otto Koellreutter.[40] According to him the concept of the *Volk* in National Socialism starts in the first place from common natural features of the people, its being marked by *Blut und Boden*. The common historical experience also contributes to shaping the people as a unitary political quantity. In Koellreutter's view, experience and formation are similarly features of a dynamical conceptualisation.

As a further example we may adduce a definition of the term by Ulrich Scheuner, who became professor for public law at the University of Jena in 1933. According to him the *Volk* is 'the living community formed of the natural bond of blood and marked by its historical destiny, in which a particular primordial law of creative development is deployed.'[41]

For all the difference in content, a common method of conceptualisation emerges as a link. Many conceptual definitions at the time use a procedure of combining conceptual features contradictory in themselves into a new definition. Let us have Scheuner speak here again: 'the new view', he says, 'reaches down into the irrational forces of human life'. It places decisive emphasis on the importance of the 'natural foundations of the *Volk*', the racial aspect. Just as strongly, it stresses the 'special nature of its soul'. It is only the two together, the essential character of nature and soul, which form the whole that is a *Volk*.[42] We again meet a concept of the *Volk* or the community diffusely established in substantive terms. Irrational cognitive procedures are explicitly brought in.

Much the same could be said about the more detailed definition of the Führer principle. Let us go back to only one example from the then standard work by Ernst Rudolf Huber. According to Huber, in the Führer the 'essential laws' of the *Volk* come into manifestation. By allowing these essential laws to emerge he sets up the great common objectives that have to be realised. The Führer 'embodies the overall will of the people as an objective historical quantity'.[43]

b) Method of conceptualisation

If the perception of National Socialist law by constitutional theorists of the time can be summarised and generalised here, the following picture emerges: with the specifically new, National Socialist principles, an openness of content with a negative consensus can be found. On the new concepts propagated by National Socialism there was no substantive agreement. What lawyers regarded

[40] Koellreutter, n 31, at 67.

[41] U Scheuner, Die nationale Revolution, 63 *Archiv des öffentlichen Rechts* 166–220, 261–344 at 273 (1934). On the emergence of this article in connection with the editorial policy of the archive for public law of taking influence on the National Socialist 'renovation of law' cf L Becker, *Schritte auf einer abschüssigen Bahn. Das Archiv des öffentlichen Rechts (AöR) und die deutsche Staatsrechtswissenschaft im Dritten Reich* (Tübingen, Mohr Siebeck, 1999) 96, 103–8.

[42] Scheuner, n 41, at 273. A similar combining of blood and soul can be found in U Scheuner, Der Gleichheitsgedanke in der völkischen Verfassungsordnung, (1939) 99 *Zeitschrift für die gesamten Staatswissenschaften* 245–78 at 256–58.

[43] n 15 Huber, above at 281.

as National Socialist was open, undefined, relative. Nonetheless, they were convinced of the correctness and bindingness of their findings. This discrepancy can be explained only by the dynamic principle in National Socialism. The perception of the core concepts of the National Socialist ideology like *Volk*, *Gemeinschaft* and Führer came about through a special cognitive procedure that dissolved dichotomies. The dynamic, not the content, is the defining feature of the conceptualisations. In this dynamic conceptualisation procedure we also find the decisive characteristic of National Socialist legal thought. National Socialist legal concepts are defined through a specific procedure marked by the transcending and synthesising of contradictory criteria. The concept of the *Volk*, for instance, was defined by a combination of spirit and nature, value and reality, blood and soil, life and history. Even the term National Socialism itself combines two contradictory components, nationalism and socialism, together into one concept, thereby alluding to a synthesis that transcends them. The term 'Third Reich' too suggests a content of expectations of salvation. If these observations can be generalised, the following conclusion may be drawn: antagonisms and dichotomies fell into a combinatory dynamic. Multiplicity of content is constitutively associated with the dynamic procedure.

The method of conceptualisation, not the substantive definition of the concepts, thus contains the specific feature that marks out National Socialist law. It is only in the method of conceptualisation that an autonomous, constructive criterion of National Socialist law can be found, while common features of content can be established at best in negative terms. I wish to call this specific method 'contradiction-transcending concept formation' (*gegensatzaufhebende Begriffsbildung*). Using it, for instance, a term like *Volk* can be redefined without having to focus on a traditional meaning. *Volk* need refer to neither ideal nor real features: it can embrace both. It is just in this that the procedure felt to be new at the time lies: it could be used to suggest that traditional bounds on thought were being overcome and a new stage of knowledge reached, by transcending antagonisms and reaching a new third level. This procedure of transcending contradictions also explains why the substantive openness and subjective arbitrariness remained concealed: if the specific feature is the transcending of traditional oppositions, then it is perfectly natural for different authors to define the traditional criteria differently. This is harmless since the new common feature lies in transcending these oppositions. The new method of concept formation also explains why the authors in National Socialism were so convinced of the rightness and compellingness of their findings. They had the impression of reaching something substantively and methodologically new, of entering a new stage of knowledge. National Socialist legal thinking revealed itself in this respect as philosophical and epistemological wishful thinking.[44]

---

[44] Cf M Leske, *Philosophen im Dritten Reich. Studie zu Hochschul- und Philosophiebetrieb im faschistischen Deutschland* (Berlin, Dietz Verlag, 1990) 117, 187. On the cult of the Führer as epistemological aristocraticism, at 154.

Conversely, this explains why so many scholars were intellectually attracted by National Socialism. Irrespective of various political preferences, National Socialism promised to establish new substance. It offered the chance to realise a philosophical and epistemological programme politically. This explains its great seductive power and the widespread willingness of German academics to collaborate in its advancement and intellectual transposition. In the dynamic procedure of contradiction-transcending concept formation, then, we see the specific feature of National Socialist law linking various authors with differing substantive views. Transcending the antagonisms in something higher concealed the subjective multiplicity of the initial concepts—presupposing a negative basic consensus on the destruction of constitutional categories.

c) Concrete order theory ('konkretes Ordnungsdenken') and concretely general concepts ('konkret-allgemeine Begriffe')

This finding is confirmed by two approaches in legal theory of the times, Carl Schmitt's 'concrete order theory'[45] and Karl Larenz's 'concretely general concepts'[46]. Schmitt and Larenz wanted to offer new methods with which the traditional legal order could be adapted to National Socialist needs.[47] Behind this lay the correct perception that National Socialist law was something qualitatively different that required a method of its own. Both perceived the change as

[45] C Schmitt, *Über die drei Arten des rechtswissenschaftlichen Denkens* (Hamburg, Hanseatische Verlagsanstalt, 1934); see also C Schmitt, 'Nationalsozialismus und Rechtsstaat', (1934) *Juristische Wochenschrift* 713–18. On the concrete order theory see K Anderbrügge, n 19, 106–20; G Balakrishnan, *The Enemy. An Intellectual Portrait of Carl Schmitt* (London, Verso, 2000), 194–7; E-W Böckenförde, Ordnungsdenken, konkretes, (1984) 6 *Historisches Wörterbuch der Philosophie* 1312–5; H Hofmann, *Legitimität gegen Legalität* (Berlin, Duncker & Humblot, 3d ed 1995) 177–87; M Kaufmann, *Recht ohne Regel? Die philosophischen Prinzipien in Carl Schmitts Staats- und Rechtslehre* (Freiburg, Alber, 1988) 355–70; C Graf von Krockow, *Die Entscheidung* (Frankfurt/Main, Campus, 2d ed 1990) 94–104; I Maus, *Bürgerliche Rechtstheorie und Faschismus* (München, Wilhelm Fink, 1980) 131–42, 159; C Möllers, n 23, at 61–64.

[46] K Larenz, *Über Gegenstand und Methode des völkischen Rechtsdenkens* (Berlin, Junker und Dünnhaupt, 1938); see also K Larenz, 'Rechtswissenschaft und Rechtsphilosophie', (1937) 143 *Archiv für die civilistische Praxis* 257–81; K Larenz, Zur Logik des konkreten Begriffs—eine Voruntersuchung zur Rechtsphilosophie, (1940) *Deutsche Rechtswissenschaft* 279–99. On the concretely general concept see: I Maus, 'Juristische Methodik und Justizfunktion im Nationalsozialismus', in H Rottleuthner (ed) *Recht, Rechtsphilosophie und Nationalsozialismus* (Wiesbaden, Steiner, 1983) 176–96 at 183–8; B Rüthers, n 8, 76–98; M La Torre, 'La „Lotta contro il diritto soggetivo". Karl Larenz e la dottrina giuridica nazionalsocialista', (Milano, Giuffré, 1988) 31–51; M La Torre, 'A National Socialist Jurist on Crime and Punishment. Karl Larenz and the so-called „Deutsche Rechtserneuerung"', (1994) 25 *Rechtstheorie* 57–86.

[47] Explicitly C Schmitt, 'Nationalsozialistisches Rechtsdenken', (1934) *Deutsches Recht* 225–9 at 228. See also C Schmitt, 'Unsere geistige Gesamtlage und unsere juristische Aufgabe', (1934) *Zeitschrift der Akademie für Deutsches Recht* 11–12; C Schmitt, 'Die Rechtswissenschaft im Führerstaat', (1935) *Zeitschrift der Akademie für Deutsches Recht* 435–40. Schmitt's objective participation in specific contexts of action in National Socialism has now been shown by D Blasius, *Carl Schmitt* (Göttingen, Vandenhoek und Rupprecht, 2001).

not just a shift in content but a metamorphosis in the basic categories of legal thinking. They sought to grasp and influence this change through thought in terms of concrete order, or the concretely general concepts. Schmitt explicitly fought for a method that could do justice to the new orders of National Socialism, and would require a 'new type of the German lawyer'.[48]

Both approaches are, moreover, an expression of basic philosophical considerations and claim to bring in a new procedure of thought. Schmitt demarcates his method from normativism (statute thinking, as he says) and decisionism (decision thinking, as he says). We can again recognise the pattern of National Socialist legal thinking: the concept of a new stage, promising an advance in knowledge by overcoming traditional contradictions. There is a similar case with Larenz's concretely general concept, which contains transcendence of contradictions in its very name and is moreover justified in Hegelian terms by a synthesis approach to proof.[49] Larenz explicitly bound up the Neo-Hegelian method with National Socialist content.[50]

Conclusions

1 Indefiniteness of content and methodical inevitability

What conclusions can now be drawn from this study of the perception of National Socialist law? At the objective level of the actual legal development we saw that the core and the specific feature of National Socialist legal development was the element of movement and dynamics. At the time it was understood as a legal principle. But it cannot be understood as a legal element, since movement and dynamicisation were outside any legal definition. It is at this point that it coincides with the National Socialist weltanschauung, which similarly had no positively definable content. Statements on the 'objective content' of the National Socialist ideology can thus hardly be made with any certainty. One can scarcely find more than a negative basic consensus and associative appeals with conceptual shells. In this way one can also explain why many interpreters sought to steer National Socialism in terms of content, or to style themselves as self-appointed pioneers of thought. The openness in content of

---

[48] n 47 C Schmitt, above at 228.

[49] On the importance of Neohegelianism for the methodological rather than substantive acceptance of National Socialism cf Lepsius, n 4, 271–86; E Topitsch, *Die Sozialphilosophie Hegels als Heilslehre und Herrschaftsideologie* (Neuwied, Luchterhandt, 1967); H Rottleuthner, 'Die Substantialisierung des Formalrechts. Zur Rolle des Neuhegelianismus in der deutschen Jurisprudenz', in O Negt (ed) *Aktualität und Folgen der Philosophie Hegels* (Frankfurt/Main, Suhrkamp, 1970) 211–64; J Kokert, Briefe, die Geschichte schrieben—Karl Larenz und die nationalsozialistische Zeit, (1999) *Zeitschrift für Neuere Rechtsgeschichte* 23–43.

[50] K Larenz, *Rechts- und Staatsphilosophie der Gegenwart*. (Berlin, Junker und Dünnhaupt, 2 ed 1935) 88, 124, 150.

central principles of National Socialism was a downright invitation to fill the ideological gaps.

At the subjective level, of attempts at scholarly interpretation, we met with a similar finding: the specific feature was not agreement on content. This could be found at best in negative respects, in what one did not want, but not in positive terms, as an objective to be reached in common. The specific feature of National Socialist constitutional theory was the contradiction-transcending method. It is the legal category corresponding to the feature of movement and dynamic in the National Socialist legal principles. It managed to transform the dynamic of National Socialism in legal terms. At the same time the contradiction-transcending method could be interpreted as a revolutionary step in knowledge even outside National Socialism, a new stage in knowledge and perception of reality that had been reached. National Socialism could then be understood as an opportunity for political implementation of an underlying intellectual goal. This is how the impetus to progress and the belief in the rightness of one's own findings can be explained: these are consequences not of closeness in substance, but of methodological procedures.

This explanatory approach, focusing more on philosophical causes, may explain why constitutional theory under Nazi rule overwhelmingly and unscrupulously sacrificed the Weimar constitutional principles. They were victims on the altar of the presumed advancement in knowledge. Faust had indeed met his Mephisto. National Socialism seemed to guarantee an illumination in ideas for the sake of which compromises were to be accepted.

2 Loss of content or loss of method?

The perception of National Socialist law by scholars of the time thus shows a wide range, reflecting the ideological structure of the law. National Socialism could combine different positions of substance because it was open and undefined in content, and even downright invited interpretation. Subjective interpretation presupposes a procedure of contradiction-transcending concept formation. Otherwise, the wide range of content and the openness would have come out. Because of the decisionism of the Führer principle, the indefiniteness of content was on the other hand not a hindrance, but enhanced the need for Führer decisions.

A comparison of the content of subjective positions of particular authors with objective statements of National Socialism meets with insuperable obstacles because of this triangle of openness of content, political decision and methodological determination.[51] Subjective views cannot be compared with objective statements, because there is no substantive basis for comparison. They might at most be found in a vague negative consensus, which however is no

---

[51] n 4, Lepsius, above at 93–97.

more than an indicator. Comparability in positive terms fails because it was in fact an essential feature of National Socialist law not to reach solidly fixed content, but to leave things hovering in an associational syncretism. Openness in principle plus occasional decisions by the Führer make substantive comparison impossible.

This means, first, that comparisons of content of subjective positions of individual authors of National Socialism can promise no decisive result. The classification of writings as National Socialist can simultaneously be affirmed and denied, according to whether agreement in negative terms is regarded as enough and comparatively crude criteria as satisfactory, or else one asks for agreement in positive terms, thereby raising a demand that is in contradiction with the structural features of National Socialism. But this also means that because of the openness in content of the National Socialist ideology, along with the negative basic consensus, positive agreement is not necessary in order to classify particular writings by content as National Socialist. Those using a particular vocabulary and sharing a particular negative consensus were not just subjectively but also objectively moving within the framework of National Socialist ideology.

If a comparative yardstick in content can be found only to a limited extent, this means, secondly, that it can be found only in methodological terms. Here was the very feature of the National Socialist ideology that transformed syncretism of content into an advance in knowledge and enabled the legal transposition of openness of content coupled with one-off decisions. It was only the contradiction-transcending concept formation that could cover differences in content and at the same time raise the impression of substantive closure and determinacy of positions, which however de facto existed neither in the ideology nor among its interpreters.

The evaluation and perception of National Socialism should accordingly pursue less substantive than methodological criteria. Methodological agreement should be established as the decisive classificatory criterion specifically in order to escape the difficulties of classifications of substance. Moreover, it can help to grasp the significant feature of National Socialist law better. Movement and dynamic prevented both canonisation of the substantive content and the fixation of forms of action. Both were preconditions of an ideology of rule based on the Führer's ultimate decision.

The special feature of the methodology of National Socialism lay in its contradiction-transcending basic nature. Typically, contradictory features were transcended and synthesised as a new unity (eg nature and spirit, value and reality, normativity and practicity, descriptive and prescriptive elements). This procedure of conceptualisation is dangerous because it helps to disguise differences in content and at the same time produces the certainty of being able to create something new. This means ruling out legal control mechanisms or subjecting them to a balance where one is ready to sacrifice them to presumed advances in knowledge.

In National Socialism, accordingly, it was not so much the object of law that got lost, but instead specifically legal methods of grasping the objects. The contradiction-transcending, synthesising style of thought concealed the differences of content, created the illusion of an advance in knowledge and sacrificed traditional legal categories. The new method thus proves key to the acceptance of the new law and the associated loss of categories. Legal objects could no longer be grasped by this method, since its very object was to go beyond the traditional constitutional categories. Those who signed on to this sort of mode of thought could no longer draw any boundaries between a legal and an ideological object.

3 Was there a constitutional theory of National Socialism?

We are now in a position to answer our initial question: was there a constitutional theory *of* National Socialism, or merely a constitutional theory *in* National Socialism, the object of which went lost in the course of the 'Third Reich'? One again sees in this question how hard it is to apply comparative criteria of substance to National Socialism. If the object of constitutional theory has got lost through the de facto development of National Socialist constitutional law, is it still possible at all to talk of a constitutional theory of National Socialism? A classification by objective criteria would have to answer this question in the negative. Classification by the subjective ideas of constitutional theorists of the time would, however, have to give the answer 'yes'. It would have to be so answered if the focus were on conceptualisation too.

This leads to an apparently contradictory result: the specific feature of National Socialist law lay in the delegalisation of content and form on the one hand and delegalisation of legal thinking on the other. One can speak of a constitutional theory on National Socialism only if its effect of destroying law is declared to be its object. To that extent a constitutional theory of National Socialism certainly existed, but we cannot define it or even delimit it by legal means.

Once again, we see that the loss of the legal method destroys the object of constitutional legal science. The constitution had deliberately been dropped as an object in National Socialism. Only the State seemed to remain in existence as an object of constitutional theory. But it could no longer be treated as a legal quantity, even if a 'National Socialist State' undoubtedly existed until liberation in 1945. That State was not a suitable object for treatment by legal science. It could only still be grasped in ideological, political, philosophical, spiritual or psychological terms, but not using the resources of law. Lawyers themselves had willingly sacrificed these resources, in the very expectation of sharing in a 'higher knowledge'. It is here that the law-destroying quality of National Socialism is manifest: the sacrifice of definable substantive values and forms in favour of a new methodological procedure had in the end to rob legal science of its object. Crossing presumed legal boundaries was seen by many protagonists of the contradiction-transcending method as its very gain. Historical experience, spiritual and mental depth, irrational folk consciousness: including these and similar factors in the substantive essence cannot be combined with legal method unless a legally definable object is to be sacrificed.

It cannot therefore be surprising if as the outcome of constitutional theory its object, whether constitution or State, had disappeared. This is only the consequence of deliberate application even by lawyers themselves of an irrational method, namely a procedure of contradiction-transcending conceptualisation. Reaching a new stage of knowledge thereby proved to be self-deception. That in the end there was no constitutional theory *of* National Socialism does not ease one's mind, nor exculpate legal scholarship. For in National Socialism, because of its law-destroying nature, there could be no constitutional theory. Having failed to recognise this or done so too late is a reproach that legal science in National Socialism cannot escape. Being able to recognise and avert this is the methodological legacy to the present.

2

LOOKING INTO THE BRIGHTLY LIT ROOM: BRAVING CARL SCHMITT IN 'EUROPE'

Navraj Singh Ghaleigh*

I was an obscure young man of modest descent . . . Neither the ruling strata nor the opposition included me . . . That meant that I, standing entirely in the dark, out of the darkness looked into a brightly lit room . . . The feeling of sadness which filled me made me more distant and awoke in others mistrust and antipathy. The ruling strata experienced anybody who was not thrilled to be involved with them as heterogeneous. It put before him the choice to adapt or to withdraw. So I remained outside.[1]

Raising Doubts, Doubts Resolved

At various points during the gestation of this work, eyebrows were raised as to its relevance, political valency and even moral qualifications. At one point, a colleague made reference to the meeting in an adjacent room, of 'Christian Joerges and his Nazis'. Perhaps barbed, but the sentiments lying beyond that remark have to be answered by every participant in such a project, and probably at some level by anyone who makes the time-investment of reading it. Why expend so much energy exploring the rancid ruminations of the legal profession's darkest luminaries? Other than opportunism and venality (at best), what are we likely to glean from the legal scholarship emerging from National Socialism and Fascism? Even if, as in the instant case, the scope of enquiry is restricted to conceptions and understandings of 'Europe', does it not beggar belief and verge on poor taste to suggest commonalities between *their* conceptual apparatus and *ours*? And this from scholars based at the *European* University Institute!

My initiation to the broad themes of this volume commenced with a series of discussions with Christian Joerges in the autumn of 1999. Then operating

* Lecturer in Public Law at Edinburgh Law School, University of Edinburgh. This chapter was written when the author was a Researcher at the European University Institute. Sincere thanks are owed to Christian Joerges for his comments on this chapter, and support and advice more generally. Errors and opinions are the author's alone.

[1] Carl Schmitt's own account of his arrival in Berlin as a student—from P Noack, *Carl Schmitt: Eine Biographie* (Frankfurt am Main, Ullstein, 1996), quoted in G Balakrishnan, *The Enemy: An Intellectual Portrait of Carl Schmitt* (London, Verso, 2000), 13.

under the title, 'The National Socialist and Fascist Heritage of Legal Thought in Europe', and envisaged as a forum for debate, there was already no denying the subversive, potent quality of an investigation into putative continuities between interwar conceptions of Europe, and contemporary ones. But at the same time, doubts existed. These were not moral doubts about engaging with the authors, apologists or in some cases, the protagonists, of the twentieth century's darkest chapters. Nor was it a fear of giving a platform to their views—the extant scholarship (only a minority of which is legal) deals with these concerns.[2] Rather, the doubts were personal, pertaining to relevance. Was this all not a little too abstruse, too abstract for one conventionally educated in Anglo-American constitutional law and legal theory? Whence the connection for a Left-Liberal British-born Sikh amongst all these Germans and other Central Europeans struggling to come to grips with *their* past, *their* traditions and *their* angst?

These doubts—which may not have exercised a mind better versed in such matters—fell away with the formation of a new Austrian government by Jörg Haider's proto-fascist Freedom Party on 1 February 2000. Suddenly, there was nothing abstract in the slightest about revisiting the concept of Europe as perceived by Fascistic lawyers in middle Europe in the mid-century. The resonances between past and present formulations of a 'European peoples', the debates over democracy, demos and homogeneity, assumed a violent pointedness in an era of European right-wing extremism. Were there other developments to be tracked, remnants to be unearthed, dark luminaries to be revisited? As the project assumed its current form—moving from a state of great expectancy prior to, and then energy after, a highly successful conference in September 2000; to a process of reorientation and reinvigoration through a new seminar series throughout that academic year; onto a sustained period of discussion between and amongst editors and contributors; and all the while against September 11 and its aftermath, and Jean-Marie Le Pen's success in the French Presidential election of 2002—the clarificatory power of this diverse body of thought was continuously reinforced. The new populists, who are surfing so successfully over European anxieties, play the familiar tunes. Fascistic legal thought can not be ignored *ipso facto*. Much of it illuminates contemporary debates, often with a disturbing luminosity, throwing up challenges to current practices that cannot be swept aside. I seek herein to light upon a number of those resonances and tease out the conceptual links between contemporary legal/political thought and its predecessors. The argument does not usefully take the form of 'the Nazis did/thought *x*, and so do some contemporaries, therefore . . .'. Such an

---

[2] See in particular the pithy remark by Baudrillard that, '[A]ll the talk is of the minimizing of Evil, the prevention of violence: nothing but security. This is the condescending and depressive power of good intentions, a power that can dream of nothing except rectitude in the world, that refuses even to consider a bending of Evil, or an intelligence of Evil.' J Baudrillard, *The Transparency of Evil: Essays on Extreme Phenomena* (London, Verso, 1992).

approach is to be found in polemical tracts such as Laughland's and need not be rehearsed here.[3] Rather, we need to pay close attention to arguments and conceptualisations, and through so doing, we are yielded both purchase to understand the operations of political/juridical authority and insights into the genuine difficulties, perhaps even the intractability, of present challenges.

General Schmittian Contributions

One of the central protagonists in this story is, of course, Carl Schmitt, whose work on constitutional law and theory is only recently sufficiently well known in the Anglo-American world as regularly to find itself in the pages of law review articles (having for a number of years been confined to political-theoretical debates). Why should such attention be warranted? Do we have anything to learn from this staggeringly objectionable man and his patchwork quilt of interventionist, often opportunistic, writings? We can move towards an answer by looking at key aspects of Schmitt's Weimar production. It should be noted that the reader who looks for consistent thought in Schmitt is doomed to disappointment. As has been pointed out by perhaps his most sensitive reader, Schmitt's intellectual practices were in accord with his (in)famous vision of politics as the zone of conflict between friends and enemies. His is not at all an *oeuvre* animated by a single hedgehog-like idea but rather is a,

> series of political interventions—partisan theoretical snapshots of the battle zones of Weimar and Nazi era Germany . . . Schmitt's formulations can only be fully grasped when they are seen as responses to positions staked out in a previous conjecture.[4]

But the fact that Schmitt's ideas never crystallised in a systematic manner ought not deter from paying them attention. His sharp engagements with contemporaries and classical political thought offer us a complex insight that hone understanding of our own political conceptualisations, their points of vulnerability and fortitude. What follows has the aim of bringing these very capacities to bear on a range of legal and political phenomena. It has been claimed that,

> one of the most peculiar features of the ongoing English language fascination with Schmitt is its limited impact on *legal* scholars . . . some of Schmitt's more provocative insights about the law have been neglected.[5]

---

[3] J Laughland, *The Tainted Source: The Undemocratic Origins of the European Idea* (London, Warner Books, 1997). Amongst his more restrained findings are the claim that Carl Schmitt's *Großraum* theory is a blueprint for the contemporary European integration project (see the contribution of Joerges in this volume for a sophisticated refutation) at 127, from which it follows (says he) that, 'to allow an entire super-state to be built on illiberal foundations is likely to only further entrench and amplify that heritage.' 162.

[4] G Balakrishnan, 'Among Enemies', *Boston Review*, Summer 2001.

[5] W Scheuerman, 'Down on Law', *Boston Review*, April–May 2001. Emphasis added.

There is doubtless much truth in that observation—indeed, like sentiments substantially animated much of this project—and through drawing on Schmitt's Weimar writings, this argument seeks to demonstrate that his thought frames important conflicts in a terse form. Some of those provocative insights apply to 'liberal law' generally, some to specifically European concerns. The latter focus will be more sustained, but it may be noted that in all cases illumination is cast upon pressing challenges.

To make the general point briefly, we may look to one of Schmitt's earliest works, in which he undertook an analysis of the nature and circumstances of 'dictatorship'.[6] Written against the backdrop of German civil war in 1919, Schmitt highlights the tensions between traditional *Rechtsstaat* doctrines and the implications of the emergency provisions contained in Article 68 of the old Imperial Constitution and Article 48 of the Weimar Constitution. This broad motif was to energise much of the early work. As a central plank of Enlightenment thought, legal liberalism has the ambition of containing the centralised coercive capacities of the modern nation-state by ensuring that state authority is exercised in a constrained manner, *ex ante* and *ex post* (by subjection to formal rules, and subjection to modes of accountability, respectively). Raw political power is hemmed in by law. Within the *Rechtsstaat* tradition, this of course requires that a written constitution establishes the ground rules, that ordinary legislation provides generally applicable and followable rules, and the presence of a separation of powers to enable, inter alia, the courts effectively to supervise governmental exercises of state power.

Schmitt probed this ideal-typical characterisation from a variety of perspectives. In the 1912 work *Gesetz und Urteil*[7] the tack taken—one not alien to Oxford jurisprudence of the 1970s and 1980s—focussed on the indeterminacy of legal rules and the importance of the internal perspective of judicial officers in the interpretive process. However, demonstrating a subtle knowledge of the history of emergency powers, Schmitt later exposed another, more profound fissure in the structure of liberal legal regimes—the prevalent use of emergency laws to afford the executive supremacy over the legislative and judicial branches under the pretext of solving 'exceptional' difficulties. In this way, the gapless conception of Kelsenian positivism is undermined as the pre-established rules are shown not to apply to all eventualities.

Drawing on classical and Renaissance models, Schmitt carefully delineates between permissible and impermissible dictatorial rule, the temporary and the permanent, that which defends and restores republican liberty, and that which terminates it.[8] This 'commissarial' form of dictatorship is to be contrasted with 'sovereign dictatorship' which rather envisages itself as the replacement of the traditional political order, not its saviour, by virtue of its identity with the

---

[6] C Schmitt, *Die Diktatur* (Leipzig, Duncker & Humblot, 1921).

[7] (Munich, CH Beck, 1968).

[8] Above n 1, Balakrishnan 32 in particular the reference to Machiavelli's *Discourses*.

pouvoir constituant which entitles it—in the name of the sovereign people—to recast the constitutional architecture. Schmitt's primary opponent is easily discernible in historical context—left-wing revolutionaries (the fear of whom was shared across almost the entirety of the remainder of the German political spectrum in 1919) embracing untrammelled popular sovereignty and the relentless re-configuration of every structure of social life.[9] Accordingly, at times when the established legal order is fundamentally threatened, a 'constitutional dictatorship' directed solely towards the re-establishment, or defence, of the established order, is justified. These extra-ordinary powers are essentially negative in that the dictator is entitled temporarily to suspend laws and take other emergency measures, but may not legislate in order to ride out exceptional events.

At first blush, to relate such situations and practices to the real world has an outlandish flavour. What *might* have been true in the violent turbulence of the early Weimar period is *surely not* now. We do not recognise our world, our constitutional orders, to be under constant mortal threat, do we? In 1974, a *US Senate Special Committee on National Emergencies* took an opposing view. It noted the presence of,

> at least 470 significant emergency statutes without time limitations delegating to the Executive extensive discretionary powers, ordinarily exercised by the Legislature, which affects the lives of American citizens in a host of all-encompassing ways. Taken together, these powers confer enough authority to rule this country without reference to normal constitutional processes.[10]

Indeed, it was even claimed that the extent of these measures was such that 'emergency government has become the norm'. And further, in the post-September 11 world, exogenous polity-shocks of this nature are not merely imaginable, but imagined to be regular events.[11] But do Schmittian analyses of emergencies bear any resemblance to 'respectable' attempts to understand this critical nexus of constitutional law, emergency powers and body-politic vulnerability? In the various criticisms to the Bush Administration's responses to the terrorist attacks of 11 September 2001, not least from a number of prominent arch-liberals of American legal academe, we find a remarkable degree of

---

[9] 'Out of [popular sovereignty's] endless, elusive, groundless power emerges ever new forms, which it can at any time shatter, never limiting itself.' C Schmitt, at n 6 above, 142. As is well known, Schmitt's formulation of emergency powers underwent an abrupt *volte-face* with the 1922 publication of C Schmitt, *Political Theology: Four Chapters on the Concept of Sovereignty* (Cambridge, MIT Press, 1985)—see Balakrishnan at n 1 above, chs 2–3 and O Gross, 'The Normless and Exceptionless Exception: Carl Schmitt's Theory of Emergency Powers and the "Norm-Exception" Dichotomy' (2000) 21 *Cardozo Law Review*, 1825.

[10] Cited in Gross, *ibid.* at 1830, n 24.

[11] See B Ackerman, 'Don't Panic', *The London Review of Books*, 7 February 2002—'Like it or not, terrorist attacks will be a recurring part of our future . . . The attack of 11 September is the prototype of similar events that will litter the 21st century.'

marching in step.[12] The response of Bruce Ackerman (Yale Law School) is of particular interest.

As might be expected from one of the leading proponents of legal liberalism, Ackerman is critical of the 'extreme actions' of the Bush administration which undermine civil liberties in exchange for the promise of greater security. Amongst the suspect measures are dragnet arrests of over 1,000 suspects in the absence of basic constitutional procedural safeguards such as the naming of those detained and attorney-client confidentiality, the now-notorious special military panels *in lieu* of the conventional judicial process and the deportation of non-citizens for under-determined 'terrorist activities'. Quite apart from their apparent violation of established constitutional norms, such a bout of lawmaking, when coupled with continued terrorist attacks, creates the likelihood, says Ackerman, of a 'destructive cycle' as,

> after each successful attack, politicians will come up with repressive laws and promise greater security—only to find that a different terrorist band manages to strike a few years later. This disaster will, in turn, create a demand for even more repressive laws, and on and on.

The challenge then is how to 'maintain popular support [and act] effectively to calm panic and [try] to prevent future terrorist strikes'. What is needed then are 'new constitutional concepts', counsels Ackerman.

> Defenders of freedom must consider a more hard-headed doctrine—one that allows short-term emergency measures, but draws the line against permanent restrictions . . . government shouldn't be permitted to run wild even during the emergency.

The parallels are, of course, striking. Indeed, Ackerman's 'new constitutional concepts' are nothing of the sort, but in fact well located within a venerable, pre-democratic tradition. In the face of extraordinary threats to the constitutional order from without (civil war in Schmitt's mind, anti-American terrorism in Ackerman's), ordinary constitutional norms are to be added to by yet higher, temporary laws ('Sunset statutes') which give authority to the executive so as to facilitate the re-establishment of constitutional normality. We could of course depart from Schmitt's conclusion that this similarity is a justification of authoritarianism in the presence of political imperatives. However, the exposure of legal liberalism's tendency to paper over these cracks (and what cracks!) is a necessary corrective. Although he does not make the point himself, Ackerman might have noted that emergency moments are more frequent than his own much vaunted 'constitutional moments', and of no small import themselves.

---

[12] Exemplary in this respect are R Dworkin's, 'The Threat to Patriotism', *The New York Review of Books*, 28 February 2002, and Ackerman *ibid*.

Injudicious Justices—A Specifically European Matter

A second aspect of Schmittian thought, and one that will consume the remainder of this chapter, is what might be termed the *Volkish* question—one that assumed the greatest prominence in the aftermath of the German *Bundesverfassungsgericht*'s Brunner decision on the *Treaty on European Union*.[13] The judgment has been prominently criticised on the ground that it amounts to 'little more than a product of a deep historical strand of pre-political illiberality within German constitutional thinking',[14] these being the 'somewhat injudicious ruminations . . . of the German justices.'[15] The nub of Weiler's well-known criticism of this judgment is that in adopting its 'No demos' thesis, the *Bundesverfassungsgericht* and in particular the author of the decision, Justice Kirchhof, has settled upon democratic prerequisites which look back (like Lot's wife, we are told) to an,

> Ethno-culturally homogenous *Volk* and the unholy Trinity of *Volk-Staat-Staatsangehöriger* as the exclusive basis for democratic authority and legitimate rule-making . . . What is interesting and, in my view, rather troubling is the basis on which the German Court's scepticism is founded.[16]

And what exactly is the troubling substance at hand? The operative author of the judgment is identified as Carl Schmitt himself,[17] and its troubling basis is the 'no demos' thesis—the understanding that the pre-conditions for democratic discourse stipulate a substantial degree of homogeneity amongst the membership of a putative polity, reflecting the pre-political predilections of the *Bundesverfassungsgericht*'s members. The notion is further specified as consisting of:

> . . . common language, common history, common cultural habits and sensibilities and—this is dealt with more discretely since the twelve years National Socialism—common ethnic origin, common religion . . . [and] one will always find allusions to some spiritual, even mystic elements as well.[18]

Taken together, the inherent objectionableness of ethno-cultural categories, the resurgence of anti-Semitism across Europe, so-called 'ethnic cleansing' in the former Yugoslavia, and the National Socialist overtones of this conceptual apparatus, give us sound reasons to reject such an argument and perforce its

---

[13] [1994] *Common Market Law Review* 57. The case has generated enormous comment—see the following citation for references to that literature.

[14] M Everson, 'Beyond the Bundesverfassungsgericht: On the Necessary Cunning of Constitutional Reasoning' (1998) 4 *European Law Journal*, 391, referring to the assessment in J Weiler, 'Does Europe Need a Constitution? Demos, Telos and the German Maastricht Decision' (1995) 1 *European Law Journal*.

[15] *Ibid*, Everson at 400.

[16] Above n 14, Weiler 223–24.

[17] Above, at n 10.

[18] Above n 10, 225–26.

principle exponent, Schmitt. But is this a faithful interpretation of Schmitt's thought? And if it is not, can it actually advance the task of shaping a meaningfully described, normatively appealing, European polity? I argue that not only is this aspect of Schmittian thought not properly characterised by Weiler, but if it were to be, we would discover that: (1) Schmitt's conception of democratic pre-conditions is perfectly consistent with contemporary 'acceptable' political theory on the matter and; (2) it brings challenges of European integration and constitutionalism to a sharp focus.

The very use of the 'no demos' thesis and its imputations of racial homogeneity instantly raises hackles in the context of a thinker not merely associated with National Socialism but who served as a legal advisor to von Papen and Goering. We can of course condemn by association, but professional considerations may also demand that we ask what exactly is meant by the notion of 'homogeneity', as used by Schmitt. Some commentators have assumed the worst. Richard Wolin, one of the most active archivists of Heideggerian thought and its influence, has recently claimed that Schmitt's insistence on the necessity of homogeneity in a demos for a state's self-preservation is an 'idea with unmistakable racial overtones'.[19] But this is a mere claim, one assumed without textual reference. Indeed, the ease of the assumption is given away when at one point Wolin translates *Artgleichheit* as 'racial homogeneity'[20] but later, translates the same word, more accurately, simply as 'homogeneity'.[21]

Further, and somewhat more decisively, when we do go to the text itself, *pace Wolin*, we find that not only is there no evidence of a racial or biological argument (in their Weimar works' rejection of biological classifications, Schmitt and Heidegger distinguished themselves from many other Nazi goons),[22] but that such classifications are explicitly rejected. In what is commonly agreed to be Schmitt's most significant contribution to constitutional theory, *Verfassungslehre*,[23] the nature of the political community is twice made out:

[19] R. Wolin, *Heidegger's Children : Hannah Arendt, Karl Löwith, Hans Jonas, and Herbert Marcuse* (Princeton, Princeton University Press, 2001), 90.

[20] Above, at 26.

[21] Above, at 90. For other instances of Wolin's own, idiosyncratic, understandings of Schmitt, see JP McCormick, *Carl Schmitt's Critique of Liberalism: Against Politics As Technology* (Cambridge, Cambridge University Press, 1997), 4 at n 8.

[22] See the remarks of George Steiner in reference to Heidegger, which substantially apply to Schmitt also:

'His own conduct towards certain Jewish colleagues when Hitler assumed power displayed a complex brew of opportunism, mendacity and nastiness. None the less, the problem of Heidegger's attitudes to Jews remains exactly that. In the works as we have them, there is no substantive trace of any biological racism. The whole issue seems to have been to Heidegger utter nonsense or simply left him indifferent. Hence the Nazi regime's early finding that Heidegger would be 'useless' to them. The ugliness remains that of Heidegger's studied silence after 1945 in regard to the Holocaust.'

'Seeing the Master Clearly', *The Times Literary Supplement*, 18 January 2002.

[23] C Schmitt, *Verfassungslehre* (Berlin, Duncker & Humblot, 1928).

'Nation' and 'Volk' are often treated as synonymous concepts, but the word 'nation' is terser, and less subject to misunderstanding. It designates, that is, the 'Volk' as a unit of political action, while the Volk that does not exist as a Nation is only some kind of ethnic or cultural group, not, however, a real political bond among human beings.

Diverse elements can contribute to the unity of the nation, and to the consciousness of this unity: common speech, common historical fates, traditions and memories, common political goals and hopes. Language, while it is an important factor, is not in itself decisive . . . Authentic revolutions and victorious wars can overcome linguistic oppositions and establish the feeling of national belonging, even when the same language is not spoken.[24]

One cannot read these extracts without being struck with their lack of fit with the content, the values and the general outlook attributed to this aspect of Schmittian thought by Weiler.[25] We have here the explicit rejection of the notion of ethnic or cultural grouping as necessary for the creation of a national bond. We have an explicit endorsement of 'diverse elements', of heterogeneity, not least of language.[26] What is important is not a common tongue, but the establishment of feelings of national belonging, through shared futures, shared values and aspirations. It is surely not objectionable then, armed with this understanding of the *Volk*/nation, to accept it as the basis for the democratic state, constituting the very polity that will then accept the coercive power of government. After all, if the common goals of a putative polity cannot be shared, one is well placed to ask whether a common government is appropriate, much less whether it is likely to succeed. There is scant evidence here of the sort of 'homogeneity, measured by . . . ethno-cultural criteria [which] is typically an important, indeed critical element of the discourse.'[27] Whilst that may well be a feature of other currents of German citizenship debates,[28] it is not one that can be imputed to Schmitt's writing on the pre-conditions for the nation state. And it may be the case that Weiler's arguments have some purchase on Kirchhof's democratic pre-requisites but such objectionable configurations are not merely absent from *Verfassungslehre* but explicitly rejected by it, supplanted by diametrically opposed energies.

For the avoidance of all doubt, it should be stated transparently that no attempt is made herein to acquit Schmitt of charges of anti-Semitism. Such an

---

[24] *Ibid* at 79 and 231.

[25] It is interesting to note that although Weiler makes a reference to the latter of these two extracts, at n 10 of his article, he does not cite from it. Nonetheless, Weiler is far from alone in imputed to Schmitt an ethnically-based conception of homogeneity—see too, Scheuerman, at n 5 above.

[26] Cf D Grimm, 'Does Europe Need a Constitution?' (1995) 1 *European Law Journal*, 282–302, which takes a markedly less heterogeneous view on linguistic diversity—Grimm was himself, of course, a Justice of the *Bundesverfassungsgericht*.

[27] Above n 14, Weiler 226.

[28] Above n 14 as Weiler himself points out, quite correctly, at 224–27.

endeavour would be futile and repugnant. We are aware of his self-serving passivity as Jewish friends and colleagues were dismissed from the universities after
April 1933. He joined the Party the following month, and ambitiously reaped
the benefits to be had from that association, by means including the revision of
earlier work. Schmitt's response to the 'Night of the Long Knives' was to pen
an appalling justificatory text—*The Führer Protects the Law*[29]—and his adoption of visceral anti-Semitism to protect his position in the Party (unsuccess-
fully) in 1936 is beneath comment. Rather, my point is that, like Heidegger,
Schmitt's anti-Semitism, was essentially opportunistic, not an intellectual commitment nor programmatic.[30] This absolves him in a moral sense not at all. But
it does give grounds for raising the burden of proof as to his racialist motiva-
tions, especially in respect of those works published well before the commencement of the Nazi era. From this, there moves a strong argument as to the
mistaken attribution of ethnic/cultural overtones to 'no demos'-type arguments, at least to the extent that they are attributable to Schmitt. This scarcely
amounts to a ringing endorsement of the argument itself, much less as one that
gives us any leverage on the task of understanding the democratic enterprise
itself. A return to contemporary legal/political theory again provides some
assistance, this time from the recent work of Philip Pettit.

In a 'first principles' approach to the architecture of a republican notion of
democracy, Pettit rejects familiar, majoritarian bases (giving voice to the will of
the people, ensuring equality between citizens etc), and argues instead that the
normative role of a system of government rests on four presumptions:

(1) if a population desires government, then that body of people will share
    certain common interests (CI)
(2) CI will be recognisable to a given population upon reflection and discus-
    sion (they are not simply 'out there')
(3) government should be oriented towards the satisfaction of these common
    recognisable interests (CRI)
(4) only CRI should guide government—it shall have no other masters

For present purposes, only the first of these presumptions is of direct relevance,
although readers will certainly profit from reading the entirety of the argument.[31] Accordingly, we note that from the first, the notion of 'common interests' bears a significant load and so it must accordingly be well specified and

---

[29] See, JP McCormick, 'Political Theory and Political Theology: The Second Wave of Carl
Schmitt in English' (1998) *Political Theory*, 830–54. For further details and references, see the
dedicated work, R Gross, *Carl Schmitt Und Die Juden : Eine Deutsche Rechtslehre* (Frankfurt am
Main, Suhrkamp, 2000).

[30] See Steiner at n 22 above, and also Balakrishnan at n 1 above, 204–8.

[31] See in particular, P Pettit, *A Theory of Freedom: From the Psychology to the Politics of
Agency* (Cambridge, Polity, 2001), ch 7. For an earlier, non-republican, version of the same argu-
ment see P Pettit, *Democracy, Electoral and Contestatory* in I Shapiro and S Macedo (eds),
Designing Democratic Institutions (New York, New York University Press, 2000), 105–44.

detailed so as to do the work sought of it. The idea, expressed abstractly, is contractarian in character—readers of Rawls will be somewhat familiar with the hypothetical bargain it invokes. Simply, *if* the populace were to engage in discussions about what it ought to cooperate in collectively providing, *then* common interests would be those considerations which could not be dismissed as irrelevant. In other words, since no participant in the debate could dismiss them as irrelevant, they are not sectional interests, and every party would have a reason to heed them.[32] This is not the same as saying that everyone will agree about everything, if only they are given the opportunity to reflect on their disagreements! It is almost inevitable that rival sets of initiatives will arise that will benefit different groups differentially, but this is not a fatal difficulty. In cases of conflicting interests, it will invariably be the case that there will be one further collectively avowable consideration—that everyone is worse off if no agreement is found between rival schemes. In such circumstances, mechanisms will be found for resolution (tossing a coin, adjudication, voting etc). In the absence of the possibility of resolution (no one is willing to compromise their position for they fear that their position would be wholly undermined by so doing), we may not unreasonably conclude that single government is not a desirable solution for that population. Specified appropriately, absent an 'ethno-cultural' framework, the requirement of homogeneity, ceases to become an objectionable democratic precondition, but instead reveals itself to be both a necessary and liberal feature of the self-governing polity. Why would we expect a collective of individuals who conceive of their interests, futures, values etc as diverse and distinct (that is, not shared) desire to exist under a common government? As Pettit puts it,

> That a group has certain interests in common does not pre-suppose that members already enjoy equal economic standing or identical cultural affiliations; the required commonality of interests is wholly consistent with economic, social and indeed ethnic diversity.[33]

To Close / Too Close?

The title of this chapter alludes to the sense of estrangement felt by the young Schmitt in the cosmopolitan splendour of Berlin. The choice (he felt) he faced, a provincial Catholic from a petit-bourgeois family, was to align and engage, or reject. He opted for the latter, although when the National Socialist revolution offered him the opportunity to become an insider, he grabbed at it. This personal vignette speaks on a couple of registers. Schmitt's position probably closely reflects that of those who come to the corpus of fascistic legal scholarship anew from the Anglo-American tradition. For legal scholars without a

---

[32] Technically put, common interests are 'cooperatively avowable considerations'.
[33] Above n 31, P Pettit, 158.

grounding in the mores of Germanic law or the political theory of that time and place, these are writings with questionable intellectual merit and of no moral appeal. The energy expended by continental scholars is a curiosity indeed and offers little transparent incentive for engagement. Those who do take this body of work seriously are viewed with 'mistrust and antipathy'—viz. 'Christian Joerges and his Nazis'. Both at the general legal level, and at the specifically European one, this chapter and others in this volume aim to offer sound reasons for such scepticism to be displaced, for gaps to be bridged. True, they can, were and occasionally are, turned to objectionable ends, but as the juxtaposition with Ackerman shows, Schmittian thought not infrequently parallels approaches we would not shirk from ourselves.

Further, and of greater moment for the undertaking of European integration, the insider/outsider motif from Schmitt's juvenile account speaks to a broader concern, and one with European particularities. The insistence on homogeneity need not, and does not when the actual text in *Verfassungslehre* is looked at, have implications that ought embarrass or trouble us. Indeed, one might ask what it is that distinguishes Schmitt's requirement that members of a polity share common aspirations and political goals that transcend their particular traditions, from Pettit's 'common interests', or even Habermasian '*Verfassungspatriotismus*'? In the context of the ongoing project European integration, an attentiveness to such questions is all the more vital. And perhaps troubling too. The widespreadedness of 'mistrust', 'choosing to withdraw' and 'remaining outside' on the part of Europeans is the most powerful force hindering the authentic creation of a European citizenry, a European polity, and a European constitutional order, meaningfully termed. The attainment of these goals appears to require that the diverse elements of Europe would need to recognise one another as sharing 'common speech, common historical fates, traditions and memories, common political goals and hopes'. If this is so, then perhaps the most potent threat of Schmitt's thought to Europe is not that it will embed illiberal traditions but rather that it will reveal the scale of that lofty aspiration.

PART II

The Era of National Socialism and Fascism

3

THE FASCIST THEORY OF CONTRACT

Pier Giuseppe Monateri* and Alessandro Somma†

Keywords and Formalisms of the Debate on Juridical Fascism

The reflection carried out by German authors on National Socialism and the law has taken on the dimension of a debate the features of which have impressed Italian scholars. First of all, it is a debate that involves a considerable number of jurists, and therefore it is not the marginal occupation of a limited circle of enthusiasts. In the second place, it is not a debate conditioned by the intent of preserving the scientific and moral integrity of the masters whose activity is under discussion or of complying with the protective instinct of their disciples. Finally, it is a debate characterised by a prominent interdisciplinary vocation and, therefore, by methods less susceptible to the charm of the formalistic approach.

In Italian literature the features of the scientific discussion regarding law in the Fascist time are different. It is carried out against the background of a dispute about the role of the relationship between intellectuals and the Fascist regime stimulated by the intent of finding its most open supporters, thus neglecting the ample circle of those who simply made the totalitarian perversion possible by attitudes that were in other respects not so markedly referable to the dominant ideology.[2] This approach becomes an expedient by which any continuity of the twenty years of Fascism with the immediately preceding or following periods can be denied. It combines with the intent of maintaining that intellectuals are substantially impervious to the regime, and that such condition concerns most of all the juridical science.[3]

* Professor of Law, University of Turin and Faculté Internationale de Droit Comparé, Strasbourg.

† Researcher, Max Planck Institut für Europäische Rechtsgeschichte and Professor, University of Genoa. Quotations translated by Iain L. Fraser.

[2] See A Somma, 'Fascismo e diritto: una ricerca sul nulla?', (2001) *Rivista trimestrale di diritto e procedura civile* at 617.

[3] Such trend is developed in particular by those scholars who adopt the conception of Crocian origin elaborated by N Bobbio, 'La cultura e il fascismo', in *Fascismo e società italiana* (Torino, Einaudi, 1973) at 209.

In the wake of these specifications it is asserted that

the regime's policy is paid extrinsic homage: 'no historian whose gaze is directed at the salient features of the two decades rather than to rare, limited episodes, will wish to talk about a fascist doctrine of private law, seeing the period as showing a break with the diplomatic method and with the tradition of our schools'.[4]

A similar opinion is expressed with regard to the codificazioni mussoliniane: The Italian codes published from 1930 to 1942 to which they wished to give a fascist stamp, draw largely on the old codes and existing doctrine, even though shaped in a different climate: instead of denying the old legislation and established doctrine, something that would have been impossible, they believed they were taking them over and merely grafting the new shoots into them, so that everything would have a new approach and a different spirit; to the extent that today it is easy to de-fascistify, so to speak, these codes, just by eliminating those new sprouts.[5]

The above quoted opinions are founded on an implied premise: that the formulas used in legal texts and in doctrinal discussion are capable of expressing univocal constructions, regardless of the cultural context in which they are used. Such premise leads to deny that the so-called lip service paid to the regime contributes to the definition of the rule. With specific reference to private law, it leads to insist blindly on a jus-rationalist assertion: namely the necessary Anti-Fascist value of a contract discipline claiming to be constructed around the principles deriving from Roman Law.[6]

The link between Roman Law and the liberal juridical culture is hinted at on different occasions, starting at least from the well-known dispute opposing the Bernhard Windscheid Romanists to the Otto Gierke Germanists in the course of drafting the German Civil Code currently in force. On the other hand such link is disproved if one examines the life of the *Bürgerliches Gesetzbuch*: this text begins in the Germany of Wilhelm II and survives the Weimar Republic. The same text remains in force during National Socialism and after the World War II it constitutes for almost three decades the core of printed law of the German Democratic Republic private law. The reference to the National Socialist experience is therefore of sure interest for studying juridical Fascism: an interest that, in fact, is justified not only on a scientific level. As the existence and the features of National Socialist private law are largely agreed upon, identifying analogies with the Fascist experience actually contributes to temper the ideological conflict that, especially in the Italian context, still accompanies the investigations devoted to the theme which is the object of these notes.

---

[4] N Irti, 'Diritto civile', in *Digesto delle discipline privatistiche—Sezione civile* VI (Torino, Utet, 1990) at 138.

[5] B Biondi, *Il diritto romano cristiano* I (Milano, Giuffré, 1952).

[6] Above. See A Somma 'Roma madre delle leggi. L'uso politico del diritto romano', (2002) *Materiali per la storia della cultura giuridica* at 149.

A Possible Way Out: The Comparison with Juridical National Socialism

There are many connections—mostly highlighted by the theories about Fascism as a European phenomenon—between the Fascist and National Socialist experiences. In particular, both regimes develop in a common economic and social background which at first feeds their revolutionary potential and later on, instead, calls for adaptation to the status quo: for this purpose they start building a productive system formally based upon co-operation among the classes but, in fact, sensitive to the request of major industry. Further, Fascism and National Socialism share the view of State organisation as a power instrument in the hands of the *leader* and therefore the construction of a legal system aimed at minimising and controlling individual action.[7]

Such circumstances lead, during the twenty years of Fascism, to a comparative study of Fascism and National Socialism, centred on themes of public and political importance in a broad sense: in particular about the idea of State developed in both experiences by the scholars who were close to the political power. The system of private law is also of interest for the scholars of the time. Besides, both National Socialists and Fascists tackle problems connected with the codification of civil law and with overcoming of the values which inspire the texts in force at the time. And this is one of the aims of the Italo-German juridical Committee—Comitato giuridico italo-germanico—constituted to co-ordinate the collaboration between the scholars of the two countries.[8]

Some passages of the *Nationalsozialistische Deutsche Arbeiterpartei* (NSDAP) program are indeed devoted to the reform of the German legal system. It says that each German citizen has the duty of acting both spiritually and materially for the common interest (item 10) and that it is up to the State, in this perspective, to fight those who act to the prejudice of the common needs (item 18). It also says that it is necessary to substitute the Roman Law 'subservient to the world-wide materialistic order' with the German common law: 'Wir fordern ersatz für das der materialistischen Weltordnung dienende römische Recht durch ein deutsches Gemeinrecht' (item 19).[9]

In private law, such intents lead to cancelling most laws and institutions based in different ways on the Kantian philosophy and therefore refusing the jus-rationalist perspective of the legal system as a complex of duties: 'if

---

[7] See AJ De Grand, *L'Italia fascista e la Germania nazista* (Bologna, Il Mulino, 1999) and N Tranfaglia, *Fascismi e modernizzazione in Europa* (Torino, Bollati Boringhieri, 2001).

[8] The Committee is mentioned in Art 7 of the Cultural Agreement between the Italian Reign and the German Reich dated 23 November 1938. In this regard S Messina, 'Origini scopi ed organizzazione del Comitato', 1938 *Lo Stato* at 387.

[9] See D Simon, 'Die deutsche Wissenschaft vom römischen Recht nach 1933', in M Stolleis and D Simon (eds), *Rechtsgeschichte im Nationalsozialismus* (Tübingen, Nomos, 1989) at 161. In the literature of the time see E Jung, 'Deutschrechtliches und Römischrechtliches zur Reform des Bürgerlichen Rechts', (1934) *Zeitschrift der Akademie für Deutsches Recht*, at 183.

National Socialism subordinates the individual to the community, it must also reverse the hierarchical relationships between law and the individual will, making the general will the master and the party's the servant.'[10]

Within the indicated perspective, the underrating of individual interests is clearly the element characterising the National Socialist experience, which identifies in the struggle against the liberal ideology the only course to reconstruct a legal system based on the duties of individuals and on the glorification of the prerogatives pertaining to the group: 'the individual is of importance not for his own sake but because of his position in the community.'[11]

It is widely known that in the National Socialist ideology the group on which the destiny of the individuals depends, has in the first place a racial connotation. However, references to its economic value often prevail, and together with them, statements regarding subordination of the individual needs to the requirements of production: 'On the National Socialist idea of law, concluding a contract is, even from the point of view of legal policy, a community matter, so that the state's action upon the conclusion of contracts may be required. All general or specific sovereign orders to this effect are guidance measures . . . these measures are an expression of the state guided economy.'[12]

As an implementation of this program, a number of special laws are developed with regard to different aspects of the discipline of the relations among individuals. Most of all, the National Socialist doctrine intends to replace the Bürgerliches Gesetzbuch with a 'popular' code: the Volksgesetzbuch.[13] This project, anyway, does not appear to be a political priority of the regime, whose interest seems rather to be directed to conditioning the application of the law and therefore to formulating keywords expressing a use of the law in force as an instrument to impose the Führer's will.[14]

Comparisons Between Fascist and National-Socialist Private Law: In Particular the Debate on the Value of Roman Law

National Socialists and Fascists are joined in the fight against the values believed to be expressed by the Liberal juridical thought. Even in Italian

---

[10] H Lange, Vom alten zum neuen Schuldrecht (Hamburg, Hanseat Verl.anst 1934).

[11] H Lange, Liberalismus Nazionalsozialismus und Bürgerliches Recht (Tübingen, Nomos, 1933). In the same way see for example G Böhmer, Einführung in das Bürgerliche Recht (Leipzig, Weicher, 1932) and H Stoll, Vertrag und unrecht, 3. Aufl., 1. Halbb. (Tübingen, Mohr, 1943).

[12] H Stoll, ibid also see among others K Larenz, Vertrag und Unrecht, Theil 1 (Hamburg, Hanseat. Verl.anst., 1936).

[13] In the literature of the time see for example HW Hedemann, 'Arbeit am Volksgesetzbuch', (1941) Deutsches Recht, at 1913 and H Lehmann, Vom Werden des Volksgesetzbuchs, (1942) Deutsches Recht at 1492.

[14] See in particular H Frank, 'Gesetzgebung und Rechtsprechung im Dritten Reich', (1936) Zeitschrift der Akademie für Deutsches Recht, at 137 and H Lange, Vom alten zum neuen Schuldrecht, loc. cit.

literature, the individualist framework of the private system inherited from the past is criticised[15] and especially those civil law codifications are attacked, which 'aimed particularly at recognising individual interests, while banning consideration of the rights of labour understood as a social function or of the objectives, including the collective ones, of the exchange of goods.'[16]

As we have already seen, the National Socialist scholars conceive the struggle against the Liberal laws as a glorification of the German juridical experience and a contextual abandoning of the Roman one. Some authors close to the Fascist Regime express themselves in the same way, demanding to give up the

> farce of the defence of roman law, which was aimed at making specific the confirmation of the liberal system in this sphere of law and the paraphrasing of the Napoleonic code as a fascist codification.[17]

On the other hand, Italian scholars of the Fascist period do not approve of such statements and, on the contrary, claim a solid link with the Roman law.[18] Actually, the Fascist authors work in a context which the traditional structures are still solid, and in this perspective they are interested in legitimating the regime by excluding a break with the past. This does not mean, however, promoting values alternative to those implied by the National Socialist reference to German law: for Fascists 'Roman-Italic law is the living law of the Roman, authoritarian, hierarchical, expansionist state.'[19] Thus, Dino Grandi was able to address the German jurists by stating:

> You National Socialist comrades seeking to achieve the purest tradition of Germanism and the German race, and we Fascists, steadfast protagonists of the Roman law that is the law of our Italian race, are closely linked by the clear unity of our future.[20]

Fascists and National Socialists also share the belief that private law is to be seen as a complex of duties assigned to the members of society for the common needs.[21] Even among Italian scholars, the underrating of individuals is further

---

[15] As appears, for instance, from G Scaduto, 'Introduzione al libro primo del nuovo codice civile', (1939) *Rivista di diritto commerciale* at 321 and FM Dominedò, 'Studi sulle fonti del diritto', (1942) *Rivista di diritto commerciale* at 1942, I, 203. See also PB Bellomo, *Dallo stato liberale alla politica corporativa* (Padova, Cedam, 1936) and C Costamagna, 'La Carta del lavoro nella Costituzione italiana', (1940) *Lo Stato* at 530.

[16] G De Semo, 'La riforma dei codici e la nuova partizione del diritto privato', (1942) *Diritto e pratica commerciale* at 166. Similarly F Maroi, 'La codificazione fascista del diritto civile', (1941) *Monitore dei tribunali* at 65 and S Panunzio, 'Il problema dei codici e i limiti della codificazione', (1936) Lo Stato at 647.

[17] [C Costamagna], 'Professori ebrei e dottrina ebraica', (1938) *Lo Stato* at 490.

[18] Among many others G Maffei, 'La concezione anti-romana razzista del diritto', (1934) Lo Stato at 674.

[19] D Grandi, *Tradizione e rivoluzione dei Codici Mussoliniani* (Roma, 1940).

[20] D Grandi, 'Diritto romano-fascista e germanico-nazista di fronte alla rivoluzione del secolo XX', in (1941) *Monitore dei tribunali* at 3.

[21] See for all A Asquini, 'Unificazione del diritto delle obbligazioni', (1938) *Lo Stato* at 413.

aimed at defending 'the race, understood as governing the Italian family, its civilisation and its law,' [22] such aim leads to establishing the rule according to which 'the limitations of legal capacity deriving from membership in certain races shall be laid down by special laws. (Art 1 of the Italian Civil Code)'[23]

However, in the Fascist literature the intent of supporting economic interests, and in particular the necessities of National production, prevails. Italian authors substantially agree in believing that such circumstance may be ascribed to the development of the corporative idea of State[24] and in underlining that it lead to exalting themes such as enterprise productivity and economic solidarity in the superior interest of the Nation.[25] For this purpose the Labour Chart states that the production objectives 'are unitary and can be summarised in the prosperity of individuals and the development of national strength' and that 'the organiser of the undertaking is responsible for guiding production vis-à-vis the state.'

Even with specific reference to the law of obligations, Fascists and National Socialists have the opportunity to draw the guidelines of a common development of the Italian and German legal systems. These aspects are dealt with in the course of a meeting of the Italo-German juridical Committee, held in Rome in the summer of 1938. On this occasion, Alberto Asquini notices that

> the determination of general principles of a binding nature by which the new law of obligations should be informed ought to be a translation of the practice of the political spirit of the reform, bringing into the new system of law of obligations, the principles of the new fascist and national socialist legal doctrine.

Similarly Hans Carl Nipperdey observes:

> while remaining loyal to the fundamental principles of private property, contractual freedom, the right to free competition and the right to private association, both nations take the view that these principles have decisively changed the meaning in the fascist and national socialist interpretation, from the influence of the principle of the individual's responsibility towards the collectivity. Both nations see the principles of private law thus characterised as a species of constitutional law in the context of private law, in the sense not of defending the individual against the excessive power of the state, but of grounding civil life in the collectivity's interests, for the good of the nation.[26]

---

[22] F Maroi, 'La codificazione fascista del diritto'.

[23] For references to the Italo-German co-operation in building a racist legal system see 'Razza e diritto al convegno italo-tedesco di Vienna', (1939) *Lo Stato* at 129.

[24] See A Aquarone, *L'organizzazione dello stato totalitario*, 2. ed. (Torino, Einaudi, 1995).

[25] In the literature of the time see among many others S Pugliatti, 'L'ordinamento corporativo e il codice civile', (1942) *Rivista di diritto commerciale* at I, 358.

[26] See 'Il comitato giuridico Italo-germanico per la riforma del diritto delle obbligazioni', (1938) *Rivista di diritto commerciale* at I, 437.

National Socialism and the Law of Contracts: From the Bilateral Juridical Transaction to the Agreement for Exchange of Goods and Services

Fascists and National Socialists devote another meeting of the Italo-German juridical Committee to the contractual matter: the one held in Vienna in the spring of 1939. On that occasion they discuss the principle of freedom of contract to affirm its value only in the 'limits of the new principles of the public order of the two nations' and to specify that the same is abused

> not only in cases of breach of express prohibitions of statutes or good custom, but also in cases of breaches of the principles of the national political order and the fundamental rules of the economy laid down by the state.[27]

Along these guidelines the law of contracts is re-examined and in particular its traditional aspects referable to the theory of individual rights are removed.

In Germany, first of all the equation identifying contracts with a bilateral juridical transaction is abandoned. In fact, the abstraction principle is criticised, and with it also the identification of contract aimed at the immediate transfer of real rights as an independent figure of the law of goods.[28] It is also specified that the cases regarding the individual position in respect of the social formations, in particular in family law and in labour law, do not constitute contracts.[29] In this way, the contract is confined to cases in which the parties exchange individual goods and services:

> Engagement, marriage, taking up employment, are not in our sense contracts, since they do not have as their object the change of individual services or goods but the incorporation of the whole personality into a community.[30]

Obviously, the limitation of contracts to the cases of exchange of goods and services depends on considerations regarding the emphasis on the act with respect to the contractual bond. Such limitation is also a means to underline subordination of the parties' interests to those promoted by the legal system. And indeed, on one hand, in the National Socialist literature the relation between debtor and creditor is qualified as a bond between co-operating parties. On the other hand, it is said that the external control on the contract derives from considerations concerning the execution of its performance according to the bona fine principle:

---

[27] G Vassalli, 'Per un diritto unico delle obbligazioni', (1939) *Lo Stato* at 206.

[28] See F Wieacker, *Zum system des deutschen Vermögensrechts. Erwägungen und Vorschläge* (Leipzig, Weicher, 1941).

[29] See for instance W Siebert, 'Ergebnisse und Vorschläge zum System des deutschen Vermögensrechts', (1941) *Deutsches Recht* at 1506.

[30] K Larenz, 'Neubau des Privatsrechts', (1939) *Archiv für die civilistische Praxis* at 93.

The community is certainly interested that the relationship of obligation no longer be a struggle between creditor and debtor, and that one party not be free to deploy any means whatever in the fight against the other.[31]

It is worth noticing that in this way the reference to good faith is not connected with the *jus-rationalist fides*: it does not lead, in fact, to suppress the principle of the freedom of contract to give prominence to the opposite principle of contractual equity. The legal system, in fact, prevails on the private act for aims placed beyond the parties' horizon and not corresponding to the intent of achieving the balance of performances:

good faith is after all not a requirement for a fair weighing of interests between the contracting parties in the sense of a secondary principle or recourse, but that this principle has to be seen as a concrete expression of the just idea of the contract.' Therefore, 'good faith is a primary and obvious basic principle, in the sense of confirming the common membership of the contracting parties in the national community, and the social function of the contract.[32]

Such formulation is insisted upon during the works for the drafting of the *Volksgesetzbuch*. On that occasion it is underlined in particular that the law of contract must be restricted to the exchange of goods and services. It is also confirmed that this institution must be reconstructed from the point of view of the bond, ignoring its formation. This latter suggestion is the maxim founding the known theory of the 'de facto' contractual relations, carried out by legal writers close to the National Socialist political power.[33] However, in the intention of its founder it is not aimed at preventing the application of the civil code, but only at avoiding recourse to legal fictions. In this sense, it would not represent an element of crisis in the traditional doctrine of contracts, but simply an integration of the same.[34]

Fascism and the Law of Contracts Between Tradition and Innovation

We have said before that Fascists and National Socialists recognise themselves in the statement according to which the free private enterprise is a value to be re-examined in the light of the maxims formulated by the regime. In the Italian context such idea causes a re-examination of the contractual matter in less strict terms than in the German formulation. And yet it leads to promote solutions

---

[31] G Vassalli, above n 27.

[32] W Siebert, 'Contrato y libertad de contratación en el nuevo sistema del Derecho alemán', (1942) *Revista de derecho privado* at 454.

[33] G Haupt, 'Über faktische Vertragsverhältnisse', in *Festschrift der Leipziger Juristenfakultät für H. Siber zum 10. April 1940*, II (Leipzig, Weicher, 1943) at 3.

[34] G Haupt, above n 33.

characterising the system of the sources of law 'in senso pubblicistico e corporativo';[35] unification of the law of obligations and of contracts is among these solutions.[36] The patterns deriving from it often laid 'the emphasis on the productivity of the undertaking, economic solidarity and the superior interests of the nation.'[37]

A selection of material regarding the codification of private law allows some traditional solutions to be found together with interventions in the opposite sense. To the former kind belong the descriptions of the law of obligations as a subject matter 'that has remained closer to the classical roman model, not wrongly described as reason put down in writing.' To the latter, instead, the glorifications of the law of contracts as a sector of the legal system in which 'the obligations are strictly bound up with general economic life.'[38]

This second remark does not account for the statements regarding the patrimonial nature of the performance (Art 1174 of the It. civil code) and of the legal relation that is the object of the contractual relation (Art 1321 of the It. civil code). In both cases such nature is included in the intent of co-ordinating the regulations of contracts with the damage compensation system centred on the principle of the patrimonial liability of the debtor.[39] Nor are there any links with the Fascist doctrine of contracts, finally, in those comments to the legal definition of the concept that seem not to exclude its equivalence to the bilateral legal transaction and that, however, highlight its 'nature' of 'a technical concept of positive law.'[40]

Different observations can be made with regard to the rule according to which 'the debtor and creditor shall comport themselves in accordance with the rules of propriety in relation to the principles of corporate solidarity.' (art. 1175). Such provision, in fact, takes up the idea of co-operation of the parties of the obligation and in this perspective it reveals 'the influence on our compilers of a certain national socialist doctrine vaguely inspired by communitarian and/or solidaristic ideologies.'[41]

Similar influences seem to inspire the reflections aimed at relinquishing the equivalence of the contract to the bilateral legal transaction: equivalence that is recurrent in the literature influenced by the German doctrine of pandectist

---

[35] L Ferrajoli, *La cultura giuridica nell'Italia del novecento* (Roma e Bari, Laterza, 1998).

[36] See mostly R Teti, *Codice civile e regime fascista* (Milano, Giuffré, 1990).

[37] P Perlingieri, 'Scuole civilistiche e dibattito ideologico: introduzione allo studio del diritto privato in Ialia', (1978) *Rivista di diritto civile* at I, 44.

[38] *Relazione della Commissione Reale al progetto del libro Obbligazioni e contratti*, n 5.

[39] See the 'Relazione del Guardasigilli al progetto ministeriale delle obbligazioni' n 17.

[40] 'Relazione del Guardasigilli al progetto ministeriale delle obbligazioni' n 156. In the same sense, among the authors of the time see F Messineo, *Manuale di diritto civile e commerciale*, 6. ed., Vol. II (Padova, Cedam, 1943).

[41] A Di Majo, *Obbligazioni in generale* (Bologna, Zanichelli, 1985), who refers to opinions expressed by Pietro Rescigno. By this latter see the Introduzione al Codice civile (Roma and Bari, Laterza, 1991).

inspiration. On the basis of such intents, in the preliminary works it is stated that the contract is the 'instrument for the exchange of goods and services upon which production is based' and that it must be governed by provisions based on the 'fascist rule of the sagacious coordination of every individual interest and the proper pre-eminence of the general interest.'[42]

Some indications about the contents of the mentioned maxim can be derived in particular from the comments to the regime of atypical contracts and from the regime of the essential elements of the contract. As regards the first aspect, the civil code provides that

> the parties may also conclude contracts not belonging to types having a specific discipline as long as they are directed towards the bringing about of interests deserving of protection (Art 1322).

In this respect it is specified that this rule intends to codify the maxim according to which the legal system acknowledges the private agreement only in as much as the effects deriving from it realise at the same time interests outside the sphere of the parties: the new obligation law is inspired by the 'concept of autonomy of the will' instead of the one of 'sovereignty of the will'[43] and sees in the equivalence of contract to law a formulation by which it can be stated that 'autonomy cannot legitimise interference in the sphere of the rights of a third party.'[44]

Similar considerations, as is well known, are the grounds of the rule that identifies 'causa' as one of the essential requisites of contracts and in particular of the formulation according to which it is 'the economic and social object the contract is intended to accomplish; the socially valuable extrinsic object of the contract.'[45] The same conclusions drawn with regard to the German experience may be inferred from the discipline of 'causa' and of atypical contracts: in the Fascist idea the supremacy of positive law on the covenant is mostly characterised as an instrument for the imposition of the will of the political power 'per se', and not as a means to affect the situation of the party whose interests the system decides to interpret. In other words: in the Fascist and National Socialist contract law 'the individual was never considered *uti singulus*, but always and only *uti civis*.'[46]

Protection of the Weaker Contracting Party in Juridical Fascism and National Socialism

Both Fascism and National Socialism develop reflections regarding protection of the weaker contracting party. On the other hand, they do not deviate from

---

[42] *Relazione del Guardasigilli al progetto ministeriale delle obbligazioni*, n 10.

[43] *Relazione al Re*, n 603.

[44] *Relazione al Re*, n 627.

[45] Above n. 42, nn 193 and 194.

[46] M Costanza, *Il contratto atipico* (Milano, Giuffré, 1981). Finally G Alpa, *La cultura delle regole* (Roma and Bari, Laterza, 2001).

the principle according to which the prevalence of the legal system on contract is a mere mark of the power of the group on the individual. The weaker contracting party, in fact, is considered as such only insofar as he is party to a bond that the outside intervention intends to examine in the perspective of the common needs and not of the balance between performances.

Such considerations are consistent in the first place with some of the proposals worked out during the drawing up of the National Socialist 'popular code', and in particular the one concerning the duty of the drafting party to formulate the general conditions of contract in accordance with the needs of society: 'in particular, agreements fixing the content of the contract for an indefinite number of contracts to be concluded in the future (series contracts) (general terms of business) must meet the requirements of community life.'[47]

In this sense, the general condition of contract assume a largely different meaning compared to the one attributed to them previously, in particular by the liberal scholars. The latter had considered such conditions as a sort of generalisation of the contents of bonds that certain categories of contracting parties would later conclude. The National Socialist scholars deem such approach not to be a sufficient break with the traditional private system and maintain that it is necessary, on the contrary, to underline the prescriptive character of the general condition of contract. Only in this way, in fact, they can be efficiently co-ordinated with the super-individual interest:

> the contractual order makes the conditions of business feasible, thereby facilitating public review and the incorporation of the business of the individual entrepreneur into the national economy and our peoples' order as such.[48]

Not all the proposals formulated by the National Socialist authors imply a discipline of mass contracts having the indicated features.[49] On the other hand, those who justify the lawmaker's intervention to subtract scope to private autonomy without carrying out considerations regarding the matter of contractual equity are definitely prevalent.[50]

Even the Fascist experience tackles the protection of the weaker contracting party with different attitudes. In the civil code some rules seem to take up models aimed at promoting values such as the balance between the performances provided for in contracts: in particular the provision stating usurious

---

[47] So par. 1 'Gesetzentwurf von Heinrich Stoll aus der Denkschrift des Ausschusses für Personen-Vereins- und Schuldrecht: Die Lehre von den Leistungsstörungen', in W Schubert (ed), *Volksgesetzbuch. Teilenwürfe, Arbeitsberichte und sonstige Materialien*, in W Schubert and J Regge (ed), *Akademie für deutsches Recht 1933–1945. Protokolle der Ausschüsse*, Bd. III.4 (Berlin and New York, Springer, 1988).

[48] W Herschel, 'Die Vertragsordnung als Rechtsnorm. Zur praktischen Bedeutung der neuen Lehre von den allgemeinen Geschäftsbedingungen', in (1942) *Deutsches Recht* at 753.

[49] See for example G Haupt, 'Vertragsfreiheit und Gesetz', (1943) *Zeitschrift der Akademei für Deutsches Recht* at 84.

[50] K Larenz, above n 12.

interests to be void (Art 1815) and the one deciding on the matter of annulment for injury, pointing out the general character of such remedy and setting aside the referability of the relevant hypothesis to the vices of agreement (art. 1448).

Quite different are some reflections devoted to protection of mass contracts parties. The authors who are close to the political power invoke in this regard a 'binding action' that would place the 'state's will above the individual's.'[51] Similar concerns seem to have inspired the discipline of the general conditions of contracts (Art 1341 of the civil code) and of contracts stipulated through forms (Art 1342 of the civil code). This latter is sometimes indicated as an instrument of protection of the contracting parties who are at a disadvantage because of the context in which the transaction is stipulated. However, the mentioned discipline is often based on the remark that mass negotiation is 'a condition for speeding up the process of production, a need to which the need for freedom of bargaining should be sacrificed.'[52]

The underlining of such aspects is a feature of the Fascist and Nationalist contract law, which refers to the economic interests of the group and in such perspective pursues objectives such as an efficient allocation of assets: 'the contract has for the community the task of working towards a rational distribution of goods and the achievement of ever higher performance.'[53] Therefore, the invectives of certain authors that in the Fascist period point out the distance of the new ideas from the Liberal theories about the *homo economicus* assume a merely propagandistic meaning, and in any case they seem to be inconsistent, as those theories are also founded on a view of the contract that sets aside the parties' horizon.[54]

The Law of Contracts in the Fascist and National Socialist Courts

A common feeling has thus been shown between the Fascist and the National Socialist literature interested in constructing a contract law alternative to the one inherited from the Liberal scholars. And we have seen that the spreading of the new ideas characterises the German experience more than the Italian one. Similar considerations concern the application of the law.

Fascists and National Socialists entrust the judiciary with the task of implementing the political programme of the regime through re-examination of pre-existing rules: such task is taken care of by some scholars during the meeting of the Italo-German Juridical Committee, held in Vienna in March 1939.[55] In this perspective, the National Socialists prepare a system of strict political control

---

[51]   FM Dominedò, 'Studi sulle fonti del diritto', loc. cit.

[52]   *Relazione al Re*, n 612.

[53]   H Stoll, *Vertrag und Unrecht*, above n 12.

[54]   See among others CE Ferri, 'Il sepolcro dell'uomo economico', (1931) *Lo Stato* at 708 and C Costamagna, 'La riforma della scienza giuridica', (1933) *Lo Stato* at 563.

[55]   See the report by C Costamagna, 'Il giudice e la legge', (1939) *Lo Stato* at 193.

extended to the whole public service.[56] The Fascists, on the contrary, issue rules aimed at favouring conditionings on the judiciary that do not lead 'to political persecutions proper,'[57] and yet affecting a system of rules that only 'assert the autonomy of the judicial order only as a mere statement of principle.'[58]

With specific reference to the law of contract the German Courts seem at first to resist the pressures of the National Socialist doctrine: in particular those regarding the use of general clauses as an instrument to emphasise the 'general interest' in construing the agreements between individuals.[59]

A different trend develops through the reference to the provision according to which 'the legal transaction in breach of good custom is null and void (par. 138 BGB)'. On one hand the good morals clause is apt to allow the introduction in contracts of the values promoted by the political power, particularly as judges apply it referring to a subsequent time with respect to the conclusion of the agreement.[60] On the other hand such clause is combined with the sanction of voidness of the private deed, thus not allowing to reform its contents. Especially National Socialists deem that such impediment is not compatible with the intent of subduing individual ends to the exigence of the legal system and therefore that it is an 'exaggerated respect for contractual freedom.'[61]

The civil code of the Kingdom of Italy also contains, obviously, provisions regarding contracts contrary to good morals. In particular Article 1119 provides that 'an obligation without cause or based upon a false or wrongful cause cannot have any effect,' and the subsequent Article 1122 specifies that 'the cause is wrongful when it is contrary to law, good morals or public order.'

However, it seems that the Courts did not develop trends inspired by the intent of accepting the guidelines of the political power. On the background of a concept of 'causa' other than the model used in the preliminary works,[62] the Courts continue interpreting such formulation with reference to the 'degree of average morality', thus establishing a continuity with the previous line of decisions.[63] And they also provide that 'for the purposes of the wrongfulness of the cause, account should be taken of the time when the parties concluded the contractual bond.'[64]

---

[56] See the Gestetz zur Wiederherstellung des Berufsbeamtentums dated 7 April 1933, in particular par. 4.

[57] According to A Aquarone, *L'organizzazione dello stato totalitario*, above n 24.

[58] G Neppi Modona, 'La magistratura e il fascismo', in *Fascismo e società italiana*, loc. cit. at 135.

[59] RG, 9 July 1935, (1935) *Entscheidungen des Reichsgerichts in Zivilsachen* at 266.

[60] RG, 8 January 1937, (1937) *Entscheidungen des Reichsgerichts in Zivilsachen* at 294.

[61] G Vassalli, above n 27.

[62] See Cass Civ., 1rs August 1936, (1936) *Repertorio della Giurisprudenza italiana*, Entry 'obbligazioni e contratti' n 44 and Cass. Civ. 23 April 1937, (1937) *Repertorio della Giurisprudenza italiana*, Entry 'Obbligazioni e contratti' n. 18. Later on see Cass civ. 11 December 1940, (1940) *Repertorio della Giurisprudenza italiana*, Entry 'Obbligazioni e contratti', n 25.

[63] See Cass. civ., 11 May 1936, (1936) *Giurisprudenza italiana* at I, 1, 626.

[64] Trib. Caltanissetta, 22 December 1933, (1934) *Repertorio della Giurisprudenza italiana*, Entry 'Obbligazioni e contratti', n 59.

The Revision of Contracts by Judges

We have already remarked that through the good morals clause the German Courts come to eliminate agreement that are not compatible with the maxims propagandised by the regime, without, however, affecting their contents. This latter result is obtained instead by recourse to certain constructions derived from application of parr. 157 and 242 BGB: ie the provisions mentioning the good faith principle respectively in the matter of contract construction and performance fulfilment. It is well known that the use of good faith for the mentioned aims is not a remedy conceived by the National Socialist literature. It was established, in fact, during previous periods and is present, for instance, in the first doctrinal formulations of the 'contractual grounds' (*Geschäfts-grundlage*) theory: the whole of the events integrating the implied foundation of a negotiable agreement, the breaking of which justifies an intervention aimed at re-balancing the transaction.

The theory in question is established in a period of German juridical history characterised by the intent of re-examining the cultural premises on which the civil codification is based, and in particular the intent of re-valuating the *rebus sic stantibus* clause. In the Italian context it is precisely the recourse to this clause that allows the Courts during the Fascist period to justify certain interventions affecting the contract contents. Nothing being contained in the civil Code of the Kingdom of Italy on this matter, the judges use to this end the provision regarding good faith in the fulfilment of contracts (Art 1124).[65] On the other hand, in this way they do not promote principles formally referable to the Fascist private law. The provision, in fact, is interpreted in the light of the 'comune intenzione delle parti' (Art 1131)[66] on the equivalence of performances and leads to solutions which do not subordinate the individual end to the general interest: as it is proved by those decisions that refuse to use the '*rebus sic stantibus* clause to find a golden clause without effect' thus damaging the regime's monetary policy[67] and by the judgement according to which a

foreign contracting party, resident in a foreign country which on the occasion of the Italy-Ethiopian conflict decreed sanctions against Italy in execution of the Geneva decisions is not liable for failure to perform a contract in favour of an Italian citizen.[68]

Even the scholars who are closest to the political power, in fact, do not seem to agree completely with the National Socialist writers' trend. Many Italian authors are not favourable to the

---

[65] See Cass. Civ., 13 July 1942, (1942) *Giurisprudenza italiana* at I, 1, 606.

[66] See App. Palermo, 29 April 1938, (1939) *Repertorio della Giurisprudenza ialiana*, Entry 'Obbligazioni e contratti', n 16 and Cass. Civ. 24 June 1940, (1940) *Giurisprudenza italiana* at I, 1, 919.

[67] See, among many others, App. Bologna, 20 July 1939, (1940) *Giurisprudenza italiana* at I, 2, 37.

[68] Cass. Civ., 10 June 1938, (1938) *Giurisprudenza italiana* at I, 1, c. 1056.

attribution to the judge of very broad powers of discretion to amend the contract in
a case where according to the traditional principles of impossibility instead the contract would instead have been declared dissolved.'

It seems, actually, that the opinion fostering the limitation of political interventions in the monetary and economic order is prevalent.[69]

In the German Courts the theory of the contractual grounds becomes, on
the contrary, an instrument used to reform contract law in the light of the principles proposed by the National Socialist literature. This latter identifies in the
use of the institution in question one of the main devices apt to strike at
Liberal individualism.[70]

The German judges do not cease to found such theory on the grounds of an
intimist character: as proved in particular by the references to the presumed
intention of the contracting parties and the discipline of error. However, they
emphasise new events capable of justifying external intervention on the act viti-
ated by loss of the 'contractual grounds'. In order to determine the social and
economic marginalisation of Jews, the changes in the racial policy of the
regime, in particular, are mentioned:

> The enhanced provenance of the race idea may . . . be a reason for reviewing earlier
> severance agreements with Jewish employees to see whether and how far they are still
> compatible with National Socialist, popular and legal perceptions.[71]

To increase political control on the productive system, on the other hand, circumstances such as the destiny of the 'sistema economico popolare' are referred
to:

> For keeping to the contract would, according to consistent caselaw, infringe good
> faith, in particular where as a consequence of error by both parties as to the existence
> of an objective basis for the transaction, a mismatch between performance and
> consideration has arisen . . . adducing the viewpoint of the national economy in this
> connection is also to be endorsed.[72]

Some Final Considerations: the Law of Contracts 'Fascist Malgré Soi'

In consulting the Italian Fascist magazines cases and on court decisions, therefore, one does not receive the impression that in the law of contract the Italian
judges have behaved simply as executors of the regime's policy: at least not with
as much zest as their German colleagues.

---

[69] Above n 21.
[70] H Lange, above n 10 K Larenz, and n 12.
[71] RG, 24 April 1940, (1940) *Deutsches Recht* at 1314.
[72] RG, 5 April 1939, (1939) *Entscheidungen des Reichsgerichts in Zivilsachen* at 257.

The same does not apply, on the other hand, with regard to scholars. Certainly, they have not adopted the regime's keywords with the same intensity as observed in the German authors: a circumstance due in part to the variety of positions in which the authors who were close to the political power have reflected themselves.

And yet the comparison with National Socialist law has allowed the highlighting of certain features characterising the Fascist doctrine on contract law. In particular, it has allowed to remark that such doctrine is based on the subordination of agreements to the legal system for aims outside the pursuit of interests ascribable to the parties. The comparison with the German experience has also made it clear that the prevalence of the legal system is often functional to promotion of the economic structure decided upon by the political power. This leads to confine the matter to the cases of exchange of goods and services, through certain devices that differentiate it from contracts of a jus-rationalist character. From this point of view the Fascist and National Socialist experiences diverge from the preceding theories about functionalisation of private action, even though they seem to imply a reconstruction of the relations between contracts and the legal system which is not always sensitive to the question of the balance between performances.

If these are indeed the characteristics of the Fascist law of contracts, it is necessary to specify, in the first place, that they have been introduced in the civil law codification in force. And it is further to be underlined that this implies the presence of a juridical doctrine in some way participating to the construction of such law, even though only 'through typical content or through the omission of established solutions.'[73] The statements of those who think that it is possible to speak of juridical Fascism only if the scholars are united and conformed to the political power, concluding that this is not the case in a context where it merely formulates 'extrinsic homage to the regime's policy' are therefore worthless. Even such homages, in fact, contribute to outline a law of contracts 'fascista malgré soi'.[74]

However, even without such express references to the Fascist contract law—for instance in the language that was substantially taken from the Liberal tradition—some constructions have emerged, capable of supporting the legal policies determined by the regime: a circumstance that was justified some time back by portraying Fascism as 'the white guard of capitalism'.[75]

---

[73] F Lucarelli, *Diritti civili e istituzioni privatistiche* (Padova, Cedam, 1983).

[74] A Somma, above n 2

[75] A Gramsci, 'I due fascismi', in R De Felice, *Il fascismo. Le interpretazioni dei contemporanei e degli storici*, 2. ed. (Roma and Bari, Laterza, 1998).

4

'SPHERES OF INFLUENCE' AND 'VÖLKISCH' LEGAL THOUGHT: REINHARD HÖHN'S NOTION OF EUROPE

*Ingo J Hueck**

Who was Reinhard Höhn (1904–2000)?

Professor of constitutional and administrative law at Berlin University (*Friedrich-Wilhelms-Universität zu Berlin, 1935–1945*), Director of the Berlin Institute for State Research (*Institut für Staatsforschung, 1936–1945*) and an influential SS lawyer (retiring as an SS *Oberführer*, Major General), Reinhard Höhn numbers amongst the ranks of the ghastly 'Third Reich' lawyers. Höhn was a decisive co-founder of *völkisch* constitutional legal theory. With his Institute for State Research he created a forum for an intellectual Nazi elite of the *völkisch* State. The centre of his academic and political work was the reshaping of the principles of constitutional and administrative law in accordance with National Socialist *völkisch* notions. Along with Otto Koellreutter and Karl August Eckhardt, Reinhard Höhn was among the fiercest opponents and rivals of Carl Schmitt and contributed decisively to removing Schmitt from power in the Nazi legal hierarchy.

In the first years after the 'seizure of power', Höhn's academic work was concerned primarily with the transformation of domestic law in accordance with *völkisch* notions. According to a basic idea, observation of the life of the State was to be used to create a stronger link with the science of constitutional law: constitutional and administrative law were to be adapted to the new social and political requirements—the new vocabulary indicated the direction: 'leadership (*Führung*)' and 'national community (*Volksgemeinschaft*)'. Legal thinking was henceforth to be governed by its utility to the 'whole'. As a radical innovator and political publicist, Höhn was already in 1933–1934 advocating the

* Permanent Research Fellow at the Max Planck Institute for European Legal History, Frankfurt am Main (http://www.mpier.uni-frankfurt.de); co-founder and co-ordinator of the institute's research project / Ph.D. programme 'The Discipline of International Law in Germany between the Foundation of the Kaiserreich and National Socialism (1870–1945)'. For further details, see IJ Hueck, 'The Discipline of the History of International Law', (2001) 3 *Journal of the History of International Law*, 194–217. http://www.ingohueck.com.

transformation in constitutional legal thinking and calling for radical departure from the sovereign State and its liberal tradition of rule of law (*Rechtsstaat*). The individualistic State was to be replaced by the national community under leadership, a community without an institutional system and with authoritarian leadership. Described as a 'community rhetorician' by Michael Stolleis,[1] Höhn was, with a community ideology inspired in this way, openly and clearly promoting the claims of the Party, and especially the SS, to rule. A special, practical relevance was initially developed by Höhn and his Berlin Institute for State Research in the area of police law. Through reports to the Ministry of the Interior, the Secret State Police (*Gestapo*) and the SS Reich leadership, Höhn supported the stiffening of police law and the legalisation of terror.

Höhn first concerned himself with questions of international law in connection with the sphere-of-influence (*Großraum*) debate. The basis was two major articles in which Höhn developed mainly the *völkisch* foundation of the sphere-of-influence concept. The same line of argument was pursued by SS lawyers like Werner Best and Herbert Lemmel, a pupil of Höhn's. By stressing the *völkisch* idea, the SS thus promoted concepts of Europe that clearly differed from Schmitt's concept of a sphere-of-influence system under international law. In the foreground, this stance served as a welcome occasion for further attacks aimed at diminishing Schmitt's power. Höhn too utilised the sphere-of-influence debate in order to further to weaken Schmitt's position in the Nazi hierarchy. Höhn's stance in the sphere-of-influence debate, however, above all strengthened the National Socialist, *völkisch* -oriented science of international law in the Third Reich. After the 'seizure of power' in 1933–1934, autonomous National Socialist positions on international law and on Europe took shape initially only very gradually. In the first years after 1933, representatives of traditionally conceived international law dominated the academic evaluation of events of relevance in international law, in particular the gradual disposal of the Versailles Treaty. What National Socialist international law was supposed to be long remained unclear from an academic viewpoint, and likewise was long irrelevant from a practical political viewpoint. Accordingly traditional institutions of international law as the Berlin Kaiser Wilhelm Institute for Comparative Public Law and International Law (1925–1945) dominated the scene. Carl Schmitt had been an academic advisor there since 1933, though without major influence on the institution and its academic programme.

With the increasing politicisation of international law and its instrumentalisation by Nazi policy and the SS, the proponents of the traditional understanding of international law moved on to the defensive, at the latest by the start of immediate preparations for war. To that extent, the sphere-of-influence debate marks, from the viewpoint of the history of science, an important turning point for international law and for the relationship between National

---

[1] M Stolleis, *Geschichte des öffentlichen Rechts in Deutschland, Dritter Band 1914–1945* (München, C.H. Beck, 1999), 361.

Socialism and Europe: the National-Socialist academic strategist Paul Ritterbusch in 1939 proclaimed the 'fight for Reich and *Lebensraum*', and foreign policy advisor and international legal politician Friedrich Berber called for the development of a 'true law of peoples', while SS lawyers like Reinhard Höhn advocated the *völkisch* idea for international law and for Europe.[2] Those who saw classical European international law of the universal type as finished and did not want to follow the racist concepts of the SS sought refuge in geopolitical concepts of the superordination and subordination of States and peoples. But such people were a small minority in German international legal science. Carl Schmitt's sphere-of-influence theory can be located here. Höhn and the SS by contrast, with their *völkisch*, racist concept of Europe and spheres of influence, proclaimed a legally unserviceable propaganda formula intended to serve solely the German claim to rule. These *völkisch* conceptions of Europe and of an international community of States denied traditional principles of international law such as universality and the equality of States. They destroyed the idea of equal rights and advocated an allegedly modern imperialism, with master peoples (*Herrenvölker*) and slave peoples (*Sklavenvölker*). The sphere-of-influence debate stimulated by Carl Schmitt was in this connection also a contribution towards splitting German international legal science. Numerous prominent figures in German international legal science, like Victor Bruns, Herbert Kraus or the *Emeritus* Heinrich Triepel, no longer engaged in the sphere-of-influence debate, but instead holding onto traditional international legal thinking, fled into teaching activity or worked in academic niches.

Reinhard Höhn died only in May 2000, at the great age of 95. Like Carl Schmitt, Höhn was dismissed from his official functions (in the civil service) immediately after the war—both lost their chairs in Berlin. Unlike Schmitt, who retreated to his birthplace Plettenberg (in the Sauerland) where he remained until his death in 1985, Reinhard Höhn disappeared only very briefly. In Bad Harzburg, he founded a management school, the '*Harzburger Akademie für Führungskräfte*' (Harzburg Academy for Executives)—'*Führung*' being the challenge in the new circumstances of the booming post-War German economy. Numerous SS colleagues worked there as lecturers and former SS comrades, who succeeded in Germany's economy, sent their promising young people. The *Akademie* developed during the early years of the Federal Republic into a leading location for the training of up-and-coming (future) leaders in the economy, associations and parties, mainly from conservative quarters, but also among social democrats and trade unions. The Cold War and a managed 'collective memory'[3] eventually ensured a pleasant retirement for Herr Professor Dr. iur.

---

[2] See P Ritterbusch, 'Die Aufgabe der Wissenschaft im Kampf um eine neue europäische Ordnung', (1939) 3 *Raumforschung und Raumordnung*, 489–95; F Berber, *Deutsche Völkerrechtswissenschaft* in *Deutsche Wissenschaft, Arbeit und Aufgabe* (Leipzig, Hirzel, 1939), 62.

[3] Cf B Rüthers, 'Reinhard Höhn, Carl Schmitt und andere—Geschichten und Legenden aus der NS-Zeit', (2000) 39 *Neue Juristische Wochenschrift*, 2866–71, at 2869.

Reinhard Höhn and even honourable obituaries.[4] The Berlin Professor and SS elite jurist was embarrassingly praised as management expert and teacher of 600, 000 economic leaders in the financial pages of the *Frankfurter Allgemeine Zeitung* and the *Süddeutsche Zeitung*, with no mention of his leading role in the ideological and scientific backing of the German expulsion and extermination policy—a fatal, but rather typical (even today), wilful blindness to historical connections.

Radical Notions of the Community under Leadership

Reinhard Höhn was an intelligent, ambitious and enormously career-conscious lawyer. He was born on 29 July 1904 in a small town in Thuringia. His father was a District Court judge (*Amtsgerichtsrat*) in the small local capital of Meiningen. After the First World War and the 'Versailles shock', Höhn studied legal science and national economics in Kiel, Munich and Jena. In Kiel, as early as 1923 in his first year of studies, Höhn took up intellectual and friendly relations with a later SS *Standartenführer*. In the same year he experienced Hitler's failed *Putsch* in Munich. These events brought Höhn into the Young German Order (*Jungdeutscher Orden*), one of the big right-wing radical movements in the Weimar Republic, opposed both politically and in armed struggle equally to Communists and Democrats. Here, as a young law student, Höhn made his first career as a political functionary. Initially he was the so-called Grand Commander of the Order for Bavaria and Austria. It was in this period that Höhn developed his first radically anti-democratic ideas, influenced by such intellectual leaders as Oswald Spengler or Othmar Spann.[5] Höhn was particularly struck in that period by Arthur Mahraun, the leader of the Young German Order and opponent of Alfred Hugenberg in the fight for dominance of policy and opinion formation in the spectrum of right-wing opinion.[6] In a document on constitutional policy of the Young German Order published in 1929 under the title 'The bourgeois State based on the rule of law and the new front', the twenty five year old Höhn engaged with great vigour and full conviction in the then much pursued research into the 'Germanic idea of the State'.[7] This was Höhn's first publication and already contained the concepts, later so decisive, of 'leadership' (*Führung*) and 'national community' (*Volksgemeinschaft*). In

---

[4] *Frankfurter Allgemeine Zeitung* (FAZ), 19 May 2000; and *Süddeutsche Zeitung* (SZ), 22 May 2000. For further details, see Rüthers, (2000) NJW, at 2867.

[5] O Spann, *Der wahre Staat* (Leipzig, Quelle & Meyer, 1921) and O Spengler, *Der Untergang des Abendlandes. Umrisse einer Morphologie der Weltgeschichte* (München, CH Beck Verlag, 1918–22).

[6] Cf A Mahraun, *Gegen getarnte Gewalten. Weg und Kampf einer Volksbewegung* (Berlin, Jungdeutscher Verlag, 1928).

[7] Details in K Sontheimer, *Antidemokratisches Denken in der Weimarer Republik* (München, Deutscher Taschenbuch Verlag, 1962, 1992), 174 ff.

this maiden work Höhn saw Germanic democracy as 'true' democracy and the source of the Germanic principles of leadership, obedience and living community. The opposite to this ideal form of State is the bourgeois democracy based on rule of law, on the Weimar model. According to Höhn it forms the sharpest contrast—'so enormous, so unbridgeable, that one can well understand how mixing and melding of varied political content has brought quite monstrous falsification of political thinking and political views'.[8] The young Reinhard Höhn vigorously sends liberal rule of law thinking where it belongs: 'together with liberal ideas and freedoms'.[9] With the same vigour Höhn advocated the *völkisch* range of ideas associated with the political demand for a fundamental transformation of the State intended to lead to destruction of the rule of law.

In 1926 Höhn went from Munich to Jena in order to take the First State Examination. Höhn was by no means an outstanding lawyer. He invested his industry and talent more in his political commitments. Thus, after the First State Examination he took up training as a trainee lawyer, but left after two years without completing it. Alongside the activities in the Young German Order, at any rate, at this stage there came a small dissertation on 'The position of the criminal judge in the laws of the period of the French Revolution', with which Höhn took his doctorate at Jena in 1928.[10] His promoter was the criminal lawyer Max Grünhut, who was expelled after the 'seizure of power' in 1933 because of his Jewish background.[11] After his doctorate and breaking off legal training, Höhn worked mainly as a law tutor. In 1930 the possibility of an academic career eventually opened up. Höhn became assistant to constitutional lawyer and legal sociologist Franz W Jerusalem in Jena. After Arthur Mahraun's Young German Order, the young Höhn received a further decisive imprint from Jerusalem's sociological seminar. By contrast with what the name might lead one to expect, Jerusalem was not of Jewish origin. Reinhard Höhn's academic teacher was a legal sociologist of 'community'.[12] Jerusalem, with whom Höhn worked for the next four years until he took his *habilitation* in Heidelberg in 1934, shaped and strengthened the 'community thinking' of Höhn. But the pupil Höhn soon far exceeded the teacher Jerusalem in radicalism and sharpness. While Jerusalem and many other thoroughly orthodox National Socialists like Otto Koellreutter or Ernst Rudolf Huber continued to seek the relationship to a State and nation, Höhn developed into a *völkisch*

---

[8] R Höhn, *Der bürgerliche Rechtsstaat und die neue Front* (Berlin, Jungdeutscher Verlag, 1929), 51.

[9] Above n 7, K Sontheimer 176.

[10] R Höhn, *Die Stellung des Strafrichters in den Gesetzen der französischen Revolutionszeit* (Berlin, de Gruyter, 1929).

[11] Cf P Landau, 'Juristen jüdischer Herkunft im Kaiserreich und in der Weimarer Republik' in H Heinrichs, H Franzki, K Schmalz & M Stolleis (eds), *Deutsche Juristen jüdischer Herkunft* (München, CH Beck, 1993), 133–213, at 188–91.

[12] See M Stolleis, *Geschichte des öffentlichen Rechts in Deutschland, Dritter Band 1914–1945* (München, CH Beck, 1999), 327 ff.

revolutionary.[13] He wanted a total break with the bourgeois rule-of-law tradition. He therefore rejected the fixation with the concept of State, and 'smelled reactionary elements wherever traditional links with legal norms were defended.'[14]

Höhn developed the basic concept of replacing the legal person of the State by the 'community'. He advocated this basic idea in his *habilitation* thesis 'The transformation in constitutional legal thinking' and especially in his article 'On the essence of community', both published in 1934.[15] Höhn here also explicitly opposed the pluralist cooperative theory of Otto von Gierke, whom he thought of as a liberal. For Höhn was pursuing what Gierke had already in 1902 called the 'war of extermination against the concept of the personality of the State'. No one else in German constitutional theory went so far in that phase of radical change. Höhn undoubtedly wanted through this radical position to differentiate himself from such rivals as Koellreuter and Schmitt and locate himself as an 'orthodox National Socialist constitutionalist'. But his radicalism also strikes one as full of conviction and faith. Sometimes in a blustering tone, he attacked National Socialist comrades like Huber and Koellreutter or Carl Bilfinger and Ulrich Scheuner.[16] On the one hand, those colleagues also had 'communitarian' feelings. On the other, he attacked their ideas about the State as half-hearted, 'liberalistic' and 'individualistic'. Here is a sample from a speech on 'The Constitutional Position':

> In the place of the individualistic principle today a different one has appeared, the principle of community. It is no longer the legal person of the State that is the basis and cornerstone of constitutional law; the national community is the new starting point. . . . The legal person and the concept of community totally exclude each other.[17]

For Höhn, then, the decisive point was whether '*Volk*' and '*Gemeinschaft*' ('people' and 'community'), and thus the *völkisch* idea, took primacy over the traditional understanding of the State. Then there would be no room for traditional binding by legal norms or principles of the rule of law. According to Höhn's notions, the State should really be henceforth only a technical apparatus, and unconstrained auxiliary for the leadership of the 'national community' (*Volksgemeinschaft*).[18] With this radical position Höhn appealed at the same

[13] See generally, FW Jerusalem, *Über den Begriff der Nation* (Jena, Fischer, 1932), and in detail ER Huber, 'Bau und Gefüge des Reiches', in *idem* (ed), *Idee und Ordnung des Reiches* (Hamburg, Hanseatische Verlags-Anstalt, 1941). Cf also M Stolleis, at n 12 above, 329.

[14] Above n 12, M Stolleis, 328.

[15] R Höhn, *Die Wandlung im staatsrechtlichen Denken* (Hamburg, Hanseatische Anstalt, 1934); *Vom Wesen der Gemeinschaft* (Berlin, Heymanns, 1934).

[16] For details see Stolleis, at above n 12, 327 ff.

[17] R Höhn, 'Die staatsrechtliche Lage' (1934/35) *Volk im Werden*, 286; cf. also *idem*, *Der individualistische Staatsbegriff und die juristische Staatsperson* (Berlin, Heymanns, 1935).

[18] See M Stolleis, 'Gemeinschaft und Volksgemeinschaft. Zur juristischen Terminologie im Nationalsozialismus', in *idem*, *Recht im Unrecht. Studien zur Rechtsgeschichte des Nationalsozialismus* (Frankfurt am Main, Suhrkamp Verlag, 1994), 94–125.

time to the Nazi regime and especially to the SS, for the Berlin security service of which he had been working since 1932. Höhn officially became an NSDAP and SS member in 1933.

The expansion of the National Socialist State through the *Anschluß* with Austria in 1938 and the creation of 'protectorates' made the vigorous debate about State and community lose importance even before the outbreak of war. Foreign policy events overwhelmed the German 'community thinkers' in constitutional and international legal science. This new central concept was the 'Reich'.[19] The fluctuating concept, used by many thoroughly heterogeneous groups ranging from the Conservative Revolution via the European Movement to unofficial National Socialism, took up elements of traditional Statehood and especially to serve the expanding National Socialist Reich. For the official National Socialist State the term 'Reich' guaranteed more openness over the incorporation of ethnic German groups abroad and rule by force over neighbouring States. From the viewpoint of constitutional and international law, the new term opened up more possibilities of engaging in imperial efforts. 'To that extent, one could really have the impression that the guiding image of the sovereign nation State of the nineteenth century had been finally dismissed', says Stolleis in his chapter on 'Destruction and self-destruction of a faculty'.[20] Reinhard Höhn contributed prominently to this development in traditional German theory of the State and constitutional law.

Master peoples and slave peoples: Reinhard Höhn's notion of Europe

Reinhard Höhn was neither a constitutional lawyer nor an international lawyer in the traditional sense. With a heady faith in National Socialism he implanted the *völkisch* idea in traditional constitutional theory. Here he acted primarily as a political publicist or 'community rhetorician' (Stolleis), rather than as an intellectual theoretician—like, say, Carl Schmitt. He was primarily concerned with underpinning the claims of the NSDAP and especially the SS to rule. Here Höhn radically departed from a major part of the equally orthodox National Socialists in German constitutional and international legal science. He sought a radical break with traditional concepts and principles, while the majority of his comrades and colleagues stuck to elements from traditional constitutional and international legal theory.

Below I shall approach the theme of National Socialism and Europe from the viewpoint of the history of science. This means that I am discussing not aspects of international law but of the academic treatment of international law.

---

[19] ER Huber, 'Bau und Gefüge des Reiches', at n 13.
[20] M Stolleis, at above n 12, 330.

This distinction is important. Although theory or doctrine is an important source of international law, they are in principle different positions, irrespective of whether I speak as a historian about international law in the 'Third Reich' or about responsibility in constitutional and international legal science in the National Socialist State, which soon developed into a regime of terror. In this connection I accordingly attempt, starting from the protagonists in the sphere-of-influence debate, not just to reconstruct the various concepts of international law and of Europe, but to deal also with questions of the profession's self-perception and responsibility in a dictatorship. This approach is in line with the conviction that political and social reality is not just interpreted and observed by science, but also changed.

The focus is on European notions of the SS in the framework of the sphere-of-influence debate sparked off by Carl Schmitt from 1939 to 1945. They can best be brought out using the three prominent SS lawyers: Werner Best, Norbert Gürke and Reinhard Höhn. On Werner Best there is already the excellent work by the historian Ulrich Herbert which I shall also deal with.[21] Norbert Gürke, who took an active part in the Second World War early on and died of a war wound in 1943, said nothing more about the sphere-of-influence theory.[22] That is why I have chosen Reinhard Höhn, hitherto not dealt with in any broader framework. This is perhaps also connected with the fact that he did not die till the year 2000, at the age of 95.[23] In analysing his role in the sphere-of-influence debate and his responsibility within constitutional and international legal science I have in particular brought in the relevant works of Dan Diner, Mathias Schmoeckel and Michael Stolleis.[24] I myself have been working for some three years on a monograph about the rise and development of the Berlin Kaiser Wilhelm Institute (KWI) for Comparative Public Law and International Law (1925–1945), today the well-known Max Planck Institute in Heidelberg. The focus in these studies is on institutional and personal development in German international legal science after 1933 and on the international law thinking of individual international lawyers from the KWI (such as Viktor Bruns, Helmuth

[21] U Herbert, *Werner Best- Radikalismus, Weltanschauung und Vernunft* (Berlin, Arenhövel, 1997); cf also *idem* (ed), *Nationalsozialistische Vernichtungspolitik 1939–1945. Neue Forschungen und Kontroversen* (Frankfurt am Main, Fischer-Taschenbuch-Verlag, 1998).

[22] Gürke was academic assistant to, and son-in-law of, the Nazi constitutional lawyer Otto Koellreutter. He was a fanatical supporter of National Socialism and active even before 1933 as a Party functionary in the NSDAP country leadership in Austria. Cf eg N Gürke, *Volk und Völkerrecht* (Tübingen, J.C.B. Mohr, 1935). Further details in Stolleis, at n 12 above, 385 ff.

[23] Cf the obituary notice by U Wesel, 'Der Letzte. Zum Tod des Juristen Reinhard Höhn', *Frankfurter Allgemeine Zeitung* (FAZ), 23 May 2000.

[24] D Diner, 'Rassistisches Völkerrecht', (1989) 37 *Vierteljahrshefte für Zeitgeschichte*, 23–56; M Schmoeckel, *Die Großraumtheorie. Ein Beitrag zur Geschichte der Völkerrechtswissenschaft im Dritten Reich, insbesondere der Kriegszeit* (Berlin, Duncker & Humblot, 1994); M Stolleis, at n 12 above, 380 ff; see further E Bristler & JH Herz, *Die Völkerrechtslehre im Nationalsozialismus* (Zürich, Europa-Verlag, 1938).

James Graf Moltke, Hermann Mosler, Hermann Raschhofer, Ulrich Scheuner, Ernst Schmitz, Bertold Schenk Graf von Stauffenberg, Wilhelm Wengler) in the Third Reich.[25]

The Großraum (sphere-of-influence) theory

On 1 April 1939, at the invitation of Paul Ritterbusch, Carl Schmitt spoke in Kiel at the Institute for (Politics and) International Law (*Institut für Internationales Recht*; today known as *Walther-Schücking-Institut*), on 'a sphere-of-influence system in international law with a ban on intervention by powers alien to the area'.[26] Ritterbusch was not only the Institute Director but especially the organiser of the 'Association for the German moral sciences', a major research project to renew German science in the National Socialist State.[27] It was again Ritterbusch who in the same year mobilised the Academy around the 'fight for Reich and Lebensraum'.[28] The same direction was taken by the endeavours of Friedrich Berber, an occasionally extremely influential international legal advisor to Nazi Foreign Minister Joachim von Ribbentrop and Director of the (Hamburg) Institute for Foreign Policy (*Institut für Auswärtige Politik*), founded by the distinguished scholar Albrecht Mendelssohn Bartholdy, who had left Germany in 1934. In 1939 Berber announced the unofficial slogan that international law ought no longer to be a 'playground for internationalist and pacifist ideologies'.[29] According to Berber the point in detail was not just to,

> trace the political, historical and ideological roots of Western European and Anglo-Saxon international law and unmask them, supply German foreign policy, in its fight for the freedom and greatness of the German people, with international-law weapons, and to find new forms, new vessels for new political thoughts and

---

[25] On the topic see: IJ Hueck, 'Die Gründung völkerrechtlicher Zeitschriften in Deutschland im internationalen Vergleich' in M Stolleis (ed), *Juristische Zeitschriften. Die neuen Medien des 18.–20. Jahrhunderts* (Frankfurt am Main, Klostermann, 1999), 379–420; *idem*, 'Die deutsche Völkerrechtswissenschaft im Nationalsozialismus. Das Berliner Kaiser-Wilhelm-Institut für ausländisches öffentliches Recht und Völkerrecht, das Hamburger Institut für Auswärtige Politik und das Kieler Institut für Internationales Recht' in D Kaufmann (ed), *Geschichte der Kaiser-Wilhelm-Gesellschaft im Nationalsozialismus. Bestandsaufnahme und Perspektiven der Forschung* (Göttingen, Wallstein, 2000), 490–527.

[26] C Schmitt, *Völkerrechtliche Großraumordnung mit Interventionsverbot für raumfremde Mächte. Ein Beitrag zum Reichsbegriff im Völkerrecht* (Berlin/Wien/Leipzig, Deutscher Rechts-Verlag, 1939, 1941); for later variants see the listing in M Stolleis, at n 12 above, 389.

[27] On this see F-R Hausmann, *'Deutsche Geisteswissenschaft' im Zweiten Weltkrieg. Die 'Aktion Ritterbusch' 1940–45* (Dresden, Dresden University Press, 1998).

[28] P Ritterbusch, 'Die Aufgabe der Wissenschaft im Kampf um eine neue europäische Ordnung', in (1939) 3 *Raumforschung und Raumordnung*, 489–95; *idem*, *Wissenschaft im Kampf um Reich und Lebensraum* (Stuttgart, Kohlhammer, 1942).

[29] F Berber, *Deutsche Völkerrechtswissenschaft* in *Deutsche Wissenschaft, Arbeit und Aufgabe* (Leipzig, Hirzel, 1939), 62.

creations; it has above all to work out the system of a genuine international legal order that is no longer a summation of more or less random and formal rules behind which any moral and dishonourable action can be concealed but is above all cut to suit owners with their gluttonous needs, but instead a system of a genuine law of peoples that constitutes an order for the community of free peoples, with equal rights, based on justice and located in the living stream of history.[30]

Carl Schmitt hardly worked out a 'genuine international law', yet in 1939 with his sphere-of-influence theory he conceived a new 'system of a genuine international legal order' in Berber's and also Ritterbusch's sense. The international law politicians Berber and Ritterbusch were calling in 1939, in the phase of the immediate preparations for war and in connection with National Socialist foreign policy, was a new system of international law that would support the imperialist aspirations of the Hitler government. Here Berber in particular made it clear that traditional European international law with its universal stamp did not constitute a 'genuine international legal order' for the National Socialist system. It was decried as a 'West European' or 'Anglo Saxon' and therefore not 'genuine' or 'Germanic' international law. What possibilities existed for international legal theory at that point in time? Those who stuck to traditional universal international law were silent. Those who did not wish to identify with the *völkisch*, racist basic ideas of the radical innovators in the SS ambience could really be involved only with geo-political approaches and thoughts about a superordination and subordination of States. In connection with National Socialist foreign policy in 1938–1939 (the incorporation of Austria, the first 'protectorate') a division into power spheres or spheres of influence suggested itself, say by dividing up the world into American, British and German spheres of influence. Carl Schmitt bundled these ideas into his sphere-of-influence speech in Kiel, which came after the foreign policy successes of 1938–1939 and directly after the crushing of Czechoslovakia.

In its basic conception the sphere-of-influence theory put forward by Schmitt displays classical features of traditionally understood international law. In his speech Schmitt explicitly adhered to an international law of the inter-State type. He started from the 'State' as his reference quantity. He called the term '*Volk*' (people) unsuitable, thus explicitly departing from *völkisch* ideas even if perhaps only from practical political considerations. It was a way to avoid discussion about a sphere-of-influence system in international law becoming fixated on questions of ethnicity and thus from the outset not being upheld internationally. But other countries saw even Schmitt's conception of a system of spheres of influence as a sign of an international law underpinning of current National Socialist foreign policy, something that after Austria and Czechoslovakia was fairly plain to see. Schmitt himself gave adequate occasion

[30] Above.

for this, considering his line of thought on the establishment of the European power spheres. Like Berber, he talked of two incompatible systems of international law, a continental European one and an 'English' one dominating the sea. Whereas the land-based system allegedly always tended to the moderate waging of war, the 'English' order was said to tend towards total war.[31] In a historically questionable structure of ideas, Schmitt thus calls the leading sea power, Britain, an international aggressor, whereas the continental European countries, including Germany, appear as upholders of the old '*ius publicum europaeum*'. From this opposition between land and sea, Schmitt developed the concept of empires and spheres of influence in Europe and internationally.[32] This made the sovereign State lose its decisive importance as the reference quantity in traditional international law. According to Schmitt's conception, the spheres of influence ought now to rule both internally and externally, and in particular be able to defend themselves externally against interventions by powers alien to the area. In this connection Schmitt made a historical reference to the US Monroe Doctrine of 1823. He also referred, however, to the current situation, namely the foreign policy interests of the German Reich in relation to Eastern and Central Europe. Schmitt even went so far as to characterise the German Reich in this relationship as a 'protective power', with the 'role of a sacred bulwark (Katechon)' against Bolshevism.[33] Lothar Gruchmann showed in 1962 in his study on the 'construction of a "German" Monroe Doctrine' how open and fluid Schmitt's transitions between historical argumentation and the instrumentalisation of international law for the purposes of National Socialist foreign policy were.[34] In favour of this position is the political context in which Schmitt developed his sphere-of-influence theory. When he later said he wished through his international law based theory of sphere of influence to uphold traditional concepts and principles of constitutional and international law, this is hardly convincing.[35]

Reinhard Höhn's Concept of a New Europe

Carl Schmitt did not advocate a *völkisch* sphere-of-influence system—it was a comrade of Reinhard Höhn's that extended the sphere-of-influence debate: Werner Best. In a small 1939 article on the '*Völkisch* sphere-of-influence system' he categorically denied the existence of any universal international

[31] Above n 26, C Schmitt.

[32] Further details on the idea of a spatial arrangement and geo-politics can be found in Schmoeckel, at n 24 above, 81 ff. Also worth reading, more broadly, on Schmitt's land-sea thinking is N Sombart, *Die deutschen Männer und ihre Feinde: Carl Schmitt—ein deutsches Schicksal zwischen Männerbund und Matriarchatsmythos* (München and Wien, Hanser, 1991), esp. 295 ff.

[33] Above n 12, M Stolleis 390.

[34] L Gruchmann, *Nationalsozialistische Großraumordnung. Die Konstruktion einer 'deutschen' Monroe-Doktrin* (Stuttgart, Deutsche Verlags-Anstalt, 1962).

[35] Above n 12, M Stolleis 390.

law.[36] The fact that SS lawyers were speaking to the sphere-of-influence debate
in order to continue denouncing Carl Schmitt too as *'unvölkisch'* or 'statist' is
shown in this connection by the way Best continued to attack Schmitt even once
he had accepted the concept of the *völkisch* sphere-of-influence system.[37] While
Best was essentially pursuing a dispute over terms, Reinhard Höhn from the
ranks of the SS dealt more exhaustively with the sphere-of-influence theory and
the idea of a Europe with a *völkisch* inspiration. His basic thoughts on this can
be found primarily in his 1941 work on 'Sphere-of-influence system and
völkisch legal thought', and then in the 1942 article 'Reich—Sphere of influence—Great power'.[38] Initially, Höhn's attack on Schmitt's sphere-of-influence
theory also bore the mark of polemic. Höhn reacted as a rival to the slogans
given out by Schmitt, and like Best called for a departure from traditional conceptualisations taken from older constitutional and international law. Höhn
saw the sphere-of-influence idea as containing above all the following main
positions:

> The idea of a sphere-of-influence system in its essence includes a departure from a
> purely statist expansion of domination, such as typified imperialism in the nineteenth-
> century sense. . .[Moreover]. . .a sphere-of-influence system means recognition of the
> fundamental idea that quite definite historically powerful peoples bear responsibility
> for quite definite areas. In Europe and the living space (*Lebensraum*) associated with
> it, it is the German idea of the Reich and the Fascist idea of the Imperium that take
> account of the history and the current importance of these peoples.[39]

Thus, Höhn initially, like other *völkisch* representatives, denies the suitability of
the sphere-of-influence concept without a *völkisch* basis. In parallel with his
work in constitutional and administrative law, he sought here too to eliminate
all traditional elements of statehood. But Höhn went further. One specific contribution is his distinction between the sphere-of-influence idea as a 'concept for
economic struggle' and a 'concept for political struggle'.[40] First, the sphere-
of-influence idea was directed against the excessive economic power that
Höhn saw in the continental policy pursued by Britain. Here Höhn set
against the chaotic, liberal, capitalist system of Britain, a 'planned, space-
organising, unitary, associative economy' in the 'Danube area'. But the second,
political dimension of the sphere-of-influence idea is more significant: it was
supposed to break through the 'narrow framework of liberal, territorial-State

---

[36] W Best, 'Völkische Großraumordnung' (1939) 9 *Deutsches Recht*, 1345–48; cf also *idem*,
Grundfragen einer deutschen Großraum-Verwaltung in *Festgabe für Heinrich Himmler*
(Darmstadt, Wittich, 1941), 33–60.

[37] On the controversy between Best and Schmitt: W Best, 'Nochmals: völkische
Großraumordnung statt ,völkerrechtliche' Großraumordnung', in (1941) 11 *Deutsches Recht*, 1533 ff.

[38] R Höhn, *Großraumordnung und völkisches Rechtsdenken* (Wittich, Darmstadt, 1941); *idem*,
'Reich—Großraum—Großmacht' (1942) 2 *Reich—Volksordnung—Lebensraum*, 97–226.

[39] Höhn, *Großraumordnung ibid.* 6 ff.

[40] Above 5–6.

thinking'[41] and reject the 'chaotic, liberal-capitalist economic principles in principle'.[42] Politically, this space-filling economic idyll was to be underpinned by the so-called ban on intervention for powers considered alien to the area. Here, according to Höhn, the basis is 'the fundamental concept of the distinction between friend and foe'. This is raised into the 'legal principle of a sphere-of-influence system'.[43] The opposition arises from 'sphere of influence' and 'universalism':

> an international law that sets sphere of influence against sphere of influence and raises the principle of non-intervention into the legal principle for a new sphere-of-influence system sees as its opponent the system of international law based on a number of small and medium-sized States acting in sovereign fashion . . .[44]

Höhn describes the detailed features of a '*völkisch* sphere-of-influence system' particularly clearly. He confines himself here to a New Order for Europe. He is not concerned with a world-wide conception for a new system of international law. Instead, he produces a Eurocentric, reactionary and utopian design for an anti-Western continental Europe under German leadership, with master peoples and slave peoples. Starting from the political and military situation following the outbreak of the war in 1939–1941, Höhn thus calls for the *de facto* position in Central and Eastern Europe, favourable to the Nazi State, to be fixed. He thus—whether intentionally or otherwise—decried Carl Schmitt's concept of an international law system of spheres of influence that contemplated not just a Europe dominated by Germany but also a new, world-wide system of international law.[45]

'Völkisch' and universal international law thought in National Socialism

The international lawyer Gustav Adolf Walz made perhaps the most wilful attempt to respond systematically to Schmitt's sphere-of-influence theory.[46] Walz starts like Schmitt by distinguishing between international law of sea and land warfare. Like Höhn and others he saw Britain, and Capitalism and

---

[41] R Diener, 'Reichsverfassung und Großraumverwaltung im Altertum', (1941) 1 *Reich—Volksordnung—Lebensraum*, 178. Diener was a pupil of Höhn's.

[42] Höhn, *Großraumordnung* at n 38 above.

[43] Above n 38 11 ff.

[44] Above n 38 17 ff.

[45] For further aspects surrounding perceptions on Europe in Germany during the 'Third Reich' see H Dreier, 'Die deutsche Staatsrechtslehre in der Zeit des Nationalsozialismus in Veröffentlichungen der Vereinigung der deutschen Staatsrechtslehrer' (Berlin, de Gruyter, 2001), 9–72.

[46] GA Walz, *Völkerrechtsordnung und Nationalsozialismus. Untersuchungen zur Erneuerung des Völkerrechts* (München, Eher, 1942).

Bolshevism, as the enemies of Europe that would destroy the old European international-law system under the cover of humanitarian values. Accordingly, said Walz, an 'international legal system conceived from the centre of Europe' had to be created.[47] The Nazi State was in a sense called on for this, as the upholder of old European and Germanic values. Walz used the term *'Urvolk'* (original people) for the German nation in order to strengthen its historical legitimation. This *'Urvolk'* was allegedly legitimated to incorporate all racially related peoples into the Reich.[48] In connection with the 'policy of *Lebensraum* and conquest', Walz ends by talking of *völkisch* land consolidation. By this he wished to make it clear that German imperialism was aimed only at Eastern and Central Europe, not at world dominance. In clear text, the adversaries ought to leave Germany a free hand in the power sphere it was aiming at. Outside this 'völkisch sphere of influence', rules of international law could be followed. Of course, by the time it appeared in 1942 this conceptual structure was already no longer particularly realistic.

Many international lawyers, even ones who in the phase of change were quite actively involved in the integration of the Nazi State internally and externally, did not engage at all in the sphere-of-influence debate. This included such varied international lawyers as Bruns, Grewe, Kraus, Schätzel, Scupin, Verdross and Verosta.[49] From an institutional viewpoint this circle included especially international lawyers in the Berlin Kaiser Wilhelm Institute for international law, namely directors Bruns and Schmitz and co-workers Moltke, Mosler, Stauffenberg and Wengler. The Berlin KWI, by contrast with the institutes in Kiel (Ritterbusch) and Hamburg (Berber), was spared *Gleichschaltung* or dissolution after 1933. The reasons are manifold, among them its international reputation and its intensive consulting activity for the Foreign Office. The majority of these international lawyers moved on to the defensive in the years after 1938–1939, even before Schmitt's sphere-of-influence idea. With the military rearmament and the increasing politicisation of international legal science, many adherents of international law on the traditional understanding fell silent. Many concentrated on teaching work, others became involved with historical topics. Many published in sharp tones, using the 'semantic recognition marks', but de facto remained on the basis of traditional international legal thinking. Heinrich Drost, a criminal lawyer and international lawyer from Münster, published a textbook of international law in 1936 that was written entirely without the spirit of National Socialism. He even nonchalantly cited all the relevant Jewish authors.[50] Ernst Schmitz, an early NSDAP member and

---

[47] *Ibid.* 79.

[48] Above n 46 104 ff

[49] See DF Vagts, 'International Law in the Third Reich' (1990) 84 *American Journal of International Law*, 661–704.

[50] H Drost, *Grundlagen des Völkerrechts* (München/Leipzig, Duncker & Humblot, 1936); on this see M Stolleis, at n 12, 398.

deputy director of the Berlin KWI, gave lectures on the international law of war as honorary professor of Berlin University shortly before the outbreak of war which treated the international law in force plainly and objectively.[51] These examples show that the destructive tendencies in international law apply to only a part of the development in the 'Third Reich'. In the Nazi State there was always also a traditional science of international law. In diplomatic connections traditional international law arguments were used right into the war phase, for instance in the international law of land and sea war, price law and law on prisoners of war. This situation enabled many international lawyers to keep away from the destructive debates about universal international law. They felt themselves responsible for international dealings, but were also helping to disguise the true intentions of National Socialism.

---

[51] E Schmitz, Course of Lectures *'Kriegsrecht'* (1938), 189 pages (typescript), Max Planck Institute for Comparative Public Law and International Law, Heidelberg, Germany.

5

'THE OUTSIDER DOES NOT SEE AL THE GAME. . .': PERCEPTIONS OF GERMAN LAW IN ANGLO-AMERICAN LEGAL SCHOLARSHIP, 1933–1940

*David Fraser**

Nazi Law, Continuity and The Stakes of The Debate

One popular and perhaps intellectually dominant jurisprudential view in the English-speaking world, after 1945, is that Nazi law was and is not law. According to this position, Nazi ideology so perverted our normal and accepted notions of right and wrong, of law and justice, that Nazi law was law in form only. Of course, this view can be refuted as a jurisprudential matter either by arguing at length, as have others, that it is based in a foundational normative view of natural law which is epistemologically unsound and historically untenable or perhaps even more basically that it confuses concepts of law and justice.

Nonetheless, the traditional post-War view of Nazi law as 'not law' remains a powerful and often necessary one.[1] If we cannot distinguish law before and after Auschwitz, what does that say about our ability, as a theoretical or principled matter, to characterise the rule of law as 'good' and desirable? If we do not live in a time and under norms which are radically discontinuous with 'Auschwitz', what does that say about our own ethical universe and about our relationship with good and evil, with justice, or at the very least with law?

This is, I believe, the vital role played by the discontinuity thesis and the key function served by the apparently widely accepted characterisation of Nazi law as not law. The 'perversion' idea, based in our belief that Nazi law was not law, would of course be central to subsequent prosecutions of German legal officials at Nuremberg. It is perhaps interesting and important to note however, that the 'new' international criminal offence created at Nuremberg—'crimes against

* Department of Law, Brunel University.

[1] See eg R Primus, 'A Brooding Omnipresence: Totalitarianism in Postwar Constitutional Thought', (1996) 106 *Yale Law Journal* 423 for the argument that anti-totalitarianism informs most important recent American jurisprudence.

humanity'—nonetheless, and unlike the other offences in the Nuremberg Charter, required a specific dispensation from the norms of domestic legality. Article 6 (c) of the Charter specifically states that acts governed by the concept of 'crimes against humanity' would be unlawful: '. . . whether or not in violation of the domestic law of the country where perpetrated.'

The drafters of the Charter were conscious therefore that 'offences' or actions including 'murder', 'extermination', 'enslavement', 'deportation' etc. could have been, (or often were) 'lawful' under domestic law. This is the trauma which continues to trouble law and lawyers in relation to the Holocaust or at the very least in relation to Nazi law. The very idea that Nazi law was law, that Nazi lawyers and judges were lawyers and judges, or even that a Nazi judge could be a 'good' judge,[2] is one which we viscerally reject but which many might find intellectually intriguing or even simply obvious.

The dilemma, which is both jurisprudential and psychological, still haunts us. Key questions remain unanswered. Is natural law a tenable position? Is there some other way of defining the jurisprudential point of no return at which an otherwise apparently legal system, or more precisely a legitimate system of law, crosses over into criminality? If so, the discontinuity thesis becomes nothing more than another element in a propaganda campaign during wartime and loses any claim to jurisprudential meaning or standing. Did some fundamental change operate in the German legal system after 1940 so that the last vestiges of 'law' or 'legality' were destroyed? If this is the case, then the discontinuity thesis can retain its jurisprudential standing, if a review of the historical facts reveals that such a dramatic change did occur in the German legal system at the time in question. Of course, such an analysis would still demand a particular periodisation of Nazi law which would require even proponents of the discontinuity thesis to acknowledge that German or Nazi law was both procedurally and substantively 'law' prior to that period. This would mean that as a matter of accepted and acceptable jurisprudential principles, the content of some of Nazi law, including the racial, biological exclusion of the unacceptable enemies of the *Volk*, was nonetheless recognisable as law. Or did German 'law' become 'not law' simply by the operation of historical circumstances ie because once America and Britain were at war with Germany, Nazi law was now a tool of the 'enemy'?

The temporal element of many well-known Anglo-American works dealing with various aspects of Nazi law explains why the discontinuity thesis was prominently displayed. America was either just about to enter the war or was at war with Germany.[3] The 'legal' system of the totalitarian enemy had to be

---

[2] D Fraser, 'South African Cricketers, Nazi Judges and Other Thoughts on (Not) Playing the Game', (2000) 38 *Osgoode Hall Law Journal* 563.

[3] See eg, AA Herzberg, 'The Situation of the Lawyer in Germany', (1941) 27 *American Bar Association Journal* 294; F Pollock, 'Is National Socialism a New Order?', (1941) 9 *Studies in Philosophy and Social Sciences* 440; EC Helmreich, 'The Return of the Baltic Germans', (1942) 36 *American Political Science Review* 711; AF Kiefer, 'Government Control of Publishing in

portrayed as completely at odds with the rule of law under democracy. This discontinuity, which again marked Nazi law as not law, could be and was addressed as a matter of jurisprudential and legal definition, most commonly by relying on some normative underpinning based in natural law theories.

A historically sensitive review of the construction of Nazi law as not law appears to be a useful field of jurisprudential inquiry. Anglo-American lawyers, in their discussions of Nazi legality, did not universally reject the German legal system after 1933 as being 'not law'. A careful examination of the legal discourse in English language countries, particularly the United States and Great Britain, indicates that the idea of a continuing law and legality operating within German society after 1933, was always present. [4] The portrayal of the Nazi state as an unlawful, illegitimate, criminal enterprise, operating outside Western understandings of law was not dominant in the period between the Nazis' coming to power in 1933 and the time of entry of the United States into the war. If coeval external understandings and constructions of the Nazi legal apparatus did not portray German law as 'not law', as completely lacking in legitimacy, as 'beyond the pale', if the irony of the phrase can be forgiven, then again basic questions about the jurisprudential nature of the Nazi state must be re-opened.

Critiques of Nazi Legality: The International Law Exception

Principled legal opposition to the Nazi regime and to Nazi jurisprudential practices was not limited to this period of imminent or actual hostilities. American international lawyers were at the forefront of academic and jurisprudential critiques of Nazi legality from the very early stages of the Hitler regime. Criticism from international law scholars ranged from discussions of the 'Reichstag fire' trial,[5] to analyses of Nazi legal theory,[6] and included attacks on the undemocratic nature of the referenda used to legitimate Nazi power,[7] racial

---

Germany', (1942) 57 *Political Science Quarterly* 73; WJ Dickman, 'An Outline of Nazi Civil Law', (1943) 15 *Mississippi Law Journal* 127; B Shartel & HJ Wolf, 'Civil Justice in Germany', (1944) 42 *Michigan Law Review* 863; JB Mason, 'The Judicial System of the Nazi Party', (1944) 38 *American Political Science Review* 96.

[4] Lawyers and legal scholars were not alone. Scholars in many fields offered similar responses to the Nazi regime. See M Lauwers-Rech, *Nazi Germany and the American Germanists*, (New York, Peter Lang, 1995).

[5] See V Hamel, 'The 'Van Der Lubbe' Case and Diplomatic Protection of Citizens Abroad', (1933–4) 19 *Iowa Law Review* 237.

[6] L Preuss, 'Germanic Law Versus Roman Law in National Socialist Legal Theory', (1934) 16 *Journal of Comparative Legislation* 269; VL Gott, 'The National Socialist Theory of International Law', (1938) 32 *American Journal of International Law* 704; JH Herz, 'The National Socialist Doctrine of International Law and the Problems of International Organization', (1939) 54 *Political Science Quarterly* 536.

[7] A J Zurcher, 'The Hitler Referenda', (1935) 29 *American Political Science Review* 91.

legislation,[8] and its impact on the annexation of Austria[9] and on the international refugee crisis.[10] There are, I believe, two main explanatory factors which would help us understand why American international law scholars were at the forefront of legal opposition to Nazi law in the English speaking world. First, the very nature of their field means that the level of knowledge and interest in the affairs of a foreign country would have been higher than that in the legal community as a whole. Secondly, international law, then as now, operates largely and by necessity, on the basis of underlying legal and moral norms. While international legal morality today may be said to find its embodiment in various formal legal instruments, at the time, the existence of something called 'international law' was not necessarily universally accepted nor was there a broadly accepted and actualised normative content of the discipline. Of all the legal academics and practitioners who had to base their understanding of the fundamental norms of 'law' in unwritten and unarticulated underlying epistemological and moral categories, international lawyers were at the forefront. It would only be natural then, that it would be they who were most aware of what was happening in Germany and who were also able to bring to their analyses of the situation, a basic moral and ethical framework for their legal critique. At some level, then, international lawyers, it could be argued, constituted an 'interpretive community' apart, a group of legal scholars and practitioners whose world view distinguished them from their municipal and inward-looking colleagues.

International law discourse of the period continued, nonetheless, to draw a distinction, vital to the issues under discussion here, between 'law' and 'morality'. Thus, in his critique of the Nuremberg Laws, Garner makes it clear that even a violation of 'the conscience of mankind' did not per se render Nazi law invalid under then existing international law norms. He wrote:

As international law now stands, it probably cannot be successfully argued that the German Citizenship law of 1935 violates any positive prescription of the law of nations. It is a municipal statute—a piece of domestic legislation—which falls within the legislative competence of any independent State, unless that competence has been limited by treaty engagements with other States. Nevertheless, it is believed that such legislation as this will meet with general disapproval, because it is an outstanding example of race discrimination, if it is not in violation of one of the fundamental

---

[8] L Preuss, 'The Position of Aliens in National Socialist Penal Law Reform', (1935) 29 *American Journal of International Law* 206; JW Garner, 'Recent German Nationality Legislation', (1936) 30 *American Journal of International Law* 96; JW Garner, 'The Nazi Proscription of German Professors of International Law', (1939) 33 *American Journal of International Law* 112.

[9] CG Fenwick, 'Editorial Comment: Fuit Austria', (1938) 32 *American Journal of International Law* 312; JW Garner, 'Questions of State Succession Raised by the German Annexation of Austria', (1938) 32 *American Journal of International Law* 421.

[10] EC Stowell, 'Intercession Against the Persecution of Jews', (1936) 30 *American Journal of International Law* 102; L W Holborn, 'The Legal Status of Political Refugees, 1920–1938', (1938) 32 *American Journal of International Law* 680.

rights of man as they are generally recognised today and generally approved by the conscience of mankind.[11]

Here we find, in the leading journal of American international legal scholarship, the clear, correct and obvious, assertion that racial discrimination within the context of domestic legislation was not at this time considered to be a violation of international law. This is important for our understanding of the construction of Nazi law in the Anglo-American literature not just because it may bring into question basic subsequent assertions about the nature and content of the substantive legal norms of international law, but equally because it points out that international legal discourse at the time did not exclude the Nazi legal regime from the category 'law'. At the time Garner wrote his commentary, the legal system was functioning under the operative legal normativity of the epoch. Furthermore, domestic, racial legislation at least as obnoxious as that found in 1930s Germany continued to be in force in the United States and in other Western democracies. Nazi legality was perfectly legal, or at least as perfectly legal as the law of many American states.

The key issue raised here is the definitional one. Not only must we decide what it is we mean by 'law', 'legality' and the 'rule of law', but we must also engage in careful analyses about various concepts, ideas and positions which are put forward by the different claimants in the rhetorical and ideological debate, both then and now. The issue becomes, to put it simply, at what point, if ever, does something which looks like law from the procedural or formal perspective, because of its substantive content, become 'not law'? Where is the point of rupture between 'law' and 'Nazi law'? More broadly, is it accurate, fair or even useful, to understand the period between 1933 and 1945 in German law, as an aberrant time, in which all normative and institutional characteristics of that nation, must be quarantined? These questions of rupture, continuity and discontinuity are vital. The very idea of definitional stability, of a *Grundnorm*, of something which is clearly 'law' and something which is clearly 'not law', is absolutely essential to determining the philosophical soundness and historical accuracy of the discontinuity thesis.

A brief survey of the attitudes expressed by legal academics and lawyers outside Germany, writing in mainstream professional and learned periodicals can prove invaluable in testing the discontinuity thesis.[12] If, as many international

---

[11] 'Recent German Nationality Legislation', at n 8 above, 99. It might also be noted here that as far as Garner is concerned certain restrictions on citizens' rights may be perfectly acceptable if they are based on other criteria which would disqualify the individual on the grounds of a real incapacity. He states: '. . . under the law of the latter States, the first category of persons usually embraces only those who for reasons of age, sex, lack of education or moral character are not deemed qualified to exercise political privileges for the best interests of the State, whereas the basis of the German distinction is primarily racial.' (98). Discrimination against women clearly was part of acceptable legality and did not shock the conscience of mankind.

[12] The survey is in fact brief, not because of some methodological weakness inherent in the project, but rather because, by and large, Anglo-American legal scholarship was, at this time at least, insular and myopic in focus and interest.

lawyers of the time seem to have claimed, Nazi law was in violation of international legal norms, then a strong argument for discontinuity can be established.
That argument would be further strengthened if other members of the legal
interpretive community shared this opinion about the correct characterisation
of Nazi law as not law. Unfortunately for the proponents of the discontinuity
thesis, the proof of a unanimous or even majority condemnation of Nazi law
among Anglo-American lawyers themselves is clearly lacking. The writings of
Anglo-American legal scholars at the time do suggest that there are strong
points of communality and continuity between the normative rules and discourses of German law after 1933 and those rules and discourses in the English-
speaking world of the period. I would suggest that we may indeed learn more
useful legal, moral and ethical lessons from an examination of these points of
continuity between legal systems than we ever will from the more comforting
view that we share nothing in common with Nazi law.

Understanding Nazi Law: Contemporary Anglo-American Accounts

An article written in 1940 by Richard Flournoy, after the invasion of Poland and
the start of World War II, and long after the exclusion of Jews from an Aryan
German *Volksgemeinschaft* had been implemented, demonstrates at a general
level the continuity thesis.[13] Published in a professional journal which was at the
forefront of condemning Nazi policies, this article deals with the history of the
various attempts to legislate with regards to American citizenship. Flournoy
writes:

> Thus the nationality laws of any state necessarily reflect its political history and
> character. An outstanding example of the fact last mentioned may be found in the
> nationality laws adopted in Germany in recent years.[14]

He then goes on to analyse German nationality law from 1914, with extensive references to the deprivation of citizenship rights of Jewish Germans contained in the *Reich Citizenship Law*. An examination of British and American
nationality legislation follows. For Flournoy, and for the editors of the most
prestigious international law journal in the United States, the Nuremberg Laws
fit comfortably not just within the historical evolution of German law under
the *Kaiserreich*, but they also serve as a useful point of comparison for developments in the two great English-speaking democracies. There is no idea here,
after the Nuremberg Laws, after the refugee crises of the previous years, and
after the beginning of the war in Europe, that German nationality legislation,

---

[13] RW Flournoy, 'Revision of Nationality Laws of the United States', (1940) 34 *American
Journal of International Law* 36.

[14] *Ibid*. See also 'Development of German Law on Nationality', (1938) 186 *Law Times* 122.

the legalised exclusion of German Jews, was anything other than the perfectly valid expression of that state's 'political history and character'.

Flournoy goes beyond a simple approbation by silence of legalised anti-Semitism as a valid legislative goal. Instead he apparently issues a call for the adoption of a worldview which is not readily distinguishable from the ideological, jurisprudential underpinnings of Nazi racial legislation. Flournoy writes:

> Laws, in their nature, require some sacrifices on the part of individuals or groups, and this is especially true with regard to nationality laws, which relate to the very substance and texture of the state itself. In the shaping of such laws, affecting profoundly, as they do, the character of the country, it is especially important to consider first and last, not only claims of special groups and individuals, who are likely to be represented by special advocates, but the welfare of the people as a whole, whose only advocates are to be found in the membership of the Congress itself.[15]

While it is possible to read this part of the text as a call for a Burkean idealisation of the functions of representative government, the rhetoric invoked by the author clearly echoes many of the themes of Nazi ideology and legal practice surrounding citizenship. Notions of sacrifice for the collective good, the idea of the nation as a whole, would not have been out of place in Nazi rhetoric about the duties of the *Reich* citizen to the *Volk*.

Again, this does not mean that Flournoy was a Nazi, nor that the United States was planning to deprive its Jewish citizens of their rights.[16] What it does mean is that even in 1940, it was not considered inappropriate to compare the goals of US nationality and citizenship law to those of Germany. One can also find many of these same themes, the threat from unchecked migrants to the national fabric and fibre, in today's debates on the subjects of immigration and national identity. Arguments that Nazi Germany was a criminal state, cast out from the community of nations because of its perversion of law generally, are belied, I believe, by the discursive reality of contemporary Anglo-American jurisprudence, of which the Flournoy article is but one example.

Concern among American scholars, many of them German natives, about events in Germany, is also evidenced in the scholarly literature of the period. The country and its political system were carefully and knowledgeably studied. Even before Hitler's formal rise to power, American scholars were examining the political situation in Germany. There is little evidence of unanimity among Germanists or comparative lawyers on events there. In 1930, three years before the beginning of what would come to be characterised as the 'criminal' Hitler

---

[15]   (1940) 34 *American Journal of International Law* 46.

[16]   Although the history of US immigration law and practice would lend support to the idea that anti-Semitism was rife among those in charge of immigration and that American Jews in particular were aware of the dangers of legalised taxonomies based on race. See J Perlmann, ''Race or People': Federal Race Classifications for Europeans in America, 1898–1913', SSRN Working Paper No 320, January 2001.

State, Carl Friedrich published an important article 'Dictatorship in Germany?'[17] Discussing the uncertain domestic political situation following the end of the occupation of the Rhineland, Friedrich carefully analysed all the political factors leading to the possible establishment of an authoritarian regime in Germany, including the invocation of emergency powers under Article 48 of the Constitution.[18] Rather than interpreting this constitutional manoeuvre as leading inevitably in the direction of a dictatorship, Friedrich saw the invocation of emergency powers as actually promoting stability and democracy. He wrote:

> In such conditions, Germany might well be congratulated for the wisdom of its constitution-makers, who included in their fundamental charter provisions which enable a responsible minority to tide the country over a temporary impasse, if it has the backing of a constitutionally elected President and a permanent civil service of high excellence and proven loyalty to the state. The advantage of such an arrangement to Germany is shared by those who deal with her internationally. For the obligations of the country are safeguarded by such a flexible constitution. Truly benevolent despotism of this sort forestalls internal chaos and a complete breakdown of the government, particularly when it is placed in the hands of a man who has grown old in unswerving loyalty and service to his country.[19]

Of course, the benefit of hindsight allows us to see now how wrong Friedrich was in his prognostications.[20] But this is not the important point. The situation in Germany in the early 1930s, while confused, was not seen to be a legal system in a position of radical rupture or of revolutionary change. It is vital to the issue of continuity/discontinuity to underline that for Friedrich, the use of the emergency provisions of Article 48 of the Weimar Constitution, was not per se contrary to a general understanding of the paradigm of constitutional governance. The history of the economic and social dislocations caused by the Great Depression in the United States, for example, also gave rise to many instances of government by emergency decree, often of a problematic constitutional nature, both at the state and national levels. Indeed, at least one American scholar urged courts to adopt interpretive mechanisms and strategies which would confirm the constitutional normality of such decrees.

---

[17] (1930) 9 *Foreign Affairs* 118.

[18] At 123.

[19] At 132. The French constitutional scholar René Brunet made similar points in his discussion of Article 48. See R Brunet, *The German Constitution*, Joseph Gollomb (trans.), (London, T. Fisher Unwin Ltd, 1923), 162–70.

[20] Although he persisted even later in insisting that Article 48 posed no threat to democracy and constitutionalism. He wrote in April 1933 that '. . . Germany will remain a constitutional, democratic state with strong socialising tendencies whose backbone will continue to be its professional civil service.' 'The Development of the Executive Power in Germany', (1933) 27 *American Political Science Review* 185. In that same month, the *Law for the Restoration of the Professional Civil Service* was passed. This statute imposed the first legal prohibitions on German Jews since their emancipation in 1871.

If we are entering upon an era of social and economic planning, legislation upheld on emergency grounds with the corollary that it would be unconstitutional in 'normal' times can only shackle real adjustments of the social framework to new economic situations and conditions. It is better openly to make such adjustment without any doctrine of emergency . . . The Constitution and the police power provide ample scope for the allowance of reasonable experimentation not only to meet the needs of the present depression but to prevent the ever-recurring cataclysmic disturbances to which our economic system has been periodically subject.[21]

It cannot be argued, then, that the invocation of a similar constitutional mechanism in 1933 by Hitler and the Nazi party, marks per se the beginning of the extralegality of the Nazi legal system. While hindsight might allow us to see this constitutional step as one committed in bad faith and as part of a broader plan to gain control of the state apparatus, such an analysis misses the central concern of the 'interpretive community' viewpoint. How did the participants in the legal system, the creators of legal discourse at the time, experience the system itself and their role therein?

Friedrich, a professor at Harvard, and Clark, from Columbia, clearly did not see strong executive government, which characterised the early days of Nazi legality, as anything other than in keeping with the political, economic, social and constitutional requirements of the time, in both the United States and Germany.

Later interventions in related fields after the Hitler regime came to power reveal a similar belief that while the Nazis were operating fundamental changes to the German state apparatus, these changes did not qualify for immediate and definitional exclusion from the concept 'law'. Thus, Fritz Marx, writing about the revolutionary reconstruction wrought upon the Civil Service, largely as a result of its politicisation under the Nazis and the removal of 'non-Aryans' under the provisions of the *Law for the Restoration of the Professional Civil Service*, could see and explain the 'logic' and even necessity of the Nazi policies.

In a spiritually homogeneous people, he can enforce the will of the leader without the formal safeguards of 'independence' through life tenure. Such logic could readily legitimise a thoroughgoing transformation of the legal status of civil servants . . .[22]

Not only did Marx assert that the changes to the basic structure of the administrative branch of government did not by definition violate democratic, legal norms, he further argued that the changes brought about in Germany could be seen to be similar to, or continuous with, certain changes brought about during recent events in the United States, He wrote:

A permanence of the one-party state will certainly ease transitional difficulties for the German civil service; for there is no more essential condition for the smooth functioning of the public service as the instrument of government than stability. And

---

[21] JP Clark, 'Emergency Powers', (1934) 49 *Political Science Quarterly* 268, 283.
[22] 'German Bureaucracy in Transition', (1934) 28 *American Political Science Review* 467, 480.

the ethical foundation of civil service ideology has much in common with the emotional pattern of the New Deal, with its emphasis on allegiance, devotion, and sacrifice and its middle-class appeals.[23]

While others did not draw such clear parallels between the politics and policies of governmental reform in the United States and Germany, neither did they assert that which was happening at the time in Germany was completely unacceptable. While they continued to be bothered by certain aspects of Nazi reform, they also saw much of what was happening as being consistent with the previous history of government reform in Germany.[24]

Nazi agricultural and land-holding policy, based in the ideology of blood and soil, was described as consistent in intent and practice with the 'Internal Colonisation' policy of the pre-World War I era and with concepts of land redistribution and social justice.[25] The exclusion of German Jews from the *volkisch* peasantry was not deemed worthy of mention. Similarly, a detailed study of the German railway system conspicuously placed the Nazi model as one which was in practice consistent with the entire history of public enterprise in modern Germany.[26] For Macmahon and Dittmar, 'German' and 'Nazi' policy were not only continuous, but Nazi practice was in some ways a marked improvement in the governance model.

The clearest example of their analysis of Nazi practice and its connections with previous policies can be seen in their discussion of personnel issues in state enterprises.

> Rigidity in the personnel of a large public undertaking is apt to be lessened by keeping down the proportion of full civil servants. In the decade before 1933, the managements of autonomous public enterprise in Germany were pushing in that direction. It is interesting to note how far the tendency has been carried since the advent of National Socialism.[27]

In addition,

> Most of this, of course, is the mere continuation of the practices of an old and progressive state industry which had been developed in the context of German social legislation. The National Socialist régime, while contracting the proportion of railway

---

[23] *Ibid.* 479.

[24] See eg F Marx, 'Germany's New Civil Service Act', (1937) 31 *American Political Science Review* 878; G Krebs, 'A Step Toward *Reichsreform* in Germany', (1938) 32 *American Political Science Review* 536; AV Boerner, 'The Position of the NSDAP in the German Constitutional Order', (1938) 32 *American Political Science Review* 1059; 'Toward Reichsreform: The Reichsgaue', (1939) 33 *American Political Science Review* 853; cf J Caplan, *Government Without Administration: State and Civil Service in Weimar and Nazi Germany*, (Oxford Clarendon, 1988).

[25] MP Jasny, 'Some Aspects of German Agricultural Settlement', (1937) 52 *Political Science Quarterly* 208.

[26] AW Macmahon & WR Dittmar, 'Autonomous Public Enterprise—The German Railways', (1939) 54 *Political Science Quarterly* 481 and Part II (1940) 55 *Political Science Quarterly* 25.

[27] *Ibid.* 506.

workers who have civil service status, has conserved and extended certain elements of security.[28]

Macmahon and Dittmar are here underlining two elements of contemporary political and legal analysis of the Nazi reforms to employment and civil service structures. First, the changes are seen to be consistent with long standing trends and practices in Germany. Secondly, the changes are constructed and interpreted as being for the good. Changes introduce greater flexibility in corporate governance and service provision while at the same time maintaining protections and benefits for the workers. The analysis of the German railway system offered here would not necessarily be out of place in literature about the administrative and corporatised state today.

The authors expressly address the legislative and legal framework for the changes brought about by the Nazis in the railway and for the employment status of railroad employees. The law in question is the statute which dealt with *'the Restoration of the Professional Civil Service'*.[29] In other words, as far as the first legislative instrument which began the slow and inexorable process of the legalised exclusion of German Jews is concerned, Macmahon and Dittmar simply describe

> The law of April 7, 1933, which declared its purpose to be the 'restoration of the professional civil service' and the supplementary decrees applied to Reichsbahn employees as regards the paragraphs relating to Aryans and to communists.[30]

For these American scholars, the exclusion of Jewish Germans and others from employment in civil service jobs was noteworthy only in so far as it could be seen to be part of the continuous improvements being made to the governance structure of the railways. The relatively late date of publication of the two-part article by Macmahon and Dittmar, 1939 and 1940, gives a stark illustration of the way in which American scholars continued, at a point in time at which the Nazi régime could no longer be said to give rise to any illusion about its true character, to construct Nazi legal mechanisms as continuous, acceptable and ordinary in the minds of members of the academic community. The changes and improvements to the German railway system and its corporate structure fit easily into a long line of structural readjustments dating back to the period of the *Kaiserreich*. The exclusion through legislation of German

---

[28] Above n 26, 509.

[29] Article I (4) of the Law stated that 'The Reich Bank and the German State Railway are empowered to make corresponding regulations.' The 11 April 1933 regulation under the Law defined those to be excluded as anyone with one grandparent who was a non-Aryan, a broader definition than would later be operative under the *Law for the Protection of German Blood and Honour*, which required three Jewish grandparents. None of this was particularly relevant or of any concern for the authors of this study.

[30] At 507. The Reichsbahn had further experience with 'the new managerialism' of Nazi racial policy. See eg AC Mierzejewski, 'A Public Enterprise in the Service of Mass Murder: The Deutsche Reichsbahn and the Holocaust', (2001) 15 *Holocaust and Genocide Studies* 33.

Jews from state employment is for these authors barely worthy of comment and hardly indicative of any radical break with the legal and administrative past.

Other reputable journals simply published descriptive articles by German lawyers about the situation in their country, including as a matter of fact and of law, the legal exclusion of German Jews from the Civil Service, without further elaboration or comment.[31] The reforms of the constitutional order in Germany brought about by Hitler, the abandonment of Parliamentary democracy, the creation of a one-party state, the abolition of civil service neutrality and legalised anti-Semitism, were not considered by Anglo-American experts in various legal fields at the time as constituting a rupture with acceptable legal norms.

Throughout the 1930s, articles continued to appear in the leading periodicals of the English-speaking legal profession and academy supporting the Nazi legal regime. Writing in the *Scottish Law Review*, on the Reichstag Fire Trial, C de B Murray, urged his readers to place themselves in the position of imagining that a similar process were occurring in Britain. In such a case, he argued, no one would dare pretend that the accused would not receive a fair trial. It would be unjust to reach the opposite conclusion where Nazi justice was concerned. After all, he wrote:

> For example, to the foreigner the feeling against the Jews appears very ugly but it must be remembered that the outsider does not see all the game, whatever the proverb may say. A strong conviction (supposing it exists in Germany) that too much power is at present in the hands of financiers is not per se an unreasonable conviction, though it may produce a very bitter feeling against the Jews.[32]

He went on:

> We are in the presence of a new civilisation, and, one hopes, a new culture. And for that reason one ought to look at the picture as a whole, not extenuating the blemishes, but to not obscuring the merits either.[33]

If one adopts the proper perspective and puts developments in their real context, then one must really attempt to understand events from the perspective of the Germans. The 'Jews', here without question assimilated to 'financiers', and by definition excluded from the status of 'Germans', are to some extent to blame for their own situation. One must expect a few rough spots in the creation of a new civilization. From its open endorsement of Nazism's underlying legalised anti-Semitism to its call for a strict analogy between the Reichstag Fire trial and an arson trial in Britain, Murray's article is a clear example of the idea that Nazi law, was not, in its early stages, so outside the norms of Western legal

---

[31] H Tasse, 'Civil Service Law in Germany', (1937) 19 *Journal of Comparative Legislation and International Law* 260.

[32] 'The Reichstag Trial', (1933) 49 *Scottish Law Review* 307, 308.

[33] *Ibid.* 309.

culture that the discontinuity thesis can look to contemporary British legal discourse at the time for complete and unqualified support.

American legal academe was likewise not totally inimical to Nazi law. Two years after Murray's article, a reputable American law review published a symposium on comparative property law. Among the articles included in the collection was one by a Germanophone Swiss law professor on the new Nazi regime of farmland holding.[34] The *Reich Farm Law* was a key, if somewhat controversial and ultimately unsuccessful, component of the Nazi legal revolution. The preamble to law stated that,

> By upholding the old German custom of entailment, the Reich Government wishes to retain the peasantry as the blood spring of the German nation.

This particular legal reform sought to integrate notions of 'duty' and 'citizenship' into the legal relations of the *Volk* by abolishing 'liberal' ideas of property and replacing them with *volkisch* and therefore more racially pure, 'blood and soil' principles. Liberal, non-German, notions of the free transfer of land, in the words of Professor Kaden are pernicious because,

> They threaten the peasantry as such and thereby endanger the existence of the nation and the State to which that peasantry belongs.[35]

Professor Kaden elaborates that proper and clear legal principles need to be established to create appropriate and acceptable qualifications for land holding.

> First of all, it is necessary, according to these (paragraphs), that the owner hold German citizenship. This is paramount, because the peasantry is to constitute the basic stock of the German people. Secondly, it is necessary that the owner of the farm be of Germanic blood. Whoever is of non-Germanic blood cannot fulfill [sic] the mission which the law imposes upon and instrusts [sic] to the owner of an hereditary peasant farm—to be the 'life fountain of the German people'.[36]

As the Professor goes on to explain, this means that Jews are by legal definition excluded, although this does leave open for him the intriguing legal question as to whether English blood, as non-German, would disqualify the putative owner. All of these issues simply come down to the fact that while some technical legal difficulties may remain, the statute,

> ... shows to what extent the law giver was concerned to master these problems and to solve them in an intelligible and just manner.[37]

---

[34] EH Kaden, 'The Peasant Inheritance Law in Germany—On the Basis of the Reich's Hereditary Peasant Farm Law of 1933', (1934–5) 20 *Iowa Law Review* 350.

[35] *Ibid*. 352. The law declared that 'Only German citizens of German blood or of that of a similar race and who are respectable are eligible to be peasants.'

[36] Above 370. See generally, G Corni, *Hitler and the Peasants: Agrarian Policy of the Third Reich*, (New York, Berg, 1990); S Baranowski, *The Sanctity of Rural Life: Nobility, Protestantism and Nazism in Weimar Prussia*, (New York and Oxford, Oxford University Press, 1995).

[37] Above n 34, 388.

This article is not the only one which allows us to see the ease with which Nazi anti-Semitic legislation fit into existing legal discourse, not just within Germany, but more importantly within the legal practice and understanding of 'law' within the Western English-speaking democracies.

The *Tulane Law Review*, noted for its strength in comparative law, was a leading journal in communicating knowledge of European legal systems among US lawyers. It published a series of reports from a leading German lawyer on developments in that country during the 1930s. These articles all deal with Nazi anti-Semitic legislation as if this type of enactment is to be expected and as if there is nothing extraordinary about the content of German law.[38] Describing the Nuremberg Laws, the German attorney simply states that the laws:

> ... inflict various legal incapacities upon the Jews affecting their civil and political status and establish special criminal offences. Thus, marriages of Jews or members of racially undesirable people, such as gypsies and negroes, with nationals of German or kindred blood are prohibited.[39]

For the editors of the *Law Review* of the segregated Tulane University, in the Deep South state of Louisiana, any discussion of 'racially undesirable people' and of legal restrictions imposed upon them, would not have struck a chord of disharmony or existential, professional self-doubt. Such ideas were part and parcel of the legal systems of many States of the United States where legalised racial discrimination was the norm, and where anti-miscegenation statutes were at the time on the books and where they remained until well after the time Nazi law had been declared 'not law' after the triumph of the forces of democracy in Europe.[40] The discursive climate in which these articles appeared was one in which anti-Semitism and legalised race-based discriminations were not unknown in the Anglo-American world. Developments in Germany, which codified and legalised the Nazi racialist worldview, were not seen to be outside the bounds of what lawyers understood as a procedurally and normatively recognisable and acceptable legal system. For them Nazi law was still clearly recognisable as 'law'. Even the anti-Jewish purge of the legal profession itself and the Aryanisation of legal education in Germany were not enough to convince Anglo-American lawyers that their German counterparts were stepping outside the boundaries of the interpretive community of law and lawyers.

---

[38] See RR Kuhlewein, 'German Legislation Since 1933', (1936) 10 *Tulane Law Review* 425; 'Recent German Legislation', (1937) 11 *Tulane Law Review* 601; 'German Legislation From 1937 to 1939', (1939–40) 14 *Tulane Law Review* 593.

[39] 'German Legislation Since 1933' 431–32.

[40] For historical examples of the legal lengths to which American courts would go to uphold the validity of legislative prohibitions on inter-racial marriage, see eg *Dupre v Executor of Boulard*, 10 La.411 (1855); *State v Tutty*, 41 F. 753 (1890); *Baker v Carter* 68 P. 2d 85 (1937); In *re Shun T. Takahashi's Estate*, 129 P. 2d 217 (1942).

Several articles published during this period dealt with changes to the legal education system in Germany, changes which would include the expulsion of Jewish German law professors and students as well as lawyers and judges. Yet, there is little, if any, overt criticism of the Nazification of the German legal academy.[41] I could find no mention of the 'Aryanisation' of legal education and of the profession in the literature on German law published between 1933–1938 in the standard periodical literature in the Anglo-American world. Instead, what one discovers is work that would easily, in hindsight, be classified as Nazi propaganda. For example, the article by the German lawyer Weniger in the *Illinois Law Review* contains the following history of the legal profession in his country:

> After National-Socialism had come to power in 1933, and new men had taken the lead in government as well as in the professional organisations, it was urgently pointed out that the profession could not be left to drift into decay.[42]

This drift into decay was dealt with in several ways but the result was a desirable one, despite some minor inconvenience.

> Whilst entry into the profession is thus restricted in many respects, its exercise is entirely free, being subject only to the law, to the rules of professional ethics, and to supervision by the professional organisation.[43]

Weniger's contribution can be read in hindsight, if it could not be so read at the time, as little more than an apologia for the Nazification of German law and the legal profession. But its interest is much deeper for present purposes. Here we have a member of the 'interpretive community' offering his view that practicing law in Germany in 1939 is just like practicing law in the United States. This view is expressed in an academic journal from a reputable law school, and is nowhere contradicted. Of course, he recognises that there are some restrictions placed upon entry into the profession but 'Jews' are not mentioned, just as the restrictions on their entry into certain American institutions of higher learning were also not mentioned at the time. Articles in the academic mainstream of American legal education easily convey the impression that Nazi law in the 1930s, with its anti-Semitism and policy of racial biology, was not considered to be completely excludable from that mainstream of American legal knowledge.

For some, the parallels were clear. Thus, Professor Max Rheinstein could write (and the *Wisconsin Law Review* could publish) as late as 1938 that as far as the academy was concerned:

---

[41] See L Loewensohn, 'Legal Education in Austria and Germany', (1939) 55 *Scottish Law Journal* 166; M Schmittoff, 'Recent Reform of Legal Education in Germany', (1936) *Society of Public Teachers of Law Journal* 34; H Weniger, 'The Profession of the Bar in Germany', (1939) 34 *Illinois Law Review* 85; M Rheinstein, 'Law Faculties and Law Schools: A Comparison of Legal Education in the United States and Germany', (1938) *Wisconsin Law Review* 5.

[42] 'The Profession of the Bar in Germany' at n 41 above, 85–86.

[43] *Ibid.* 87.

If a man who has been a member of a German law faculty has, like the writer of this article, the thrilling experience of being appointed to the staff of an American law school, he is struck by the similarity of his new and his old surroundings. He finds an impressive illustration of the essential unity of Western civilization and its institutions. He moves in a familiar atmosphere; he has little difficulty in feeling himself at home. There are differences, of course, and they will be emphasised in the following, as in any comparison. We should not forget, however, that they are less important than the essential unity of common traditions, common aims, common social functions, and a common spirit.[44]

Once more we find a leading law journal publishing an article which proposes a clear parallel between the systems of legal education in the United States and in Nazi Germany, a parallel strengthened by the points of commonality and continuity in Western civilisation. Law, German and/or American, is a foundation stone in the bulwark of the common traditions which unite the two nations as members of Western civilisation. This article, which reproduces in an appendix the translated statutes dealing with legal education under Hitler,[45] makes and is able to make, these claims of commonality and continuity at such a late date without any sense of self-doubt. Not a word is written about purges or expulsions from the academy or the profession. No mention of the Aryanisation of University faculties in Germany is made. These are apparently only minor concerns, unworthy of note as compared to the continuity of the great traditions of American and German culture and law, and all this despite Rheinstein's biography and his experience of discrimination.

German Criminal Law and the Nazi Criminal State in Anglo-American Legal Scholarship

Criminal law best embodies the practical experience and ideology of legal Nazism with its centralisation of the State/Criminal Law/Police bureaucracy functions under a racial state ideology. At the same time, the characterisation of this key governmental arrangement of Nazism as itself 'criminal' is central to the idea that Nazi law was not law and that the Hitler state was in fact a 'criminal state'. An examination of the discourse circulating in the interpretative community of Anglo-American legal thought and practice will perhaps offer us invaluable clues as to the status of Nazi criminal law within Western legal tradition and culture.

The general field of criminal law offers perhaps the clearest example of Nazi ideology in its legal form. This area of law, characterised in all jurisdictions by the manifestation and implementation of the repressive power of the State, under the Nazis, incorporated two of the most important elements of the Nazi

---

[44] Above n 41, 5.
[45] Above n 41, 29.

Weltanschauung: the identity and identification of the Nazi party, the State and the *Volk*, on the one hand and the centrality of racial bio-ideology on the other hand. These two elements, while perhaps analytically separable, are, in fact, part and parcel of an overriding legal vision.

That such an ideological vision is in clear conflict with the ideals of individual freedom and autonomy which characterise traditional Western versions of the rule of law is clear. In the field of criminal law, for example, a basic principle is that of *nulla poenem sine lege*, ie that no one may be found guilty of criminal offence unless that offence is previously clearly defined and public. Lawrence Preuss is one author who consistently criticised Nazi law in the strongest terms.[46] Preuss offers this summary of the Nazi position which for him abandoned the principle of *nulla poena sine lege*.

> The principle of the non-retroactivity of the criminal law stands at the beginning of the *Reichsstrafgesestzbuch*, and is among the fundamental rights guaranteed by the Weimar Constitution. That it is the product of the liberal, humanitarian thought of the *Aufklärungzeit* apparently suffices to condemn it, however, in nationalist eyes.[47]

However, at this stage, even a critic of the Nazi regime like Preuss was not willing or able to dismiss the system of Nazi legality in the criminal law arena with its vast array of repressive mechanisms as outside 'law'. At this most vital definitional point of Nazi legality, the criminal justice system and the repressive state apparatus, even critics were forced to recognise that a high degree of continuity existed with numerous aspects of previous embodiments of German criminal law. Preuss himself states that:

> When the National Socialists came to power, they found at their disposal a well-stocked armoury of legal weapons with which to combat their enemies. There remained only the tasks of filling certain gaps, of increasing the severity of penalties, and of applying the law in the spirit of the authoritarian state.[48]

Even Otto Kirchheimer was compelled to construct his attacks in terms which to a reader today might seem conceptually problematic. For him, the ideological underpinnings of Nazi criminal law could be found in the complete shift,

> . . . from the objective characteristics of the criminal act to its subjective elements. It is suggested that the state is justified in demanding greater self-control from the individual as the main object of the offensive action of the authorities.'[49]

---

[46] Above n 6

[47] 'The Position of Aliens in National Socialist Penal Law Reform', (1935) 29 *American Journal of International Law* 206, 216.

[48] *Ibid*. 209. Footnote omitted.

[49] 'Criminal Law in National-Socialist Germany', (1939) 8 *Studies in Philosophy and Social Sciences* 444. See more generally, K Lowenstein, 'Law in the Third Reich', (1938) 45 *Yale Law Journal* 779.

Current debates in the Western democracies about penal and criminal justice policies also place a renewed emphasis on the individual responsibility of those engaging in anti-social behaviour. This does not mean that we are seeing a resurgence of Nazi-inspired criminology. It does mean, however, that simplistic assertions about the criminality of Nazi law as epitomised in Hitler's criminal justice system need to be more carefully and explicitly articulated in light of contemporary understandings about what was happening in Germany.

A brief survey of Anglo-American legal literature indicates that as far as many members of the legal interpretive community were concerned, Nazi theory and practice fitted clearly and identifiably within the mainstream of criminal law and criminological discourse. As in the case of law more generally, some legal scholars seem to have been content to offer uncritical exegeses of Nazi criminal law theory and practice. A Canadian scholar, for example, wrote,

> The significant figure in the new criminal law is not the unworthy member of society, but society itself. The criminal law is to be built up on broad lines of defence of the strong and proved and capable element of the German people as against the morally ill and unworthy element of social decadence. The identity of law and morals must be restored, that is, it must replace the un-German contrast between morality on the one hand and the feeling for law on the other. The wrongdoer in a criminal sense must be the wrongdoer in a social sense. In particular, factors of social security must be built up; society must not any longer wait to act until an unworthy member of its group has begun a wrongful act; the dangerous element in society must, as early as possible, be forestalled by preventive measures. The ideal of racial security must be made operative.[50]

A close reading of this text describing German criminal law reveals quickly why English-language scholars by and large could not and did not exclude Nazi criminal law from the category 'law'. All of the goals of Nazi legality, prevention of criminality, the creation of a nexus between law and morality and the like, can be identified within the traditions of Western jurisprudence. Debates about the law/morality nexus, the struggle to balance the rights of individuals and the rights of society as a whole, the social responsibility of offenders, are all elements of historic and current criminological study and discourses.

The contemporary English-language literature in the field of criminology and criminal justice evidences the same uncertainties and debates about German law as was found in other learned discussions of different aspects of post-1933 legality. For each example of criticism of German and Nazi penal policy and practice, we can find one lauding or at the very least refusing to condemn Nazi law as outside the accepted definitions of the 'rule of law'.

---

[50] FC Auld, 'Law Reform in Germany', (1934) *Canadian Bar Review* 26.

EAM Wedderburn dismissed criticisms of the 'new' German criminal law by arguing:

> The Nationalist Socialist view is that *all* behaviour worthy of punishment shall meet with its just reward and that there shall be no evasion of the meshes of the law. Henceforward in Germany the ruling maxim is *nullum crimen sine poena,* and it is the arduous duty of the judge to realise true justice. Revolutionary as this may sound, anyone familiar with the fictions, distinctions, and interpretations resorted to in the development of the Criminal Law of many other nations will agree that the principle at least is not new.[51]

He then goes on to argue that Nazi legality is indeed at least partly consistent with some idea of the 'rule of law':

> With these new duties it is clear that judges will in future have to create as well as administer law. This is contrary to the democratic doctrine of the division of authority in the sphere of judiciary and legislature, but it is not a complete negation of the idea.[52]

Anyone familiar with current jurisprudential debates will indeed recognise the familiar tension between those who argue that judges should simply apply the law and those who argue that the very principle of judicial decision-making requires that judges 'make' law within certain boundaries. But the important point here is not so much that one can recognise recurrent themes in present day debates over jurisprudential basics, but rather that at the time, these debates took place within a context which did not automatically, at least for some of the participants, eliminate Nazi legality from consideration. While some contemporaries were extremely critical of developments within the criminal justice system in Germany from 1933 onwards, others were nonetheless willing to consider that these changes were not totally unacceptable or that they fell completely outside the realm of what was then recognised as 'law'.

In the pre-war period, from the Nazi seizure of power, it is clear that Western legal discourse considered the changes operating in Germany under Nazi legality to be changes occurring within a continuous context of Western, or at least recognisably German, legality. While there was disagreement about the nature of the changes and the dangers they posed to some basic principles of the 'rule of law', there was never a dominant discourse within the Western legal and academic community which completely rejected Nazi legality and placed it outside the realm of 'law'.

Furthermore, it is clear from many of the analyses of the Nazi penal system that the continuity existed not just at this broader level of discourse about 'law' in the West, but that developments under the Nazis could find their roots and sources within the historical evolution of German legality.

---

[51] 'Criminal Law in the Third Reich', 48 *Juridical Review* 373, 378–79.
[52] *Ibid*. 380.

A discussion in a leading English-language journal of the first major reforms to the penal law under the Nazis highlights this aspect of the continuity issue. As Professor Hermann Mannheim makes clear, reform within the German criminal law system was influenced by earlier, non-Nazi developments in the field of criminology. [53] In conclusion, Mannheim argues that while the system may operate as a threat to the liberty of the individual, the reforms had a positive aspect as well.

> The advantages of the new Act are that it has introduced for the first time into German Criminal Law important measures of protection of society and has strengthened the power of the Criminal Courts instead of that of the Administrative Authorities. [54]

One of the key themes developed by Mannheim is the historical, ideological and jurisprudential bases of the various conflicts between different schools of thought within criminology, particularly about causation of crime. [55] In Nazi criminology, with its bio-racial roots, biological explanations clearly predominated, although, as the literature also makes clear, such views had not yet achieved hegemonic status in the German legal system.

For Mannheim, the introduction of legislation within the German penal system dealing with the problems of habitual and mentally ill criminals, was by and large a good and potentially progressive step. He placed German debates and legislative provisions dealing with preventive detention within the broader context of public safety and order, and argued that much of the German system could be said to be based in English law reform proposals. [56] Further he argued that one of the problems with the German ie Nazi, preventative detention system, in 1938–1939, after *Kristallnacht* and the institutional development of the concentration camp system, was its failure to adequately distinguish between ordinary prison establishments and preventive detention facilities and practices.

> It is, however, questionable whether these differences, will in the whole, be practically important enough to be appreciated by the inmates, all the more since the Preventive Detention Establishment, as mentioned before, can be connected with the ordinary prison. If the differentiation is imperceptible, then the transfer of the prisoners from prison to the Preventive Detention Establishments would mean only a change of name, not of aim, and the whole double-track system becomes useless. [57]

---

[53] H Mannheim, 'The German Prevention of Crime Act, 1933', (1935–36) 26 *Journal of Criminal Law and Criminology* 517.

[54] *Ibid*. 537.

[55] See also, WS Landecker, 'Criminology in Germany', (1940–41) 31 *Journal of Criminal Law and Criminology* 551. For a case specific study see, O Kirchheimer, 'Recent Trends in German Treatment of Juvenile Delinquency', (1938–1939) 29 *Journal of Criminal Law and Criminology* 362.

[56] Above n 53, 523–24.

[57] Above 526.

The key issue was not the existence of preventive detention establishments, concentration camps, but the failure to physically and institutionally separate them from ordinary prisons. While hindsight permits us to see the tragic under-estimation of the efficiency of the German criminal law apparatus which characterises Mannheim's analysis, his article offers clear evidence that con-temporary scholars, even those in exile, did not, when they had grave doubts about the racial biological worldview which informed Nazi law, seek to under-stand German law after 1933 as discontinuous in a radical sense with what had gone before or with the legal systems of other 'civilized' countries. [58]

In so far as the introduction of measures aimed at 'dangerous sexual offend-ers' was concerned, Mannheim wrote that,

> The provisions dealing with the *castration of dangerous sexual offenders*, may, per-haps, be interesting especially for the American reader, since just in the whole of this sphere the example of the United States has been suggestive for Germany. For many decades the German criminal and biological science has devoted its deepest attention to the United States legislation and practice.[59]

For Mannheim, as for others, a central element of Nazi criminal policy, a eugenic crime prevention practice, which would lead ultimately to the murder of millions of asocial and anti-social 'elements', found its inspiration in the United States. Clearly, any idea that the body of Nazi law, even in its most vital conceptual elements, informed by the bio-politics of the *Volksgemeinschaft*, was (or can be) understood as inimical to other ideals or practices inherent in democratic rule of law notions or in rule of law nations, is refuted here.

Indeed, other writers saw the emergence of biological explanations of the origins of crime and criminals as a corrective antidote to what they perceived as an unhealthy American obsession with psychological constructions of criminal behaviour.[60] It is at the juncture of the issues of causation and treatment that the discourses of the English-speaking West and of Nazi legality come together in the clearest example of the continuity between Western legal practice and Nazi legality. In the eugenic world-view according to which criminals and asocials are born, not made, and in which society can only protect itself by tak-ing proactive measures, Nazi legality and other understandings of law as we know it live in almost total harmony.

---

[58] Mannheim himself simply asserted that the criminal justice system was ill suited to implement racial and biologically informed notions of national improvement. He wrote, '[p]ersonally, I should think that criminal justice should rather content itself with the protection of the public against crime and should leave the racial improvement of the people to other institutions which are better fitted for this work.' *Ibid.*, 536.

[59] *Ibid.*, 530.

[60] See N Cantor, 'Recent Tendencies in Criminological Research in Germany', (1936–1937) 27 *Journal of Criminal Law and Criminology* 782. But cf N Cantor, 'Prison Reform in Germany 1933', (1934–35) 25 *Journal of Criminal Law and Criminology* 84 and Cantor, 'Untermassfeld—An Experiment in Prison Education', *ibid.*, 721.

At the point at which the coercive power of the state can be and is brought
to bear on the most intimate aspects of its citizens and subjects, in a concrete
manifestation of a eugenic aspiration for a perfectible society, Nazi law and our
law most clearly resembled one another. Here the body of the law and the law
of the body inscribe, create and destroy the embodied *homo sacer*.[61] If it is true
that the Nazi state was at its epitome a racial state,[62] characterised by a bio-
racial view of the world and the social order, then the program whereby the
state ordered and organised the compulsory sterilisation of those who did not
conform to the accepted and decreed standard, must surely be the most clear
legal embodiment of that Nazi ideology, according to the discontinuity thesis,
which distorted and destroyed the rule of law. However, if we can find evidence
that our own legal system permitted and compelled similar practices for similar reasons, then we must begin once more to question the very idea and ideology of discontinuity. Exactly where, if at all, can we situate and locate the point
at which Nazi law diverges so radically from our own legal system that we may
once more comfortably assert our difference? When the camp, which segregates
and excludes the Other,[63] and the physical mutilation and later elimination of
that Other, come to epitomise and embody the law in its sovereign function,
where can we even begin to imagine an epistemological circumstance separat-
ing our law from Nazi law?

Others have examined in detail both the history of compulsory sterilisation
in the United States and Germany, and the connections between the two.[64]
Oliver Wendell Holmes' judgment in the Supreme Court case of *Buck v Bell*
remains an infamous paradigm of progressive and democratic legal acceptance
of the same eugenic principles which would later drive Nazi legality.[65] Ideas of
inherited criminality were central to many criminological and policy debates in
the 1930s, and today we are witnessing a revival of many of the same issues in
slightly more sophisticated scientific guises. I shall limit my discussion of the
question of continuity/discontinuity in this context to one important example
taken from Anglo-American legal literature.

Here, a leading expert on the world of law and politics under the new Nazi
regime in Germany brought his insights to an elite American legal audience.
Karl Loewenstein, in his article describing the Nazi legal system in otherwise
less than laudatory terms, said about one aspect of Nazi law:

---

[61] See G Agamben, Homo Sacer: *Sovereign Power and Bare Life*, (Stanford, Stanford University
Press, 1998).

[62] See eg M Burleigh and W Wipperman, *The Racial State: Germany 1933–45*, (Cambridge,
Cambridge University Press, 1991).

[63] See D Fraser, 'To Belong or Not To Belong: The Roma, State Violence and the New Europe in
the House of Lords', (2001) 21 *Legal Studies* 569.

[64] See Stefan Kühl, *The Nazi Connection*, (New York and Oxford, Oxford University Press,
1994).

[65] 274 US 200 (1927). See also, ML Dudziak, 'Oliver Wendell Holmes as a Eugenic Reformer:
Rhetoric in the Writing of Constitutional Law', (1986) 71 *Iowa Law Review* 833.

Other legislation from the race myth attempts to weed out the physically unfit and to provide for a healthy progeny in the future. Despite the vagueness and uncertainty of underlying biological and anthropological theories, they constitute, on the whole, a commendable effort to promote eugenics and national hygiene.[66]

He adds in a footnote:

The public health offices take care of many questions of biological hygiene. Stripped of its racial exaggerations the public health legislation seems soundly conceived.[67]

Loewenstein's comments are important for several reasons. The article itself is, in all other respects, highly critical of Nazi legal theory and practice. It is dismissive and contemptuous of what Loewenstein refers to as the basic Nazi 'race myth'. Loewenstein, a former Professor at Munich, later became a key player in the legal program set up by the United States for the administration of justice in Occupied Germany. Nonetheless, at this time, Loewenstein clearly believed not just that compulsory sterilisation formed a valuable part of any public health legislation, but also that readers of the *Yale Law Journal* would not be shocked to their moral or legal core by reading these assertions. In other words, an opponent of the Nazi regime, who would spend much of his career trying to (re)establish the rule of law after years of Nazi (il)legality, found, in 1936, parts of a legal system based on racial hygiene to be perfectly sound and quite worthy functions of a law-bound state.

Of course, Loewenstein rejected many of the racial 'exaggerations' of Nazi racial theory and legal practice, but the basic idea of 'eugenic' principles being applied in a coercive legal setting was for him, and for many of his fellow members of the American legal interpretive community, not outside the realm of the acceptable or normal. While these positions may seem problematic to many of us in hindsight, it is important to remember that part of that hindsight is for us informed by the historical facticity of the Holocaust and by the ideological juridical construction of the Nazi state as a 'criminal state'. Loewenstein's analysis of the state of German law underlines the fact of the continuity between what lawyers then understood as being acceptable within the broader construct of 'the rule of law' and some key aspects of Nazi legality.

Eugenic discourse and legislative practice around the issue of compulsory sterilisation of 'asocials' and of the 'mentally defective' were clearly on the agenda of Western industrialised countries in the early part of this century. The fact that such discourses and practices of sterilisation were on the 'legal' agenda of the Western democracies must cause us to question the 'illegality' of a central component of Nazi law.

---

[66] 'Law in the Third Reich', above n 49 at 797.
[67] *Ibid.* at fn 61.

An examination of the self-understanding of participants in the policies and practices of eugenic sterilisation at the time demonstrates once again that any critique of Nazi law as radically discontinuous with law as we understand (or at least understood) it in Anglo-American democracies, must be brought into question. If lawyers in the United States, for example, considered 'eugenics', or 'racial hygiene' to be an acceptable normative underpinning for operative and operating legal measures within and upon the body politic, then it simply cannot be asserted, *tout court*, that Nazi law, with its *Grundnorm* insuring the health and survival of the *Volksgemeinschaft,* was a criminal aberration, unworthy of the name 'law'.

Conclusion

It appears that there was, on this key, characteristic issue of compulsory eugenic sterilisation little, if anything, which would have permitted one to distinguish between American legal practice and German, or more precisely Nazi, law. Indeed, very few at the time sought to make the distinction and any who did, did not go so far as to characterise what was happening in Germany as not recognisable as law. When American legislators, doctors and lawyers were actively pursuing the eugenic sterilisation of their own citizens within the context of democracy and the rule of law, German doctors and lawyers were pursuing the same policies and practices within the context of a 'criminal state'. At this level, it was difficult then, as it appears to be now, to know where one began and the other ended.

Eugenic sterilisation was not the only element of Nazi law to have found a counterpart in Anglo-American jurisdictions. Nor was it the only central element of Nazi legal ideology to have been contemplated and accepted by English-speaking jurists or by Anglophone learned journals. Jews were excluded from the civil service and German civil service reforms were seen by some as being beneficial to the country. Jews were forbidden from owning agricultural property and Nazi 'blood and soil' ideology was portrayed as essential to national survival. German Jewish professors were removed from their positions, students were expelled because they were Jews and American readers of leading law publications were told that German and American culture, civilization and law sprang from and preserved common values. For many, if not most, lawyers in the English-speaking world at the time, the question of whether German law had crossed over the line into the territory of 'not law', much less the realm of the morally unacceptable, did not seem to arise at all. Legal memory has been distorted by the passage of time and more crucially by the post-1945 construction of Hitler's Germany as a 'criminal state'. It seems clear, however, that the English-speaking interpretive community, whether dealing with Nazi land law, penal law, legal education or the compulsory sterilisation of 'defectives' never conceived of Nazi law as 'not law'.

Contemporary lawyers and legal academics understood and constructed law under the Hitler regime as more or less normal. For them, German law was often interesting, developments were sometimes innovative, sometimes merely the continuation in different circumstances of long-standing German practices, but never particularly problematic because of an utterly unacceptable breach of normative standards. For non-Germans, and especially for those of us from the Anglo-American legal tradition, our own legal history relating to Nazi law has much to teach us. Whether the present day interpretive community is willing or able to learn the lessons and face the demons of our own past is a vital existential question for us all to face up to.

6

'A DISTORTED IMAGE OF OURSELVES': NAZISM, 'LIBERAL' SOCIETIES AND THE QUALITIES OF DIFFERENCE

*Laurence Lustgarten**

I

In his attempt to understand the extraordinary chemical attack on the Tokyo subway in 1995 by members of a cult called Aum Shinrikyo, the Japanese novelist Haruki Murakami, having interviewed cult members as well as survivors, concludes that the killers should not be seen as an alien 'them', but as a 'distorted image of ourselves'.[1] Confronted with undoubted moral horror, it is easy to denounce, and even easier to deny any resemblance between the doer, the deed, and what we ourselves might have done. Much ink and energy was expended during the Cold War on arguments about similarities between Nazi and Fascist movements and Communism, but those were politically-driven disputes. Either (in their American form) they were attempts at shoring up the 'free world's' view of its own superiority or (in their German form much later) attempts to minimise the sense of guilt or need for reparation on the part of the West German state by arguing that Stalin's crimes were at least as great as Hitler's. Neither made any serious effort to grapple with the morally more difficult and ambiguous question of the distance between Nazism and the philosophy or ideology of the victorious Western allies. We may call the latter Liberalism, although that word covers a multitude of meanings, and of sins. The term is not harmful however if the user defines its intended meaning at the outset. I use it to incorporate two key ideas. The first is that the liberal political order is one of constitutionalism—a state which respects the principle of limited government, those limits to be patrolled by a legal system insulated from political pressure. The second is that the fundamental unit of value in a liberal society is the human person, rather than the community/people/majority, or dominant ideology or religion. In the contemporary era, there is also a close

* Professor of Law, Faculty of Law, University of Southampton.
[1] H Murakami, *Underground* (London, Harvill Press, 2000).

relation between liberalism and representative democracy. This is entirely contingent and, if claimed as a universal truth, false. Britain, the archetypal and arguably the first liberal society, was one of the least democratic in Europe, as measured by the proportion of the population permitted to vote.[2] Nonetheless the connection is today so close that liberalism also subsumes a commitment to the values and institutions of representative democracy.

To say this is to see at once that Nazism was, as indeed it proclaimed, an absolute rejection of liberalism. But that is only one side of the story, one which leaves two key questions unanswered. The first is whether the self-styled liberal states in fact adhered to their purported principles. The second is the extent to which those principles as practised truly differed from the policies adopted by the Nazis during the peacetime period of 1933–1939. In doing so it is worth remembering that at this time nothing like a majority of states in the world proclaimed themselves liberal, and many fewer came close to the practice.

There are a number of directions from which one might approach these questions. One is to look at the continuities and ruptures between the policies of the Nazis and those of their Weimar predecessors, and also in the ideas and values which supported and drove them. This line of inquiry would place the Nazis in the context of specifically German culture, politics and history. Most probably the closest connections—how close would be a matter of great importance and no doubt great controversy—would be with conservative-nationalist movements and philosophical currents, but even more revealing would be evidence of continuities or similarities over a wider range of the political spectrum. Perhaps the pre-eminent scholar who has worked this vein and whose works are available in English is the late Detlev Peukert. His study of Nazi criminal and penal policy concluded that it

> was a radicalised version of schemes of social policy that had been advocated, sometimes on optimistic, progressive grounds since the turn of the century. The practice of terror by the national socialists thus made apparent the repressive features that were inherent in the normative and disciplinary methods of these schemes.[3]

Peukert and others[4] have developed this line of argument persuasively and depth, so in this paper I will focus on the more unsettling and controversial issue of analogies and connections between Nazi policies in a particular area, and those adopted in 'liberal' states. Practices which were imbued with Nazi rhetoric may on examination prove to reflect more widely-shared political choices.

---

[2] In the period leading up to World War I, Britain had the smallest male electorate of the parliamentary states of Europe, with the sole exception of Hungary. See Blewitt, 'The Franchise in the UK, 1885–1918', (1965) *Past and Present*, 31 December.

[3] D Peukert, *Inside Nazi Germany* (London, Batsford, 1987), 248.

[4] Notably N Wachsmann, *Reform and Repression: Prisons and Penal Policy in Germany, 1918–1939*, (Unpublished Ph.D Thesis, Univ. of London, 2000). I am grateful to Dr Wachsmann for making a copy of this work available to me.

Conversely, one might look at influences from outside Germany and from intellectual sources apparently removed from Nazism, on policies adopted after 1933. To what extent, in other words, were the Nazis part of, or at least attuned to, wider intellectual and political trends or influences? One much studied example is eugenic theory and the advocacy of sterilisation of the unfit. David Fraser's paper documents fully and well the similarities of thought on this issue between German and American lawyers,[5] whilst Stefan Kuhl[6] and Robert Proctor[7] have traced the links between American organisations advocating compulsory sterilisation, usually on racist grounds, and their Nazi counterparts in and out of power, to whom they provided support and inspiration.

Another angle of vision is to look at the Nazi conceptualisation and perception of 'problems', or conversely at their formulation of desirable social ends or aims. What did these have in common with analogous understandings put forward by other political or intellectual movements, both within and outside Germany? It hardly needs saying, for example, that the great majority of Germans shared an anger at the terms of the Versailles Treaty and that many of Hitler's foreign policy objectives were widely shared; it is however worth recalling that British 'appeasement' at least in part grew out of the view that the German complaints had merit.[8] Shifting the focus to internal matters on which one would normally expect less consensus, to what extent did the Nazi diagnosis of the ills of German society draw upon or resemble other critiques? Were there similar themes—the need for restoration of 'order', a sense that society's moral foundations were in peril, etc.—and similar solutions advocated elsewhere, especially on the political Right? Turning this round and also looking more widely, what parallel conceptualisations of problems, and solutions to these, were offered by non-Nazi political leaders, legal institutions and broad intellectual currents in liberal societies at the time? If one finds notable parallels which did not lead to equally horrific resolutions, is that because the German attachment to liberalism was much more problematic, and its democratic institutions more fragile, if only due to the absence of longstanding practice and associated traditions? Or did the absence of institutional constraints which operated elsewhere as a result of those traditions free the Nazis to take to the logical limit and implement measures that in other states could only remain in the realm of ideas? Were some Nazi policies at least the [patho]logical working out of the implications of ideas shared by more mainstream movements and thinkers? Could it be said also that in some sense the Nazis had the courage of others' convictions?

---

[5] D Fraser, '"The Outsider Does Not See Al the Game . . .": Perceptions of German law in Anglo-American Legal Scholarship, 1933–1940', in this volume, 87–111.

[6] S Kuhl, *The Nazi Connection* (New York, Oxford University Press, 1994).

[7] R Proctor, *Racial Hygiene* (Cambridge, Mass., Harvard University Press, 1988), 97–101 ('the American connection').

[8] This was the core argument of AJP Taylor's famous study of the *Origins of the Second World War* (London, Hamish Hamilton, 1961).

These lines of inquiry all focus on the past, and have a value in themselves as part of our understanding of ourselves. More controversial is the search for parallels between Nazi thought and policy and that found in liberal societies today. Dr Mahlmann declares that 'it is plainly a question of responsibility for the future to understand clearly what went wrong in the past.'[9] So it is; and there is if anything an even graver responsibility to inquire whether at the present time we are in the process of replicating the mistakes of the past. The comparison across time is not for purposes of crude political or philosophical name-calling: 'so-and-so is advocating Nazi policies' as a way of denigrating an opponent. Rather there are two justifiable purposes. The first would enrich historical understanding: if some solution to a purported problem adopted by the Nazis continues to command adherence despite the odour of the association and passage of time, their similarities to the mainstream of Western politics would appear more marked and the thesis that they were a pariah or aberrational movement is correspondingly weakened. Further, the existence of such similarities would tell us hard truths about the dark side of our proclaimed Liberalism, or call into question the depth of our commitment to it. Similarity does not mean identity, but it is in assessing the degree of similarity that the hard and uncomfortable questions have to be faced. The existence of continuum rather than chasm is a frontal challenge to the morality of contemporary politics.

II

The values of liberal democracy come under the severest pressure when faced with demands for the control of individuals or groups regarded as in some way threatening to public safety or public order. The particular flashpoint is the extent to which the restraints demanded by the liberal values, notably the concept of legality, are dispensed with in the name of public protection. Among lawyers, social scientists and historians this has most often been discussed in the context of high politics, of supposed threats to state security or stability and the corresponding dangers of dictatorship. Perhaps the most famous example in Europe is the use of Article 48 of the Weimar Constitution and the conflict between Carl Schmitt and his critics over the proper invocation of emergency powers. However, an equally important dimension, indeed one of much greater impact on the daily life of any society, has tended to be overlooked. I would suggest that the greatest commonality between Nazism and Liberalism can be seen in dealing with perceived problems of crime, disorder, 'social breakdown', and more generally the problem of what in Victorian England were called the 'dangerous classes'.

---

[9] M Mahlmann 'The European Order in Fascist and Nazi Legal Thought', *EUI Review* Autumn 2000, 14–17, available at http://www.iue.it/General/EUI-review/

To support this thesis I propose to compare several aspects of criminal law and criminal justice in liberal societies of the 1930s and the present time, with their corresponding practices in Hitler's peacetime regime. Through all the specific case studies, one dominant theme consistently emerges: the idea and practice of *pre-emptive intervention and control*. Classical criminal law limits the intervention of state authorities to the punishment of specific conduct after it has been committed. Moreover, the form and severity of sanction is highly particularistic, being based at least partly on the motive of the offender and the circumstances of the offence. The sanction is also imposed by a judicial authority independent of the executive, which must follow a set of procedures which is supposed to permit the accused person a fair hearing. All these principles and institutions of legality meet with frenzied impatience from those who claim that they obstruct measures necessary to protect the needs of the community or certain sections of supposedly deserving people within it. Sterilisation as the extreme eugenic measure of course takes prevention to its logical conclusion: 'three generations of imbeciles are enough', as Mr Justice Holmes asserted with callous pithiness.[10] Unsurprisingly, though, most pre-emptive intervention is directed at the living, and the examples I shall discuss are those involving measures within the system of state punishment or confinement—as opposed to welfare-orientated measures designed to assist the elevation of those whose bad behaviour is seen as a response to degrading social conditions.[11]

Preventative measures share certain characteristics: they are implemented by a bureaucratic agency rather than through the judicial system, and are intended to counter future behaviour rather than being a response to past misconduct. Moreover, although such future behaviour is said to be accurately predictable by the enlistment of scientific knowledge, by definition it cannot be personalised or individualised: it can only be based on models derived from analysis of patterns of the behaviour of others. Judicial punishment by contrast requires proof to a high standard that a particular individual has violated a specific legal norm. The guiding strategy that can be seen at work in all the measures to be discussed is the evasion or short-circuiting of legal norms and procedures normally required before someone can be deprived of their liberty. The supposed justification is that they will present a future threat to general well-being so grave as to override their normal rights; sometimes this is coupled with an attack on the idea of individual or 'subjective' rights as itself contrary to the general interest. This strategy is adopted regardless of when, where or by whom these measures are promoted.

---

[10] See Fraser, at n 5 above, for a discussion of the case from which this quotation is taken, *Buck v Bell*, 274 US 200, 207 (1927).

[11] For a study of this school of thought in Germany, see R Mocek, 'The Programme of Proletarian *Rassenhygiene*', (1988) 11 *Science in Context* 609–17.

The Nulla Poena Principle

One of the most notorious innovations in criminal law effected by the Nazis was the enactment, soon after they came to power, of the so-called analogy principle. This abandoned the requirement that an act is only punishable if it had been proscribed by a law in force when it was committed. Instead, both Public Prosecutor and Judge were enjoined that,

> 'If an act which, according to sound popular feeling, is deserving of penalty [but] is not made punishable by law, [they] shall consider whether the fundamental conception of a penal law covers the said act, and whether it is possible to cause justice to prevail by the application of such law by analogy.'

This is the English translation of the identical provision enacted in Danzig in 1935 by the Nazi-controlled Senate. Unusually, the fact that the Constitution of the Free City was guaranteed by the League of Nations under the Treaty of Versailles permitted opponents to challenge the Decree before the Permanent Court of International Justice. In a remarkable Advisory Opinion,[12] the first instance of international judicial review of a national enactment in the sphere of fundamental human rights,[13] a majority of the Court held that the law violated the Constitution, which proclaimed that the Free City was a *Rechtsstaat* and that its citizens were guaranteed certain fundamental rights. They rejected the argument that the provision would bring about 'real' justice and not merely 'formal' justice, and that 'sound popular feeling' corresponded to the basic demands of morality, which could provide a widely-recognised and acceptable standard of criminal liability. Laws which gave such vast discretion to public officials and judges did not comply with the constitutional command, derived by the Court from the *Rechtsstaat* principle, that citizens know specifically when their liberties may be restricted.

This Advisory Opinion, though it had no practical effect in Danzig nor of course in Germany itself, expresses the longstanding and predominant view in European legal thinking that fair warning is a fundamental precept of the rule of law: *nulla poena, nullem crimen, sine lege.*[14] Use of the analogy principle was widely condemned as an example of totalitarian abuse of power, and the revulsion against it influenced the drafting of the European Convention on Human Rights after the War. Article 7, entitled 'No punishment without law',

---

[12] *Consistency of Certain Danzig Legislative Decrees with the Constitution of the Free City,* PCIJ Series A/B 65 (1935), from which the translation of the statute is taken.

[13] H Lauterpacht, *The Development of International Law by the International Court* (London, Stevens and Sons, 1958), 107, n 50. I am grateful to Mr Justice Kenneth Keith of the New Zealand Court of Appeal for this reference.

[14] The Nazis made great political capital of their rejection of this principle, in the name of combating crime. They coined a new catchy alternative Latin phrase, *nullum crimen sine poena* (no crime without punishment), popularised it in the press and even printed it on small posters that were glued to court dossiers, for the inspiration of judges and lawyers: see R Gellately, *Backing Hitler: Consent and Coercion in Nazi Germany* (Oxford, Oxford University Press, 2001), 38.

forbids retrospective criminal law (and also retrospectively increased punishment). This is one of the very few provisions of the ECHR which is both absolute and from which derogation by signatory states is forbidden even in time of war or emergency.

In light of the universal obloquy attached to the use of the analogy principle, what is one to make of the English common law of crime? For centuries judges, not Parliament, defined criminality and did so with little regard for clarity and precision. In 1801 it was declared that all acts prejudicial to the community were indictable (ie. were prosecutable as serious crimes),[15] an assertion which merely reflected past practice. Although by the end of the century it appeared that judicial creation of new offences was on the wane as Parliament devoted greater attention to criminal law, the principle was never disapproved and was then given fresh authority by the Lord Chief Justice in (quite coincidentally) the fateful year 1933.[16]

Piggy-backed onto this principle was the even more extraordinary common law crime of conspiracy. In the formulation that governed most of its history, conspiracy was defined as the agreement by two or more persons to commit an unlawful act.[17] Unlawful did not mean criminal, but could include a civil wrong. This is what enabled the laws of criminal conspiracy to be used against strikes and especially picketing, which were technically collective breaches of contract or tortious [ie delictual] attempts to interfere with others' performance of their contracts of employment.

As social and political conflict began in the 1960s and early 1970s to replace the consensus and uniformity that had for so long distinguished English life, conspiracy also provided an extraordinary weapon of social control. It was revived and used vigorously by police and compliant judges to regulate public morality in a manner strongly redolent of the 'sound sense of the people'.

In one of the most severely-criticised cases in modern English legal history, the House of Lords held in 1961 that a man who had compiled adverts for prostitutes and sold them openly in a magazine could be prosecuted for the offence of conspiracy to corrupt public morals.[18] This offence was previously unknown; it was in fact created by the judges to, in the well-worn phrase, 'fill the gap' in the law so as to prevent what was strongly felt to be immoral conduct escaping punishment.[19] No one gave a thought to the European Convention at

---

[15] R. v Higgins, (1801) 2 East 5, 21, per Lawrence J.

[16] R. v Manley (1933) 1 KB 529.

[17] Most textbooks of English criminal law provide the history. The standard work is J Smith and B Hogan, *Criminal Law* (London, Butterworths, 1999), ch 11.

[18] *Shaw v DPP*, [1962] AC 220

[19] A flavour of the dominant judicial attitude of 40 years ago can be gained from an extract from the lead judgment of the majority: 'Let it be supposed that at some future, perhaps early, date homosexual practices between adult consenting males are no longer a crime [NB: this in fact occurred six years later]. Would it not be an offence if even without obscenity, such practices were publicly advocated and encouraged by pamphlet and advertisement?': [1962] AC at 268, per Viscount Simonds.

the time, but counsel for the defendant did argue that it was beyond the power of the courts to create new offences. This was met by the robust assertion that,

> In the sphere of criminal law I entertain no doubt that there remains in the courts of law a residual power to enforce the supreme and fundamental purposes of the law, to conserve not only the safety and order but also the moral welfare of the State, and that it is their duty to guard it against attacks which may be all the more insidious because they are novel and unprepared for . . . if the common law is powerless in such an event, then we should no longer do her reverence.[20]

The quaintly old-fashioned phrases masked the harsh reality that followed. Since the object of a conspiracy need not itself be criminal, and with any act 'prejudicial to the community' potentially a crime, the authorities did not trouble themselves unduly as to how they framed the amorphous, catch-all charges they laid. In one case, conspiracy to outrage public decency was used to convict publishers of sexually explicit material so as to circumvent the defence that would have been available under the statutory definition of obscenity.[21] Then a group of students who had organised a sit-in in their home country's embassy were convicted of conspiracy to trespass.[22] Finally came the straw that broke the camel's back. Prosecutors had begun with increasing frequency to lay charges of conspiracy to effect a public mischief. In one case the jury was directed that they should find the defendants guilty if they had agreed to do 'deceitful acts which would cause extreme injury to the general well-being of the community as a whole'. It took no less than six days of oral argument to persuade the House of Lords to rule that the offence of conspiracy to effect a public mischief was unknown to the law, and further to reaffirm that the judges no longer had the power to create new offences.[23] That decision, however, did not overrule the practice, or question the principle, of using recognised categories or heads of conspiracy to criminalise civil conduct that the police (and judges) found distasteful or threatening. It took political pressure from trade unions on the Labour government then in office to bring about legislation in the Criminal Law Act 1977 which removed most civil wrongs from the scope of criminal conspiracy. This has largely curbed authoritarian uses of the offence.[24] Statistics are impossible to obtain, but there is every reason to think that in the 1960s and 1970s at any rate, prosecutions of the kind discussed here[25] were more common in England than was the use of the analogy principle in Hitler's Germany.

[20] *Ibid.* at 267–68.

[21] *Knuller v DPP*, [1973] AC 435

[22] *Kamara v DPP*, [1974] AC104

[23] *DPP v Withers*, [1975] AC 842, 860, per Lord Dilhorne.

[24] Moral offences were excluded from the statute, so *Knuller* and *Shaw* technically remain good authority, although such prosecutions are no longer brought today. It is doubtful that they could survive scrutiny under ECHR standards.

[25] As distinct from defensible uses of the charge such as prosecuting as conspirators those participating in a scheme to sell non-existent securities or foreign property to investors.

The treatment of 'habitual criminals'

There is no single agreed liberal approach to the aims, forms and appropriate severity of punishment. Those on the Left have tended to emphasise the possibility of reform of the offender and relatively humane treatment of those in custody, whilst the tendency on the Right is to stress the evil character of offenders and the necessity for confinement in relatively harsh conditions. This debate was played out in full in Weimar Germany.[26] Upon coming to power, the Nazis very soon enacted the Habitual Criminals Law, which was based on a draft prepared in 1927 by conservative civil servants in the Ministry of Justice who were unable to gain the backing of their political masters. It required judges, in the case of anyone who had already been sentenced twice to terms of at least six months, to pass harsher sentences up to 15 years penitentiary for the third offence. The court was also given a discretion to impose harsher sentences in the case of someone who had previously committed three or more minor offences, even though none had led to imprisonment. More drastic still were the so-called Preventive and Rehabilitative Measures, under which judges could lock up 'dangerous habitual criminals' after the completion of their sentence for an indefinite period. This category remained undefined, and what one senior Ministry of Justice official called 'the evidence of modern criminal-biology' [27] was often presented to the courts to support of the detention of the alleged 'incorrigible'. Estimates vary, but at least 4,000 and possibly as many as 11,000 people, almost all men, had been made subject to this regime of 'security confinement' by 1939.[28]

It may be argued that the Nazis pioneered practices that have subsequently become respectable.[29] If not the direct inspiration, they were certainly the harbinger of the kind of law and order politics that has had such depressing influence in the English speaking countries in recent years. Robert Gellately's excellent recent study has shown that, notwithstanding their erasure of parliamentary institutions, political parties and a free press, the Nazis worked assiduously to cultivate popular support for the dictatorship among 'ordinary'

---

[26] W Wachsmann above n 4, chs 6 and 7.

[27] Criminal biology was not a Nazi invention, having been part of the programme adopted by certain Lander and popular with influential eugenic-minded doctors and psychiatrists in the Weimar era. See Weindling, *Eugenics and the Welfare State* in W Lee and E Rosenhaft (eds), *The State and Social Change in Germany, 1880–1980* (New York, Berg Press, 1990).

[28] W Wachsmann above n 4, offers the lower estimate; Gellately, at n 14 above, 94 and n 30 at 295 provides figures for various forms of confinement from which the higher total may be deduced.

[29] To say this is not to ignore the movement in England in the three decades before the First World War for the incarceration of 'habitual offenders' and the attempts, in part influenced by eugenic theory, at pre-emptive state control of 'inebriates', 'lunatics', and others of the social 'residuum' who, in the words of a prominent social reformer, 'degrade whatever they touch'. Pressure from various quarters produced no less than six Acts of Parliament in fifteen years, including those authorising severe added punishment for 'habitual criminals' and detention of the

Germans. A central element in this non-democratic politics was the claim that they had taken firm but necessary measures which successfully reduced crime.[30] This was linked with a strident emphasis on pre-emptive action, with the ordinary criminal police (Kripo) boasting that 'the days were gone when police only arrived after a crime was committed', and that they were now able to protect the community by refusing to be bound by 'the dead letter' of the law and instead following 'the spirit of the law and the Fuhrer'. This was used to justify preventive detention of criminal elements in what were called 'educative camps'.[31]

It is hard to imagine a greater contrast than the spirit which animated English sentencing policy at the same time, politically one of overwhelming Conservative domination during which the number of people in prison did not rise for twenty years. It was well illustrated by the view expressed by an influential Prison Commissioner that the average man could not spent more than 10 years continuously in prison without deteriorating in character and in mind.[32] The distance has narrowed dramatically, and all the movement has been in one direction. Increasingly the Anglo-Saxon countries[33] have been dominated by what my colleague Andrew Rutherford has called the 'eliminative ideal'. By this he does not mean extermination, but rather the attempt 'to solve present and emerging problems by getting rid of troublesome and disagreeable people with methods which are lawful and widely supported.'[34] Britain once led the way in

---

'feeble-minded'. However, most remarkable are the limitations built in to this legislation—in significant part to overcome strong opposition—and even more, the speed with which their effect was undermined by refusal of Ministers in charge of their administration either to apply them rigorously or to authorise expenditure that would have enabled the necessary carcerative institutions to function. Most of the statutory provisions were either repealed or simply ignored by the authorities within a few years after the end of the War. For details, see L Radzinowicz and R Hood, *A History of English Criminal Law* (London: Stevens & Sons, 1986), vol 5, Part 4 and 775–78; and Rutherford, 'Boundaries of English Penal Policy', (1988) 8 *Oxford Journal of Legal Studies* 132–41. A further striking difference compared to the measures of the 1930s is the preoccupation of pre-War policy with female deviance: see L Zedner, *Women, Crime and Custody in Victorian England* (Oxford: Oxford University Press, 1991), especially chs 6 and 7.

[30] Above n 14, 87–89. His own careful analysis casts doubts on the accuracy of the claims, but they were undoubtedly credited by the public at the time, as he shows.

[31] Above n 14, 94–95. This of course was tightly linked with the new slogan, *nullum crimen sine poena:*.

[32] Quoted in RM Jackson, *Enforcing the Law* (London, Macmillan, 1967), 159.

[33] A fascinating and difficult question is whether the English-speaking countries have more in common in their attitudes and practices of punishment than do the nations of Continental Europe, and if so, why. Put very crudely, I would argue that the USA is in matters like capital punishment, prison conditions and sentencing practice quite close to 1930s Germany whilst Britain, Canada and Australia most often occupy a point somewhere between contemporary Western Europe and the USA, though more influenced on many issues, except the death penalty, by American models. Fortunately, resolving this issue, worthy of a major study in itself, is something I need not attempt here.

[34] A Rutherford, 'Criminal Policy and the Eliminative Ideal', (1997) 32 *Social Policy and Administration*, 116–35, 116.

this respect, having eliminated the possibility of recurrent petty crime by thousands of poor offenders by physically transporting them, first to America and then 20,000 kilometres to Australia. Today the method of exclusion is long-term imprisonment. The most notorious example is what the Americans, borrowing the jargon of baseball, call the 'three strikes' rule. Enacted in more than half the states, it requires astonishingly long—25 years to life—mandatory sentences on anyone with two earlier convictions for violent offences when convicted of a third offence; in some states, notably California, the final 'strike' can be an offence of the most trivial nature.[35] England is moving in the same direction. Ten years ago an attempt was made, in unfortunately drafted language, to enact the principle that whilst a good record may serve to lessen a guilty person's sentence, a history of offending should not lead to a disproportionately aggravated penalty (Criminal Justice Act 1991, s 29). This was the highwater mark of attempts to limit imprisonment to a class of very serious offences, whilst dealing with those committing minor offences, even if repeatedly, outside custodial institutions. A combination of judicial dislike, press attack, and the outrage spilling over into hysteria that followed the killing in 1993 of two-year old James Bulger by two youths aged 10 led not only to the repeal of that legislation, but opened the floodgates to a series of punitive outbursts. The two main parties have since attempted to outbid each other to prove that they are 'tough on crime'. One result is a recent Sentencing Review, endorsed in principle by the new Home Secretary, which when enacted will create a statutory presumption of increasing severity of sentence where the defendant has a recent criminal record. The aim is to target the so-called 'hard core' of repeat offenders, and to overcome judicial reluctance by removing sentencing discretion by means of codified sentencing guidelines.[36] The language of 'habitual criminals' and 'incorrigibles' has been carefully avoided, but the message, and the impact, is unmistakably the same. And on the theoretical plane, the most interesting feature is the rejection of individualised desert as the commanding principle of sentencing. It has been replaced an untidy combination of denunciation, crime prevention, and 'maintaining public confidence in the criminal justice system'—no attempt being made to question how public attitudes have been shaped and whether they accurately reflect the practice of the courts and the prisons. England already has the highest rate of imprisonment of any of the larger countries in Western Europe,[37] and the likely result of these proposals, even taking into account the accompanying recommendation that sentences under one year be used much more sparingly, will be to increase the overall use of imprisonment still further. They will also mark off a growing number of men as Outsiders unfit to participate in civil society.

[35] *Ibid.* 2. For a detailed study of the American statutes see Austin *et al.*, 'The Impact of "Three Strikes and You're Out"' (1999) *Punishment & Society*, 131–62.

[36] At the time of writing, the Report is only available on the Internet: www.homeoffice.gov.uk/cpg/halliday.htm

[37] Portugal alone has a higher one.

The elevation of social protection at the expense of all other considerations is manifest in even more extreme form in proposals for confinement of those with so-called Dangerous Severe Personality Disorders (DSPD) whose presence among the general population is considered to pose a threat. This is a category unknown to medical science: it is an administrative—or even political—label. Some of the people who fall within it will have been convicted of a serious crime, and denial of early release on parole on the basis of an assessed risk to public safety in light of their behaviour and attitudes in prison would raise no legitimate complaint. Further detention after the expiration of sentence on the basis of predicted dangerousness is a major invasion of liberty, hitherto used only when the person in question is considered 'treatable' by psychiatrists. It is now proposed in England to redefine and broaden the treatability criterion and forcibly intern people under a regime designed 'to manage the consequences of their mental disorder in a therapeutic environment'.[38] The basis of the deprivation of the freedom will be a risk assessment conducted by psychiatrists. In effect the Nazi category of 'dangerous habitual criminal' and the practice of 'security confinement' have been renamed and given a more pleasant public face, with psychiatry replacing 'modern criminal-biology' as the scientific expertise justifying and guiding state power.[39]

Yet the English proposals go even further. By the White Paper's estimate, between 2,100–2,400 men who are currently not serving any sentence—in plain language, free men—will be subject to a civil commitment regime as DSPDs. In other words, confinement—described of course as treatment—does not require conviction for a specific offence if an 'expert' assessment of your personality decides that you are likely to present a serious danger. They are remarkably close to a law proposed in 1944 by Heinrich Himmler, entitled 'Law for the Treatment of Community Aliens'. Several criteria were laid down to define these undesirables, including persons 'showing themselves in their personality or in the conduct of their life, mentally disposed towards the commission of serious offences (community-hostile criminals and criminals by inclination)'.[40] Against persons of such 'mental disposition' a series of police supervisory measures could be undertaken. Treatment was not among them, but neither is there an effective guarantee that those branded as DSPDs will receive meaningful and effective assistance.

Like Himmler's projected measure, the recent English proposals, most egregiously in their civil commitment aspect, dispense with what for centuries has been regarded as a fundamental element of criminal liability and therefore a precondition for the deprivation of liberty, namely an *actus reus*. Only by

[38] The proposals are contained in a White Paper, unusually co-produced by the Home Office and the Department of Health, 'Reforming the Mental Health Act', issued in December 1999.

[39] It should be emphasised that psychiatrists' associations have expressed strong objections to the proposals, and many psychiatrists may refuse to co-operate. Other professionals, notably psychologists, may however be employed to fill the gap.

[40] The translation is Peukert's, above n 3, 220–21.

claiming that public protection and some ill-defined regime of care justify a sort of pre-emptive attack on 'dangerous' people can such a regime purport to satisfy elementary standards of legality. (Human rights standards pose another and perhaps more difficult obstacle.) Indeed the importance of the care element may be in doubt. Just what dangers lurk down this road can be seen from the United States, whose Supreme Court has not only upheld compulsory civil commitment following the end of imprisonment but also more recently ruled that it is *not* necessary that treatment be provided for detention of this kind to satisfy constitutional principles.[41]

Eugenics and Compulsory Sterilisation

Perhaps because of its extreme nature and closeness to the appalling 'experiments' performed by doctors in the death camps, this subject has attracted a great deal of historical attention. There are at least a dozen books and articles in English alone[42] which are at least partly concerned with forcible sterilisation of 'incorrigibles', the 'feeble-minded' and certain 'inferior' peoples like the Roma that preceded the extermination of the Jews and others begun during the War. As Fraser's paper shows,[43] there is also a substantial literature on the equivalent American practice. Nor were these two nations alone in pursuing the biological improvement of the nation through barbaric means: approximately a dozen nations, or jurisdictions within them, adopted compulsory sterilisation laws.[44] Rather than tread again on well-worn ground, I would simply pray in aid this extensive scholarship to support the following propositions:

1) Nothing in the values of a significant number of liberal societies was offended by compulsory sterilisation in what were deemed to be appropriate cases;

2) These societies implemented them through legal procedures, not by any sort of extra-legal arbitrary power. Exalted principles of legality and the right of recourse to the courts failed to protect the vulnerable, indeed largely legitimated their victimisation. Where attempts to introduce compulsory sterilisation failed, as in England, this was not due to the influence of law and lawyers but to the force of moral, philosophical and policy arguments which prevailed in the political arena;

3) The Nazis were in this respect no different. A sterilisation law was enacted in the summer of 1933 which allowed for compulsory sterilisation on 'genetic indications'. These were not carried out arbitrarily: special courts, called Genetic

---

[41] *Seling v Young,* 121 US 727 (2001); the earlier case is *Kansas v Hendricks,* 117 US 2072 (1997).

[42] Of which the best that I have found is M Burleigh, *Death and Deliverance: Euthanasia in Germany c.1900–1945* (Cambridge, Cambridge University Press, 1994).

[43] Fraser, above n 5, 87–111.

[44] Proctor, above n 7, 97. Another marked difference between the England of the 1930s and Germany and the USA at that time was the virtual absence of support for compulsory sterilisation in England. Even the campaign for voluntary sterilisation failed badly in the face of 'the dominant discourse of morality and rights': M Thomson, *The Problem of Mental Deficiency: Eugenics, Democracy and Social Policy in Britain, c.1870–1959* (Oxford, Clarendon, 1998), 205 and ch 5 *passim.*

Health Courts were established, to which those affected might appeal, and by no means all appeals failed.[45] All this was done by what Wachsmann calls the 'legal state', not by the SS;[46]

4) It seems to have taken the experience of war against Germany, and its transformation into an ideological struggle against Nazism, to cause a revulsion against this practice. Fraser supports this view through his examination of the reactions of American lawyers before the War to the racial legislation and purge of Jews and to forcible sterilisation. He shows that none of these measures were criticised as putting Hitler's regime beyond the pale of legality.[47]

Perhaps another indication is that shortly after the United States belatedly entered the War, its Supreme Court began to retreat from the position it took in the notorious *Buck v Bell* case from which he quotes.[48] In *Skinner v Oklahoma*,[49] a statute which provided for the compulsory sterilisation of those convicted three times of felonies involving 'moral turpitude' whilst specifically exempting embezzlement and other offences of equal or even greater seriousness, was held to violate the Constitution's guarantee of equal protection of the laws. The majority's reasoning is rather disingenuous in avoiding direct repudiation of *Buck v Bell*, but importance of the judgment lies in the recognition of the 'fundamental' and 'basic' liberties involved— phrases that had never previously been applied to personal and dignitary interests of this kind—and the recognition of the 'irreparable injury' inflicted, which served to trigger a heightened standard of judicial review in light of constitutional norms. This judgment was delivered before the Americans had become seriously engaged in Europe, but it seems likely that at least some of the Justices were in advance of most of their countrymen in reacting to events of the preceding decade.

The qualitative similarities, legal and ideological, are therefore strong. However the quantative impact on society was radically different. Proctor quotes figures for the USA of somewhat over 30,000 sterilisations committed upon the mentally ill and criminally insane, mostly of whom were in institutions, in the thirty years up to 1939.[50] As against this, the Nazi programme led to approximately 400,000 compulsory sterilisations authorised and legitimated by legal process, most of them enforced in the first four years of the new legislation, 1934–1937.[51]

---

[45] Proctor, *ibid*, 101ff. One should not exaggerate the value or impartiality of these courts, which upheld only 3% of appeals against sterilisation, but thousands of people did bring their cases to them (for statistics see *id.*, 106–7).

[46] Above n 4, 192; he translates the title of these bodies as 'Hereditary Health Courts'.

[47] Above n 5, Fraser, *passim*.

[48] *Ibid*. 44.

[49] 316 US 535 (1942).

[50] Above n 7, 97.

[51] *Ibid*. 108, drawing upon the work of the Bielefeld historian Gisela Bock. Her work has not been translated but was reviewed by Paul Weindling in the journal *German History*, No.5, 10–24 (Autumn 1987).

Of course even one violation of humanity is too many, but it is clear that in the hands of the Nazis the brutality inherent in the ideas of their predecessors and the practices of liberal regimes elsewhere was transported to a totally different plane. This brings us full circle to the questions posed at the start of this paper concerning the true distance between Nazism in its pre-War manifestations and the practices of liberal societies.

III

One line of argument needs to be disposed of at the start. It is that the evil was limited elsewhere because there was something radically different, and morally degraded, about Germany. This will not sustain serious examination. If it were true, why did implementation have to await the coming of the Nazis, and why were ideas that they put into effect rejected during the Weimar period?[52] It is also clear from research into occupied France[53] and the Channel Islands[54] that lawyers, administrators and judges in liberal societies, who were not acting in fear of their lives, had no professional difficulties in putting into practice Nazi-imposed racial laws, including the deportation of Jews to a likely death. To locate any explanation in the deficiencies of 'national character' is to indulge in a form of self-serving racist myth-making which also conveniently obfuscates the real issues.

I would suggest instead that Nazi-like potentialities existed and exist almost everywhere, but are normally reined in due to influences that were unable to make themselves felt in the Germany of the 1930s, let alone once the War had been unleashed.[55] These influences were in part economic—the severity of the Depression in Germany, equalled only in the USA—but above all, political in the broadest sense. Germany lacked stable democratic institutions, and had no tradition of attachment to democratic ideals. For numerous well-known reasons, the Weimar Republic lacked legitimacy in the eyes of most Conservative opinion in Germany, whose political leaders were directly responsible for Hitler's constitutional accession to power. There existed no political elite capable or willing to contain the sense of irredeemable crisis and breakdown of social order that was widely felt among the middle and lower middle classes

---

[52] One particularly pertinent example: sterilisation was illegal in Germany before 1933 (Gellately, n 14, p.93), whereas it was well established in many American jurisdictions.

[53] V Curran, this volume; R Weisberg, *Vichy Law and the Holocaust in France* (New York, New York University Press, 1996).

[54] D Fraser, *The Jews of the Channel Islands and the Rule of Law, 1940–1945* (Brighton, Sussex Academic Press, 2000).

[55] In Gellately's striking phrase (at n 14 above, 2) 'the war revolutionised the revolution' the Nazis had implemented in German society. His study argues persuasively that although wartime atrocities built on what had gone before, they were radically and qualitatively different, in matters ranging from initiating the Genocide to summary execution of those denounced for grumbling about the regime.

amidst the ever-present political violence. The way was open for the Nazis to draw upon very widely shared anxieties and dissatisfactions, and they responded in ways that commanded widespread approval and even greater acquiescence, which endured to the bitter end of the regime.[56]

IV

If, to recall Dr Mahlmann's phrase[57], we are to take seriously our responsibility for the future—our future as citizens of free and democratic European societies—we must ask two related questions about our own societies:

1) what similarities with Nazism do we find, and how can we avoid further convergence? and
2) what are the enduring differences, and how can we preserve them?

Clearly those questions open vistas too vast and require answers too complex even to attempt a full discussion of them here. What follows is a sort of epilogue, a brief sketch of the outlines of a response.

Perhaps the most important similarity emerges when it is recalled that the attack on criminals, 'asocials', the mentally handicapped and, of course, the Jews and the Roma, were not the starting point of Nazi persecution. Arbitrary state power was legitimated by action taken against the 'threatening' presence of Communists, who were the initial target of the police in February 1933. This was popular among middle class Germans, and began the process of habituating them to viewing violent repression as normal and acceptable action by the state, even when carried out by a newly-established political police (the Gestapo) which operated outside ordinary law.[58]

In post-War liberal societies a much more attenuated version of the same process has occurred. The Cold War led to the permanent imposition and steady expansion of security agencies and political policing and in some states —notably the USA with its McCarthyism, 'unAmerican activities' committees and loyalty oaths and West Germany with its *berufsverbot*—various forms of persecution of political dissidents. The need to counter violent domestic movements in Britain produced legislation that sharply increased police powers, did away with protections for suspects in custody and allowed administrative imposition of a form of internal exile (so-called 'exclusion orders') on persons suspected but not convicted of criminal offences. In a classic illustration of the irreversible dynamic of such measures, these and other extraordinary powers, described in statute for over two decades as 'temporary provisions', have now been made permanent. Moreover, they have been extended to all forms of

---

[56] Gellately's fundamental thesis, to my mind demonstrated convincingly, is precisely the endurance of the backing for Hitler, and that it was not maintained only by terror.

[57] Above n 9.

[58] Above n 14 Gellately, 17–21.

political violence regardless of subject or source, so that people who assist rebellions against dictatorships anywhere in the world are now considered 'terrorists' or supporters of 'terrorism' within the UK.[59]

Most dramatic of all, however, in terms of incursions on liberty and the growth of the power of repressive agencies of the state has been the impact of the 'war on drugs'. The language itself should be a warning, and not only because it was frequently employed by the Nazis. The use of the symbols and emotions of militarism implies a disregard for the normal civil restraints on government action. Although Americans have a tendency to use this language more generally—as in the 'War on Poverty' in the 1960s—certainly in Britain this metaphor is always used in the context of demands for greater powers of surveillance, harsher sentencing, more central government control over policing, and more preventive powers over personal movement and property. Use of the rhetoric of war, with the implication that the traditional values and limits of civil society can no longer be respected, should be an automatic danger signal for citizens of liberal societies. Britain is by no means unique in this respect, as the controversy over the amendment of the *G-10-Gesetz* in Germany has illustrated.[60] It is a signal to which most people have unfortunately remained blind. Indeed in Britain certainly and probably elsewhere, the distortion of constitutional or libertarian principles, and the alteration of legal provisions and norms in the direction of removing individual rights has been far greater as a result of the (largely ineffective) efforts to prevent commerce in drugs than from the reaction to serious, sometimes deadly, political violence. We have come to regard as normal restrictions, institutions and laws that would have been greeted with incredulity thirty or even twenty years ago, a habit of mind which will make resistance to further developments along this path even harder to sustain.

Secondly, although nothing could be more remote from official policy and pronouncements than the biologically-based murderous racism of the Nazis, the fact remains that racial bigotry remains strong and politically influential in all European states. Not only are there thousands of racist attacks, some of them fatal, every year in Britain alone, but policies on immigration, asylum and foreign relations are influenced if not dominated by various forms of fear and animosity towards people from the Third World. The new legitimating discourse is not biology but culture. This appears at a grand level on which we are warned of an inevitable 'clash of civilisations'[61] between the superior West and the benighted Muslim world, and equally in day to day politics and social life where the language of exclusion is that of cultural difference.[62] Throw into the

---

[59] Terrorism Act 2000, which does abolish exclusion orders so that movement between Northern Ireland and mainland Britain can no longer be restrained.

[60] For details, see *Statewatch*, vol. Vol.11 (3/4) May–July 2001, 16–18.

[61] The title of the influential Islamophobic tract by the American political scientist Samuel Huntington (New York, Simon & Schuster, 1996).

[62] See M Barker, *The New Racism* (London, Junction Books, 1981). It must be said that some arguments offered in support of 'multiculturalism' are decidedly unhelpful in this respect.

mix fear, vengeance, and political conflict, expose to a white heat of media hysteria, and there can readily emerge a half-baked dog's dinner of poisonous repression and violence very like Germany of the 1930s. This is written in the immediate aftermath of the suicide attacks on the United States; we can only cross our fingers and hope that our leaders will have the courage to act to avoid these dangers.

Flowing naturally from their racially-centred view of the world, the Nazis also believed that human behaviour, particularly undesirable behaviour, was biologically-based. This was by no means original or unique to them: the search to identify the 'criminal type' had been central to the rudimentary 'science' of criminology since the work of Cesare Lombroso in the 1870s. Most obviously it underpinned the sterilisation campaigns, and it also came to shape ordinary policing. The Kripo were increasingly subject to the influence of the Racial Hygiene Office, with whom they were required to co-operate by investigating the racial-biological and antecedents of criminal suspects.[63] This particular strand of 'modern criminal biology' was discredited permanently after 1945, but that does not mean that the tendency to look for 'natural'—as opposed to social and/or economic—causes of unacceptable conduct has vanished with it. In particular, the astonishingly rapid growth of human genetics over the past decade has already begun to stir popular discussion of whether there are 'genes for crime'. It is a safe bet that conservative writers will begin to plough this potentially fertile field to nurture arguments for preventive confinement of those 'born bad'—and, logically, for their sterilisation to prevent passing on the 'dysfunction' to future generations. The uses of modern genetics may well become one of the most bitterly-contested areas of our developing politics.

Turning to differences that require sustaining, the first is one that has perhaps received inadequate attention. The professional classes in Germany—lawyers, doctors, professors, civil servants, ministers—overwhelmingly supported the Nazis. This was true both politically and more sinisterly, in their willing participation in the execution of various unsavoury programmes during the 1930s and—particularly among the medical profession—in acts of mass murder once the War began. Those professions, and not only in Germany, were historically bastions of conservatism, and it was not necessary for the Nazis, once they had purged them of the relatively small number of Jews, to curb their independence by direct or legal measures. In recent decades in many Western countries, there has been a strong liberal or Left element in several of these professions, who have often been a thorn in the side of governments in a wide range of political, moral, and intellectual disputes. It is therefore particularly important that the traditional independence of the professions in matters such as clinical judgment, academic freedom, and the like are resolutely defended and remain unrestricted. Since it is easy for incompetence and economic self-interest

---

[63] Above n 7, 202–3.

to hide behind such freedoms this is not a popular or easy position to maintain in a time in when 'accountability' has become a great mantra. The alternative, however, is much worse: doctors who act in the purported interests of 'the community' or the state rather than those of their patients, or lawyers who try to pacify their clients or compromise their interests rather than fight their corner against state power[64] become potent accomplices in tyranny. The same is true of intellectuals who devote their energies to agendas set for them by officials, rather than exercise their own critical faculties.

A second institution, which the Nazis quickly overcame and which remains a distinctive feature of liberal states, is a free press. Sustained criticism of political and commercial elites, even if undertaken for the most self-interested reasons, is perhaps the strongest bulwark against oppression in its various forms. Debates about concentration of media ownership and the requirements of public service broadcasting are not primarily about markets, profits, and competition but ultimately about the quality of political life. This is especially true in relation to newspapers and journals, which remain more important as a source of knowledge and extended analysis of public affairs than television. That these same organs often invade privacy and offer sensationalist pap does not negate that fact that at some critical moments, some of them offer the only effective—because widely disseminated—critical responses to government attempts to control information and establish an official version of public truth. It is not necessary to swallow the American First Amendment approach to freedom of expression—in particular, there is compelling need to curb unwarranted intrusions into privacy—to protect freedom of the press and correlative rights such as the journalists' ability to protect the anonymity of their sources. This remains well understood in the legislation of several European states and, with a few exceptions, in the Article 10 jurisprudence of European Court of Human Rights. It is also a position to which the English courts, partly under the influence of that jurisprudence, have moved after sharp resistance in the 1980s.

Finally, there remains the obvious point that Germany after 1933 was neither a democracy nor a state based on the rule of law. It is however less clear what follows from that. The Nazis did not destroy legal institutions; indeed they worked through them, and received overwhelming support from the judiciary.[65] As Fraser's paper emphasises, all the repressive and racist measures of the 1930s—mostly famously the Nuremberg Laws stripping Jews of their German citizenship—were enacted through legislation under normal procedures and

---

[64] The Nazis' transformation of the 'peace of law' movement of the 1920s into 'National Socialist Legal Care' is a good example of the use of lawyers to pacify people with grievances rather than pursuing their legal rights. See Reifner, *The Theory and Practice of Legal Advice for Workers in Prefascist Germany* in R Abel (ed) *The Politics of Informal Justice* (London, Academic Press, 1982), vol 2, 110–14, which discusses the Nazi period.

[65] See generally on this point Michael Stolleis' excellent collection of essays: *The Law Under the Swastika* (London & Chicago, University of Chicago Press, 1998).

were recognised as valid by foreign legal systems for decades thereafter.[66] With fewer exceptions than one might think (eg the Night of the Long Knives), the Nazis ruled through a state which observed the forms of law. Even Himmler's plans for 'community aliens' was intended for implementation in legal form. Nor will it do to claim that Nazi legislation was somehow not law. This can only be maintained by a tautology in which law is defined as having some determinate substantive content. Yet the content of law is pre-eminently a political matter on which there are no universally accepted principles. Laws may be opposed and discredited as unjust and immoral, but that is not at all the same thing as claiming that they are somehow not 'real' law.[67]

Nor is democracy as such any guarantee against tyrannous measures, though it may serve to prevent permanent tyranny. Democratic authoritarianism, particularly in relation to minority groups which can never prevail against a united ethnic majority, is both the logical corollary of absolute majority rule and the observable practice of a growing number of states.[68] It is also something that has long been a serious problem in Britain, with its unwritten constitution and *grundnorm* of parliamentary supremacy. To take but one example, recently very well documented: wartime legislation carried over into peacetime with the barest whimper of parliamentary dissent, (and interpreted by a judiciary dangerously close to the political leadership) served to legitimate persecution through the legal process of various dissenting movements in the 1920s and 1930s.[69] Serious students of the British constitution have long been aware of this danger, though divided over its likelihood. It moved from the academy to centre stage of political life in the 1980s, when Margaret Thatcher enjoyed an overwhelming parliamentary majority which she used imperiously to override opposition to her regime. (Out of the reaction to this came the movement for constitutional reform, which eventually led, among other things, to enactment in domestic law of the European Convention on Human Rights.)

Legality as such cannot guarantee freedom; democracy can as easily imperil as preserve it. It is in the synergy of both, in the institutions and ideals of democratic constitutionalism, that liberal societies are at their best in preserving freedom, equality and self-government. Democratic constitutionalism means majority rule, constrained by substantive norms designed to protect political and personal freedoms. These norms moreover must be legally enforceable. Only insofar as they can demonstrate real attachment to that praxis can liberal societies claim to be genuinely distinct from the Nazis.

---

[66] See also the discussion earlier in this paper of the legislation on sterilisation and the preventive detention of 'habitual criminals'.

[67] For a further elaboration of this view, see the present author's review of Stolleis' work (above n 65), 'Taking Nazi Law Seriously', (2000) 63 *Modern Law Review* 128.

[68] This point is made very well in a thoughtful essay by F Zakaria, 'Democratic Tyranny', 76(6) *Foreign Affairs*, (1997) 22–42.

[69] See K Ewing and C Gearty, *The Struggle for Civil Liberties: Political Freedom and the Rule of Law in Britain, 1914–1945* (Oxford, Oxford University Press, 2000), *passim*.

PART III

Continuity and Reconfiguration

7

CARL SCHMITT'S EUROPE: CULTURAL, IMPERIAL AND SPATIAL PROPOSALS FOR EUROPEAN INTEGRATION, 1923–1955

*John P McCormick**

Fascism is generally understood as a fundamentally nationalist phenomenon. And rightly so: there are vast literatures confirming this point.[1] For all the idiosyncrasies that make Carl Schmitt an unconventional—that is, substantively interesting—fascist, he certainly qualifies as a German nationalist.[2] However, common to fascism generally, and Schmitt in particular, is a much less discussed vision of regions.[3] In Schmitt's case, I will treat this as an, if you will, evolving vision of European integration. Originally, this research project was organised to pursue the following question: does the post-war development of the EC and EU share, or even owe, anything to this darker legacy of regional integration? In this paper, I approach this question by sketching out Schmitt's vision of Europe from the early 1920s through to the mid-1950s.

On the one hand, Schmitt should be of only limited interest: his unmitigated antipathy to Russia, his brooding, often paranoid Catholicism and his highly abstract conceptual categorisations set him apart from most twentieth century theorists of a more unified Europe. On the other hand, the remarkable extent of Schmitt's intellectual influence in postwar policy circles, as emphasised most

---

* Yale University. Successive drafts of this paper were presented at the European University Institute, Florence, 17 June 1999 and 29 September 2000 as part of the Research Project: 'Perceptions of a European Legal Order During the Fascist and National Socialist Era.' The first two sections elaborate on ch 2 of my *Carl Schmitt's Critique of Liberalism* (Cambridge, Cambridge University Press, 1997); the balance of the paper was composed specifically for this project.

[1] As just one recent example of this tradition of scholarship, see R Thurlow, *Fascism* (Cambridge, Cambridge University Press, 1997).

[2] Helmut Quaritsch perhaps most extensively treats Schmitt's nationalism in *Positionen und Begriffe Carl Schmitts* (Berlin, Duncker & Humblot, 1989).

[3] Notable exceptions in this regard, at least pertaining to Schmitt, are: M Schmoeckel, *Die Großraumtheorie: Ein Beitrag zur Geschicte der Völkerrechtswissenschaft im Dritten Reich, insbesondere der Kriegszeit* (Berlin, Duncker & Humblot, 1994), and F Blindow, *Carl Schmitts Reichsordnung: Strategie fuer einen europaeischen Grossraum* (Berlin, Akademie Verlag, 1999).

immediately in Christian Joerges's contribution to this volume,[4] renders his thought unavoidable. Then there is, of course, the issue of the alluring and tantalising quality of his thought, idiosyncratic or not, politically palatable or not.

In the early 1920s Schmitt adhered to a conception of Europe as neo-Christendom in *Roman Catholicism and Political Form*. As his thought becomes more secular, this gives way to a preoccupation with Europe as specifically *Central* Europe [*Mitteleuropa*] in the 1929 essay, 'The Age of Neutralizations and Depoliticisations.' During his National Socialist career, Schmitt formulated a *Großraum* theory of Central Europe dominated by the German *Reich*. And finally, in post war writings such as *The Nomos of The Earth*, Schmitt identifies Europe as the source of a rational, juridical international order—an order disrupted by the emergence of the intercontinental empires of the United States and the Soviet Union.

Europe as Christendom, 1923

Political Form expresses the young Schmitt's clerico-conservative vision of Europe.[5] At this time, Schmitt, still a confessing Catholic, promotes the Church as a tent under which Europeans might unite against the common enemy of Soviet Russia. What could possibly give the Catholic Church such authority in an apparently post-Catholic, even post-Christian era? Schmitt contends that since liberalism, Protestantism and romanticism have sacralised privacy in Europe, these movements have inhibited the public acknowledgment and display of what is important. The European public sphere was once an arena for the representation of substantive principles like authority, community, justice, even democracy, but, especially 'humanity.' In response to the passive retreat from the social world engendered by developments such as liberalism, Schmitt offers a Catholicism whose public and objective, not private and subjective, disposition manifests itself in politics rather than a domestic or economic realm. According to Schmitt, Catholicism is faithful to the essence of European civilisation, that is, the public assertion and representation of substantive values.

This separates Europe, to Schmitt's mind, from the odd amalgam that resides beyond Europe's Eastern frontier: Byzantine Christianity, communism and anarchism. Schmitt supposes that the Catholic capacity for representation of values inspires a full-scale revolt by Russian radicals, whether of Eastern Orthodox, anarchist or communist stripe. They revolt against the very notion of the 'Idea.' For Catholicism, 'humanity' is the notion that human beings exist

---

[4] See C Joerges, *Europe A Großraum? Ruptures, continuities and re-configurations in the Legal Conceptualisations of the Integration Project*, in this volume.

[5] C Schmitt, *Römischer Katholizismus und politische Form* (Stuttgart, Klett-Cotta, 1984); *Roman Catholicism and Political Form*, trans. G.L. Ulmen (Westport, Greenwood Press, 1996).

as more than biology; they are capable of good, but need guidance intellectually. Humanity for the Russians, according to Schmitt, is mere material to be manipulated technologically. Catholicism, is the juridical heir to Roman jurisprudence; the rational-institutional reminder that human beings possess a divine component.

Schmitt avers that European liberals and Western socialists are complicitous in the promotion of the economic rationality radicalised in Russia, and are embarrassed of the substantive rationality claimed for Europe by Catholicism. But they are nonetheless, in the last instance, friends of Catholicism and enemies of the Soviets. European liberals and socialists are inclined to fight for substantive, universal conceptions of humanity, but they need Catholicism to remind them of how to wage these battles properly. The Catholic Church, as a 'complex of opposites', has embodied all political forms, knows when to ally with some, and when to confront others. Schmitt notes that contemporary Catholics are unsure about who constitutes the immediate enemy: French Catholics like Tocqueville, Montalembert and Lacordaire took liberal stands 'at a time when many of their fellow Catholics still saw in liberalism the Antichrist.' One of the main thrusts of the book is to clarify exactly *who* the common enemy is for Catholic intellectual elites, and their erstwhile liberal adversaries. Who in 1923 really represents an opponent with the stature of the Antichrist? Here, Schmitt finds the mythic enemy of Catholicism, not in liberalism or Western socialism, but, rather, in Russia.

However different, Dostoyevsky, Lenin and Bakunin—that is, Orthodox, Communist and Anarchist—all manifest a particularly Russian antipathy to idea, to form and to authority: Schmitt claims that the fable of the Grand Inquisitor demonstrates how Dostoyevsky understands as evil anyone holding an office or exercising intellectual leadership. Schmitt predicts that the rebellion against order, against form per se, can only lead to the greatest abuses of order, as it already had in Soviet Russia. For Schmitt, Bolshevik Russia is the seat of both a technical *rationality* in communism, as well as an anarchic *irrational* counter-force to order of any kind that is the logical outgrowth of radical Eastern Christianity. The Russian anarchist Bakunin, that 'naive beserker,' waged battles against metaphysics, religion, politics, jurisprudence and the 'the idea' as such. Schmitt claims that, in this regard, the spirit of the Soviet Union moves in distinct opposition to that of its ideological fathers, Marx and Engels. They were fundamentally *Europeans* and *intellectuals* who had faith in moral *authority*. They detested the likes of Bakunin, and were, vice versa, despised by him.

Schmitt claims that the antagonism between Marx and Engels, on the one hand, and Bakunin, on the other, 'sets the stage whereon . . . Catholicism stands as a political force.' Because of this antipathy, Catholicism and Europeans can make their political choice. According to Schmitt, despite Catholicism's past and present difficulties with liberalism or Western Socialism, the two must ally together against the Soviets. He concludes this 1923 work with the imperative that Catholicism stands 'on the side of the *idea* and West European civilization' and *against* 'the atheistic socialism of the Russian anarchist.' Catholicism stands as the reminder that Europe is the home of the Idea, of values, and of the institutional forms that embody them. From the Roman imperium through Christendom to liberalism and Western Socialism, Europe *champions* substantive human content. Soviet Russia is the greatest historical threat to such content, and its physical host, Europe.

Central Europe as Anti-Russia, 1929

Four years later, Schmitt has fully developed his thesis concerning 'the political'. He stops speaking in terms of political Catholicism and his vision of Europe no longer includes France. Thus, in the 'Age of Neutralizations' essay,[6] Schmitt describes Europe less theologically, and also in less pan-continental terms—that is, in more Germanic terms. Ideas or values are no longer the main difference between Europe and Soviet Russia. Instead, the difference seems to rest with the relationship of elites to masses, in general, and elites and masses to technology, particularly, in both Europe and Russia. Now, Schmitt's Europe seems to have little substantive content apart from being simply an existential *other* to Soviet Russia.

The 'political' intent of the 'Neutralizations' piece is expressed in its very first sentence: 'We in Central Europe live under the eyes of the Russians.' The point of the essay is to convince its European audience that the Soviet Union is the enemy and must be recognised as such. The grounds for this 'political' position vis-à-vis the Russians reside with technology, specifically weapons. Why does the Soviet Union and its orientation toward technology pose a threat to Central Europe? Because while Europe is predisposed toward the status quo in the wake of the 'Great War' of 1914, Russia recognises the changes underlying historical circumstances and seeks to appropriate the moment. Just as the Soviets stunned Europe with the Revolution of 1917, Schmitt intimates that they are again poised to shatter the veneer of neutrality in League of Nations Europe a decade later.

According to Schmitt, the dynamic of modern European history is driven by the search for a *neutral sphere*—a sphere completely free from violent conflict and intellectual contestation. In response to the strife of the religious civil wars, Europe since the sixteenth century has sought in each successive century a different fundamental organising principle—a central sphere, which might serve as the source of peace and agreement. Schmitt contends that

---

[6] C Schmitt, 'Das Zeitalter der Neutralisierungen und Entpolitisierungen,' reprinted in Schmitt, *Der Begriff des Politischen: Text von 1932 mit einem Vorwort und drei Corollarien* (Berlin, Duncker & Humblot, 1963); C Schmitt, 'The Age of Neutralizations and Depoliticizations,' trans. M Konzett and JP McCormick, (1993) 96 *Telos*.

neutrality could not be maintained due to the inevitable return of the repressed human inclination toward conflict. In the twentieth century, technology is the sought-after neutral area, but Schmitt claims that it actually becomes a new and definitive source of conflict: 'Every strong politics will make use of it.'

Soviet Russia is possessed, bewitched, by the spirit of technicity, the compulsion toward mastery for mastery's sake. Schmitt starkly contrasts this technicity [*Technizität*] with the neutrality and passivity of European elites who are overwhelmed by mere technology [*Technik*]. A whole generation of German intellectuals feels supplanted by engineers and technicians who know nothing of culture, politics and, most importantly, nothing of *myth*. Reminiscent of the earlier *Political Form* book, Schmitt claims that Soviet Russia (he never refers to it in either work as the Soviet Union) is the embodiment of seemingly contradictory characteristics: (1) socialistic economic rationality; (2) anarchism, or the irrational revolt against all form and order; and (3) Slavism, an ecstatic nationalism. Despite what European elites might think, Russia is not just a formal, mechanical, lifeless technological state. Schmitt emphasises the expressly life-like, spiritual, willful, even *satanic* quality of the Soviets. The Soviet elite commands technology rather than vice versa and is capable of motivating the masses in unprecedented ways.

Thus, Europe 'lives under the gaze of the more radical brother who compels one to drive practical conclusions to the end.' The Russians are the new 'ascetics' who are willing to forego the 'comfort' of the present for control of the future. They will dominate their own nature for the sake of dominating external nature and the nature in others. If European intellectuals continue to indulge their passively aesthetic enrapture with the status quo, they abdicate their duty and privilege to lead, and they invite domination by their more radical brother. A decade later, in the service of a movement that would energetically and murderously mobilise Central Europe against the Soviets, Schmitt formulates a plan to control the *space* between Europe and Russia.

The German Großraum, 1939

Schmitt unveiled his infamous *Großraum* theory in an April 1939 lecture.[7] He had been a member of the Nazi party since 1933, although his prominence had been under sharp challenge since 1936. The lecture continues certain trends in Schmitt's conception of Europe that we can trace from the previous works discussed. For one, Schmitt continues to move eastward: *Political Form*

---

[7] C Schmitt, 'Völkerrechtliche Großraumordnung mit Interventionsverbot für raumfremde Mächte: Ein Beitrag zum Reichsbegriff im Völkerrecht,' published in 1941 and reprinted in ed. G Maschke (ed) *Carl Schmitt, Staat, Großraum, Nomos: Arbeiten aus den Jahren 1916–1969* (Berlin, Duncker & Humblot, 1995).

envisioned a Europe that included France and, perhaps, even Britain. The 'Neutralizations' essay is preoccupied with *Central* Europe, but one defined in opposition to the Soviets, exclusively. The Soviets are still of grave concern in the *Großraum* lecture, but so too is a Western order dominated by Britain and the United States.

Schmitt insists that Western Europe has been absorbed into the US *Großraum*, a greater territorial sphere of influence, through the Monroe cum Wilson doctrine. He brilliantly exposes the hypocrisies of the League of Nations and the Monroe doctrine, but this does not prevent him from developing a specifically German 'Monroe doctrine.' In this sense, substantive content has returned to the European order that Schmitt promotes: German ethnicity now serves as a content that was absent in the 'Neutralizations' essay of a decade before. But even this ethnicity is described rather vaguely; it is never consistently described in cultural, linguistic, or racial terms. Schmitt leaves undefined how ethnic distinctions will be made let alone specifically enforced within the German *Großraum*.

The actual governance of the *Großraum* is also elucidated in only the sketchiest terms: Germany's Monroe doctrine will share with its US counterpart the prohibition on external intervention into its space. As in the US doctrine, foreign entities within this geographical sphere will not be directly subsumed under, or annexed to, the dominant state or *Reich*, which Schmitt describes as the intermediary regime between a state and the greater *Großraum*. However, the defining internal principle of the German *Großraum* differs from US policy in Central and South America: self-determination and civil liberties will *not* prevail for entities within this sphere of influence as they do at least theoretically in the US paradigm. Rather, so-called respect of ethnic nationalities will be observed. This is a qualified 'respect' to be sure since, on the one hand, Jews are completely exempt from such respect, and, on the other, German nationality is granted greater respect over all other nationalities within the *Großraum*.

Thus, Schmitt's German *Großraum* is explicitly *not* universalist in the way claimed by the US doctrine, even if hypocritically. According to Schmitt, the *Reich* will intervene explicitly on behalf of German ethnicities within its *Großraum* against other ethnicities that might threaten them. Again, what that means in specific policy terms is left unstated by Schmitt. Here, I leave aside the controversial issue of the relationship of Schmitt's *Großraum* theory to Hitler's policy of *Lebensraum*. In this context, it might be more interesting to explore whether Schmitt's post-war conception of Europe retains anything from his National Socialist *Großraum* theory, or whether, on the contrary, it hearkens back to Schmitt's earlier Weimar vision of Europe.

Europe as Origin of International Law and Spatial Order, 1950

In his book, *The Nomos of the Earth*,[8] written in the largely self-imposed, internal exile of the post-war years, Schmitt still privileges Europe vis-à-vis the rest of the world. However, this privileging is no longer based on notions of humanity, or on Europe as the opposite number to Russia, or on its status as the seat of Germanic culture. Rather, Europe is the ground, the territory, the *space* in which the geo-political arrangement most conducive to world peace developed. Only Europe developed the concept and practice of independent, sovereign, and explicitly Christian nation states who balanced each other's lethal military power through international law. This law evolved out of Roman law, was nurtured by the medieval church, and definitively articulated by early-modern natural law thinkers. This law was 'Eurocentric' because it developed in Europe, but was universally rational because it could be applied to the rest of the globe.

In the history of this development, Britain plays an ambivalent part: it was by adopting the viewpoint of Britain—that is, as both part of, and apart from, Europe—that Europe could conceive of itself in terms of the whole globe. Europe could sufficiently abstract away from itself to observe and contemplate its place in the globe, in a way that other cultures, regions and regimes hitherto could not. Thus did Europe develop a doctrine and practice of world-historical significance, rather than one of merely local, parochial or regional importance. But England's somewhat remote relationship to continental Europe—an estrangement reinforced by the former's seafaring nature—is the source of the dissolution of European public law and order.

Britain's control of the sea, in Schmitt's view, her ability to hold the world as a sphere in her hand, initiates the contest for overseas colonies. This retards the development of a world of sovereign nation states, accelerates the emergence of hemispheric empires, and encourages *extraterrestrial* means of travel and conquest. The latter, in particular—sea travel, air travel and, Schmitt gestures, even space travel—rule out an order of independent states governed by international law. When travel and the threat of military force is no longer bound to the land, sovereign integrity is not secured by geographical space. Rather, it evaporates in the limitlessness of, literally, *unearthly* interaction, surveillance and conquest. Consequently, Europe's significance and power shrink between the weight and reach of the intercontinental, inter-hemispheric, even intergalactic, Soviet and American empires. Schmitt, himself, of course, was complicitous in this decline of state sovereignty: his attempt to formulate a Central European hemispheric empire for Germany under the Nazis results in the arrested development of potential independent states within that sphere of influence.

---

[8] C Schmitt, *Der Nomos der Erde im Völkerrecht des Jus Publicum Europaeum* (Berlin, Duncker & Humblot, 1974).

Despite the pessimistic tone of the volume, the book and related essays[9] leave open the question of whether a European *Großraum* might rectify the excesses of a world dominated by American and Soviet empires. Could Europe once again produce the specifically European, yet universally world-historical, grounds for a peaceful global order? After the collapse of the Soviet empire this is a question worth confronting, if we are not to capitulate to one of the other alternatives that Schmitt invokes: US global hegemony. I will conclude with a few remarks along these lines.

Preliminary Conclusions

Do any of Schmitt's visions of Europe survive in the EU's self-understanding today? Do any of them help us think about a contemporary or future European *Großraum*? Certainly the view of Europe as reconstructed Christendom had resonance in Adenauer's and Monnet's understanding of what animated the post-war Community.[10] On the other hand, the technocratic interpretation of the EU certainly replays many of the themes found in the 'Neutralizations' essay: specifically, the sense that Europe must use its technology—albeit economic and *not* military technology—to distinguish and strengthen itself vis-à-vis the US, the Soviet Union and, eventually, Asia.[11] Fortunately, Germany's post-war cultural and political self-understanding facilitates its membership in a *European*, not *Central* European *Großraum*.[12] In this regard, the EU is thankfully *not* a Schmittian *Großraum* in several hopefully obvious senses: It is (1) a *Großraum* without a center, (2) a *Großraum* with affection toward the West, and without imperial ambitions in the East, and (3) a *Großraum* that embraces equanimity among European peoples.

But Schmitt still prompts us to question what *specifically* characterises Europe's internal commonality and its distinction from the outside world today. He compels us to ponder the means by which such a supranational union might be administered. In a resoundingly un-Schmittian move, Jürgen Habermas, for instance, has suggested that the common experience of having happily—albeit with great difficulty—overcome nationalism provides a unify-

---

[9] Especially, C Schmitt, 'Der Neue Nomos der Erde,' (1955) 3 *Gemeinschaft und Politik: Zeitschrift für soziale und politische Gestalt.*

[10] On the cultural disposition of the EC's framers, see AS Milward, *The European Rescue of the Nation State* (London, Routledge, 2000).

[11] On the centrality of economic issues in the evolution of the EU, see A Moravcsik, *The Choice for Europe: Social Purpose and State Power from Messina to Maastricht* (Ithaca, Cornell University Press, 1998).

[12] See the recent collections: PJ Katzenstein (ed), *Tamed Power: Germany in Europe* (Ithaca, Cornell University Press, 1998); and AS Markovits and S Reich (eds), *The German Predicament: Memory and Power in the New Europe* (Ithaca, Cornell University Press, 1997).

ing principle and a cautionary lesson against future excesses in Europe.[13] He promotes a system of governance by which deliberating publics constituting a European civil society that sustains a continental party and parliamentary system generates law that is rational and responsive to the popular will. But Habermas has not answered what might definitively justify the very demarcation of a European *Großraum* from the rest of the world; and his plan for legal-democratic governance in the EU is hardly operational at the present time. Until these questions and problems are addressed, Schmitt's work and career, like a specter, haunts the study of European integration.

---

[13] See several of the essays contained in J Habermas, *The Inclusion of the Other: Studies in Political Theory*, (eds C Cronin and P de Grieff) (Cambridge, MA, MIT Press, 1998) and M Pensky (ed) *The Postnational Constellation: Political Essays* (Cambridge, MA, MIT Press, 2001).

8

CULTURE AND THE RATIONALITY OF LAW FROM WEIMAR TO MAASTRICHT

J Peter Burgess

Introduction

At the dawn of the twenty first century, the late modern *ethos* of Weimar social and political organisation reproduces itself in the post-modern *ethos* of the European Union.[1] The Treaty of the European Union at Maastricht witnesses the return of the unresolved crisis of the modern constitution, which erupted even before the dust had settled over the struggles to find a political compromise at the close of 1919. The weakness and indecisiveness of the Weimar Constitution, its blind homogenisation of the disparate components of the German Empire, its transformation of a richly layered legal and institutional history into a bureaucratic black box, and its rote collectivisation of diverse sub-national traditions and ethnic particularity in the name of an empty concept of 'republicanism', is not singular, but symptomatic of a phase in the history of constitutionalism. Not in the history of constitutional law, but rather in the history of the *concept* of the constitution, its place is in a reference network that organises the relation of that concept to its subject, its content, its legitimacy and its own implicit ambiguity.[2] The recent debates concerning the constitutionality of the European Union, its state-oid appearance, and its democratic aspirations re-open an analogous if radically different constellation of questions and problems, categories and paradigms, which are required for a thorough understanding of the Weimar episode.

What is the function of the modern constitution? Does it have a *function*? Or does its *ontos*, its very existence, constitute its function? What is its *conceptual* status? Is it normative? That is, does it describe the order of rules and regulations, institutions and procedures that form the political basis for a programme

---

[1] Many thanks to Wilfried Spohn for his thoughtful commentary on an earlier version of this piece.

[2] The work of JHH Weiler has gone farther than any in the reconstruction of this conceptual history, and my debts to his work in the following will soon become clear. See in particular, JHH Weiler, 'The Transformation of Europe,' (1991) 100 *Yale Law Journal* 2403, which is integrated into JHH Weiler, *The Constitution of Europe* (Cambridge, Cambridge University Press, 1999).

of change, progress and realisation? Or is it descriptive, that is merely an image, a record and legitimisation of the social, political, cultural order of what is? According to what norms and measures does it engage the question of validity and applicability, of who belongs to the constitutional state and who decides who belongs to the constitutional state? On what conceptual plane can the tension between disparate components of one unified entity be resolved? What is the meaning of the tension of interests which make up the inner fabric of constitutional compromise?

The task of this paper is to develop a hypothesis not about the *historical* continuity between Weimar and Maastricht, but rather about the *conceptual* continuity between them, to chart its sometimes-severe limitations, to analyse its excesses, and map its deficiencies. It is our hope that this process of moulding and melding will produce a set of conceptual *vases communicantes*, the basis for a certain continuity of juridical and political thinking capable of connecting two realities nearly a century apart. It will thus produce a certain number of conclusions about the nature of the legal categories that organise both the early twentieth century self-understanding of the Weimar Republic, and the early twenty first century self-understanding of the European Union.

The following discussion begins with the presentation of a contemporary conceptual issue: the legitimacy crisis of the European Union. It then explores the most notable legitimacy crisis of the twentieth century—the debate surrounding the Weimar constitution, and one of the central antagonists of that crisis, Carl Schmitt. It then returns to the present in the light of the findings from Weimar. It is a fundamental presupposition of this paper that the terms and categories of the critique, which the Weimar jurist Carl Schmitt brings to the debate around the Weimar Constitution of 1919, can cast light upon the debate about the European constitution. We will not try to suggest that the European 'peoples' of the late twentieth century are in a social, political or legal position identical to that of the German 'peoples' at the beginning of the twentieth century. However we will suppose that they are not so far away as to make uninteresting the project of bringing them into conceptual communication with one another. Carl Schmitt is not the analytic key to the conundrum of the European constitution. He is our conduit to an understanding of the European present. More than any other legal thinker of the twentieth century, his categories and concepts, queries, incoherencies and paranoia's expose the irreducible problems of late modernity, both in the historiographical and juridical terms.

'"The King of Prussia" is not an Acceptable Partner at Versailles'

The immediate pre-conditions of the Weimar constitutions—its accessible form and acceptable categories—were determined through the formal impositions made in the 'negotiations' led by the allies in mid-October 1917. President Wilson and the Americans dominated the process. Indeed the conditions of peace imposed by the Allies were never formally recognised by France and Italy.[3] It was not until 5 November, one month after the de facto armistice, that the 'official' armistice was 'enacted'. Indeed de facto peace was not peace at all. Peace in the eyes of Wilson was not a state attained after a cessation of hostilities. It was rather a principle or set of principles. Wilson's famous 'Fourteen Points', which he subsequently presented in several political speeches, confirmed that peace was a *formal*, not *empirical* state. In other words, the very modalities and categories available to those negotiating the Treaty of Versailles—18 months later—were prepared in advance. The most dramatic consequence of this 'pre-conditioning' of the treaty negotiations, was that Imperial Germany, *strictu senso* was excluded from negotiation. Wilson declared that neither the 'military autocrats' nor the 'King of Prussia' were acceptable partners at the table of peace negotiations.[4] Obviously it is not Wilhelm II who is at issue. It is rather the *identification* of the German people with one man, *according to the logic of monarchy*. The *formal* requirement of the Versailles negotiations is that the logic of embodiment, the entire nature of the relation between *people* and *person*, is being radically transformed, revolutionarised. Germany was not excluded in the sense that the vanquished part was not allowed to participate, to represent its own subjective position and to recognise—and thereby legitimise—the charges made against it. An integral part of the judgment was 'which Germany?'. Which 'figure' could politically represent the German 'people' in a politically 'acceptable' form while at the same time embodying the German identity? Wilson ridiculed the monarchy, virtually decapitating the King of Prussia, and the German Empire was left to make massive identity changes in order to legitimate itself in the international symbolic dialogue. Imperial Germany had to *change* its symbolic identity in order to represent itself.

Obviously there were clear revolutionary moments in the pre-history of the Weimar Republic. The military revolts in Kiel on 4 November 1918, preceded by the famous submariner mutiny a few days before, as well as the public uprisings in Munich on 7 November 1918, combined with a newly opened public sphere, helped to lead the Empire to a collective mood of change. Furthermore, both the Independent Socialist Party (USPD) and the Spartakists played

---

[3] H Holborn, *Deutsche Geschichte in der Neuzeit. Band II: Das Zeitalter des Imperialismus (1871–1945)*, trans. A Holborn (Frankfurt am Main, Fischer, 1981) 287.

[4] *Ibid.* 292.

important roles in determining the tone of the first attempts at a new constitution. But an undeniable novelty in the 'revolutionary' events is the *formal* revolution, which shadows the material one. From the first actual cessation of hostilities until his 'retirement' from Berlin to Spa on 10 November 1918, Wilhelm II was pathetically drained of his legitimacy, to a large degree because of disagreement with his military advisors on the *legitimacy* concerning the cessation of hostilities, but also in part because of Wilson's simple refusal to acknowledge that a king, any king, could legitimately represent a people or a nation.

This de-coupling of the *people* from its formal logic of *collectivity* explains in part the weakness of the constitutional formulations of the Weimar Republic. Where the Bismarckian constitution of 1871 is based on a reciprocal relation between a *popular* representative body—the Reichstag—and the king, the presuppositions given to the architects and theorists of the Weimar constitution—Preuß, Weber, Jellinek, Meinecke, and others—were required to strike delicate balances along several registers, between Prussian hegemony, liberal and anti-liberal tendencies, revolutionary and anti-revolutionary movements, economic interests, etc.[5]

It is customary to insert the Weimar Constitution of 1919 either into a general European tradition of constitutional law or a particular Germanic legal tradition dating from the early nineteenth century—say from the Deutsche Bundesakte of 1815 or the Wiener Schlußakte of 1820. Such genealogies have distinct advantages, and in what follows we will build in part on historical reconstructions of a number of conceptual constellations. Still, the political and legal run-up to the Weimar Republic in 1919, and its extraordinarily turbulent fifteen year life make it a singular object of study. What sets Weimar Republic apart, and at the same time makes it an instructive case for our understanding of contemporary European questions, is the weave of tensions that traverse and organise it: monarchy and republic; novelty and tradition; revolution and democracy; bureaucracy and pre-bureaucracy.[6] These tensions are echoed by the conceptual construction of the Treaty of European Union.

To narrow the point of entry for this unorthodox comparison, we will focus on the constitutional theory of Carl Schmitt. More than any other theorist, Schmitt opened up theoretical reflection on the notions of constitutionalism, representation, identity, and legitimacy, and contributed a generalised set of categories for prying apart the antimonies of modern democracy. It is our intention both to explicate those categories, which seem pertinent to the question of European constitutionalism, and to measure the extent of their portability to the legal, political and ethical questions of the beginning of the twenty-first century.

---

[5] W Apelt, *Geschichte der Weimarer Verfassung* (München & Berlin, Beck'sche Verlagsbuchhandlung, 1964); H Schulz, *Weimar. Deutschland 1917–1933* (Berlin, Siedler, 1982) 90–91.
   [6] P Gay, *Weimar Culture. The Outsider as Insider* (London, Penguin, 1968) 1–8.

'The German Empire is a Republic.'[7] / 'Citizenship of the Union is Hereby Established.'[8]

Conventional wisdom holds that the unification of the German Empire under Bismarck and the Imperial Constitution of 1871 was significantly weakened and indeed endangered by its successor, the Weimar Constitution.[9] The various forms of quasi-revolutionary turbulence, separatist movements, general social unrest and dissatisfaction put into question the entire consciousness of the Germanic peoples as a *Schicksalsgemeinschaft*, as it had been cultivated through the second half of the nineteenth century. The crisis of the immediate post-war period had two aspects—the material military catastrophe, and its immediate consequences for the material well being of the German Empire, on the one hand, and an *identity* crisis, on the other. This identity crisis can be mapped on several levels. It traverses social strata, cultural groups, and institutional matrixes. On the conceptual level, which is our primary interest, the crisis involves revisiting the question of the *unity* of the people(s) of the German empire.

For despite ideological dogma, and popular perception (both domestic and international), the German Empire at the end of the Bismarckian era was remarkably heterogeneous. Indeed the most noteworthy *political* achievement ascribed to Bismarck, and carried forth by Wilhelm II, was the *unification*, of the relatively diverse German peoples. The Frankfurt Constitution, born out of the Paris uprisings in 1848, although a grand opportunity for the German Empire Parliament to enter the ranks of liberal democracies in the early nineteenth century, ended in failure. When the Frankfurt Parliament collapsed in 1862, the baton was past from bourgeois liberalism to aristocratic militancy, within a discourse of culture, soul, and not the least body. The Empire was once again unified under the famous sign of blood and iron. As Bismarck remarked in 1862:

> Germany does not look to Prussia's liberalism but to her power. The south German States—Bavaria, Würtemberg, and Baden—would like to indulge in liberalism, and because of that no one will assign Prussia's role to them. [. . .] Not by speeches and majorities will the great questions of the day be decided—that was the mistake of 1848 and 1849—but by iron and blood.[10]

Both Article I of the Constitution of Weimar, ('The German Empire is a Republic') and Article 8 of the Treaty of European Union ('Citizenship of the Union is hereby established') are far rhetorical cries from more noteworthy

---

[7] H Hildebrandt (ed), *Die deutschen Verfassungen des 19. und 20. Jahrhunderts* (Münch/Wien/Zürich, Schöningh, 1992) 69.

[8] 'Treaty on European Union,' European Commission (1992) Article 8.

[9] Above n 5, Apelt, 369.

[10] M Viorst (ed), *The Great Documents of Western Civilization* (New York, Barnes and Noble Books, 1994), 265.

constitutional precedents, say the French Constitution with its poignantly deep
and necessary enmeshing of state and right, or the American Constitution with
its rhetoric of religiosity, freedom, and independence, or even the Frankfurt
Constitution of 1849. Both Weimar and Maastricht conspicuously avoid
poignancy, taking aim at the kind of instrumentality which assures their landmark rhetorical dryness. The Wilsonian democratic moral *ethos* and the utter
failure of the politically embodied force of Wilhelm II or the other princes,
made republican instrumental neutrality unavoidable.[11]

The naked, skeletal rhetoric of citizenship in the TEU European construction is also inseparable from a desire to avoid the politically ungainly questions
of ethnicity and ethics in history. In this sense Germany's dominant position in
the processes of European integration is inseparable from a certain political
posturing towards a renewal of its political *ethos*. Both the Weimar
Constitution and the Treaty of European Union grow out of political situations
in which cultural politics grew burdensome, difficult, unprofitable, and even
dangerous. At Weimar the result was schematic republicanism, at Maastricht
econometric populism. The first inaugurates, the second reproduces, albeit in a
different way, within a different context, a kind of transparent constitutionalism: the constitution as simple form, the modern antinomies of cultural unification resolved as juridical formalism.[12]

Not at all gratuitously, the self-transforming *ethos* of the transparent constitution, the conceptual history of the modern constitution has gone full cycle.
We must underscore the modernity of the constitution since, as is well known,
polity is also the central constitutional concept of Athenian democracy.
Distinctively *modern* conceptual history reveals however that constitution
enters the second half of the eighteenth century—the very dawn of synthesis of
natural rights and individuality—as an experiential concept, which reproduces
the political and judicial situation of a given state. Constitutional debates are
empirical. Opponents of the modern consolidation of constitutionalism not
satisfied with the pragmatic consequences of the constitution interrogate and
attack its juridical backgrounds, thus opening a toward a tradition of political
and social analysis, which parallels the more romantically inspired imperial
traditions of the nineteenth century.[13]

---

[11] Indeed the strongest critique of the Weimar Constitution came from the southern German
and Prussian 'federalists', who felt that the side of national unity was not strengthened to an acceptable level against the variety of regional particularity. Apelt at n 5 above, 371.

[12] Thus when Article A of the Common Provisions of Maastricht proclaims, 'This Treaty marks
a new stage in the process of creating an ever closer union among the peoples of Europe, in which
decisions are taken as closely as possible to the citizen . . .', a Pandora's box of constitutional antinomies is opened: 'union', 'people(s), 'citizen' must all be analysed in this same light.

[13] D Grimm, *Verfassung II* in R Kosellek et al. (eds), *Geschichtliche Grundbegriffe* (Stuttgart,
Klettverlag, 1990).

The Constitutionality of the European Constitution

In the opening reflections of his landmark work, *The Constitution of Europe*, JHH Weiler attempts to articulate an abiding general definition of a 'constitution', or even of *the* constitution of Europe as it is promised in the determinate form of his title. Indeed, glancing at the comprehensive index of the volume we find that the entry 'constitution' promises only a meagre handful of direct references. Instead of focusing on a fixed definition of a constitution, or even *the* constitution of Europe, Weiler begins by evoking the memorable '"constitutional moments" associated in the collective mind with important changes in the constitutional order'.[14] He thus shies away from a substantial definition of the constitution, moving instead toward the notion of constitutionalism as a kind of *phenomenology* of the constitution. In other words, he focuses, in most of *The Constitution of Europe* not on what the European constitution is, was or should be, but rather on the what *happens* when constitutionalism happens, what are the backgrounds, structures, and newly articulated models that become visible when the constitution of Europe 'constitutions'. He regards such 'constitutional moments' of European construction and integration as the key situations in which the logical, legal, cultural coherence of Europe is put to the test and brought to the fore. Some 'obvious candidates', he suggests are the Schuman Declaration, the entry into force of the Treaty of Rome, the declaration of the European Court on the supremacy of Community law, the 1985 White Paper, etc. For all his theoretical sophistication, Weiler never explicitly theorises this approach, and that is perhaps one of its great advantages. Weiler's theory of European constitutionalism is a synthetic one, articulating and consolidating itself through the examination and analysis of the existing legal situation or reality.

This synthetic approach is instructive for a theoretical understanding of the nature and function of legal scholarship. The immense advantage of a legal-theoretical approach to European construction, compared, say, to a political scientific one, is that juridical science is accustomed to understanding the legal 'meaning' of juridical documents to be the object of a process of their own interpretation and testing. No legal scholar would claim that the legal sense of Maastricht is fixed at the moment of its signing. Its meaning is phenomenological, it emerges and evolves in and through a kind of logic of speech act, of 'doing things with words' to borrow Austin's illustrious phrase. Legal thought does not produce legal sense until it 'does' law, until it deploys the material and institutional mechanisms at its disposal, themselves produced within the limits of the legal system.

Through this institutional phenomenology a number of the tensions inherent in any constitution—and in the notion of constitutionalism—come forth.

---

[14] JHH Weiler, *The Constitution of Europe* (Cambridge, Cambridge University Press, 1999), 3.

The most tenacious of these is closely related to the paradigm of legal-theoretical thinking as we just evoked it. Legality, and legitimacy, become active, indeed thinkable and analysable, only after the legal system whose legality and legitimacy is in question, closes the door on precisely these questions. The legitimacy of a legal system is created at the very moment when the origin or basis of that legitimacy withdraws into self-evidence. Thus the primordiality of the constitution obeys a very strange logic indeed. Any constitution or fundamental document of a legal order is composed and authorised by actors who not only do not belong to the legal order they are creating, but are not destined to belong to it. The legitimate, authorised creators of a constitution or constitutional order function necessarily *outside* and *prior* to the existence of the constitution. All constitutions are un-authorised, or in other words, authorised before authorisation was legitimately possible. The constitution is understood as the organisation structure and norms ('tenets') of the 'political and civic culture' of the polity, while at the same time dependent upon that polity for its constitutionality.

Conceptual Logic of the Constitution According to Carl Schmitt

As we have already suggested, the genesis of the Weimar Constitution draws together the extremes of the political spectrum. No true revolution was necessary: the Empire collapsed by implosion under the strain of the revolutionary atmosphere of the times and the real shock of general strike on German soil. The precedence of constitutional republicanism widely occupied the consciousness of the continent. The German Empire stood prominently in the line of the similar quasi-revolution conjunctures.

In the eyes of Carl Schmitt, the military, political and social security of the Bismarckian Empire bred a constitution replete with juridical weakness and loopholes. This political arrogance was corroborated by the dominant paradigm of legal positivism, which tended to repress or simply displace theoretical questions of constitutionality, constitutional legitimacy and juridical coherence.[15] *Verfassungslehre* (1927) is in this context intended as a first of its kind study. Neither a commentary, nor an analytic study of individual articles, it is intended much more as a deeper conceptual reflection on the essence of the notion of the constitution in general. It refers actively but not exclusively to the living Weimar Constitution, seeking instead to present a general framework of the concept of constitution. It is thus a general theory of the constitution, in both historical and analytical perspective, an analysis of the networks and models in intellectual history that serve as origins and models for the *possibility* of thinking about the constitution today.

---

[15] C Schmitt, *Verfassungslehre* (Berlin, Duncker & Humblot, 1993), 3.

In the perspective of a treatment of the question of Europe, the situation of Schmitt's text opens many doors, but must at the same time be treated somewhat delicately. On the one hand, the generality of Schmitt's treatment of the concept of constitution provides a considerable body of indexes for revisiting the question of European construction in general and of a European constitution in particular. On the other hand, the political unity of Europe, not unheard of in 1927, is far from being submitted to an informed analysis, and farther still from the insights gained through the pragmatic attempts at construction of a European house. We will in what follows attempt to play on both registers, as it were. We will on the one hand deepen and exploit Schmitt's theory of constitutionality as it might possibly relate to some un-thought-of political entity with the possibility of being politically organised in a constitutional manner. On the other hand, we will attempt to bring the more speculative contemporary theory of European statehood and federalism into orbit with Schmitt's more narrow considerations of a constitutional state (*Rechststaat*).

Unity and Constitution

Schmitt's first insight in the *Verfassungslehre* carries the argument of the entire work: the term 'constitution' is polyvalent. It denotes not only a number of different contents or notions, but also connotes a certain ontological *status*. A constitution in the latter sense (in English as in German) is the fundamental essence of a thing. In the most general sense, any thing that has being has a *constitution*. The constitutionality of any given thing is its position against the background of the *hic et nunc* of the cultural, social, historical order. It is its opposition to the general fabric of existence. It is a kind of assertion of existence against the forces which would cause the thing to wither or disappear. It is the irreducible kernel of the thing, that which cannot be dissolved either by conceptualisation, rationalisation, institutionalisation, or politicisation. We will retain this open, ontological sense of the word constitution as *statu*, for it will serve as a key to the mysterious and politically and ideologically charged concept of 'people'.

Schmitt, however, sees the need to concretise the object of his constitutional theory within the domain of traditional political forms in order to render it, as he puts it 'understandable'. He thus begins by narrowing his focus to the constitution of the State, defined as 'the political unity of a people'.[16] In this context a 'state' refers to 'the political unity or as a particular, concrete manner and form of state existence, and in this sense it can be understood as synonymous with 'the general state of political *unity* and *order*'. At the same time, he hastens to add, 'constitution' can refer to a 'system of norms' and must thus be

---

[16] *Ibid.* 3.

considered not a concrete, political unity, but rather an 'ideal unity'. Common to both conceptions of a constitution is the notion of a unified *whole*. In other words, both the political unity of a people and the unity of norms are based on an implicit coherence, a closed system of norms values and references. Both aspects of the conception of constitution belong to what Schmitt calls the 'absolute concept of constitution' as contrasted with the 'relative concept of constitution'. The former is best understood in opposition to the latter.

The 'relative' concept of constitution is, according to Schmitt, based on a conception of the relationship between individual laws of political entity and the total and general constitution of the same. The relative concept sees the constitution as *summun partes*. The constitution is neither more nor less than the totality of the rules, regulations, and norms that organise the polity that it encompasses. The constitution in this sense has no metaphysical dimension, no meaning, be it political, social, cultural or spiritual, which might transcend the empirical laws in effect. 'Constitution' in the 'absolute' sense seeks to comprise the notion of political *unity* in the broadest sense. It refers to the 'mode of existence (*Daseinsweise*)' of any given political unity. This mode of existence can be conceptualised on three levels: (1) as the concrete 'general status of political unity and social order of a particular state', (2) as a particular manner (*Art*) of political and social order, and (3) as the 'principle of *dynamic becoming* of political unity'. The conceptual frameworks of all three levels surpass in important ways the *summun partes* of the positivistic legal-constitutional model.

In the *first* sense the constitution *is* the State. It is the real, existing State in its present form, in all its possible dimensions. Constitution—which can only be named in the indefinite form—is not something the State possesses, it is rather the very State-ness of the State, its essence or irreducible substance. Constitution is prior to any notion of sovereign or sovereignty, any idea of monarchical or popular will, any constitution in the narrow sense of 'fundamental law'. Constitution, says Schmitt, is a *status* of 'unity and order': 'The State would cease to exist if this constitution, that is this unity and order ceased'.[17] The constitution of a State is not the mere fact that there is unity and order in a material sense. By 'order', Schmitt refers in part to the Aristotelian sense of a naturally given cohabitation of people in a city or a region. Far from the modern police-technical notion of 'law and order', Schmitt seeks to underscore the cultural or cosmic order. In the same vein, 'unity' is an organic belonging, an irreducible common ground, which resists the instrumentalisation of modern forms of systematic conceptualisation—and at the limit, democratic forms of instrumentalisation. This organic or cultural connotation of unity and order represented by constitution possess a spiritual dimension. 'The constitution is [the State's] *soul*, its concrete life, and its individual existence'.[18] The

---

[17] Above n 15, 4.
[18] Above n 15, 4.

State is a gathering point or nexus of a number of groups and individuals, common in certain respects, different in others. The fabric of commonality, the substance of the common belonging is its constitution, the spiritual common ground, the motivation for the laws and institutions which otherwise serve to organise in a concrete or pragmatic fashion the spiritual constitution of the collectivity.

In the *second* sense, Schmitt understands a partial concretisation of the political and social order. 'Constitution', in this regard, is still indeterminate, still inseparable from the existence or being of the State, still far from being one contingent property among others, but Schmitt attaches it to a determinate form of governance. The constitution of the State makes its imprint on the social and historical reality by determining the forms of governance available to and in part utilised by the State. Constitution in this sense corresponds to what is more commonly called the *form* of the State, be it monarchy, democracy or otherwise. In as far as constitution in this meaning represents a particular state form it is still an existential form, profoundly related to the very *being* of the state. The constitution is the *forma formarum*. This *being*, this *status* can be and is the object of evolution, of change. In a kind of historical State-paradigm shift, revolution can bring about a change in a State in the sense of a change in form of existence of the State. Indeed with the November Revolution of 1919 fresh in mind, Schmitt is obliged to explain historical change in terms of both continuity and rupture. Revolutionary change obeys both logics. This change, according to Schmitt is not merely a continuous change, a shift from one institutional or legal structure to another. It is rather a shift in the form of *being*, in the form of existence in which a new kind of 'soul' becomes the foundation for the new State.

Finally, in the *third* sense, Schmitt sees this *status* as a situation in constant development, or to use the more existential terminology, as constant in becoming. The analysis of the static, existential nature of constitution is thus opened to include this same cosmology in terms of genesis (*Entstehung*) and 'dynamic becoming' (*dynamisches Werden*). Here too Schmitt calls upon the dynamic reason in Aristotle's *Politics* in order to reconcile the notion of the organic unity of a political collectivity with its implicit, necessary, and equally organic self-transformation.

The conflation and concentration of these three aspects in the modern notion of 'constitution', such as it appears in the Constitution of Weimar of 1919 is far from simple. Yet a number of particularities of the Schmittian conception may be underscored, in view of a dialogue with the contemporary discourse of European constitutionalism. The guiding question that indeed receives some prospective answers concerns the nature of the unity, which can serve as the basis for the 'institution' of a State or a State-like entity. In his existential reflections on the nature of constitution, Schmitt suggests that the fundament of constitutional belonging is to be in a situation prior to the constitution as a positive document prescribing rights and obligations to those technically belonging to the state. The ontological prioritisation of the 'classical' model conceives of the relationship between State, belonging, and constitution, in an entirely different manner. For the 'classical' model, the 'belonging' is more or less primordial, the State is conceived as an appropriate form of organisation for those who 'belong', and the constitution is then the final administrative tool for organising those who belong within the State-form. By reading both 'constitution' and 'State' in their strong, existential forms, Schmitt opens the dimension of the primordiality of the constitution, of 'the' constitution as 'constitution', of 'constitution' and 'state' *qua status*, as the ground existential forms of collective self-organisation.

Legal Implications of the Existential Constitution

Schmitt points out that 'constitution' in this 'absolute' conceptual sense likewise signifies a 'unified, closed *system* of greatest and last norms'.[19] The constitution in its existential sense is thus also the most general, most comprehensive normative dimension of a collectivity's self-organisation. The organic unity of constitution provides the organic pre-State—and thus pre-legal—basis for law. The ontological *status* is that of the 'shall (*Sollen*)'.

Schmitt emphasises that this system is *closed*. Yet as we have remarked before, this closure is not a summation of the parts. It is in effect the sum of the components of a legal order, plus the bonds between the components, plus the sense of the cohesion, plus the origin of the cohesion. 'Unity and order' are not purely technocratic or bureaucratic as, for example Weber would argue. On the contrary, order is a metaphysical term, far closer to the notion of *cosmos* than perhaps Schmitt is at liberty to suggest in his legal treatise.

This implicit normative essence has clear consequences for the notion of State as *status*, and Schmitt hastens to underscore them. For norms are by essence dynamic. Norms refer to a *status*, to a state of affairs, which does not yet exist, but which *should* exist. They thus implicitly point elsewhere, to a kind of potential development, the attainment of which requires that the *status* at hand be abandoned.

To further this reflection, Schmitt once again makes use of the foundational formula 'the constitution *is* the state', which we discussed above. In this context however the implication is that the State is always *already* normative. Such a position is in clear opposition to Weber and other modern theorists of the State, who understand it as a transparent, bureaucratic scaffolding in which the individual is more or less accessory.[20] Schmitt's view of the normative character of the State considers normativity as inseparable in some primordial way from the

---

[19] Above n 15, 7.
[20] Cf M Weber, *Wirtschaft und Gesellschaft* (Tübingen, JCB Mohr, 1972), 125–26.

essence of the State. The State is considered, *in its very being* as something implicitly normative (*'als etwas normgemäß Sein-Sollendes'*). Consequently a system of constitutional rights is already implicit in the State, quite simply because it *constitutes* the State (once again in the broad sense of the term.)

What prevents Schmitt from taking recourse to the most primitive moral essentialism? A Heideggerian existentialist response to this question would be: the being of normativity would precede any given normative code. A simple determination of norms in the direction of interests moral or otherwise would be derivative or secondary. Schmitt's response is less rigorous and perhaps more in tune with the modern history of political ideas. In order to re-associate the normative essence of the constitution-*qua*-State with a modern political subject more or less unified with the 'will of the people', Schmitt makes recourse to more classical principles of natural law and distances himself from the legal positivism of his time. A constitution is valid because it has its origin in some constitutive power (*verfassunggebenden Gewalt*).[21] This power is either identical to or a derivative of *will*. This will is associated with the people or peoples represented by the constitution.

> A constitution reposes not on a norm whose correctness would be the basis of its validity. It reposes upon a political decision arising from political being about the kind and norm of its own being.[22]

Norms, whose correctness is based on the internal coherence of a *closed* system, must after all be *posited*. This positing is performed by the political will, nominally defined in a similar existential manner as the existing (*seinsmäßig*) dimension as the origin of normativity (*Sollen*).[23]

This brings Schmitt's argument full circle, and at the same time leads back to the European present. There is no such thing as a closed constitutional system of a purely normative kind. Once again the 'unity and order' of a political system lies not in its legal system, nor in rules and laws or normative dictates, but in the political *being* of the State. The *will* of s/he who was the origin of the constitution (in the narrow sense) is equally primordial as the state. The 'will' refers to, and in contrast to any 'independence from a normative or abstract correctness'—the 'essential *existential aspect* of the basis of validity'.[24] To extrapolate on Schmitt, the will of law makers *is* the State. The unity and order of a constitution does not refer to the internal coherence of its rules and norms. The question for the notion of European self-governance at the beginning of the twenty first century is what the 'closed system' in which both existential norms and existential will orbit and mutual refer to each other as a basis for the 'rule of law' of the system. The constitutionality of the constitution, be it the

---

[21] Above n 15, 9.
[22] Above n 15, 76.
[23] Above n 15, 9.
[24] Above n 15, 76.

'European constitution' or any other, lies in its primordial Europeanness, a substance—for those who cry 'essentialism'—which is disinterested, which precedes interests. The constitutionality of the European constitution must and shall transcend all the systematic internal contradictions, discontinuities and obscurity of the bureaucratic processes.

Legitimacy of a Constitutional Collectivity

The problem of legitimacy of a European legal order may be pursued by following further the thread already exposed: that of the closed constitutional system and of the nature of such closure. This concept of closure is essential both to Schmitt's critique of the Weimar legal order and to our extrapolation of some of Schmitt's principles to the European present.[25] It is also this distinction which structures Schmitt's distinction between 'legality' and 'legitimacy'. In the long essay 'Legality and Legitimacy' (1932) he introduces the central distinction between the constitutional state in its legislative capacity (*Gesetzgebungsstaat*) and the constitutional state in its juridical, governmental, and administrative capacity. The former is characterised by a 'closed system of legality' which stands in contrast to the system of legitimisation of the latter. Never has the difference been so marked, says Schmitt, as today: '. . . today the normativistic fiction of a closed system of legality enters into a striking and undeniable opposition to the legitimacy of a truly present, legal (*rechtmäßigen*) will'.[26]

In more or less Weberian spirit, Schmitt criticises the tendency towards understanding the State as a purely administrative entity, concerned more or less with matters of economic management and administration all of whose motivation and 'legality' resides in the immense technical regulations that organise them. For Schmitt it is not a question of whether such bureaucratic activities are legitimate or not. The correctness of their activities are simply never reduced to questions of legitimacy. In this sense the legislative State is a mere vehicle, containing no inner substance, no existential significance, no place for the ethical forces that bind and separate the individuals assembled in the name of the State.

---

[25] 'End' is to be understood within the logical opposition between finitude and infinity. The end of something is the completion of a finite series of elements, finite from the inception. The process or task is understood in terms of and with reference to its completion and thus to its finitude. 'Finitude' is simply the contrary of infinitude. Closure, on the other hand, belongs to a dialectical logic. Closure is both the 'end', in the sense of 'finitude', and the exhaustion or completion of the notion of infinity. End is the stopping point against the backdrop of infinite possible continuation. Closure is the 'end', beyond which there is nothing more. Closure transcends the opposition finite-infinite. The opposition between closure and end is a recurring theme in Derrida's philosophical anthropology.

[26] C Schmitt, *Legalität und Legitimität* (Berlin, Duncker & Humblot, 1998) 10.

Schmitt evokes the jurist Rudolf Smend, who in his own writing had complained of a missing *pathos* in the claim to the constitutional validity of values (*Wertgeltungsanspruch*). Schmitt agrees of course. Still with the help of some Weberian tactics his critique goes even further. Schmitt sees progressive disjunction from the feudal states of the Middle Ages, to the absolutism that preceded the French Revolution, to the constitutional systems of the Restoration, to the July Revolution 1830, to the German Revolution of 1848, and finally to the November Revolution of 1918, when the conditions were set for the emergence of the most modern edition of the Weimar constitution.[27] All these phases of European history are marked not only by renegotiations of constitutional documents, re-negotiations of relations of power between the sovereign and the ruled. They also constitute transformations in the very notion of the legitimacy necessary to constitute a sovereign and a state, of the minimum sufficient conditions to establish governance in the ideal (or absolute) sense, but also in terms of the pragmatic, policing functions of the State. Schmitt's analysis parallels Weber's in its agreement on the bureaucratisation of State authority and the transformation of legitimacy into floating legality.

The history of constitutional thinking has lead to a point where the ideal of a closed, self-reflexive system of legality is the standard by which to measure the degree of legitimacy.[28] Legality has taken over the roll played by legitimacy. Legitimacy is henceforth an expression or a derivative of legality. 'Legitimacy and legality are reduced to one common concept of legitimacy, when in effect legality actually means the opposite of legality'.[29] It is far from Schmitt's claim that nothing has legitimacy any more. Rather he means that legitimacy as a concept has been refilled with a new concept, that is, as legality.

The conflict that Schmitt and others see is that this displacement of legality to legitimacy, though it may be in pact with a certain political *Zeitgeist*, is nonetheless not in pact with the people intended as the sovereign subjects of the constitutional system. The state will not be successful as pure administration as long as there is popular aspiration for the ideals of a constitutional *ethos*.

> As long as the belief in the rationality and ideality of its normativity is alive and well, in times and in peoples who still have the capacity to assert a (typical Cartesian) belief in the *idées générales*, it appears as something higher and more ideal.[30]

The measure of the conceptual and political need for the cultivation of a legitimising *ethos* is the popular ability to imagine it. The *ethos* that Schmitt suggests German citizens still know how to invoke is not proper to Weimar. It is a *European ethos*. It is the 'thousand years old' difference between *nomos* and

---

[27] Above n 15, 44–57.
[28] G Teubner & Z Bankowski, *Law as an Autopoietic System* (Oxford, Blackwell, 1993).
[29] Above n 26, 13–14.
[30] *Ibid.* 15.

phesmos, between *ratio* and *volontas,* intelligence instead of blind, indifferent will, rights against the instrumentality of simple commands.[31]

The same classical questions may be asked of the legal components of European construction. On what do the claims of validity of European law repose? What is the origin of the legitimacy of the European Union in general and of the system European law and the European Court of Justice in general? To re-pose these questions in a Schmittian (or Smendian) fashion would be to seek the site (and historical moment) or rupture between legality and legitimacy. At what juncture in the history of the rise and fall of the nation-state as universal basis of collective identity, does the legality of collective systems break free from the deeply rooted *ethos* of legitimacy? What is the extent of the *pathos* of European belonging? To what degree can this *pathos* provide the legitimating basis for a constitution? And does the presence of a European *pathos* override the alleged absence of a European *demos*?

EU and the Political Constitution of Union

Schmitt concludes his *Verfassungslehre* with an overview of the different forms of interstate political organisation, with particular focus on the constitutional nature of *union* (*Bund*). Already in 1919 Europe had seen the birth of the League of Nations, conceived as a vehicle to collective understanding, and the hindrance of further world war. But without any strenuous reciprocal obligations, it represented a weak model for the kind of visionary concept of 'union' that Schmitt felt to be a natural continuation of his *Verfassungslehre*. Indeed, in his taxonomy of interstate relations Schmitt situates the *union* at the terminus of a progression from the least binding to the most binding types of relations.

Firstly, and in general, *accessory relations* between states are commonplace, reposing on the notion of coexistence as a 'right of peoples'. States that share an appreciation of these rights share also a common sense of belonging together. The principle of the other State is the basis for a logic of belonging. Here there is no constitution of any kind, only the 'pluriversum' of shared principles. *Secondly, contractual relations* between individual States represent the next level in the hierarchy of formalisation of international cohesion. Such agreements are binding, but do not but into play the existence of the State. *Thirdly,* the *alliance* (*Bündnis*) is a contractual relation between individual States in which war is a potential reprisal against violation. The conclusion of an alliance thus invokes a far more complex system of values and an existential *ethos*. The alliance is not an internal political act, does not require modification of the political identity of the individual actor, but nonetheless appeals to notions of justice and fairness in its relations toward those with which the

---

[31] Above n 26.

accords are made. Lastly, the *union* (*Bund*) sets itself apart from the other types of association by the fact that it puts into play the existential *status* of the political organisation involved. Not only does its conclusion imply a potential modification of the political architecture of the very State, but also violation of the union pact can have existential consequences for the parts involved.[32]

In this regard the European Union concluded at Maastricht and partially realised through Phase III of financial and monetary union, is a union in Schmitt's way of thinking. This is most marked by the fact that the Treaty of European Union is *irreversible*. There are no provisions for failure. Should it fail, it will not simply entail the locking up the doors of countless institutions in Brussels and in the various European capitals. Failure would introduce not only political but also structural crisis into each of the European member-States, and revolutionise the very architecture of European politics.

As Schmitt conceives it, the most essential determination of a union is the political unity that organises it. The union is conceived as a long duration project and its contract aims at the preservation of all the constituent members. In the same way, a union, in Schmitt's view, implies the commitment to protect any and all members from external military aggression. To this end, there can be no union without the possibility of intervention in the internal affairs of individual members. Lastly, there is no union without at the same time the possibility, indeed the international right, to go to war *as a union*. Now the European Union is a completely original creation, and we share the point of view of those who claim that it will only find a final political form that is *sui generis*. Still, we once again approach common ground with the provisions of the TEU, which as it were may be said to meet the criteria such as Schmitt understands them. The only grey zone is clearly the final criterion concerning 'union war' Article J4, goes reasonably far in opening for the possibility of an orchestrated European defence policy and military action with the aim of upholding it.[33]

With these categories and determinations in place Schmitt examines the contours and limits of the legal structure of the union. He arrives at three 'antinomies', all of which have direct interest for the question of European construction.

(1) The first antinomy concerns *the right to individual self-preservation*. On the one hand, by definition, each member of the union is interested in the preservation of sovereignty and independence of each of the other members of the union. On the other, the preservation of the independence of other members necessarily weakens one's own sovereignty and independence.

(2) The second antinomy concerns *the right to individual self-determination*. On the one hand, each member seeks, through the union, to preserve its own independence. On the other, the union in general is interested in the

[32] Above n 15, 363–66.
[33] *Ibid*. 367–70.

well-being of each of its members, and thus there is a tendency to intervention, thereby cancelling out the right to self-determination of each member.

(3) The most general—and most interesting for our purposes—antimony concerns *the question of the homogeneity of the union*.[34]

Schmitt's understanding of the union's homogeneity, or lack thereof, builds upon two previously explored themes from the *Verfassungslehre*, namely those of 'will' and 'existence'. Both are to be understood in their deep-organic ontological sense. The 'common will' and 'political existence' of the individual members of the union are kernels, guarantors of the individuality of the individual members, irreducible to the will and existence of the collective union. In this sense there is also an irreducible political cohabitation within the union: the general existence of the union, and the individual existence of each member. They constitute to diverse forms of political existence, which, though fundamentally incompatible, because fundamentally, necessarily heterogeneous— that being the very definition of a union. The *degree* of heterogeneity, or inversely, homogeneity is also the key to Schmitt's 'solution' of the antinomy. Any union must repose upon an essential precondition: the homogeneity of its members, that is, a substantial equanimity (*Gleichartigkeit*) which founds a concrete and essential agreement and thus hinders situations of extreme conflict. This homogeneity, says Schmitt, can be 'national', religious, 'civilisational', social or class-oriented, or otherwise.[35] The political union can exist only in a contradictory situation. Any union must exist within the limitations of its double subjectivity, one based on the nation-State constitution, the other based on the rights of peoples.

The Euopean *Nomos*: Cultural and Legal Geography

In his 1944 article 'The Situation of European Legal Science' and more systematically in his post-war book *The Nomos of the Earth* (1950), Schmitt prolongs his critique of legality masquerading as legitimacy, which we have already underscored in his pre-war writings.

Some comments on the term *nomos* are indispensable. From a certain point of view the entire book *The Nomos of the Earth* is little more than a prolonged historical reconstruction and interpretation of this term. Either explicitly or

---

[34] The matter of homogeneity is a crucial component in the argumentation of the German Constitutional Court in its famous finding against the constitutionality of the Maastricht Treaty of the European Union. The absence of a European *demos*, among other things, excludes its constitution from legitimate recognition. JHH Weiler, 'Der Staat über alles—Demos, Telos und die Maastricht Entscheidung des Bundesverfassungsgerichts,' *Harvard Jean Monnet* WP no 7 (1995) 3 and JHH Weiler, *The Constitution of Europe* (Cambridge, Cambridge University Press, 1999) 268–70.

[35] Above n 15, 376.

implicitly, it is central to the majority of Schmitt's reflections on culture, law and economics in the European context. When Schmitt thinks internationally, his particular understanding of the concept of *nomos* makes itself felt. *Nomos* is the copula that makes possible the thought of the transnational. It is the common 'ground' of the concept of Europe, and in this sense it is essential for our speculations on the meaning and future of European construction. The abiding critique through virtually all of his writings on international law is against an impoverished determination of the concept of the 'European' through a too narrow understanding of the roll of space and thus geo-politics, on the one hand, and the mutations in the categories of the *Volk* and international law, on the other. For Schmitt's sometimes virulent attacks on legal and political scholarship is an attack on the *discourse* of Europe. By this I mean the notion of a certain legal rationality that pretends to capture adequately and exhaust the question of Europe. In this sense, Schmitt is already an anti-postmodernist. This does not mean that he is simply a modernist—here in the Lyotardian sense of implicitly adopting the 'master narratives' of progress, individuality, technology, etc. These too fail to grasp the metamorphoses of the European conceptual universe, made 'visible' in the metamorphosis of the European *space*. Schmitt refuses the abiding and canonical discursive-construction of Europe created in and through the discourse of international law.

It is thus not incorrect, but somewhat myopic to translate *nomos* with 'law'. *Nomos* does indeed translate to law, but only in its most technical-rational modern sense, precisely the sense that is the object of Schmitt's ire. Schmitt's work clearly indicates that *nomos*, has deep pre-discursive roots, or that in some sense 'law' is also the law of the earth, not simply the object of legislation, execution, or judgment, it is a transposition of ontological nature of Europe. Not merely the moving of borders from A to B on the surface of one self-same continent, but a change in the nature of the surface, in the nature of the border, in the relation of individuals—real, living bodies, with concomitant physical borders and limitations, and States, 'legally' constituted 'bodies' which in turn, as we have tried to show above, are not simply pronouncements ('legality', as Schmitt himself would say) but certain, specific kinds of *being*.

Here is Schmitt's definition in the early pages of *The Nomos of the Earth*:

> Nomos [. . .] comes from *nemein*, a word which means both 'to divide' and 'to pasture'. *Nomos* is accordingly the immediate form in which the political and social order of a people makes itself spatially visible, the first measuring and division of the pasture, that is the partitioning of land and also the concrete order which lies in it and follows from it. [. . .] *Nomos* is the *measure* that divides and spatialises the ground and soil of the earth in a particular order, and thereby in the given form of the political, social and religious order.[36]

---

[36] 'Nomos dagegen kommt von *nemein*, einem Wort, das sowohl 'Teilen' wie auch 'Weiden' bedeutet. Der Nomos ist demnach die unmittelbare Gestalt, in der die politische und soziale Ordnung eines Volkes raumhaft sichtbar wird, [40] die erste Messung und Teilung der Weide, d.h. die

Schmitt's historical reconstruction begins in the sixteenth century when the notion of *jus gentium* could not refer to a plurality of peoples to whom an equally plural system of law would apply. The notions of *self* and *other*, as they are often used today were in some sense applicable, but the *topology* of otherness was not yet differentiated. The spatial order, which associates people and space, was not global in the sense that the term can be understood today, nor was it 'local' in the sense that place and varying place were real dimensions. Schmitt uses the term *terran*. This original 'terrane world' first underwent change in the fifteenth century age of discovery, when the first evidence of 'global consciousness' appears.[37] In this context, 'people' is not understood as a given group to whom a set of rights might be applied. It is the *singular* origin of the notion of right. The expression *jus gentium*, thus implies a powerful double genitive. Right comes *from* the people and is applicable *to* the people. There exists no people for whom it might be a *question* of the applicability of *jus gentium*. The meaningfulness of the legal system reposes on the singularity of the people.

The historical progression, which Schmitt carefully charts out in *The Nomos of the Earth* traces the effects of the de-coupling of the legal system from this singular origin, and its transformation into a plural system based on an application to 'peoples' in the plural. The final phase of this transformation corresponds to the definitive disappearance of European *Völkerrecht* and its modernised incarnation as 'international law'. This innovation simultaneously renders the differentiation between *Völkerrecht* and *Staatsrecht*. To this delineation, can be added a number of others, such as *Privatrecht, Wissenschaftsrecht, öffentliches Recht*.

Against this background, Schmitt paints the picture of the new *nomos* of the earth. The central element in the new European topological situation is the domination of the global economy, or to use the contemporary term, *globalisation,* which clearly has always only meant *economic* globalisation. The historical turning point is the period from 1890 to 1939, from the Monroe Doctrine to the 'Wilson Doctrine'.[38] Until the 1890s, says Schmitt, the dominant perception was that *Völkerrecht* was a particularly European *Völkerrecht*, based on the classical notions of humanity, civilisation and progress.[39]

Landnahme und die sowohl in ihr liegende wie aus ihr folgende konkrete Ordnung [. . .] Nomos ist das den Grund und Boden der Erden in einer bestimmten Ordnung einteilende und verortende *Maß* und die damit gegebene Gestalt der politischen, sozialen und religiösen Ordnung.' C Schmitt, *Der Nomos der Erde im Völkerrecht des Jus Publicum Europaeum* (Berlin, Buncker & Humblot, 1988) 39–40.

[37] *Ibid.* 19.

[38] 'Die 1823 verkündete amerikanische "Monroe Doctrine" ist in der neueren Geschichte des Völkerrecths das erste und das bisher erfolgreichste Beispiel eines völkerrechtlichen Großraumprinzips. Sie ist daher für uns ein einzigartiger, wichtiger "precedent". Von ihr, nicht von der Lehre der "natürlichen Grenzen" oder dem "Recht auf Land" oder gar den eben erwähnten Regionalpakten, ist auszugehen, wenn der Rechtsgedanke eines völkerrechtlichen Großraumprinzips zur Erörterung steht.' C Schmitt, *Völkerrechtliche Großraumordnung mit Interventionsverbot für raumfremde Mächte* (Berlin, Duncker & Humblot, 1991) 22.

[39] Above n 36, 201.

Simultaneously these principles began to find themselves detached from their previous topology, by and through the advances in globalisation. The distinction between *peoples,* between *jus inters gentes* and *jus gentium* disappeared from the discourse of international law, and consequently the problem of a spatial order disappeared with it.[40] This process is what Schmitt calls *Entortung*— both displacement and detachment from spatiality in general. The general *Entortung,* which Schmitt sees taking place in Europe in the 1950s has put it into a whole new constellation of powers and doctrines, for which legal positivism of the day has no influence at all. Schmitt's analysis of the European present shows that it has completely lost its relationship to any *Raumordnung.*

The most pregnant illustration of this tendency in its institutionalised form are the attempts at European unification. Schmitt attributes, for example, the geopolitical failures of the League of Nations precisely to its absence of a concrete *Raumordnung.* And the seeming lack of *nomological* vision in Briand's notion of the Union Européenne, suffers from the same weaknesses. These problems are exacerbated by the entire problem of war reparations, by the intervention of a freshly constituted global community in the 'internal' affairs of the European continent.[41] In the same way, Schmitt sees the Treaty of Versailles as a further illustration of the domination of an 'empty legal and contractual positivism, which was nothing more than the juridical instrument of the legality and legitimacy of the status quo, and indeed principally the status of Versailles'.[42] Within the logic of *nomos* the central question for Schmitt is which new *Raumordning* will become dominant in the period to come.[43]

Conclusion: Contentious Europe or the Dialectic of Resistance

As is well known and already exhaustively debated, in its decision of 14 October 1994 the German Constitutional Court found that the European Union could not be considered a federal entity into which the German Federal Republic could *legally* be integrated according to the terms of the Maastricht Treaty. Its reasoning was based on a certain notion of democracy, which the Court found to be absent from the European empirical picture. 'Democracy', according to the Court, is based on the existence of a democratic polity, itself by nature based on an observable *demos* emitted by and empirically observable people (*Volk*). The amalgamation of the European 'peoples' cannot, according to the Court, be considered a people. Since the principle of democracy would be unacceptably emptied of content if it were to exercise state power without

---

[40] *Ibid.* 203.
[41] C Schmitt, '*Der Begriff des Politischen*' (Berlin, Duncker & Humblot GmbH, 1996) 56.
[42] Above n 38, 15.
[43] *Ibid.* 214–17.

reference to a 'relatively homogenous' civil population (*Staatsvolk*). Thus the entry into full of the GFR is judged unconstitutional.[44]

We have already dealt with the central complaint of the GCC—the notion of homogeneity as a condition for the legitimisation of a Union—in our discussion of Carl Schmitt. In an oft-cited paper, Weiler opens a parallel set of questions about the conditions of possibility for the establishment of a *demos* and its relationship, in the history of constitutionalism to the notion of constitution, and what he calls the GCC's 'No Demos Thesis'.[45] Weiler's criticism of the German Court's decision correctly takes its point of departure in a *conceptual* problematisation of the terms used by the Court. A certain 'organic' idea of *Volk*, affirms Weiler, is the basis for the modern-nation state, in the sense that it forms the polity, which is the basis for the constitution. Ethnicity, he admits, has a roll to play in the notion of national belonging. Still, argues Weiler, by formulating the conceptual constellation as the Court does, (*demos* = *Volk* = polity), it both definitively denies the prospect of European democracy and proclaims a kind of de facto European internal alienation. Weiler answers by challenging and then re-formulating both the notion of demos, such as it is used by the Court, and the notion of polity. What is most compelling about Weiler's argument is the nuance with which he reconstructs the concept of *Volk*, refusing, in the end to de-mystify it, to debunk it as a residue of nineteenth century political romanticism.

Weiler's critique is two-pronged. On the one hand, it argues that from an empirical point of view, the charge of 'no *demos*' is simply not accurate. A look at the 'European anthropological map' reveals significant pockets of 'social cohesion', 'shared identity' and 'collective self'. On the other hand, Weiler points to the juridical antinomy that informs not only the Court's decision, but the constitutions of national democracies in general, namely that the demos-nation link is circular. The *demos*, this un-definable amorphous ethnic-organic-cultural entity, is practically speaking defined by members of the nation. The nation constitutes its *demos*, which in turn gives substance to the nation, which constitutes the *demos*, etc. Weiler's critique is convincing, but by way of conclusion, we would add a voice to the chorus of critique of the GCC finding, in the form of two remarks.

The first remark is to some extent parasitic upon Weiler's reflection on the actual, empirical existence of a European *demos*, an observation, which flies in the face of the GCC ruling. There is indeed a clear and empirically observable European *ethnos*. For better or worse, the empirical measure of this *ethnos* is, on the one hand, the rainbow of political conflicts on the national level sur-

---

[44] EuGRZ (1993) 439.

[45] JHH Weiler sets the tone for the most engaging debate on the legal philosophy of the European Union. His oft cited 1995 working paper on the German decision: http://www.law.harvard.edu/programs/JeanMonnet/papers/95/9506ind.html) and its reworking in *The Constitution of Europe* are the basis for these comments.

rounding immigration policy, national language, cultural heritage, social support, minority rights, religious freedom, culturally and religiously marked content of school curriculum, etc. On the other hand, the presence of a European *ethnos* is present in the transnational or European debates on coordinating immigration policies. The Schengen Agreement has served to Europeanise to some extent these national traits by Europeanising the legal guidelines for immigration. There is a clear empirically observable European ethnicity. But more importantly this ethnicity is in particular observable in the political *conflicts* which arise within the framework of each nation-state around the question of immigration and migration. Ethnicity as a perceivable substance arises in moments of conflict, insecurity, and political strife. The *concept* of ethnicity erupts in border disputes. And yet the conceptual twist on the traditional logic of border disputes is that the borders are no longer simply identical with the frontiers of nation-state territories. They traverse territory, institutions, groups and collectivities. They demarcate the cultural consciousness of any given collectivity, divided, regroup and reform the self understanding of all social and cultural formations—most of all that of the modern nation-state. Ethnicity is thus structurally identical to the constitution such as it is thematised by Weiler in *The Constitution of Europe*. It is *phenomenal*. Its essence is its appearance. And this appearance is inseparable from conflict and contention. Schmitt's critique of European conceptual territoritoriality meets the phenomenality of ethnicity.

The second remark concerns the evolutionary nature of the *concept* of constitution. Just as the ethnic fabric of Europe is in a state of change, and just as the concept of ethnicity is in constant evolution, so the very notion of constitution is in a state of change. To understand the present situation of European constitutionalism requires that one understand the relation between *ethnos* and constitution in a dialectic. In other words, both the present state and the evolution of the one is implicitly dependent on the other. As the European ethnic topology changes, the European 'constitution', which pretends to have institutionalised it also changes. But what is more, the concept, the self-understanding of constitution evolves as well. This is Schmitt's second fundamental contribution to this discussion. The cultural-spiritual topology implies an evolution in the very notion of what a constitution is.

Belonging cannot be utterly and timelessly institutionalised in the form of a constitution. The European collectivity is not a sack of identical marbles, which can be seamlessly conceptualised and thus constitutionalised. It is rather a set of heterogeneous individuals and groups which by nature *resist* collectivisation, or which 'accept' constitutional collectivisation dialectically as part of the logic of recognition, adopting the rule of collectivisation in order to achieve the right to dispute it. The *resistance* to homogenisation, among the populous, among the political elite, and among the constitutional theorists, in the German or other national courts is the basis of dialectical substance of the European polity. The European mode of constitutional existence is the production, contention, and renewal of a European polity. This understanding calls upon both the deepest European tradition of the public sphere, and an understanding of that tradition as one of debate and dissent. This is the most profound democratic impulse and doubtless the greatest hope for Europe. The task for those who would construct a European institutional scaffold is to relocate polity in resistance to polity, to recognise polity in the form of the *question* of polity.

9

EUROPE A *GROßRAUM*[†]? SHIFTING LEGAL CONCEPTUALISATIONS OF THE INTEGRATION PROJECT

*Christian Joerges**

Queries

A nasty topic! Numerous queries obtrude. Why deal with Europe from such perspectives? There are many answers to this sort of question, some of which are easy. The integration project is a response to the bitter experiences of the past for all Europeans, and for the Germans, in particular. It is a way of *Vergangenheitsbewältigung,* as Germans call their efforts to face the past. This is true of a manifold range of topics, which encompass the shape of the European institutions and include many individual policy sectors, both old and new, such as the return of neo-nationalist and xenophobic movements, and even the sad destiny of the German language. Everywhere and at every moment, Germany, its culture as a whole, its academic disciplines, political moves and ambitions, come up against German history. Such encounters are, indeed, often nasty, polemic or, at the very least, unpleasant.[1] And this will remain so, especially in the more immediate future as the EU's eastern enlargement recalls

---

[†] 'Großraum', literally, 'greater space', was a term in use in a variety of contexts long before its adoption by Carl Schmitt. The connotations of the concept that Schmitt intended are better captured by a term like 'sphere of influence'. We use italics and leave it untranslated.

[*] Florence/Bremen. I am grateful for many suggestions, warnings and corrections. Since the list is so long, I shall make explicit mention only of Bardo Fassbender (Berlin), Ingo Hueck (Berlin), Oliver Lepsius (Heidelberg), Jean-Victor Louis (Brussels), Philip Manow (Cologne), and John P McCormick (New Haven), who helpfully criticised the first draft of this paper. A subsequent revision was written and published in German ('Europa ein Großraum? Zäsuren, Kontinuitäten, Re-Konfigurationen in der rechtlichen Konzeptualisierung des Integrationsprojekts', in M Jachtenfuch, M Knodt (eds), *Regieren in internationalen Institutionen*, (Opladen, Leske & Budrich, 2002) 53–78. That version was then again revised and translated by Iain L Fraser.

[1] Sometimes it is all of these things at once, eg J Laughland, *The Tainted Source: The Undemocratic Origins of the European Idea* (London, Warner, 1997), 11 ff, and 142 ff.

disturbing old notions of '*Mitteleuropa*', and arouses concerns about Germany's role in the enlarged and enlarging *Großraum* economy.[2]

The past will not lie down, nor, indeed should it be allowed to. It is, of course, true that the competence to discuss the consequences of history fall more to historians, political scientists and politicians than to lawyers. And yet, *Vergangenheitsbewältigung*, cannot be left to particular disciplines. National Socialist and Fascist ideologies and practices had an impact on the whole of social and human science; their impact on law was particularly strong and is embarrassing because of the involvement of both the law and lawyers in the exercise of state authority. The 'duty to remember',[3] which follows from such involvement, implies the task of following and deciphering the traces that the past has, or may have, left in the individual disciplines. Europe is, one should add, a special case in important respects. Ideas resonating from National Socialism cannot be directly relevant in a discipline which constituted itself only after the founding of the European Communities in the late 1950s. But what about more indirect, and more subtle undercurrents? All of the legal disciplines that later contributed to the legal conceptualisation of the European Community had been infected by '*völkisch*' legal thinking in Germany. There was a National Socialist practice of international law and a National Socialist-inspired theory of it, the striving for a '*völkisch*' 'legal renewal' [*Rechtserneuerung*] permeated Germany's *Staatsrecht,* constitutional law, administrative law and the whole body of private and economic law. Both vague and elaborate visions of the historical role and/or position and mission of Europe in general, and Germany in particular,[4] complement the picture. And, to be sure, scholars who documented their allegiance more or less industriously made themselves heard.[5]

Europe, nevertheless, remains a special case—in a very special sense even for the *völkisch* movement. The notion of Europe had been widely discussed in the 1920s in many variants. There was a European radical right with projects of their own. After the National Socialist seizure of power, 'Europe' was to remain

---

[2] On the notion of *Mitteleuropa* and its complex history, cf. PMR Stirk. 'Ideas of Economic Integration in Interwar Mitteleuropa', in *idem, Mitteleuropa. History and Prospects*, (Edinburgh, Edinburgh University Press, 1994) 86–111; J Brechtefeld, *Mitteleuropa and German Politics. 1848 to the Present*, (Houndmills-London, Macmillan, 1996). B Kletzin, *Europa aus Rasse und Raum. Die nationalsozialistische Idee der Neuen Ordnung*, 2nd ed. (Münster, Lit, 2002), 13 ff; P Chiantera-Stutte, 'Das Europa der Anti-Europäer; Ein vergleich von Legen Nord und FPÖ', Working Paper 2002/9, SPS Department, (EUI Florence 2002).

[3] P De Greiff, 'Redeeming the Claims of Justice in Transitions to Democracy', unpublished manuscript, Princeton, NJ 2001.

[4] For the quasi official (Nazi party) position, cf FA Six, *Das Reich und Europa—eine poltisch-historische Skizze* (Schriftenreihe der NSDAP. Gruppe 4. vol 5, 1943); FA Six, *Europa—Tradition und Zukunft* (Hamburg, Hanseatische Verlagsanstalt, 1944).

[5] Not just in law; suffice it here to mention the so-called *Kriegseinsatz* of German human and social sciences, organised by international lawyer Paul Ritterbusch, cf F-R Hausmann, *Deutsche Geisteswissenschaft' im Zweiten Weltkrieg. Die 'Aktion Ritterbusch' (1940–1945)*, (Dresden-München, Dresden University Press, 1998); 172 ff below.

a political issue. All thoughts about a future common Europe were, however, gradually abolished and then more or less radically rejected.[6] They were first overlaid by the grand National Socialist project to conquer the continent militarily, and, as defeat in the war became clear, became obsolete and downright undesirable politically.[7] All this may explain why the European integration project attracted scarcely any attention in the *Vergangenheitsbewältigung* of legal historians and in other disciplines. Nevertheless, the more indirect impact, as already hinted at, of the anti-liberal and anti-democratic legal concepts so highly rated in National Socialism represent a disquieting heritage. These elements did not simply emerge from nothing only after 1933, nor did they simply disappear without trace after 1945. We should be prepared to reckon not just with ruptures in legal thinking, but, equally, with continuity. This observation cannot, of course, claim any originality. But its implications are complex. For the years after 1933, MR Lepsius[8] distinguishes between three German academic cultures:

the one that dominated under National Socialism; the one that was oppressed and silenced in Germany; and the one in emigration.

In the latter, political attitudes and theoretical orientations remained alive in the German tradition that had represented 'modernity' and were, until 1933, able to come out openly against the anti-individualism and anti-democratic strands. The protagonists of these traditions, who had often welcomed the new regime with great hopes and in much naïvety, were now, after the National Socialist seizure of power, looking forward to the acceptance and flourishing of their ideas under the *aegis* of the new regime.[9]

---

[6] Cf the documents in M Salewski, 'Ideas of the National Socialist Government and Party', in W Lipgens (ed), *Documents on the History of European Integration*, vol 1, (*Continental plans for European Union 1939–1945*), (Berlin-New York, de Gruyter, 1985), 37–178; see also the references in n 12 below.

[7] E Siebert, 'Entstehung und Struktur der Auslandswissenschaftlichen Fakultät an der Universität Berlin (1940–1945)', in (1996) 15 *Wissenschaftliche Zeitschrift der Humboldt-Universität zu Berlin. Gesellschafts- und Sprachwissenschaftliche Reihe*, 19–34, at 33.

[8] MR Lepsius, 'Juristen in der sozialwissenschaftlichen Emigration' in M Lutter, CE Stiefel & MH Hoeflich (eds), *Der Einfluß deutschsprachiger Emigranten auf die Rechtsentwicklung in den USA und in Deutschland*, (Tübingen, Mohr, 1993), 19–31, at 30; cf MR Lepsius, 'Kultur und Wissenschaft in Deutschland unter der Herrschaft des Nationalsozialismus', in idem, *Demokratie in Deutschland* (Göttingen, Vandenhoeck & Ruprecht 1995), 119–32.

[9] For the interesting case of the history of constitutional thought, cf A Lübbe, 'Die deutsche Verfassungsgeschichtsschreibung unter dem Einfluß des Nationalsozialismus', in M Stolleis & D Simon (eds), *Rechtsgeschichte im Nationalsozialismus. Beiträge zur Geschichte einer Disziplin*, (Tübingen, Mohr, 1989), 63–78. It took more than half a century until the Association of German Teachers of Public Law ('*Staatsrecht*') dedicated a meeting to contemporaneous responses to, and reflections on, the *Machtergreifung*; cf. the two reports by H Dreier and W. Pauly, 'Die deutsche Staatsrechtslehre in der Zeit des Nationalsozialismus', (2001) 60 *Veröffentlichungen der Vereinigung der Deutschen Staatsrechtslehrer*, 9–72 and 70–101—and the comment by B Schlink, 'Unfähigkeit der Staatsrechtswissenschaft zu trauern?', in *idem*, *Vergangenheitsschuld und gegenwärtiges Recht*, (Frankfurt a.M., Suhrkamp 2002), 124–44.

It is these contrasts, parallels, continuities and re-configurations in legal thinking and their impact upon the conceptualisation of Europe in legal science that have to be discussed below. This is a highly complex venture. In searching for traces in the German legal tradition, distinctions between 'modernity' and 'anti-modernism', as used by MR Lepsius, are helpful, yet do not provide a sufficiently reliable yardstick. This dichotomy has proven to be illuminating in political philosophy, sociology and constitutional law.[10] It is normatively committed to the biding idea of the democratic constitutional state. That yardstick, the end of the 'German exceptionalism' (Germany's so-called political and intellectual *Sonderwege*) is valuable and yet insufficient when it comes to the construction of Europe if, and indeed because, the European integration project is bound to establish an unprecedented polity.

Concomitant uncertainties determine today's debates. However, even these uncertainties have their traditions. Europe's *faiblesse*, the complaint about its political and social diversity, the hopes invested in its unification, have long been talked about: 'it's reputation as poor, its social order decried . . . let Europe unify, become a legal unity'—runs a 1929 kind of Euro-barometer.[11] This paper will, however, refrain from any attempt to sift through the errors and confusion of the movements of thought about Europe which circulated in the 1920s, and were first selectively taken up and then abandoned under National Socialism.[12] It will rather seek to reconstruct the origins and the content of ideas on the ordering of Europe; it will be concerned with what M Rainer Lepsius has called the 'institutionalising of rationality criteria'.[13] That looks like an impossible, at best paradoxical, effort for two interrelated reasons. First, its problematic to apply a label like 'rationality' to the thinking influenced by, or trying to grasp intellectually, National Socialist ideologies.[14] Secondly, it is particularly unlikely, that there will be any space left for thoughts about the proper ordering under a regime seeking to conquest the whole of Europe. And indeed, the only intellectual contribution worth mentioning stems from the *Third Reich's* 'crown jurist'[15] Carl Schmitt. And even that contribution is only indirectly

---

[10] Cf famously, K Sontheimer, *Antidemokratisches Denken in der Weimarer Republik*, (München, Nymphenburger, 1962).

[11] H Jahrreiß, *Europa als Rechtseinheit*, (Leipzig, Robert Noske, 1929), preface.

[12] n 4–6 above; P Kluke, 'Nationalsozialistische Eruropaideologie', (1955) 3 *Vierteljahreshefte für Zeitgeschichte*, 240–75; J Elvert, '"Germanen" und "Imperialisten"—Zwei Europakonzepte aus nationalsozialistischer Zeit', in (1992) 5 *Historische Mitteilungen der Ranke-Gesellschaft*, 161–84; F-R Hausmann, *Aktion Ritterbusch* (n 5), 84 ff.

[13] MR Lepsius, 'Max Weber und das Programm einer Institutionenpolitik', (1995) 5 *Berliner Journal für Soziologie*, 327–33.

[14] Cf on this *problématique* the contribution of O Lepsius to this volume.

[15] On that title, A-M Gräfin von Lösch, *Der nackte Geist. Die Juristische Fakultät der Berliner Universität im Umbruch von 1933*, (Tübingen, Mohr, 1999) 430; B Rüthers, 'Reinhard Höhn, Carl Schmitt und andere—Geschichten und Legenden aus der NS-Zeit', (2000) 53 *Neue Juristische Wochenschrift*, 2866–71 at 2868.

pertinent. The *Großraum* debate Carl Schmitt sparked off in 1939 was, first of all, about the destruction of classical international law. And even if one acknowledges a constructive dimension in Carl Schmitt's 'European Monroe doctrine', it is nevertheless striking that he himself remained largely silent as to the *internal order* of the *Großraum*. However, the Schmitt of the *Großraum* theory is not the whole Schmitt. In his diagnoses and theses on the erosion of the international law system of states by spheres of influence—the *Großräume*—Schmitt referred briefly, albeit rather apocryphally, to general developments that were affecting traditional understandings of state constitutions and governance. These diagnoses were written before the *Machtergreifung*; they dealt with what Schmitt perceived as the crises of the Weimar Republic. It is hence through the linkages between Schmitt's *Großraum* concept and his writings that this paper seeks to shed light on the continuities and discontinuities of legal thinking. All this may make this paper look overly concerned with Schmittian ideas. Yet, it is not just the general paucity of pertinent contributions from the National Socialist period that necessitate a discussion of the *Großraum* theory. Schmitt is the weightiest exponent of anti-liberal thought in the German tradition—and this is in itself reason enough for taking both his ideas and their impact seriously.[16]

Rupture: Carl Schmitt's *Großraum*-theory

In the years following the seizure of power, the *Third Reich*, despite its withdrawal from the League of Nations and other international organisations, did not simply disregard international law in its external presentations. Furthermore, international law was more intensively observed and commented upon in the outside world than other disciplines.[17] For these reasons, the discipline continued to enjoy some protection against the *völkisch* renewal of legal thought.[18] Schmitt paid attention to international law very soon after the

[16] This concern is different from JP McCormick's who deals in his contribution to this volume with Schmitt's visions of Europe, which he presented from 1923 to 1955 in ever new variants.

[17] Cf VL Gott, 'The National Socialist Theory of International Law', (1938) 32 *American Journal of International Law*, 704–18; JW Garner, 'The Nazi Proscription of International Law', (1939) 33 *American Journal of International Law*, 112–19; JH Herz, 'The National Socialist Doctrine of International Law and the Problems of International Organization', (1939) *Political Science Quarterly* 54, 536–54 and analyses by D Fraser, '"the outsider does not see al the game . . .":': Perceptions of German Law in Anglo-American Legal Scholarship, 1933–1940', in this volume; revealing the indignant responses to Garner in C Schmitt, *Völkerrechtliche Großraumordnung mit Interventionsverbot für raumfremde Mächte. Ein Beitrag zum Reichsbegriff im Völkerrecht*, 4th edn.1941, reprinted in G Maschke, (ed), *Carl Schmitt, Staat, Großraum, Nomos. Arbeiten aus den Jahren 1916–1969*, (Berlin, Duncker & Humblot 1995), 269–320 at 302. Maschke's reprint is very carefully annotated (321–41) and contains an annex on the impact of Schmitt's essay (341–87).

[18] Cf R Wolfrum, 'Nationalsozialismus und Völkerrecht', in FJ Säcker (ed), *Recht und Rechtswissenschaft im Nationalsozialismus*, (Baden-Baden, Nomos, 1992), 89–102, at 95; M Stolleis,

Machtergreifung,[19] although his really intensive concern with it commenced, however, only after he had fallen out of official, albeit not of Hermann Göhring's, favour. Tragedy, irony, justice? Schmitt had broken with the former German legal culture, without establishing himself safely enough in the new hierarchies. Despite its '*situativem*' opportunism, the impact of the *Großraum* theory was to be limited both in the political arena and in contemporary academic international law.[20]

The Theory

From 29 March to 1 April 1939, ie after the *Anschluß* of Austria until the invasion of Bohemia and Moravia, but before the war against Poland, the '*Reichsgruppe Hochschullehrer des Nationalsozialistischen Rechtswahrer-Bundes*' [Reich section of professors in the National Socialist Association of Lawyers] met in Kiel. At the same time, the Institute for Politics and International Law was celebrating its twenty-fifth anniversary. Paul Ritterbusch, was both the chairman of the professorial league and the rector of Kiel University.[21] This was the setting in which Carl Schmitt presented his new theory of international 'law':[22] the '*Großraum* order in international law, with a ban on intervention for powers from outside the sphere. A contribution on the concept of the *Reich* in international law.'[23] The paper appeared in the Institute's publications series as early as April 1939, and, in 1941, had its fourth edition.[24]

Geschichte des öffentlichen Rechts in Deutschland, vol 3, *Staats- und Verwaltungsrechtswissenschaft in Republik und Diktatur 1914–1945*, (München, CH Beck, 1999), 382, 384; I Hueck, 'Die deutsche Völkerrechtswissenschaft im Nationalsozialismus', in D Kaufmann (ed), *Geschichte der Kaiser-Wilhelm-Gesellschaft im Nationalsozialismus. Bestandsaufnahme und Perspektiven der Forschung*, (Göttingen, Wallstein, 2000) 490–527; B Fassbender, 'Stories of War and Peace. The Writing of the History of International Law in the "Third Reich" and After', (2002) 13 *European Journal of International Law*, 479–512, at 492 ff.

[19] C Schmitt, *Nationalsozialismus und Völkerrecht*, (Berlin, 1934).

[20] For comprehensive analyses, cf L Gruchmann, *Nationalsozialistische Großraumordnung. Die Konstruktion einer deutschen Monroe-Doktrin*, (Stuttgart, Deutsche Verlags-Anstalt, 1962); M Schmoeckel, *Die Großraumtheorie. Ein Beitrag zur Geschichte der Völkerrechtswissenschaft im Dritten Reich, insbesondere der Kriegszeit*, (Berlin, Duncker & Humblot, 1994).

[21] Ritterbusch was soon entrusted with organizing the '*Kriegseinsatz*' of the human and social sciences, an effort to document the usefulness of academic work for the *Reich* in its war; cf F-R Hausmann, *Aktion Ritterbusch* at n 5, 11.

[22] The quotation marks are not intended merely to indicate taking a distance, but to point to a problem that affects Carl Schmitt's jurisprudence as a whole, mainly his rejection of a concept of law involving general validity claims: in international law he indicated this with his '*quis judicabit*' question, and otherwise most sharply with his distinction between friend and foe.

[23] For the orginal German title of the *Völkerrechtliche Großraumordnung* see n 17 above.

[24] Maschke's reprint is the fourth edition; on the context of Schmitt's lecture, cf F-R Hausmann, *Aktion Rittersbusch* at n 5, 44 f, 253 ff; 'Carl Schmitt und die deutschen Romanisten', (1999) 23 *Romanistische Zeitschrift für Literaturgeschichte*, 409 ff, 419 ff; G. Balakrishnan, *The Enemy. An Intellectual Portrait of Carl Schmitt*, (London-New York, Verso, 2000), 226 ff.

The core ideas of the lecture were that the *jus publicum europaeum,* which had made the sovereign state its central concept, was no longer in line with the de facto spatial order of Europe. Referring to the example of the American Monroe Doctrine, Schmitt explained that a specific 'sphere/space' had to become the conceptual basis for international law, with the *Reich* constituting the order of that space. Self-confidently, Schmitt declared:

> When, in autumn 1937, I presented my report on the turn to a discriminating concept of war, the overall political situation was still markedly different from today's . . . . Having delivered my report, I was asked to substantiate what new order was to substitute the state order . . . Today, I can give the answer. The new ordering concept for a new international law is our concept of the *Reich*, with its *Volk* based, *völkisch Großraum* order.[25]

The German *Reich* had been introduced by Schmitt a page earlier as

> a *Großraum order* dominated by particular ideological ideas and principles that exclude intervention by powers foreign to the area, whose guarantor and guardian is a people that has proved itself capable of this task.[26]

The only people that came into question as a 'guarantor and guardian' were the Germans. This meant acknowledging de jure a *Großraum* in which states could no longer claim equal respect, a situation, which Germany had just set in motion de facto. And Schmitt went on praising the *Führer*, who had 'given the idea of our *Reich* political reality, historical truth and a great international future.'[27] The political success of such an exemplary demonstration of *konkretes Ordnungsdenken* á la Schmitt seemed predestined. Yet, although the echoes to Schmitt's messages were considerable,[28] they did not find political acclaim.

Controversies

Opponents, like those who had, in 1936, already halted Schmitt's career as 'crown jurist', made themselves heard again.[29] Objection was taken to his statement that 'the new international law approach, its reference to the concept of the *Volk* notwithstanding, retained elements of order stemming from the state concept'. In his brief review, Werner Best explained that the *Völker* [peoples, national communities] with their 'supra-personal, supra-temporal overall

---

[25] C Schmitt, *Großraum* above n 17, 306.

[26] Above, n 17, 305.

[27] Above n 17, 306.

[28] Cf the annotations by G Maschke at n 17 above, 321 ff and the references in M Schmoeckel at n 20, 152; J Brechtefeld at n 2, 55 ff.

[29] Cf B Rüthers, 'Reinhard Höhn' at n 15 above; *idem, Carl Schmitt im Dritten Reich. Wissenschaft als Zeitgeist-Verstärkung,* 2nd edn. (München, CH Beck, 1990), 81 ff; A-M v. Lösch, *Der nackte Geist* at n 15 above, 429 ff, 448 ff.

essentialities' were to replace the 'concept of the abstract state' or 'economic interest formations', and to understand the *Großraum* as an 'order of *volks*' orders [national communities]'.[30]

This criticism was taken seriously—so seriously that Schmoeckel, is able use this dichotomy of '*völkisch*' as against 'statist' to reconstruct the whole contemporary debate.[31] The contrast between the two reference points is theoretically important and politically nothing less than dramatic. Schmitt's reminder that the existing concept of the state contains a minimum of reliable organisation and internal discipline, and that this organisational minimum constitutes the real basis of everything that has been seen as the concrete order of the 'international community' appeals to values which Schmitt himself had substantially discredited but which he, having fallen in disgrace, seems to have rediscovered.[32]

The support Schmitt found, particularly from Ernst Rudolf Huber, goes in a similar direction. Schmitt's statements on how both of his quests, for the preservation of the basic elements of international law on the one hand, and for the legal recognition of the new power structure of Germany's power politics in the *Großraum* on the other, could co-exist had remained ambiguous. Schmitt[33] had previously ventured ideas on a consolidation of both elements somewhat provisionally in a review essay on the second edition of Heinrich Triepel's '*Hegemonie. Ein Buch von führenden Staaten*' [Hegemony: a manual on states that lead].[34] He refrained from further elaborating his idea in his *Großraum* essay, but contented himself with underlining the elasticity of the notion of international law, which, as he explained, could also cover 'inter-*völkische* relations within a *Großraum*'. His famous disciple, Huber, however, took the key National Socialist concept of *Führung* much more seriously as a legal concept.[35] *Führung*, he argued, was to be understood as a concept of general significance

---

[30] W Best, 'Völkische Großraumordnung', (1940) 10 *Deutsches Recht*, 1006–7; in more detail *idem*, 'Grundfragen einer deutschen Großraumverwaltung', in *Festschrift für Heinrich Himmler zum 40. Geburtstag* (Darmstadt, Wittlich, 1941), 33–60.

[31] M Schmoeckel at n 20 above, 174 ff; cf the documentation in G Maschke at n 17, 343–48 and on contemporary 'state law' [*Staatsrecht*] M Stolleis *Geschichte des öffentlichen Rechts in Deutschland. vol. 3* at n 16, 361f; W Pauly at n 9, 76 ff.

[32] Cf D Dyzenhaus, 'Leviathan in the 1930s: The Reception of Hobbes in the Third Reich', in JP McCormick (ed), *Mass Democracy and Industrial Technology. Political and Social Theory from Nietzsche to Habermas*, (Durham/London, Duke UP, 2002), 163–94 at 171 ff.

[33] C Schmitt, 'Führung und Hegemonie' (1939), reprinted in G Maschke at n 17, 225–33.

[34] (Stuttgart/Berlin, Kohlhammer, 1938); see, also, M Schmoeckel at n 20, 117 ff.

[35] ER Huber, 'Herrschaft und Führung', (1941) 11 *Deutsches Recht* , 2017–24. Cf on the broader discussion, O Lepsius, *Die gegensatzaufhebende Begriffsbildung. Methodenentwicklungen in der Weimarer Republik Lepsius und ihr Verhältnis zur Ideologisierung der Rechtswissenschaft unter dem Nationalsozialismus*, (München, CH Beck, 1994), 93 ff and for a sociological analysis, drawing upon Weber's concept of charismatic domination and leadership cf RM Lepsius, 'Das Modell der charismatischen Herrschaft und seine Anwendbarkeit auf den "Führerstaat" Adolf Hitlers', in *idem*, *Demokratie in Deutschland* (n 8 above), 95–118.

in the new order, which offered an alternative to such categories as power and rule:

> *Führung* implies rule, but it is more: it goes further by setting people moving from within . . . .the awakening of the inward urge to action on one's own responsibility within a pre-designed action plan is the distinguishing feature of true leadership.

This applied between peoples [*Völkern,* ethnic communities] no less than between individuals [as *Volksgenossen*]:

> Political leadership is, then, the responsible determination of a closed unity of life, growing directly out of the basic forces of the community and based on a symbiosis of authority and power.[36]

This sounds, as is characteristic for this author, quite conciliatory.[37] The difference between a *völkisch* order entirely devoid of law and the proponents of a state-structured international legal system is indeed important, even terribly so. The writings of the radical *völkisch* school—Werner Best, Reinhard Höhn, and Wilhelm Stuckart, a group which contributed prominently to the Himmler *Festschrift* of 1941—are not merely a disaster in academic terms. Werner Best[38] did not shrink from explaining the necessity, as a law of life, for the *Führungsvolk* to 'totally destroy (or totally expel from its sphere)' undesired peoples. 'Annihilation and expulsion' do not, 'according to historical experience, contradict the laws of life if it is done totally.'[39] Best's contemporaries and comrades did not, apparently, ever publish such sentences, neither before nor after 1941 or 1942.[40] So, the dichotomy was merely ideological when Schmitt set to minimise his differences with Best: '[It] . . . can be left open whether the relationships emerging between a *Reich* and a *Großraum* can still be called "international law", whether other words and designations are more proper, and whether the inter-people [*zwischenvölkische*] relationships developing within a *Großraum* had not, as Werner Best suggested, more properly to be termed as the '*völkisch* (instead of international law) order of the *Großraum*'.[41] Huber once again managed to find a pleasant formula for the new order:

---

[36] The tone of his conclusion (ER Huber, *ibidem* at 31) does not survive translation into a living language: 'Politische *Führung* ist sonach: *die aus den Grundkräften der Gemeinschaft unmittelbar erwachsende, auf der Verbindung von Autorität und Macht beruhende verantwortliche Bestimmung einer geschloßenen Lebenseinheit*'.

[37] And must be read in the context of Huber's efforts to identify a 'constitution' of the National Socialist state (cf comprehensively R Walkenhaus, *Konservatives Staatsdenken. Eine wissenssoziologische Studie zu Ernst Rudolf Huber* (Berlin: Akademie Verlag, 1995), esp. at 234 ff.

[38] On his biography, cf U Herbert, *Best. Biographische Studien über Radikalismus, Weltanschauung und Vernunft, 1903–1989*, 3rd edn. (Bonn, JHW Dietz, 1996).

[39] W Best, 'Grundfragen' at n 28, 42; in the same sense, *idem*, 'Großraumordnung und Großraumverwaltung', (1942) 32 *Zeitschrift für Politik*, 406–12; cf U. Herbert at n 33, at 283.

[40] Cf H Dreier at n 9, 39 (Best is not cited there, but Dreier's observation is neither surprising nor illuminating anyway).

[41] Above n 33.

For political theory as for legal theory, the decisive problem is how the idea of the Reich, in its adaptation to the Großraum principle, differs from the imperialism of the others against whom we have honourably and uprightly fought . . . .The vital difference can only lie in the fact that the old imperialism was a formation of pure power and naked interest, concealed behind the high sounding talk of the equal rights of all nations; for the concept of the Reich, what must, instead, be decisive is that it is a structure of graduated order in which the leading power takes over open responsibility for the preservation of the overall order and the existence of all the members. For power becomes Law only by being understood as a responsibility boned function vis à vis a living whole entrusted to it . . . .The most important aspect of the Reich's task will thus be to make German leading power [Führungsgewalt] responsible for solving prime European questions beyond the state boundaries of the Reich.[42]

In the dark shadow of such artistic linguistic exercises, the internal shape of the *Großraum* remains well discernible. If, in contrast with the uncompromisingly *völkisch* school, the 'order' of the *Großraum* is not presented as a naked power structure,[43] the implications of a graded legal capacity of the 'states' in the *Großraum* and also for its inhabitants are drastic enough:[44] in line with the 'existential determination of the people by its natural biological vitality and its spiritual and historical character', which distinguishes the '*Volk* comrade' [*Volksgenosse*] and his 'German or species-related [*artverwandtes*] blood'. In consequence, the old category of citizenship, which had once included alien racial groups, is to be replaced by that of the '*Reich* citizen' [*Reichsbürger*]; below this species, we find mere '*Reich* members', who enjoy a status of 'protection and obligations' and therefore owe obedience but not 'loyalty' and military service. Among the *Reich* members—we are to distinguish further between '*Volk* members' and the 'racially alien'—there is 'citizenship' for '*Volk* groups' (who owe the German *Volk* and *Reich* obedience); and there is *Reich* citizenship for groups with a 'culture of their own'. Then, there are *Volk* members living outside the *Reich* frontiers to whom the *Reich* owes duties of protection.[45] 'No theoretician presupposed that the governments or inhabitants of the *Großraum* "states" would have to consent to the new order', observes Schmoeckel.[46] This aspect of the *Großraum* should be taken into account by

---

[42] ER Huber, 'Bau und Gefüge des Reiches', (1941) 6 *Deutsche Rechtswissenschaft*, 22–33, at 31.

[43] Above n 30: 'The *Großraum* order is, then, neither a "state" nor "international law" phenomenon in the sense hitherto usual. Accordingly, the "legal" forms in which the rules for the lasting relationships between the peoples of the *Großraum* are expressed. and also without real importance, and can be applied as one will'.

[44] Huber's summary is reprinted in AJ Jacobson & B Schlink (eds), *Weimar: A Jurisprudence of Crisis*, (Berkeley-Los Angeles, University of California Press, 2000), 330–31.

[45] Above n 42, 26.—It should be added that Huber did not adopt the anti-Semitic phraseology. And in his relentless search for conciliatory formula he suggested a '*Kriegsverfassung*' (war constitution), which would 'govern' the creation of the *Großraum* (cf. R Walkenhaus, *Konservatives Staatsdenken* at n 37, 242 ff.

[46] *Großraum* at n 17 above, 274.

those who present Carl Schmitt's position as actually being in contrast to the purely *völkisch* concepts.[47]

Franz Neumann, in his *Behemoth*,[48] presented the *Großraum* theory as a toolkit for the regime. However, very soon after its presentation at the 'Aktion Ritterbusch' in spring 1939, this new instrument was already outdated. Schmitt, the *'situative'* thinker, responded in the 1941 edition, when Germany occupied ever-greater spaces, by adding an epigraph to his paper: 'We are like mariners on a continuing journey, and no book can be more than a log book.' He was well aware of the implications of the changed situation within the *Großraum*.

Continuities: elements of internal ordering

In his reply to Best and his *völkisch* admonitions, Carl Schmitt had presented his *Großraum* as a 'concrete, historical and politically contemporary concept' [*konkreten geschichtlich-politischen Gegenwartsbegriff*] rooted 'essentially not in the state but in the technical, industrial and economic sphere'.[49] The revised editions of the Kiel lecture contain corresponding passages.[50] Schmitt was now referring, albeit apocryphally, to debates and theorems which lend support to his theses on the erosion of the territorial state, a harbinger of the necessity to adapt international law to the factual restructuring of international relations and the replacement of classical international law by norm systems which one would call governance structures today. Schmitt referred specifically to two phenomena, namely, the economic interdependencies beyond state frontiers [an emerging *'Großraum* economy'] and the valueless rationality of technology driven developments, which further the dictatorship of 'technicity' [*Technizität*].[51] He could have linked his pre-1933 writings with the *Großraum* theory when he designed it. But he did not—and had to let them remain as they were in view of the changed 'situation' in 1941. He also failed to consider a third alternative to international law, namely, its replacement by administrative law—even though, here, too, Carl Schmitt had delivered pertinent contributions.

---

[47] Cf JH Kaiser, 'Europäisches Großraumdenken. Die Steigerung geschichtlicher Größen als Rechtsproblem', in H Barion, E-W Böckenförde, E Forsthoff & W Weber (eds), *Epirrhosis. Festgabe für Carl Schmitt* vol. 2 (Berlin, Duncker & Humblot, 1968), 319–31.

[48] F Neumann, *Behemoth. Struktur und Praxis des Nationalsozialismus 1933–1944*, G Schäfer (ed), (Frankfurt, Fischer 1984), 198 ff.

[49] C Schmitt, *Großraum* at n 17 above, 305.

[50] Above at n 17, 307.

[51] On this term cf JP McCormick, *Carl Schmitt's Critique of Liberalism. Against Politics as Technology*, (Cambridge, Cambridge University Press, 1997), 122 ff and 180 f below.

Economy

The theorising on private law and economic law during the Weimar era has received much less attention than the debates on state law [*Staatsrecht*] and constitutional law; although, despite being much less visible, private law jurisprudence is scarcely less interesting. The type of economic policy and law actually practiced mirrored, as Knut-Wolfgang Nörr has argued in two monographs,[52] the 'organised economy'; Nörr's notion recalls what the Bielefeld social historians described as nineteenth century German 'organized capitalism',[53] a configuration, which was to survive the end of the Monarchy.[54] The theoretical debate, however, was much richer and the gamut of concepts between industrial society and economic democracy had a— more or less powerful—backing in the political world.[55] The alternative model, of which Nörr, in particular, is interested, is '*ordo*-liberalism', developed by such economists as Walter Eucken, Alexander Rüstow, and Wilhelm Röpke, who were joined by the lawyer Franz Böhm, at the end of the 20s and in the early 1930s.[56] Both, Carl Schmitt[57] and the *ordo*-liberals, advocated a strong state.[58] At the same time, Alfred Müller-Armack[59] and Carl Schmitt

---

[52] KW Nörr, *Die Leiden des Privatrechts. Kartelle in Deutschland von der Holzstoffkartellentscheidung bis zum Gesetz gegen Wettbewerbsbeschränkungen*, (Tübingen, Mohr, 1994); KW Nörr, *Die Republik der Wirtschaft. Teil I: Von der Besatzungszeit bis zur Großen Koalition*, (Tübingen, Mohr, 1999).

[53] See, eg, J Kocka, 'Organisierter Kapitalismus oder Staatsmonopolistischer Kapitalismus', in HA Winkler (ed), *Organisierter Kapitalismus: Voraussetzungen und Anfänge*, (Göttingen, Vandenhoeck & Ruprecht, 1974), 19 ff.

[54] Cf J Bast, *Totalitärer Pluralismus,* (Tübingen, Mohr, 1999), 200 ff; Ph Manow '"Modell Deutschland" as an inter-denominational Compromise', (Centre for European Studies, Harvard University. CES Working Paper, Program for the Study of Germany and Europe, No 003).

[55] G Brüggemeier, *Entwicklung des Rechts im organisierten Kapitalismus, Band 1* (Frankfurt a.M., Syndikat, 1977) 239 ff; D Wielsch, *Freiheit und Funktion. Zur Struktur- und Theoriegeschichte des Rechts der Wirtschaftsgesellschaft*, (Baden-Baden, Nomos, 2001), 103 ff.

[56] R Wiethölter, *Franz Böhm (1895–1977)*, in B Diestelkamp & Michael Stolleis (eds), *Juristen an der Universität Frankfurt a.M.*, (Baden-Baden, Nomos), 208–52, at 215 ff; D Haselbach, *Autoritärer Liberalismus und Soziale Marktwirtschaft. Gesellschaft und Politik im Ordoliberalismus*, (Baden-Baden, Nomos, 1991); Ph Manow above n 54.

[57] C Schmitt, 'Starker Staat und gesunde Wirtschaft. Ein Vortrag vor Wirtschaftsführern' (Lecture of 23 Nov 1932), in (1933) *Volk und Reich*, 81–94, reprinted in G Maschke at n 17, 71–94.

[58] A Rüstow, 'Freie Wirtschaft—starker Staat', in *Schriften des Vereins für Socialpolitik*, vol 187 (ed Boese) *Deutschland und die Weltkrise*, (München, Duncker & Humblot, 1932), 62–9.; F Böhm, *Wettbewerb und Monopolkampf*, (Berlin, Carl Heymanns, 1933); F Böhm, *Die Ordnung der Wirtschaft als geschichtliche Aufgabe und rechtsschöpferische Leistung*, (Stuttgart und Berlin, Kohlhammer, 1937); D Haselbach above n 56, 40 ff; D Wielsch above n 55, 83 ff; Ph Manow, 'Ordoliberalismus als ökonomische Ordnungstheologie', (2001) *Leviathan*, 179–98.

[59] A Müller-Armack, *Entwicklungsgesetze des Kapitalismus. Ökonomische, geschichtstheoretische und soziologische Studien zur modernen Wirtschaftsverfassung* (Berlin, 1932); A Müller-Armack, *Staatsidee und Wirtschaftsordnung im neuen Reich* (Berlin, Juncker & Dünnhaupt, 1933).

himself[60] showed their fascination with Mussolini's Fascism. For this—and other—reasons, Hermann Heller[61] criticised *ordo*-liberalism as 'authoritarian' liberalism. This qualification applies to the common critique of a pluralism in which the conflict of interests determines the contents of state policy. Yet, the 'order' of the economy that the *ordo*-liberals hoped for differed from the ideas of Schmitt and his successors in one very important respect. Carl Schmitt had very clearly indicated in his talk of the 'strong state' and the 'healthy economy'[62] that he was advocating the primacy of politics over a politically obedient self-administration' of the economy.[63] The primacy of the political over the economic, Ernst Forsthoff was to explain some years later, is a specific feature of the '*Führer* constitution'.[64] This primacy finds its expression in the 'plan', the 'specific action form of the *Führer* state . . . in the spheres of the economy and technology'. 'Order' and 'plan' are opposing concepts, even if both call for a 'strong state'.[65] And even with the pleas for this 'plan', interpretive caution is called for. Hans Freyer[66] to whom Forsthoff refers,[67] discusses the notion of 'plan' without National Socialist connotations.

Research on the implications of the primacy of the political in economic law after the *Machtergreifung* in 1933 is gradually intensifying.[68] However, on the question of how the economy of the *Großraum* might be legally structured, there is very little to be found—and maybe very little worth looking at. Werner Daitz, probably the best known exponent of economic *Großraum* thinking,[69] is

[60] C Schmitt, 'Die Wendung zum totalen Staat' (1931), in *idem, Positionen und Begriffe im Kampf mit Weimar—Genf—Versailles, 1923–1939*, (Berlin, Duncker & Humblot, 1988), 146–57.

[61] H Heller, 'Autoritärer Liberalismus', (1933) 44 *Die Neue Rundschau*, 289–98.

[62] n 53 above.

[63] See the analysis by I Maus, 'Existierten zwei Nationalsozialismen?', in *idem, Rechtstheorie und politische Theorie im Industriekapitalismus*, (München, Fink, 1986), 83–92.

[64] E Forsthoff, 'Führung und Planung', (1937) 7 *Deutsches Recht*, 48–9, at 48.

[65] Specifically on the distinct positions of Franz Böhm cf R Wiethölter at n 56 above, 232. The often cited contacts by the *Reich* Ministry for the Economy which, at the end of the regime, sought economic advice from exponents of *ordo*-liberalism for an economic policy concept beyond classical liberalism and socialist planned economy. See L Herbst, *Der totale Krieg und die Ordnung der Wirtschaft*, (Stuttgart, Deutsche Verlagsanstalt, 1982), 144 ff, 133 ff, are no proof to the contrary.

[66] H Freyer, *Herrschaft und Planung. Zwei Grundbegriffe der politischen Ethik*, (Hamburg, 1933), reprinted in E Üner, *Hans Freyer. Herrschaft, Planung und Technik. Aufsätze zur politischen Soziologie*, (Weinheim, VCH, 1987), 17–44.

[67] 'Führung und Planung' at n 64, 48, n 1.

[68] D Gosewinkel, 'Wirtschaftspolitische Rechtsetzung im Nationalsozialismus', (ms. Frankfurt a.M., Max-Planck-Institut für Europäische Rechtsgeschichte, 2000); W Seibel, 'Steuerung durch Recht im Nationalsozialismus?', Contribution to the Workshop 'Wirtschaftskontrolle und Recht im Nationalsozialismus—Zwischen Entrechtlichung und Modernisierung. Bilanz und Perspektiven der Forschung', Berlin-Brandenburgische Akademie der Wissenschaften, Studiengruppe 'Das Europa der Diktaturen. Wirtschaftssteuerung und Recht', Blankensee, 14–16 June 2001; cf much earlier G Brüggemeier, *Entwicklung des Rechts im organisierten Kapitalismus, vol. 2: Vom Faschismus bis zur Gegenwart*, (Frankfurt a.M., Syndikat, 1979), 32 ff, 69 ff.

[69] Cf M Salewski, 'Ideas of the National Socialist Government and Party' at n 6 above, 37–178; G Maschke at n 17, 364, 465 ff.

mentioned by Schmitt for the first time in a follow-up essay to the *Großraum* lecture of 1939.[70] This is difficult to understand, but, at the same time, illuminating: Daitz's writings document obedience to the regime and are of disastrous quality. This writer had first advocated a retreat from the world economy to a national economy, for the autarchy first of the national economy and then of the *Großraum* economy of the European 'family of peoples' as a whole.[71] More realistic contemporaries saw the *Großraum* economically as merely an emergency solution.[72] At any rate, Justus Wilhelm Hedemann, who was prominent in German economic law long before 1933, and heavily involved in the *Akademie für Deutsches Recht,* in working out the new *Volksgesetzbuch* from 1939, took up the theme, in 1941 and 1943, in two essays which have received practically no attention.[73] He was looking for a leadership model for the economy, which would leave the economic actors and the citizens in the *Großraum* with some autonomy. The peoples [*Völkerschaften*] of Europe were perceived as the bases of law; self-administration, corporatist structures and planning were to complement each other—vagueness everywhere; but why and how could he seek clarification in what had become a war economy?[74]

Technicity

Carl Schmitt[75] had complemented his plea for the 'strong state' in which politics was to assert its priority over the economy with a polemic against all technocratic endeavours and promises to decide all questions of the polity by relying on technical and economic expertise, 'according to allegedly purely practical, purely technical and purely economic viewpoints'. In contrast with the US, where *'The Technocrats'* praised the welfare prosperity enhancing potential of

---

[70] C Schmitt, *Großraum und Völkerrecht* (1940), reprinted in G Maschke at n 17, 234 ff, at 237.

[71] W Daitz, *Der Weg zur Volkswirtschaft, Großraumwirtschaft und Großraumpolitik,* (Dresden, Meinhold Verlagsgesellschaft, 1943); cf B Kletzin, *Europa aus Rasse und Raum* at n 2, 129 ff, 163 ff.

[72] W Abelshauser, '"Mitteleuropa" und die deutsche Außenwirtschaftspolitik', in C Buchheim, M Hutter & H James (eds), *Zerrissene Zwischenkriegszeit. Wirtschaftshistorische Beiträge. Knut Borchardt zum 65. Geburtstag,* (Baden-Baden, Nomos 1994), 263 ff, 279 ff.

[73] Cf H Mohnhaupt, 'Justus Wilhelm Hedemann als Rechtsdenker und Zivilrechtler vor und während der Epoche des Nationalsozialismus', in M Stolleis & D Simon (eds), *Rechtsgeschichte im Nationalsozialismus. Beiträge zur Geschichte einer Disziplin* (Tübingen, Mohr, 1989), 107–59, 156, n 259; M Schmoeckel at n 20, 224.

[74] On the 'scientific' tasks and activities of the German Institute for Foreign Studies cf R Eisfeld, *Ausgebürgert und doch angebräunt. Deutsche Politikwissencahft 1920–1945,* (Baden-Baden, Nomos, 1991), 152 ff; Siebert at n 7; on the foreign trade continuities of *Großraum* ideas, cf. VR Berghahn, *German Big Business and the Quest for a European Economic Empire in the Twentieth Century,* in *idem* (ed), *Quest for Economic Empire: the European Strategies of German Business in the Twentieth Century,* (Providence-Oxford, Berghahn Books, 1996), 1 ff, 5 ff.

[75] Above n 57, 73; the diagnosis of a turn towards the 'quantitatively' (but politically rather weak!) total state, also C Schmitt at n 60 above.

technologically and economically underpinned expertise,[76] many of the conservative intellectuals who set the tone of the Weimar Republic saw the dominance of soulless technical machinery arriving, against which most cultural values could be mobilised, while it seemed hopeless to trust in the creative possibilities of Weimar democracy.[77]

In his counter revolutionary Barcelona manifesto,[78] Carl Schmitt had identified the Soviet Union as the institutional incarnation of a quasi-religious, soulless technicity.[79] Does this mean that the 'particularly strong' and 'qualitively total' state should lead not just the economy; should this state be able to ensure the primacy of the political over 'technicity', and thus accomplish what a powerless culture could not achieve? A frightening notion. Hans Freyer,[80] who, with good reason, counted among the conservative techno-pessimists who impressed, for instance, Ernst Forsthoff,[81] argued, in comfortingly Weberian terms, that technical formations become a reality only through the 'plan'; behind the plan stands 'political power'; power, however, presupposes 'rule' [*Herrschaft*]; but *Herrschaft* is of lasting duration, because and in so far as it is comprehensive ... *Herrschaft* essentially seeks legitimacy, and its duration depends on the solidity of the legitimacy bases it finds ready-made or manages to create.[82] It seems simply impossible to fit the positions of the conservative technology critique into the National Socialist domination fantasies.

Administration

Schmoeckel[83] finds the most original contemporary elaboration of Schmitt's *Großraum* theory in what seems, at first sight, an inconspicuous article by Hans

---

[76] See C Radaelli, *Technocracy in the EU* (Essex/New York, Longman, 1999), esp. at 24 ff; see, also, A Mohler, 'Der Weg der "Technokratie" von Amerika nach Frankreich', in H Barion, E-W Böckenförde, E Forsthoff & W Weber (eds), *Epirrhosis. Festgabe für Carl Schmitt*, (Berlin, Duncker & Humblot, 1968), vol. 2, 579–96.

[77] T Vesting, *Politische Einheitsbildung und technische Realisation. Über die Expansion der Technik und die Grenzen der Demokratie*, (Baden-Baden, Nomos, 1994), 9 ff; N Stehr, *Arbeit, Eigentum und Wissen. Zur Theorie von Wissensgesellschaften*, (Frankfurt a.M., Suhrkamp, 1994), 278 ff; JP McCormick at n 51, 31 ff, 83 ff.

[78] C Schmitt, 'Das Zeitalter der Neutralisierungen und Entpolitisierungen' (1929), reprinted in *idem, Positionen und Begriffe im Kampf um Weimar—Genf—Versaillles 1923–1939*, (Berlin, Duncker & Humblot, 1988), 120–33.

[79] *Ibid.* at 120 f: ' ... its vitality is strong enough to wield knowledge and technology as weapons; its courage for rationalism and opposite ... are overwhelming.'

[80] H Freyer, 'Zur Philosophie der Technik', reprinted in E Üner, *Hans Freyer* at n 66 above, 7 ff, 9.

[81] See M Vec, 'Aushöhlung des Staates? Selbst-Normierung im Staat der Industriegesellschaft als historisches Problem', 2000 (19) *Rechtshistorisches Journal*, 517–32.

[82] Above n 66, 20, 28, 38; cf *idem*, 'Das Politische als Problem der Philosophie', (1935), reprinted in E Üner, *Hans Freyer* at n 66, 45–64; *idem*, (1940) 'Beiträge zur Theorie der Herrschaft', reprinted in E Üner, *Hans Freyer* at n 66, 65–83.

[83] *Großraumtheorie* at n 20 above, 225.

Peter Ipsen on the 'External administration of the *Reich*' [*Reichsaußen-verwaltung*], with the explanatory subtitle: 'the German administration looks after [sic!] 145 million people outside the *Reich* frontiers'.[84] This external administration, explained Ipsen, is 'concrete, objective, and functional' in its orientation. It presupposed the continued existence of 'country specific administrations', but claims unconditional supremacy. This idea, says Schmoeckel,[85] is 'near genius' and, at the same time, has 'something downright diabolical'. In fact, Ipsen's idea is to be differentiated from the rather dry classificatory exercises in the writings on the administrative practices in occupied Europe.[86] His concept precisely mirrored the *Reich's* power claims. Ipsen retained a legal form while freeing rule from any legal constraint. And this was not just simply written down off the top of his head. In his 1937 Hamburg *Habilitation* thesis in its comparative chapters, scholarly and by the same token in its substance depressing study, Ipsen had developed the conceptual preliminary.[87] This study dealt, as its subtitle announces, with 'judiciary free sovereign acts' [*justizlose Hoheitsakte*]. It offered, as a review of the study by no less than Ernst Rudolf Huber emphasised, an accurate 'internal interpretation of the essence' [*innere Wesensdeutung*] of those acts in distinguishing them from the familiar discretionary acts and establishing their 'complete freedom from judicial control'.[88] But Huber also discovers and defends another dimension of the argument. Ipsen is praised for basing himself—against Reinhard Höhn—on the continuing existence, in principle, of a control of the administration in the new state, which implies a protection of individual rights.[89] Yet, higher than this latter principle is the genuine norm-setting power of the National Socialist government. This power is not derived from some legislative power, the government is the bearer of government power,[90] which embraces legislative power.[91]

This is unadulterated Schmittianism.[92] In his essay on 'Legality and Legitimacy', Schmitt had already proclaimed the end of the 'legislative state', a

---

[84] HP Ipsen, 'Reichsaußenverwaltung' (1942) *Reichsverwaltungsblatt*, 64 ff, reprinted in HW Neulen, *Europa und das 3. Reich, Einigungsbestrebungen im deutschen Machtbereich 1939–1945* (München, Universitas 1987), 111–15.

[85] *Großraumtheorie* at n 20, 226.

[86] D Majer, 'NS-Verwaltung im besetzten Europa', (1999) 90 *Verwaltungs-Archiv*, 163–86.

[87] HP Ipsen, *Politik und Justiz. Das Problem der justizlosen Hoheitsakte*, (Hamburg, Hanseatische Verlagsanstalt, 1937); on this book see also n 92 below.

[88] ER Huber, '"Politik und Justiz": Zu Hans Peter Ipsens Schrift über das Problem der "justizlosen Hoheitsakte"', (1937/38) 98 *Zeitschrift für die gesamte Staatswissenschaft*, 193–200, at 195.

[89] *Ibid.*

[90] *Ibid.* at 196 (and suggesting the use of 'leadership power' [*Führungsgewalt*] as the more adequate term).

[91] Above n 87, 180.

[92] Biographical remarks are in principal beyond the scope of this essay. The importance of Hans Peter Ipsen for European legal scholarship in Germany seems to warrant an exception. His *vita* and academic career illuminate the intellectual continuity/discontinuity *problématique* and

Germany's 'reluctance to glance back in the mirror' (the 'Prologue' to this book by M Stolleis) in an exemplary way. Ipsen, born in 1907 in Hamburg, was already a highly respected professor of public law when he focused on the new European Communities and became the *doyen* of European law in Germany: a successful supervisor of—according to M Hilf, *Eurparechit* 1998, 107 ff—some 150 PhD students and no less then 8 *Habilitations*; for good reasons, an admired author of the first great 1092 page textbook in German on European law (*Europäisches Gemeinschaftsrecht*, Tübingen: Mohr 1972), of some 30 monographs and of some 150 articles, one of which [his 1964 Bensheim lecture on 'Das Verhältnis des Rechts der europäischen Gemeinschaften zum nationalen Recht' ('The relationship between the law of the European Communities and national law'), published, *i.a.* in *Aktuelle Fragen des europäischen Gemeinschaftsrechts, Europarechtliches Kolloquium*, Bensheim 1964 and in (1965) 2 *CMLRev* 397–409] suggested the '*Durchgriffswirkung*' (supremacy) of European law and is said to have been taken into consideration by the ECJ judges who attended the lecture and handed down, only 5 days later, on 15 July 1964, the seminal *Costa v ENEL* judgment (Case 6/64, ECR [1964] 1251; Th Oppermann, 'Hans Peter Ipsen und das Europarecht', in Fachbereich Rechtswissenschaft der Universität Hamburg (ed), *Hans Peter Ipsen. 1907–1998*, (Münster-Hamburg-London, Lit 2001), 21–32 at 27 f; G Nicolaysen, 'Lebensbild Hans Peter Ipsen', *ibidem*, 33–48 at 44 f.

Ipsen was 25 years old when the Nazis seized power in 1933. Having published his *Dissertation* on *Widerruf gültiger Verwaltungsakte* in 1932, he handed in his *Habilitation* in 1936 and published it a year later (*Politik und Justiz. Das Problem der justizlosen Hoheitsakte* at n. 87). In the same year 1937, he was appointed *Dozent* [H. Quaritsch, 'Hans Peter Ipsen zum Gedenken', (1998) 123 *Archiv des öffentlichen Rechts*, 1–20 at 19: only in 1939] and joined the Nazi party on 1 May 1937 (according to a response by Ipsen, written in impeccable French, to a letter of 2 March 1960 from Professor Hames of the Faculté du Droit Comparé in Luxembourg; the letter— 'Prise de position au sujet de la lettre de la Faculté de Droit de l'Université Libre de Bruxelles du 27 Février 1960: mémoires, 12/11/1941–27/2/1960' HP Ipsen.—Hambourg, 6/1960.—22 p.: dact.—is being kept at the Studiecentrum Oorlog en hedendaagse Maatschappij, Wetstr. 155/2, B-1040 Brussel, België). He was appointed Professor in Hamburg on 9 February 1940. As Ipsen himself in the letter cited and G Nicolaysen ('Lebensbild Hans Peter Ipsen', in Fachbereich Rechtswissenschaft, *ibidem* 13–48, at 39), underline, the local section of the National Socialist *Rechtswahrerbund* had resisted an earlier appointment. Still in 1940, the German Military Administration of Brussels appointed Ipsen, Commissioner of the Colonial University of Antwerp and subsequently, in May 1941, *Commissaire of the Université Libre de Bruxelles*—according to many reports of the German Military Administration in their eyes a masonic, leftist, anti-germanic institution. He was in charge when the University decided to close its doors rather than accept the appointment of three collaborators as professors. In 1945 Ipsen was dismissed from his professorial position by the military government of Hamburg, but soon, in December 1946, returned to his University position.

No mention of all this, not even of the subtitle of the *Habilitation*, in Rolf Stödter's *laudatio* in *Hamburg-Deutschland*-Europa, *the Festschrift für Hans Peter Ipsen zum 70. Geburtstag*, (Tübingen: Mohr 1977, 1–8) or in the (1998) 123 *Archiv des öffentlichen Rechts* memorial by Helmut Quaritsch. And indeed, an assessment of Ipsen's activities as a commissioner of the Free University of Brussels is not so easy. G Nicolaysen, 'Zu Leben und Werk', in Fachbereich Rechtswissenschaft (ed), *ibidem*, 5–8, writes at 7 (my translation): 'When I applied for a position to work with Ipsen, he himself handed over to me in 1960 things that had been written on him, in Belgium and elsewhere . . . Had I found anything compromising, I would not have accepted the position'. In his 'Lebensbild Hans Peter Ipsen', *ibidem* at 39 f, G Nicolaysen presents a more detailed defence of the activities in Belgium. The Belgium documents and publications, however, which Professor David Fraser from Sydney has made available to me, are not at all that favourable. In a publication for the Belgian Government Information Center in New York of 1947, 'Commissioner Ipsen of Hamburg University' is called 'a henchman of the Nazi party' ['The Universities under the Occupation', in J-A Goris (ed), *Belgium under Occupation*, Moretus Press;

'turn to the total state' with its inevitable trend towards the 'plan' (rather than, as a hundred years ago, to freedom). It was characteristic of the actual moment, Schmitt continued, that this turn presents itself as the establishment of the 'administrative state'.[93] This state, he added shortly before Hitler's seizure of power, was exposed to the influence of pluralist interests; it was out of this weakness that it penetrated ever more spheres of existence and hence became total in the 'quantative' sense. This state was particularly strong, however, in that it used all new technical means to enhance its power.[94] Ernst Forsthoff seconded this:

> Under the Weimar constitution, the German state decayed because it became prey to social pluralism. This total state which has now become a reality cannot see the old executive power as sufficing. Now, alongside state officials, the *Berufsbeamtentum*, the 'commissar' enters in, not as a neutral but as a politically-motivated and decisive

similarly in her assessment M-R Thielemans, 'Un commissaire allemand pour l'Université', in A Despy-Meyer, A Dierkens & F Scheelings (eds), 25.11.1941. *l'Université Libre de Bruxelles ferme ses portes*, Bruxelles: archives de l'ULB 1991, 25–41; see also H Liebrecht, *L'Université de Bruxelles et la guerre*, Brussels: La renaissance du livre (no year), esp. at 35, 93]. In 1960, when Ipsen was invited to lecture in Luxembourg, a letter of Professor Hames of 2 March 1960 opined that 'cette nouvelle . . . souleva une revolte'. In his response Ipsen called the accusation that he was an ardent partisan of the Nazis 'absurd'.

   This is a case of exemplary importance for two reasons. Our factual knowledge is imperfect. It could be improved, but, so I have been told by Sebastian Remus, *Dokumentar* for Military History in Freiburg i.Br., uncertainties are likely to remain. And even if we would find out more, how are we to assess Ipsen's political attitudes and his behaviour? What remains possible is to read what Ipsen has published. And then we see: His *Politik und Justiz* of 1937 is not just a comparative study. It is an analysis of the ideological and political background of the separation of powers ideas with a quite emphatic defence of Germany's New Order (esp. at 200; see M Stolleis, *Geschichte des öffentlichen Rechts in Deutschland* at n 16. at 336–8). Among the acts that are to be removed from judicial Schutzpowers of review are (see 218): the 'Schutzhaftanordnung' (internment in a concentration camp); the 'Säuberung des Beamtentums' (cleansing of the *Reich's* civil service); the 'Reinigung der von der Deutschen Arbeitsfront beseitigten Gewerkschaften von politisch Unzuverlässigen' (cleansing of the trade unions). Nothing but a study in comparative 'law'? Ipsen clearly pays tribute to the political context that generated such ideas. Did he have to? Does it make a difference that his study cites Jewish authors as G Nicolaysen emphasises (*ibidem*, at 37)? At that point, our argument is again confronted with 'contextual' considerations: Ipsen could not, surely, be expected to give up his career. Perhaps, what he wrote can be read more benevolently and did not really reflect his inner beliefs anyway. Be that as it may, this much is sure: *Justiz und Politik* is a bad book. I am not aware of any theoretical and methodological standard which would provide us with a defence of the type of thinking presented in this *Habilitation*.

   [93] C Schmitt, *Legalität und Legitimität*, (München, Duncker & Humblot, 1932), cited from the reprint in *idem, Verfassungsrechtliche Aufsätze aus den Jahren 1924–1945. Materialien zu einer Verfassungslehre* (Berlin, Duncker & Humblot, 1973) 2nd edn., 265–93, 266; cf the interpretation by JP McCormick, *Identifying or Exploiting the Paradoxes of Constitutional Democracy? An Introduction to Carl Schmitt's Legality and Legitimacy*, in C Schmitt, *Legality and Legitimacy*, (Durham, Duke UP, forthcoming).

   [94] C Schmitt, 'Weiterentwicklung des totalen Staats in Deutschland', reprinted in *idem, Verfassungsrechtliche Aufsätze aus den Jahren 1924–1945*, at n 91), 359–66, 361, 365.

functionary, 'an exponent of political will'.[95] What applies internally no doubt has to apply all the more 'externally'.[96]

An interim observation

Carl Schmitt's *Großraum*, although loaded with state elements, remains internally empty. This discrepancy has its logic. The National Socialist vision of Europe, which sees a *Großraum* uniting racially-akin, fascist-led peoples from the North Cape to Sicily, and from Brittany to the Urals under German leadership, was not concerned with institutionalising any sort of economic, technical or political rationality patterns. With the rupture that Schmitt's theory made with traditional international law, a second one went hand in hand: Schmitt was not capable of identifying, and his opponents did not even want to identify, the structures that would replace the autonomy which the sovereignty principle in international law had protected.

The renewal of the first legal culture in the integration process

The European unification efforts that started with the 1950 Schuman plan and led to the Treaty of Rome in 1957 meant a very deliberate overcoming of the racist imperialism of the Nazi regime. The situation differed radically from the one which existed after the First World War—both politically and academically. There had indeed, as Dreier notes,

> not been any noteworthy attempt at factual or legitimatory linkage back to the Third Reich, nor any substantive study of the further effects of National Socialist modes of thought in constitutional theory.[97]

Nor were there any preservations, in principle, against the Basic Law's openness towards Europe. Instead, there were intensive debates about the legal nature of

---

[95] E Forsthoff, *Der totale Staat*, (Hamburg, Hanseatische Verlagsanstalt, 1933) 28; 36; see also, E Forsthoff, 'Das neue Gesicht der Verwaltung und die Verwaltungsrechtswissenschaft', (1935) 5 *Deutsches Recht*, 331–3; idem, 'Führung und Bürokratie—Einige grundsätzliche Erwägungen', (1935) *Deutsches Adelsblatt*, 1339–40.

[96] For Forsthoff's further development after 1933, see E Forsthoff, 'Daseinsvorsorge als Aufgabe der modernen Verwaltung' in *idem Die Verwaltung als Leistungsträger* (Stuttgart und Berlin, Kohlhammer, 1938), partly reprinted in *idem, Rechtsfragen der leistenden Verwaltung*, (Stuttgart, Kohlhammer, 1959), 23–34; M Stolleis, *Geschichte, des öffentlichen Rechts in Deutschland. vol. 3* at n 16, 352 f and 366.; R Mehring, 'Epilogue. The Decline of Theory—Introduction', in AJ Jacobson & B Schlink (eds), *Weimar* at n 44 above, 313–20, 316 f; W Pauly at n 9, 60, 70 ff, 81 f, 98 ff; on the continuity in Forsthoff's thinking cf V Neumann, 'Der harte Weg zum sanften Ziel. Ernst Forsthoffs Rechts- und Staatstheorie als Paradigma konservativer Technikkritik', in A Rossnagel (ed), *Recht und Technik im Spannungsfeld der Kernenergiekontroverse*, (Opladen, Westdeutscher Verlag, 1984), 88–99; I Staff, 'Die Wahrung staatlicher Ordnung. Ein Beitrag zum technologischen Staat und seinen rechten Propheten Carl Schmitt und Ernst Forsthoff', (1987) *Leviathan*, 141–62, 151 ff; M Vec, 'Aushöhlung des Staates? Selbst-Normierung im Staat der Industriegesellschaft als historisches Problem', (2000) 19 *Rechtshistorisches Journal*, 517–32.

[97] H Dreier, at n 9 above, 69.

the European Economic Community, in which the representatives of *Staatsrecht* [constitutional law], of international law, of public international and of economic law took part.

Focus

The histories of these discussions, which moved toward the twofold demarcation of the law of the European Economic Communities against international law on the one hand, and *Staatsrecht* and constitutional law on the other, thus establishing European law as an autonomous discipline, cannot, and need not, be retold in any detail here. The focus of the following section is on the continuities and discontinuities of legal concepts, on the necessity and difficulty to grasp a new situation conceptually, and, in so doing, to differentiate between discredited, undamaged and renewable elements of a complex legal heritage. The post-war situation of the young Federal Republic was very clear: democracy was to be established in the new polity. And, in addition, co-operation and trust were to be achieved with the former enemies (in the West). The German European law debate is marked by seeing the tensions between the integration process very early on the one hand, and the political autonomy of the Member States on the other, as a problem for the democracy that it had only just attained domestically, without on that account falling back into *völkisch* national nostalgias. Admittedly, this sort of openness towards Europe had, with a certain inevitability, or, at any rate, with striking historical 'logic', made the effort to mediate between democracy and integration in order to lead to the revival of the pre-democratic elements from Germany's 'first culture' in particular.

This was no easy task. As a reminder: all spheres of society—in the economy, technology, the administration—had been subjected to the leadership claim of National Socialist policy. This subjection was, after 1945, outdated in every conceivable sense. Yet, the problems of the order of the economy, of the exposure of society to technological possibilities and necessities, and the difficulty of ensuring the political and social accountability of the administration did not resolve themselves with the disappearance of National Socialism. This was true domestically in the new republic (see below). And, paradoxically enough, it was the integration project in particular, that responded so convincingly to the militant past of the nation state, which was to give rise to new concerns about the legitimacy of European governance.

Ordo-liberalism, organised capitalism and the State of the industrial society

In his above-mentioned[98] studies on the recent history of private and economic law, Knut Wolfgang Nörr has described the history of the operation of the con-

---

[98] Above n 52.

cepts of the 'organised economy' and the 'social market economy' under the Basic Law.[99] The so-called 'organised economy'—antitrust law was not to exist until 1958—was the concept that (implicitly) prevailed in *Staatsrecht* and constitutional law: the inherited practices were, once again, tolerated or even promoted, this time by parliamentary majoritarian legislation, and hence understood as *ipso facto* constitutionally legitimate. In private law and economic law thinking, in contrast, *ordo*-liberalism dominated, postulating that the ordinary legislator be bound by principles of a liberal, competitive market constitution.[100] *Ordo*-liberalism became influential in practical political terms because—in contrast with its early form, which Hermann Heller had called 'authoritarian liberalism',[101]—it entered into an alliance with exponents of the new 'social market economy'.[102]

Carl Schmitt's gloomy vision of a 'strong state' and a 'healthy economy' had been left behind by each school of thought in its own way, without considerably irritating the praxis of politics with their theoretical queries and differences. The Federal Republic did both, it officiously cultivated ideas, conceptions and institutionalisations in the *ordo*-liberal sense; at the same time, however, it displayed ideological indifference, in line with the mainstream view in public law, thus allowing legislative policy to come to terms with, or even re-establish, the patterns of the 'organised economy'. Nörr accordingly diagnoses:

> *a basic phenomenon in the history of the emergence of the Bonn Republic . . . [a] dual line, in economic policy and economic constitutional law [And] for the economic order that was to characterise the new State, we have even to talk about a dual mise en scène, two stagings of the same play that took no notice of one another.*[103]

In Nörr's description, which concentrates on economic law, the position of Ernst Forsthoff is missing. It is interesting here not so much because of its importance for German administrative and constitutional law, but in the light of its transferability to the European context—and the continuity that marks Forsthoff's thinking. When, in 1933, Forsthoff welcomed 'the total state', it seemed to him, in all seriousness, a bulwark against the robberies of the 'societal pluralism' of the Weimar Republic.[104] This enthusiasm had already evaporated in the 1930s.[105] It is remarkable that Forsthoff, in his *Der Staat der*

---

[99] Above n 52, *Die Republik der Wirtschaft*, 5 ff.

[100] Ch Joerges, 'The Science of Private Law and the Nation-State', in F Snyder (ed), *The Europeanization of Law. The Legal Effects of European Integration*, (Oxford, Hart, 2000), 47–82, at 51 ff; cf KW Nörr, *Die Republik der Wirtschaft, ibid.* at 58 ff, 81 ff.

[101] Above n 61.

[102] See W Abelshauser, *Die Langen Fünfziger Jahre. Wirtschaft und Gesellschaft der Bundesrepublik Deutschland 1949–1966*, (Düsseldorf, Schwan, 1987); D Haselbach at n 56, 117 ff; Ph Manow at n 54 and n 58.

[103] n 52, KW Nörr, *Die Republik der Wirtschaft*, 84.

[104] n 95, E Forsthoff, *Der totale Staat*, 28.

[105] Above n 95–6.

Industriegesellschaft ['The State of the industrial society'], referred to his early writings; and it was by no means post-war opportunism which motivated his characterisation of the control of the state by totalitarian political movements, a 'degeneration [*Entartung*] of the state'.[106] Even by 1938, Forsthoff had—quite in the style of conservative criticism of the 1920s[107]—in a seminal study which concentrated on the 'technicization' of all relationships, found something which he complained of, yet also placed hopes in for taming the demon of the political: it was a consequence of 'industrial and technical development' and the associated 'mass forms of life' that 'modern man' could enhance his 'effective living area' and, at the same time, fall into new 'social need'.[108]

> The measures taken to meet appropriation needs, I call *Daseinsfürsorge* ['provision of subsistence'][109] existential security ... The responsibility for meeting these appropriation needs, I call *Daseinsverantwortung* [individual responsibility for one's subsistence].[110]

Forsthoff thus established existential security as a sort of fact of the matter of life, not as such up for disposal. Accordingly, in the post-war debate on the social state clause in Article 20 (1) of the Basic Law, he was able to classify social matters as belonging to an extra-constitutional realm, a factual sphere 'driven and determined to the utmost by social impulses'; it was these constraints which forced politics, legislation and the administration into supplementing the *Rechtsstaat* by material content, namely, the social state.[111]

The same type of argument, which guided his understanding of the social dimension of the modern state [*soziale Realisation*], he now used in his analyses of 'technical realization' [*technische Realisation*]. Just as Carl Schmitt had demonised 'technicity' in his Barcelona lecture of 1929,[112] Forsthoff perceived a freedom-threatening potential inherent in the technical processes. The frontlines were still the same:[113] '[I]mmediately after taking power, Bolshevism had identified itself with technology', Forsthoff explained in an accompanying essay; but the 'free state, too, will have a partial identification with technology forced on it through the conditions of the technical process'.[114] All this had led

---

[106] E Forsthoff, *Der Staat der Industriegesellschaft. Dargestellt am Beispiel der Bundesrepublik Deutschland*, (München, CH Beck, 1971), 53.

[107] Above n 95.

[108] E Forsthoff, 'Daseinsvorsorge' at n 96 above, 25, 32; cf the analysis by V Neumann at n 90.

[109] Above n 9. On the origin of this term, cf W Pauly, 98, n 114.

[110] 'Daseinsvorsorge' at n 96, 26.

[111] E Forsthoff, 'Begriff und Wesen des sozialen Rechtsstaats', (1954) 12 *Veröffentlichungen der Vereinigung der Deutschen Staatsrechtslehrer*, 8–36, at 24, 29, 31.

[112] Above n 78.

[113] Above n 78, 120 ff.

[114] E Forsthoff, 'Technischer Prozess und politische Ordnung', (1969) 22 *Studium Generale*, 849–56, at 852; WE Scheuerman, 'Unsolved Paradoxes: Conservative Political Thought in Adenauer's Germany', in JP McCormick (ed), *Mass Democracy and Industrial Technology. Political and Social Theory from Nietzsche to Habermas*, (Durham/London, Duke UP, 2002), 221–44 at 228.

to the point where 'technical and proper decisions' could often be taken only in ever decreasing circles that possessed the necessary 'technical knowledge', while government and administration could no longer be controlled by the 'rule of law normative system'.[115] 'This is the situation that the politicians have not yet understood, and is beyond the horizon of contemporary legal thought that has shrunk down from *Staatsrechts*-science to *Rechtsstaats*-science operating inside its normative cage'.[116]

If such notions may have gone beyond the normative horizon of *Rechtsstaats*-science, Forsthoff was by no means alone here. We find similarly, for instance, in Helmut Schelsky:

> political norms and laws are replaced by the objective regularities of the scientific and technical civilization ... which cannot be taken as political decisions and are not comprehensible as philosophical or ideological norms.[117]

In the middle of the so-called technocracy debate, the 'technicity' tradition was markedly prevalent.[118]

The technocracy debate did not concern itself with Europe. Forsthoff saw very well that 'the technical process' had burst the bounds of the state and was not to be controlled domestically. It was, then, 'not wrong' to think about the development of an 'international organization', 'able to accompany the further course of the technical process as an effective guardian of humanity'.[119] Forsthoff did not reveal the source of these so unexpectedly sown hopes for humanity. He apparently took scarcely any account of the EEC; but the conceptual apparatus which he employed was, nonetheless, to become important in that new sphere.

The Heritage of the German Tradition in Europe

In *ordo*-liberalism and Forsthoff's theory of the industrial society, two concepts which promised to master the tensions between the democracy principle and the integration project were available. The *ordo*-liberal school saw this very early. The freedoms guaranteed in the EEC treaty, the order of the national economies, the bans on discrimination and the competition rules, were understood as a common decision for an economic constitution that went to meet the *ordo*-liberal concepts of the framework conditions for a market economy system (if only the many departures from that model were treated as mere

---

[115] Above n 106, 84, 105, 158 ff.

[116] *Ibid*. 46.

[117] H Schelsky, *Der Mensch in der wissenschaftlichen Zivilisation*, (Köln-Opladen, Westdeutscher Verlag, 1961) (reprinted in *idem*, *Auf der Suche nach Wirklichkeit. Gesammelte Aufsätze* (Düsseldorf, Diederichs, 1964), 439–80, at 453.

[118] For a famous contemporary critique, see J Habermas, 'Technik und Wissenschaft als "Ideologie"', in *idem*, *Technik und Wissenschaft als 'Ideologie'*, (Frankfurt a.M., Suhrkamp, 1968), 48–103.

[119] aAbove n 106, 169.

exceptions, and a blind eye could be turned to the original sin of agricultural policy). And the very fact that Europe had started its integrationist path as a mere economic community lent plausibility to *ordo*-liberal arguments: the Community acquired a legitimacy of its own by interpreting the economic-law provisions of the European Community as a law-based order committed to guaranteeing economic freedoms. This legitimacy was independent of the State's democratic constitutional institutions and thus placed limits upon the political powers of the Community.[120]

Yet, despite its orientation as an economic community, Europe fell within the disciplinary confines of public law. The concept of a supranational system of economic law that binds sovereign constitutional States was not exactly current in international law or *Staatsrecht* and constitutional law.[121] Nonetheless, someone as close to Carl Schmitt as Joseph H Kaiser was able to take up the *maître-penseur's* vague references to the triad of *Großraum* economy, technology and administration in order to categorise European public power in Forsthoff's sense as factually adequate and expedient, and entrust it to 'socially independent intelligence' [*einer sozial freischwebenden Intelligenz*].[122]

Similar statements can be found even earlier.[123] They were, however, deployed most fundamentally and systematically by Hans Peter Ipsen (first probably in 1964) in terming the (three) European communities 'purposive associations of functional integration' [*Zweckverbände funktionaler Integration*]. The concept 'purposive association' opened up Community law to tasks that had no place in an *ordo*-liberal world—without exposing it, on that account, to democratic requirements. As a purposive association, Europe was to deal with questions of 'technical realization', ie, with administrative tasks that could—and had to be—conveyed to a supranational bureaucracy.[124]

How thoroughly thought out the conception was can be seen in the very fact that Ipsen decisively differed from Forsthoff in his understanding of the Basic Law.[125] While wishing to root technocratic rationality in the EEC, at the same

---

[120] Significant, here, is A Müller-Armack, 'Die Wirtschaftsordnung des Gemeinsamen Marktes', in *idem, Wirtschaftsordnung und Wirtschaftspolitik*, (Freiburg, Rombach, 1966), 401–15; for a comprehensive account W Mussler, *Die Wirtschaftsverfassung der Europäischen Gemeinschaft im Wandel. Von Rom nach Masstricht* (Baden-Baden, Nomos, 1998), 94 ff, 113 ff.

[121] Cf Ch Joerges, 'Vorüberlegungen zu einer Theorie des Internationalen Wirtschaftsrechts', (1979) 43 *Rabels Zeitschrift für ausländisches und internationales Privatrecht*, 6–79, at 6 ff.

[122] JH Kaiser, 'Bewahrung und Veränderung demokratischer und rechtsstaatlicher Verfassungsstruktur in den internationalen Gemeinschaften', (1966) 23 *Veröffentlichungen der Vereinigung der Deutschen Staatsrechtslehrer*, 1–33, at 28 and 23.

[123] H Bülck, 'Zur Systematik der Europäischen Wirtschaftsgemeinschaften', (1959) 6 *Berichte der Deutschen Gesellschaft für Völkerrecht*, 66–118, at 105–7.

[124] HP Ipsen, *Europäisches Gemeinschaftsrecht* at n 92, 176 ff.

[125] Cf only HP Ipsen, *Über das Grundgesetz* (Hamburg 1950), reprinted in E Forsthoff (ed), *Rechtsstaatlichkeit und Sozialstaatlichkeit* (Darmstadt, Wissenschaftliche Buchgesellschaft, 1968), 16–41, on the one hand, E. Forsthoff, 'Begriff und Wesen des sozialen Rechtsstaats' at n 111, 9 f, 28, 32 on the other.

time, he wanted to restrict its sphere of action: the Communities were to confine themselves to administering questions of 'knowledge', but leave truly 'political' questions to democratic and legitimated bodies.[126] With his theory of the purposive association, Ipsen rejected both further-reaching federal integration notions and earlier interpretations of the community as a mere international organisation.[127] He saw Community law as a *tertium* between (federal) state law and international law, constituted by its 'objective tasks' and adequately legitimised by their solution.[128]

Concluding remarks

Ordo-liberalism and functionalism promised answers to the European legitimation dilemma which do without parliamentary democratic affirmation in the sense of the national constitutional state. Both conceptions had their *fundamentum in re*. They offered not just abstract legal doctrinal interpretations, but rationality criteria that could be institutionalised and applied in practice. Neither of these approaches needed to hide; on the contrary, in the total gamut of the contemporary debate, they represent exceptional achievements at least, because they faced the challenges inherent in the EEC's *Sonderweg* beyond international law and domestic legal systems. Both of them perceived and justified a new form of supranational governance that could not have been adequately legitimised by referring to the assent of the governments of the Member States alone even under the unanimity rule. Both positions have, also, to be sure, to see their limits. Here, the continuity with pre-democratic heritages of German legal culture is striking, but that, after all, is not very surprising. Ironically and fortunately, it is the successes of the European project that fundamentally challenge those traditions: Europe has developed in such a way that it needs a constitution that structures and legitimises its politics. If this constitution cannot copy those of nation state democracies, this does not mean it has to content itself with inherited alternatives.

---

[126] *Europäisches Gemeinschaftsrecht* at n 92, 1045.

[127] Ipsen's famous 'Bensheim lecture' (n 92 above) and *idem*, 'Der deutsche Jurist und das europäische Gemeinschaftsrecht', (1964) *Verhandlungen des 43. Deutschen Juristentages*, vol. 2, Part L, 3 ff. (München, CH Beck); *idem*, *Verfassungsperspektiven der Europäischen Gemeinschaften*, (Berlin, de Gruyter, 1970).

[128] HP Ipsen, *Verfassungsperspektiven* at 8 ff and the interpretation by M Kaufmann, *Europäische Integration und Demokratieprinzip*, (Baden-Baden, Nomos 1997), 300 ff, 312 ff; see, also, M Bach, *Die Bürokratisierung Europas. Verwaltungseliten, Experten und politische Legitimation in Europa*, (Frankfurt a.M., Campus, 1999), 38 ff.

10

FROM *GROßRAUM* TO CONDOMINIUM
A COMMENT

*Neil Walker**

I am not a theorist of National Socialism, still less an expert on the work of Carl Schmitt. What I share with Christian Joerges, however, is an interest in supranational governance in the modern EU—in its roots, in the best conceptualisation of its contemporary structure, and in its prospects. As Joerges makes clear in his subtle treatment of the inadequately explored yet deeply controversial question of Germany's contribution to the late twentieth century European legal imagination, and as I also endorse, these three themes are closely related. More specifically, the roots of the modern idea of European supranationalism, which are clearly to be found in a diverse range of cultural sources— German and otherwise—appear relevant to its present and future in two ways.

First, these roots are relevant in terms of historical causality, or to put it more technically, in terms of a diachronic sociology of knowledge and of the relationship between knowledge and power (or ideology). As Max Weber said, political ideas and related cultural sensibilities run in 'switchlines'[1] between generations, intersecting in complex patterns and often veering off in new directions. Joerges claims that two of the major formative influences of supranationalism—ordo-liberalism and what might loosely be called technocratic functionalism—have roots in the Germany of the 1920s and 1930s, and in the more general climate of Weimar and post-Weimar critique of the supposed limits and paradoxes of Parliamentary democracy and of classical liberalism in which Schmitt's was clearly a prominent voice. Yet as Joerges emphatically demonstrates, both of these traditions are deeply antithetical to National Socialist thought in general and to Schmitt's thought in particular, most tellingly in their rejection of its insistence on the primacy of the political, whether the shield against naked political power be the rule of law and individual rights—as in ordo-liberalism—or the prominence of bureaucratic and/or technocratic expertise, as in functionalism. Nevertheless, for reasons developed below, we can agree with Joerges that while the links between Schmittian thought and the pre-war German roots of the modern supranational

---

* Professor of Law, Department of Law, European University Institute, Florence.
[1] M Weber, *The Methodology of the Social Sciences* (Glencoe, Free Press, 1949).

idea are highly tenuous and complexly attenuated, these links remain important, albeit at a high level of abstraction.

As regards the other aspect, or 'second leg', of his thesis in historical sociology, namely the connection between the two streams of pre-war thought on the
one hand, and the condition of the renewed post-war German *Rechtstaat* under
the 1948 Basic Law, and the gradual flowering of the modern supranational idea
on the other, again Joerges's position is quite persuasive in general, although the
weight and decisiveness of the German influence remains an open question.
Certainly, Joerges is correct to reaffirm the importance of the ordo-liberal tradition, a factor often neglected in the Anglo-American literature.[2] The importance of the German contribution to the technocracy debate and the
development of functionalist thinking—and here Joerges stresses the importance of Forsthoff and Ipsen—is more questionable. From the outset the
Monnet-Schuman strategy, as laid down in the foundations of the European
Coal and Steel Community in the Treaty of Paris of 1951, displayed elements of
'functionalist' thinking as broadly conceived, particularly in its emphasis upon
an initially modest integration in areas of 'low politics' but key economic function, the creation of a High Authority staffed by a technocratic elite and relatively immune from national political pressures to oversee integration, the
subsequent accumulation of pressure to integrate in 'spillover' policy functions
in order better to achieve the initial functional goals, and the secular shift of
loyalty by key social interests towards the supranational level as the more significant site of political authority. In turn, this foundational architecture is
closely bound up with the development of a certain strain of academic thought
most fully developed in the Anglo-American world—famously in the neo-
functionalism of Haas[3] and Lindberg[4]—which for its part owes much to the
earlier 'simple' functionalism of Mitrany.[5] Of course, the received version of the
symbiosis of the intellectual movement of neo-functionalism and the practical

---

[2] Two recent examples of this neglect, in otherwise comprehensive treatments of the theoretical
background to the European Union are DN Chryssochou, *Theorizing European Integration*
(London, Sage, 2001) and B Rosamund, *Theories of European Integration* (Palgrave, Basingstoke,
2000). For an interesting exception in the legal literature, see D Chalmers, *The Single Market: From
Prima Donna to Journeyman* in J Shaw and G More (eds) *New Legal Dynamics of European Union*
(Oxford, Clarendon Press) 55–74.

[3] See in particular, EB Haas, *The Uniting of Europe. Political, Social and Economic Forces,
1950–57* (Stanford, Stanford University Press, 1958); *Beyond the Nation State: Functionalism and
International Organisation* (Stanford, Stanford University Press, 1964). Of course, Haas, too, has
an intimate connection with the German tradition, as a German Jew who emigrated to the United
States in 1938 aged fourteen. For interesting biographical information, including Haas's thoughts
on the influence of his early experience on his mature intellectual concerns, see H Kreisler, *Science
and Progress in International Relations: Conversation with Ernst B Haas* (University of California
at Berkeley, 2000), http://globetrotter.berkeley.edu/people/Haas/haas-con0.html

[4] See in particular, LN Lindberg, *The Political Dynamics of European Economic Integration*
(Stanford, Stanford University Press, 1963).

[5] See eg D Mitraney, *The Functional Theory of Politics* (London, Martin Robertson, 1975).

development of the Community method tends towards oversimplification, and again Joerges performs a useful corrective in pointing to the importance of the German influence; yet that influence itself remains but one strand of uncertain significance in a more complex narrative.

The second way in which the roots of the European supranational idea may be relevant to its present and future form, and the one that I concentrate upon in the remainder of this comment, is in the realm of the history of ideas. Here we are concerned with the influence of history not as the flow of causal forces but as a series of templates to be drawn upon, adapted or avoided—as a series of utopias, suggestive frameworks or dystopias—when making judgements about the present and choices about the future. To add to the complexity of influence, and also reinforcing the significance of the past as a reservoir of ideas for the present, the diachronic sociology of knowledge and power on the one hand and the history of ideas on the other are closely related. There are two aspects to this relationship. In the first place, powerful actors may appropriate historical ideas and this process itself becomes part and parcel of the sociology of knowledge. This is particularly true in the age of what writers such as Anthony Giddens and Ulrich Beck call 'reflexive modernisation'[6]—in a 'post-traditional' world in which choices, including the grand choices associated with polity formation, political mandate and institutional design, are no longer so closely affected by the restrictions of local knowledge, immemorial practice or even strong ideology.[7] In the second place, and most pertinently for present purposes, the reflexive appropriation of ideas and of the historical experience associated with the implementation of these ideas is more relevant between, and so more likely to take place across periods and contexts which have certain features in common. That is to say, where the objective social, economic and political conditions which obtain in one setting display certain similarities to those which obtain in another, the puzzle-solutions proffered in the earlier setting assume a closer significance to those concerned with the later setting. This, I believe, is the main justification for the project in which Joerges is engaged, and, indeed, provides the main thrust of his essay. In the spirit of this understanding, in what follows I make a modest attempt to build on some of the foundations laid by Joerges.

Within the context of the history of twentieth century European political thought and its increasingly influential place in the *praxis* of the present, Schmitt's idea of the *Grossraum* takes its place as a relevant dystopia for the European Union. Its dystopian qualities are self-evident, its relevance perhaps

---

[6] See eg U Beck, A Giddens and S Lash, *Reflexive Modernization* (Cambridge, Polity, 1994).

[7] So, for example, one of the striking characteristics of the so-called Third Way which has recently become fashionable in European centre-left politics, particularly though the influence of Tony Blair and New Labour in the UK, is its self-conscious and self-proclaimed distance from received ideological categories, and the way in which it makes a virtue of its pragmatism and eclecticism. For a schematic overview, see A Giddens, *The Third Way and its Critics* (Cambridge, Polity, 2000).

requires more careful elaboration than it sometime receives. One of the major services of Joerges's paper is that it indicates two strands of objective continuity between the *Grossraum* and the EU which were hardly appreciated previously. For Joerges, the area of objective continuity and common *problematique* lies not only in the reconceptualisation of international law required by the *Grossraum*/EU, but also, and relatedly, in the search for a new type of internal governance structures of the *Grossraum*/EU. The two themes—the external and internal dimensions—are closely related.

First, then, let is consider the status of international law in both designs. Schmitt's *Grossraum* pays lip-service to the continuation of the normal discourse of international law within the *Grossraum* zone (albeit, with the onset of war, with increasing ambivalence as both the *subjective* situation of Schmitt, the archetypal 'situational thinker' and the *objective* situation which he sought to dignify in legal terms deteriorated)[8] just as international law may still be stretched (although with ever-decreasing returns) to make sense of the EU.[9] In both cases, the idea that the nature of the relevant legal space is adequately conceptualised in terms of international relations and international law, as merely the external legal relations between formally equal states, is deficient. Of course the reasons for this deficiency are radically different. In the case of the *Grossraum*, the structure in question is a particularly—perhaps uniquely— egregious example of the type of imperialism which has so often exposed the selective logic of the Westphalian conception of the international order of states which has dominated in the modern age. The Westphalian order, and the understandings of international relations and international law which accompanied it, was supposedly premised upon a *societas* of mutually tolerant independent states rather than, as in the pre-Westphalian phase, the imposition (however imperfectly and contingently) of a *universitas*—a form of rule in accordance with a universal or transcendental imperative which did not recognise or respect territorial boundaries.[10] The Westphalian order was always an instructive example of European double standards, as the logic of the *universitas*, although increasingly redundant in the European context, was remorselessly exported in the name of the imperial powers to the territories of their overseas empires. In that 'age of extremes, the short twentieth Century'[11] we witness a chilling homecoming of the *universitas*—in both fascist and communist manifestations—in two major territorial blocs of the European continent.

---

[8] See Joerges, present volume.

[9] On the limits of the international law paradigm as a way of making sense of supranationalism, see eg N Walker, *Flexibility in a Metaconstitutional Frame: Reflections on the Future of Legal Authority in the EU* in G de Búrca and J Scott (eds) *Constitutional Change in the EU: From Uniformity to Flexibility?* (Oxford, Hart, 2000).

[10] See. R Jackson, 'Introduction: Sovereignty at the Millennium' (1999) 47 *Political Studies*, 423.

[11] See E Hobsbawm, *The Age of Extremes: The Short Twentieth Century. 1914–91* (London, Michael Joseph, 1994).

If the *Grossraum* exposed the fragility of the Westphalian order, and the absence of effective alternative principles of international governance in the event of its transgression, the EU involves, if not the systematic transcendence of the Westphalian order, then at least the beginning of a new relational pattern which does not pivot exclusively on the state. Instead, what we have in place of the one-dimensional order of states is a new multi-dimensional or pluralist order[12]—a Condominium[13] to continue with the disarmingly homely building metaphor—in which state legal orders overlap with, co-operate with and compete with other levels of legal order—in particular the supranational order of the EU—in a shifting, uneven and continuously negotiated relationship based upon a fragile demarcation of functional competences.

In both cases—*Grossraum* and the EU—our understanding of sovereign equality, non-interference, reciprocity and the whole conceptual armoury of international law is challenged. In the first case, this is announced by the stark asymmetry of power within the *Grossraum*, by the stripping of effective autonomy of non-German states and peoples within the zone of influence and their deference to the overriding sovereignty of Germany in accordance with the *Fuhrung* principle. In the second case, international law is challenged by the overlap, intersection and competition of sovereign claims within the EU legal space. In other words, international law is confounded in the first case by the *deficiency* of sovereignty within the system, and in the second case by its *surfeit*.

Furthermore, because international law is concerned with external rather than internal relations, and because in both systems of 'multi-level governance'—*Grossraum* and EU—the previously 'external' *becomes* 'internal' to the new transnational order—international law cannot provide answers to the new questions of governance which arise within these orders. That is to say, in both cases, international law simply has too little to contribute. In the *Grossraum* case, in the absence of an effective system of enforcement of international law in general and of its principle of recognition in particular, the entire regime is reduced by default to the single imperative of German authority. In the EU, international law, given its indifference to anything other than inter-*national* relations and the norms which govern these, begs all the difficult

---

[12] See eg N Walker, 'The Idea of Constitutional Pluralism,' *Modern Law Review* (2002, forthcoming).

[13] Historically, the idea of Condominium, at least in the English language, has been used to describe circumstances of joint sovereignty, where two sovereign states share authority over a third territory. As to the use of the term in the present paper, however, Philippe Schmitter's characterisation of condominium, or *condominio*, as the sharing of sovereign authority between EU and member states in a multi-level governance entity marked by an advanced framework of flexible or differentiated integration, with different territorial pooling of authority for different functions, is a more apposite model. See PC Schmitter, *Imagining the Future of the Euro-Polity with the Help of New Concepts* in G Marks, F Scharpf, PC Schmitter and W Streeck (eds) *Governance in the European Union* (London, Sage, 1996).

question as to the terms on which and the mechanisms through which state and EU, and indeed other overlapping non-state polities or putative polities,[14] should be mutually accommodated.

Yet, as Joerges crucially shows, for all the inadequacy of international law to the task, and for all the differences in the reasons for this, the objective problems of internal governance which confront both regimes display certain similarities. As he says,

> the problems of the order of the economy, of the exposure of society to technological problems and necessities, and of the difficulty of ensuring the political and social accountability of the administration did not resolve themselves with the disappearance of National Socialism.[15]

The problems in question may be paraphrased as follows. First, as regards the economy, how to ensure the *relative* insulation of an increasingly complex transnational economy from protectionist or otherwise market-jeopardising interventionist political forces? Secondly, as regards technology, how to ensure that the increasing range of questions of modern governance which require technical knowledge in areas such as environmental impact, product safety standards and public health are treated with the requisite expertise while preserving the scope for open political contestation over those associated normative choices which are not reducible to merely technical considerations? Thirdly, as regards administration, how to ensure fairness, consistency and calculability of administration in an era of increasingly 'big government' without succumbing to the pathologies of bureaucracy's 'iron cage'[16]—where legality descends into mere legalism[17] and public administration becomes insensitive to differing social needs and unsusceptible to supervision, guidance or transformation in accordance with a legitimate normative vision.

These problems are of course staples of modern politics and are not peculiar to systems of multi-level governance. Yet in its recognition that the complexities and potential of transnational economic circuits and the boundary-transgressing ramifications of new technological processes may be usefully addressed through political mechanisms other than the state, multi-level governance can be seen both as a particular response, or at least as a reaction to the problems in question, and also as a setting in which these problems, through bring reconfigured, are as likely to be exacerbated as resolved. The explanation for such a perverse possibility is not hard to seek, for the various problems speak to the significance and delicate balance of a plurality of values

---

[14] Such as the World Trade Organisation or the Council of Europe.

[15] Joerges, present volume.

[16] In Weber's famous metaphor. See M Weber, *The Theory of Social and Economic Organisation* (Glencoe, Free Press, 1947).

[17] For a recent discussion of this distinction, see Z Bankowski, *Living Lawfully: Love in Law and Law in Love* (Dordrecht, Kluwer, 2001) esp. ch 3.

which are in tension with one another, and where often the prioritisation of one value may be to the unhealthy detriment of others. So the relentless Nazi emphasis on the primacy of the political, and Schmitt's apologia for this strategy,[18] seek to exorcise the demons of soulless technocracy and rudderless bureaucracy, but do so at the expense not only of the virtues of independent expertise and unbiased and non-arbitrary administration but also of any conception of the political sphere itself as democratically pluralist and so 'weak' rather than authoritarian and ideologically 'strong'. In the context of the European Union both ordo-liberalism and functionalism stand in stark contrast to fascist doctrine in terms both of the moral defensibility of their intentions and their explicit *defence* of economic and technical rationality patterns in an economic constitution protected from the vicissitudes of politics, whether quotidian or millenarian. Yet, as Joerges indicates in his essay, and as he elaborates elsewhere,[19] these approaches may err too much in the other direction and create an opposite imbalance, even if profoundly less dangerous in consequence. For, as the European Union, through an increasingly deep-rooted and wide-ranging process of positive integration, is transformed from a mere 'internal market into a polity',[20] the relationship between the economic, the technocratic and the political logics which inform decision-making and regulation within the Union increasingly defy any simple demarcation into different compartments, while the traditional indirect, state-centred democratic legitimation of the expanding Union mandate looks ever more threadbare.

How then, armed with this general understanding of the objective conditions of governance of the contemporary multi-level polity, do we begin to appreciate the nature of institutional pathology and fashion optimal institutional solutions? How, if at all, do we avoid, or at least minimise tragic choices between competing governance values? Joerges himself has made a significant contribution in this area. In particular his views on the ever-expanding EU committee system as an arena for the deliberative reconciliation of technical, administrative and normative dimensions in a hybrid structure which includes different national, supranational and otherwise aligned voices, are well-known and influential.[21] This is not the place to add to the considerable literature which that thesis has generated, but rather to take a step back and try, in the light of the contrasting experiences of Nazi Germany and contemporary Europe, to deepen our appreciation of just what is at stake in the governance debate.

---

[18] Even though, as Joerges points out, there was much in Schmitt's pre-*Grossraum* writings which could have been drawn upon to mitigate this emphasis.

[19] See, most recently, '"Good Governance" in the European Internal market: An Essay in Honour of Claus-Dieter Ehlermann,' EUI Working Papers, RSC No. 2001/29.

[20] *Ibid.* 40

[21] See eg C Joerges and J Neyer, 'From Intergovernmental Bargaining to Deliberative Political Processes', (1997) 3 *European Law Journal* 273.

For behind the governance values that Joerges astutely identifies and places in mutual tension lie other even more fundamental political values and an even more fundamental set of objective tensions concerning the reconciliation of these values. This point has been well made by the social theorist Ralf Dahrendorf in recent work.[22] For him, the great problem of modern political thought in Europe and elsewhere is the reconciliation of the three virtues of economic well-being, social cohesion and political freedom. Affluence, community and (personal and political) liberty, in other words, are the often inarticulate major premises on which we base our political visions. From Dahrendorf there is the melancholy message that the twentieth Century has witnessed the gradual disconnection of these three *eigen*values. This uncoupling may be precipitated knowingly and in bad faith, as in Nazi Germany, where political freedom, and, if less blatantly, the conditions of economic affluence were sacrificed to the imperative of 'community', defined in unforgivingly 'thick,' authoritarian and exclusionary terms.

But even good faith architects, including the many who see the European Union as a community of value rather than simply a site for the exploitation of parochial interests, find it increasingly difficult to fashion a satisfactory reconciliation of the values in question. Partly this is a question of tensions *within* each of the values, and also the absence or elusiveness of conditions for the flourishing of these values. So economic affluence must be coupled with a politics of redistribution if that affluence is to be equitably shared, a task made harder by the increasing modesty of pooled resources in an eastward-enlarging Union. Equally, discussion of the value of community in modern Europe often seems caught between the rock of myopic ethnic or cultural nationalism, and the hard place of social fragmentation and the attenuation or dissolution of all solidary bonds. How, then, to forge a wider, supranational community of attachment in which risks and resources are willingly shared? Finally, while personal freedom, as intimated by the growing—if uneven and always fragile[23]— attachment to individual rights in the legal and political discourse of the EU, may be one of its more conspicuous successes, meaningful political freedom in the sense of effective participation in and account-holding of the complex mosaic of institutions which make up its multi-level governance system, has proven much more elusive.

The problems are compounded if we look at the relationship between the core values. Without effective political freedom and voice it is difficult to generate a meaningful sense of political community on a transnational scale, yet in the proverbial chicken-and-egg of contemporary European constitutional

---

[22] R Dahrendorf, 'A Precarious Balance: Economic Opportunity, Civil Society and Political Liberty' (1995) 5(3) *The Responsive Community,* 13.

[23] As the new emphasis upon security at the expense of rights of liberty, due process and privacy in some of the post-September 11th policy proposals of the EU indicate. For an early overview, see *Statewatch* vol.11 No.6 November–December 2001.

politics, the converse also threatens to hold.[24] Similar conundrums apply as regards the relationship of these values of community and effective political freedom to the dimension of economic value.[25] So without a politically responsive community of attachment, it is difficult to carve out a legitimate space for a technically-informed politics of risk allocation, or to guarantee broad allegiance to the rigours of a single market which, after all, produces many short-term losers. Yet, conversely, without the requisite conformity to a common regulatory framework which can produce real economic gains, it is likewise difficult to generate support for a transnational level of governance with the wherewithal and regulatory power to undertake its own community-reinforcing politics of redistribution and risk-allocation.

This is only the most superficial rendition of the problems associated with the articulation and reconciliation of the core political values in the contemporary European Union. Yet it provides, in however skeletal a form, a deep structure which alerts us to what is fundamentally at stake in the reconciliation of the governance values addressed in Joerges's triumvirate of economy, technology and administration. Obviously, it is a complex and lengthy task, and one well beyond the confines of this short comment, to investigate contemporary European governance values and their institutional implications in the round in the light of these core values. Instead, by way of conclusion, I will make three modest points of more immediate relevance to the concerns which animate Joerges's essay.

In the first place, identification of the core values which underpin the complex of governance values allows us better to appreciate the pathology of the Nazi solution, and even something of its warped attraction. At the level of core values, the subordination of economy, technology and administration to the primacy of the political is reflected in an equally uncompromising preoccupation with an exclusionary conception of social cohesion propagated at the expense of the other core values. Yet just as it is misguided to emphasise some governance values at the expense of others, so at the more basic level it is dangerous, and in this extreme cases disastrous, to emphasise one core value at the expense of the others. Not only does this lead to the neglect of values which must figure in any defensible ethic of political organisation, but it also encourages—or reflects—the corruption of the very value which is accorded priority. The idea of balance between core values, then, as indeed between governance values, is not just an unavoidable incident of the diverse plurality of values necessarily accommodated and articulated in any defensible polity and in the

[24] Of course, there are many constructivist perspectives which deny the second premise and assert the plausibility of building strong political institutions without strong pre-existing cultural bonds. See eg J Habermas, 'So Why do We Need a European Constitution?' Robert Schuman Centre Working Paper, 2001.

[25] For a magisterial treatment of these issues, see F Scharpf, *Governing in Europe: Effective and Democratic?* (Oxford, OUP, 1999).

institutions of that polity, but is also a necessary corrective to the excesses immanent in any particular core value. In other words, the solution which allows unconditional precedence to one value is culpable not only in its sacrifice of other values, but offers false gold even in its own distortedly simplified terms—fashioning a mere parody of the value it claims to celebrate.

Secondly, if we leave behind the extreme case, even in the very different scenario of the European Union it is worth reminding ourselves of the necessity to resist the temptation to focus too closely on one or more core values, and on the institutional implications of the pursuit of these values, to the neglect of others. Even the very best work on the legal and political theory of European Union—indeed perhaps *especially* the best work—has a tendency to bracket some of the core values at the expense of others, whether the emphasis is on political freedom and the democratic deficit, or on the meaning and mutual articulation of national and supranational identity, or on the regulatory structure necessary to achieve an effective internal market without neglecting the importance of retaining a problem-solving capacity which can fairly distribute the risks and resources associated with an affluent economy.[26] Yet however understandable this selectiveness is, the complex political puzzle which lies at the core of the European Union, as of any multi-level polity, means that in the final analysis *all* the relevant values must be held equally in focus.

Finally, to return to questions of governance, the institutional implications of the balancing of core values are themselves deeply complex. In the last analysis, the overall institutional architecture of the Union can only usefully be approached and evaluated as an integrated system of mechanisms for achieving an optimal balancing of the core values of political organisation. Particular institutional forms and levels cannot be regarded in isolation, and not just because, as a trite truth of institutional design, the shape and operation of one institution will always 'have consequences' for others in the same overall framework. More profoundly, each institution must address from a particular simple or compound constituency perspective—regional, national, Union, functional group, expert—and in a particular simple or compound governance modality—legislative, executive, administrative, judicial executive—the same complex puzzle involving the balance of core values, while also always bearing in mind the need to complement the contribution of each of the other differently constituted and tasked institutions. Institutional design, then, and the theorisation of governance which informs such design is essentially a derivative exercise, always at the service of the core values and, notwithstanding the broad

---

[26] To take but two examples, Scharpf's work (see eg *ibid*) is a powerful analysis of the economic and political dimension of the problems of European integration, but places less emphasis on the cultural or community dimension, while Joseph Weiler's work (see, in particular, *The Constitution of Europe* (Cambridge, CUP, 1999)) is a seminal treatment of the cultural or community dimension and related problems of political freedom and accountability, but with less emphasis on the economic dimension.

similarity of objective conditions between different periods alluded to earlier, always sensitive to the changing detail of material and cultural conditions which influence the articulation and optimal balance of these core values. Joerges is correct, then—and correct as a matter of general principle and not just on account of the particular failings or redundancy of ordo-liberalism or technocratic functionalism—to conclude that contemporary Europe cannot content itself in the choice of governance tools with 'inherited alternatives.'[27] The lessons of experience and of political theory are that that there is no timeless key to good governance, nor even any 'master institutions'[28] or defining mechanisms[29] within a particular governance complex. Rather, good governance depends first and foremost upon a critical reflexivity—upon a healthy awareness of the contingent and provisional quality of its multi-faceted and intricately interdependent solutions to the unending puzzle of the balance of the core values of political organisation.

[27] Joerges, present volume.

[28] Joerges, n 19, at 46, discussing the role of Comitology. To be fair, here Joerges is at best ambivalent about the attribution of such an exalted status to Comitology within the Union's institutional architecture.

[29] So in the context of the present debate about institutional reform in the Union, we should be wary of claims which invest too much in any one mechanism of reform, whether it be the new Charter of Fundamental Rights, the post-Nice process of 'constitutional' deliberation and innovation, or the Commission's recent 'good governance' initiative. For fuller discussion, see N Walker, *The White Paper in Constitutional Context* in C Joerges, Y Meny and J Weiler (eds) *Responses to the Commission White Paper* (Florence, Robert Schuman Centre, 2002).

11

FORMALISM AND ANTI-FORMALISM IN FRENCH AND GERMAN JUDICIAL METHODOLOGY

*Vivian Grosswald Curran**

The French and German judicial systems traditionally have had significant differences in their methodological approaches, despite being civil-law systems with numerous fundamental similarities. French private law courts have tended to adhere to a tradition of formalism in their interpretive processes, while German courts have enjoyed considerably more interpretive freedoms. In the ongoing debate about whether judicial formalism or positivism was responsible for the injustice meted out by the courts of France and Germany during their fascist periods, it is my position that, *grosso modo,* the judicial injustice in the two countries was comparable, despite the differences in their respective traditional national judicial methodologies, and despite the fact that both countries' judiciaries during their fascist eras continued their nation's traditional methodological approaches. I conclude that judicial methodological approach correlated weakly with substantive outcome in France and Germany during the fascist period.

Although in my opinion the post-fascist tendency to attribute responsibility for judicial injustice to positivism was erroneous, nevertheless the post-war analytical focus on methodology's implication in substantive judicial outcome in and of itself was justified and important in terms of recognising the dynamic of indissociable mutual influence that ties methodology to substance in law. Nothing in these pages should be interpreted as implying that the two are conceptually separable. Indeed, decontextualising judicial methodology as though it were not part of the fabric of substantive law, and vice versa, would be a highly misleading point of departure for legal analysis.[1]

* Professor of Law, University of Pittsburgh. My thanks to the participants of the conference on *Perceptions of Europe and Perspectives on a European Order in Legal Scholarship During the Era of Fascism and National Socialism,* European University Institute, September, 2000, for their helpful comments on my oral presentation of many of the ideas expressed here. A longer version of this essay has been published under the title 'Fear of Formalism: Indications from the Fascist Period in France and Germany of Judicial Methodology's Impact on Substantive Law' in 35 *Cornell International Law Journal* 101 (Nov. 2001–Feb. 2002). Except as otherwise noted, translations are mine.

[1] My sense is that Habermas' analysis suffers from decontextualising procedure from substance in *Between Facts and Norms*, inasmuch as his belief in the potential of procedure as the solution

Moreover, while I conclude that judicial positivism or formalism was not a significant culprit for the courts' injustice during French or German fascism (for different reasons with respect to each of those countries), I do believe that positivism, in conjunction with more fundamental overriding causes, played, and continues to play, some role in encouraging substantive outcomes that comply with the texts of enacted law. Similarly, I believe that, in conjunction with more fundamental overriding causes of compliance with fascist-era laws, the mere fact that there were such laws was a contributing, although not primordial, factor in popular obedience to the laws.

The view that judicial positivism is not correlated strongly in a causal paradigm with the judicial propensity to countenance and implement unjust enacted laws, which I argue here, has been described as nihilistic by more than one legal scholar.[2] I hope it is not too petty to quibble over a single word, but I do not agree that the view expressed in these pages properly can be called 'nihilistic.' I prefer to think of it not only as primarily realistic in nature, but as realistic with the constructive purpose of seeking to understand the actual, rather than the desirable, state of affairs, with an ultimate view to determining if there may be ways, even if other than through the reform of judicial methodology, to increase the likelihood that judges in times of political and social crises will resist the temptation of abandoning constitutional, democratic principles and values.

To the extent that our purpose is to focus on the past for the sake of Europe's developing legal order, the question of formalism's role, and, more largely, of judicial methodology's relation to substantive outcome and to justice, is of continuing and crucial importance. The accusation of nihilism leveled at my perspective springs from the correct understanding by its critics that, if judicial methodology is not much related to substantive outcome, and was not responsible for the rabid injustice of courts from 1933 to 1945 in Germany, and from 1940 to 1944 in France, then the project of repairing or remedying judicial methodology also cannot be held out as a repository of hope for ensuring safety in the future, for ensuring the rendering of predictable and reliable judicial justice even in times of political crisis.

There is reason nonetheless to hope that the lessons of fascism may be instructive for the European Union's developing legal order. An examination of the evidence leads one to conclude that Europe's focus might better be diverted from judicial methodology, that a shift in the terrain of the debate may be more productive. In my opinion, that 'elsewhere' is the battleground between pluralism

---

to heterogeneity of substantive values suggests an insufficient accounting of the inevitably profound intermeshing of procedure and substance. I discuss this issue at greater length in VG Curran, 'Romantic Common Law, Enlightened Civil Law: Legal Uniformity and the Homogenisation of the European Union', (2001) 7 *Columbia Journal of European Law* 63.

[2] Among them David Dyzenhaus in his book, *Legality and Legitimacy: Carl Schmitt, Hans Kelsen, and Hermann Heller in Weimar* (Oxford, Clarendon, 1997), 1–17.

and unicity; between diversity and uniformity; between the complications and inefficiencies of multivocality on many levels, and an encroaching monolinguism, temptingly sanitary, but levelling, and potentially repressive and suppressive. I hope to be able to justify this suggestion for displacing the area of future study through my focus on formalism and anti-formalism.

Indeed, it may be that one can best see why it is the question of pluralism that lies at the heart of the real challenges to the future of the European legal order by seeing first why it is *not* the issue of formalism that is the crux of the problem. The question of formalism versus anti-formalism thus in one sense may be the wrong question to ask, but, in another sense, the right place to start, because addressing it may be the most illuminating way of obtaining direction as to how to reorient the analytical focus in order to increase its constructive potential.

This is especially so because the judicial orders in both France and Germany during their respective periods of fascism were orders permeated by unicity, by univocality, features that also challenge contemporary Europe's future development. It is not as though the formalism or anti-formalism of the French and German judiciaries during the fascist period existed in isolation from other aspects of the judicial context. They existed as relatively uninfluential elements substantively in terms of fascistic results within societies that rejected multiplicity and difference, and whose rejection of multiplicity and difference permeated all of their institutions, extending into the entrails of their judicial systems.

When one leaves the terrain of methodology to step into that of pluralism, however, one vastly increases the inchoate nature of the elements to be analysed, and indeed enters into that most inchoate of worlds which is the world of values. In the final analysis, the value of pluralism, and, more specifically, the value of *value pluralism*, the concept Isaiah Berlin advanced throughout his life's work as essential to liberal societies, provides the best hope for a continuous rejection of the quintessentially fascistic value of oneness, of the willed erasure of difference, multiplicity and otherness.[3] Much that is built into the institutional structures of the European Union militates against multiplicity, such that retaining value pluralism may be a challenge that will grow, rather than diminish, as time passes. On the other hand, pluralism in and of itself is not a panacea, and may result in strident conflict rather than in inclusiveness. Just as where methodology is at issue, one needs to be careful in considering unicity versus multiplicity to avoid a blanket condemnation of unicity because of its historical association with fascism.

Substantive values inevitably fluctuate with changing circumstances over time, and there can be no assured future to the values that future courts as

---

[3] See A Sen, *Development as Freedom* (New York, Knopf, 1999), 65, as to how the 'liberties of different people [within a society] are interlinked'; and *id*. at 77 on the disadvantages of homogeneity in values. *Accord*, M Horkheimer & T W Adorno, *Dialectic of Enlightenment*, trans. John Cumming (New York, Conitinuum, 1997) (originally *Dialektik der Aufklärung*, 1944).

institutions, or future judges as individuals, will hold and implement. As the American constitutional law scholar, JM Balkin, has shown so well, and captured so effectively with his coining of the term 'ideological drift,' even values which appear to be frozen into an immutable format on the surface evolve and change in political, social and economic valence with the passage of time and with the development of society, such that surface, rhetorical identity in court decisions, legislation and other legal texts, masks inexorable shifts in underlying concepts as times change.[4] One might think in this context of the considerable irony that the French Civil Code, that hallmark of Republican democracy, was enacted as part of a highly authoritarian régime, by an authoritarian leader who, in the words of Jean Carbonnier, considered the code a means of continuing war.[5]

The dilemma of trying to ensure for the future the values of the past was conveyed as follows by Ernst Cassirer, writing in *The Myth of the State*, published in 1946, after having experienced personally the political vicissitudes of states that had hounded him from his native Germany to Sweden, and finally to the United States. In a passage in which he reflected on Plato's political thought, he wrote that

> [t]he self-preservation of the state cannot be secured by its material prosperity nor can it be guaranteed by the maintenance of certain constitutional laws. Written constitutions or charters have no real binding force, if they are not the expression of a constitution that is written in the citizens' minds. Without this moral support the very strength of a state becomes its inherent danger.[6]

---

[4] See JM Balkin, 'The Footnote', (1989) 83 *North Western University Law Review* 275; and JM Balkin, 'Ideological Drift and the Struggle Over Meaning in Legal and Political Theory', (1993) 25 *Conn. Law Review* 869. *Accord*, J Rawls, *Political Liberalism* (New York, Columbia Univ. Press, 1993); and J Habermas, *Between Facts and Norms: Contributions to a Discourse Theory of Law and Democracy* trans. William Rehg, (Cambridge, MIT, 1996) , see n 1.

[5] J Carbonnier, *le Code civil,* in Nora, *Les Lieux de mèmoire* (Paris, Gallimard, 1977), 1331,1335 ('*une continuation de la guerre par d'autres moyens*').

[6] E Cassirer, *The Myth of the State* (New Haven, Yale University Press, 1946), 76. Cf A Sen, n 3 at 9, 'The exercise of freedom is mediated by values, but the values in turn are influenced by public discussions and social interactions . . .' See also *id.* at 31, 'individual conceptions of justice and propriety . . . depend on social associations—particularly on the interactive formation of public perceptions and on collaborative comprehension of problems and remedies'; N MacCormick, *Questioning Sovereignty: Law, State, and Nation in the European Commonwealth* (Oxford, Oxford University Press, 1999), 114, 'it is both true that the laws make the institutions, and yet also true that the institutions make the laws . . .'; and G Del Vecchio, 'Les bases du droit comparé et les principes généraux du droit', (1960) 12 *Revue internationale de droit comparé*, 493, 495, '*Tous les phénomènes de la vie sociale sont complexes entre eux; et l'on ne peut comprendre pleinement un système juridique dans sa réalité historique qu'en se référant aux conditions de vie du peuple chez lequel il est né. Si ces conditions changent, le droit lui aussi doit être modifié*'.

France

One of the difficulties of examining the extent to which a judiciary's method-ology or philosophy is positivistic is the extreme difficulty of defining the term.[7] On one level, the French private law judicial tradition has been highly positivistic from the time of the Revolution inasmuch as the French judiciary has been the most averse among the western constitutional democracies to any overt challenging of the legislative text or to pronouncements that might be interpreted as judicial law-creation. The legal requirement that it refrain from law creation continues today to be explicit in Article 5 of the *Code civil: 'Il est défendu aux juges de prononcer par voie de disposition générale et réglemen-taire sur les causes qui leur sont soumises.'* On the other hand, French judges also have tended to indulge in unacknowledged creativity by questionable selec-tions of the enacted law allegedly applicable to the pending case. As Professors Ghestin and Goubeaux put it in their *Traité de droit civil*, French judges create law, but they do so under the cover of interpretation (*'sous le couvert de l'interprétation de la loi'*).[8]

A challenge to the very concept of positivism and formalism during the fascist periods in both France and Germany, moreover, arises from the coexis-tence of mutually contradictory enacted laws. Both Germany and France experienced the enactment of a very large number of laws during their fascist eras that coexisted with a virtually untouched amalgam of enactments from before Hitler's rise to power in Germany and Pétain's in France.[9] Which laws, then, were the ones whose strict judicial application would justify a condemna-tion of positivism? In Germany, for instance, why were not the ever-valid pre-fascist laws prohibiting murder and requiring that assistance be given to a target for murder by anyone possessing the knowledge of premeditated murder, not

---

[7] For related difficulties that I do not analyse, including that of 'competing versions of legal positivism,' see SL Paulson, 'Lon L. Fuller, Gustav Radbruch, and the 'Positivist' Theses', (1994) 13 *Law & Philosophy* 313.

[8] J Ghestin & G Goubeaux, *Traité de droit civil: Introduction générale*, (Paris, Librairie générale de droit et de jurisprudence, 1977), 318. Ghestin and Goubeaux illustrate how the French courts create law while maintaining an appearance of merely applying it, as where they take a rule of proof and interpret it as one of substance. See *id.* at 322–23; and *id.* at 326 (in principle, no case rule may have a *'portée générale,'* ie, be generalised into a new norm to be applied in the future, but in prac-tice judicially-created rules are generalised). See also J Boulanger, *Principes généraux du droit et droit positif* in *Le droit français au milieu du Xxe siècle: études offertes à Georges Ripert* (vol.1), (Paris, Librairie générale de droit et de jurisprudence,1951), 68. France's courts are known to inter-pret enacted law as meaning something completely different from what the legislator intended. See also *id.* at 63 (decrying the problem of the 'false principle' [*'le faux principe'*], in which the French exegetical school fabricated principles they alleged to find in the Civil code, but which the Code did not contain). *Accord*, JH Merryman, 'The French Deviation', (1966) 44 *American Journal of Comparative Law* 109.

[9] With respect to this issue solely in Germany, see M Zimmermann, *Foreword*, vii–xiii, in M Stolleis, *The Law Under the Swastika: Studies on Legal History in Nazi Germany* (Chicago, University of Chicago Press, 1998).

evoked? Bishop von Galen of Münster, for one, did raise them with the authorities, and recounted the futility of his efforts to do so in his sermon of 3 August
1941.[10] Indeed, after the war, the courts struggled with whether defendants
should be convicted for having denounced fellow citizens, in indisputable compliance with Nazi-enacted law, but also in clear contravention of law from the
pre-Nazi era that had remained in effect at all relevant times. Both Radbruch
and Hart discuss such cases.[11]

In France, the rights to private property had been sacrosanct at least since the
1804 enactment of the *Code civil*, and, as has been documented persuasively,
that concept was not newly endorsed even in 1804, but had been codified by the
republican state, which took much for its new code that, like private property
rights, had deep roots in pre-revolutionary French legal thought.[12] Why then
were not the long-established property rights of French citizens effective to
protect the property ownership of French citizens from 1940 to 1944?[13]

Vichy legislation was couched in reassuringly familiar legal rhetoric,
designed for somnolescence, not awakening.[14] Hannah Arendt explored the
importance of used, familiar, clichéd language in connection with Eichmann's
testimony during his Jerusalem trial with respect to his role in effectuating the

---

[10] For my English translation of relevant portions of his sermon, see VG Curran, 'The
Legalization of Racism in a Constitutional State: Democracy's Suicide in Vichy France', (1998) 50
Hastings Law Journal, 1, 37. A more extensive French translation of von Galen's sermon was pub-
lished in 'Documents', in 160 *Revue d'histoire de la shoah*, 64–5. Bishop von Galen was referring to
Articles 211 and 139 of the German Criminal Code, the full texts of which appear in *id*. But see B
Mendelsohn, 'Les infractions commises sous le régime nazi sont-elles des 'crimes' au sens du droit
commun?', (1996) 43 *Revue de droit internationale des sciences diplomatiques et politiques* 333,
emphasising that, except for murder and assassination, national law before the end of the Second
World War *failed* to criminalise what later would be classified under the rubric of crimes against
humanity, such as deportation and human servitude.

[11] See *Positivism and the Separation of Law and Morals* in HLA Hart, *Essays in Jurisprudence
and Philosophy*, (Oxford, Clarendon Press, 1983), esp 74–8; For an overview of Radbruch's analysis of this issue, see T Mertens, 'Radbruch and Hart on the Grudge Informer: A Reconsideration',
(2002) 15 *Ratio Juris*, and sources cited therein.

[12] See J Gordley, 'Myths of the French Civil Code', (1994) 42 *American Journal of Comparative
Law* 459; JH Merryman et al., *The Civil Law Tradition* (Charlottesville, Va., Michie Co., 1994),
450; and J Carbonnier, *le Code civil*, in Nora, at n 5, 1332–3 describing the French Civil Code as
a repository of memory. Indeed, in 1805, an annotated *Code civil* was published, correlating
Code articles with their pre-Revolutionary legal sources. See H Dard, *Code civil des Français avec
des notes indicatives des lois romaines, coutumes, ordonnances, édits et déclarations qui ont rap-
port avec chaque article ou Conférence ou Code civil avec les lois anciennes* (Paris, J.A.
Commaille,1805).

[13] Interestingly, when the initial *statut des juifs* was enacted in October, 1940, the official government press release insisted that the new law did not pose a threat either to ' the physical persons'
or to 'the property of the Jews.' The original text of the official press release is reprinted in J Billig,
Le Commissariat général aux questions juives 1941–1944 (Paris, Editions du centre, 1955), at 32.

[14] See RH Weisberg, *Vichy Law and the Holocaust in France* (New York, New York University
Press, 1996).

murder of six million Jews.[15] When decades later, in her last and posthumously published book, *The Life of the Mind*, she tried to explain the much-misunderstood concept of the 'banality of evil' that she had introduced in her Eichmann account to describe the apparently infinite chasm between the evils perpetrated and the defendant perpetrator, she noted the irony, and perhaps even paradox, of the fact that the word 'morals comes from *mores* and ethics from *thos*, the Latin and the Greek word for customs and habits . . .'[16]

Arendt suggested that the ordinary, commonplace language of the past does not invite thought to depart from the ordinary habits of past thought, and indeed speculated that much of the evil perpetrated by the Nazis was due to what she described as a kind of 'thoughtlessness.'[17] In a similar vein, where laws such as the Vichy enactments incorporate both the terms and style of previously well-established legal norms, that very attribute enhances the ease for the legal community to experience them as unremarkable, rather than as an abrupt and profound departure from prior norms.[18]

Among the legal scholars in France of the view that positivism bears substantial responsibility for the Vichy-era court decisions, the principal proponent has been Danièle Lochak.[19] Lochak's analysis of the situation in France is in substantial agreement with the gist of the post-war German tendency to blame judicial positivism in Germany for the Nazi era court decisions.[20] While I disagree with Professor Lochak's assignment of culpability to judicial positivism, I agree with her view that the French judiciary was positivistic and formalistic in approach. On the other hand, French legal theory was mixed, with theorists such as François Gény rejecting traditional judicial positivism, taking inspiration from the German historical school, and engaging in a mutually influential relation with the German Free Law and Sociological School theorists (Kantorowicz, Ehrlich, etc.). For this reason, Marie-Claire Belleau has argued against viewing French legal theory as positivistic.[21] While it is true that France had an anti-positivistic legal school of thought, for the purposes of a discussion about the judicial injustice wrought by France's courts under fascism, it is more

---

[15] See H Arendt, *Eichmann in Jerusalem* (New York, Viking Press, 1963).

[16] H Arendt, *Life of the Mind* (New York, Harcourt Brace Javonovich, 1978) at 5.

[17] Above; and H Arendt, at n 15.

[18] For a more general and theoretical discussion of cognitive limitations on the acquisition of newness, see Peirce's concept of 'trace.' N House & C Kloesel (eds) *The Essential Peirce: Selected Philosophical Writings* (Bloomington, Indiana University Press, c1992–c1998), 24, 30. Ricœur also discusses trace in P Ricœur, *Temps et récit III: Le temps raconté* 177–83 (Paris, Seuil, 1985).

[19] See D Lochak, *La doctrine sous Vichy ou les mésaventures du positivisme*, in D Lochak (ed), *Les usages sociaux du droit* (Paris, Presses universitaires de France,1989); D Lochak, *La légitimation de la politique antisémite, in Écrire, se taire . . . Réflexions sur l'attitude de la doctrine française*, in M Olender (ed), *Le droit antisémite de Vichy* (Paris, Seuil, 1996) 436; D Lochak, Le juge doit-il appliquer une loi inique?, in M Olender (ed) *Juger sous Vichy* (Paris, Seuil,1994), 29–39.

[20] Above.

[21] See M-C Belleau, 'Les juristes inquiets: classicisme juridique et critique du droit au début du XXe siècle en France', (1999) 40 *Cahiers de droit* 507.

significant to note, however, that the anti-positivists in France by and large did *not* succeed in persuading the courts to follow their advice (in contrast to their German counterparts).[22]

Nor did the French maverick theorists persuade even the majority of other French legal theorists. Despite a considerable trend away from legal formalism in France, particularly since the end of the Second World War, even current French legal theory reflects a continuing reluctance, and even refusal, to accept the interpretive methods Saleilles and Gény advocated.[23] The evidence appears compelling that while France had some theoreticians who fully agreed with the German Free Law School in recognising the importance of judicial discretion as a dimension of law, in France those scholars' views penetrated into mainstream legal culture principally only after the Second World War, and even then continued to be diluted and limited through interpretation, as they still continue to be to the present.

An interesting difference between France and Germany during the fascist period was the activity of legal scholars. Generally influential in both countries, especially when compared to their common-law counterparts, legal academics' contemporaneous responses to the fascist-inspired laws were very different in France and Germany. While German legal theorists openly and profusely discussed the theoretical underpinnings of the new German legal concepts and conceptions, including extensive references justifying the rejection of Jews from national life, French legal scholars on the whole meekly accepted and indirectly endorsed the new legal order, but tended to avoid evaluative commentary on the new enactments.[24]

---

[22] See F Terré, Introduction générale au droit, 475 (Paris, Dalloz, 4th edn., 1998); and Curran, *Romantic Common Law*, at n 1.

[23] A most illustrative recent example of this phenomenon can be seen in the portrayal of Saleilles' theory in a textbook for French law students published in 1999. The author quotes from Saleilles' introduction to Gény's *Méthode d'interprétation et sources en droit privé positif* to the effect that gaps in statutory law are to be filled by judges in accordance with the spirit of the Code: 'Beyond the Civil Code but by means of the Civil Code' ('*Au-delà du Code civil, mais par le Code civil*'). The key point is that Professor Courbe, writing in 1999, presents Saleilles' theory as if it insisted primarily on the judicial obligation to *adhere* to the Code, on the judge's duty to fill gaps in law *by means of* the Code, when in fact Saleilles had stressed exactly the converse. See P Courbe, *Introduction au droit* (Paris, Dalloz, 6th edn., 1999), 52. For the Saleilles text in question, see R Saleilles, *in* F Gény, *Méthode d'interprétation et sources en droit privé positif*, (Paris, Librairie générale de droit et de jurisprudence,1919), xxv (originally published in 1899).

[24] For an excellent portrayal of German legal discourse during the Third Reich, including its open and plentiful discussions of anti-Jewish animus, see B Rüthers, *Entartetes Recht: Rechtslehren und Kronjuristen im Dritten Reich* (Munchen, Beck, 1989) and E Fraenkel, *The Dual State: A Contribution to the Theory of Dictatorship,* trans. A. Shils et al. (New York, London, Oxford University Press, 1941). Rüthers' choice of the word '*entartetes*' ('degenerate') in his title to designate Nazi law echoes the abundant Nazi use of that word when describing the 'non-Aryan' world. Among others, the painting and music of Jews was so designated, and Nazi Germany and occupied France went so far as to hold exhibits of such allegedly 'degenerate art' ('*entartete Kunst*'), B Manz, *A Mind in Prison: The Memoir of a Son and Soldier of the Third Reich*, (Washington D.C.,

The substance of the scholarly commentary to which the new legislation in France gave rise tended to focus on the minutiae of applying the new laws, such that legal journals developed new categories of law ('*Jews;*' '*Jewish matters;*' *Jewish issues*') that discussed the literal and legally technical applications of the texts with virtually no attempts to address their philosophical import within the framework of the French legal universe.[25]

Scholarly legal commentary in France shared with the courts an approach that skirted the larger significance of the newly-enacted discriminatory laws. In France, the tendency was to downplay the racial discrimination, and to emphasise the allegedly protective function of exclusionary laws. While German legal theorists also portrayed discriminatory laws as protective of the German *Volk*, the German rendition of the theoretical bases of the new laws included far more underscoring of the inimical nature of all Jews.[26] Thus, in his *German Legal Science at War with the Jewish Spirit*, Carl Schmitt wrote that '[w]e must free the German spirit from all Jewish falsifications/fabrications' ['*Fälschungen*'].[27] Schmitt also wrote of a 'holy exorcism' of Jews,[28] on the basis of which Rüthers has observed that Schmitt was equating Jews with the devil.[29]

Indeed, in a brilliant work on totalitarian language, Jean-Pierre Faye has argued compellingly that both German fascist law and legal theory used the term 'race' as synonymous with 'species,' rather than in the traditional meaning of 'race,' thus laying the ground through rhetorical device for the conceptual relegation of Jews to non-human status.[30] French fascism as manifested in Vichy legal discourse, and in such scant French legal theory as existed, did not extend that far, despite such apparent anomalies in Vichy French law as a more

---

Brassey's, 2000), 85. It should be noted that the French scholarly avoidance of evaluative commentary and the French dearth of racist legal theory had its counterpart in Germany. Ingo Hueck refers to Victor Bruns and Herbert Kraus as representative of German legal scholars who chose to bury themselves in teaching or other legal endeavors that did not involve them in Nazi legal theory. *See* IJ Hueck, *Sphere of influence and 'Völkisch' legal thought': Reinhard Höhn's Notion of Europe*, 3 (this volume). The difference was, rather, that racist legal theory abounded in Germany, as it did not in France.

[25] For the role of the French legal community, including both eminent law professors and members of the *Conseil d'État*, in supporting Vichy's antisemitic measures, endowing them with the appearance of legality, see P Birnbaum, *Grégoire, Dreyfus, Drancy, et Copernic,* in Nora, *Les Lieux de mémoire,* at note 5, 2679, 2705, 'le rôle très actif joué par les membres des grands corps, et en particulier ceux du Conseil d'État qui aux côtés de célèbres professeurs des facultés de droit, comme Joseph-Barthélemy, Achille Mestre, Julien Laferrière, Georges Ripert et bien d'autres, donnèrent un fondement juridique aux mesures d'exclusion et de répression des juifs'); and Joseph-Barthélemy, Ministre de la Justice: Vichy 1941–43 (Paris, Pygmalion, 1989).

[26] See, eg., C Schmitt, 'Die Deutsche Rechtswisssenschaft im Kamp gegen den jüdischen Geist', (1936) 41 *Deutsche Juristen-Zeitung*, 1193.

[27] Above at 15 ('*Wir müssen den deutschen Geist von allen jüdsichen Fälschungen befreien'*).

[28] Above at 30.

[29] See Rüthers, *Entartes Recht,* at n 24, 138.

[30] J-P Faye, *Langages Toylaitaires* (Paris, Hermann,1972). See in particular Faye's discussion of Carl Schmitt at 366–7.

inclusive definition of who was Jewish than was to be found in Hitler's Nuremberg laws.[31]

Lochak's view of positivism's responsibility for French judicial injustice is very similar to the criticism heard in post-war German circles in the immediate aftermath of the war: 'Positivism categorically rejects any reference to an alleged natural law and correlatively refuses to subordinate the validity of a legal order to a judgment about its moral worth.'[32] Interestingly, although Lochak concludes that it was due to positivism's influence that the French legal community and judiciary automatically accepted the antisemitic legislation, rather than question its moral validity, Lochak herself points out that the same legal scholars who failed to challenge antisemitic enactments did in fact challenge other legislation on moral grounds.[33]

An explanation capable of accommodating the apparently incompatible conduct of the same legal actors with respect to differing sorts of legislation lies in the all-important values which those actors held, as Cassirer's comment about the constitutions written in the citizens' minds would suggest. As numerous students of Vichy law and society have concluded in recent years, France as a whole, including its legal community, which in turn included legal academics, judges and practicing lawyers, approved of Vichy's antisemitic laws, particularly initially, due to widespread, deep-seated hostility principally towards foreign Jews.[34]

---

[31] See Curran *Legalization of Racism,* at n 10, 5, n 7; 27, n 77.

[32] D Lochak, *La légitimation de la politique antisémite, in Écrire, se taire ... Réflexions sur l'attitude de la doctrine française, in* Le droit antisémite, at n 19, 436, 'Le positivisme rejette catégoriquement toute référence à un prétendu droit naturel et refuse corrélativement de subordonner la validité d'un ordre juridique à un jugement porté sur sa valeur morale'. See also E Bodenheimer, 'Significant Developments in German Legal Philosophy Since 1945', (1954) 3 *American Journal of Comparative Law,* 379, on post-war Germany's interest in natural law and rejection of positivism.

[33] Above at 437.

[34] Above, n 14, Weisberg, *Vichy Law*; R Badinter, *Peut-on être avocat lorsqu'on est juif en 1940–1944?, in* Le droit antisémite, at n 19; R Badinter, *Un antisémitisme ordinaire* (Fayard, Paris,1997); MR Marrus & RO Paxton, *Vichy France and the Jews* (Stanford, Stanford University Press, 1995); P Laborie, *L'Opinion française sous* Vichy (Paris, Seuil, 1990); S Klarsfeld, *Vichy-Auschwitz: le rôle de Vichy dans la solution finale de la question juive en France, 1943–1944* (Fayard, Paris, 1985); N Levin, *The Holocaust; the Destruction of European Jewry, 1933–1945* (New York, T.Y. Crowell, 1968) 429; Curran, *The Legalization of Racism,* at n 10. It is also of interest to note that while French antisemitism appeared to target foreign Jews, see *ibid.* at 55–7, German publications reflect a greater hatred for the assimilated Jew, on the theory that the assimilated are harder to detect and therefore more nefarious. See C Schmitt, *Glossarium. Aufzeichnungen der Jahre 1947–51,* (Berlin, Duncker & Humblot, 1991) 18 (1958), quoted in Dyzenhaus, *Legality and Legitimacy,* at n 2, 93, note 189.('*Gerade der assimilierte Jude ist der wahre Feind*'). For ruminations on whether the human tribalist tendency is to persecute the different, the almost-different, or the similar-to-identical, see the superb works of V Jankélévitch (who coined the term '*le presque-semblable*'), especially V Jankélévitch & B Berlowitz, *Quelque part dans l'inachevé,* (Paris, Gallimard, 1978), 69, arguing that the most intense hostility is elicited by those who are minimally different, the 'almost-the-same'; and R Girard, *La Violence et le sacré* (Paris, Bernard Grasset, 1972), arguing that, contrary to general belief, it is identity and not difference that elicits hatred.

While German legal commentary also is, and was, influential for judicial developments, the French judicial branch had far more of a tradition of refraining from independent evaluation than its German counterpart.[35] It was the least likely branch to offer resistance even to a repugnant turn in the law's development.[36] The French political theorist, Raymond Aron, noted that even the *Conseil d'État*, the tribunal from which one might have expected more of a critical stance than from lower courts or from the French private law judicial system, also commented and applied the *statut des juifs* as though it were a law comparable to any other, and as though its violation of the fundamental laws of the Republic, what in the United States and perhaps in contemporary Germany would tend to be described as constitutional principles, could be adopted and accepted without further ado by the legal community, merely because the law had originated in an act of state power.[37]

Recent scholarly work on the decisions reached by French courts during Vichy is to be found in Richard Weisberg's *Vichy Law and the Holocaust in France*; in his essay, *Legal Rhetoric Under Stress*, in *Poethics,* and in the studies contained in two volumes of work edited by Maurice Olender, *le Droit antisémite de Vichy*, published in 1996, and *Juger sous Vichy*, published in 1994.[38] The French judiciary may be said to have resisted in its own way, a way that also harked back to its time-honored tradition of silent, unacknowledged conduct

---

[35] See generally, R David, *French Law: Its Structure, Sources and Methodology,* trans. Michael Kindred (Baton Rouge, Louisiana State University Press, 1972).

[36] Although the judiciary in France was subdued, the bar was far less so. In their recent books, both Weisberg and former French Minister of Justice Robert Badinter document the proud tradition of independence of the bars of France, particularly of Paris. See Weisberg, at n 14; and Badinter, at n 34. *Accord,* L Karpik, *La profession libérale, Un cas, le barreau, in* 3 Nora, at n 5, 3278 ('la profession [d'avocat], loin de s'inscrire dans les mécanismes sociaux et les institutions existantes, manifeste, depuis l'Ancien Régime, un irrédentisme qui s'affirme dans la revendication de libertés particulières'). See also above at 3285 (solidarity of profession harks back to pre-Revolutionary times).

[37] R Aron, *Mémoires: 50 ans de réflexion politique,* (Paris, Julliard,1983) 709: 'Le Conseil d'État commenta et appliqua le statut des Juifs, comme s'il s'agissait d'une loi comparable aux autres, comme si la violation des principes de la République pouvait être acceptée par les juristes à l'instar d'une décision quelconque du pouvoir.' Of course, the Republic no longer existed at that time, the '*République française*' having been replaced in both substance and nomenclature by Pétain's '*État français.*' Indeed, killing the Republic was a major motivating force among many who opted for collaboration, inspired as much or more by their hatred for the Third Republic as by any other consideration, in a sentiment reminiscent of the widespread revulsion against Weimar in Germany a decade earlier. In his account of the parliamentary debates that led to Pétain's takeover, Emmanuel Berl recounts how the death of the Republic was already understood by France's members of parliament at the infamous July 1940 assembly, when Marcel Astier, one of the few who had voted against the turn to dictatorship, had called out a last '*Vive la République quand même!*' His was an isolated voice in the instantaneously-altered rallying cry of simply '*Vive la France,*' the *Pétainistes'* omitting reference already, *avant la lettre*, to the soon-to-be-defunct Republic. See E Berl, *La fin de la troisième République: 10 juillet 1940* (Paris, Gallimard, 1968).

[38] See Weisberg, *Vichy Law,* at n 14; R Weisberg, *Poethics* (New York, Columbia University Press, 1992), *Le droit antisémite*, at n 19, and *Juger sous Vichy*, at n 19.

where overt conduct might have reflected impermissible judicial liberties with enacted law. Notwithstanding numerous cases to the contrary,[39] French courts sometimes showed leniency towards Jews who sought judicial relief from the strictures of Vichy's antisemitic laws. In failing to challenge or even to address the *validity* of enacted laws, the courts were following the tradition they had followed since the Revolution of 1789, according to which the judge's sole tasks are to identify the governing legal text, and then to apply it. Thus, even when lenient, Vichy-era judges purported to reach substantive results in full compliance with governing enacted law.

It has been pointed out by numerous scholars that French judges have a long tradition of skirting legislation when they deem it necessary to do so in order to reach the results they believe to be correct in the pending case.[40] Since they do this in a way that may be described as covert, by applying code provisions whose relation to the issues of the pending case are not apparent, or by allowing for interpretations of legislative texts that bear little resemblance to any plausible rendition of those texts, such conduct well might be viewed as *non-positivistic*. On the other hand, however, it also is profoundly positivistic, precisely inasmuch as it refrains from challenging the legislative text, and purports to apply it.

The ethics of judicial activity that undermines evil law through the interpretive powers of judges, and more specifically the issue of whether an inevitable complicity with evil arises, even when the courts use their powers to mitigate the injustice of enacted law, has been a subject of some controversy, and figures within the debate about positivism. Following one view, perhaps best represented by such figures as Lon Fuller and Gustav Radbruch, at some point law must cease to be considered law when it contravenes the basic requirements of justice, and judges should declare such enactments not to constitute law, and therefore not to warrant judicial interpretation or application at all.[41]

The positivist response, articulated perhaps most clearly by HLA Hart, rejects this view in the measure in which it concerns the definition of law, but Hart emphatically did *not* endorse judicial (or popular) compliance with evil laws.[42] In other words, Hart insisted that laws are laws, no matter how evil, when they

---

[39] For an account of some of those cases, see, eg Curran, *Legalization of Racism,* at n 10, n 97.

[40] See, eg JP Dawson, *The Oracles of the Law,* (Ann Arbor, University of Michigan Law School, 1968), 431; JH Merryman at n 9, 109. Modern French law textbooks also discuss this. See Ghestin & Goubeaux, at n 8, 318; and Terré, at n 22.

[41] See LL Fuller, 'Positivism and Fidelity to Law', (1958) 71 *Harvard Law Review* 593; G Radbruch, 'Rechtsphilosophie: "Gesetzliches Unrecht und (bürgesetzliches Recht"' (1946) 1 *Süddeutsche Zeitung,* 105–8.(An English translation of Radbruch's declaration, so famous in Germany as to be known as 'Radbruch's formula' ('die *Radbruchsche Formel')* appears in S Paulson, 'Lon. L. Fuller, Gustav Radbruch, and the 'Positivist Theses,' (1994) 13 *Law and Philosophy,* 313, 317.

[42] See *Positivism and the Separation of Law and Morals* in HLA Hart, *Essays in Jurisprudence and Philosophy,* 49–87, especially above at 77, 'we say that laws may be law but too evil to be obeyed', and continuing passage, above at 77–8, 82.

are generated by the authorised law-making authorities, but he insisted with equal vigor that a duty of conscience requires violating laws that do not deserve to be obeyed, and that to say that something is a law is not tantamount to saying that it should be obeyed.[43] Hart's position thus stands in sharp contradistinction to Lochak's rendition of positivism as 'refus[ing] to subordinate the validity of a legal order to a judgment about its moral worth.'[44]

Hart was quite critical of Radbruch,[45] but what emerges from their disagreement often seems to suggest less substantive disagreement than different focuses of attention. While to Hart it was vital to call law by its proper name, my reading of Radbruch suggests that he was less worried about nomenclature than about the power of legal enactments to command obedience, and in this matter he and Hart were not in conflict.

In more recent times, JHH Weiler's analysis of legitimacy in terms of *social* versus *political* legitimacy, although not addressing the specific debate we are discussing, indicates a way to bridge some of the differences that separated Radbruch and Fuller from Hart. Weiler concludes that

'[t]o suggest that the legitimacy of the polity, or some of its features, may be called into question is not to say that the polity is to become illegitimate, either in the strict legal sense or in the court of public opinion.'[46]

This statement is in keeping with Hart's definition of the legal as that which is an act of state power within the processes internally envisaged as official and legitimate; but it also suggests, in keeping with Radbruch and Fuller's optic, that social legitimacy is a crucial factor in the success of enacted law, and that when popular opinion does view technically legitimate acts as illegitimate, they eventually lose their claim to legitimacy independently of technical internal categories of legitimacy.

Weisberg argues that the French judiciary was to blame for not having resisted openly, because the court decisions of even the most liberal, personally compassionate, judge who saved the individual party in the case at bar by engaging in the French judicial tradition of semantic casuistry in his judicial

---

[43] See above, Hart, *Positivism* at 77–82. *Accord,* W Twining, 'The Path of the Law 100 Years Later: Holmes's Influence on Modern Jurisprudence: Holmes and English and German Jurisprudence: Other People's Power: The Bad Man and English Positivism, 1897–1997', (1997) 63 *Brooklyn Law Review* 189, 203. Thomas Mertens argues that Kant's philosophy also mandates against '[s]trict obedience to immoral duties' imposed by the sovereign. T Mertens, 'Arendt's Judgement and Eichmann's Evil,' (1998) 2 *Finnish Yearbook of Political Thought* , 58, 68.

[44] See D Lochak, *Écrire, se taire* in *Le Droit antisémite*, at n 19 above.

[45] See Hart, at n 42, at 75.

[46] JHH Weiler, 'Does Europe Need a Constitution? Reflections on Demos, Telos and the German Maastricht Decision', (1995) 1 *European Law Journal*, 219. See also JHH Weiler, 'Parlement européen, intégration européenne, démocratie et légitimité', in J-V Louis et al.(eds) *Le Parlement européen dans l'évolution constitutionnelle* (Bruxelles, Éditions de l'Université de Bruxelles,1988), 325.

interpretation, nevertheless was reinforcing and supporting the very laws he simultaneously was subverting.[47] According to Weisberg, such judges inevitably, even if unwittingly, sent the message to the public at large, to their professional colleagues, and to the authorities, that fascist laws deserved the respect, deference and application of the judiciary.[48]

Contrary to Weisberg, however, David Dyzenhaus has endorsed the idea of judges' resisting evil legislation by attempting to do justice from the bench. In the context of apartheid South Africa, Dyzenhaus explores the dilemma of liberal judges, condoning the idea of judges' working from within the system that generated evil legislation, rather than going underground.[49] One might object to comparing Vichy France with apartheid South Africa on the basis of the profound differences between common-law and civil-law courts. Indeed, Dyzenhaus himself insists that the South African judges' ability to rely on what he calls common-law principles is precisely a distinguishing feature of the common-law legal world that would have permitted judges to reject unjust enacted law from the bench, and therefore from within the system, thus not just saving individual defendants, but also effectively reforming the system.[50]

My own sense is that nothing Dyzenhaus discusses is by nature a feature so exclusive to common-law legal systems as to render the South African example incommensurable with the European fascist situation. More specifically, what Dyzenhaus refers to as common-law principles contain strong parallels to the general principles doctrines that do and did exist in Continental European civil-law systems: the *principes généraux* of France and the *Generalklauseln* of Germany.[51]

In France, history, tradition and habit conspired to make the judicial branch the least suited in Vichy France to call legislation into question. The judicial branch's status had been of an unequal and inferior branch of government in France since the time of the Revolution, a status unchanged by Vichy, or, incidentally, by the Republics that preceded or succeeded Vichy. Meanwhile, the legislature, traditionally France's most powerful branch, had legislated itself out of existence in its suicidal sessions of July, 1940, in a display of collaborationist zeal. Those members of parliament who had not voted for change in July of 1940 were methodically hunted down, imprisoned and often murdered in the months and years that followed.

---

[47] See Weisberg, *Vichy Law*, at n 14.

[48] Above.

[49] See D Dyzenhaus, *Judging the Judges, Judging Ourselves: Truth, Reconciliation and the Apartheid Legal Order* (Oxford, Hart, 1998). Dyzenhaus goes to considerable pains to be clear that he does not condemn those who made the decision to go underground, however, and indeed discusses one such case at some length and admiringly.

[50] Above.

[51] Moreover, while I have been a proponent of taking care to consider how significant the differences are between the common-law and civil-law legal perspectives, Carl Schmitt's writings (*Gesetz und Urteil*, in particular), make clear that at least German judicial decision-making for almost a century has involved many attributes we tend to associate with common-law processes.

One path of resistance arguably open to France's courts would have been to apply the *principes généraux* ('general principles'), a judicial doctrine that would have allowed judges to comply with the spirit of France's civil code while interpreting specific enacted law. Jacques Ghestin and Gilles Goubeaux describe the function of *principes généraux* in *Traité de droit civil* as having the capacity to allow 'the introduction into positive law of moral rules or of principles of natural law.'[52] Ghestin and Goubeaux suggest that *principes généraux* are suitable particularly where the judiciary is handling new law, as was the case for Vichy enactments.[53]

Since the *principes généraux* are a judicial doctrine, they are not officially amenable to application to private law legislation inasmuch as French courts do not have judicial review over legislative acts.[54] Not surprisingly, given the inferiority endemic to France's conception of the judiciary's place within the branches of government, an inferiority that was codified into legal nomenclature in Articles 64–66 of the 1958 Constitution, in which the judicial branch is described as a mere '*autorité*' ('authority') while the other two are '*pouvoirs,*' ('powers')[55] the French courts traditionally have not been prepared to indulge in open application of their *principes généraux*.

Article 4 requires that judges decide all cases, and prohibits them from abstaining from judgment on the ground that enacted law is ambiguous or non-existent.[56] Such directions within positive law, obliging judges to depart from positive law, create a paradoxical situation in terms of what positivism signifies,

---

[52] J Ghestin & G Goubeaux, *Traité de droit civil* at n 8, 338. See also A Lajoie et al., 'Pluralisme juridique à Kahnawahe?', (1998) 39 *Les cahiers de droit*, 681, 685, associating *principes généraux* with tacit governing social presumptions.

[53] Ghestin & Goubeaux, above 339.

[54] The *Conseil constitutionnel* has acquired judicial review in recent times, and now the *Cour de cassation* has acquired a sort of judicial review, and indirectly all French national courts have acquired another variant of judicial review through their power to refer national cases to the European Court of Justice in order to ensure compliance with European law. See *The Reviewing Powers of the Court of Cassation and the Conseil d'État* in A von Mehren & JR Gordley, *The Civil Law System* (Boston, Little Brown, 1977) 307–9. On the fledgling powers of legislative review of the Cour de cassation, see MA Rogoff, 'A Comparison of Constitutionalism in France and the United States', (1997) 49 *Maine Law Review*, 21, 77–8. See also JHH Weiler, 'The Transformation of Europe', (1991) 100 *Yale Law Journal*, 2403 the national judiciaries of European Union Member States have gained in power internally through their effective power to review national legislation in terms of compliance with European legal standards.

[55] But see M-L Rassat, *La Justice en France* (Paris, Presses Universitaires de France, 1985), disagreeing that this nomenclature was intended to reflect the judiciary's inferiority, and challenging the widespread view of the French judiciary in this light.

[56] See Article 4, Code civil: 'Le juge qui refusera de juger, sous prétexte de silence, de l'obscurité ou de l'insuffisance de la loi, pourra être poursuivi comme coupable de déni de justice.' Professor Boulanger sees in Article 4 an implicit reference to judicial recourse to *principes généraux*. See Boulanger, at n 8, 64 ('*L'article 4 du Code civil impose au juge, sous peine de déni de justice, de rendre une décision malgré le silence de la loi . . . Nous constaterons que la découverte, puis la mise en œuvre, des principes lui apportent un puissant secours*').

since they may be seen as a positivistic instruction to engage in anti-positivism. In France, one might consider the issue as that of the '*principes généraux* of the *principes généraux*,' somewhat analogous to the '*Kompetenz-Kompetenz*' problem of the European Court of Justice.

Given the traditional French judicial antipathy against the vague, the unwritten, as well as against the appearance of judicial law-creation, and given the judiciary's self-understanding as a subservient branch within the governmental separation of powers, it is not surprising that the courts of Vichy France eschewed the use of *principes généraux* as they grappled with the interpretation in an altered legal universe.

The reaction against judicial positivism that arose in France after the war, and that Danièle Lochak espouses, also became internalised by the courts. France's association of positivism as a cause of judicial injustice, because it was synchronous with the substantive judicial injustice of the Vichy period, is nowhere more strongly evidenced than in the fact that the *principes généraux* finally did obtain favour in France after the end of the Second World War, as a reaction against the Vichy period, a development all the more momentous because French judicial formalism had not been a phenomenon just of the war years, but, as discussed above, was a tradition deeply entrenched in the history and politics of the country.

It is tempting to infer a dynamic of causality between the French judicial approach from 1940 to 1944, and substantive outcomes that disregarded larger issues of justice and constitutionality. Judicial positivism and formalism seem to imply a judicially-wrought self-referentiality in enacted law, which in turn would seem to provide the explanation for how the courts of France from 1940 to 1944 saw their way to effecting the robbing of citizens through the implementation and application of property 'aryanization' laws, and ultimately enabling the rounding up and deportation of some 75,000 people through the judicially sanctioned progressive deprivation of individual rights, rights that had seemed well-established in pre-war French legal culture.[57]

It is precisely the contrast of Germany's anti-positivism that gives one pause before concluding too quickly that formalistic, positivistic judicial methodology, with its effect of making enacted law self-referential and beyond challenge, necessitated the results that the courts of Vichy France reached. The German judicial tradition and practice of applying *Generalklauseln* illustrate how the *principes généraux* could have been used in France to perpetrate judicial outcomes as rabidly unjust as those which the French courts did realise through their positivistic applications of antisemitic laws, and through their rejection of *principes généraux*.

Once the causal link between methodology and substantive outcome is called into question, one also may become more receptive to the ever-present

---

[57] The texts of the principal 'aryanization' measures are reprinted in Appendix 4 in *Le droit antisémite*, at n 19 above, 591–8.

possibilities, even during Vichy France, for France's courts to have entertained traditionally accepted judicial methods for reaching results they wanted to reach, regardless of whether they violated enacted law in the process. Under the traditional judicial methodology, the *principes généraux* would not have been necessary, since judicial departures from enacted law often were undeclared, under the 'cover of interpretation,' as Ghestin and Goubeaux put it. The role of political ideology in conjunction with the values held by the judges as individuals and as parts of the judicial institutions, rendered the different styles that typified France and Germany's respective national judiciary of limited influence.

In addition, once one is prepared to challenge the concept of a causal connection between judicial methodology and substantive legal outcome, it also becomes easier to view the judiciary in its larger context as part of a country in crisis, and to consider that the causes of substantive judicial injustice may have had less to do with judicial methodology and philosophy than with the judiciary's participation in the nation-wide receptivity to collaboration for purposes of national survival, a reaction that occurred throughout France not just after its unexpected and psychologically devastating military defeat, but that also was situated in the aftermath of national exhaustion from still lingering effects of the previous world war's catastrophic losses.

Germany

The German experience in some ways was almost diametrically opposed to the French experience, despite initial appearances of similarity. The outcry after the Second World War against judicial positivism in Germany succumbed to growing compelling evidence that German courts during the Nazi era had largely been anti-positivistic in their methodology, and that in this they had continued an anti-formalistic, *anti-positivistic* judicial tradition that dated from well before the Nazi era.[58]

The work of Bernd Rüthers, Ingo Müller and Michael Stolleis has documented extensively the anti-positivism characteristic of Nazi Germany's judiciary, as well as its predecessor,[59] and in the United States John Dawson also has shown the pre-war judicial acceptance, endorsement and implementation of Germany's *Generalklauseln*, the 'general clauses' that were comparable in role

---

[58] See B Rüthers, *Die unbegrenzte Auslegung: zum Wandel der Privatrechts im Nationalsozialismus* (T(bingen, Mohr-Sibeck, 1968); I Maus, *'Gesetzesbindung' der Justiz und die Struktur der nationalsozialistischen Rechtsnormen*, in R Dreier & W Sellert (eds), *Recht und Justiz im 'Dritten Reich'* (Frankfurt am Main, Suhrkamp, 1989); and W Ott & F Buob, Did Legal Formalism Render German Jurists Defenceless During the Third Reich?, (1993) 2 *Social & Legal Studies*, 91.

[59] Neither the German nor the French judiciary was changed in its members when fascist régimes came to power, other than the removal of its Jewish judges. This continuity in personnel was itself a powerful element in realising judicial methodological continuity.

and nature to the French *principes généraux* which France's judiciary tradition-ally had rejected.[60]

A striking similarity between Germany and France was in post-war reaction. Germany's post-war response represents a mirror image of France's, a move-ment in reverse, but both of their reactions shared an underlying tenacity to dwell on the terrain of methodology, and to refrain from challenging their fun-damental assumption that methodology was the culprit. Each country repudi-ated the particular methodological approach it believed its judiciary had practiced in its fascist period, tainting that methodology by its association with fascism and terror.[61] Thus, in Germany, when it became more generally accepted that the German judiciary had been anti-formalistic in methodology, and that much of the attack levelled against formalism had been on the part of judges hoping to exculpate their own past actions, the objections tended to switch their target from formalism to anti-formalism, but, just as in France, the debate itself continued to be argued within the framework of methodology.[62]

Well before Hitler's accession to power, German legal theory had strayed from the traditional civil-law reliance on codes as a guiding force preclusive of judicial law-creation. The view of the judge as restricted to mechanically apply-ing enacted law, however, prevailed before inroads against it gradually appeared. The Enlightenment eroded this mentality more than three centuries before the time we are discussing, and the transformation of the conception of law in that time was dramatic in Germany, but German law and legal theory nevertheless retained residues of the past.

Major inroads against the view of law as a closed system from which logical deduction could provide correct answers to all legal issues were made by Jhering already in the nineteenth century, with his departure from the views of Savigny and Puchta, the *Pandektentheorie* and *Begriffsjurisprudenz* (conceptual theory of law), which had emphasised the role of logic in legal resolutions, even going so far as to suggest a pyramidal structure of legal reasoning that Jhering was to criticise for its divorce from the realities of practice. Jhering attacked the view that all answers were obtainable from the cumulative body of enacted law,

---

[60] See JP Dawson, 'The General Clauses Viewed From a Distance' (1997) 41 *Rabels* Zeitschrift, 441.

[61] See B Rüthers, *Die unbegrenzte Auslegung* at n 58; M Stolleis, at n 9; H Schorn, *Der Richter im Dritten Reich* (Frankfurt am Main, V. Klostermann, 1959); and S Paulson, at n 41, 315—'the exoneration thesis [ie, exoneration by blaming positivism for judicial injustice] has been substan-tially discredited.'

[62] The attack on positivism was not formulated solely by those who were attempting to excul-pate themselves from personal responsibility. The prime counterexample was Radbruch, whose motives were unimpeachable and who had had no participation in furthering or endorsing Nazi law. His challenge to positivism on the other hand did militate in favor of exculpating from personal responsibility the members of the Nazi-era German judiciary, since his view was that they did noth-ing worse than follow an interpretive tradition which, in light of recent history, proved to have cat-astrophic potential. Professor Paulson has clarified this consequence (though not motive) of Radbruch's position. See S Paulson, at n 41.

or that the judge's duty was to deduce the solution through the rigorous logic of his analysis, or that the process of legal reasoning was a mathematical-like undertaking, with a corollary promise of mathematical correctness, precision, or even the possibility of unassailable logic.[63]

After Jhering, the sociological school of Eugen Ehrlich and the Free Law School of Kantorowicz continued to develop concepts that rejected a minor, merely mechanical role for the judiciary. Ehrlich, like Kantorowicz and Gény, rejected literalism, or what Ehrlich called 'legal technicalism,' in the judicial approach to interpreting textual law.[64] Like Kantorowicz and Gény, Ehrlich believed that judicial discretion is an inevitable player in the equally inevitable gaps of enacted law. According to Ehrlich, where legal technicalism prevails, with its accompanying illusion of gapless enacted law, judicial discretion not only persists, but tends to degenerate into arbitrariness, precisely because the discretionary processes must be covert.[65] Ehrlich's insight was very close to Professor Merryman's evaluation that in France the net effect of the enduring mythology that judicial discretion is unnecessary and contrary to the appropriate role of the judiciary, has been to lower the quality of the judiciary, rather than to diminish judicial discretion.[66]

Free law not only was inextricably bound to the high quality of the judge, and the latter was central to the viability of justice.[67] Ehrlich saw in France's *Cour de cassation* an illustrative example of how judicial technicalism does not prevent a court from infusing its own ideas into a legal system even where technicalism is the mandated judicial methodology, because legislatures are not able to control how law is applied, no matter the mandates methodological approach.[68] Habermas has discussed this issue in terms of 'the Aristotelian insight that no rule is able to regulate its own application.'[69]

---

[63] See R von Jhering, *Der Geist des römischen Rechts auf den verschiedenen Stufen seiner Entwicklung* (Darmstadt, Scientia Verlag Aalen, 10th edn., 1968); *Scherz und Ernst in der Jurisprudenz* (Leipzig, Breitkopf and Härtel, 1884); *Der Kampf um's Recht* (Wien, Manz, 1872). For an overview of the traditional *Begriffsjurisprudenz* in German legal theory, see *Die Begriffsjurisprudenz*, in A. Kaufmann & W. Hassemer (eds) *Einführung in Rechtsphilosophie und Rechtstheorie der Gegenwart*, 140–5 (Heidelberg, CF Müller Juristischer Verlag, 1994). On the pyramidal structure mentioned above, see F Wieacker, *A History of Private Law in Europe*, trans. Tony Weir (Oxford, Clarendon Press, New York, Oxford University Press, 1995) 345, also explaining the key concept of nineteenth-century German legal science as a gaplessness of law. above at n 14 above, 344–5. For the concept-pyramid ('*Begriffspyramid*'), see GF Puchta, *Cursus der Institutionen* (Leipzig, Breitkopf und Härtel,1841).

[64] E Ehrlich, *Judicial Freedom of Decision: Its Principles and Objects* in E Bruncken & LB Register *Science of Legal Method* (New York, A.M. Kelley, 1969), 47 at 63.

[65] Above at 63.

[66] See Merryman, 'The French Deviation' at n 8 above.

[67] Ehrlich, at n 64 above, 73.

[68] Above at 70.

[69] Habermas, *Between Facts and Norms*, at n 4 above, 199.

Nazi theorists such as Schmitt and Larenz (including Schmitt in pre-Nazi times) opposed positivism because they associated it with individualism, a primary hallmark of the liberal political state to which they were opposed above all.[70] They thus viewed judicial positivism as a decadent approach to law that neglected the community interest by purporting to apply neutral legal principles based on the governing legal texts. The better judicial approach, according to Schmitt and Larenz, was to evaluate the individual's claims under law with respect to how the result would affect the society as a whole (a society defined in terms of an ethnically homogeneous *Volk*.)

An illustrative example of the two countries' traditionally different attitudes towards judicial formalism of Germany and France lies in the pre-war inflation cases, in which German courts went so far as to modify concrete contractual terms in order to remedy the tremendous hardship and injustice that a formalistic interpretation would have wrought during a time of hyper-inflation. Significantly and characteristically, the French courts did not follow that path, retaining the shibboleth that 'a franc is a franc' ('*un franc est un franc*') in the exact quantity specified in the relevant contract, and never more nor less than that.[71]

Conclusion

The issue of formalism and anti-formalism in the French and German judicial methodology of the fascist era first demands a lucid assessment of which category accurately describes the practices of those judiciaries. The answers depend

---

[70] See C Schmitt, *Über die drei Arten des rechtswissenschaftlichen Denkens* (Berlin, Duncker & Humblot, 1993) 44. Schmitt's criticism of legal positivism is extremely interesting inasmuch as he deftly underscored the dilemma inherent in judicial decision-making. Paradoxically, his analysis implies the illusory nature of the closed-system (*Geschlossenheit*) theory Kantorowicz also sought to debunk, yet Nazi legal theorists *advocated Geschlossenheit*, since an entirely self-referential system facilitated Nazism. See ER Huber, 'Die Einheit des Staatsgewalt', (1934) 15 *Deutsche Juristen-Zeitung* 950; and C Schmitt, *Nationalsozialismus und Völkerrecht*, (1934), 18, defining law ('*Recht*') as a closed, self-contained system. While, as noted above, Schmitt principally took aim at positivism for furthering individualism, he also criticised it by associating it with the Versailles peace treaty. above [Nationalsozialsmus u. Völkerrecht], at 12. Schmitt also rejected positivism as a Jewish outlook, associating it with the Talmudic emphasis on the letter of the law. This criticism involves ignoring the line of thinkers, both Jewish and non-Jewish, who followed Spinoza's rejection of such literal legalism three centuries before the time in which Schmitt wrote, and which, among others, was the inspiration for the Reform Movement within Judaism. See, eg B Spinoza, The Ethics of Spinoza (ed. Dagobert D. Runes, New York, Carol Publishing Group, 1995). For an excellent discussion of Schmitt's anti-formalism, see WE Scheuerman, *Carl Schmitt: The End of Law* (Lanham, Md, Rowman & Littlefield, 1999).

[71] On the German courts, see Rüthers, *Unbegrenzte Auslegung*, at note 58, 213 et seq; and JP Dawson, 'Specific Performance in France and Germany,' (1959) 57 *Michigan Law Review*, 495. On the contrasting results reached by French courts, see generally Section III, *La révision du contrat*, in J Flour & J-L Aubert, *Les obligations. Sources: L'acte juridique* (Paris, Armand Colin, 1988).

on how one approaches the question. We have seen that the French judiciary was more formalistic in overt tradition than its German counterpart, but that its practices would allow for a characterisation of lack of formalism if one considers the numerous ways in which the courts traditionally also carved out paths to reach substantive results they deemed desirable, with far less deference to enacted law than they claimed or than appeared on the surface of the texts of court decisions. On the other hand, their overt deference to the letter of textual law itself bespeaks of positivism, particularly in a system in which case precedents are not binding on future adjudication, since the purported implementation of the enacted law confirms the judiciary's duty to adhere to it.

With respect to Germany, we saw a shift in the perception of whether the courts in fact had adhered to a formalistic outlook during the Third Reich, or merely claimed after the war to have done so. A history of anti-formalism existed in the German judicial approach before Hitler's rise to power, and was related to the important role that the courts of Germany played officially and in their self-understanding of that role as crucial to the moral life of the nation. On the other hand, a two-track system of judicial methodology coexisted in Nazi Germany, depending on whether the law to be applied was pre- or a post-Hitler law, thus allowing one to conclude that both formalism and anti-formalism were the German judicial approach.

While the contrasts between the judicial approaches of Germany and France, coupled with grave injustice in substantive results in both countries, allow one to question whether causality linked the specific methodologies to the substantive nature of case results, the uncertain role of methodology in terms of substantive outcome may be most starkly visible by the example of Germany alone. The post-war about-face from initially criticising judicial formalism to subsequently criticising anti-formalism, when the view that German courts had been positivistic changed to a view that they had not been positivistic, signals starkly the strength of the impetus to blame the particular methodology that had been tainted by association with Nazism, and casts doubt on the validity of the conclusion that either methodology by nature mandates injustice in substantive result.

In addition, the German judicial use of *Generalklauseln* yielded results as terrible in kind as France's judicial positivism, with its rejection of *principes généraux,* France's version of general clauses. The accumulated evidence demonstrates that we will not be able to identify the responsible culprit for fascist-era judicial injustice in France or Germany in the methodological distinctions that separate positivism from anti-positivism, or formalism from anti-formalism.

The driving force behind court decisions in both Germany and France was political ideology, and the particulars of judicial methodology were far less important to the outcomes of cases. If we can learn from the fascist era's judicial experience, it is perhaps to beware of that pervasive facet of the era that also permeated law: namely, unicity. The fascist judicial experience suggests that, even in legal methodology, the European Union should avoid listening to one voice alone, at the risk of moving in the direction of what in Germany was called the 'total State' ('*der totale Staat*').

In Germany, the ideas of *Volk* as conceived by Herder and Savigny before the twentieth century had held genuine promise for a flowering of human particularity in the context of mutual respect among communities.[72] In the European Union's goals of maintaining cultural diversity, early German theories of *Volk* may be positive and productive after all. Fascist legal theory nullified the concept of *Volk* that had animated Herder, Savigny and others, however, even while it purported to exalt it, inasmuch as fascist theorists allowed only for the initial legitimation of the political system through its selection of the *Führer*. In a context that rejected popular elections, the *Volk* and state became one, but, in lieu of an ineffable fusion entailing communal well-being, as the theory maintained, the *Volk* de facto was at the mercy of an all-powerful, single person. This then, of necessity entailed loss of voice and vanishing of *Volk*.[73]

The European Union should develop from this history a resolve to prevent its constituents from merging into oneness, even at a sacrifice of some efficiency. The temptation to opt for efficiency through a levelling absorption of the many into one was at the basis of Schmitt's theory. He argued that the will of the people, '*der Volkswille*,' could not be realised if it was dispersed into various channels of expressions, as where multiple parties express conflicting views, impeding political action of any kind.[74] The flaw in his reasoning was not in his critique of the liberal pitfall of inefficiency, and its ultimate potential for political paralysis due to multiplicity. It was, rather, in equating the reduction of the many with a realisation of the *Volkswille*.

The fascist theoretical conceptualisation did not allow for a *Volkswille* that aspired to more than a fictitious or illusory realisation. It may be, as Schmitt observed, that empowering the *Volkswille* creates momentous, sometimes insuperable, challenges where it is not channeled into a single articulation, such that multiplicity threatens to nullify its very objective. It also may be that liberalism carries by nature the paradoxical potential of degenerating into meaninglessness through an excess of proposed political agendas, such that a large *quantity* of meanings impinges on *quality*, eventually nullifying the possibility of meaning itself.

---

[72] The issue has arisen with some frequency since the Second World War as to whether German Romanticism was responsible for the virulent turn in German nationalism under Hitler. The view on this issue expressed above is discussed at greater length in VG Curran, *Herder and the Holocaust: A Debate About Difference and Determinism in the Context of Comparative Law*, in FC DeCoste & B Schwartz (eds) *The Holocaust's Ghost: Writings on Art, Politics, Law and Education* (Edmonton, Alberta, Alberta University Press, 2000).

[73] Cf Carl Schmitt, complaining during the Hitler period that Germany still enjoyed too broad a freedom of the press, and advising against free expression of opinion. See C Schmitt, *Weiterentwicklung des totalen Staat in Deutschland (Januar 1933)*, in C Schmitt, *Positionen und Begriffe im Kampf mit Weimar-Genf-Versailles*, (Berlin, Duncker & Humblot, 1988), 186.

[74] See C Schmitt, above at 189.

From this, however, it cannot be deduced that the challenge of determining a viable expression of the people's will can be resolved by the elimination of multiplicity. Schmitt's solution of the 'total State' thus succeeds in ridding the problem of its symptom, but does not, and cannot, resolve the problem of plural voices by silencing all but one. Pluralism and its corollaries of open conflict and cacophony can be eliminated by allowing for only a single expression, as where an authoritarian state eliminates rival parties and free legislative elections. The surviving residue of one, however, will bear no logically necessary connection to any authentic version of the will of the people, unless a viable process exists for the people to offer continuing information as to the nature of its will through some organism empowered to initiate change that is politically responsive to ongoing indications of popular sentiment.

The fascist belief that individualism was the decadent residue of Weimar (and of the French Revolution)[75] could justify dismissing the value of individual disagreements with the leader's decisions; nevertheless, however one differentiated the communal concept of the people from its individual constituent members, even that communal entity of necessity would remain an unknown factor in practice, so long as the *Führer* was deemed to be organically able to embody its will without needing to respond to any continuing political control exerted on its behalf as a check on the *Führer*.

The modern world, far beyond the European Union, and still farther beyond the specifics of its legal order, is challenged today by a threat of encroaching unicity. A prime example concerns the rapidity with which languages are disappearing from the earth. Recent studies show disconcerting parallels between language disappearance, often taken to be an anodyne stepping-stone to economic prosperity, and progressive biological impoverishment of the ecosystem.[76]

Legal pluralism in and of itself is not likely to be a panacea to the problem of globalisation or to what sometimes appears to be the European Union's inexorably increasing erasure of differences.[77] One should be careful to avoid condemning unicity wholesale because it coincided with Nazi theory and practice.

Legal methodology may acquire a new sort of significance as part of the diversification paradigm. While we have seen that particular legal methodologies are unlikely have a strong causal correlation with substantive justice or injustice, it may well be that a convergence of methodologies culminating in a

---

[75] Hitler and Nazi legal theorists had German antecedents also critical of the French Revolution for excessive individualism. For nineteenth-century Prussian criticism of the *Code Napoléon* on those grounds, see A-W Rehberg, *Über dem Code Napoleon und dessen Einführung in Deutschland* (Hanover, Hahn, 1814) (cited in Carbonnier, at n 5 above, 1350, n 13.

[76] See D Nettle & S Romaine, *Vanishing Voices: The Extinction of the World's Languages* (Oxford, New York, Oxford University Press, 2000).

[77] See L Sheleff, *The Future of Tradition: Customary Law, Common Law and Legal Pluralism*, (London, Portland, or, F. Cass, 1999), 432–62, pluralism in and of itself neither necessarily beneficial or detrimental.

homogenised European legal methodology is likely to militate indirectly against justice and democracy, in accordance with Isaiah Berlin's insight that 'a unified answer in human affairs is likely to be ruinous . . .'[78]

Methodological pluralism has value in offering choices to the European Court of Justice, hallowed not so much by time or history as by accumulated judicial insights and perspectives, no doubt some to be rejected, but others that may well illuminate the path by enhancing judicial imagination in the future. In this sense, the European Court of Justice should seek insights not just from the formalist and anti-formalist methodologies discussed above, but also from the wealth of judicial tradition of its common-law constituent judiciaries. Europe, after all, in embarking on the most exciting adventure of our times, and arguably also of her history, should not cease to be a locus of memory, a *lieu de mémoire*.[79]

At the extreme end of pluralism lie chaos, disharmony and paralysis. On the other hand, the European fascist experience suggests that if the loss of pluralism in legal methodology is part of an increasing, perhaps even inexorable, motion towards uniformisation, it may entail sacrifice in a plenitude of vision that depends on diversity, and that may be extinguished irretrievably in its absence. Paradoxically, pluralism may be indispensable not just for cultural autonomy and diversity, but also for achieving an integrative, inclusive unification that encourages human independence, freedom and individuality, and that can continue to inspire those who live in the European Union to have confidence that it is worth preserving, developing and vigilantly safeguarding.

[78] I Berlin, *The Roots of Romanticism*, (Princeton, Princeton University Press, 1999) 146.
[79] See Nora, at n 5.

12

JUDICIAL METHODOLOGY AND FASCIST AND NAZI LAW

Matthias Mahlmann[*]

Dark legacies of the past demand many things from their heirs, especially because there is no disclaimer: to face what has been bequeathed, to remember the victims and to alleviate their suffering if still possible, to do justice to the perpetrators of the crimes, to make the very human effort to understand what has happened and to provide for the even more urgent human need to draw lessons from the past to prevent a future cataclysm. All this is or at least should be on the agenda of the countries to whose history a Fascist or Nazi past belongs, most notably of course, Germany. It should also be of great concern to anybody who cares for the course of human affairs. Within this context of great questions and tasks, the following remarks will address a problem which is at first view of a rather technical nature but that leads to important issues at the foundations of legal systems and that has been consequently much contested in scientific debates about Fascism and Nazism and the law:[1] what role did judicial methodology play in the facilitation of the establishment of Fascist or Nazi legal orders and what lessons can be drawn from the answer of this question for legal science at large and more concretely for the evolving European legal order?

The starting point of the following observations are some findings about the role methodology actually did play in the history of Fascist and Nazi legal systems. The second part of the paper will consist in an attempt—given these

[*] Assistant Professor of Public Law, Legal Philosophy and Legal Sociology, Law Faculty, Freie Universität Berlin.

[1] Vivian Curran raises all of these issues in her contribution to this volume. For more discussion, see V Curran, 'Fear of Formalism: Indications from the Fascist Period in France and Germany of Judicial Methodology's Impact on Substantive Law', (2001) *Cornell International Law Journal*.

Curran's main theses may be summarised as follows: (1) ideology and not legal methodology is the main causal factor for the development of a Fascist legal system; (2) as a consequence, both formalism and anti-formalism can serve such a system depending on circumstance and historical background. This was the case in France and Germany, respectively; (3) the lesson to be learned from the past is to aim for a culture of diversity of methods, cultures and values against the 'fascist value of oneness, the willed erasure of difference, multiplicity and otherness' as Curran puts it in her introduction. These theses will be commented on in this paper.

Thanks to Miriam Aziz, Vivian Curran, Navraj Singh Ghaleigh, Christian Joerges and Hubert Rottleuthner for comments.

findings—to defend moderate positivism as legal methodology of good
hermeneutic merits and best suited for democratic needs. The final part of the
paper will be devoted to a question the methodological considerations invariably lead to: what normative basis does the law have, if any, and if there is some
such foundation—what kind of value-system is defensible? This clearly leads to
one of the most contentious topics of practical philosophy. Thus, no surprisingly
insightful new answers can be expected in this paper. Nevertheless, some brief
remarks will be made to defend the view that a quite rational choice would be a
value system that has nothing to do with contingent national borders and imag-
inary collective essences of historically changing, often ideologically constructed
entities—such as nations, 'the Occident', the 'Judeo-Christian tradition', the
'Asian culture' and the like—but which is concerned with the only entity which
is properly of any real interest in moral questions, namely humanity itself: the
universalistic, international, cosmopolitan culture of human rights.

The impact of legal methodology on legal systems

a) The theoretical framework

There is a great intellectual tradition of legal hermeneutics. This comes as no
surprise for a quite obvious reason: modern legal cultures are invariably based on
texts like bills, statutes, constitutions, legal codes etc. These texts—unlike other
texts such as romantic poems to the moon—have very clear practical impact
(even though sometimes not great beauty). Understanding legal texts determines
as a consequence how to decide cases—in which considerable interests are regularly at stake. The question of methodology is thus not only of theoretical interest. There have been many schools of legal methodology.[2] There are numerous
hard questions involved, of which two are possibly the most difficult. The first
goes to the heart of the philosophy of language and the question of the *meaning*
of a word or sentence that forms perhaps the most contested issue of the

---

[2] On varieties of legal positivism: J Austin, *The Province of Jurisprudence Determined* (New
York, Burt Franklin, 1970) and HLA Hart, *The Concept of Law* (Oxford, Clarendon Press, 1961);
H Kelsen, *Reine Rechtslehre* (Wien, Franz Deuticke, 1960); legal realism: J Frank, *Law and the
Modern Mind* (New York, Anchor, 1966); critical legal studies: RM Unger, *The Critical Legal Studies
Movement* (Harvard University Press, Cambridge, 1983); constructive interpretation: R Dworkin,
Law's Empire (London, Fontana, 1986). In Germany, accounts of legal methodology for the 19th
century and the first half of the 20th century list conventionally *Historische Rechtsschule*, FC v
Savigny, *Vom Beruf unserer Zeit für Gesetzgebung und Rechtswissenschaft* (reprint of the edition
of 1840, Hildesheim, 1967); above, *System des heutigen römischen Rechts*, Band 1 (Aalen, Scientia,
1981); *Begriffsjurisprudenz*, Puchta, *Cursus der Institutionen*, 1. Buch (Leipzig, 1841);
Interessenjurisprudenz, P Heck *Das Problem der Rechtsgewinnung* (Bad Homburg, Gehlen, 1912);
Freie Rechtsschule, eg Kantorowicz *Der Kampf um die Rechtswissenschaft* (Heidelberg, 1906). The
post-war era is supposed to be dominated by the *Wertungsjurisprudenz*: K Larenz, *Methodenlehre
der Rechtswissenschaft* (Berlin, Springer, 1991), 119.

reflection about language in the twentieth century. Accordingly, depending on the outlook adopted in this respect the theories of legal methodology vary considerably—there are adherents to the hermeneutic tradition inspired by Gadamer's work,[3] to modern analytical philosophy of semantics formed by the later work of Wittgenstein[4] or Quine[5] among other important contributions or—a recent consequence of the mentalist revolution in linguistics[6]—the first tentative and very interesting mentalist accounts of legal methodology.[7] The second core question of legal methodology concerns the minimum moral content of the law—is there any? If so—what role does it play in solving concrete cases?

The different methodological schools are often divided into two main groups, with some injustice being rendered to the different point of views.[8] The formalist or positivist tradition is identified with the doctrine that the source of legal decisions are positive legal texts and authoritative legal decisions and nothing else. The law to be taken in consideration is positive law irrespective of its content, more specifically, irrespective of its moral merits. The anti-formalist or natural law tradition might be described as the doctrine that legal texts and authoritative legal decisions are not enough to determine a legal decision and that as a consequence one has to have recourse to considerations that are not part of the written law such as interests and, most importantly, basic values, to decide at least hard cases and possibly even most cases to be solved by legal practice. In addition, only those rules are law that embody a minimal content of morality. Certain meta-ethical positions are regularly associated with these methodological schools: positivism is supposed to be accompanied with some variety of ethical relativism according to which there is no universal, intersubjective ethical standard that could be applied legitimately by legal practitioners above and beyond the law. Anti-formalism in contrast is regarded to defend such an objective normative moral standard.

There is some debate of course whether one can actually choose between these methods—some anti-formalists would surely argue that they just admit to do what the positivists only pretend not to do because the reliance on extra-legal sources is simply inevitable and thus also deployed by the positivists while they are claiming to do otherwise. But there are many voices that stick to the view that there is an element of choice and for the sake of the normative argument contained in these remarks let us assume that there is some truth in this view.

---

[3] H-G Gadamer, *Wahrheit und Methode* (Tübingen, Mohr, 1972).

[4] L Wittgenstein, *Philosophische Untersuchungen* (Frankfurt/M, Suhrkamp, 1984).

[5] WVO Quine, *Word and Object* (Cambridge, The MIT Press, 1960).

[6] N Chomsky, *Aspects of the Theory of Syntax* (Cambridge, The MIT Press, 1965); above *Reflections on Language* (London, Temple Smith, 1976); above *Knowledge of Language* (Westport, Praeger, 1986).

[7] L Solan, 'Why Laws Work Pretty Well but Not Great: Words and Rules in Legal Interpretation', (2001) 26 *Law & Social Inquiry*, 243.

[8] Alternative distinctions are of course possible, eg R Dworkin, *Law's Empire* (London, Fontana, 1986), 33 distinguishes positivism, the school of natural law and legal realism.

b) The historical record

As far as the historical record of the effects of judicial methodology is concerned the best researched example is Germany. There has been extensive discussion on the question which role the different methodological schools played in establishing the perverted, barbarian Nazi legal order, with some findings that are—after long debate—not contested any more.[9] The famous beginning of this debate was Radbruch's thesis, that positivism had made German lawyers defenceless against the onslaught of Nazi law—they just applied it without consideration for the content.[10] This view has interesting implications, most importantly perhaps that the legal community became a victim of the Nazi legislator and of a bad methodology. It becomes a justification for the role of the legal community played during the Third Reich. This Radbruch-thesis has been refuted through closer historical studies on two accounts. Firstly, the German lawyers were not particularly positivistic in their outlook. There is ample evidence, that during the First German Republic of Weimar the judiciary actively circumvented legal regulations when it seemed justified according to their predominantly anti-republican outlook.[11] Secondly, it became clear that the judiciary played a quite active role in establishing the Nazi legal order, anticipating regulations that were not yet enacted often by clearly circumventing the written law by material considerations, reference to Nazi ideology and the like.[12] To take an example, one commentator and drafter of the Nürnberg-Race laws of 1935, Lösener, commented on the legal situation of certain aspects

---

[9] There are of course important influences on the judiciary beyond methodology that played a crucial role in creating the conformity to the Nazi legal system—fears of sanctions, direct intervention by authorities, creation of insecurity in the judiciary, making the judiciary an accomplice of illegal action as a test of loyalty and the like. For detailed analyses, see H Rottleuthner, *Die Konformität des Rechtsstabes*, (manuscript on file with author), 17.

[10] G Radbruch 'Gesetzliches Unrecht und übergesetzliches Recht', (1946) *Süddeutsche Juristenzeitung* 105 at 107. 'Der Positivismus hat in der Tat mit seiner Überzeugung "Gesetz ist Gesetz" den deutschen Juristenstand wehrlos gemacht gegen Gesetze willkürlichen und verbrecherischen Inhalts'. Cf O Lepsius, *Die gegensatzaufhebende Begriffsbildung* (München, Beck, 1994), 320.

[11] A classical example for the bias of the judiciary in die Republic of Weimar are the convictions for political murder. According to the statistics of J Gumbel, from 1919 to 1922 for 354 right-wing killings the perpetrators were convicted to one lifelong imprisonment and 90 years of imprisonment and some pecuniary penalties. The perpetrators of 22 left-wing killings were in contrast convicted to 10 death sentences, three life long imprisonments and 248 years of imprisonment, EJ Gumbel, *Vier Jahre politischer Mord* (Berlin, Verlag der Neuen Gesellschaft, 1922). See on this matter H Rottleuthner 'Rechtspositivismus und Nationalsozialismus', (1983) 19 *Recht und Politik* 195; above 'Rechtspositivismus und Nationalsozialismus: Bausteine zu einer Theorie der Rechtsentwicklung', (1987) *Demokratie und Recht* 373; M Walther, 'Hat der juristische Positivismus die deutschen Juristen im "Dritten Reich" wehrlos gemacht?' in R Dreier & W Sellert (ed.), *Recht und Justiz im 'Dritten Reich'* (Frankfurt/M, Suhrkamp 1989).

[12] I Müller, *Furchtbare Juristen* (München, Kindler, 1987); B Rüthers, *Entartetes Recht* (München, Beck, 1989); Bundesministerium der Justiz, *Im Namen des Deutschen Volkes. Justiz und Nationalsozialismus* (Köln, Wissenschaft und Politik, 1989).

of family law before 1935 that—through the actions of the judiciary—there was a 'Stillstand der staatlichen Rechtspflege,' (a stagnation of the due process of law).[13] The background was that parts of the judiciary had taken the initiative to nullify marriages which were of mixed race according to Nazi ideology on the demand of one of the spouses that wanted to circumvent divorce or shared the Nazi ideology and marriage registrars refused to marry couples on these grounds.[14] This happened before any specialised legislation was enacted. As a consequence, one of the reasons for the concrete content of Nürnberg-Race laws of 1935 was the activity of the judiciary.[15] The legal community was not a tool or even a victim of the Nazi state and its positivist methodology but part of the social groups that established it. It was not made helpless by positivism but rather made anti-formalism a sharp tool for the racist and anti-human aims many of its members actively pursued.

As a consequence, it seems that many early excesses would have not been possible if the German lawyers had been as positivist as assumed by Radbruch. In addition, some signs of the dissolution of the law in the Nazi state would have been more obvious for the legal community as positivism is not only about the application of norms. It sets standards for the form of the norms applied as well. According to these standards, such as the principle of clarity and definiteness of the wording of enactments, much of what passed for law in Nazi Germany[16] and possibly elsewhere like France[17] was no law at all.

---

[13] B Lösener, 'Als Rassereferent im Reichsministerium des Innern', (1961) *Vierteljahreshefte für Zeitgeschichte* 262 at 278.

[14] A Rethmeier, *'Nürnberger Rassegesetze' und Entrechtung der Juden im Zivilrecht* (Frankfurt/M, 1995) 38, 54; Müller note 12 98 ff.

[15] For further comments on the genesis of the Nürnberg-Race laws and some proposals for possible theoretical lessons of this genesis for the understanding of the evolution of law compare M Mahlmann 'Katastrophen der Rechtsgeschichte und die autopoietische Evolution des Rechts', in G Teubner (eds), *Paradoxien des Rechts*, (2000) 21 Zeitschrift für Rechtssoziologie 247.

[16] For detailed comments compare Rottleuthner (1987) note 11 388; I Maus 'Gesetzesbindung' der Justiz und die Struktur der nationalsozialistischen Rechtsnormen, in R Dreier/W Sellert, n 11 80, 93. Much discussed examples are the ministerial order on the punishment of Poles and Jews (Verordnung über die Strafrechtspflege gegen Polen und Juden in den eingegliederten Ostgebieten vom 4.12.1941, RGBl. I, 759) or the retroactive legalisation of the killings during the 'Röhm-Putsch' in 1934 by the Gesetz über Maßnahmen der Staatsnotwehr vom 3.7.1934, (RGBl I, 529). Other properties of the Nazi legal system are open to a positivist critique as well, eg the lack of prosecution of formally illegal acts by the Nazis—from violence against dissenters to the crimes of the concentration camps or the legality of the system established contrary to the provisions of the Constitution of Weimar. Radbruch commented in a letter of 26 April 1939, that given the situation Germany was in at that time, positivism seemed to him to be an 'ideal': 'Und jetzt will mir der Positivismus sogar als ein Ideal erscheinen', G Radbruch *Gesamtausgabe* Band 13 (Heidelberg, Müller, 1995) 154.

[17] The formalistic tradition of French legal thought has been often emphasised—as its tradition to decide *praeter* or *contra legem* if the need arose, eg M Troper, C Grzegoczyk & J-L Gardies, *Statuory Interpretation in France* in DN MacCormick & RS Summers (eds), *Interpreting Statutes* (Aldershot, Dartmouth, 1991) 172. As to the application of anti-semitic Vichy law, studies have emphasised the formalist features of legal methodology, eg RH Weisberg, *Vichy Law and the Holocaust in France* (Amsterdam, Harwood, 1996) 401 (though arguing for the existence of an

The Radbruch thesis thus is widely taken to be refuted.[18] As a consequence it seems unavoidable to conclude that not the legal methodology but the ideological beliefs current in the societies of that time and more concretely of the legal communities itself are core factors for an explanation of the evolution of the legal systems in the Nazi and Fascist orders.[19]

This observation leads to the next question these remarks want to address: what lessons are to be learned from these findings which have not been made for the sake of pure historical analysis alone but are supposed—as indicated above—to inform the discussion about which judicial methodology is recommendable for the evolving European legal order? Can positivism really serve as such a methodology? Is there not a problem that positivism cannot solve? What if a society enacts very clear and definite racist norms? Is this not the real shortcoming of positivism even if one admits, as it is widely done, its relative merits as a barrier to perversions of the law? Is positivism not without methodological remedy against such norms because it has renounced the import of extra-legal norms within the legal system, most importantly by erecting a minimal moral standard for any law to be actually law? Is exactly this not the real lesson of the past: the need to erect absolute barriers to the perversion of the law by applying only law that matches this minimal moral standard? Is Radbruch's famous formula[20] proposing exactly this not rightly

---

antiformalist 'other side of the Vichy hermeneutic coin, the *non-statutory* flexibility of the Vichy community' as well, above 402 (emphasis in the original). Some questions that have been asked about the Nazi law might be asked for the Vichy law as well, including the very fundamental one concerning the constitutional legality of the whole regime: 'Avant de considérer la place de l'administration et des juges dans l'application des lois antijuives sous le régime de Vichy, il faut considérer la source initiale de ces lois: le seul organe législative reconnu par les lois de 1875, l'Assemblée nationale, s'était démis de ses functions. Les chambres réunies renonçaient à la compétence des compétences, en légiférant contre elles-mêmes. Elles décidaient . . . de ne plus rien décider, en cessant de délibérer et d'adopter les lois. N'etait-ce pas contraire, pourtant, à l'article 8 de la loi du 25 février 1875, selon lequel "la forme républicaine du gouvernement ne peut faire l'objet d'une proposition de révision"?' D Gros, 'Un droit monstrueux?' in Le droit antisémite de Vichy, 30, 31 *Le Genre Humain* (1996). For some critical remarks on positivism Danièle Lochak, *Écrire, se taire . . . Réflexions sur l'attitude de la doctrine française* in Le droit antisémite de Vichy, 454.

[18] In her conclusion Curran sums up her ambivalent findings of the French methodology in which numerous incidents of anti-formalist applications of the law are mentioned as follows: 'We have seen that the French judiciary was more formalistic in overt tradition than its German counterpart, but that its practices would allow for a characterisation of lack of formalism if one considers the numerous ways in which the courts traditionally also carved out paths to reach substantive results they deemed desirable, with far less deference to enacted law than they claimed or than appeared on the surface of the text of court decisions. On the other hand, their overt deference to the letter of textual law itself bespeaks of positivism'. All of this—the ambivalence of French methodology, the anti-formalism in the application of Fascist laws in Vichy (see n 17)—seems to suggest reluctance to formulate a Radbruch-thesis for the French case as well.

[19] As Curran very convincingly points out.

[20] G Radbruch 'Gesetzliches Unrecht und übergesetzliches Recht', (1946) *Süddeutsche Juristenzeitung* 105 at 107.

regarded, in theoretical reflection[21] and judicial practice,[22] to be without alternative?

To answer these questions, one has to consider what positivism actually means, what relation it has to meta-ethical positions and whether it is compatible with the necessity of absolute barriers against the perversion of the law anew and beyond the simplistic and common picture painted above about the two methodological schools.

Positivism, universalism and democracy

a) The merits of positivism

The first question to be answered for reassessing the respective merits of different schools of judicial methodology is rather fundamental, namely: is there actually anything like a *meaning* of a norm, or more precisely, the sentence formulating a norm? If that is not the case, if such a sentence can mean anything, positivism is senseless as there is nothing positive to be applied. Positivism clearly presupposes the possibility to fix the meaning of a norm.

Let us consider a simple example. The norm 'dogs are not allowed in the park' might pose all kinds of familiar interpretative problems, some easier, some more difficult to solve: Are cats allowed in the park? what about bears? what about dogs for blind people? etc. For core cases, however, the norm seems clear enough. If James enters the park at noon with his German Shepherd for a stroll, the norm clearly applies. For most norms there are clear cases like this and this should not be forgotten. Not only hard cases provide philosophical insights as often is assumed in philosophical reflection, simple cases do too. The accounts for the basis of understanding the meaning of norms like this will be different according to the semantic theory applied—a Gadamerian might refer to some kind of 'Vorverständnis'[23] shared by a cultural community whilst a Wittgensteinian might point to a 'Sprachspiel'[24] that established a certain way to understand this norm. Most promisingly, perhaps, the recent findings of mentalist linguistics might be applied that base understanding of a language on a common 'language faculty' of human beings that is relevant for semantics, too.[25] There is a lot to say about the respective merits of these schools and there

---

[21] Eg R Alexy *Begriff und Geltung des Rechts* (Alber, Freiburg/Br, 1992) 201.

[22] The German courts applied it both after 1945 and after 1989: BGHSt 2, 234, BGHSt 39, 1; BVerfGE 95, 96. For some comments C Laage 'Die Auseinandersetzung um den Begriff des gesetzlichen Unrechts nach 1945' (1989) *Kritische Justiz* 409.

[23] H-G Gadamer, *Wahrheit und Methode* (Tübingen, Mohr, 1972), 252 ff. Gadamer emphasises, however, the historical relativity of understanding at 277 ff.

[24] L Wittgenstein, *Philosophische Untersuchungen* (Frankfurt/M, Suhrkamp, 1984), 7.

[25] N Chomsky, *New Horizons in the Study of Language and Mind* (Cambridge, Cambridge University Press, 2000).

is of course an enormous literature on these questions. In the context of these short remarks, however, it must suffice to note that it is not senseless to speak of norms with a fixed meaning for core cases and that there are serious philosophical and linguistic theories to account for this observation. Positivism is as a consequence contrary to radical legal scepticism[26] not without necessary semantic preconditions.

The next question concerns the role of extra-legal consideration for legal systems. This is another very difficult question that merits further scrutiny. Here a crude form of positivism is surely untenable that asserts that it is possible to solve any case without any reference to any extra-legal normative standards in the process of legal interpretation. To take just one but very important example: the adjudication of human rights. In these human rights, the classical content of enlightened (and for a period, revolutionary) natural law is positivised.[27] Again, contentious issues arise as to the methods of the interpretation of human rights catalogues that have been widely discussed. It seems, however, that there is a consensus that to a certain degree this adjudication necessarily draws from normative standards that are not derivable from positive law as such.[28] Take the example of human dignity which now stands as a central norm of the European Union by the Charter of Fundamental Human Rights.[29] To determine what this concept concretely means, any interpreter and any court has to make choices between a great variety of possible contents—Thomas Aquinas theological, community orientated concept of human dignity[30] is for example quite different from Immanuel Kant's individualistic formula.[31] The choice between conceptions of dignity is surely of a different difficulty than the choice between different concepts of 'dog' or 'park' that is the precondition of understanding the norm mentioned above. This choice of any of these possible contents is not determined by the law itself—it cannot be so because this choice

---

[26] Compare the assertion that the limits of interpretation are themselves a question of interpretation, N Luhmann, *Das Recht der Gesellschaft* (Frankfurt/M, Suhrkamp, 1993) 256.

[27] R Dreier, *Recht—Moral—Ideologie* (Frankfurt/M, Suhrkamp, 1981) 124.

[28] R Alexy, *Theorie der Grundrechte* (Frankfurt/M, Suhrkamp, 1985) 19, 494. One might be able to narrow down the space for these kinds of choices by the classical interpretational methods of genetic, systemic or teleological interpretation. But there is a wide perception that—at least in a considerable number of cases—the solution of the case determines the choice of the methods and not vice versa. The same seems true for classical legal arguments like *e contrario* or *per analogiam* by which opposite results can be justified.

[29] For some comments compare M Mahlmann, 'Die Grundrechtscharta der Europäischen Union', (2000) *Zeitschrift für Europarechtliche Studien*, 419.

[30] 'homo peccando ab ordine rationis recedit; et ideo decidit a dignitate humana, prout scilicet homo est naturaliter liber et propter seipsum existens (cf Eth. 3, 3), et incidit quodammodo in servitutem bestiarum, ut scilicet de ipso ordinetur secundum quod est utile aliis (. . .). Et ideo quamvis hominem in sua dignitate manentem occidere sit secundum se malum, tamen hominem peccatorem occidere potest esse bonum, sicut occidere bestiam: pejor enim est malus homo bestia, et plus nocet, ut Philosophus dicit (. . .)', Thomas Aquinas, *summa theologica*, II-II, q. 64, 2.

[31] I Kant *Grundlegung der Metaphysik der Sitten*, Akademie Ausgabe, vol. IV, 434 ff.

is the precondition of understanding what the law actually is in the first place. Consequently, the choices between interpretive possibilities are determined by many factors that will not play a role when interpreting the concepts 'dog' or 'park'—among others certain theories of the state, of the good organisation of societies, concepts of humans or moral values. There are influences beyond the written law that thus play an important role in the interpretation of norms and whose influence should not be denied by any theory of legal methodology and which are real enough in any practical adjudication of norms. If any variety of positivism is supposed to be taken seriously it should acknowledge these facts.[32]

The third question asks whether positivism is necessarily connected with certain meta-ethical positions, more precisely with relativism of some sort. In discussions about positivism the question of the relationship of law and morals appears in two respects. First, the relation of law and morals plays a role for the problem of whether law—to be valid law—actually has to conform to a minimum standard of morality. This is the problem of the identification of law. Secondly,—as discussed above—the relation of law and morals is problematic as to the application of law.

Clearly, if one considers the history of ideas, it has mostly been the case that positivists tended to be moral relativists. The thinkers that developed positivist doctrines regularly embraced some kind of scepticism as to the possibility of a universalistic foundation of values.[33] Often positivism was even a consequence of a relativist outlook—if one holds the view that there are no universal values but perceives the necessity of some kind of normative order, the law is the last resort. Law plays the role morality cannot play anymore—the balancing of interests, the creation of a minimal normative foundation of society. As a consequence of these sceptical views, the concept of law is purified by legal theorists from any moral content—law is regarded as a set of rules generated according to certain procedures.[34] Whatever its content—a rule generated in this manner still has the character of law. Adequately, the application of law is purified of any moral considerations, too—as we have seen to certain degree falsely so.

It is worthwhile to note that there is, however, no necessary connection between a positivist outlook and moral relativism or even scepticism. The first

---

[32] Positivists have emphasised the indeterminacy of norms. Kelsen for example argued that the point of legal interpretation is the delineation of the possible applications of a norm. Within these limits the applicator of the norm is in his view completely free. The attempts of classical interpretative theories to narrow down this freedom was regarded by him as mere legal politics, H Kelsen, *Zur Theorie der Interpretation* in H Klecatsky, R Marcic & H Schambeck (eds), *Die Wiener rechtstheoretische Schule* (Wien, Europa, 1968), 1363 at 1366, 1368. This is perhaps a too pessimistic view about the range of rationality in legal interpretation.

[33] H Kelsen, *Reine Rechtslehre* (Wien, Franz Deuticke, 1960), 65 ff.

[34] Eg a Grundnorm, H Kelsen, above; or a rule of recognition, HLA Hart, *The Concept of Law* (Oxford, Clarendon Press, 1961).

step to clarify this is by recalling Hart's important remark on the relationship of positive law and morals taking up some insights Austin had formulated a century before that started the famous debate between Herbert Hart and Lon Fuller. Austin insisted—quite convincingly it seems—on the distinction of the existence of law and its evaluation:

> The *existence* of a law is one thing: its *merits* or *demerits* are another thing. Whether a law *be*, in one inquiry: whether it *ought* to be, or whether it agrees with a given or assumed test, is another and distinct inquiry.[35]

Hart pointed out that this analysis has some advantages:

> There are (. . .) two dangers between which insistence on this distinction will help us to steer: the danger that law and its authority may be dissolved in man's conception of what law ought to be and the danger that the existing law may supplant morality as a final test of conduct and so escape criticism.[36]

The important point of this argument for the context pursued here is that it clarifies that positivism is compatible with the view that there are normative standards beyond the law.[37] One might regard law in a formal and pragmatic way independently of the content and still be able to criticise law on moral grounds because morality forms a different and actually more important standard for conduct than positive law.[38] The question that arises next, is what kind of morality is defended as 'final test of conduct'. This is however, a question completely independent from the question of adhering to a positivist tradition in the sense outlined or not. The 'final test of conduct' might be based on a relativist outlook or a universalistic one. This will depend on the personal convictions concerning moral epistemology but not on the question whether one adheres to positivism or not. There is no necessary connection between positivism and a certain meta-ethical belief.

Given these findings on the question of the semantic preconditions of legal interpretation, the extra-legal influences on legal interpretation and the

---

[35] J Austin, *The Province of Jurisprudence Determined* (New York, 1970), 233.

[36] HLA Hart *Positivism and the Separation of Law and Morals* in *Essays in Jurisprudence and Philosophy*, (Oxford, Clarendon Press, 1983) 54.

[37] This is of course a very contested view. According to Habermas for example the conception of a hierarchy of morality and law belongs to the pre-modern world, J Habermas *Faktizität und Geltung* (Frankfurt, M, Suhrkamp, 1992) 137, 286. On the other hand, legal validity is—according to him—still dependent on morality, above 137. It is not clear how this is possible without assuming a hierarchy between morality and law.

[38] There are even good reasons to assume that a formal concept of law clearly distinguished from morals can help to keep the moral conscience of citizens alive: 'What surely is most needed in order to make men clear sighted in confronting the official abuse of power, is that they should preserve the sense that the certification of something as legally valid is not conclusive of the question of obedience, and that, however great the aura of majesty or authority which the official system may have, its demands must in the end be submitted to a moral scrutiny', HLA Hart, *The Concept of Law* (Oxford, Clarendon Press, 1961) at 206.

relationship of law and morals, it is quite clear that some sort of crude positivism that assumes, that first, any norm has a clear fixed meaning, that secondly from this meaning the solution for any case can be deduced by a couple of logical inferences without reference to any other than legal consideration and that thirdly there is no higher instance than the law as final test of human conduct is untenable. But some moderate, pragmatic positivism that avoids these mistakes might still make a lot of sense. This moderate, pragmatic positivism holds that for core cases norms have a fixed meaning without denying that there are important extra-legal influences on the interpretation of law. It holds that there is a burden of proof for any interpreter, that—given any norm—the norm cannot be interpreted without recourse to such extra-legal considerations. Legal doctrine has to make these influences transparent, open to criticism and has to try to develop and defend standards of rationality for the evaluation of these influential extra-legal considerations.[39] It insists, thus, that norms are actually a constraint for legal interpretation and practice—a lesson especially important given findings outlined above about legal voluntarism in the Fascist and Nazi past.[40] It holds further, that there are good reasons for a formal concept of law *and* that morality is the final test for human conduct and thus for legal rules as well.

The most important reason for this kind of moderate, pragmatic positivism is that it seems to be the legal methodology best suited for democracies. Democracies presuppose the possibility to regulate a society according to the will of the majority by legal rules. A legal methodology that increases the binding power of legal norms thus might help to transfer the will of the citizens into legal practice. In contrast, the more interpretative leeway is given to the legal professions, the more they tend to become legislators in judicial disguise. This is, to a certain degree unavoidable as explained above but should be limited as far as possible if one is interested in the rule of people instead of the rule of judges. Pragmatic, moderate positivisms aims to do exactly that.

b) The philosophical plausibility and political necessity of Universalism

The last question to be answered in these remarks concerns the question of the value system the judicial methodology is supposed to be embedded in. As

---

[39] For example: Conceptions of humanity play an important role for the interpretation of human rights. Some theories of (philosophical) anthropology are, however, worse than others. There are rational standards to assess these merits. For some comments eg on A Gehlen's highly influential theory and its connections to Nazi ideology compare M Mahlmann *Rationalismus in der praktischen Theorie* (Baden-Baden, Nomos, 1999) 348.

[40] As Curran remarks in her introduction: 'I do believe that positivism, in conjunction with more fundamental overriding causes, played, and continues to play, some role in encouraging substantive outcomes that comply with the texts of enacted law'. This seems to be a desirable effect of legal methodology.

explained, the proposed moderate, pragmatic positivism acknowledges the importance of such a value system for legal interpretation and underscores its social relevance as final test for questions of human conduct.

One of the clear lessons of the totalitarian system of Fascism and National Socialism is the categorical imperative of modern times to defend tolerance and plurality in every sphere of life. One of the sources of the post-modern culture of diversity, of discussions about the 'Other' and pluralism is surely the perception of this imperative. It is presumably not too farfetched to assume that part of the appeal of post-modern writing is derived from its apparently radical opposition to any kind of totalitarianism. The strong tendency in post-modern thought to be mistrustful of any kind of universalism, is, however, philosophically not very convincing and politically rather dangerous. Let us consider one clarificatory example: the diversity of people and the diversity of values which are intricately connected in post-modern discourse.

It is regarded as a truism by cultural relativists that there are clearly defined collective entities like nations, the 'western culture' and the like. It is even possibly the standard argument in philosophical debates about the foundations of values that they originate from such homogenous contingent cultural traditions.[41] German values are as a consequence opposed to French ones, European to American, Western values to Asian ones and so on, in ever new constellations.

The problems of these post-modern varieties of cultural essentialism are, however, firstly that these models of thought overlook the role of individuals for moral judgments. Moral judgments are always the judgments of concrete human beings. Cultures and other entities do not judge morally, only persons do.[42] Thus, the moral judgments of individuals are at the core of any system of values. Cultural traditions are a secondary product of these judgments (which of course might in turn influence them to a certain degree). But people are able to transcend any given tradition and are constantly doing so. This is the reason for moral innovation and change, sometimes for the better, sometimes for the worse. Secondly, there are good philosophical theories to make the assumption plausible that there are universal standards for moral judgment—the most plausible perhaps a mentalist account of ethics and law that continues the project of enlightened moral philosophy with the conceptual means of the modern post-metaphysical theory of the mind. From this perspective, there is a promising explanatory theory for a universal basis for moral understanding: a *moral sense*[43]

---

[41] A classic statement of this view is offered by R Rorty *Human Rights, Rationality and Sentimentality* in S Shute & S Hurley (ed), *On Human Rights* (New York, Basic Books, 1993) 111 ff.

[42] Judgments of individuals might be taken as judgments of an entity due to institutional arrangements that make these persons and their decisions represent the collective body, eg in a parliament. The agents of moral judgment are, however, always concrete individuals.

[43] F Hutcheson *An Inquiry into the Original of Our Ideas of Beauty and Virtue* (New York, Garland Publishing, 1971); above *Illustrations on the Moral Sense* (Cambridge MA, Belknapp, 1971).

or *practical reason*[44] in enlightened, a *moral faculty* in modern terminology that generates moral judgements and forms the basis for human core intuitions of freedom, solidarity and justice.[45]

As a consequence, there is a plausible philosophical foundation for the claim, that the categorical imperative of tolerance has cross-cultural foundations, that the defence of human dignity, freedom and equality are values for any human culture. The positive aim of the counter-culture of tolerance is thus not plurality as such, but pluralism with a firm universalistic basis, in modern times in essential parts codified in human rights.

This view is a practical necessity, too. Without this basis, the culture of tolerance is defenceless against the attempts to disguise conventional power politics with the veil of impenetrable cultural traditions. The claim of any authoritarian ruler that his violations of human rights are actually no violation at all but just the embodiment of a certain cultural tradition not to be criticised by another equally contingent cultural tradition could not be challenged if one embraces the principles of radical pluralism so popular today. It should however not be taken more seriously than the claim of Louis XVI that Absolutism is an embodiment of the values of France.

In this sense, there appears to be nothing wrong with a unified human culture. Quite to the contrary, it is a great but rather remote hope in a world pursuing energetically and with determination a quite different course.

---

[44] On the relation of this approach to Kant's practical philosophy and to moral sense theories compare M Mahlmann *Rationalismus in der praktischen Theorie* (Baden-Baden, Nomos, 1999).

[45] For some work on ethical mentalism see N Chomsky *Language and Problems of Knowledge* (MIT Press, Cambridge, 1988) 152; M Bierwisch, *Recht linguistsch gesehen* in G Grewendorf (ed), *Rechtskultur als Sprachkultur* (Frankfurt/M, Suhrkamp, 1992) 42; S Stich, *Moral Philosophy and Mental Representation* in M Hechter, L Nadel & RE Michod (eds), *The Origin of Values* (New York, Aldine de Gruyter; 1993), 215; G Harman, *Explaining Value* (Oxford, Oxford University Press, 2000); R Jackendoff, *The Natural Logic of Rights and Obligations* in R Jackendoff, P Bloom & K Wynn (eds), *Language, Logic and Concepts* (Cambridge, The MIT Press, 1999); S Dwyer, *Moral Competence* in K Murasagi & R Stainton (eds), *Philosophy and Linguistics* (Boulder, Westview Press) 169; M Mahlmann n 44. Especially illuminating and innovative J Mikhail, *Rawls' Linguistic analogy*, Cornell Ph.D. dissertation, 2000. Universalism is not to all of these authors the consequence of a mentalistic approach. This is, however, not very convincing.

13

ON NAZI 'HONOUR' AND THE NEW EUROPEAN 'DIGNITY'

*James Q Whitman**

The new Europe is founded on a forthright rejection of the fascist past. This is a commonplace. It is commonplace that we repeat when we describe the European repudiation of nationalism and militarism. Perhaps most of all it is a commonplace that we repeat when we discuss the European embrace of the values of 'dignity,' and 'dignity''s imposing cousin, '*human* dignity.' In the wake of World War II, 'human dignity' was sanctified in number of constitutions—most significantly in those of post-Fascist Italy and post-Nazi Germany. Since then, the campaign for 'dignity' or 'human dignity' has swept through wide regions of post-war European law, both public and private, from bioethics to pornography to criminal punishment to the protection of personality. In the literature on all these areas of law we find forthright rejection of the legacy of the fascist era, and especially of the horrors of Nazism. This drive for 'dignity' has given a distinctive shape to European law, setting it sharply apart from the law of the United States in particular. Indeed, if we were looking for one phrase to capture the last fifty years of European legal history—or at least of *continental* legal history; Britain's place in this tale is very uncertain—we might call it the high era of 'dignity.' And if we accept the commonplace view of continental lawyers, we should credit the triumph of the values of 'dignity' precisely to the widespread disgust Europeans have felt for the practices of the era of Mussolini and Hitler.

But does contemporary European 'dignity' really represent such a clear break with those with the awful days of what I will call, for the sake of convenience, the 'fascist era'?[1] When we look closely at the record, the story is messier than one might wish. The truth is that important threads of continuity connect the fascist era, horrific as it was, with the subsequent era of dignity. To

* Yale Law School. My thanks for comments to participants in the original EUI workshop, and to participants at presentations at the American Association of Law Schools and Cardozo Law School, as well as to Rainer Schröder and Henry Turner.

[1] I choose this term in order to avoid some of the difficulties raised by the question of the relationship between Nazism and Fascism. Certainly, from the point of view of the self-understanding of contemporary European jurists, it is not necessary to distinguish carefully between the two as historical phenomena: to jurists, both represent a kind of generic 'fascism.'

be sure, there are prominent aspects of the contemporary law of 'dignity' or 'human dignity' that are best understood as the products of a reaction against fascist-era coldbloodedness. The abolition of the death penalty, at least in Germany and Italy, is one case. The characterisation of many harsh punishment practices as 'torture' is another. The relatively easy-going internal regulation of the military everywhere in continental Europe is a third. The continental attitude toward questions of bioethics may represent a fourth example. Most of all, the determination of continental jurists to find ways to integrate racial and other minorities into their societies represents an unmistakeable break with the appalling work of the Nazis. Yet at the same time, the unpalatable truth is that certain other prominent aspects of the contemporary European law of dignity rest on practices whose histories reach well back into the fascist period, and even into the Nazi darkness.

Let me tick off a few examples of this unpalatable truth, some familiar, some unfamiliar, concentrating on Germany. One example is the protection of 'personality'—the rubric under which German law provides extensive safeguards for the right of privacy and a variety of other individual dignitary interests. The protection of personality is regarded as the core body of doctrine dedicated to the preservation of dignity in German private law; and the rise of the protection of personality is widely described as a triumph of the humane German jurisprudence of the 1950s. Yet in fact the protection of personality was proclaimed in sources from the Nazi era—notably the 1941 *Volksgesetzbuch*, the draft 'People's Code' of the Nazis, and the first, 1939, edition of Palandt's still-standard commentary on the *BGB*, the German Civil Code.[2] This fact is not unknown, but those who mention it seem to it treat it simply as a curiosity. Much the same is true of another major institution of contemporary dignitary law. Regularized probation, *Strafaussetzung zur Bewährung*, is universally regarded as the central institution of post-fascist, humane, punishment practice. The standard literature generally describes probation as having been introduced in 1953, as part of a grand reaction against the harsh punishment practices of the Nazis. Yet in fact regularized probation too was first introduced *by* the Nazis, in 1935. German lawyers were still quite conscious of this unexpected and troubling truth in the early 1950s, and they commented on it then; but it has since been, carelessly or wilfully, forgotten.[3] The law of collective insult, another institution of central importance for the German law of human dignity, similarly rests on jurisprudence of the Nazi era—most notably on decisions aimed at protecting the honour of the SA and the SS. This strange fact was noted by no less a figure than Arthur Kaufmann in 1960;[4] but since then,

---

[2] See generally S Gottwald, *Das allgemeine Persönlichkeitsrecht. Ein zeitgeschichtliches Erklärungsmodell* (Berlin, 1996), 47–57.

[3] Discussed in my forthcoming book, *Harsh Justice*, ch IV (forthcoming from Oxford University Press, 2003).

[4] A Kaufmann, 'Zur Frage der Beleidigung von Kollektivpersönlichkeiten', (1960) 72 *Zeitschrift f. die gesamte Strafrechtswissenschaft* 419–20.

other authors seem to have been deemed it unworthy of comment. Many other examples can be offered, especially from the world of the social welfare state. From health care, to paid vacations, to protection from arbitrary discharge, the regulation of the contemporary social welfare state—the real practical home, for most Europeans, of 'human dignity'—owes a great deal to the work of the 1930s.

What should we say about this? Are these just bizarre trivia of legal history, without any ultimate significance for the understanding of contemporary Europe? Or do they tell us something more important about the continuities between the fascist era and the present?

In this chapter, I am going to defend the proposition that these facts do indeed tell us something important about real continuities between the Nazi era and the German world of today. 'Dignity' as it is protected in contemporary German law is not just the product of a reaction against Nazism; seen in proper sociological perspective, 'dignity' as it is protected today, is the product of an evolution that partly took place *during* the fascist era. This is a case that has to be made with care, of course, and with some philosophical subtlety; only an idiot would give the Nazis any share of credit for the invention of 'dignity.' But as the Nazi period recedes slowly into the past, it is a case that has to be made. The twentieth century has ended, and we should be ready to reflect a little more soberly, and a little more open-mindedly, on the place of the fascist period in the history of the continuous development of European law. For of course the history of the development of European law is largely a history of continuities, just as all human history is largely a history of continuities. What Tocqueville famously demonstrated about the French Revolution—that it represented not a simple rupture in French history, but a step in an unbroken march—is also true of the fascist era, and it is time that legal historians acknowledged as much.

The case that I want to make, stated briefly, is this. The many, various and disturbing instances in which we discover Nazi origins of modern practices of 'human dignity' have something in common: they are, for the most part, cases in which Nazi law aimed to vindicate claims of 'honour,' of *Ehre*. Correspondingly, the right way to understand the connection between the Nazi period and the high era of 'dignity' that followed it, is to focus on the connection between contemporary values of 'dignity' and older values of 'honour.' And those values are indeed connected: *modern 'dignity,' as we see it in continental legal cultures, is in fact often best understood, from the sociological point of view, as a generalisation of old norms of social honour.* European dignitary law, as it exists today, is largely founded on doctrinal sources and fundamental concepts that are drawn from the old law of social honour, dating back to an older era of continental social hierarchy. What has happened, in continental Europe, is indeed fundamentally this: old norms of 'honour,' norms that applied only to aristocrats and a few other high-status categories of persons in the seventeenth and eighteenth centuries, have gradually been extended to the entire population. As I have argued at length elsewhere, what we observe in the contemporary dignitary law of continental Europe is a striking pattern of *levelling up*: a pattern, of the kind analysed by such sociologists as Elias and Bourdieu, by which high-status patterns of behaviour are generalised throughout the lower strata of the population.[5] The rise of the contemporary culture of generalised 'dignity' is the latest stage in this long process of the social extension of norms of honour: 'human dignity' for everybody, as it exists at the end of the twentieth century, means definitive admission to high social status for everybody.

Now that is a large and complex thesis, which I cannot fully prove in this paper. Nevertheless, I hope my readers will accept it, at least provisionally. For it is in light of this long history of levelling up that we can best interpret the continuities that are my topic. The aspect of Nazi ideology that matters most for my purposes is precisely the commitment to extending the claim to 'honour' to low strata of the population. The 'Brown Revolution' claimed to engineer a considerable broadening of the base of persons with a claim to social honour. Everybody who counted as a member of the *Volk*-community was a person of 'honour,' in Nazi ideology; and, repulsive as that ideology was, it established some of the doctrinal framework for the broad extension of a claim to 'dignity' that characterises contemporary Germany. It may even have laid some of the attitudinal foundations for the culture of human dignity that we observe a half-century after the collapse of the Nazi regime. Low-status Germans who learned to believe that they were 'honourable' persons in the 1930s became Europeans who believed they persons were entitled to 'human dignity' after 1945.

It is important to emphasise that the claim I am offering is a *sociological* claim, and thus a very different kind of claim from the usual claims made in the German juristic literature. German jurists who write about 'human dignity' generally write about the *philosophical* sources of that concept as it is discussed in the theoretical literature today—sources that lie, especially, in the philosophy of Kant. For my purposes here, those philosophical sources are, at best, of very limited interest. The question that I pose here is not the question of which philosophers jurists customarily cite or discuss. The question that I pose here is the question of the *social* basis of human dignity.[6] I want to ask, not about the *philosophy* of dignity, but about the *culture* of dignity—to ask what it is that has made 'dignity' a value that seems meaningful and important to ordinary Europeans. As we shall see, inquiring into the sources of the culture of 'dignity,' rather than the philosophy, puts the Nazi era in quite a new light.

Trying to stay with the limits of the manageable in this short paper, I am going to focus on two examples. The first is the criminal law of insult,

---

[5] Whitman, 'Enforcing Civility and Respect: Three Societies', (2000) Yale Law Journal 109, 1279–1398.

[6] Gerald Neuman observes to me that the cult of Kant in Germany is itself a social phenomenon, sociologically analysable. This is entirely true. Nevertheless, I believe it is a social phenomenon that has had a far less formative influence on German law than jurists commonly claim.

Beleidigung. Drawing on earlier research, I will argue briefly that the law of insult reveals much about the connection between 'dignity' and 'honour,' and about the place of the Nazi era in the development of current culture. My second example will involve the dignity of workers in particular. Here I will focus on the so-called 'courts of social honour' established under Nazi labour law, as well as on certain issues in labour law more broadly. At the close of the chapter, I will try to give a careful philosophical assessment of the admittedly disturbing argument I have to offer.

I

Nazi law revolved around the value of 'honour.' This fact is hard to miss, since Nazi authors proclaimed the supreme value of 'honour' all the time; and historians of Nazi law have not failed to note it. Nevertheless, I think it is fair to say that historians have not taken Nazi talk of 'honour' quite seriously. It has seemed to belong to the typical repertoire of Nazi *Quatsch*—to the predictable rhetoric of Nazi militarism, and the bogus grandeur of Nazi millenarianism. Even Ute Frevert—a wonderful historian, whose *Ehrenmänner* is fundamental to my topic—does not make all that much of Nazi 'honour.' Frevert notes one of the oddest, and most revealing, bits of Nazi culture: the idea that all Germans, even low-status ones, ought to *duel*.[7] As Frevert shows in her fine book, the history of duelling is a barometer of the history of changes in social hierarchy in Germany. The practice of duelling was the great marker of high social status in pre-twentieth century Germany. At first the province exclusively of military officers and the aristocracy, duelling slowly worked its way down the social scale, into the bourgeoisie, during the nineteenth century. The Nazi notion that *everyone* was 'satisfaktionsfähig,' was honourable enough to engage in a duel, was thus the dramatic culmination of a very long process of German social change. Frevert has, in the end, though, little to say about this Nazi development. Even to Frevert, the business of Nazi 'honour' seems beneath sustained consideration, seems like typically vacuous Fascist chest-thumping. As for the literature on the Nazi legal theory of honour: it is for the most part limited to a little book by Markus Brezina[8]—also a fine book, but one without much interpretive ambition.

Nevertheless, if *we* find it hard to take Nazi 'honour' seriously, that does not mean that ordinary Germans did not take it seriously in the 1930s. We must remember that people cared a great deal about their honour in the early decades of the twentieth century, and particularly about their *social* honour. Continental society was sharply stratified, right through the nineteenth century.

---

[7] U Frevert, *Ehrenmänner. Das Duell in der bürgerlichen Gesellschaft* (Munich, Beck, 1991), 256–63.

[8] M Brezina, *Ehre und Ehrenschütz im nationalsozialistischen Recht* (Augsburg, 1987).

Differences of dress and manner distinguished social status groups, and low status persons routinely received harshly disrespectful treatment. While this stratification had begun to break down, in the early decades of the twentieth century, it was by no means dead. Continental society—especially German society—remained stratified not only economically, but also in terms of norms of deference. Some people could expect to be treated more respectfully than others. This was a fact of life, and a fact of life that was painfully important to people—as we all know, even if only from watching the American films of the era, in which the Marx Brothers so often manipulated their social betters in high-toned settings. What was true of America was far truer of continental Europe. Money was not all that counted in this world—deference counted too and social mobility was largely social *climbing*: it involved the effort, not just to get rich, but to be treated deferentially. It involved the effort to be treated as a person of *honour*—as, for example, Felix Krull, Thomas Mann's classic anti-hero of twentieth century social hierarchy, tried to be treated as a person of honour through his *Hochstapelei*, his pretence to be a socially 'better' person than he really was.

These old forms of stratification are still with us, to some extent. But they have crumbled enough that we have lost much of our capacity to really empathise with the yearning for respectability that gripped people eighty years ago. This makes it very hard for us to grasp the power of what the Nazis said, when they spoke, as they did so incessantly, about 'honour' for all Germans. People cared intensely about whether they were treated as persons of 'honour' or not; and a political formula, like the Nazi formula, that promised honour for everybody had real potency. Indeed, as the late George Mosse insisted, offering honour for everybody may have counted for much more, in the interwar world, than offering financial well-being. As Mosse observed:

> 'We know that real wages fell in Germany and that the Italian workers and peasants did not materially benefit from the fascist régime. But it would seem that, to many of them, this mattered less than the gain in status. Those who have tried to prove otherwise apparently believe that material interests alone determine men's actions.'[9]

One can raise some doubt about what Mosse says: even if real wages fell in Germany, the unemployment rate fell too. Nevertheless, he is entirely right that gains in status matter, and that they mattered especially in the still-stratified world of the 1920s and 1930s.

Certainly, it is against the background of this world of deference and social hierarchy that we must understand the ideological import of 'honour' within Nazi law. If we have the patience to see Nazi law in social context, and in long historical perspective, we very frequently discover that it operated precisely to extend old high-status norms to low-status persons. What was true of Nazi

---

[9] G Mosse, *The Fascist Revolution: Toward a General Theory of Fascism* (New York, Fertig, 1999), 38–9.

rhetoric about duelling was much more broadly true of honour in Nazi law. Just as the Nazis proclaimed that the duel, once the privilege of high-status persons alone, was now the privilege of all, so they proclaimed that a variety of forms of high-status legal honour were now to be accorded to all Germans—at least, to all Germans as the Nazis chose to define them.

II

It is best to begin, indeed, with a species of law that was very closely associated with the duel: the law of insult, of *Beleidigung*. The history of the connection between duelling and the law of insult is one that I have explored at very great length elsewhere,[10] and I will simply summarise some of my results here. As I have tried to show, it is a history that carries us far back into the *ancien régime*; and it is also a history that allows to see important aspects of the social basis of the 'human dignity' as it exists in Germany today.

The law of insult leads a rich life in the popular mind of ordinary Germans today: Germans who have been insulted believe that they have criminal cause of action against those who insult them and indeed often show a very lively awareness of their right, as persons of 'honour,' not to be insulted. The result is a culture of insult that foreigners find little short of bizarre, a culture in which Germans threaten criminal actions against people who have committed such offences as calling them 'du' (the familiar 'thou' form) or using mildly obscene hand gestures. Ordinary Germans believe that the criminal law should protect their 'honour' against anyone who has shown them, in the formula of German insult law, lack of *Achtung*, lack of respect. German scholars generally have little to say about this popular culture of insult, treating it mostly as a source of amusing anecdotes about obscene hand gestures. Yet the everyday legal culture of insult is deeply revealing about German society: it suggests how widespread and intensely felt the attachment to personal 'honour' is in Germany. Indeed, it provides our best evidence for a phenomenon of great importance: the existence of a popular culture of 'dignity' that underlies the great theoretical jurisprudence of 'dignity' that we can read about in German juristic articles and commentaries.

What are the historical origins of this strange German culture of insult? The answer is that the historical roots of the current law of insult lie, in large part, precisely in the law of duelling. The law of insult has a complicated history, but as it exists today it is the doctrinal descendant of law that was intended to bring duellists into court. Early nineteenth century jurists were eager to create a law of insult that could be deployed in the great social war against duelling: rather than drawing swords or guns, duellists were supposed to come to court when

---

[10] This section summarizes arguments offered in my 'Enforcing Civility and Respect: Three Societies', (2000) 109 *Yale Law Journal*, at 1313–32.

they were insulted. Correspondingly, the law of insult, as it developed in the nineteenth century, closely tracked duelling norms. The justiciability of insults, in the law of the early nineteenth century, came to be associated precisely with the *Satisfaktionsfähigkeit* of the litigants—with the question, once again, of whether they were persons honourable enough to duel. The 'insults' that found their way into the standard commentaries were thus classic *duelling* insults: words like 'Lump!' ('rascal!') and gestures like the *Ohrfeige*, the box on the ear. As a matter of procedure, an action in insult came to require a *Privatklage*, a private criminal prosecution. After all, men of honour settled their disputes for themselves. The history of the law of insult in Germany is history during which these older legal norms, and indeed older behavioural norms, have gradually been extended throughout the German population. When ordinary Germans believe they have been criminally insulted today, they are, in fact, acting in the way that duelling aristocrats and military officers once acted: over the course of the last couple of centuries, the *right to take offence* has slowly been generalised throughout German society.

Now, these historical roots of the law of insult are of special interest for the large history of 'human dignity' in Germany. For a central aspect of human dignitary law—law against what we in the United States call 'hate speech,' protecting minorities from insulting or degrading treatment—has grown directly out of these same traditions of the law of insult. This is something that goes occasionally forgotten in the German literature, but it is so. German hate speech protections today extend beyond the narrow law of insult, to include prohibitions on 'Volksverhetzung,' on inciting popular hatred. Nevertheless, those contemporary protections are all derived from, and still closely associated with, the old law of insult. As I have tried to show, German minorities today are protected by rules that were once intended to apply to *duellists*; and patterns of thought that grew up in the world of duelling continue to haunt German hate speech jurisprudence.

And what is the place of the Nazi era in the development of this German culture of insult? The answer is that the Nazi chapter was central to the long-term tale of *levelling up*, the tale of the extension of high-status duelling norms of behaviour to the lower orders of German society. It was in many ways during the Nazi period that low-status Germans came to benefit from the modern law of insult; and in consequence the tale of the making of the current culture of everyday dignity in Germany cannot be told without many pages on the Nazi era, and especially on the 1930s. The nineteenth century law of insult was careful to distinguish between the claims of persons who were 'satisfaktionsfähig' and persons who were not. This tradition did not end even in Weimar. Rather, the shift came largely during the Nazi period. I will not recite the history in any detail here; readers can consult my earlier article:[11] suffice it to say that the

---

[11] Above.

generalised culture of insult that we observe today in Germany, and that is so closely linked to the dignitary norms of hate speech, is largely a product of the Nazi period, and specifically of a Nazi-era commitment to the *Satisfaktions-fähigkeit* of low-status Germans—of their right to take to take offence. What is more, the Nazi insistence on adjudicating claims of 'honour' in court resulted in one particularly bizarre irony: the law of hate speech itself has Nazi-era roots. For, just as Kaufmann observed, the law of collective insult, which now protects German Jews, was originally developed to protect two very different collectivities: the SA and the SS.[12]

III

Indeed, the Nazi era produced some remarkable insult jurisprudence— jurisprudence that laid some of the social foundations for the German culture of insult today. Some of this involved the ordinary courts—though in some extraordinary cases. One is astounded, for example, to discover a successful insult prosecution brought in 1935 by a man who had been castrated under Nazi congenital defect laws.[13] As Nazi-era courts saw it, this victim of Nazi horror could be castrated, but he could not be insulted by his neighbours for having been castrated! Even a person who stood near the bottom of biologised scale of social honour in Germany could expect his honour to be protected in court. The most revealing Nazi-era cases do not come from the ordinary courts at all, though. They come from a different species of court, established by the Nazis in 1934: the *Ehrengerichte*, the 'courts of social honour' created as part of Nazi labour law.

Everyone who studies Nazi social policy knows that labour law is an area in which nasty fascist ideology mixed with practices that even today look socially progressive. On the nasty ideological side, Nazi labour law is associated above all with the smashing of unionised labour, with the introduction of the *Führer* principle into the workplace, and with the promulgation of the ideology of cor-poratism. (There were also, as we might expect, plenty of labour-law decisions that reflected the horror of the regime.[14]) Under the *Führer* principle, intro-duced through enactments of the early 1930s, what had been workplace bosses were to become workplace *Führers*: leaders, on the model of Hitler himself, who could expect *Treue und Gehorsam*, loyalty and obedience, from their employees. As for those employees, they were now to be a *Gefolgschaft*, a com-pany of followers. The introduction of the *Führer* principle was obviously

---

[12] Above n 4.

[13] (1935) 27 *Deutsche Richterzeitung* 686.

[14] Eg B Michel, *Die Entwicklung der Arbeitsgerichtsbarkeit in den Faschismus*, in U Reifner (ed) *Das Recht des Unrechtsstaates. Arbeitsrecht und Staatsrechtswissenschaften im Faschismus* (Frankfurt, Campus, 1981) 154–77.

intended to bring a dramatic new style of fascist discipline to the workplace, and historians have taken it quite seriously. (The ideology of corporatism, on the other hand, was embraced by the Nazis much less whole-heartedly, and historians have played it down a bit.[15])

Führer principle and corporatism introduced a spirit of fascism into labour law that all historians have commented upon. At the same time, they have also all felt obliged to comment on a variety of measures that seem less purely fascist in inspiration. These include such durable innovations as the introduction of legally mandated paid vacation, and the expansion of protection against arbitrary discharge (*Kündigungsschutz*), as well as the *Mutterschutzgesetz*, the Law for the Protection of Mothers. The connection between these facially 'progressive' measures and the larger programmatic drive of the Nazis has been the subject of intense debate.[16]

Both the unproblematically fascist aspects of Nazi labour law, and the problematically 'progressive' aspects, have thus gotten plenty of attention. But what has sometimes been called the most original and striking innovation[17] of Nazi labour law has gotten almost no analytic attention at all: the so-called 'courts of social honour.'

The 'courts of social honour' were established by the centrepiece legislation of Nazi social planning: the *Gesetz zur Ordnung der nationalen Arbeit* (AOG), the Law on the Organization of National Labour, of 1934. This statute, which followed months of vicious programmatic efforts to destroy organised labour in Germany, introduced *soziale Ehrengerichtsbarkeit*, the principle that workplace conflicts and difficulties were to be subject to the jurisdiction of 'courts of honour,' associated with the ordinary labour courts, and staffed by one officer of law and two lay judges. The statute also established an appellate instance, the *Reichsehrengerichtshof*, the Reich Court of Honour, in Berlin. This system of honour courts was to penalise 'gröbliche Verstöße gegen die sich aus der Betriebsgemeinschaft ergebenden Pflichten,' 'gross offences against the duties established by the workplace community,' whether committed by management or by labour. The statute purported in particular to regulate relations of respect, *Achtung*, within the workplace:

§ 35 AOG. Every member of a workplace community bears the responsibility of fulfilling conscientiously the duties incumbent upon him by virtue of his position within

---

[15] For a convenient English language account, see M Linder, *The Supreme Labor Court in Nazi Germany:A Jurisprudential Analysis* (Frankfurt, Klostermann, 1987) 108–18.

[16] For literature struggling with these problems:R Hachtmann, *Industriearbeit im 'Dritten Reich'* (Göttingen, Vandenhoeck & Ruprecht, 1989); O Radke, Nachwirkungen des 'Gesetzes zur Ordnung der nationalen Arbeit,' (1965) 13 *Arbeit und Recht*, 302–8.

[17] T Ramm, *Nazionalsocialismo e diritto del Lavoro*, in Ramm, *Per una Storia della Costituzione del lavoro Tedesco* (Milan, Giuffrè, 1989), 114 (orig. German version, 1968); A Kranig, *Lockung und Zwang. Zur Arbeitsverfassung im Dritten Reich* (Stuttgart, Deutsche Verlags-Anstalt, 1983), 232: '[e]ine der auffälligsten Neuerungen.'

the workplace community. Through his conduct, he is to show himself worthy of the respect that arises from his position in the workplace community. In particular he is to dedicate his full energies to the service of the enterprise, and subordinate himself to the common good, in constant consciousness of his responsibility.[18]

Offences against workplace duties were to meet with 'Ehrenstrafen,' honour punishments:

§38 AOG. The punishments administered by the courts of honour are:
1. Warning,
2. Rebuke,
3. An administrative fine of up to ten thousand marks,
4. Deprivation of the capacity to be *Führer* of an enterprise . . . or to exercise the office of a shop steward [*Vertrauensmann*—a worker serving effectively as an official representative of the Nazi party],
5. Removal from the workplace in which the offender has been serving; in this regard the court of honour may prescribe a period of notice diverging from the period specified statutorily or by contract.

Most historians have simply viewed these honour courts as insignificant window-dressing—as having led, in the words of Tim Mason, 'a miserable existence on the fringes of the most important developments in social and labour policy.'[19] The 'honour punishments' that they administered have, in particular, often been described as 'merely symbolic' or 'merely educational.' Few scholars have taken these 'honour courts' to be anything worthy of much discussion.[20] Yet even to read the letter of the text is to see that the penalties issued by the courts of social honour had real bite, especially the noteworthy penalty of 'deprivation of the capacity to be *Führer* of an enterprise.' Moreover, to read the jurisprudence of the courts of honour is to discover that these were penalties that were really applied. More than that: to read the jurisprudence of these 'honour courts' is to discover a world of real, if episodic, social upheaval; and to see them in legal historical context is to penetrate into important corners of the Nazi ideological world.

---

[18] § 35 AOG. 'Jeder Angehörige einer Betriebsgemeinschaft trägt die Verantwortung für die gewissenhafte Erfüllung der ihm nach seiner Stellung innerhalb der Betriebsgemeinschaft obliegenden Pflichten. Er hat sich durch sein Verhalten der Achtung würdig zu erweisen, die sich aus seiner Stellung in der Betriebsgemeinschaft ergibt. Insbesondere hat er im steten Bewußtsein seiner Verantwortung seine volle Kraft dem Dienst des Betriebes zu widmen und sich dem gemeinen Wohle unterzuordnen.'

[19] *Nazism, Fascism and the Working Class* (Cambridge, Cambridge University Press, 1995), 82.

[20] Exceptions: Ramm, *Nazionalsocialismo e diritto del lavoro*, see n 17 above; W Spohn, *Betriebsgemeinschaft und Volksgemeinschaft. Die rechtliche und institutionelle Regelung der Arbeitsbeziehungen im NS-Staat* (Berlin, Quorum, 1987) 121–23. For a brief account of the interpretation of these courts, whose significance has been generally 'bagatellisiert' since Neumann, see R Wahsner, *Arbeitsrecht unter'm Hakenkreuz. Instrument des faschistischen Terrors und der Legitimation der Unternehmerwillkür* (Baden-Baden, Nomos, 1994) 118–20.

Indeed it is very strange that historians have not found the decisions of the courts of social honour more interesting for even the barest facts about them seem to cry out for deeper investigation. This is especially true because the targets of prosecution in these courts were overwhelmingly *employers and managers*. This fact is noted by historians such as Andreas Kranig, who observes that 'from the beginning, the proceedings in the courts of honour rested overwhelmingly' on two charges aimed specifically at employers and managers: 'malicious exploitation of labour' and 'affronts to the honour' of employees. 'Thus,' Kranig observes, 'of a total of 223 persons against whom a complaint was filed in 1935, 170 had to respond to charges involving these offences.'[21] Yet Kranig has little to say about this, on its face rather revolutionary, business of attacking bosses in Nazi courts. Nor, surprisingly, does David Schoenbaum, who observes that, of 65 prosecutions in the last five months of 1934, no fewer than 60 were against employers, and three more against other managerial personnel. Indeed, by Schoenbaum's reckoning, the figure for 1935 was not 170/223, but 205/223![22] To be sure, these actions did not all result in the ultimate sanction of deprivation of the capacity to serve as *Führer*—what I will call 'deprivation' for short. Full-scale deprivation was ordered in only 23 cases during the period 1934–1937, and sixteen more by 1942.[23] Yet it is misleading to focus on those figures. Other, 'merely symbolic,' honour penalties must have had great significance indeed in the economy of honour of German workplaces. An employer who was publicly rebuked by a Nazi court for showing lack of respect to his workers was an employer who had been subjected to a truly revolutionary sanction. As for the 'educational' penalties, one must think of them as 'educational' in something like the sense that the milder penalties of the Chinese cultural revolution were 'educational.' It is occasionally observed that these penalties were principally applied to the 'Führer' of smaller enterprises.[24] This observation is true enough; but it hardly diminishes the high symbolism of those penalties, or their importance in the lives of workers who did find themselves in small enterprises. Indeed, the phenomenon of the courts of social honour is one that, in any other historical context, no one hesitate to describe as 'revolutionary'; if we had a database of this kind for the French Revolution, for example, we would investigate it with intense interest. Yet essentially all historians have chosen to treat these courts as of wholly minor importance.[25]

What went on in the cases before the 'courts of social honour'? Wolfgang Spohn, the one scholar who has looked closely at the cases, is content to sum-

---

[21] *Lockung und Zwang* at n 17, 235.

[22] Schoenbaum, *Hitler's Social Revolution: Class and Status in Nazi Germany, 1933–1939* (Garden City, Doubleday, 1966) 90. This corresponds to the figure in Kranig's table in n 17 at 234.

[23] Table in Kranig, above.

[24] Eg, Linder, Supreme Labor Court, at n 15, 90.

[25] For some observations parallel to my own, see Mai, '"Warum steht der deutsche Arbeiter zu Hitler?". Zur Rolle der Deutschen Arbeitsfront im Herrschaftssystem des Dritten Reiches', (1986) 12 *Geschichte und Gesellschaft*, 212–34, esp. 216–17.

marise them as follows. Cases of 'exploitation of labour,' accordingly to Spohn, generally had little effect, leaving employer prerogative untouched; the successful actions instead involved 'affronts to honour,' which included above all 'insults, abusive language, insulting physical touchings [*Tätlichkeiten*—i.e. slapping or similar acts that show disrespect without causing serious physical harm], ill treatment, sexual improprieties, etc.'[26] Now, this account is a shade misleading: 'Exploitation of labour' was in fact a charge with some real significance, invoked in many successful prosecutions involving wage, hours, and accommodations litigation: the terms of employment *did* change, and in ways that distinctly disfavoured employers. Nevertheless, it is true that cases involving insults, disrespectful touchings and the like—the classic affronts to 'honour'—featured prominently indeed; as did, very noticeably, cases of what we would now call 'sexual harassment.' The dramatic fact is that the 'courts of social honour' endorsed something that German social history had simply not seen: full-scale protection for the 'honour' of German workers—and even for the 'honour' of German women.

To get a full sense of how worker 'honour' was handled in these courts, we must read some of the caselaw in some of its remarkable detail. I have chosen to do that by reading the published cases from the years of hot revolution, 1934 and 1935. Reading those cases, we discover that the 'courts of honour' were sometimes used to eliminate Jewish bosses[27]—no surprise there. Most of the time, though 'Aryans' were the targets. In case after case, abusive bosses, especially in smaller enterprises, were called to account in the courts of honour; and what they were called to account for was failing to treat their employees respectfully—whether through beatings or through abusive language.

Many of these cases involved violence or the threat of violence: 'A *Führer* of an enterprise,' as the headnote of one typical 1934 case involving a Königsberg farm reads, 'who threatens to beat the members of his company of followers [*Gefolgschaftsangehörigen*], maliciously affronts their social honour.'[28] Decisions like this really must have meant something in the East Prussian world of overweening and brutal rural bosses. Indeed, throughout Germany, many of the cases before the courts of honour seem to have involved a crackdown on the traditional right of bosses to beat their low-level, and especially their young, employees. Part of what the courts of social honour were about was an attack on the traditional employer's prerogative of violence.

---

[26] W Spohn, *Betriebsgemeinschaft und innerbetriebliche Herrschaft*, in C Sachse, et al (eds), *Angst, Belohnung, Zucht und Ordnung. Herrschaftsmechanismen im Nationalsozialismus* (Opladen, Westdeutscher Verlag, 1982) 198–9; Spohn, *Betriebsgemeinschaft und Volksgemeinschaft* at n 20, 121–23.

[27] (1935) 23 *Arbeitsrechtssammlung*, 142.

[28] (1935) 22 *Arbeitsrechtssammlung*, 117: 'Ein Betriebsführer der seinen Gefolgschaftsangehörigen Prügel anbietet, kränkt sie böswillig in ihrer sozialen Ehre.'

But they were also about an attack on the traditional employer's prerogative of showing disrespect to his employees and it is here that the caselaw of the courts of social honour joins the great river of the history of insult in Germany. Subjecting employers to anything like the law of insult was a change. In pre-1933 Germany, employers and managers famously benefited from the 'Herr-im-Hause' tradition—from the tradition that held that they were 'master of the house' in their enterprise, with all of the prerogatives of a traditional German paterfamilias. The weight of this tradition made itself felt in the Weimar law of insult. While it was not unambiguous, Weimar law classed employers and managers, for purposes of the law of insult, alongside heads of households: bosses and fathers both were presumptively shielded from prosecution for insult by their underlings; it was an aspect of their hierarchical superiority that they were permitted to treat underlings disrespectfully. It was this 'master of the house' tradition that came, strikingly, under repeated attack in the new courts of social honour. In a sense the new 'Führerprinzip' was simply the doctrinal descendant of the 'master of the house' concept. But taken seriously, it could dictate some meaningful limits indeed to the hierarchical prerogatives of disrespect.[29]

The direction and power of attacks on those traditional prerogatives is something we can best grasp if we go into the details of a typical case. I take as an example a 1934 dispute from Essen, which ended in a 300 Mark fine against an employer. Both the facts, and the court's discussion of the appropriate penalty, deserve to be quoted at length:

> The defendant has a clothing factory enterprise, in which he employs on average some 18–20 persons. The employee [Angestellte—white-collar worker] P.J. belonged to his company of followers [Gefolgschaft] since 1922, having begun as an apprentice and eventually risen to a position as cutter, which placed him high in the ranks of the workforce. The relationship between the defendant and the plaintiff was such that the defendant still addressed the plaintiff as 'thou,' just as he had done during the period of J.'s apprenticeship.

Addressing one's employee as 'thou' in this way was very disrespectful: this was hardball deference behaviour, of a kind that Americans will not find it easy to appreciate. Calling an employee 'thou' in this way would have had some of the bite that calling an American employee 'boy' would have. This boss clearly belonged to the tough old German world of status hierarchy. The case involved some vague wage and vacation allegations:

> In recent years there had been numerous disputes between J. and the defendant; indeed J. had twice been given notice. The defendant says that he had given J. notice because he was 'hard to get along with.' J. testified under oath that he was given notice the first time, on the 30th of September 1933, merely because he had insisted on the vacation time to which he was entitled under standard industry regulations,

---

[29] Cf Spohn, at n 20, 122: 'Die nationalsozialistische Auffassung, die neue Arbeitsverfassung sei unvereinbar mit dem "Herr im Hause"-Standpunkt. . .hatte einen durchaus zutreffenden Kern.'

and that he was given notice the second time, in the Spring of 1934, because he demanded to be paid according to standard industry regulations.

The second firing had led to a labour court action, which settled the dispute. Further difficulties followed though. Finally, in September of 1934, the defendant called J into his office, and made a number of accusations of misfeasance. What followed was a little *contretemps* of the kind we all have seen in human society:

> J rejected the accusations that the defendant made against him. In particular he responded ironically to the accusation that he was not producing nearly as much as before, and did not work half as hard as he had two years before: *That was undoubtedly true*, he said, *since he stood around the entire day with hands in his pockets.* [Presumably because the factory had little work in the depressed economy of the time].

It is worth observing that, in the hierarchically minded law of the nineteenth century, J might well have been criminally prosecuted for this piece of smart backtalk.[30] A boss of the traditionalist kind we can guess the defendant here was would have been enraged. At any rate, the dispute continued:

> After further agitated exchange of words, which included terms of abuse like 'rascal' ['Schuft'] and 'idiot,' J. finally demanded his papers as of the 30th of September, adding that if he had put all of his affairs in order by then, the defendant's 'funny business' would 'become public knowledge.' These words of J. caused the defendant to become visibly agitated, and he demanded an explanation of what J. meant. When J. responded that he meant the 'K. matter,' the defendant leapt up and hit J. in the face with his fist, exclaiming 'thou damned scoundrel!' ['Du verdammter Lump'] (as he himself admits), in consequence of which J. suffered (according to the certificate of a medical examination) a pronounced swelling of the upper lip, with light bleeding in the skin of the lip. In self-defence, J. also struck the defendant.

It is certainly to be regretted that the published case report omits the description of the 'K. matter.' At any rate, this is an account of a typical sort of human set-to. It is not easy to say who is the most at fault here—though it seems fairly certain that in the nineteenth century, and perhaps even in the Weimar era, if German courts had punished either of the parties, it is the employee that they would punished. In any case, insulting words were flung from both sides, and both men struck blows. Nevertheless, the court of social honour seized the opportunity to chastise and fine the boss:

> Be the K. matter as it may, it does not excuse the defendant's actions against J. Even if we admit the truth of the defendant's pleadings, as *Führer* of an enterprise, he should not by any means have allowed himself to get so carried away that he engaged in this sort of dishonourable treatment of a member of his company of followers.

---

[30] Cf the sources discussed in Whitman, Enforcing Civility and Respect, at n 5 above, 1320–321.

According to J's sworn testimony, the defendant heaped J. with terms of abuse like 'rascal' and 'idiot' even before the K. matter was mentioned, and added the insulting phrase 'thou damned scoundrel' when he struck his blow. These facts compel the conclusion that the defendant did not act merely out of a forgivable sudden impulse, but out of a *sentiment of disrespect* [*Gefühl der Mißachtung*], that is to say with malicious intent and through abuse of his position of power. . . .

The Court of Honour has accordingly determined that the defendant, on the 5th of September 1934, in his capacity as *Führer* of an enterprise, maliciously affronted the honour of a member of his company of followers through abuse of his position of power. He thereby made himself guilty of a gross violation of the social duties arising out of the communal relationship of the enterprise, and therefore became liable to punishment for an offence against social honour in accordance with § 36 Abs. 1 Ziff. 1 AOG. An affront to honour through words alone might have been adequately penalized through a warning or a rebuke. However the insulting physical touching [*die tätliche Beleidigung*] which the defendant permitted to accompany his worlds demands a punishment which be felt more severely.[31]

Accordingly the court imposed a fine of 300 Reichmarks. Let me emphasise that this is not a case, in my view, in which the boss was by any means clearly the most at fault; and that it is a case in which the courts of the nineteenth century (and perhaps the courts of Weimar) might have treated the employee harshly. What then was going on here? I think the correct interpretation has to give full weight to the deep social changes at work in the case. This is a case in which an old-style, hard-line employer was fined and rebuked for acting in exactly the way that old-style, hard-line employers had always acted. It was a case that ostentatiously rejected norms of social hierarchy that were very deeply rooted in Germany—and that were emblematised, in this case, by the boss's rough use of the 'thou.' This was a case that emphasised that workers who had always been on the very low end of the status ladder were entitled to respect.

There are many, many other cases of the same kind in the published reports, too, and from all over Germany,[32] and they heralded a real attack on traditional hierarchical norms in the workplace. As one 1934 case put it, the new norms of 'honour' for workers were, at least under certain circumstances, inconsistent with the 'obsolete *Herr-im-Hause* point of view.'[33] They are evidence that something dramatic was afoot, at least in the first few years of the Nazi regime, and at least on the local level. Nor are these cases the only ones of significance. Of especially notable interest is the large number of cases involving what we would now call 'sexual harassment.' There are many, many of these, too. To cite a few headnotes:

---

[31] (1934) 22 *Arbeitsrechtssammlung*, 133–35.

[32] For an example with a detailed discussion by the Reichsehrengerichtshof and commentary by Mansfeld, see (1935) 23 Arbeitsrechtssammlung, 43–52.

[33] (1934) 22 *Arbeitsrechtssammlung*, 190.

'Indecent amorous advances made by the owner of an enterprise constitute a malicious affront to the honour of members of his company of followers';[34] 'Malicious affront to honour through putting immoral pressures [*unsittliche Zudringlichkeit*] on female members of the company of followers';[35] 'The *Führer* of an enterprise ought also to set his company of followers an example of irreproachable moral conduct of his life. He affronts the honour of a female employee when he has sexual intercourse with her, even with her consent.'[36]

Caselaw of this kind simply flourished in the courts of social honour. Indeed, if we read a summary of the jurisprudence of the courts of honour from the 1943 edition of the Hueck/Nipperdey/Dietz standard commentary on labour law, we can see how much the activity of those courts aimed to protect the two vulnerable classes of women and apprentices:

> The courts have limited [the penalties called for by the statute] in a variety of other ways. Thus the Court of Honour for the Middle Elbe . . . limited the punishment of deprivation by decreeing that the condemned defendant could not be *Führer* of an enterprise that employed minors; similarly, the Court of Honour for Silesia . . . decreed that a defendant could not be *Führer* of an enterprise in which women were members of the company of followers. The Court of Honour for Saxony went yet further . . ., recrafting the penalty of deprivation of the capacity to be *Führer* of an enterprise so as to deny the defendant the right to employ apprentices . . . .[37]

The commentators disagreed with such decisions—but only because they thought that 'Führer' who abused women or minors, rather than being subjected to restrictions on whom they could hire, should be banned entirely as bosses:

> 'Anybody who fails to control himself when dealing with minors or with female members of the company of followers displays such bad qualities of character, that he cannot be a *Führer* of German workers, and he must be wholly deprived of his capacity.'[38]

'Honourable' Nazi labour law was partly about protecting women, and the class of younger workers who are now notably represented by trainees, often regarded as specially in need of the protections of sexual harassment law in Germany.

---

[34] Above, 221. 'Unzüchtige Annäherungsversuche des Betriebsinhabers sind eine böswillige Ehrenkränkung der Gefolgschaftsmitglieder'

[35] (1935) 23 *Arbeitsrechtssammlung*, 132. 'Böswillige Ehrenkränkung durch unsittliche Zudringlichkeiten gegenüber weiblichen Gefolgschaftsmitgliedern'

[36] (1935) 23 *Arbeitsrechtssammlung*, 53ff. 'Der Führer des Betriebes soll seiner Gefolgschaft ein Beispiel auch von einwandfreien sittlichen Lebenswandel geben. Er kränkt die Ehre einer weiblichen Angestellten, wenn er—auch mit ihrem Einverständnis—geschlechtlich mit ihr verkehrt.'

[37] A Hueck, HC Nipperdey and R Dietz, *Gesetz zur Ordnung der national Arbeit*, 4th edn. (Munich, Beck, 1943), 572.

[38] Above.

All of this is pretty darn interesting, and it is hard to make excuses for a historical profession that has not studied these courts more carefully. These cases introduced into German labour law, for the first time, the principle that employees have a right to respectful treatment in the workplace. This is a right that German workers still enjoy—by contrast with American workers, whose protections against disrespectful treatment are extremely limited at best.[39] Now, to be sure, there were certainly important limits to the activity of the Nazi courts of social honour. First of all, it is my impression (gleaned only from the reading of published decisions) that the really revolutionary activity of the courts of social honour went on at the *local* level. Where decisions of the Reich Court of Honour are reported, they generally aim to cut back on the revolutionary fervour of the lower courts. In one notable case, for example, the Reich Court of Honour quashed the conviction of a boss who had sexually harassed a female employee.[40] My guess is that, here as elsewhere in the early years of the Nazi regime, the authorities in Berlin were sometimes confronted with radical applications of Nazi doctrine of which they did not approve. Second of all, it is clear that the activity of the social honour courts declined after the early years of the regime. This is something that had a number of possible causes, as Kranig has observed.[41] Perhaps the most important cause for the decline is that the aims of the regime turned increasingly to war, and interest in internal social revolution correspondingly waned. The achievement of full employment, and indeed the arrival of a labour shortage, may have had some impact too: perhaps employees who had gained the option of moving on were no longer subjected to the same kinds of depredations. One should not neglect a third possibility, though: it may be that employer behaviour, under the pressure of several years of Nazi rule, began to change somewhat. At any rate, the years of really intense activity by the social honour courts cannot be dated beyond 1936 or 1937.

Nevertheless, it is foolish scholarship to write the courts of social honour off: they heralded significant, and lasting, changes in the German workplace. Maybe in some sense Tim Mason is correct in saying that this all happened 'on the fringes of the most important developments'; but within the enterprises and towns in which bosses were thrown out or chastised, the activity of the courts of honour certainly must have seemed thoroughly revolutionary. Indeed, these courts administered, in general, serious sanctions, for forms of misbehaviour that represented a serious threat to the dignity of low-status German workers. Of course, they must have touched only a small minority of the instances of abusive behaviour in the German working world of the 1930s—just as contem-

---

[39] See R Austin, 'Employer Abuse, Worker Resistance, and the Tort of Intentional Infliction of Emotional Distress', (1988) 44 *Stanford Law Review* , 1.

[40] (1935) 23 *Arbeitsrechtssammlung*, 209.

[41] Kranig, *Das Gesetz zur Ordnung der nationalen Arbeit (AOG): Grundgesetz der national-sozialistischen Arbeitsverfassung?*, in H Steindl (ed), *Wege zur Arbeitsrechtsgeschichte* (Frankfurt, Klostermann, 1984), 486.

porary jurisprudence touches only a minority of even the worst instances. Yet, like contemporary jurisprudence, the jurisprudence of the Nazi courts of honour will have had symbolic significance even for persons who were not directly involved in any particular proceeding. The caselaw of the courts of honour proclaimed that ordinary German workers were, in the telling terms of the statute, 'worthy of respect'—that they were, as one 1934 commentator put it, no longer 'second-class human beings';[42] and for persons hungry for respect, this must have meant something. The jurisprudence of the courts of social honour thus marked a step toward lifting the status expectations of German workers. Legal historians should be ready to recognise that this was a shift in attitudes of no small significance. As Mahlmann and Paul put it in their 1991 close study of industrial relations, Nazi labour policy saw 'a revolution of ways of viewing the world, patterns of behaviour, and forms of perception—a brown cultural revolution of the mind.'[43] This was a revolution in the very way of perceiving human relations, one that set some of the terms for the new dignitary order that would fully descend over Germany by the 1960s and 1970s.

The drive, or at least the rhetorical promise, to lift workers up in social status is something we can find, moreover, in other corners of Nazi labour law, too. It is a claim made symbolically by the very structure of the courts of social honour themselves, for example, what did it mean to say that ordinary German workers were subject to an 'Ehrengerichtsbarkeit,' a 'jurisdiction of honour'? In part, it symbolically located them in a quasi-feudal restructuring of the world of labour. Guilds had long had 'Courts of Honour'; and introducing Courts of Honour into factories was partly of way of symbolising the resurgence of a premodern guild order. But there was more to it than that. The structure of the courts of honour established by the AOG was not in fact modelled on the structure of the old guild courts; and the word 'Ehrengerichtsbarkeit' was not particularly associated with guild jurisprudence. The term 'Ehrengerichtsbarkeit' and use of the 'honour punishments' administered by the new courts were associated with a different set of traditions: with *military* courts of honour and *professional* courts of honour. Courts of honour, as they primarily developed in the German nineteenth century, began as courts for military officers—courts that were, inevitably, heavily concerned with the most important matter of honour, the duel. Over the course of the century, 'Ehrengerichtsbarkeit,' subjection to such courts, also appeared in the higher bourgeoisie, just as duelling itself did. Lawyers, doctors and others fell increasingly under the jurisdiction of their own 'courts of honour,' which judged both matters of professional conduct,

---

[42] Deneke, Die soziale Ehrengerichtsbarkeit, (1934) *JW*, 1009.

[43] K-M Mahlmann and G Paul, *Herrschaft und Alltag. Ein Industrierevier im Dritten Recht* (Bonn, Dietz, 1991), 162: 'eine Revolution der Sichtweisen, Einstellungsmuster und Wahrnehmungsformen—eine braune Kulturrevolution der Köpfe.' The authors see, however, no 'Umwälzung der gesellschaftlichen . . . Verhältnisse.' I am not convinced that that formulation is correct.

and questions about duelling. This history is of capital importance for interpreting the social meaning of courts of honour for workers in the Nazi era.
Clearly enough, the introduction of *Ehrengerichtsbarkeit* for workers meant
much the same thing as the proclamation of their *Satisfaktionsfähigkeit*, their
capacity to duel: it moved them up into the higher reaches of society; it included
them in a world of high-status honour.[44]

The same is true, in varying degrees, of some of the other measures of Nazi
labour law, which also need to be understood against a background of social
status stratification. In particular, if *Ehrengerichtsbarkeit* tended to symbolically identify all workers with the professionals of the *haute bourgeoisie*, other
measures tended to identify one, relatively lowly, status group, *Arbeiter*, blue-
collar workers, with another, higher status group, *Angestellte*, white-collar
workers.

Here it is important to bear in mind some basic facts about status stratification within the German workforce. Traditionally, German working people have
been classified in socially revealing ways. In particular, Germans have made
charged distinctions between *Beamte*—government officials, including both
bureaucrats and academics—*Angestellte*—employees of a status higher than
blue-collar workers—and *Arbeiter*—blue-collar workers. These are distinctions
that have carried a lot of social baggage at various periods. To become *ver-
beamtet*, to become a government official, has carried special status and honour for a long time, and it continues to do so. To be an *Angestellter* has also
carried connotations of special respectability for a very long time in German
society. Especially in the earlier part of the twentieth century, *Angestellte* were
sharply aware of the social distinction between themselves and *Arbeiter*.
Angestellte were *respectable* people, persons of middling high status whose
great marker was the starched white collar that features so prominently in the
caricatures of George Grosz. Significantly, they were people who could expect
relatively respectful treatment in their everyday interactions. Thus according to
the survey evidence of Erich Fromm's 1929 study of the psychology of labour,
Angestellte, unlike *Arbeiter*, felt that they could treat their bosses in the same
way that they treated their co-workers.[45] *Angestellte* were not ordinarily social
inferiors of their bosses in the way that *Arbeiter* were. It was part and parcel of
this that *Angestellte* were people for whom the loss of respectability was a terrible prospect. The gnawing fear of loss of respectability that could be felt by

---

[44] The importance of this resemblance to older forms of *Ehrengerichtsbarkeit* can be detected in
the commentary of Hueck, Nipperdey & Dietz, at n 37, 523–4, which distinguishes the *soziale
Ehrengerichtsbarkeit* from *ständische Ehrengerichtsbarkeit* by observing that the former was not
limited to any particular *Stand*. This care to distinguish the two is the result of their close similarity, of course. For a broader survey of the law, H Hochtritt, *Die Berufsgerichtsbarkeit. Eine verfassungsrechtliche Untersuchung über die Verfassung und das Verfahren der Berufsgerichte* (Cologne,
Deutscher Artze-Verlag, 1969).

[45] Fromm, *Arbeiter und Angestellte am Vorabend des Dritten Reiches. Eine sozialpsychologische
Untersuchung* (Stuttgart, Deutsche Verlags-Anstalt, 1980), 199–206 (English original 1929).

Angestellte is accordingly a theme of early Depression-era literature like Hans Fallada's wonderful novel, *Kleiner Mann, Was Nun?* Fallada's hero, a small-time *Angestellter* who loses his job, ends totally bereft of respectability, as his collar becomes so frayed and his suit so threadbare that he is casually mistreated by a police officer.

The distinction between *Angestellte* and *Arbeiter* was about 'distinction' in Bourdieu's sense of the word: it was about a *status* difference, signalised by dress and patterns of behaviour, in a world in which status differences counted for a lot. This distinction was faithfully reflected in German labour law, and in the culture of German work. In the 1920s, it was reflected in the law of *Kündigungsschutz*, of protection against arbitrary discharge. Ordinary *Arbeiter* had protections of a certain kind against discharge after 1919—if they worked in large enterprises in which organised labour had succeeded in setting up a *Betriebsrat*, a factory council.[46] *Angestellte* had, after 1926, protections against discharge of a different, somewhat more far-reaching kind. *Angestellte* were also the beneficiaries of special insurance requirements, which directly foreshadowed, and indeed were the ultimate source of, many of the provisions of the modern social welfare.[47] As a matter of the sociology of leisure, *Angestellte* were distinguished from *Arbeiter* in one further important way: *Angestellte* took vacations, and were indeed (along with *Beamte*) the first to benefit from a culture of tourism that has since become such a consuming passion for Germans of all social classifications.

Many Nazi labour law innovations have to be seen against the backdrop of these social distinctions of the 1920s. For their drive—especially in such matters as arbitrary discharge and paid vacation—was largely to assimilate *Arbeiter* to the status of *Angestellte*. As David Schoenbaum has elegantly argued, Nazi labour law tended, very broadly speaking, to treat *Arbeiter* more the way *Angestellte* had been treated in the previous decade.[48] This is not to say that the

---

[46] See A Hueck & J Nipperdey, *Lehrbuch des Arbeitsrechts* (Mannheim, Bensheimer, 1931), 1: 362–77.

[47] For the special insurance treatment of *Angestellte*, see above, 64–6; and for the extension of insurance coverage as the 'Grundstein' for the rise of relatively uniform treatment of all classes of employees in the welfare state, R Richardi and O Wlotzke, *Münchener Handbuch zum Arbeitsrecht* (Munich, Beck, 1992), 1: 21.

[48] Esp. Schoenbaum, n 22 at 109–10. For the assimilation of *Arbeiter* to *Angestellte* in *Kündigungsschutz*, see AOG § 56 (1); and for a brief general history, A Hueck, G Hueck, G v. Hoyningen-Huene, R Linck, *Kündigungsschutzgesetz*, 12th edn. (Munich, Beck, 1997), 18–31. For the example of paid vacation, already gradually being extended to some *Arbeiter* in the Weimar era, see Hueck and Nipperdey, n 46 at 1: 268; W Oppermann, 'Das Recht auf Urlaub', JW 1935, 3136; K Ihmels, *Das Recht auf Urlaub. Sozialgeschichte, Rechtsdogmatik, Gesetzgebung* (Königstein, 1981), 40–56; and for the cultural/political significance in the Nazi period, G Fromann, *Reisen im Dienste politischer Zielsetzungen. Arbeiter-Reisen und 'Kraft durch Freude'-Fahrten* (Diss Stuttgart, 1992). For the (in some ways limited) range of extensions of insurance coverage during the Nazi period, G Wannagat, *Lehrbuch des Sozialversicherungsrechts* (Tübingen, Mohr, 1965), 1: 87–93 and W Gitter, *Sozialrecht. Ein Studienbuch* (Munich, 1996), 18–20; for continuing distinction

differences between the two statuses were fully eliminated. It is only to say that the basic drift of these labour law innovations was much the basic drift of Nazi ideology more broadly. At least one passage of Schoenbaum's deserves to be quoted at length:

> 'Equality was a key word, not economic but, as it were, spiritual equality. In a characteristically ideological treatment . . . an instructor in the "Department of German Socialism" of the University of Cologne sketched the example of a white-collar employee at a factory celebration asking a dance of the owner's daughter. "The owner's wife is delighted with the courage and dash of the clerk." Supposing, the writer asks, it had been a worker who requested the dance. How would the wife react? "She would regard it as presumption," is the answer. The snobbery implicit in the answer was the target of the labour ideology. Did the worker resent the discrimination that obliged him but not the foreman of the white-collar worker to punch a clock? The recommended solution: a universal obligation to punch the clock . . . .'[49]

Snobbery was the target of Nazi ideology; and legal historians should be able to acknowledge that the same is true of their subject-matter: Nazi labour law, too, was intended, expressively, to undermine *snobbery*. The Nazi period represents indeed an important phase in a long-term German trend toward assimilation of the two statuses of *Arbeiter* and *Angestellte*.[50] Correspondingly, it is underdescriptive, and a shade misleading, to describe these various measures of Nazi labour law simply as 'socially progressive.' They represented progress of a particular kind, for a particular social status group: they tended, symbolically, to lift blue-collar workers one rung up on the social status ladder, making their lives a little more like the lives of the *Angestellte* who had previously stood just above them.

Conclusion

These examples are limited in scope; a full account of the role of fascist-era 'honour' in the making of European dignitary norms would require the study of many more areas of the law than my space limitations permit. Acknowledging that this study is too limited to sustain any grand conclusions, let me offer some grand conclusions nevertheless:

The Nazi era did not bring 'dignity' to Germany. 'Dignity,' as I have suggested throughout, is a much older value than that. It is a value that rests on norms of hierarchical honour whose history reaches well back into the early modern period. What we see in the complex, and often very admirable, culture

---

between *Arbeiter* and *Angestellte* in the Nazi period, L Richter, *Grundriß der Reichsversicherung* (Stuttgart, 1935), 28.

[49] See n 22, 77.

[50] For the constitutional assimilation of the two with regard to *Kündigungsfristen* as late as 1990, see (1990) *NJW*, 2246–47.

of dignity that reigns in Germany today is the product of many generations of development—generations of *slow* development, during which German society has only *gradually* embraced the notion that *all* Germans are high-status persons, that all Germans deserve full and unencumbered respect. Norms of high-status treatment began to spread in German society before the Nazi period, and they have continued to spread since.

Nevertheless, the fascist era played a manifestly important role in what is a history of slow, *continuous* development. Much of the Nazi ideological program in particular promised precisely a levelling up—a systematic effort to include low-status Germans in a world of high-status honour. Indeed, the competition between German Nazism and German Communism can in part be captured by saying that where Communists promised primarily a redistribution of wealth, Nazis promised primarily a redistribution of honour.[51] This was a promise that undoubtedly yielded the fruit of some real social change in Germany. Certainly it was a promise that produced some important innovations in legal doctrine, innovations whose place in the history of German law cannot be neglected.

But can one really speak in an intelligible way about the Nazi heritage of European dignitary law? The very phrase seems paradoxical to the point of the bizarre, if not to the point of the offensive. Well, there is indeed a paradox in the phrase. But the paradox is a paradox in 'dignity' itself, as 'dignity' plays itself out in the realities of human psychological and social structures. Intellectuals and politicians of good will like to talk, in our Kantianized post-war world, as though 'dignity' were something that could easily be extended to all 'humans.' But if are honest about it, I think we can all acknowledge that the humans themselves tend to think of their 'dignity' differently. Very much of human society, as Erving Goffmann so powerfully argued, involves treading on others and asserting one's own right to deference. Humans are animals constituted in such a way that they often take offence, and their societies often rest on distinctions of status. For most people, most of the time, the promise of 'dignity' is accordingly a promise that they will be regarded as better than somebody else. The promise that the Nazis made—if I may try to capture in a phrase the force of the Nazi ideology of honour—was of course precisely that all Germans would be better than somebody else. That promise, which turned out to be murderous, was integral to the making of a Nazi dignitary order. There is no surprise in the fact that German workers who had been told they were 'Aryans' were more ready to insist on respectful treatment in the workplace; nor is there any surprise that women who were told they were 'Aryans' were more ready to fight back when their bosses groped them. In this sense, the worst horrors of Nazism were thoroughly compatible with the creation of a dignitary law for all 'Germans' as the Nazis defined them. If 'Germans' were all to be

[51] Compare the discussion of the proclaimed mission of the DAF in Mai, at n 25, 213.

high-status persons, this had to come at the cost of defining a new class of low-status, and indeed supremely low-status, persons. There is no mystery in this: human beings do not easily think of themselves as belonging to the 'in' group if there is no one who belongs to the 'outs.' If we do not like to contemplate the idea that 'human dignity,' as it exists today, grew partly out of the Nazi dignitary order, that is only because we do not like to think too hard about how the human psyche works.

Now, of course, 'human dignity' as it exists today in Europe grew at best only *partly* out of the fascist-era dignitary order. The fascist dignitary norms that matter most directly for the formation of contemporary dignitary law have to do with one aspect of the dignitary life: dignity for ordinary, average Europeans—dignity for persons who already possess some basic claim to membership in society. Nazi dignity in particular was dignity for people who, by Nazi reckoning, were unambiguous Germans; and the legacy of Nazi dignity is a legacy of dignity for people who are unambiguous Europeans. Dignitary protections for others obviously have been powerfully driven by revulsion against the Nazis. When contemporary European law extends a claim to dignity to persons the Nazis deemed sub-human, it is manifestly a reaction against Nazism that is at work. Certainly it is true that viewed up close, from the perspective of contemporary dignitary jurisprudence, dignity means anti-Nazi dignity.

Nevertheless, up close is not the only way to view things. Seen in more distant perspective, the contemporary era seems simply to be pressing forward with something that the Nazis were attempting to do too. The Nazis extended a claim to honour to the lowest-status 'Aryans': they pushed honour down toward the bottom of the social hierarchy. Contemporary jurisprudence has simply continued to push the claim to honour down, reaching at last what were formerly the most despised sectors of the population. In both eras, we see the twentieth-century culmination of a process of social change that extends back to the eighteenth century in Germany, and to the seventeenth century in France. Continental law has been drawing low-status persons up the social scale for generations. The really hard question about this process is not whether the fascist era fits in the history of European law: it does. The really hard question is whether the contemporary era is attaining results that can be sustained. Is it really going to be possible to maintain *everybody* at the top of the social scale?

14

ON FASCIST HONOUR AND HUMAN DIGNITY: A SCEPTICAL RESPONSE

Gerald L Neuman*

Professor Whitman's nuanced investigation of the role of honour in the Nazi legal system raises many interesting questions and opens a variety of avenues for further exploration. In these brief comments, made from a less sociological perspective, I will attempt to clarify some issues relating to the contemporary significance of the argument, and state some hesitations about the breadth of the conclusions that could be justified by the evidence it describes. Thus far, I see grounds for scepticism about the contribution of the Nazi policies to modern European conceptions of human dignity.

Dignity

It is important to begin by clarifying the term 'human dignity' and its relation to the more generic term 'dignity.' In post-War discourse, 'human dignity' refers to a dignity that is intrinsic to humanity, that is shared by every individual human being.[1] Not all claims to dignity are claims to human dignity—some are claims to considerably more. The dignity of heads of state, of judges, sometimes even of professors, illustrate a form of differential dignity that persists despite the abolition of aristocratic privilege and the enfranchisement of the working class. Aside from these status distinctions, 'dignity' also describes a heightened standard of behaviour, and there may be reciprocal obligations of respectful conduct toward those who engage in dignified behaviour. Human dignity, by contrast, is inalienable, and not earned or forfeited by conduct.

Within this framework, I agree that historically the modern commitment to human dignity derives from interaction of egalitarianism with the differential

* Herbert Wechsler Professor of Federal Jurisprudence, Columbia Law School.

[1] See GL Neuman, *Human Dignity in United States Constitutional Law* in D Simon & M Weiss (eds), *Zur Autonomie des Individuums: Liber Amicorum Spiros Simitis* (Baden-Baden, Nomos, 2000), 249; O Schachter, 'Human Dignity as a Normative Concept', (1983) 77 *American Journal of International Law* 848 at 853. For Germany, see G Dürig, *Art. 1* in T Maunz et al., *Grundgesetz Kommentar* (München, CH Beck, 1976) at 10–13; K Stern, *Das Staatsrecht der Bundesrepublik Deutschland*, vol. 3/1 (München, CH Beck, 1988) at 6, 15, 22–3, 27.

dignity of a stratified society, and that it involves a degree of 'levelling up.' Within an appropriate domain (an important qualification), human dignity implies equality of status for all human beings, and elevates them above the animal world. Human dignity is universal, inalienable and inviolable. It entails mandatory limits on the action of the state, which exists for the sake of human beings and not vice versa.

This specification of some of the content of the concept 'human dignity' is consistent with the usage of the term in international human rights law, and with the concept employed under the post-War German Constitution (*Grundgesetz*). It is, of course, radically inconsistent with Nazi ideology, and Professor Whitman rightly notes the prevailing assumption that the post-War ascendancy of the value of human dignity resulted from a reaction against Fascism. Human dignity (*Menschenwürde*) is an important operative concept within German constitutional law, although the specific consequences that it entails are much debated. Professor Whitman's broader category of 'dignitary law' is perhaps less clearly defined, and I will confine these comments to human dignity.

Continuity

In partial contrast to conventional wisdom, Professor Whitman appears to argue that the effects of the law of the Third Reich on the modern European law of human dignity were not limited to the reaction against Nazi practices. He states that 'important threads of continuity connect the fascist era, horrific as it was, with the subsequent era of dignity,' and that there are 'many, various and disturbing instances' in which modern practices of human dignity grow out of Nazi practices. He attempts to account for this 'unpalatable truth' by discussing the relationship between honour and dignity.

It may be useful to distinguish among several different kinds of continuity in legal history. Some threads of continuity could reflect nothing more than that laws of the Wilhelmine or Weimar periods remained in force under the Nazis and survived into the post-War era. In these relatively common cases, we may still need to investigate how the Nazi period affected the evolution of the interpretation of such laws. Other threads of continuity may reflect Nazi appropriation of reforms proposed but unaccomplished—or unaccomplished *in Germany*—in earlier periods by liberals and social democrats. Some of Professor Whitman's examples appear to have that character. Again, such a history might alert us to examine how Nazi ideology inflected the manner in which the reform was implemented, and whether such inflections persisted after the war. Other continuities may result from technical innovation: certain regulations concerning aviation or broadcasting might have become relevant in the 1930s, and might have been adopted first, or first for Germany, by the Nazi regime. The most shocking example, I assume, would be a genuine moral insight that the Nazis were first to perceive and act upon, and that has become part of the modern law of human dignity.

National and Transnational Legal History

Paradoxes sometimes dissolve after a shift in perspective. In evaluating the contribution of Nazi honour to modern European human dignity—or even to modern German law—a broader range of evidence than national legal sources may be relevant.[2] I will attempt to provide a concrete example in the next comment.

The express commitment to human dignity in Article 1 of the *Grundgesetz* was preceded by other constitutive international acts in which Germany played no part. Thus, the Preamble to the United Nations Charter declares as one goal of the organisation 'to reaffirm faith in fundamental rights [and] in the dignity and worth of the human person . . . .' The preamble of the Universal Declaration of Human Rights opens with the assertion that

> recognition of the inherent dignity and of the equal and inalienable rights of all members of the human family is the foundation of freedom, justice and peace in the world,

and four further invocations of human dignity follow.[3] The positive contribution of Nazi honour to this opening affirmation of human dignity was nil.

Although the drafters of the *Grundgesetz* had ample local reasons for seeking a new order in which human dignity would be fundamental, they were also acting under the watchful eyes of the post-War international order, and within its context. The drafting history of its Article 1 includes express reference to the Universal Declaration.[4]

Nazi Labour Law and Paid Vacations

The example of annual vacations with pay, mentioned very briefly by Professor Whitman, may illustrate the risk of a narrow focus. The example is particularly interesting because it recalls the controversial provision of the Universal Declaration asserting a universal human right to 'periodic holidays with pay.'[5]

---

[2] In stating this point, I do not mean to suggest that so gifted a comparatist as Professor Whitman has overlooked it. Indeed, the earlier article on which his current paper draws conducted such an inquiry with regard to the law of insult. See JQ Whitman, 'Enforcing Civility and Respect: Three Societies', (2000) *109 Yale Law Journal* 1279. Rather, I wish to emphasise this point for the general reader, in relation to the broader thesis of the current paper.

[3] See Universal Declaration of Human Rights, G.A. Res. 217A, UN GAOR 3rd Sess., pt. I, at 71, UN Doc. A/810, preamble, pars. 1 & 5, Arts 1, 22, 23 (10 Dec. 1948). Article 22 declares everyone's entitlement to (progressive) realisation 'of the economic, social and cultural rights indispensable for his dignity and the free development of his personality.'

[4] See Stern n 1 at 16–17.

[5] See Universal Declaration, n 3, Article 24. 'Everyone has the right to rest and leisure, including reasonable limitation of working hours and periodic holidays with pay.'

Professor Whitman notes that the Third Reich extended the privilege of paid vacations from white-collar employees (*Angestellte*) to blue-collar workers (*Arbeiter*) as part of a 'levelling up' of their status. This may be correct as far as it goes. But in fuller context, Nazi vacation policy does not cohere well with post-War notions of human dignity, and it may be misleading to call it a 'durable innovation' of that regime.

First, the policy favouring annual paid vacations for workers apparently represented the appropriation of a trade union project of the Weimar period. Although paid annual vacations were rare for workers (*Arbeiter*) before the First World War, Weimar trade unions negotiated annual vacations for the vast majority of the workers covered by collective bargaining agreements.[6] These vacation rights were limited in coverage and duration, and they were not necessarily respected in practice.[7] Nonetheless, they indicate the attention of the German labour movement. Nazi labour policy provided for paid vacations after destroying the trade unions that had previously negotiated them.

Secondly, the evolution of German vacation policy should be seen in the context of international labour goals. Restriction of working hours, guarantee of weekly rest, and finally minimum annual vacations with pay were policies pursued both locally and through the International Labour Organisation (ILO), created in 1919.[8] The vacation issue was first raised at the ILO in 1919, and was the subject of a report published in 1925.[9] According to that report, the first country to adopt general legislation requiring paid annual vacations for workers was Austria (1919), followed by Finland, Latvia, Poland and Soviet Russia. Fascist Italy included the right to paid vacations in its programmatic Charter of Labour, proclaimed in 1927.[10] Reportedly, by 1935, '14 countries and two Swiss cantons had enacted legislation conferring the right to an annual holiday with pay on manual workers and salaried employees in general.'[11] The ILO adopted a Holidays with Pay convention in 1936,[12] and although only a few countries

---

[6] See H Spode, *Arbeiterurlaub im Dritten Reich* in C Sachse, et al, *Angst, Belohnung, Zucht und Ordnung: Herrschaftsmechanismen im Nationalsozialismus* (Opladen, Westdeutscher Verlag, 1982) 275, 277–8, citing estimates of 82% of workers covered by collective bargaining agreements in 1920, and 98% in 1929.

[7] Above at 278–9.

[8] See GA Johnston, *The International Labour Organisation: Its Work for Social and Economic Progress* 163–70 (London, Europa Publications, 1970).

[9] See A Thomas (ed), *The International Labour Organisation: The First Decade* (London, Allen & Unwin, 1931) 117; 'Legislation on Annual Holidays for Workers', (1925) 11 *International Labour Review* 60, 63.

[10] See *The Charter of Labor*, Art xvi, in WG Welk, *Fascist Economic Policy: An Analysis of Italy's Economic Experiment* (New York, Russell & Russell, 1968) 290, 'After a year of uninterrupted service the employee of enterprises whose work is continuous is entitled to an annual vacation with pay.'

[11] See International Labour Office, 'Facilities for the Use of Workers' Leisure During Holidays', (1939) *Studies and Reports, Series G (Housing and Welfare)* No 5, at 9 [hereinafter cited as Facilities].

[12] See ILO Convention No 52, Holidays with Pay Convention, 1936, entered into force 22 Sept 1939.

ratified that convention before the Second World War,[13] the International Labour Office counted twenty-three countries with 'general statutory schemes covering all or practically all workers and salaried employees' in 1938.[14] At a minimum, these data provide a substantial non-Fascist pedigree for the post-War right to periodic holidays with pay.

Third, in other respects the post-War approach to workers' vacations more closely resembles the practices of inter-war liberals than Nazi vacation policy. Although, as Professor Whitman emphasises, much of the rhetoric surrounding Nazi vacation policy emphasised the equalisation of blue-collar and white-collar workers, the policy was also accompanied by rhetoric and measures less consistent with the human dignity of the workers. Leisure was not justified by the importance of permitting workers an opportunity to engage in private pursuits, but rather as a necessary pause for the recovery of strength, a strength owed to the *Volk*.[15] The Nazis perceived the workers' use of their leisure as potentially subversive, and sought to monopolise the provision of leisure activities in order to prevent autonomous recreation. The Nazis borrowed this strategy from Fascist Italy, but intensified its totalitarian character.[16] Discussions within the ILO concerning workers' use of their time exhibit a conflict between the Fascist model of state-dominated recreation and a pluralistic model that respected workers' autonomy. The ILO's 1924 Recommendation on Facilities for the Utilisation of Workers' Spare Time observed that 'the workers in the great industrial countries have always sought to ensure that they may live their lives outside the factory or workshop in complete freedom and independence,' and recommended 'that every care should be taken to avoid any encroachment on the liberty of those for whose use such institutions are intended.'[17] A Resolution adopted in 1938 by an ILO committee reiterated that action to facilitate workers' holidays 'should respect individual liberty and leave each

[13] See <http://webfusion.ilo.org/public/db/standards/normes/appl/index.cfm?lang=EN>, listing ratifications of Convention No 52, including by Brazil, Denmark, France and Mexico in 1938 and 1939.

[14] See Facilities n 11 at 10, listing Belgium, Brazil, Bulgaria, Chile, Cuba, Denmark, Finland, France, Hungary, Ireland, Italy, Latvia, Luxemburg, Mexico, Norway, Peru, Poland, Portugal, Rumania, Spain, Sweden, U.S.S.R. and Venezuela. The ILO did not view the German rules as embodied in legislation. Cf Spode n 6 at 280–81, characterising the principal vacation policies as nonbinding guidelines.

[15] See Spode n 6 at 285–87; D Schoenbaum, *Hitler's Social Revolution: Class and Status in Nazi Germany 1933–1939* (New York, Doubleday, 1967) at 106–7. The International Labour Office also emphasised health and efficiency justifications for vacations, but described these as secondary to 'the principle that the worker, like any other member of the community, is entitled to his fair share of leisure, and to the time and opportunity to develop his personality.' Facilities n 11 at 7–8.

[16] See Spode n 6 at 288–93; V DeGrazia, *The Culture of Consent: Mass Organization of Leisure in Fascist Italy* (Cambridge, Cambridge University Press, 1981) 239–42.

[17] ILO Recommendation No 21, part V, in *International Labour Conventions and Recommendations 1919–1951* (Geneva, International Labour Office, 1996), at 69, 72.

person free to use his holiday in conformity with his own preferences, tastes and aspirations, and according to his own particular position.'[18]

In short, the ILO Convention provides a more likely model for the inclusion of paid vacations in the post-War discourse of economic and social rights grounded in human dignity than Nazi vacation policy.

'Levelling Up,' Social Honour, and Human Dignity

The example of paid vacations in Nazi labour law may illustrate a more general problem regarding the relationship between social honour (Fascist or otherwise) and human dignity. Admittedly, the extension of paid vacations to workers was accompanied by a rhetoric of raising their class status (while destroying their individual liberties). The question remains how such rhetoric relates to post-War conceptions of human dignity.

It is unclear how strong an explanatory force Professor Whitman claims for his central thesis, *how much* of human dignity would be 'best understood, from the sociological point of view, as a generalization of old norms of social honour.' Undoubtedly there is *some* connection between human dignity and honour. Indeed, the Universal Declaration of Human Rights recognises everyone's right to protection against 'attacks upon his honour or reputation.'[19] Moreover, some of the interpretation of the prohibition against 'degrading treatment' may be informed by older norms of honour (though not necessarily by duellers' punctilio). Rather than attempt to quantify the scope of the thesis, I will state some concerns that would arise if it were overextended.

First, as Professor Whitman recognises, Nazi labour law did not abolish all distinctions between *Arbeiter* and *Angestellte*. It did not equalise their treatment even with regard to the length of paid vacations.[20] Thus, the 'levelling up' did not entail the total abolition of legal privilege and the extension of all material benefits of the favoured class to the disfavoured class. Under these circumstances, we need an account of how the partial 'levelling up' sufficed to provide social honour, despite the continued maintenance of a former status distinction with persisting material consequences. We may also need an account of why the particular benefits that were (partially) extended were salient in terms of honour. Professor Whitman tells us that these reforms 'tended, symbolically, to lift blue-collar workers one rung up on the social status ladder.' But one might still

[18] Facilities n 11 at 81.

[19] Universal Declaration, n 3, Art 12. Interestingly, the drafters of the European Convention on Human Rights, designed to enforce 'certain of the rights stated in the Universal Declaration,' deliberately omitted the protection of honour or reputation from its equivalent of Art 12. See J Velu, *The European Convention on Human Rights and the Right to Respect for Private Life, the Home and Communications* in AH Robertson (ed), *Privacy and Human Rights* (Manchester, Manchester University Press, 1973), 12, 15–16, 42–3.

[20] See Spode n 6 at 286.

ask whether these benefits were prized by the workers because of their status implications rather than because of their material effects, and whether post-War guarantees of similar benefits are motivated by their status implications.

More generally, in post-War discourse, the obligation to respect human dignity signifies a *minimum level* of treatment owing to all persons by virtue of their humanity. It does not require equalisation of incomes, of housing conditions, of medical treatment, or of paid vacations. To fully explain human dignity in terms of social honour would require an account of how the older norms identify the areas of government action and inaction addressed by human dignity, and how the obligatory levels of treatment can be derived.[21] I doubt that older norms of social honour can provide better guidance for this purpose—either descriptively or normatively—across the relevant range of activity, than inquiry into the basic material and spiritual needs of autonomous human beings.

[21] I understand Professor Whitman to be arguing at a level of concrete detail, and not at a level of abstraction. One could instead argue generally that social honour requires the treatment of the individual with full concern and respect, and then proceed without any further reference to specific older norms of social honour. This abstract move would not add much to the already contested concept of human dignity.

15

CORPORATIST DOCTRINE AND THE 'NEW EUROPEAN ORDER'

Luca Nogler[*]

I 'European' Labour Law and the 'proud victory of the National Socialist ideal'

The aim of this paper is to analyse how the problem of the new European order could be—and actually was—presented in the late 1930s from the specific view-point of Italian labour law. The term labour law is meant in the modern sense. It includes issues relating both to individual labour contracts and relationships on the one hand, and the phenomenon of collective protection on the other, apart from the public-law context of collective bargaining that envolved in Italy and Germany during the inter-war period.[1]

In the first issue in 1940 of the most authoritative labour law journal of Italy's two decade fascist period, Celestino Arena published an article on the organisation of labour in the new European order,[2] stating first and foremost that:

> In Germany scholars and ministerial offices themselves already have plans, naturally systematic and inspired by the victorious pride of the national socialist idea, already under way. But there is no ignoring the important part Italy must play in the recon-struction, in order to realise new ideals of political and social life. And in the reaffir-mation of National Socialist principles we are delighted to see reappearing ideas that are essential to Italian, corporatist Fascism. For instance, this concept: 'the hard

[*] Professor of Comparative Labour Law, Faculty of Law, University of Trento. Translated by Iain L Fraser.

[1] The university discipline of corporate law, first taught by Carlo Costamagna in the University of Ferrara in 1927, was subsequently generalised in an invitation from the Minister for Public Administration Guiseppe Belluzzo to Italian universities to differentiate corporate law from labour law when amending their statutes (circular of 9 February 1929). On competition for university posts in corporate law see F Lanchester, 'Dottrina e politica nell'università italiana: Carlo Costamagna e il primo corcorso di diritto corporativo', (1994) *Lavoro e diritto* 49 ff.

[2] C Arena, 'L'organizzazione del lavoro nel nuovo ordine europeo', (1940) *Diritto del lavoro* 157. On Germany plans for the new European Order see PF Drucker, 'Germany's plans for Europe', (1940) *Harper's Magazine* 597 ff and L Gruchmann, *Nationalsozialistische Grossraumordnung*, (Stuttgart, Deutsche Verlagsaustelt, 1962).

problem that has to be solved in Europe in the near future by the state and by businessmen will be to bring about the best and least bureaucratic possible combination between official guidance of the economy and the private initiative essential to the full development of Europe's productive forces.' A more general concept is the other one that the sign of the reconstruction has to be work, and that 'the right to work' has to resolve the crisis of the capitalist system previously founded upon gold, that is, on the initiative of financial speculators.

If this programme is to be given one of the many possible practical meanings, associated, for instance, with the previous one of harmonising state initiative and private initiative in the productive sphere, we come up against the great problem of the technical and legal organisation of work. This is more legal than technical since, as we know, no system needs legal constraints more than the labour law system. And we know the reason: it has to do much less with the technical fact of a mere combination of production coefficients and much more with the human and social fact of performing an activity that commits the personality of man, who is a world, and of masses of men, who are the world of work. This problem of labour will be the crucial one for the period after this war.

What did this authoritative economist mean when he said that 'scholars and ministerial offices themselves already have plans, naturally systematic and inspired by the victorious pride of the national socialist idea, already under way'? The use of quotation marks indicates that Arena was referring to a specific document, which we have however, lacking further indications, not been able to trace.

What is certain is that, in the same year Arena was writing, the so-called *Aktion Ritterbusch* began in Germany. It took its name from the rector (from 1936 to 1941) of Kiel University—lawyer Paul Ritterbusch—who had been given a mandate by the *Reichsministerium für Erziehung, Wissenschaft und Volksbildung* to organise a sort of academic *Kreigseinsatz* in 13 different disciplinary areas, three of which were legal (private law, private international law and *Staatsrecht*). In short, a group of no less than five hundred scholars was to shape the future new European order—the true objective of the war that had just begun—in such a way as to make it correspond in academically impeccable fashion with the 'truth and reality' of the life of the European peoples.[3] In particular, the new European order was both to fit a *Schicksalsgemeinschaft* of the European peoples that would end the plurality of state orders accused of causing the European nations' chaos that had arisen during the 1930s. In practice, remaining within the area of the legal disciplines, Germany's presumed military superiority was more 'simply' to correspond to an equally well founded academic superiority of the German model justifying its forced expansion. In short, the work done by the *Aktion Ritterbusch* was inspired by the

---

[3] The whole matter has been reconstructed in detail in FR Hausmann, *Deutsche Geisteswissenschaft im Zweiten Weltkrieg. Die Aktion Ritterbusch (1940–1945)*, (Dresden-München, Dresden University Press, 1998); an effective summary is in FR Hausmann, 'Die Aktion Ritterbusch', 13 May 1999 *Frankfurter Allgemeine Zeitung*.

very 'victorious pride of the national socialist idea' to which Arena referred in the passage cited earlier.

Labour law was dealt with by both the disciplinary sector of private law, directed by Karl Michaelis and Alfred Hueck, and by that for *Staatsrecht,* directed by Ernst Rudolf Huber. Though no specific traces have survived of the labour law activity in the first sphere, which was contributed to also by Hans Carl Nipperdey and Wolfgang Siebert, the publicists edited two volumes, on *Idee und Ordnung des Reiches,* which included Siebert's own Die *Deutsche Arbeitsverfassung,* also published separately in two successive editions.[4]

Yet in the hundred and ten pages of Siebert's little volume—the (extreme) positions of which were basically identified in Italy (wrongly) as the *herrschende Meinung* of German legal scholars—the Italian system is not even mentioned. Moreover, this author merely wrote propaganda for the main points of his national socialist conception of the employment relationship, which he understood as a personal relation (status) of the worker, in belonging to the community of the firm (*Betriebsgemeinschaft*), in turn part of the *völkische Gemeinwirtschaft* inspired by the *Führerprinzip.*[5]

Indeed, though there was no shortage of works in German on the corporatist system,[6] as well as translations of Italian works,[7] Italian labour and corporate law played no part in the German academic debate, whether during the Weimar Republic or the Nazi period, which was, if anything, affected by the British debate. The British system was also the only one mentioned by Siebert, who set against it the successes obtained by German labour law, not hesitating

---

[4] W Siebert, *Die Deutsche Arbeitsverfassung,* (Hamburg, Hanseatische Verlagsanstalt, 1942); of the minority position of this author Siebert within national socialist legal scholarship, see n 116 below. In Italy, Siebert published 'Principi fondamentali dell'ordine nazionalsocialista del lavoro', (1938) *Lo Stato* 323 ff. He was very popular in francoist doctrine.

[5] In this context it would be out of place to give a detailed summary of national socialist legislation and scholarship relating to employment. There is now an immense literature on this point. In order not to make the footnote too long, we shall refer to just a few main works, in which other sources can be found: R Wahsner, *Arbeitsrecht unter'm Hakenkreuz,* (Baden-Baden, Nomos, 1994); A Kranig, *Arbeitsrecht im NS-Staat,* (Köln, Jess, 1984); U Reifner (ed), *Das Recht des Unrechtsstaates. Arbeitsrecht und Staatsrechtswissenschaft im Faschismus,* (Frankfurt a. M.-New York, Campus, 1981); U Hientzsch, *Arbeitsrechtslehren im Dritten Reich und ihre historische Vorbereitung,* (Marburg, Elwert, 1970); T Ramm, 'Nationalsozialismus und Arbeitsrecht', (1968) *Kritische Justiz* 108 ff; T Ramm Die 'Regelung der Arbeit' (1942), das 'Volksgesetzbuch' und der Arbeitrechtsausschuss der Akedemie fuer Deutsches Recht, (1990) *Zeitschrift für Arbeitsrecht* 407 ff. Specifically, in relation to the theory of the employment relationship, it is very useful to consult S Simitis, *Die faktischen Vertragsverhältnisse als Ausdruck der gewandelten sozialen Funktion der Rechtsinstitute des Privatrechts,* (Frankfurt am Main, Klostermann, 1957) 273 ff.

[6] Including the close critique in H Heller, *Europa und der Faschismus,* (Berlin-Leipzig, De Gruyter & Co., 1931).

[7] Cf G Bottai, *Der italienische Faschismus* in C Landauer, H Honegger (ed), *Internationaler Faschismus* (Karlsruhe, Braun, 1928) 18 ff; S Panunzio, *Allgemeine Theorie des Faschistischen Staates* (Berlin, de Gruyter, 1934); C Costamagna, *Faschismus: Entwicklung und Lehre,* (Berlin/ Wien, Limbach, 1939).

to refer to the initial development of the area, more specifically the activity of the *Verein für Socialpolitik*, that is, the social-democratic labour law tradition of the late empire and the Weimar Republic (!).[8] It is no coincidence that Siebert, again in the context of the *Aktion Ritterbusch,* also took a part in developing the series *England und Europa,* with a treatise—written with considerable help from his assistant (and future judge in the *Bundesarbeitsgericht*) Marie Luise Hilger—on British social policy relating to working hours, which was also published as a separate volume.[9] It goes without saying that the main objective of this volume was to show that the British system had now long lost what Mayer Maly had called the 'exemplary' function (in the European context) of British *Arbeitsschutzrecht*.[10] Siebert concluded his analysis by stating that 'the time gain that British protective legislation initially had was caught up shortly after by our law on safety at work'. But from the viewpoint taken by him the British system was criticised particularly because it had remained tied to the postulate of the free employment contract, entailing as a consistent corollary the fact that the protective intervention of the legislature (and hence the obligations imposed on the employer) represented an exception, to be interpreted restrictively, and not a natural pre-requisite for this area of law.[11]

Before considering the merits of the labour law issues, we should point out that it was particularly Guiseppe Bottai—the editor, as we know, of the journal that had printed (and commissioned?) Arena's article—who recognised the dangers of Germany's acquiring a monopoly in the area of the New European Order. In his memorandum to Mussolini on 19 July 1940,[12] originating from news of a congress of German university teachers on the topic 'Economic Science in Revolutionary War' that had been held in Weimar earlier that July, the former minister for corporations wrote inter alia:

> Our timely collaboration in this work on strict doctrine might be very useful once the material has been gathered and considered nationally. Scholars of ethnic, geographical, cultural and historical problems might be able to offer important elements for the

---

[8] See W Siebert, *Die Deutsche Arbeitsverfassung* at n 4, 28, who continues his own argument that the successes of German labour law are not diminished by the fact that the new national socialist criteria of assessment induce criticism of them as being a stage of development that has become an integral part of the *nationalsozialistische Weltanschauung* which is now having to face a completely different economic situation, requiring the introduction of a 'new order'.

[9] W Siebert, *Englische Sozialpolitik im Arbeitszeitrecht* (Stuttgart-Berlin, Kohlhammer Verlag, 1941); cf favourable review by R Höhn, (1942) *Reich, Volksordnung, Lebensraum* 436 at 440.

[10] A basic study in this connection is T Mayer-Maly, *Die exemplarische Bedeutung des englischen Arbeitsrecht* in *In memoriam Sir Otto Kahn-Freund* (München, Beck, 1980) 563 ff; a very important role was played by the studies on the British system by Lujo Brentano; for a summary, see his 'Die Gewerkvereine in England', IV *Handwörterbuch der Staatswissenschaften* 1127 ff.

[11] W Siebert, *Englische Sozialpolitik*, at n 9, 75 at 76.

[12] Published as an appendix to R De Felice, *Mussolini il duce. Lo stato totalitario 1936–1940,* (Torino, Einaudi, 1981 reprint. 1996) 922 at 923, along with a similar memorandum of 13 July to Ciano.

reconstruction. In the economic and legal area, the balance of trade, price, customs barriers, social justice, currency, finance, banking, the mass, autarky, the colonial system and especially the corporate system, considered from the viewpoint of the Axis victory, might give rise to new theoretical considerations not devoid of usefulness for practical application.

Italian university teachers would consider it as their most esteemed privilege to join, under your guidelines, in a general survey of Fascist doctrine, bringing it together into sectors, and setting out, from a rigorously theoretical viewpoint, the possible approaches. The themes would be previously brought before you for your judgement, and the work ought not, I believe, to take the external form of the congress. It would be accomplished in extremely rapid stages, in composed silence, in a sheltered academic atmosphere, and you would then be presented with the conclusions, which could remain reserved as long as you might see fit; or also be considered or discussed by other sectors of the Regime.

(. . .) If, as I consider, the experiment bears fruit, you might go on to consider the appropriateness of bringing the best elements into contact with our German teacher comrades in order, in fruitful and loyal collaboration, to bring together some theoretical principles emerging from the study that you may have found to conform to the spirit of Fascist doctrine.

Was this the Italian response to the *Aktion Ritterbusch*? Very likely. This is confirmed by the insistence with which a report in a letter handed 'without great illusions'[13] to Mussolini by Bottai on 12 August 1940 stressed the fact that the Germans were 'methodically' tackling all the problems of the future European order.[14] Indeed, the answer came very quickly, and Bottai noted in his journal the following day (13 August 1940) that Mussolini had called him in, and, with his 'letter before him . . . answered him point by point'. Again according to Bottai, Mussolini answered the question of what Europe's new economic pattern would be by saying that,

> we shall have to see what the United States and Russia do. In particular will Russia be with Europe or against it? We will have to see. What can culture do while we are waiting? Not much, he seemed to conclude. But he accepted my proposal to create broad university debate on the themes of the new Europe; a debate, I explained,

Bottai's note continues,

> that would be internal, with no publicity, 'in cells', as in a monastery. We agreed that we would see what good might come of it.

However, as far as we know at present, there was nothing in Italy comparable to the systematic German initiative, and the sole sector where the debate on the Italian contribution to European civilisation seriously took off was in the area of arts and literature, thanks in particular to the fortnightly *Primato* edited

---

[13] See G Bottai, *Diario 1935–1944*, (Milano, Rizzoli, 1982) 221.

[14] This subsequent letter was also published as an appendix to R De Felice, *Mussolini il duce. Lo stato totalitario*, at n 12, 925 ff.

by Bottai himself and Giorgio Vecchietti. Additionally, as we shall see in detail in section IV, the theme of the new European order was discussed chiefly in the economic context, and much more timidly, often likely encouraged again by Bottai, in the legal area. However, the most important event—the Volta Congress on the New European Law prepared in 1942 by the Italian Royal Academy—was not able actually to take place. In the editorial contained in the penultimate issue of *Primato*, which was devoted specifically to *Studies on the new order*—possibly the final statement of this Italian debate on the new European order—Bottai, having once again noted 'the continuing widespread mistrust by the European peoples of the plans for continental unification and collaboration', wondered why 'here too (. . .) Fascism stopped at a certain point, and did not purse all its ferment of ideas'.[15]

To support this analysis, it is significant that the *Deutsche Arbeitsfront* (*DAF*), a nerve centre of the national socialist party the main function of which was to organise leisure activities, had set up the *Zentralamt für Internationale Sozialgestaltung* in Berlin. This office's main task was to publish, in several languages including Italian, the periodical bulletin 'New International Survey of Labour', intended to replace the journal of the International Labour Organization. In this case too Mussolini was asked by Riccardo Del Giudice, President of the Italian Confederation of Commercial Workers, to 'instigate an organization of legislative and doctrinal information to disseminate abroad the principles, methods and institutions of corporatism', in part because the DAF journal mentioned published 'patchy, superficial information' on Italy.[16] Nothing, however, was done, just as there was no follow-up to the trade union aspiration to persuade the DAF itself that the new international labour bodies ought to have their headquarters in the country where the 'corporatist revolution' had been formed (on this see below, section III).

II Italy and Germany: different labour laws for different economic worlds

The absence in Siebert's monograph cited of references to Italy should not cause any surprise. No one can fail to see that the two labour law systems—Italian and German—were seriously out of step with each other, something in line with the differing degree of economic development of the two countries. In the second half of the 1930s, Italy was still centred around an essentially agricultural society that had undergone extremely limited industrialisation during the earlier years of fascism's two decades (1920–1940). By the end of that period, there was a

---

[15] G Bottai, 'Studi sull'ordine nuovo', 1 July 1943 *Primato* 229.

[16] As Del Giudice says in a letter to Mussolini of 9 February 1942, published in G Parlato, 'Polemica antiborghese, antigermanesimo e questione razziale nel sindacalismo fascista', (1988) *Storia contemporanea* 1214.

modest increase of 4.4 per cent of the active male population in non-agricultural employment, which reached around 50 per cent only in 1931 (taking the female population into account too, this figure was not reached until 1935). It is, moreover, now usual to classify Italy among the twelve European non-industrialised countries in the inter-war period; these countries were particularly exposed to the world agricultural crisis of the late 1920s.

Indeed, both the 1927 option for stabilising the lire at a rate (ninety to the pound) out of line with productive capacities,[17] and the failure immediately to devalue the currency when the 1929 crisis happened—two economic policy decisions involving the adoption of painful deflationary policies—radically compromised the (structural and widespread) take-off in the industrial sector pursued in the regime's early years by financing the most important monopoly sectors of the Italian economy,[18] thanks particularly to loans coming from the United States.

It is significant that one of the protagonists of the regime's first corporate policy plan considered in 1940 that 'one of the best-founded objections to the law' no 563 of 3 April 1926 was that

> it was too rigidly inspired by industrial types of employment, neglecting the forms of life of agricultural labour, though it is of *prevalent* importance in the Italian economy.[19]

Just because of this, Italy in the 1930s still showed very strong resistance towards the collectivism that had already become rooted in Germany. In short, private law was firmly tied to an individualistic view of social relationships. A large number of legal scholars, moreover, were still working with the conviction, typical of the pandectist view, that society was a factor external to—or else 'a natural consequence of'—law, and hence to the allocation of individual rights and duties made by the system. The fully 'jurisdictionalist' view of law, perspicaciously attributed by Arnaldo Volpicelli and Adolfo Ravà in 1932 to Francesco Carnelutti (which also perfectly fitted Lodovico Barassi) dominated.[20] But there is more. In many authors even a natural law approach still

---

[17] See D Preti, *Fascismo, grande capitale e classi sociali* in *Storia della società italiana. V. La dittatura fascista*, (Milano, Teti editore, 1983) 86, which goes on to state that 'the position the regime's currency options and the industrial expansion it had stimulated had driven the country into was anything but encouraging on the eve of the great crisis'; on this point see the comparative study CH Feinstein, P Temin, G Toniolo, *The European Economy Between the Wars* (Oxford, University Press, 1997) 76 ff.

[18] See again D Preti, *Fascismo* at n 17, 65 ff, which retells the story of the over thirty million dollar loan granted between the second half of 1925 and late 1927 which 'benefited the big leader companies in the mechanical, chemical, textile (rayon) and rubber sector (viz. Fiat, Montecatini, Snia, Pirelli etc.), and especially, the biggest proportion (some 30% of the total), the electrical industry' (71).

[19] Thus C Costamagna in *Atti della Commissione delle assemblee legislative, Libro delle obbligazioni* (Roma, Tipografia del Senato, 1940) 315. Our emphasis.

[20] L Volpicelli, *I presupposti scientifici dell'ordinamento corporativo* in *Atti del secondo Convegno di studi sindacali e corporativi: Ferrara 5–8 maggio 1932 I. Relazioni*, (Roma, Tipografia del Senato, 1932) 125.

survived. In a noted polemic of the mid-1930s, for instance, Gino Arias asserted bluntly that 'private property is a complement to the human personality', and is 'specifically a universal need, bound to impose itself, and to arise again should it, as has historically occurred and may occur, be underestimated or denied'.[21]

To the contrary in Germany, particularly thanks to Sinzheimer, the main function of labour law consisted, right from the late imperial period—and still more during the Weimar Republic—in (actually) governing social reality according to axiological parameters of overthrowing the commodifying logic of managing industrial work. In short, what was affirmed was a new awareness that law, consistently understood in a statist sense, can and must, through rules obviously unknown to traditional civil law, affect the social structure in which individuals operate, and hence also the power relationship set up in an industrial production system between employer and employee.[22]

Undeniably, German legal scholarship in the inter-war period was operating in a completely different environment from Italy's, given the high industrialisation (71 per cent non-agricultural employment in 1931), and hence with decidedly higher per capita incomes.[23] In particular, the phenomenon of collective bargaining was already firmly rooted in German society as from the first decade of the twentieth century, ie even before the point (the First World War) when the state recognised the role of trade union associations.[24] In Italy, by contrast, the collective (hetero-, certainly not self-) regulation of work relations ought to have developed following the 1926 law, but for lack of the basic instrument of the collective dispute, fascist trade unionism did not even manage to implement the (in no way revolutionary)[25] minimum guarantees protecting employees laid

---

[21] G Arias, 'La proprietà privata nel diritto fascista', (1935) *Lo Stato* 333 at 335; this article provoked a prompt reply by C Costamagna, 'Scienza antifascista e politica fascista', (1935) *Lo Stato* 335 ff, who however, significantly, maintained that the difference was confined to the fact that he held that 'in order to demonstrate the need for individual property in the context of fascist doctrine . . . it suffices to refer to the principles of the very doctrine of fascism, and to its function as a political and national doctrine'. Both articles are part of a broader debate, summarised in D Carbone, 'La proprietà nella dottrina fascista (Concludendo i Discorsi sul metodo)', (1936) *Lo Stato* 6 ff, where it is significantly affirmed that 'all the writers taking part in this debate on the right of property agreed on acknowledging that property is retained in fascist doctrine. I do not believe that there can be any doubt on this point'.

[22] H Sinzheimer, *Ein Arbeitstarifgesetz. Die Idee der sozialen Selbstbestimmung im Recht* (Berlin, D. & H., 1916 reprint 1977) 187; this work remained basically unknown in Italy until 1960, specifically until publication of the book by G Giugni, *Introduzione allo studio dell'autonomia collettiva* (Milano, Giuffrè, 1960). On this point see also the excellent summary in H Sinzheimer, *Über einige Grundfragen des Arbeitstarifrechtes*, in *Die Reichsgerichtspraxis im deutschen Rechtsleben* (Berlin-Leipzig, Walter de Gruyter & Co, 1929) 1 ff.

[23] These statistics are taken from C H Feinstein, P Temin, G Toniolo, *The European Economy* at n 17, 61 ff.

[24] Cf D Cofrancesco, 'Il mito europeo del fascismo (1939–1945)', (1983) *Storia contemporanea* 5 ff.

[25] This is the verdict, with which I fully agree, in R De Felice, *Mussolini il fascista, L'organizzazione dello Stato fascista 1925–1929* (Torino, Einaudi, 1968 reprint 1995) 296, which adds that the principles of the charter represented a logic brought by the social development of a

down in the Labour Charter (*Carta del lavoro*). This was approved on 21 April 1927 in a session lasting all night by a body (the Grand Council) which though at the highest rank, never possessed, whether before or after 1927, independent legislative powers. The Charter was published in the Italian Official Gazette for 30 April 1927, though not in the section for legislative acts, and was then followed by a law (law 2834 of 13 December 1928) which, by delegating implementation to the government, seemed to be specially made to confirm that the various declarations contained in the Labour Charter itself had no direct applicability.

In taking stock of application of the most controversial guarantee, the fascist collective bargaining provided for by Declaration XVII on the indemnity in the event of cessation of the relationship,[26] it was, moreover, already recognised that the collective corporate contracts had had to

> take account of the conditions of the firms, still patterned according to old prejudices, which is why it was countered that sizeable indemnities would have had harmful repercussions on an unprepared environment. Accordingly, the indemnity in question had to be contained within very narrow limits.[27]

The annual period of paid holiday provided for by Declaration XVI was set for workers at six days per year, and the pay set at nearly the basic wage.[28] In other respects the standard of protection provided for by the Labour Charter was even lowered, for instance in terms of compensatory leave, where additional derogations were introduced to the ones already provided for by law 370 of 22 February 1934 implementing Declaration XV of the Labour Charter.

It is no coincidence that the trade union movement sought protection from the courts. However, in response to a judgment in this connection that had doubled the small amount of dismissal allowance provided for in the collective agreement, the Court of Cassation, chaired by Carlo Costamagna, started the line according to which 'the declarations in the Labour Charter' in the second part of the document, entitled 'of the collective employment contract and the employment guarantees', while legal norms, are, as being structural provisions,

---

country in (slow, to be sure) transformation. I am not convinced by the position of G Pera, 'Per una ridefinizione dei corporativismi in Europa tra le due guerre' in G Vardaro (ed), *Diritto del lavoro e corporativismi in Europa: ieri e oggi* (Milano, F. Angeli, 1988) 123 ff, according to whom the trade union phase of the fascist two decades, which coincided with the more favourable European economic cycle (particularly thanks to the loans coming from the United States), brought a 'mass of results' that allowed various kinds of progress to be achieved earlier than other States.

[26] 'In undertakings with continuous working, the worker is entitled in the event of the termination of the employment relationships by dismissal without fault to an indemnity proportionate to years of service. This indemnity is due also in the event of the worker's death.'

[27] From the anonymous survey 'L'attuazione delle garanzie minime del lavoro' in Confederazione fascista dei lavoratori dell'industria (CFLI) (ed), *I 10 anni della Carta del lavoro* (Roma, CFLI, 1937) 149.

[28] 'L'attuazione . . .' at note 27, 147 at 148; white collar workers started at 10 days, rising to 30 days with at least 20 years seniority in the firm.

'aimed at laying down the competences for the exercise of the powers assigned to the organs of the corporate system' and 'do not contain any specific determination of the worker's rights'.[29] Moreover, a little thought will make it clear that conferring direct effect on the guarantees mentioned would have meant calling in question the Regime's founding pact (of Palazzo Vidoni)—to which we shall return below in section IV.1. It was accordingly not 'sabotage' as the idealist Lorenzo Mossa maintained,[30] nor is it tenable that on this point there was scholarly dissent from the legal policy pursued by the regime.[31]

Notwithstanding the countless other ways in which the economic structures of the two countries did not correspond, we shall consider that the historian Karl Dietrich Bracher recently drew attention to the fact that the Weimar state nonetheless managed to survive the crisis of the first post-war period, and especially the attack on parliamentary democracy, ten years longer than did Italy.[32] Those were ten very important years for all the legal disciplines, which had in common the problem of 'interiorising' collective phenomena and their democratic function of supporting the individual's participatory needs. Indeed, in the labour law area thinking about many of these aspects was marked by heavy burdens that 'bent' the individual worker to the needs imposed by collective phenomena (so-called collectivism). As a few minimal examples, there were the impossibility of derogating from the collective contract, understood as nullifying individual derogations, the constitutional protection of trade union liberty, conceived of in the fashion of Schmitt as an institutional guarantee (not 'for the purpose of' but) 'prior to' individual freedom,[33] and especially the organisation of work. The latter was seen as a collective phenomenon, or order (hierarchy), independent of the will of the individual, who is subject to it in consequence of not owning the means of production[34] or else, according to the approach that was to dominate the 1930s, as a community phenomenon constitutive of social reality.

It should to be borne in mind in this connection that, in the German system, as well as there being full development of collective forms of participation,

---

[29] Corte di Cassazione 28 marzo 1938 n. 1005, (1938) *Rivista del lavoro* 371; see also P Greco, *Il contratto di lavoro* (Torino, Utet, 1939) 72, concluding that 'the content of the labour charter can become an objective norm only if taken over into legislative or equivalent acts'.

[30] L Mossa, 'Il diritto del lavoro nel codice civile', (1942) *Archivio di studi corporativi* 100.

[31] It is no coincidence that the declarations referring to the structure of the State were without particular dissent treated as constitutional norms on the fascist totalitarian State (see C Costamagna, 'Caratteri costituzionali della Carta del lavoro', (1927) *Diritto del lavoro* 384 ff; D Donati, 'L'efficacia costituzionale della Carta del lavoro', (1931) *Archivio di studi corporativi* 163 ff and especially S Panunzio, *Teoria generale dello Stato fascista. Appunti di lezioni* (Padova, Cedam, 1937) 36 ff).

[32] This reference is to Bracher's paper to the Congress *80 Jahre Weimarer Reichsverfassung* organised by the Deutsche Nationalstiftung at Weimar on 14 April 1999.

[33] Cf L Nogler, 'Die unfruchtbaren Weimarer Wurzeln des Grundrechts auf Koalitionsfreiheit', (1996) *Arbeit und Recht* 206 ff.

[34] The well-known thesis of H Sinzheimer, *Grundzüge des Arbeitsrechts* (Jena, Gustav Fischer, 1927) 12; see also n 37 below.

scientific work organisation was now rooted, and had been from the mid 1920s. If the first—and more traditional, though often neglected—function of labour law consisted in legally formalising (and hence legitimising) the power relationships characteristic of the mode of production that emerged with the industrial revolution, the evolution of industrial capitalism thus imposed, already during the 1920s, adoption of legal categories that further broadened the ranks of subordinate workers in the firm, to the point of making them co-responsible for the course of business. The German system met this requirement—which in Italy emerged particularly (if not exclusively) in the context of the war industry[35]—by adopting the concept of community. In fact Sinzheimer had already distinguished the contractual sphere[36] from the organisational sphere,[37] but his approach kept totally away from seeing this organisational sphere as a relationship of a community nature.[38] However, by contrast with a widespread opinion (strongly upheld by the émigrés, among them, first and foremost, Franz Neumann, Ernst Fraenkel, and Frieda Wunderlich), which overestimates the actual capacity for social change of the new Nazi regime, this latter ideology did not represent an absolute novelty forged by the theorists of National Socialist legal doctrine, but a line of interpretation going back to the first years of activity of the *Reichsarbeitsgericht* (RAG), and in particular to a June 1928 decision.[39] The most important line in the case law concerned

[35] In fact, after the great crisis of 1929, the industrial policy most seriously pursued by the Italian government was that of disarmament 'which shortly after, following the Ethiopian was, turned into a downright war industry policy' (D Preti, 'Fascismo . . .' at n 17, 93; see also CH Feinstein, P Temin & G Toniolo, *The European Economy* at n 17, 196–7). On the 'archaic production structures' in Italy, cf A Aquarone, *L'organizzazione dello Stato totalitario* (Torino, Einaudi, 1965) 215.

[36] It is significant that Franz Neumann, rethinking the position his school had taken towards employment relationships in the Weimar period, stressed that 'there is no doubt that the importance of *Arbeitsvertragsrecht* was underestimated', and particularly that seeing the employment relationship as generated by an exchange contract allowed the mutual performance between the parties to be determined and rationalised with exactitude ('Das Arbeitsrecht in der modernen Gesellschaft', (1951) *Recht der Arbeit* 1).

[37] Sinzheimer's treatment of the 'powers' of the employer (see n 34) was inspired, counter to totally contractual approaches, by the attempt to juridify the asymmetrical positions encountered in the 'organisation'; the positions necessarily remained outside the 'contract' understood in pandectist terms as the exclusive source of the rights and duties in the inter-individual relationship between organiser and organised.

[38] Cf again F Neumann, 'Das Arbeitsrecht . . .' at n 36, 2, where Sinzheimer's pupil highlights extremely clearly how seeing the employment relationship as a power relationship excludes the community of interests required by the logic of the *Gemeinschaft*.

[39] The dispute originated in refusal by the employer to pay a salary for down time at the firm caused by a strike at a supplier. The BGB (s 323) restricts itself to laying down the principle that the consequences of impossibility of performance should be allocated to the party in whose legal sphere the relevant risk arises. To decide the distribution of this risk, accordingly, reference must be made to § 242 BGB, and in the case in point this distribution sprang according to the RAG from the 'modern' conception of employment relationships centring round the 'idea of the social community of labour and enterprise' (*Gedanke der sozialen Arbeits– und Betriebsgemeinschaft*), while the different individualist conception of the *Dienstverhältnis*, codified in the BGB, had now lost

Betriebsstörungen caused by a strike by the supplier's workers, in relation to which the RAG held that the worker could not simply adduce the fact that he had still made his own labour power available. The opposite was rather the case. That is, the Weimar case law created the rule that the consequences of events caused by the workers (*Arbeiterschaft*) fell also upon individual workers not directly participating in the events themselves spring from the overall bond of workers.

At the turn of the 1920s and 1930s the relevance of the enterprise community certainly kept within the formal limits of integration of the range of obligations imposed on workers as a function of their employment relationship under § 242 BGB. However, it is undeniable that the decisive step in the direction of the mental habit of *unbegrenzte Auslegung* in the case law[40] had already essentially been taken.

It was not until the year Cofrancesco identifies as the start of the debate on Euro-fascism (1939),[41] that the first true deeper treatment of industrial labour appears in Italy, almost as an unintentional effect of that debate—even though it contributed to making Italian legal scholarship less provincial.[42] We refer here to *Il contratto di lavoro* by Paolo Greco.[43] What should particularly be noted here is that although this was already the end of the 1930s Greco tackled almost exclusively the labour law doctrine of Weimar, taking over Sinzheimer's thesis —his works had in the meantime been banned in Germany—of non-ownership of the means of production as the basis for the subordination of the worker. The Italian author, however, denied that the hierarchical institution in which the latter was included had autonomous existence in relation to the fundamental relationship 'which is the property one of obligation, from which the credit and debit of employment derive'.[44]

---

meaning. The new conception changed the worker's role in the firm: he was no longer regarded as an individual making his own labour power available, but as a subject setting up a particular link with a specific enterprise, undertaking to serve its purposes [RAG 20 June 1928, in *Entscheidungen des Reichsarbeitsgerichts (ER)*, 2, 74]. However that may be, on the statement made in the text cf the fundamental contribution of O Kahn Freund, *Das soziale Ideal des Reichsarbeitsgerichts. Eine kritische Untersuchung zur Rechtsprechung des Reichsarbeitsgerichts* (Mannheim-Berlin-Leipzig, Bensheimer, 1931).

[40] B Rüthers, *Die unbegrenzte Auslegung—Zum Wandel der Privatrechtsordnung im Nationalsozialismus*, (Frankfurt am Main, CF Müller, 1973).

[41] D Cofrancesco, *Il mito europeo* . . . at n 24, 5 ff.

[42] On the attitude of repressing Weimar legal culture during the fascist two decades cf P Grossi, *Scienza giuridica italiana. Un profilo storico 1860–1950* (Milano, Giuffrè, 2000) 219.

[43] P Greco, *Il contratto* . . . at n 29 defined by Romagnoli as 'one of the few works' of the corporatist period 'that deserved to appear on the shelves of a modern library'—see U Romagnoli, *Il diritto del lavoro in Italia nel periodo fra le due guerre* in G Vardaro (ed), *Diritto del lavoro* . . . at n 25, 165.

[44] P Greco, *Il contratto* . . . at n 29, 56 at 57, where he consistently criticises the German theory of the incorporation of the worker into the enterprise community, with the consequent shift to the logic of personal status. This position, though still critical towards German methodological collectivism, was partly superseded in P Greco, 'Impresa Profilo dell'impresa economica nel nuovo Codice civile', 1940 *Atti della Reale accademia delle Scienze di Torino* 364 ff.

III The common reaction to the great crisis of 1929: totalitarianism v. individualisation

It is not surprising that, despite the differences outlined in the foregoing section, there was a sizeable area of disagreement between corporatist doctrine and National Socialist doctrine. To understand this, one has to look closer, even if in summary, at the repercussions on labour law of the great crisis of 1929.

In this context, it is useful to refer to an editorial in which, in January 1933— a few months before being compelled to emigrate to Amsterdam—Hugo Sinzheimer opened the last year of publication of his journal *Arbeit und Recht*.[45] In this article, marked by the bitter tone of a sort of labour law *Welt von Gestern*,[46] Sinzheimer started out from the premise that Weimar labour law[47] had increased the cost of labour by preventing the worker being left at the mercy of chance. Furthermore, Weimar *Arbeitsrecht* had decisively contributed to the development of a new responsibility oriented not 'only' to formal liberty but extending to the actual being of the person of the worker. However, the state of the German economy in the early 1930s was no longer compatible with the new 'value' that the labour force had reached in Weimar labour law. In this regard, Sinzheimer did not hesitate to discuss a return to the period and the situation of the 'free labour contract'.

Having established that point, the illustrious German labour lawyer went on to add a series of further considerations regarding the new social order, in the process of affirming itself in the decisive year of the article's publication on the ground left, so to speak, freed by the abolition of labour law brought about by the economic crisis. In summary, Sinzheimer held that the economic situation had evoked an ideological response of a romantic flavour that emerges in all historical periods when dominant strata of society have their existence threatened. The positional incomes they lose in terms of real function are compensated for in declining phases through *Gestalformen*—recall the glorification of the hierarchy in Ernst Jünger's 1932 *Arbeiter*[48]—that may satisfy the mind but

---

[45] The journal was forced to shut down in July 1933, but the last issue already no longer displayed the name of one of its founders (Sinzheimer). The termination of the journal's activities was formally justified by the argument that labour law was such an important topic for the fate of the Nazi Reich as to require all relevant publications to be brought together in a single journal, H Göppinger, *Juristen jüdischer Abstammung im 'Dritten Reich'* (München, Beck, 1990), 377.

[46] H Sinzheimer, 'Die Krisis des Arbeitsrechtes. Zum XX Jahrgang der Zeitschrift Arbeitsrecht', (1933) *Arbeitsrecht* 1 ff.

[47] It must in fact be acknowledged, as stated in the first years after the Second World War with notable pride by Franz Neumann, 'Das Arbeitsrecht . . .' at n 36, 1, that 'no other country contributed so much to the development of labour law and its science than Weimar Germany'.

[48] E Jünger, *Der Arbeiter. Herrschaft und Gestalt* (Hamburg, Hanseatischen Verlags-Anstalt, 1932 reprint 1963). The pars destruens of the book by contrast constitutes one of the most effective critiques of the formal liberty, devoid of actual content, that bourgeois law has granted the worker; these pages grasp the insufficient development of welfare structures in those times. There are also

have no counterpart in concrete reality.[49] These forms constitute part of a total-itarian vision of society, allowing them to be assigned an actual function.[50] This function in fact represents the negation of the value of the individuality of human beings. This is a mental *habitus* that Sinzheimer associates with the technological spirit of the times, tending to attribute greater value to the instrument than to the human person.

These words may prima facie seem to refer to the corporatist theories that Sinzheimer had opposed within the social-democratic movement.[51] None-theless, the *Gestaltformen* the author refers to are in particular those of totali-tarianism, which was taking shape in Germany in the wake of the first Italian experiments. In Italian corporatism too, the individual in fact yielded (or bet-ter, disappeared) before the function allotted to him by the system. The employ-ees' and employers' primary interest consists specifically in belonging through the mechanism of individual placing (*inquadramento individuale*) to their own category, and this was protected as a subjective right.

All this happened on the assumption that it is

> in the nation, an organism with higher ends than those of the separate individuals, that the place and function of the individuals are exactly those befitting the nationally useful activity of each carried out in order to reach those higher ends.[52]

---

thought-provoking pages criticising the bourgeois concept of society which represses elementary instincts into the realm of error and dreams, which recall contemporary psycho-analytical treatments and grasp, in the area of interest to us here, an essential aspect of modern and contemporary labour law, that in the period after the Second World War managed to internalise the positive value, in terms of evolution of society itself, of social conflict (in the specific case of labour law, collective conflict).

[49] On the other hand, the artificial nature of these legal forms in relation to the real social dynamics now constitutes a fixed point in contemporary historiography. As highlighted from the forties onward, at the very time when the legal construction became totalising, the biggest break between the legal model and actual reality came. Hence Ernst Fraenkel's theory of the double State, *Der Doppelstaat* (Frankfurt am Main, Köln, Europäische Verlagsanstalt, 1974), Franz Neumann's totalitarian pluralism—*Behemoth. The Structure and Practice of National Socialism* (New York, Oxford Univ. Press, 1942). On this point see J Bast, *Totalitärer Pluralismus* (Tübingen, Mohr Siebeck, 1999), but also Paolo Greco's more circumscribed considerations on diffuse illegality, *Legalità e libertà, in Maestri della Facoltà di giurisprudenza torinese. Paolo Greco* (Milano, Giuffrè, 1991) 63 ff.

[50] On the authoritarian nature of so-called functionalism, cf EA Tiryaakian, 'Typologies', (1968) 16 *International Encyclopaedia of Social Science* 182.

[51] Sinzheimer, cf *Arbeitsrecht und Rechtssoziologie.I* (F.a.M., Europäische Verlagsanstalt, 1976) 182, opposed both the corporatist reform of the Verordnung on the collective contract of 23 December 1918 proposed by Lujo Brentano (in (1919) 28 *Soziale Praxis* 576), and the corporatist approach of Max Cohen Reuß and Julius Kaliski, who entered the debate on the formulation of Art 165 of the Weimar Constitution. Be that as it may, during his exile in Holland he tackled the point directly in (1936) *Arbeitsrecht und Rechtssoziologie*. I, 307 ff.

[52] W Cesarini Sforza, 'Il lavoro produttivo come servizio sociale', in CFLI (ed), *I 10 anni . . .* at n 28, 58; the functional approach also comes out very clearly in S Panunzio, *Teoria generale . . .* at n 31, 141.

The preamble to the Labour Charter itself stated that the Italian nation 'is a moral, political and economic unity', accomplished 'integrally in the fascist state'. And according to Mussolini's famous motto ('everything in the state, nothing outside the state, nothing against the state'), the Fascist state was to absorb 'the whole of society into itself',[53] that is, to be 'totalitarian'.[54] It must nonetheless be recognised that this organicist view, congenial to the German mentality, met with considerable resistance, which emerged particularly when corporatist doctrine came to discuss the basis of one of the founding concepts of Fascist corporatism: the 'professional category' (*categoria professionale*).

Be that as it may, for several years the bluff[55] of Italian totalitarian corporatism, which was supposed to enable individuals to rise above the crisis (of means and of real roles) taught by liberalism, managed to work. Particularly in the stage of 'corporatism' in the strict sense (1930–1934), which coincided with the blackest economic period in the whole two decades, Italy even managed to capture international attention:[56] first with the state intervention in support of the banking system; then with the reform of the National Council of the Corporations (law 206 of 30 March 1930), which the propaganda called 'the future brain' of the Italian economy;[57] and then with law 834 of 16 June 1942 on obligatory consortia; in the following year with the creation of the *Istituto per la ricostruzione industriale* (IRI); and finally with the setting up of the twenty-two corporations (law 163 of 5 February 1934, and successive decrees of the head of government). Many had the illusion that an economic model alternative to both liberalism and socialism (and German-type state capitalism)

---

[53] M Maraviglia, 'Nazione, Stato e Lavoro' in CFLI (ed), *I 10 anni . . .* at n 28, 38.

[54] C Costamagna, 'Il nuovo Stato fascista' in CFLI (ed), *I 10 anni . . .* at n 28, 51.

[55] E Rossi, *Padroni del vapore* (Bari, La Terza, 1955) 198; for more details on the purely ideological nature of fascist totalitarianism cf A Aquarone, *L'organizzazione . . .* at note, 35 XIII. On the exemplary character that national socialist doctrine initially attributed to Italian totalitarian theory, which it sought to trace back 'to previous Italian experience', see however F Neumann, *Behemoth . . .* at n 49, 58 at 59. Moving from the theoretical to the actual practical plane, there is much debate as to whether the fascist regime really was a totalitarian one; for the opposite position see H Arendt, *The Origins of Totalitarianism* (New York, Harcourt, 1966); for a position essentially in favour see, by contrast, E Collotti, *Fascismo, fascismi* (Milano, Sansoni, 2000).

[56] An ample account of the burgeoning foreign studies of corporatism can be found in L Ornaghi, *Stato e corporazione. Storia di una dottrina nella crisi del sistema politico contemporaneo* (Milano, Giuffrè, 1984) 38 at 39. On the interest aroused by the Italian corporate model in the United States see L Villari, 'Mussolini scrive a Roosevelt', 15 September 2000 *La Repubblica* 47 and especially JQ Whitman, 'Of Corporatism, Fascism, and the First New Deal', (1991) 39 *American Journal of Comparative Law* 747, who stresses that the interest lasted until the 1935 invasion of Ethiopia. For France see the memories of L Franck, *Il corporativismo e l'economia dell'Italia fascista* (Torino, Bollati, 1990). Finally, for England see M Palla, *Fascismo e stato corporativo* (Milano, F Angeli, 1991).

[57] As Mussolini said in the speech inaugurating the Council on 21 April 1930. In fact even after the 1932 reform the council remained 'a consultative body, in general heard once the decisions are already taken, to show they were taken correctly and to lessen the responsibility of the dictatorship' (L Franck, *Il corporativismo . . .* at n 36, 117.

had been invented, and this sparked off the regime's nationalistic *folie de grandeur.*

But right from the second half of the 1930s there was a clear gap between the dictatorship's theorisation and the practical realisation—stressed almost daily by the exiles (with Salvemini, Rosselli and Tasca to the fore)—and clear, too, was the stated[58] solely 'programmatic' nature[59] of the corporate institutions, and still earlier, their positive theoretical inconsistency. Today we know that Fascist corporatism was marked exclusively negatively as a critique of liberalism and socialism, given 'the extreme vagueness of the positive content of the corporatist economy'.[60]

IV The Italian debate on the new European order

The preliminaries set out in the two previous sections now allow us to turn to the theme—the debate on the new European order[61]—that is of most interest here. Among the most important aspects of this debate worth recalling are undoubtedly the congress to study the economic problems of the new order organised in the year 1942 by Bottai's training school in the corporate disciplines at the University of Pisa (which also saw to publication of the proceedings) as well as the convention on the idea of Europe organised on 23–26 November, again in 1942, by the director of the National Institute for Fascist Culture, Camillo Pellizi (the proceedings of which were partly published later in the journal *Intervento*, 1980/41).

However, it was no coincidence that the first of a not very long series of articles[62] was written in Bottai's legal journal by none other than an economist. Though the new order constantly kept the features of 'an imprecise concept . . .

---

[58] A significant speech was given by Mussolini on 10 November 1934, inaugurating at the Capitol in Rome the proceedings of the newly formed corporation. He stated that 'the great machine is starting to move. No immediate miracles should be expected. Miracles do not happen in economics. To politics, of which the economy is an element and a strength, there belong will, organisation, method. We must be ready for a more or less long experimental stage, and we must rely for the outcome on both the efficiency of the things and the essential rectifications of the mentality of men.'

[59] V Panunzio, *Il 'secondo fascismo' 1936–1943. La reazione della nuova generazione alla crisi del movimento e del regime* (Milano, Mursia, 1988) 172; on the failure of the corporations to work, already clear as from the second half of the thirties, see A Aquarone, *L'organizzazione* . . . at n 35, 215.

[60] E Zagari, *Introduzione* in O Mancini, F. Perillo, E Zagari (ed), *La teoria economica del corporativismo* (Napoli, ESI, 1982) 24.

[61] Cf D Cofrancesco, *Il mito europeo* . . . at n 24, 5, certainly the main standard reference for the theme discussed in the text, containing on p 17 a valuable bibliography on the theme itself. See also G Longo (ed), *Il Fascismo e l'idea d'Europa* (Roma, Fondazione Ugo Spirito, 2000) and G Melis, *Fascismo e pianificazione. Il Ronvegno sul piano economico (1942–1943)*, (Roma, Fondazione Ugo Spirito, 1997).

[62] G Stammati, 'Contributo del principio corporativo sul nuovo ordine europeo', (1940) *Diritto del lavoro* 308 ff; A Guarnieri-Ventimiglia, 'Il nuovo diritto europeo', (1942) *Diritto del lavoro* 186 ff.

with vague outlines, more felt as a spiritual and political requirement than thought out in rigorous terms',[63] the economists discussed, much more thoroughly than the more somnolent lawyers, a series of alternatives I shall now attempt to summarise. In this connection it is worth recalling that in the late 1930s the background economic context was decisively changing. In fact, after the failure of the proposals to co-ordinate economic policies with the other countries that remained (unfortunately) tied to the gold standard and hence pursued the stability of their currency at existing parities, Italy was progressively drawn into the Nazi commercial area because Germany paid 'prices between twenty and forty per cent higher than those of the rest of the world for Italian farm products'.[64]

1 The theory of the two autarchic European units

The 'pact of steel' signed by Ciano at Berlin on 22 May 1939[65] was, as we know, concluded on the assumption the *novus ordo* would be based on two distinct political and economic systems (the German and the Mediterranean), which were to collaborate 'to assure the foundations of European civilisation'. Moreover, in trade union terms, the prospect of the Rome-Berlin Axis, embarked on with the meeting between Ciano and Hitler on 24 October 1936, brought only the (very timid) agreement between Cianetti and Ley on 24 June 1937. Significantly, the first noted that the

> negotiations were laborious since each of the parties sought to allege the priority of their own system. For us Italians it was inconceivable to grant the German method a universalistic nature, while we knew that once the political prejudice had been overcome the corporate system would have been unobjectionable to very many countries, with which we intended to liberally seek further knowledge and collaboration.[66]

In the agreement the Fascist Confederation of Industrial Workers and the German Labour Front (*Deutsche Arbeitsfront=DAF*) agreed the proposal to 'carry out common work aimed at benefiting both countries equally', founded on 'common faith and mutual trust' but—and this is the decisive point—inspired by the firm objective to 'rigidly respect the features of both peoples'.

---

[63] G Brugier Pacini, *Il problema dei rapporti economici internazionali, in Convegno per lo studio dei problemi economici dell'ordine nuovo.I* (Pisa, Mariotti, 1942) 2.

[64] For a more complete discussion see CH Feinstein, P Temin, G Toniolo, *The European Economy* ... at n 17, 182; the share of German imports from South East Europe rose from 11% to 21% between 1929 and 1938.

[65] This position is supported by J Mazzei, 'Relazione conclusiva' in *Convegno per lo studio* ... at n 63, 459 ff. The Catholic debate also converges on these positions: see D Cofrancesco, at n 24, 13; on the 'New Mediterranean Order' cf D Rodogmo, *Il nuovo ordine mediterraneo* (Milano, Bollati, 2002).

[66] T Cianetti, *Memorie dal carcere di Verona* (Milano, Rizzoli, 1983) 264; the text of the agreement can be read in July 1937 *Lavoro poligrafico*.

Against the background of this scenario, the contracting parties explicitly included in the agreement the clarification—undoubtedly sought by the fascist trade union movement—that it excluded 'any comparison between the corporate system of fascism and the cellular one of the German Labour Front'. The nationalist stamp thus dominated this episode, which moreover served chiefly as a support to the propaganda phenomenon of so-called workers' tourism.

In later years, too, the decisively more credited position was the one defending the corporate model, and hence the division of Europe into two areas of influence, one German, the other Italian. This first approach—openly hostile to the German model—in fact brought together authors inspired by very different motives.

First, and *pour cause,* were the supporters of a nationalist conception of law, first and foremost among them Sergio Panunzio. One ought not in this connection to underestimate the important role played by nationalist conceptions of law in legitimising the regime's totalitarian legislation. Thus, for instance, the nation was conceived of as 'that people, privileged and aristocratic in the hierarchy and in the scale of historical values' that is united by nationalising factors including the country's very economic structure (and hence the trade union phenomenon).[67] It thus represented a specific form of society[68] that became 'ruling' with the realisation of the state; the traditional relationship between state and society was overthrown. Thus the legal figure itself of the single trade union, called in Article 1 of law 563 of 1926 the 'vital cell of the fascist state',[69] could be 'blatantly' presented as the outcome of mere legislative 'recording' of a reality already present, in its exclusivity, in the body social (in the nation), and hence not as what it really was: the authoritarian imposition of the particular social movement which, born as national trade unionism, subsequently took on the more mature, more violent forms of Fascist syndicalism. The nationalist position then played a very important part in relation also to the final stage of reform of the Italian civil code, when the approach that prevailed was the one

---

[67] S Panunzio, *Popolo Nazione e Stato,* (Firenze, La Nuova Italia, 1933) 28; *idem, Teoria generale* ... at n 31, 21: 'the nation is not any people, but only that people, with a particular soul, its own individual spiritual temperament, its own particular culture and education, its own particular ideal history'.

[68] Society represented the broadest genus of Panunzio's conceptual construction; since its logical essence consisted in 'being a collectivity, a coming together, a co-operation of subjects, the con-subjectivity indeed, with a view to a common purpose transcending the subjects themselves'; this passage too is taken from S Panunzio, *Popolo* ... at n 67, 17 at 18.

[69] T Cianetti, 'Tappe della Corporazione e polemiche sul Sindacato', (1937) 1 *Rivista del lavoro* 11. The trade union organisations recognised were regarded as (public) auxiliary bodies to the state (S Romano, *Corso di diritto costituzionale* (Milano, Giuffrè, 1940) 143); the government appointed the president of the Confederation, while the outcomes of the elections of secretaries of provincial trade unions had to be approved by the president of the Confederation and then ratified by ministerial decree. The recognised trade union had conferred on it (Royal Decree no.1644 of 1 December 1930) the so-called tributary power, ie the power to impose on all those in the category represented payment of a contribution, the proceeds of which were to be distributed in accordance with law 856 of 18 June 1931, which assigned 10% to the state anyway.

that the reform itself constituted an extremely important opportunity to 'present all the peoples with the lines of our system, as complete and definite as possible'.[70]

A second group of authors taking this approach was by contrast, inspired by motives associated with the instinctive defence of their role as 'monopolists' of the interpretation of positive law, including the totalitarian law of the regime. This was essentially a group of eminent civil law theorists—with Lodovico Barassi and Francesco Carnelutti to the fore—who had accompanied the first doctrinal development of labour law and who regarded (monopoly) interpretative power as obviously the more seriously legitimated the more they could manage to adapt their (civilist) categories to the new totalitarian normative material of the regime. In this last connection, it is clear that the publicist approach favoured by the *nationalsozialistische arbeitsrechtliche Lehre* would have represented a serious danger to their leadership.

Faced with the various theories, of Carli, Ferri and Fovel to the fore, of *homo corporativus*—which did not however succeed in their aim of solving the 'problem of the co-existence (without loss of efficiency) of individual and collective choices'[71]—the more traditional Barassi, who however expressed better than any other author a position located within the dominant culture of the period (see below section IV.3) in turn stated that,

> it is very true [that a settlement between capital and labour] will be more easy to implement the more vivid is the corporative awareness in each individual, the more the state (as an ethical state) will live again within each of them, *in interiore homine*. But at the first moment the individual impulse is valuable: it is the ferment, it is the life, and it is the means the state employs to the collective welfare.[72]

Moreover, Declaration VII in the Labour Charter solemnly affirmed that 'the corporate state considers private initiative in the sphere of production as the most effective and most useful instrument in the interests of the nation'. In Romagnoli's always colourful language, this is reflected in the synthesis whereby the *homo economicus* 'was not dead. However, if he were, *homo corporativus* would have wept on his grave'.[73]

That said, it is hardly surprising if the noted jurist concluded without further ado that the 'enterprise community sketched in the 1934 German law is alien to the Fascist order'.[74] If we accept Ugo Spirito, who saw the *Gesetz zur Ordnung der nationalen Arbeit* of 20 January 1934 as confirmation of the importance of the enterprise corporation[75] (and hence indirectly of his theory

[70] From S Panunzio, 'Verso un nuovo libro del codice civile: il lavoro', 7 September 1940 *Il lavoro fascista* XVIII.

[71] E Zagari, *Introduzione* at n 60, 40.

[72] L Barassi, *Diritto sindacale e corporativo* (Milano, Giuffrè, 1938) 23.

[73] U Romagnoli, *Il diritto del lavoro* ... at n 43, 170.

[74] Above n 72, 20.

[75] U Spirito, ' Il corporativismo nazionalsocialista', (1934) *Archivio di studi corporativi*, 92 ff.

of the 'proprietary corporation' which, as we know, polarised debate at the second Congress of Corporate Studies in Ferrara in 1932),[76] the German law was, moreover, criticised from various viewpoints; particularly for its suppression of all trade union activity in the labour sphere[77] and for the failure to recognise 'the existence of divergent interests animating on the one hand the mass of workers . . . on the other the entrepreneurs'.[78]

Even the preparatory work for the Civil Code—to repeat this for a last time—shows conscious rejection of the 'administrative' nature that the national socialist order conferred on the theme of work, and reaffirmation of the Italian conception centred on the 'privatist nature of economic and social institutions in principle, that is, in obedience to the principle of individual initiative'.[79] As we have already seen, even Paolo Greco, who had considerable influence on the final formulation of the provisions of book V of the Civil Code, paid tribute to the Weimar institutionalist theories more then to the communitarian ones of National Socialist origin. Above all, he based his institutional theory on the full recognition of employer's private economic freedom, questioning 'only' the liberal *topos* according to which private law is related only to individual action.[80]

It is true at any rate that, despite the homages that corporatist law paid the German conception, corporatist doctrine consistently differed both from the communitarian version of Weimar origin, and a fortiori from Nazi doctrine. If anything, in fact, it emphasised employer authority, connecting it directly with the position of entrepreneur bearing the enterprise risk, in the light of the 'unitary interest of the national economy': 'he is head of the undertaking, on whom his collaborators hierarchically depend' (article 2086 of the *codice civile*). The entrepreneur was regarded as responsible to the state because of the organisation of his company (Declaration VII in the Labour Charter), since the management of each individual firm was to come within the unitary national objective (Declaration II of the Labour Charter). And it was indeed this 'publicist objective' that was ultimately, once the resistance of the civilists had been overcome, treated as the source of his powers, primarily the disciplinary power.[81] In other words, from the public function of private initiative there

---

[76] Cf only U Spirito, 'Individuo e Stato nella concezione corporativae', in *Atti del secondo* at note 20 181, where the author maintains that corporate property is not private property nor public property but 'the transvaluation whereby individualist economy and state economy become identified'. In fact, he already considerably modified his positions in U Spirito, *Capitalismo e corporativismo* (Firenze, Sansoni, 1933) XIII.

[77] LA Miglioranzi, 'La nuova legge tedesca sui rapporti di lavoro', (1934) *Diritto del lavoro* 78.

[78] L Barassi, 'L'ordinamento sindacale in Italia', (1934) *Vita e pensiero* 311.

[79] Above n 19, 314.

[80] Above n 44, 382.

[81] This is the approach adopted by Corte di Cassazione 30 giugno 1943, (1943) *Diritto del lavoro* 262.

followed the

> conception of the employer's power as expression of a sovereign power and of the
> hierarchical organisation of the enterprise, in which the worker loses his position as
> party to an essentially contractual relationship (. . .) to take on that of *subiectus*.[82]

Finally, a third group of authors was directly moved by the objective of protecting the concrete economic interests protected by the corporate order. Those
interests seriously risked being called in question by adoption of the National
Socialist model. In this connection one must particularly bear in mind the fact
that the fundamental difference between the Italian and the German system concerned first and foremost the representation of workers in the firm. In Italy, as we
know, the so called Palazzo Vidoni Pact of 2 October 1925, concluded on an initial impulse from Agnelli, concerned at the Communist victory in the elections
for the Fiat internal committees in 1924, brought an exchange between
Confindustria (which at the end of 1925 was officially to take on the description
of fascist) and the Confederation of Fascist Corporations Confindustria recognised the Confederation's 'exclusive representation of the workforces'; in
exchange it secured the 'abolition of internal factory commissions, with their
functions passed to the local trade union, which will exercise them only in
relation to the relevant industrial organization', as well as the dropping of
Rossoni's project for a single corporation of industry, to organise employers and
employees simultaneously.[83] In consequence, the new Fascist trade union 'was
born devoid of any organic relationship with the factory and the world of
production', and the individual labour relationship came to form part of an
'authoritarian structure of the enterprise'.[84]

On the contrary, the idea of economic democracy was part of the gene code
of the Weimar Republic, laid down in Article 165 of its Constitution and (albeit
reductively) achieved through the *Betriebsrätengesetz* of 4 February 1920. These
were admittedly measures challenged by the communist wing of the political
spectrum—and among labour lawyers, in particular by the isolated (in Weimar
labour law doctrine) Karl Korsch—but at any rate rooted collective representation of workers in the enterprise.[85] In the points of principle dictated by

---

[82] So put, critically, by U Natoli, *Limiti costituzionali dell'autonomia privata nel rapporto di lavoro* (Milano, Giuffrè, 1955), 178 at 179.

[83] 15 November 1925 saw adoption of the Royal Decree-law (regio decreto legge) 2069, laying down that 'notwithstanding any contrary agreement, clauses in labour contracts relating to worker representation stipulated prior to 1 October 1925 may be denounced with immediate effect'. On the various stages culminating finally in law 563 of 1926 see A Aquarone, n 35, 111 ff.

[84] G Giugni, 'Esperienze corporative e post-corporative nei rapporti collettivi di lavoro in Italia', (1956) 51 *Il Mulino* 3 ff.

[85] Cf also because it is a pointer to the way the question was experienced in Italy, T Cianetti., 'Relazione sulla visita alle istituzioni politiche e del fronte del lavoro tedeschi', (1939) *Ricerche storiche* 186, which states that 'the standard of living attained by the workers, in part through trade union action led by socialists and communists, has become consolidated as a position that cannot

Mussolini on 11 February 1927 to the Commission mandated to draw up the Labour Charter, this participatory logic was solemnly rejected:

> fascism is the first regime that values workers by calling on them to participate in regulating production, not at the control of individual enterprises as anarchical syndicalism, but at the control of the entire national enterprise.[86]

Two years later, the case of the Milan metal workers' trade union arose. The workers announced they intended to appoint a delegate in each factory charged with relations between workers and the firm. To the protest by Benni's Confindustria, claiming respect for the Palazzo Vidoni Pact and the support the Confederation of Industrial Workers had given the initiative on factory trustees, the inter-syndical committee chaired by Mussolini replied on 9 September 1929 by adopting the motion by Augusto Turati and Giuseppe Bottai, providing for the 'more modest solution of enterprise correspondents with no representation vis-à-vis the employer, passing merely through the trade union and workers for translation of directives and complaints'.[87] In principle, then, the regime, while contributing through the reform of the Civil Code (*codice civile*) to the full legitimation of employer powers- a departure from the ordinary law (with its pandectist imprint) but instrumental to the capitalist running of the firm—it constantly opposed the real development of the instrument typically mandated to solve the main function of modern labour law, namely effective protection for the person of the workers subject to exercise of the powers themselves.

Finally, to confirm this point, a large volume of historical research has made it clear that a whole series of public choices—starting with creation of the Ministry of Corporations (*regio decreto* 2 luglio 1926 n 1131)[88] via the unblocking decree of 21 November 1928 that dissolved the single confederation, replaced by the sector trade union confederations, the affair of enterprise trustees already mentioned, and finally the creation of the corporations—had in common the red thread of low approval of the trade union at institutional level, which they endeavoured uselessly to mask by suppressing the chamber of deputies and setting up the chamber of Fasci and Corporations (law of 19 January 1929).

To these well known reasons for employers to oppose abandonment of the generous labour law legislation of these two decades, it is obvious that the

---

be retreated from'; by standard of living Cianetti means also, and especially, the participatory prerogatives granted workers through the Council of Trust, which in his eyes exercises 'very effective defence of worker interests.'

[86] Published in CFLI (ed), *I 10 anni . . .* at n 27, 9 at 10.

[87] Above n 34, 30; on the difficulties fascist trade unionists encountered cf A Aquarone, *L'organizzazione . . .* at n 35, 230 ff.

[88] On trade union diffidence about the creation of the Ministry for Corporations cf T Cianetti, *Memorie . . .* at n 66, 147 ff, criticising also the Ministry's tendency to 'want always, at whatever cost, to split the wrongs and the rights in half.'

Fascist trade union organisations themselves had no interest in supporting a normative model (the National Socialist one) that would have meant their disappearance. There is no doubt that the German 1934 reform aroused basic rejection by the Fascist trade union movement,[89] and indeed the younger part of the movement itself displayed an open attitude of competitive challenge towards it. For this purpose the trade union slogan was created that in Germany, by contrast with Italy, the absence of trade union organisations had left the workers at the mercy of the entrepreneurs. This slogan artfully suppressed the two truths of the marginalisation of the Fascist trade union movement by the factories, and the presence in Germany of the participatory mechanism of the 'Council of Trust'.

2 The theory of international corporations

As early as 1940, Giuseppe Bottai pointed out to Mussolini, 'the danger of the formation of two or more autonomous economic units'—of 'two separate spheres of influence, two autarkic economic units'—something that would undoubtedly have brought the full dependency of the Italian (agricultural) area on the much more sizeable and industrialised German economy.

The terminology used by Bottai—and hence by corporatist doctrine setting about the problem of the New European Order—clearly drew on the theory of the *Grossraum* developed in 1939 by Carl Schmitt[90] and circulated in Italy particularly thanks to a translation produced in 1941 by the National Institute for Fascist Culture. The *Grossraum* was a territory—consisting of several states or nations—subject to the control of an empire (Reich) in the sense of the 'domination of its political ideas' and in the sense that it did not allow 'foreign interventions'. The guarantor and protector of the empire was, finally, to be the nation that had shown itself in practice to be the most worthy and able to handle the task.[91] Without going into details, it is arguable that Schmitt was thus projecting his organicist conception of the state into the international context. Properly considered, legitimisation of the empire in fact resided in the very

---

[89] For a detailed reconstruction of the trade union positions see G Parlato, *La sinistra fascista. Storia di un progetto mancato* (Bologna, Il Mulino, 2000) 116 ff, both reviewing the trade union literature and covering the results of visits by the most important fascist trade union leaders to Germany.

[90] C Schmitt, *Völkerrechtliche Grossraumordnung mit Interventionsverbot für raumfremde Mächte* (Berlin-Wien-Leipzig, Deutscher Rechtsverlag, 1939). The memorandum from Bottai to Mussolini of 20 July 1940 was prepared by Ugo Spirito, as showed by R De Felice, *Mussolini l'alleato. 1.2 Guigi e agonia del regime*, (Torino, Eimandi, 1990 reprint (1996), 851. The theory of mediterranean economic unit was also much criticised by G Pietra in *Il Fascismo e l'idea d'Europa* ... at n 61, 65 ff.

[91] C Schmitt, *Il concetto d'impero nel diritto internazionale. Ordinamento dei grandi spazi con esclusione delle potenze estranee* (Roma, Istituto nazionale di cultura fascista, 1941), 71–2, 90. It is very important to note that the 'new' concept of empire was located alongside rather than against the traditional one of state or nation.

'political union of the people' that in Schmitt's own general theory of law represented both the essential component in the 'normal situation' that he regarded as a constitutive factor of the 'legal' and the precondition for achieving the 'democratic identity between ruler and ruled':[92] any democracy is based on the assumption that the people are an 'homogeneous, unitary, undivided entity'.[93] On the contrary, the affirmation of 'social pluralism' in juxtaposition to 'state unity'—a combination that reappears in the Grossraum theory as state pluralism versus imperial unity—involved 'sovereignty of the social groups, not freedom and autonomy of the individual'.[94] This argument was to be taken up by the theorists of the Nazi regime, for whom those associations and pluralism had led to the destruction of the state. Hence the historical necessity of the National Socialist party which, by expressing this homogeneity, had brought the relation between state and people back to life, thus acquiring the role of guiding light of the German system.[95]

Schmitt's theory was certainly instrumental to the legitimation—through the concept of empire—of German annexationist policy in the late 1930s, aimed at taking over manufacturing installations, sources of raw materials and commodities, as well as people to be employed as forced labour. However, the principle of the bar on intervention in the Grossraum at least allowed an international order to crystallise where a plurality of great areas could co-exist, including the Mediterranean one where it was intended that Fascism would exercise control. This position—which at least limited the German propensity to expansionism—was subjected to detailed criticism by other Nazi legal scholars, first and foremost Reinhard Höhn[96] in the journal Reich, Volksordnung,

---

[92] C Schmitt, Die geistesgeschichtliche Lage des heutigen Parlamentarismus (München, D. & H., 1926 now reprinted Berlin, D. & H., 1991, 7[h] ed.) 20. From Schmitt's position to the theory of the totalität des politischen Volkes, for whom 'the rights of freedom of the individual must disappear, not being reconcilable with the principle of the völkisches Reich' (ER Huber, Verfassung (Hamburg, Hanseatische Verlagsanstalt, 1937) 213; see also C Schmitt, 'Nationalsozialismus und Rechtstaat', 1934 Juristische Wochenschrift 713, the step was a very short one.

[93] C Schmitt, Legalität und Legitimität (Berlin, D. & H., 1933 reprint 5th edn, 1993) 29. It has been convincingly shown that this paradigm implicitly derives from Rosseau's doctrine of the general will 'the social substrate of which perhaps tended to be a reality once in the peasant communities of the Swiss cantons', but in modern nation states represents a pure 'utopia' (cf E Fraenkel, Um die Verfassung, (1932) Die Gesellschaft 109; in fact the connection between Schmitt and Rousseau is clear from a passage in an important article by the former, C Schmitt, Die geistesgeschichtliche . . . at n 92, 19). Really, democratic thought assumes 'relativism', and hence 'pluralism'. And social pluralism, far from making impossible, as Carl Schmitt held, the 'normality' assumed by the very concept of legal 'norm' instead contributes to making normality itself implementable.

[94] C Schmitt, 'Staatethik und pluralistischer Staat', XXXV Kant Studien 28; however, see also C Schmitt, Der Begriff des Politischen, (Berlin, D. & H., 1932).

[95] C Schmitt, Staat, Bewegung, Volk. Die Dreigliederung der politischen Einheit, Hanseatische (Hamburg, Verlagsanstalt, 1933).

[96] His theories were very well illustrated in Italy by C Lavagna, La dottrina nazionalsocialista del diritto e dello Stato (Milano, Giuffrè, 1938) 150.

Lebensraum, in the context of a vision that 'recognised one right alone: the right of the stronger'.[97]

Against that background, it is evident why Italian legal scholars used Schmittian language, well beyond the bounds of the journal *Lo Stato,* directed by Carlo Costamagna and Carlo Curcio, which had previously offered Carl Schmitt's *nationalsozialistische Lehre* the most generous hospitality, and strongly supported the line that the theory of great areas or imperial conglomerates was 'decisive for the new European order'.[98]

Yet Bottai clearly saw that the problem of the great areas—the living space for the individual states—had 'an essentially dynamic nature'[99] meaning that any static solution of territorial redistribution could only be provisional. In short, it could merely suppress the problem, which was inevitably destined to surface again a few years later.

On the positive side, Bottai countered the theory of the separation of economic and political spaces with the conception that 'the criterion of complementarity implies maximum industrial development of the whole of Europe'. The point was, then, to persuade Germany to favour the strengthening of Italian industry on the basis of close collaboration inspired by a common (revolutionary) corporatist plan. This clearly presupposed loss of part of national sovereignty in areas of economic policy in favour of a joint body, almost always called the 'International Corporation'.[100] In particular, it was pointed out that the instrument of bilateral trade clearing, whereby credits and debits were balanced at national level, left 'manufacturers in both countries in perpetual uncertainty'.[101]

It must however be acknowledged that, had corporatist doctrine drawn the necessary corollaries from this critical premise regarding the 'producers', it would have been at serious risk of short-circuiting. Having for years theorised

---

[97] FR Hausmann, 'Die Aktion . . .' at n 3; this double soul of national socialist legal scholarship makes the diatribe on whether Nazism was totally irrational or not sterile: it recurs in P Lacoue-Labarthe, JL Nancy, *Le mythe nazi,* (Paris, Editiond de l'Aube, 1991).

[98] J Evola, 'Per un vero diritto europeo', (1941) *Lo Stato* 28.

[99] Cf L Robbins, *Economic Aspects of Federation,* in *Federal Union. A Symposium* (London, Jonathan Cape, 1940).

[100] A position upheld by V Travaglini, *Gli scambi internazionali nell'ordine nuovo,* in *Convegno* . . . at n 63, 172, who assigned the supranational bodies the task of 'promoting, to the benefit of each and all, a shift in the initial positions of the individual national economic systems and an increase in the transferability of products and of mobile factors of production'. In short, the transferability of mobile factors of production was presented as a factor attenuating the diversity of average income and average living standards of economic subjects belonging to different national economic systems. This approach can also be seen as the position of M Govi, *La necessaria cooperazione internazionale per gli interessi economici generali e i suoi necessari organi in Convegno* . . . at n 63, 101, who proposed the creation of national economic councils that were to co-operate internationally to identify the guidelines for an economic policy inspired by the principle of European economic solidarity. The need to create international corporations was upheld by P D'Agata, 'I principi corporativi e l'ordine economico internazionale', in *Convegno* . . . at n 63, 38.

[101] FM Pacces, 'Verso un'economia corporativa europea', 15 December 1941 *Critica fascista* 5.

the need for a totalitarian organisation of society, corporatist doctrine could not manage to argue, within these totalitarian premises, the sole dynamic remedy that fits a necessary transitional economic system: an international structure to limit—instead of reproducing—the sphere of action of the nation state, preventing it from pursuing policies of restricting free movement of goods and services. For it was only in this way that the objective—shared by Bottai— of 'creating a structure in which the German *Geist* can give Europe the best it has, instead of its worst' could be achieved.[102]

Respect for the ideology of the regime and for the interests protected by the corporate system prevented, however, this objective from being realised. Moreover, the internal debate too was marked by the paradoxical position that, faced with 'Italian economic life' that was 'basically non-corporate', it was necessary to 'pretend that were not so'.[103] This was the case even though it was undeniable that, in the late 1930s, when the debate on the new European order was in its infancy, there was a widespread awareness of the inefficacy of the system of collective protection. The experience of the Fascist trade union had not turned into a participatory vehicle in the proper sense;[104] collective regulation was, as we saw in section II, playing a secondary role; finally the corporations, constantly opposed by the trade union movement, which lost no opportunity to invoke 'creative graduality' in the 'action of the corporations'. These corporations[105] constituted a new, privileged stratum through which the captains of industry were forming increasingly intimate bonds with the upper bureaucracy of the state, enabling them to strengthen their economic position since on the Council of the Corporations, facing qualified representatives of capital, there were, as formal representatives of the workers (or more exactly of their categories), 'worthies' of the Fascist cause.

Nonetheless, Bottai was obliged again to advance the totalitarian category of the corporation again in the context of the debate on the New European Order. He accordingly made reference to a category marked by a congenital inability to support the need for limitation of the nation state mentioned: conceiving the so-called collective bodies as means for strengthening the sphere of individual liberty of the productive class.[106] And finally, given the inconsistency

---

[102] L Robbins, *The Economic Cause of War* (London, Jonathan Cape, 1939).

[103] P Barucci, 'Il contributo degli economisti italiani (1921–1936)', in P Plures, *Banca e industria fra le due guerre. L'economia e il pensiero economico* (Bologna, Il Mulino, 1981) 243.

[104] D Preti, 'La politica interna e l'organizzazione del consenso', in *Storia della società . . .* at n 17, 61, who extends the discourse to all the mass organisations of fascism. In the trade union context, the polemic sparked off by a series of articles by Vito Panunzio was pointed out; they were republished as an appendix to V Panunzio, *Il 'secondo fascismo' . . .* at n 59.

[105] T Cianetti, *Tappe . . .* at n 69, 5; in reality the reform of the corporations by no means produced enthusiasm in trade union contexts.

[106] On this different view, European economic unity represented the indirect effect of the strengthening of the sphere of individual action; on this point cf P Jannaccone, *Le forzi vitali d'Europa*, in *Reale accademia d'Italia*, Fondazione Alessandro Volta (ed), *Convegno di scienze morali e storiche (14–20 novembre 1932), Tema: l'Europa* (Roma, Reale accademia d'Italia, 1933) 286, who concluded

in practice of the institution of the corporation, there was no other way than fundamentally to acknowledge, willy nilly, the superiority of the German communitarian model.[107]

3 The theory of the unitary state of the new European 'civilisation'

It remains for us to examine the third and last alternative that emerged from the debate on the new European order, advocating unification, not merely economic but also political, between Italy and Germany. Suddenly, in the late 1930s, part of the Fascist movement began to discover 'a surprising and almost miraculous community of principles and methods' between the Latin and the Germanic civilisation.[108] For instance, there was a common (totalitarian) conception of trade union activity.[109] In fact directive XXX of the Labour Charter stated that 'education and training, particularly professional training, of their representatives, associates and non-associates, is one of the main duties of professional associations'.

The decisive debate took place, however, on the basis of, or perhaps more precisely 'aping'[110] theories of the common Aryan race or 'European civilization'.[111] The traditional position of Fascist doctrine that it was the state that made the people was replaced by the view characteristic of National Socialist doctrine, that it is the characteristics of the people and its social structures that determine the legal categories.

National Socialist doctrine (with Carl Schmitt as its leading advocate) blended diffuse communitarian thought with a racist view of law, assigning historical superiority to the concreteness of this 'Germanic' thought, as against the abstractness of Jewish origin that had inspired the pandectist method. Considering the very theories of *Eingliederung im Betrieb* of Arthur

his report by claiming that 'the formation of a European economic unity . . . will more easily be secured as an unconscious outcome, but always continuing and in growth, of abandonment of an impossible economic autonomy and continued good understanding between each state and every other, than as the realisation of a collectively agreed plan previously defined in every detail.'

[107] In essence the position, though with much reluctance, of C Arena, 'L'organizzazione' . . . at n 2.

[108] Cited from one of Bottai's closest collaborators, U D'Andrea, 'Decadenza e rinascita della civiltà europea. Un anno decisivo', (1938) *Rivista del lavoro* 34. Obviously, those who remained faithful to the nationalist ideology branded these views 'a highly forced and highly false demonstration regarding the identity of methods and objectives', see V Panunzio, *Il 'secondo fascismo'* . . . at n 59, 55.

[109] See T Cianetti, 'I lavoratori dell'industria e gli sviluppi di attuazione sindacale della Carta del lavoro' in CFLI (ed), *I 10 anni* . . . at n 27, 504.

[110] V Panunzio, *Il 'secondo fascismo'* . . . at n 59, 61; the symbol of this attitude was represented by the 'passo romano (Roman pace)', a ridiculous copy of the Prussian 'goose step'.

[111] See especially the Report by C Costamagna, 'La relazione italiana', (1939) *Lo Stato* 135 to the Italy—German Congress in Vienna on 7–12 March 1939, which concludes with a call for the new European civilisation.

Nikisch[112] ('incorporation into the enterprise') and of *Zugehörigkeit zur Betriebsgemeinschaft* (membership in the entrerpriise community) of Siebert,[113] though opposed by another part of National Socialist legal scholars who regarded them as dangerous to the security of law.[114] They denied that the 'contract' had any relevance whatsoever, not so much because it had lost its regulatory capacity,[115] but rather because the legal category of the 'contract' was regarded as an individualist degeneration that the Jewish legal *intelligèntsia* had created in opposition to the community spirit of Germanic tradition (the famous German *Sonderweg*).

In Italy the racist nature of Nazi labour law met with consensus chiefly in the context of (Fascist) trade unionism[116] as well as from the isolated[117] Costamagna, who nonetheless imposed this view within the Italo-German legal committee.[118]

However, the German jurisprudential excesses that, making reference *more solito* to *Generalklauseln,* made the employment relationship subject to achievement of the National Socialist project, were never noted. This was not just in relation to the particular view of the labour relationship that the project criticised assumed, but more generally to the underlying racist and communitarian conception of the individual and of relationships between individuals. It could

---

[112] See A Nikisch, *Arbeitsvertrag und Arbeitsverhältnis* (Berlin-Leipzig-Wien, Bensheimer, 1941).

[113] W Siebert, *Das Arbeitsverhältnis in der Ordnung der nationalen Arbeit,* (Hamburg, Haseatische Verlagsanstalt, 1935) 60, dwelling on showing that the individualist view of the labour contract had been replaced by membership of the Betriebsgemeinschaft, so that the discipline of the employment relationship could not be derived from the BGB.

[114] In particular, Siebert's theory was opposed by Werner Mansfeld, director of the Labour Ministry and supporter of the contractual theory (cf W Mansfeld, 'Die Buße', (1934) *Deutsches Arbeitsrecht* 273), see the careful reconstruction by A Kranig, 'Arbeitsrecht und Nationalsozialismus', in (1983) *Archiv für Rechts- und Sozialphilosophie* 114. Hueck, Dietz and Nipperdey instead supported the more traditional theory, followed also by the *Reicharbeitsgericht,* according to which the relationship had a contractual basis, but the content of the relationship depended also on the *Betriebsgemeinschaft* created within the enterprise, cf A Hueck, HC Nipperdey, R Dietz, *Gesetz zur Ordnung der nationalen Arbeit und Gesetz zur Ordnung der Arbeit in öffentlichen Verwaltungen und Betrieben* (München-Berlin, Beck, 1943, 4th edn).

[115] Loss of regulatory capacity was all the clearer because German doctrine was firmly tied to the pandectist conception of the contract as an agreement (rather than a regulation). It was from this view alone that some corporatist legal scholars called in question the contractual origin of the employment relationship and gave origin to the energetic reaction by L Barassi, 'Il rapporto di lavoro e la sua contrattualità', (1939) *Diritto del lavoro* 69.

[116] Cf G Parlato, 'Polemica' . . . at n 16, 1194, who states that 'for the trade union circles, who however . . . discussed the matter occasionally and with unease, the race question was nothing but the specification, the detailing . . . of the broader bourgeois question.'

[117] So much so that Volpicelli publicly calls him an author 'prey to ceaseless agitation' (A Volpicelli, above n 20, 128).

[118] See especially the report by Giovanni Petraccone, counsellor to the *Court of Cassation,* in 'Rapporto di impiego pubblico e rapporto di impiego privato' in *Atti del I° Convegno* (Roma 21–5 giugno 1938) (Roma, Istituto poligrafico dello Stato, 1939) 202 at 203, according to whom in Italy too the conception of the employment relationship as 'a relationship of a personal nature emanating from the actual personality of the worker' ought to have prevailed in Italy too.

thus happen—to take just one example—that case law could treat as legitimate the dismissal of a manager whose wife had bought things in a shop belonging to citizens of Jewish race. The foundations were laid, step by step, for Jews to be 'excluded not only from working life, but also from labour law'.[119]

But there is no need to dwell longer on practical examples of how labour law reflected the 'religiosity of the race'[120] that permeated Nazi totalitarianism. The 'neo-pagan' nature of National Socialist doctrine was hard to reconcile with the role played by part of the Catholic world during the two Fascist decades. In this context we have even recently seen assigned to the consensus that marked the relationship between Catholic church and Fascism a significance going beyond mere opportunism, to bring out a

> deeper political harmony based on an identical authoritarian conception of power, visceral anti-communism, the common desire to block social mobility and the evolution of the nation towards greater urbanisation and industrialisation.[121]

At its root, Barassi's 'authoritarian paternalism'[122]—the object of polemics that were as insistent as they were inconsistent—as well as that of Carnelutti and

---

[119] For more details see T Mayer Maly, *Die Arbeitsgerichtsbarkeit und der Nationalsozialismus, in Die Arbeitsgerichtsbarkeit. Festschrift zum 100jähringen Bestehen des Deutschen Arbeitsgerichtsverbandes* (Neuwied-Kriftel-Berlin, Luchterhand, 1994) 99. The central question was instead to decide whether membership in the Jewish race might represent valid grounds for simply terminating the labour relationship (§ 626 BGB), or be a just cause of termination itself. The approach initially taken was that merely belonging to the Jewish race was not sufficient (RAG 28 October 1933, 13 *ER* 174; RAG 25 November 1933, 13 *ER* 185; RAG 7 October 1936, cit. which excluded the legitimacy of firing on the spot because the worker, as well as being a Jew, had taken part in the First World War) to justify firing, it being necessary instead to prove why in the individual concrete case the presence of Jewish workers might bring the employer the possibility of harm. Subsequently it was instead held that membership undoubtedly legitimated the worker's dismissal, since by now the 'racist principles upheld by the national socialist party' were 'evidently supported also among those sectors of the population who did not belong to the party itself' (RAG 20 March 1937, 18 *ER* 132), so that one could not 'require' the employer to continue employing Jewish workers. In the national socialist state one could not even 'require' any employer to 'continue to give work, even for a single day, to a communist employee, while thousands of worthy national socialists, old fighters and other consciously nationalist men were on the streets in a condition of unemployment' (LAG Frankfurt 17 September 1934, 22 *ARS* 16 with added note by A Hueck).

[120] D Cantimori, 'Note sul nazionalsocialismo', (1934) *Archivio di studi corporativi* 320.

[121] See GA Borgese, *Goliath: the march of fascism* (New York, Viking, 1937). This thesis is confirmed in the opinions of L Barassi, 'L'ordinamento' . . . at n 78, 308, according to which 'national power is, in fascism as in national socialism, the ultimate goal: but fascism reaches it through union of the spirits, through harmonious collaboration in production, through moral as well as physical improvement of the Italians: and to this end the Catholic religion is a prodigious force, recognised and protected by the regime'.

[122] U Romagnoli, *Lavoratori e sindacati tra vecchio e nuovo diritto* (Bologna, Il Mulino, 1974) 187; however, adopting the (over-) simplistic thesis of the continuity between the pre-corporative and corporative legal experience led this author to underestimate the radical shift in political position that distinguishes Barassi, who had started from clearly liberal positions.

many others, was more closely adapted to the policy actually pursued by the regime than any other position.[123]

---

[123] See L Barassi, 'L'ordinamento . . .' at n 78, 308, where he theorises the insoluble link between Catholic doctrine and the regime's totalitarian policy, simultaneously rejecting the 'neo-pagan and anti-religious character' of the national socialist conception, which 'essentially proposes the hegemony of the German race in the world.'

PART IV

Responses to National Socialism and Fascism in National Legal Cultures

16

THE GERMAN IMPACT ON FASCIST PUBLIC LAW DOCTRINE— COSTANTINO MORTATI'S 'MATERIAL CONSTITUTION'

Massimo La Torre

I

In my paper I would like first to raise a few questions I believe to be funda-mental to our discussion. What is Fascism? Or rather, is there a Fascist culture or doctrine? And, if there is, what are its pillars or 'theses'? Could we say, or does it make sense to say, that there is law in Fascism? Could we really say that a Fascist regime is a rule of law, even in the barest understanding of that term?

To try to begin answering those questions I shall focus on the work of one constitutional lawyer of Fascist Italy, Costantino Mortati. The author of an important criticism against formalism in law, Mortati was much influenced by the so-called institutional theory, a product of Santi Romano, an influential public lawyer in the 'Ventennio' (the twenty years of Mussolini's dictatorship, during which he was the president of *Consiglio di Stato*, the supreme adminis-trative court). Mortati is the founding father of the concept of the 'material constitution', a notion which has enjoyed a successful career in post-fascist republican Italy. Both Mortati and Romano were involved in the elaboration of a special Fascist third way between Liberal formalism and Socialist (and National Socialist) communitarianism.

Another question to be raised is the extent to which German public law the-ories had an impact on Fascist doctrine. Here the story is not a linear one. Nor is it only a one way relationship we have to deal with but rather a dialogical one. Not only did German doctrine have an impact on the Italian, but Fascist public law had fascinated several influential German public lawyers and influenced the whole discussion in Germany in the turbulent years of Weimar Republic. Gerhard Leibholz wrote a booklet in 1928 on Fascist public law;[1] in 1931

---

[1] *Zu den problemen des fascistischen Verfassungsrechts; Akademische antrittsvorlesung* (Berlin, W de Gruyter & Co., 1928)

Hermann Heller, after six months spent travelling in Italy, published a mono-graph on the Fascist political regime.[2] Neither book was strongly critical against Mussolini's regime, which in the case of Heller (a socialist) is particu-larly surprising (Gustav Radbruch wrote a letter to his friend Heller, mali-ciously asking whether he had been converted to the black shirts' creed). Rudolf Smend's book 'Verfassung und Verfassungsrecht'[3] is full of references to Fascist Italy and the same holds for Schmitt's Verfassungslehre published in the same year.[4] The Austrian situation, notwithstanding Kelsen's Wiener Schule, was not too different—Othmar Spann's Catholic corporatism was imbued with sympathies for Fascists.

Accordingly we can legitimately speak of an Italian impact on German or 'Germanic' Fascist public law. We should not however squeeze every authori-tarian current in German law into the box of National Socialism. Though the latter is also the outcome of a more traditional authoritarian outcry and 'need' for dictatorship, we ought not ignore that until 1933, Schmitt's model or Julius Binder's authoritarian State were not exactly equivalent to Ernst Forstoff's totaler Staat or later Reinhardt Höhn's Volksgemeinschaft.

A typology of the main German doctrines might be of help. We could find four models, which I would label respectively: decisionism, communitarianism, elitism, and formalism. Schmitt's theory is self-styled as decisionist, with some later institutionalist corrections. Smend's Integrationslehre is exemplary as a communitarian approach to law, whereas much of the geisteswissenschaftliche Richtung in public law was obsessed by the notion of leadership (Führerschaft) and selection of leaders (Führerauslese). Formalism of course was the main-stream in German public law doctrine, whose epistemology was merely the product of the reception of Begriffsjurisprudenz, an approach originally reserved to private law. This reception was the great achievement of the Gerber-Laband-Jellinek school. Hans Kelsen, though subject to the attack of the geis-teswissenschaftliche Richtung, and a sincere democratic thinker, was in many senses and especially in the domain of legal epistemology, the heir to that authoritarian mainstream.

Now, none of these four ideal types were fully democratic, and they all had a more or less strong impact on the construction of a Fascist public law theory. Decisionism inspired the idea of a fourth branch of power, government, mean-ing by this something much stronger than mere executive power, and the doc-trine of its primacy. Communitarianism was used to refer to a legal stratum ontologically superior to the formal universal law. Elitism suggested a Weltanschauung centred around social hierarchy and Rangordnung. Formalism, though apparently a target of much Fascist critique, survived in the stress Fascist lawyers gave to the ideas of system and organisation.

---

[2] Europa und der Fascismus (Berlin, Walter de Gruyter, 1931)
[3] (München, Duncker & Humblot, 1928)
[4] Above

Contrary to what Norberto Bobbio has more than once affirmed, I think we can single out elements of a fascist *common* 'culture' or 'thought': the very occasionalism or cynicism of this political attitude and its several incoherences can be interpreted as a cultural, ideological trait. This is somehow recognised by Bobbio himself, when he labels Fascism a 'negative ideology'[5], meaning that Fascism was a bundle of several different positions which could only instrumentally and contingently find a common denominator. Bobbio is right in stressing the 'relativist' and opportunist character of Fascist programmes; nevertheless this is something which can in a sense not only be practised, or just rhetorically proclaimed, but also theorised. In this sense Bobbio partakes in the same mistake as Carl Schmitt when analysing political romanticism in the early 1920s.[6] Schmitt saw the core of romanticism in its being fully occasionalist, being a way of thinking in which the subject is only limited by his own intellectual productivity. This renders it possible for the romanticist to hold a complete freedom (and arbitrariness) in intellectual positions, so that logical contradictions or other incoherences might be solved through the reference to a superior 'third' stage or concept by which he is then able to make coherent the incoherent. According to Schmitt, such an attitude is only possible if it has not to cope with (social) reality. In this sense romantic occasionalism is said to be apolitical, in so far as it does not refer to, nor does it imply, any material decision. By being occasionalist—runs Schmitt's argument—romanticism could not be decisionist; and by not being decisionist, the romanticist (Adam Müller or Friedrich August Schlegel, paradigmatically) was not permitted to act politically.

Now, this analysis underplays the strong connection between occasionalism and decisionism. As a matter of fact the picture of the romanticist given by Schmitt fits perfectly well Schmitt's own later political attitude and biography. What he says of Adam Müller,

> that he was in everything only the diligent servant of any system whatever, always prepared to drop any part of his ideas standing in the way of unobstructed operation, and to adapt it to the others,[7]

seems to be a kind of anticipation of his own destiny and instrumentalist legal doctrine. If Schmitt indeed is, as he was labelled by Michael Stolleis, a 'situativ' thinker[8], that puts him not very far from the occasionalist political romanticist.

His attitude however cannot simply be dismissed as the moral weakness of a dubious character. It can instead be interpreted as a 'theoretical' feature (and failure). The same argument a fortiori holds as far as the question of Fascism's

---

[5] See N Bobbio, *Profilo ideologico del Novecento italiano* (Torino, Einaudi, 1986), 129.

[6] See C Schmitt, *Politische Romantik*, (München, Duncker & Humblot, 1925).

[7] Above 74.

[8] See M Stolleis, *Carl Schmitt*, in MJ Sattler (ed), *Staat und Recht. Die deutsche Staatslehre im 19. und 20. Jahrhundert*, (München, List, 1972).

'nature' is concerned. This is not only a degeneration of human spirit and polit-ical morality , but it is also the outcome of a particular idea of the relationship between normality and decision, where decision gets the upper hand, the one which consequently connects the law to the latter, not the former. It is important in this respect to remember that Schmitt's conclusion about political romanti-cism is the following: 'Normality is unromantic in the very concept, since any rule disrupts the one-at-a-time unboundedness of the romantic.'[9] It is perhaps a sign of romantic 'Ungebundenheit' ['unboundedness'] that a few years later Schmitt had to vindicate the same freedom in the political domain and to see the essence of politics not in norms or rules but in exceptions and arbitrariness.

Behind the romantic 'Ungebundenheit' we get a glimpse of a different and stronger idea. One feels to be 'ungebunden' by normality and norms, not sim-ply because of a failure to submit oneself to the discipline of normality. The *Ungebundenheit* is rooted into a sentiment of superiority. One feels not to be bound to norms, because these are thought to apply to normal cases whereas I myself am an *exception*. I am different, I am not like the other cases, I am not equal to the others to whom the rules apply. Indeed, I am 'superior', since I am *excepted* from compliance; but the other ('der Fremde') is not, who remains constrained by the rule. Being 'ungebunden' can be easily reformulated as being 'unique', 'einzigartig', and this privilege can be seen as the exception with regard to the normal human being who keeps being submitted to normal laws. (*Einzigartigkeit* is then played against *Gleichartigkeit* (equality) to be later reshaped by, among others, Schmitt in the racist notion of *Artgleichheit*, or common ethnic descent).

In this way a declaration of *Ungebundenheit* is a vindication for unequal concern: I am 'ungebunden', not because all are 'ungebunden', but rather because the others are not my fellows in this respect, because they are still con-strained by normality, because the rest of human beings are equal, that is *equally* 'gebunden'. As Wittgenstein once remarked, there is in the notion of the rule a reference to a context of *equality*. *Ungebundenheit*, the refusal of sub-mission to a rule, implies in this way not only egocentric freedom but also and above all hierarchy, *Rangordnung*. *Ungebundenheit* becomes nearly without being aware of it an anti-liberal and antidemocratic attitude. Its main enemy is quite immediately majority rule, based as it is on the notion that each and every human being should be given one and only one vote with no difference and graduation in its respective weight. Majority rule is therefore abhorred as an institutional equivalent to the moral principle of equal concern, and is refor-mulated as *Herrschaft der Minderwertigen*, the rule of the less worthy people.[10]

---

[9] C Schmitt, at n 6 above, 226.

[10] *Die Hersschaft der Minderwertigen* is actually the title of a book by Edgar J Jung, a 'revolu-tionary conservative', whose second edition was published in Berlin in 1930. Jung, a member of *Herrenklub*, and an adviser to Franz von Papen and general Julius von Schleicher, was killed on 1 July 1934 by the SS in the course of the 'night of the long knives'.

The summing up of our case is made by Nietzsche: 'I am compelled in the age of "suffrage universel"', ie when anyone is allowed to adjudicate about anyone and anything, to restore hierarchical order.'[11]

II

Though I have referred both to Santi Romano and Costantino Mortati as examples of the Fascist approach to legal theory, I will presently deal only with Mortati's ideas. This I do because Romano is both a more difficult case and also a less paradigmatic one. Romano's constitutional theory—such as it is presented in his *Corso di diritto costituzionale*[12]—is very keen to maintain a strong connection with traditional liberal doctrine. Reading his *Corso*, one can very often forget that what the Sicilian scholar is talking about is not a liberal but an authoritarian régime. In a sense, though he soon perceived the transformations of the State machinery due to the irruption of mass society into the political arena,[13] Romano was all his life long a man of *die Welt von gestern*, a jurist of the golden nineteenth century.

Mortati's case is different and clearer.[14] He matured as a scholar in the atmosphere of Fascism. His academic mentors were first Romano but then and more significantly for our discussion the theoretician of Fascist corporatism, Sergio Panunzio. Mortati was a student of Panunzio, and the latter supported the commencement of Mortati's academic career. Moreover, Mortati's intellectual debt towards the elder corporatist thinker is unmistakable and undeniable. Therefore, though Mortati cannot be labelled and considered as an influential lawyer of Fascist régime (in the same way as, for instance, Carlo Costamagna, not to speak of Alfredo Rocco), his scholarly production certainly is one of the more refined products of Fascist legal culture. He does not make propaganda or just pay lip service. His ambitions are higher: he is delivering an alternative both to the liberal and National Socialist State and constitutional doctrines. In this sense, for our discussion his ideas are of the greatest relevance.

---

[11] *Wille zur Macht*, § 854.

[12] S Romano, *Corso di diritto costituzionale*, (Padova, CEDAM, 1933).

[13] See for instance his essay of 1910 *Lo Stato moderno e la sua crisi* in G Zanobini (ed), *S Romano: Scritti minori vol. 1*, (Milano, Giuffrè, 1950), 310.

[14] Mortati's thought has recently been the subject of several studies. Compare the two collections of articles, F Lanchester (ed), *Costantino Mortati costituzionalista calabrese*, (Napoli, Edizioni Scientifiche Italiane, 1989), and M Galizia and P Grossi (ed), *Il pensiero giuridico di Costantino Mortati*,(Milano, Giuffrè, 1990). Very useful and intelligent, especially in its assessment of the Fascist side of Mortati's thought, are two essays by I Staff: 'Verfassungstheoretische Probleme in der demokratischen Republik Italien. Ein Beitrag zur Staatstheorie Costantino Mortatis', (1996) *Der Staat*, and 'Costantino Mortati: Verfassung in materiellen Sinn: Ein Beitrag zur Rechtsentwicklung im faschistischen Italien und im Deutschland der Weimarer Zeit und im Nationalsozialismus', (1994) 23 *Quaderni fiorentini per la storia del pensiero giuridico*, 265.

In the first chapter of his *Costituzione in senso materiale*, the work in which he gives a full account of his constitutional theory, Mortati develops the polemical side of his conception. Here he takes into account the main contemporary theories of constitutional law and subjects them to criticism. The first position to be criticised is legal positivism. This is rejected on the ground that it is unable to conceive of the legal order as a substantive coherent unity. From the narrow point of view according to which the fundamental piece of the legal domain is the single rule, or the single act of legislation, the *Satzung* of German doctrine, it is impossible to deduce a significant or meaningful system of legal propositions. The 'logical' method proposed by scholars like Paul Laband and the Italian Vittorio Emanuele Orlando is not reported to be successful in this respect. General principles of law either are deductively inferred from the various sets of legislative rules or they should be assumed as a sort of precondition of legislation. Legal positivism cherishes the first horn of this dilemma, without however succeeding in building up a system in purely logical terms. Gaps in the law can be filled in, as it is stressed by Mortati, only by means of substantive criteria, which are just what legal positivism does not want to offer in a mistaken attempt at methodological rigour.

To Kelsen's revision of legal positivism Mortati replies that the Austrian is trapped in the unsolved tension between a highly hypothetical *Grundnorm* and the assumption of a legal order's effectiveness, which only makes operative the transcendental *Grundnorm* argument.[15] On the other hand, the proclaimed purity of Kelsen's 'pure theory' is branded as a mere delusion, since it is based on one of those very ideological assumptions which the theory should supposedly fight against. As a matter of fact, the centrality of a concept of general law, as it is raised according to Mortati through the notion of *Grundnorm*, ideologically corresponds to the liberal idea of a *Rechtsstaat*, of the rule of law. Kelsen's *reine Rechtslehre* is consequently labelled as irremediably liberal and judged self-defeating.[16]

Particularly interesting for our discussion is Mortati's attitude towards the constitutional theories of both Rudolf Smend and Carl Schmitt. To Smend's *Integrationslehre* he objects that, although his idea of society as a dynamic process should be shared, Smend does not explain how the dynamic social process can reach or bring about the sufficient institutional normality which is required in order to have an effective political community. In Smend's integration theory the stability problem remains unsolved. His theory is also flawed in Mortati's view by another usual weakness of communitarian theories. Its concept of community is too diffuse and informal, in a sense too anti-institutional, to be able to offer a foundation for a normative structure such as the modern State. In such a perspective the legal dimension either disappears in the enthu-

---

[15] See C Mortati, *La costituzione in senso materiale* (Milano, Giuffrè, 1998), 22–3. First published in 1940.

[16] Above 26. Here Mortati is actually echoing a point raised in Schmitt's *Verfassungslehre*. 8–9.

siastic theatre of community or remains lost as a foreign body in the organic whole of social relations—the latter criticism Mortati explicitly applies to the National Socialist *Volksgemeinschaft*. This cannot be a legal concept. Nor can it be used as a justification or a source for a legal institution. The irony of such an idea—says Mortati—is that it would rather justify an anarchist political attitude than a *Führerprinzip*. If the spontaneity of societal relations is sufficient to rule and stabilise them, it is quite difficult to see why we need a supreme authority and a totalitarian regulation forbidding the plurality of political views and parties.

Finally, Mortati is critical towards Carl Schmitt as well. Decisionism according to him suffers from a problem similar to that which confronts *Integrationslehre*. It is incapable of founding and explaining stability. If the foundational constitutional act is a decision *ex nihilo* which has not been previously constrained by inner principles and rules, it is difficult to see how such act could produce a stable institutional reality. (It might be noted that Walter Benjamin's ideas as expressed in his celebrated essay *Zur Kritik der Gewalt* are a nice reformulation of that extreme decisionist thesis). The *Volk*, the people,—so runs Mortati's objection—does not hold as an existential entity the instruments required to elaborate a normative, principled unity. That unity can only be held by a State.

> The people taken in its generality, even if it develops a series of legal convictions concerning particular relationships, cannot supply the general principle of unification which serves to bring clashing interests to compromise and set the State moving towards a definite goal.[17]

'The people' is never a homogenous entity; it is always driven by conflicting interests and political ideals. But even if the people were of a common ethnicity, this would not suffice to render it as a sort of *Grundnorm*. 'What exists as a political quantity is, considered legally, worthy of existing,' says Carl Schmitt in his *Verfassungslehre*.[18] Too simple, objects Mortati, especially once one takes into account the epistemological vacuity of the so-called 'normative Kraft des Faktischen'.[19] Facticity is much too fractured and plural to express a clear guideline for social conduct. Moreover, if one adopt the 'geisteswissenschaftliche Richtung' common to Smend and Schmitt (according to which the science of law should imply a strong complex of 'sense' and is irremediably value- and theory-laden), then facticity can be meaningful only if we already possess a structured system of values and ideas.

The conclusion by Mortati is the following: 'A particular State[. . .]cannot be thought of as existing except as the legal organization of a collectivity ordered in accordance with a political idea.'[20] This community order according to a

---

[17] Above 138.
[18] Above n 3, 22.
[19] Above n 15,140.
[20] Above 51.

political idea is for Mortati the *political party*. It is the latter which makes possible the sought after reconciliation between Smend's communitarianism and Schmitt's decisionism. In short, the Constitution will be here conceived as decision (as it is by Schmitt), but not *ex nihilo*. The decision is taken on the basis of a particular political conception and of an already existing institutional reality holder of that ideology. This move by Mortati is in a sense also a solution to the problem in which Hermann Heller was trapped. On the one hand he affirmed that the law was (whatever) *decision* of a legislative assembly, not necessarily a general universalisable rule (as was objected to him instead by Schmitt), but on the other side he, together with other Socialist lawyers such as Franz Neumann or Otto Kirchheimer, held a sceptical attitude towards parliamentarism or the legislative assembly, as a homogeneous body unified through a strong common social and ideological essence. Mortati's party as a matter of fact is that legislative (in the sense of decisionist) assembly without parliamentarism, that is, without that very pluralism of interests and confrontation of ideological positions in which Heller was in search.

According to Mortati the decision-maker is not a 'ungebundener' individual hero, not a romanticised Machiavellian Prince, but a new Prince, the Gramscian collective Prince rather, the ruling party. When writing his book, Mortati was likely not to know a word of Gramsci's political considerations. Nevertheless his notion of the 'constitution in a material sense' is not too far from Gramsci's concept of *hegemony*, shifted perhaps a little more from the cultural into the legal domain. This closeness, I am inclined to think, might explain Mortati's later great popularity among Communist professors of law and reminds us that Mortati's thought is deeply rooted in what I have elsewhere called the 'Italian ideology'[21].

There are thus two main traits of Mortati's doctrine: (i) anti-liberalism, and (ii) anti-formalism. Anti-liberalism is unfolded along three main theses which I only sketch here.

(a) Firstly there is the pitiless critique of parliamentarism and majority rule. The latter is condemned as formal and individualist, an expression of *Sinnlosigkeit*; the former is assessed as possible only against the background of political and social homogeneity and effective only for a non-interventionist State as was the case of the classical liberal nineteenth century state. Parliamentarism could work on the assumption of a political struggle which was in fact a fight of different factions of only one big party, the Bourgeois. And it could offer practical solutions only in a society in which the State played a minimal, night watchman, role—more a simple observer than a real guardian. This argument echoes Carl Schmitt's analysis of general laws' decline on behalf of special administrative measures and his attempt to equate the social State and authoritarian régime.

---

[21] See M La Torre, 'Cittadinanza, democrazia europea e 'ideologia italiana'. Per la critica del realismo politico', (1998) 3 *Sociologia del diritto*, 5.

(b) The second point is the critique of egalitarian individualism and its purportedly disruptive social consequence: class struggle. The loss of hierarchical structure in society feeds civil strife and brings the political community to the verge of self-destruction. Here again we might perceive an echo of a Schmittian thesis, the concept of 'the political' as a friend-foe relationship. (c) Finally, liberalism is considered obsolete because, as a régime of discussion, it is unable to cope with the challenge of modernity. Modernity, says Rathenau in his book *Zur Kritik der Zeit* (1912), is 'Entgermanisierung' and 'Technisierung'. Mortati does not care much about *Entgermanisierung* or the correlative possible 'Entitalienisierung'. The are no racist tones in his fascist works. Mortati is himself a member of an ethnic minority among the Italian population: the Albanians. He is on the contrary very much concerned with *Technisierung*. Which means to him also mass society and a need for a strong social and economic intervention by the State. Parliament and its products (general laws and subjective rights) are completely unable to meet this challenge.

Modernity however is praised and vindicated as an evolutionary achievement but it is reinterpreted fully as *Technisierung* and mass society, that is, as an escalation of brute power and material forces in a futuristic mood. This escalation requires not discursive but functional rationality. Mortati's view of contemporary industrial society recalls very much Fritz Lang's *Metropolis* (which was influenced by Rathenau's views) and thus points the way to a new form of State, the 'Stato nuovo'. The last three points seen from a constructive approach can be reformulated respectively as (a) the proposal of a modernized 'monarchical principle', (b) a theory of corporatism, and (c) the centrality of mass totalitarian party.

The other strong trait of Mortati's theory of material constitution is *antiformalism*. This is firstly developed on behalf of a special radical concept of positive law, as (a) effectiveness, (b) command and power, and (c) outcome of a set of values or holding a 'sense'.

(a) If 'positivity' as effectiveness is the only possible criterion for legal bindingness, the really binding constitution is not the written one, but the one which is 'actually in force'.[22] The relationship between formal and material constitution is conceived by Mortati not in Marxian terms as a dynamics between a superstructure and a structure, but as a functional relationship driven by the need for the rationalisation of power.[23] Lassalle's definition of a constitution in this sense is closer to Mortati's view of law than Marx's. The material constitution here is already a *political* fact. The 'original constitution', which is the outcome of the victory by a ruling party over its opponents and enemies, has an autonomous legal character. It might need a further rationalisation in the form of a written formal constitution, but maintains in any case a strict normative character. It is never fully absorbed in the formal constitution, so that the

---

[22] Above n 21 117.
[23] Above 120.

validity of the latter can at any moment be assessed through its degree of adequacy to the originating constitution. However, this not being formal does not imply that the original constitution is a constitution without forms and norms of its own. It can therefore have direct legal effects[24].

It is not a *Volksgemeinschaft*, an enthusiastic and orgiastic fusion of individuals in a higher Being, but a well organised structure which solely by this good organisation is capable of affirming and maintaining its power. It is a 'Roman', classical' *form*, not a 'Germanic', 'romantic' *sentiment*. This institution is intrinsically formal; it cannot however be entirely constitutionalised. This is because the realisation of the fundamental values which it is called to pursue could well require conduct which has not been previously considered by the formal rule, or even action inconsistent with it.[25] The exceptional situation is a normal case in the implementation process of values.

The originating constitution is legally valid before there is a formal constitution, whenever at least it is effective with regard to its own ends.[26] The material constitution prevails over the formal as both the source of validity and the condition of effective implementation of the former. Being the law defined through its being positive, to the domain of law belong not only normative propositions but also context and the means of implementation. Among both contexts and means of implementation in modern times a special role is played by political groups or parties, which is why we cannot ignore them from a legal point of view and are obliged rather to recognise them as fully legal institutions.

The material constitution, Mortati writes,

> Acts above all as a source of validity or positivization of the formal constitution. We have already said that positivity or being in force is an essential feature of law, and that the features that serve to make the prediction of actual realization of the norms sound must be regarded not as mere assumptions but as constitutive parts of the legal system. Today it is the political forces which, through the organization they imprint on the society they operate in, guarantee fulfillment of that prediction.[27]

According to Mortati and his view of a material constitution, the political forms (political parties) are *directly* organs, agencies and institutions of the State. Their acts have an *immediate* legal value, because without them the formal constitution could not be given real positivity.

> The political forces act not just through organs belonging to the State system in a strict sense, but directly also outside any particular formal discipline, as an autonomous source of validity of the legal order, a factor and mechanism necessary to ensuring the order, without which the system of norms and the relations between the powers constituted could not attain the objectives they are intended for.[28]

---

[24] Above 122.
[25] Above 121.
[26] Above 111–22.
[27] Above 124.
[28] Above 129.

This 'anti-formalist' approach also makes possible a critique of parliamentary representation as mechanical and abstract and the extension of the notion of 'rappresentazione'. In the same way that Schmitt's and Leibholz's *Vertretung* (reflexive delegation of power) is opposed to *Repräsentation*, an existential link exists between 'representative' and 'represented', according to which even a dictatorship can be reshaped as a 'representative' régime.

> In essence Fascism, from both a legal and a political viewpoint, tends not only to maintain but indeed to strengthen one characteristic feature of the modern State, customarily referred to by the term 'representative'. In the fascist conception, however, the interpenetration of society and State that expresses the very content that is to be considered specific to the term 'representative' understood in the broad sense is on the one hand conceived not in purely formal fashion, but as embracing all the economic, cultural, religious etc. relationships regarded as important, and on the other, is so designed as to succeed not in annihilating but in effectively enhancing and strengthening the action of the State, understood as an organism superior to the individual social groups.[29]

(b) As already noted, there is a strong imperativistic feature in Mortati's anti-formalism. One should not forget that his first book, *L'ordinamento del governo nel nuovo diritto pubblico italiano* is a vindication and a reformulation of Smend's theory of a fourth branch of state power, that of government, which actually prevails over the traditional anodyne executive power and as a matter of fact makes the unity of the State possible and overshadows all three of the remaining powers of the liberal tradition.[30] The material constitution is far from being a sanctionless norm. This is one of the points where Mortati's concept of material constitution clearly departs from those Institutional theories proposed by Hauriou or Gurvitch but also from the notion of a legal order developed by Santi Romano. If law is command and action, and Mortati shares this opinion, the conclusion is that a legal constitution should be able to issue concrete orders and apply sanctions. This will not be the case, if the constitution is considered exclusively (i) as a set of general principles, or (ii) as a set of rules which have to control and limit the authoritative agencies.

As a set of general principles, in order to be implemented, the constitution should refer to an authority able to guarantee the required correspondence between the general principles and the features and the needs of the particular case. A principle and even a rule cannot do without prudential and authoritative intervention by a virtuous and strong personality or agency. 'One must bear in mind the necessarily incomplete nature of the formal constitution.'[31] This

---

[29] C Mortati, *L'ordinamento del governo nel nuovo diritto pubblico italiano* (Milano, Giuffrè, 2000), 224. First published in 1931.

[30] Above ch 1. See also C Mortati, *Esecutivo e legislativo nell'attuale fase del diritto costituzionale italiano*, in *Annali della Università di Macerata*, Vol. 14, 1941, republished in C Mortati, *Raccolta di scritti, Problemi di politica costituzionale (vol. 4)* (Milano, Giuffrè, 1972), 444.

[31] Above n 15, 117.

personality or agency will have to fulfill the task of realising and implementing constitution principles and rules according to the fundamental end or value which lies at the bottom of the constitution itself. This end or big value is what makes of the constitution a coherent normative scheme.

However, whence could we take or deduce this end or value? Mortati's answer is that there is an institution in society which is the privileged holder of constitutional values—the 'ruling party'.[32] This role of 'values holder' cannot be complied with or carried out by 'mechanical' institutional engineering, by a simple constitutional devise such as, for instance, the liberal division of powers. That is untenable, in so far as it cannot guarantee unity in the legal order. Powers which limit each other in a reciprocal exercise of suspicion and separation end up limiting their own institutional functioning and disrupting the fundamental unity of the State.

The alternative is then to consider as fundamental element of the legal order the supreme power's action and the social, material institution on which this is based and through which it has been achieving the supremacy within the State. The real constitutional power is the one which is able to represent not a *plébiscite de tous les jours* but rather a *pouvoir constituant de tous les jours*, that institution or agency which by its own dynamics reproduces the foundational act of that particular form of State.[33] The necessity of going beyond the liberal and formal theory of separation of powers, replacing the liberal technique of separation with a communitarian art of ruling, points out to the emergence of a new fourth power which is typical of *governing*, the power by which the various State activities get their unifying direction and the sanctioning needed to be effective.

(c) If the law is holder of a set of values or of a 'sense', if it is—using Smend's terminology—'sinnhaftig', then the State cannot be neutral; it is itself the product and the author of a political conception.

> Each individual State arises on the basis of assumptions that are the purpose and raison d'être of its founding and interpenetrate with its structure arranged so as to implement that foundation. The State derives this purpose from sociological factors [. . .] but once it has emerged it makes it its own in the way we have seen, so that it then ceases to be a *de facto* prerequisite, to become the true validity condition for acting; a limit intrinsic to the system, so that once the latter has adopted it, it could not be denied without contradicting its own essence.

So writes Mortati in his second book *La volontà e la causa nell'atto amministrativo e nella legge*.[34] This view has important implications. First of all, not only is the general law charged with normative evaluative features but so too is the entirety of State activity. They are all, (being 'sinnhaftig', highly political),

---

[32] Above 118.
[33] Above 119.
[34] (Roma, Edizione provvisoria, 1935), 150.

not neutral; nor is their sense to be found only in the general law. Judges and administrative agencies therefore are not subject only to the law but more specifically to the founding political conception.

> The activities of the organs themselves, carried out in large part in an area not disciplined by law but left to the discretion of the subjects, must be arranged in such a way as to fit the ends to which it is directed: which requires of those persons who have to carry out the activity itself not the capacity to be impersonal interpreters, but *conformity with a type that is harmonious with a given ideology.*[35]

It should be noted that Mortati here refers to a kind of *Typenlehre*, a doctrine of 'types', which substitutes 'types' of actors to the rules as criteria of conduct, in an attempt to 'ethicise' the conduct required for a case, and to make it dependent upon and assessed from the acceptance of a special body of values. The 'type theory' has the further consequence of reinforcing the *Rangordnung* concept of the polity as a fixed hierarchy, by making of it a diffuse structure in society and, what is more, something anchored in the very constitution of human beings. We might then have the 'type' of the leader, the 'type' of the judge, the 'type' of the manager, down to types such as the 'soldier', the 'father', or of the 'farmer'. Mortati does however not elaborate further this notion of 'type', perhaps because of his continuing fidelity to a normative conception as a *pendant* to institutionalist communitarianism. Only when rules are said to be condemned to wither away is it possible to draw a 'type theory' to its extreme consequences, which is the case of some National Socialist legal theorists such as Georg Dahm, Friedrich Schaffstein, and Karl Larenz.[36]

Being subject to basic political conceptions, judges and administrative agencies are, according to Mortati, also called upon to follow the guidelines laid down by the institution which is the holder of such conceptions. Such an institution however is not plural or diffuse; neither can it be democratic, which would mean to reproduce those vices of liberal State which is its task to correct— vices such as majority rule, empty discussion, and the division of powers. It must be an authoritarian agency; it is the *partito dominante*. Accordingly *stricto sensu* legal become those moments which prepare the position of those few general laws still required to organise the State and filter the interests and values expressed in them. Political parties (actually the big one political party) assume in this perspective a central constitutional relevance. This is ironically the feature of Mortati's theory which allows its extraordinarily successful reception in post-fascist Italy. It will suffice to forget only that originally the 'material constitution' was tailored to *only one* party, and to reinterpret it in a pluralist fashion, so as to make it palatable to the new republican constitutional lawyers.

---

[35] Above 126. My italics.
[36] Cf M La Torre, La *'lotta contro il diritto soggettivo'. Karl Larenz e la dottrina giuridica nazionalsocialista*, (Milano, Giuffrè, 1988).

III

Now, what was the German impact on the construction of fascist public law? Such impact was undoubtedly great, and coming from three different corners. A first important influence was the one deriving from a Labandian concept of law and the State as moments of supreme *Herrschaft*. The shift in the Italian doctrine from the French constitutionalist public law, from *science de la liberté*, to the German *Staatrechtswissenschaft* meant a dramatic change of intellectual paradigm, not only methodologically but also ideologically. The constitution once seen as a compact and a bill of fundamental rights becomes now the expression of *Herrschaft*, of power, better a rationalisation of this. Vittorio Emanuele Orlando is the scholar who succeeded in postulating and making operative this shift. It is no mere coincidence that Santi Roman was a student of his.

Secondly, in more general terms Fascism as a political attitude is in great debt with the rise of what Fritz Stern has called the 'Germanic ideology'.[37] What the harbingers of Fascism such as Enrico Corradini, or Giovanni Gentile, or Alfredo Rocco recognised, is the product of a mixture given by a particular irrational interpretation of a specific Italian ideology and several suggestions coming from *Mitteleuropa*. Nietzsche is central in this story, as well as Hegel, Fichte and Stahl. In short, whereas Fascism as a theory of political *action* has to do with Italian nationalism, as a doctrine of political *community* it is also the outcome of the modern revision of two pillars of 'Germanic thought': 'monarchisches Prinzip', and 'Ständestaat'. The first is then radicalised in a *Führerprinzip*, the second rendered palatable to mass societies as *corporatism*.

Thirdly, Fascist public law especially in its later theoretical developments is strongly influenced by the so-called 'geisteswissenschaftliche Richtung', a major theme in the German constitutional and legal philosophical debates during the turbulent years of the Weimar Republic. As we have seen, Mortati's ideas cannot be understood and explained without reference to scholars such as Schmitt, Smend, or Kaufmann.[38] Moreover, in the late 1930s, fascist public law stresses its own peculiarities in a confrontation with the views of Nazi lawyers. It is its refusal to accept the *Volksgemeinschaft* as material constitution which is one of the main points made by Mortati in his book *La costituzione in senso materiale*.[39]

---

[37] See F Stern, *The Politics of Cultural Despair: A Study in the Rise of the Germanic Ideology*, (Berkeley, University of California Press, 1961).

[38] It may be significant that the first book written by Mortati after the fall of the Fascist régime was a booklet on the Weimar constitution published in Rome in 1945.

[39] A similarly critical stance towards National Socialist public law theory, more particularly towards Schmitt, is taken by an other fascist legal philosopher, Felice Battaglia; see C Faralli and M La Torre, 'Profili filosofico-giuridici dell'opera di Felice Battaglia nella Rivista internazionale di filosofia del diritto', (1990) 4 *Rivista internazionale di filosofia del diritto*, 618. There were nevertheless fascist scholars who acted in a much more sympathetic way towards Nazi *Volksgemeinschaft* and *Deutsche Rechtserneurung*, including criminal lawyers such as Giuseppe

Before concluding, two further questions must be raised and tried to be answered. In the first section I attempted to give an outline of what I considered to represent the core of fascist political doctrine, that is, its *occasionalism*. Now, Mortati's constitutional theory seems to falsify my assumption. Mortati's concept of 'constitution' and 'law' is conceived as a polemical criticism against romantic and irrational versions of sociological jurisprudence or of imperativism. He stresses the rationality value of law and its stabilising function. But, if this is so, and we still insist on seeing Fascism as an occasionalist political attitude, we are then confronted with an alternative: either Mortati is not a typical fascist legal theorist; or we are obliged to revise our understanding of Fascism as the political expression of *Ungebundenheit* and admit that Fascism is not occasionalist.

My reaction to such a dilemma is the following. I still consider Fascism strongly connected with occasionalism. The so-called 'mistica del fascismo', a new discipline in Italian universities during Mussolini's régime, is a clear confirmation of such a thesis. In this discipline a kind of new secularised religion is outlined which is entirely based on the cult of a special personality, of a Hero, a 'demiurgo', of Him, the *Duce*, whose characters are strongly *ungebunden*. One should not forget the increasing influence of Julius Evola's mysticism in the fascist political philosophy, as witnessed in Lo Stato, the journal edited by Costamagna. Nevertheless, Mortati's worldview is quite at odds with Evola's 'religious' racism. Mortati however defends a version of the *Führerprinzip*. The new régime he says is only possible, because it is based on an exceptional *Persönlichkeit*: 'The very concentration of a huge quantity of powers in the Head of Government presupposes that the person invested with that office possess *superior political capacity.*'[40] The new Fascist form of State is so exceptional and unique that Mortati positively gives up any attempt to classify it according to traditional public law categories and has to admit that, to define it, 'there is no other more unambiguous denomination than that of Fascist Regime.'[41] There is however some doubt as to whether he would have repeated Martin Heidegger's words: 'Der Führer und nur Er ist das Recht'.[42]

On the other hand, Mortati's ruling party is, like the New Prince that it represents, a dynamic actor whose principles do not have any deontological character. Though the party is the holder of a specific set of political values, these

Maggiore, who, following scholars like Dahm, Schaffstein, and Wolf enthusiastically pleaded for the abrogation of the analogy prohibition in the field of penal law.

[40] C Mortati, *L'ordinamento del governo nel nuovo diritto pubblico italiano*, (Milano, Giuffrè, 2000), 226. My italics.

[41] Above 224.

[42] When discussing the powers held by the *Gran Consiglio del Fascismo*, Mortati seemed suggestively to say that such body, in case of a conflict on the general policies of the State, might have the upper hand over single will of the *Duce*. See above n 30. C Mortati, 'Esecutivo . . .' 460 ff. Cf F Lanchester, *Costantino Mortati e la 'dottrina' degli anni Trenta*, in F. Lanchester (ed), *Costantino Mortati costituzionalista calabrese*, (Napoli, Edizioni Scientifiche Italiane, 1989), 101–02.

are strongly instrumental to the self-affirmation of the party. Its values can never be universal, thus deontological, since the party is what it is, just *one* party, an institution of partiality, a party in a (violent) conflict and in a changing context of power relations. Though the '*partito dominante*' seems sometimes to be able to do without a *Führerprinzip* and tries to present itself as a double of the State, or as a State *in nuce*, or even better as an 'organ' of the State,[43] its deeper character is quite different. Its radical partiality instrumentalises the values of which it is the holder, making of them sheer policies, and such potent instrumentality makes of itself an occasionalist actor. *Ungebundenheit* is one of its hidden vices.

---

[43] See C Mortati, 'Sulla posizione del partito nello Stato', (1941) *Stato e Diritto*, now in C Mortati, *Raccolta di scritti, Problemi di politica costituzionale (vol. 4)*, (Milano, Giuffrè, 1972), 497.

17

MORTATI AND THE SCIENCE OF PUBLIC LAW: A COMMENT ON LA TORRE

*Giacinto della Cananea**

1 A reconstruction of Mortati's legal works: issues of method and merit

Those seeking to understand the routes and trends that the science of Public Law followed during the Fascist period and how it interacted with German legal culture will find Costantino Mortati's scientific works of particular importance. This is so primarily because, between 1931 and 1940, he published three treatises that confronted the greatest problems of his era whilst entering into dialogue with major academics in Italy, France and Germany. In addition to dedicating himself to the science of constitutional law, Mortati also cultivated interests in subjects somewhat neglected by constitutional lawyers, such as discretionary power and judicial review.[1] Lastly, one cannot fail to take account of the success of his textbook on public law, *Istituzioni di diritto pubblico* which has been a point of reference for generations of Italian university students.

One can therefore agree with Massimo La Torre's hypothesis, namely, that Mortati's juridical thought (and his concept of the 'material constitution', in particular) constitutes a vantage point for those wishing to explore the 'course' taken by legal science and, more generally, Italian culture during the Fascist period.[2]

* Professor of Administrative Law, Faculty of Political Science, University of Urbino. This short paper owes a debt of gratitude to the following: Christian Joerges, who invited me to take part in this project; Sabino Cassese, Fulco Lanchester and Giovanna Montella, for their comments on an earlier draft; Manuela Veronelli, who helped me with the preliminary research in the libraries of 'La Sapienza' University, Rome; and Catharine de Rienzo, for her valuable translation. Any errors or omissions are nevertheless entirely my own responsibility.

[1] It is not by chance that detailed studies have recently been dedicated to Mortati: M Galizia and P Grossi (eds) *Il pensiero giuridico di Costantino Mortati*, (Milan, Giuffrè, 1990), 187; F Lanchester (ed), *Costantino Mortati costituzionalista calabrese*, (Naples, Edizioni scientifici italiane, 1989). P Grossi, *La scienza giuridica italiana—Un profilo storico 1860–1950*, (Milan, Giuffrè, 2000) also pauses to consider Mortati at various points.

[2] The negative theory, frequently expressed by Norberto Bobbio (for example in *La cultura e il fascismo*, in *Fascismo e società italiana*, G Guazza (ed), (Turin, Einaudi, 1973), 229 is opposed by those who highlight the existence of a Fascist doctrine of the State, such as P Ungari, *Alfredo Rocco el'ideologia giuridica del fascismo*, (Brescia, Morcelliana, 1973) and L Ferrajoli, *La cultura giuridica nell'Italia del Novecento*, (Bari, Laterza, 1999), 39.

Precisely for this reason, however, the ways in which this hypothesis has been tested are only partly satisfactory, primarily because figures from the past cannot be studied simply by examining their most important works. Indeed, it is often in their minor works or the activities they perform outside their universities that the key to an understanding their most original ideas (and, at the same time, the 'debts' they owed to the cultural climate in which they lived) is to be found. It is therefore necessary to expand upon a textual analysis. Moreover, in order fully to grasp the novelty and originality in the thinking of an academic such as Mortati (who was on close terms both with Santi Romano and Sergio Panunzio—the former was the most authoritative representative of the 'liberal' tradition in the study of public law, the latter proposed the adoption of a new dogmatic, more apt to the Fascist State), it is necessary also to examine his context and attempt a comparison with other academics. Indeed, an investigation of this sort would require a comparison not only with the most important academics of his era but also the lesser ones as well because. As Sabino Cassese has recently recalled, 'There is no better way of understanding the stature of some men than by comparing them to the mediocrity of the others with whom they lived.'[3] Lastly, precisely on account of the 'realist' orientation that distinguished Mortati's works (he himself noted this in the last edition of *Istituzioni*), one cannot disregard a consideration that places them within the perspective of the order of real events, ie the changes occurring within the institutional framework which were numerous, far-reaching and not always easy to decipher.[4]

Of course, one cannot exclude the possibility that, despite differences regarding the route this analysis will follow, the conclusions may be, for the best part, in agreement with those drawn by La Torre, according to whom Mortati's works during the period under consideration are distinguished, in brief, by: 1) anti-liberalism, as is shown in his pitiless criticism not only of parliamentarianism but also of egalitarian individualism; 2) anti-formalism, expressed in his insistent calls for legal effectiveness and the concept he had of law as a body of values; 3) original aspects as well as some analogies with theories put forward by critics of the Weimar democracy (Rudolf Smend and, in particular, Carl Schmitt).

In order to evaluate Mortati's place within the legal culture of his time as well as the kind of contact he had with German doctrine, the following pages are dedicated to a consideration of the themes central to his thought during the fourth decade of the twentieth century: the concept of the State, the new form of government and the theory of discretion.

---

[3] S Cassese, *Oreste Ranelletti e il suo tempo*, in *Scritti in memoria di Gino Gorla*, (Milan, Giuffrè, 1995), 2678.

[4] Born in 1891, Mortati studied during the first quarter of the twentieth century. He produced his greatest works between 1931 and 1940, during the Fascist period. He was elected to the Constituent Assembly and helped to formulate the 1948 Constitution. He then continued his academic activities after it came into effect.

2 From a formal concept of the State to an analysis of interests and groups

During the period under consideration, the academics who had 're-founded' the science of public law at the end of the nineteenth century, by purifying it of philosophical and sociological interference, were (like Vittorio Emanuele Orlando) either coming towards the end of their scientific activities or (like Santi Romano) had come to the end of their most innovative period. Thus the image they gave of the State neglected the changes that had occurred in the country's social foundations and even within the structure of political representation.

Indeed, extended franchise meant that the two million voters in 1882 became eight million in 1912 and seven years later the vote was granted to everyone through proportional representation, thereby eroding the conditions that had allowed the formation of elective assemblies composed of 'eminent notables'.[5] Furthermore, growing public intervention in the economic field (already evident under Giolitti in the form of public enterprises and institutions) had assumed ever-increasing proportions during the Fascist period: the State acted as planner and enterprise. At the same time, with the introduction of the 'Work Charter' and legislation governing collective contracts, the construction of the corporate State was under way.

Orlando nevertheless remained substantially faithful to the originally German concept of the holistic, person-State. This had been useful for consolidating the new political regime which was in conflict with those supporting the *ancien régime*; he therefore saw the civil servants' trade-unions as a sign that the State was in crisis. For his part, Romano had made the most progressive effort to bring pluralism into the analysis of legal institutions as early as 1917, with his *L'ordinamento giuridico,* but he then took a step backwards, advocating that the interests of public authorities operating within government confines must, necessarily, find a moment of synthesis eventually.[6] So, despite profound differences regarding positivistic theories, Italian academics ended up expounding (to borrow an expression used by Mario Nigro) a 'desiccated and devitalised' concept of the State.[7] Apparently detached from space and time, the science of public law placed the perfecting of methodological rigour over and above the representation of real events. In reality, its (false) representation of

[5] M Fioravanti, *Dottrina dello Stato—persona e dottrina della costituzione. Costantino Mortati e la tradizione giuspubblicistica italiana,* in *Il pensiero giuridico di Costantino Mortati,* n 1, 59.

[6] S Romano, *L'ordinamento giuridico,* (Florence, Sansoni, 1946 2nd edn.); *Gli interessi dei soggetti autarchici e l'interesse dello Stato* (1930), republished in *Scritti minori, II,* (Milan, Giuffrè, 1950), 299. See A Mazzacane (ed), *I giuristi e la crisi dello stato liberale,* (Naples, Liguori, 1986) on this. Regarding the 'U-turn' Orlando advocated, see G Cianferotti, *Storia della letteratura amministrativistica italiana. I. Dall'Unità alla fine dell'Ottocento,* (Milan, Giuffrè, 1998).

[7] M Nigro, *Carl Schmitt fra diritto e politica* (1986), now in *Scritti giuridici, vol III,* (Milan, Giuffrè, 1996), 1791.

itself as a non-evaluative science was no less than an operation to de-politicise the State and its institutions, which were to be seen in an exclusively juridical perspective.

Mortati's formulation is radically different. Even in his first serious work (dedicated to the new order of governmental power),[8] his aim is to set governmental powers within the legal system, with the objective of outlining the foundations of the 'Modern State'. He then devotes himself to an analysis of the practical execution of the legislative and administrative functions, namely, the law and administrative action and, in the first place, the way in which the discretionary powers that have an impact on the hierarchy of interests are revealed. Lastly, completing the route he has embarked upon, he prepares his theory of the constitution in a material sense.[9]

In comparison with the traditional formulation, Mortati's abandons the purely formal configuration of the constitution and its provisions by affirming most resolutely that the order is 'juridical, insofar as it is linked not to a simple, formal ordering of powers but, rather, to an organisation of social forces which is capable of investing it with effect'.

The connection between society and the State, moreover, acts under a teleological profile in the sense that, over and above having generic objectives proper to every state entity such as keeping the peace and preserving public order, the State adopts numerous 'particular interests deemed to merit protection', thereby having an impact on the correlative 'social relations' which become 'the object of state regulation'. So, the State's political nature manifests itself, on the one hand, in the 'indeterminate and changeable nature of the particular objectives' it adopts and, on the other, in its ability to 'consider all the different social relations as a whole and . . . to reduce the state organs' varied behaviour to a form of unity'. It follows, in particular, that state action in the field of economic relations can, in certain cases, either be limited to guaranteeing that public order is respected, allowing 'the free emergence of conflicting interests' or 'head towards the aim of realising collaboration between the classes . . . in conditions of equality or inequality and either directed from outside or achieved spontaneously from the inside.'[10]

After bringing particular objectives (or interests) within the stronghold of the State institutions, Mortati turns his attention to the groups representing them. These are the subjects that, even purely within the limits derived from the *idem sentire de re publica*, compete between themselves to direct its actions and determine its political direction. To the extent to which the concept of constitution (rather than legal order) is used to unify the social framework, the

---

[8] C Mortati, *L'ordinamento del governo nel nuovo diritto pubblico italiano*, (Rome, Anonima editoriale, 1931).

[9] C Mortati, *La Costituzione in senso materiale*, (Milan, Giuffrè, 1940) (reprinted unaltered in 1998).

[10] Above, 77, 92–3, 96.

objectives and the powers directed at realising them (up until then expunged from the horizon of legal science) are integrated into the legal system. Indeed, the prominence assumed by the political parties is decisive: it is their business to give interests a framework by making choices related to the hierarchy of objectives and the means directed at satisfying them.

The State that Mortati describes, then, is no longer the State in the sense of a person or apolitical, juridical creation kept separate from society. On the contrary, it expresses society's government, determining its directions in social and economic fields, assuming the role of mediator between interests concerned with the sphere of production and affecting the very configuration of social structures.

This point of view is reasserted a few years later in his writing dedicated to the Weimar Constitution (destined for the collection of studies promoted by the Ministry for the Constituent Assembly).[11] Mortati observed the

> waning centre of unity in the old state which rested on the wealth and culture of the upper classes and which had put itself and the ideology of free trade forward as the foundations of the new State, assigning to Parliament (constituted without organic links with the underlying society) the function of sovereign organ of the general will.

Afterwards, however,

> so that classes other than the dominant class could acquire an awareness of the autonomy of their interests, the formation of groups representing those interests took place, overcoming legal prohibitions. These groups found themselves, if not always in contrast with the State, at least deprived of contact and co-ordination with the State's activities. The realisation of universal suffrage could not fail to reflect such a changed situation.[12]

This gave rise to a weakening of parliaments when facing 'the pluralism of various institutions on a territorial, economic, professional and political level'. It is at this point that 'totalitarianism (whether of the Left or Right) appears . . . as the necessary way out of a situation that everyone declares to be unsustainable', so as to allow the State to 'assume its proper function of maintaining social order', safeguarding liberty and at the same time intervening to support interests, assuming tasks of planning and conferring 'on individuals the right to public services of a positive nature directed at achieving a substantial equality or guaranteeing particular forms of assistance'. [13]

---

[11] *La Costituzione di Weimar*, C Mortati (ed), (Florence, Sansoni, 1946), 82–4. Similar considerations are expressed in the work *Costituzione (dottrine generali)*, in *Enciclopedia del diritto, vol.* X, (Milan, Giuffrè, 1962), 215: 'The liberal State . . . had seen its solidity compromised by the rupture arising between different parts of the population. 'The Rule of Law' . . . had revealed its incapacity to maintain the least social cohesion.'

[12] C Mortati, above 81.

[13] Above, 83.

In short, the change in the State's constitutional premises is matched by a corresponding change, on the one hand, in the system of relationships that are established between individuals and the groups to which they belong and, on the other, in the framework of institutions having the task of realising the new programme sanctioned by the primary political decision. The descriptive part was flanked by a more properly prescriptive part regarding the formation of the

> new constitution (. . . that) must not be considered as the beginning but rather as the terminal, settling phase of a process of transformation of the preceding system of social relations . . . in other words, the *stabilimentum* of a previous political decision.[14]

The outline of the social State can, therefore, already be glimpsed. The fact that Mortati laid the methodological premises for a broadening of the notion of the constitution (by indicating the extension of the franchise as the basis of the State's broader social foundation and thus re-opening the passage for osmosis between society and institutions) later permitted Massimo Severo Giannini to unite this acquisition with that (owed to Santi Romano) of the priority of the subjective element for the purpose of identifying a legal order. In this way, and precisely on the basis of the extended number of people participating in the choice of those ruling the *res publica,* it is possible to define a succession of con-stitutional frameworks: the oligarchic one (1861–1900), the democratic liberal one (1900–1922), the Fascist one (1922–1943) and the Republican one and to take this as a starting point for elaborating a notion of the multi-class State.[15]

3 The new form of government

The other theme of capital importance concerns the new form of government and the Calabrian jurist cultivated this at great length. Apart from dedicating his 1931 treatise to it, he continued to be involved with it both during the course of the subsequent decade and during the Republican period.

In this case, too, it is as well briefly to recall the prevalent directions that the science of public law was taking. The 'constitutional' events of 1922–1923[16] and the coming into effect of Law no 100 of 1926 (on the Government's organisa-tion) and Law no 2693 of 1928 (on the powers of the Fascist Grand Council) had dissolved not only the dualism between Crown and Parliament on which Vittorio Emanuele Orlando had seen the form of government as hinging

---

[14] Above.

[15] MS Giannini, *Parlamento e amministrazione* (1961), now in S Cassese (ed), *L'amministrazione pubblica in Italia,* (Bologna, Il Mulino, 1974), 81; S Cassese, *Lo 'Stato pluriclasse' in Massimo Severo Giannini,* in *L'unità del diritto. Massimo Severo Giannini e la teoria giuridica,* (Bologna, Il Mulino, 1994), 33.

[16] R De Felice, *Mussolini il fascista. L'organizzazione dello Stato fascista (1925–1929),* (Turin, Einaudi, 1968), 3.

(although he refused to recognise the political value of representation), but also the Cabinet government which the Sicilian academic had defined, in contrast to that part of German culture which relegated parliamentary government amongst the organs enjoying a merely factual existence. He no longer adhered either to the order of real events or to the theoretical representation that Santi Romano gave of them. Only in 1930, with his *Corso di diritto amministrativo*, did Romano emphasise the importance governmental activity had assumed but he nevertheless neglected the role of the political parties.[17] On the contrary, it was precisely the importance of the party (soon to be the only one) that was accentuated by the jurists intent on constructing the new political order and its correlated institutional framework.

In this case, too, the course Mortati took is an original one and marked by realism. Following Smend and Schmitt, he distinguishes the function of political leadership from the other functions of the State. Indeed, he gives it preference on account of its capacity to impress a unitary order on multiple interests ('unfettered discretion . . . the aim of realising a uniformity of State action immediately'). Furthermore, he draws the conclusion that governmental power is pre-eminent and, in comparison with the other constitutional organs in relation to which it is exercised, is attributed with 'a driving and controlling action'.[18]

This order of ideas is then developed, some years later, in the essay on the material constitution. Here, after identifying the political party as the 'organisational means that is characteristic of the Modern State' ('should only one party be admitted to act'— noted Mortati—'diversity in the appreciation of interests will be translated into changes that follow one another in time regarding the way in which the secondary objectives to pursue are to be understood'), he emphasises how it offers (on a theoretical as well as a practical level) the necessary elements for determining the content of the fundamental constitution ('including all the political forces and the objectives that they represent and that inspire the body of law'). This fundamental constitution does not have a merely sociological or political character but a genuinely legal one. It is not by chance that the failure on the part of the public offices to conform to political choices regarding 'social needs' gives rise to a real responsibility that takes the concrete form of 'an indirect repression of invalidity' in addition to the 'slackening on the part of the official covered by the office'.[19]

In this way, Mortati brings political and social forces within the constitution. This is in contrast to the apolitical valency that the jurists of the preceding generation had attributed to the State. Furthermore, he expresses a notion of political direction that plays on the concept of decision, understood as the will

---

[17] S Romano, *Corso di diritto amministrativo,* (Padua, Cedam, 1930). For the order of ideas set out in the text, see A Massera, 'Orlando, Romano, Mortati e la forma di governo. Profili storico-dogmatici' (1996) *Rivista trimestrale di diritto pubblico*, 220.

[18] C Mortati, *L'ordinamento del governo nel nuovo diritto pubblico italiano,* (Rome, Anonima Editoriale, 1931), 68.

[19] C Mortati, *La Costituzione in senso materiale,* n 9, 70, 102 and 104.

to impress a change (as much in the balance between objectives as in the choice of means) on the framework of interests emerging from the social sphere, ie the electorate, in which, precisely by virtue of its extension, formerly absent conflicts are becoming manifest. It is precisely so as to render the State capable of carrying out its new tasks in the social and economic field that the need for strong institutions arises: institutions equipped with a unitary direction that can only be determined by governmental power and, chiefly, by the organ at its apex—the Head of Government. The overcoming of the dualism between Parliament and the Crown as well as the typical product of their competition, namely, law (expressed by the representative body—which Schmitt recognised as a 'social theatre'—and 'sanctioned' by the monarch) derives from this. The registering of the change in the type of State gives rise, therefore, to the formulation of an innovative theory on the actions of its organs. This coincides with the investigation carried out by Vezio Crisafulli, who puts Government action on the level of legal materiality, whilst moving away from the positions expressed by Panunzio and other academics active in the Roman university.

The configuration of the role the Fascist party assumed and, above all, the Crown's constitutional position offer equally significant confirmation of this divergence. In open contrast to those seeking to incorporate the Fascist party within the State, Mortati first relegates it amongst the pre-juridical conditions for the regime's functioning as a public institution[20] and then recognises (in the same way as Oreste Ranelletti) its juridical relevance within the constitution without, however, indulging the opinion that the State is none other than an instrument of the single party. Even his recognition of the Government's preeminent position is tempered by the observation that the Crown maintains its right to choose as its 'Head . . . the person it deems most suited to interpreting collective requirements'.[21] So, precisely thanks to an adherence to the concept of decisionism anchored to exceptional events, Mortati adopts a reconstruction of the constitutional framework that is distinct and distanced from that of the 'regime's jurists' by assigning to the Crown an importance that few would have grasped three years on from 25 July 1943, insofar as it supposed that the sovereign had the capacity and the necessary strength to take the political decisions that circumstances dictated. In conclusion, what Mortati is advancing is an institutional framework founded on 'a balance between the State's powers' in which the Government's primacy (and that of its organ at the top) is limited by the monarchy, as if the latter were invested with the sole power to choose and make exceptional decisions.[22]

[20] Above, n 18, 186.

[21] Above, 77.

[22] It is not by chance that during these years, Mortati emphasised (in contrast to the 'regime's jurists') the juridical nature of the directives emanating from the Fascist Grand Council and its autonomy in relation to the Head of Government (*Sulle attribuzioni del Gran Consiglio del fascismo* (1941), now in *Raccolta di scritti, vol. IV,* 517. The quote is taken from M Fioravanti, *Dottrina dello Stato,* n 5, 118.

These observations suggest the following hypothetical reconstruction: although considered 'conservative' by the jurists (such as Carlo Costamagna) most committed to the attempt at constructing a physiognomy for the regime that was in contrast to the liberal one, Mortati's scientific 'programme' achieves an original synthesis of the rigour of the juridical approach (inherited from the Sicilian school) and an attention to real facts (in particular, the innovations the Fascist 'regime' introduced to the institutional framework which are transcribed amongst the categories of public law). In other words, Mortati does not follow traditional doctrine in his passive resistance to the new institutions but, rather, dedicates his studies precisely to them, without abandoning, however, the systematics developed in relation to the 'Modern State' and its variations.

4 The theory of discretionary power

If the validity of this hypothesis is to be tested, it is useful to examine briefly the studies in which Mortati set about reassessing the conceptual systems concerned with discretionary power. This subject was of central importance to Massimo Severo Giannini at more or less the same time. Indeed, these studies assume a considerable importance in relation to the theory of decisionism and the related nexus between law and politics.

The first important study, from this point of view, is the 1935 treatise on *La volontà e la causa nell'atto amministrativo e nella legge*. The choice of subject was in line with a clearly perceptible trend in the science of public law: between 1930 and 1945

> no less than thirty-five treatises were dedicated ... to individual categories of administrative acts or to elements or series of measures, which cannot be explained if not by a (politically motivated) refusal to take account of Fascism's political orientation.[23]

Mortati devotes himself to examining discretionary power so as then to analyse the characteristics of will and grounds in both private and public law. This he takes as his starting point for vigorously criticising the ideal of a rigorous legality attaching to all activities carried out by public authorities. (This ideal was typical of the nineteenth-century rule of law and reasserted by Guido Zanobini during the crisis the democratic liberal constitution—in a literal sense—suffered).

> The activity of the very organs,' notes Mortati, 'that operate to a considerable extent in a field not sanctioned by the law but, rather, entrusted to the authorities' discretionary power, must be ordered in such a way as to correspond to the objectives towards which it is directed: this requires of the people obliged to perform the said

---

[23] S Cassese, *Cultura e politica del diritto amministrativo* (Bologna, Il Mulino, 1972), 51.

activity not the ability to interpret in an impersonal manner but, rather, to conform to a norm that agrees with a given ideology.[24]

Mortati emphasises how difficult it is in the abstract to demonstrate the thesis that administrative action is bound by law and, above all, how lacking this thesis is of concrete proof:

> the complexity, multiple nature and unforeseeability of state action all make the predetermination of the terms and conditions of individual actions through precise legal rules unforeseeable: . . . it is from this that the need to entrust the choice regarding the time, manner or quality of the action to the individual functionary stems.[25] Ultimately, the public administration has and cannot fail to have wide discretionary powers.

In his next essay on discretionary power, Mortati returns to this point and clarifies the institutional implications. Once the idea that the administration also enacts regulations that integrate the legal order has been accepted, there arises the need for a connective tissue and the latter cannot be found within the law that acts as a source bestowing competence. It must therefore be found within the constitution which 'determines the objectives and interests of a given order and supplies the criterion that must serve as a measure for evaluating the exercise of discretionary power.'[26]

A variety of public interests within the State and competition between them; the abandonment of the idea that the administration is the executive apparatus of political power and a connected recognition that it makes choices between more than one solution; the call from jurists to question the reality of their era by examining its laws and jurisprudence: all this reveals how, even in relation to the theory of discretionary power, Mortati forced himself (beyond the subject-matter of the science) to renew his theoretical categories (even if, subsequently, his studies on discretionary power did not reach conclusions comparable to those drawn in Germany and, above all, in the United States, on account of the lack of criteria and parameters aimed at containing discretionary power and rendering its exercise controllable).

The originality of this reconstruction of discretionary power can be appreciated in three different ways. In the first place, it abandons the concept—stated by Guido Zanobini—according to which administrative action's objectives and also, in good part, its means are determined by Parliament so that the administration is only responsible for their execution.[27] In the second place, he also

---

[24] C Mortati, *La volontà e la causa nell'atto amministrativo e nella legge,* (Milan, Giuffrè, 1935), 126.

[25] Above, 529.

[26] C Mortati, 'Potere discrezionale', in *Nuovo digesto italiano*, vol X, Turin, Utet, 1936, 976. In this sense, see also M Fioravanti, *Dottrina dello Stato, n 5, 1001.

[27] G Zanobini, *L'attività amministrativa e la legge* (1923), now in *Scritti di diritto pubblico,* (Milan, Giuffrè, 1955), 210.

moves away from the idea (widespread in German legal culture) that the margin of judgment concretely exercised by holders of public office must be traced back to the activity of interpretation since it is of an intellectual rather than a volitional nature. Under both profiles, Mortati's position is in many respects (although not in others) in agreement with Giannini's theory (to become the *communis opinio* after 1940) that discretionary power consists of 'appraising the opportunity within a determined margin for possible solutions regarding the administrative provision to be put into effect', therefore giving rise to 'a political appraisal of discretionary power, . . . (that) consists of a comparison . . . between public and private interests.'[28] Finally, like Giannini, Mortati rejects the liberal paradigm which saw the local authorities as nothing more than a collection of de-politicised apparatuses. He shows more than one point of affinity with Schmitt's criticism of bureaucracy's neutrality (and that of technical corps). However, whereas for Schmitt administrative decisions belong to a category distinct from that of political ones (because they are not an expression of political autonomy),[29] for both Mortati and Giannini discretionary power led to a choice between interests which was not relegated to the intellectual sphere but rather distinguished by a volitional component. Therefore, if it is important (from the realist's viewpoint) to establish *who* decides, it follows that the administration too must participate in determining the framework of interests and impress them with a development that has certain characteristics as opposed to others. It is this, on the one hand, that gives the constitution its fundamental role as the source of limitation on the actions of all public authorities and, on the other, (as a consequence of this) its right to impose checks on government.[30]

5 Mortati and legal culture during the Fascist period: a dissenting view

The information that has emerged so far during the course of this analysis now permits a response to the questions posed at the beginning; namely, what is Mortati's place within the science of public law during the Fascist period and

[28] MS Giannini, *Il potere discrezionale della pubblica amministrazione,* (Milan, Giuffrè, 1939), 81. It is precisely this work to which Mortati refers in order to assess the responsibility of the administration's agents in the case where political directives are ignored: *La Costituzione in senso materiale,* n 9, 103, no 80. On the differences between the two academics, see G Azzariti, 'Discrezionalità, merito e regole non giuridiche nel pensiero di Costantino Mortati e la polemica con Massimo Severo Giannini, in *Il pensiero giuridico di Costantino Mortati,* n 1, 408.

[29] The observation is M Nigro's: *Carl Schmitt fra diritto e politica,* n 7, 1806. He takes this as a starting point for noting how the German academic reduced the decision-making's legal specificity to almost no account.

[30] S Cassese, *I controlli sulla pubblica amministrazione in Mortati,* in *Il pensiero giuridico di Costantino Mortati,* n 1, 403.

what clues may be found in his works for an understanding of the intercurrent connections between Italian and German legal cultures?

In order to answer the first question, it is necessary briefly to recall two matters. The first concerns the state that the science of political writing was in and the other regards the course Mortati's academic career had taken. The science of public law found itself at the end of the Thirties in a period of transition. It was divided (to borrow Paolo Grossi's expression) between 'legal liberalism's epigones' and those following the Weimar republic's theorists.[31] But there were also academics (such as Giannini) who, despite their position as heirs of the first category, did not hesitate to study the works of the Weimar jurists. Unlike Giannini, Mortati was not a direct pupil of Santi Romano's but he was certainly not outside his sphere of influence, as is shown by the fact that his book on the material constitution is actually dedicated to Romano. This is due to the fact that, apart from their common southern roots, it was the Sicilian academic and his theory of legal order that had broken 'the spiral of normativist positivism by broadening the study of law from that of norms to the reality of the system.'[32] At the same time, Mortati worked under Sergio Panunzio's direction and was called by him in 1936 to run the teaching of Constitutional law in the Roman faculty of political science, where the 'official wing of the regime's committed legal/political writers . . . committed to constructing its physiognomy'[33] operated. Moreover, it was none other than Panunzio who had harshly criticised Vittorio Emanuele Orlando during the Twenties for the latter's reluctance to recognise the new forces (such as the trades unions) acting within society.

In this context, Mortati does not confine himself to taking up the issues formerly left to one side by the jurists who followed well-beaten paths. He expresses his dissatisfaction with legal method in the strict sense and counters it with an openly 'realist' orientation, bringing 'concreteness to the study of law and intellectual rigour to the reconstruction of the institutions.'[34] He therefore engages his efforts in freeing the Italian science of the pandectists' issues, that is, those issues on which Orlando and Romano (together with Oreste Ranelletti and Federico Cammeo) had erected the new science of public law.[35] Unlike the other academics who, maintaining a position of neutrality as regarded the regime's political character, took no interest in the growth (after

---

[31] P Grossi, *Scienza giuridica italiana*, n 1, 257. M. Galizia's work, 'Profili storico-comparativi della scienza del diritto costituzionale in Italia' (1963) *Archivio giuridico*, 103 remains essential for a reconstruction of the directions the science of constitutional law took.

[32] S Cassese, 'Martines e le due tradizioni del diritto costituzionale italiano' (2001) *Rassegna parlamentare*, 257.

[33] F Lanchester, *Il periodo formativo di Costantino Mortati*, in *Il pensiero giuridico di Costantino Mortati*, n 1, 200.

[34] Above, n 32, 257.

[35] MS Giannini, *Profili storici della scienxa del diritto amministrativo* (1940), republished (with the addition of a *Postilla 1973*) in (1973) *Quaderni fiorentini per la storia del pensiero giuridico moderno*, 540.

1930) of the administrative State, Mortati rejects the idea of being able to keep the science 'pure' at the cost of detachment from the facts of the institutional reality, which was basically manifesting 'the most ancient tradition of opposition to the real facts emerging within the order . . . and therefore of adherence to a reactionary image of society.'[36] This is because its exponents were fully aware of the new institutions' weakness and feared that they would not have survived an over-rapid opening up to society, riddled as it was with strong centrifugal forces. The result was that the 'abstract and static nature of research techniques' employed by legal science were further accentuated.[37]

Nevertheless, it cannot be said that Mortati's legal works mirror the positions adopted by Panunzio (as appears from La Torre's article/contribution). Whilst sharing his general realist approach, he does not share his theorisations about the Fascist party. Moreover, and above all, precisely because he had criticised that methodology's inadequacy for understanding the legal institutions' historical and political reality, Mortati follows the far more difficult path of forming new theoretical categories for the modern State. For this reason, one could go so far as to say that Mortati was a critic of liberalism but was so with regard to the national version of liberalism (of which the jurists of the preceding generation had been the standard bearers), closed as it had been to society's blossoming interests and its very evolution. Moreover, his disapproval of the regime's jurists emerges quite clearly in the context of subjective legal situations: in his essay on executive and legislative powers,[38] Mortati emphasises the persistence within the Italian constitutional order of a 'sphere of autonomy for private parties', even in their dealings with the State and with this adheres to the position deeming the institutions which express the idea the rule of law to remain unabrogated. So, if it is true that, like Panunzio, Mortati criticised formalism and liberalism, the former was motivated by his intention to realise a 'corporate' State, whereas the latter was aiming at scientifically re-founding the concept of the modern State in keeping with the liberal one. That is to say, they constitute two completely different faces of the legal and political doctrine of the State.

The gap between Mortati's works and Fascist culture is also manifest in the context of his theory of the material constitution. Indeed, whilst it is misleading to say that the Mortatian construction 'rationalised' the Fascist political order, it is equally misleading to criticise its application to the multiparty framework introduced as a result of the republican Constitution, 'forgetting'— as La Torre sustains—that originally, the material constitution was suited to a single party, so as to reinterpret it in a pluralistic fashion. Although Mortati had formulated this theory in a political system distinguished by the (legal) existence of a single party, this was only by chance: it had equal value, indeed, 'in

---

[36] Above, n 23, 49.

[37] M Galizia, n 31, 103.

[38] *Esecutivo e legislativo nell'attuale fase del diritto costituzionale italiano* (1940), now in *Scritti*, n 22, IV, 429.

the case of several parties', that is, 'political forces, each one of which tends to represent and assert certain secondary objectives as relevant, over and above other ones' (whence the necessity for 'coalition governments'[39]). That this idea was in no way an isolated one is demonstrated by the attention consequently reserved to the 'so-called constitutional conventions which establish and assert themselves by virtue of the very forces' (ie political ones) that have an 'institutional character.'[40] One can object to this set-up on the grounds that ascribing social forces to public institutions leads, in a certain measure, to a weakening of individual and group liberties which are better guaranteed by an exclusively private law configuration. However, as Gustavo Zagrebelesky accurately stated, 'the material constitution is not a Fascist concept of the State but, rather, a concept of the State that was applicable and applied to the Fascist state.'[41]

Certainly, contradictions are not lacking: 'Not everything is . . . consistent, nor can every aspect of Mortati's position in this period be systematically contained.'[42] However, the academics of the past cannot be judged in a manner that detaches them from the context in which they operated (partly because they were not only academics): 'one runs the risk of betraying them if they are placed outside their own era, far from all its concrete interests, idealities and passions.'[43] It therefore seems preferable to say, as has been suggested by Mario Nigro,[44] that

> the various forms of Fascism have made those academics studying public law who wanted to learn the lesson face the reality of a framework that, however it presents itself and whatever flag it flies, is still the expression of certain ideas and interests.

It is from precisely this fact that Mortati set out, contributing in a determining manner to debunking the myth of the neutral State and following a route that was different both from that of those who (like Panunzio and Costamagna) adhered to the Fascist regime's authoritarian (or, according to another point of view, totalitarian) direction and those (such as Orlando and Piero Calamandrei) who saw legal methodology as a 'protective wall' against Fascism.[45]

These conclusions also come in useful for answering the second question regarding Mortati's relations with German legal culture. Like Smend and

---

[39] Above, n 9, 101–2.

[40] Above, 152.

[41] G Zagrebelsky, *Premessa* to C Mortati, *La Costituzione in senso materiale*, above, Part XIII; in a similar sense, P Grossi, *La scienza giuridica italiana*, n 1, 220.

[42] F Lanchester, *Il periodo formativo di Costantino Mortati*, in *Il pensiero gfiuridico di Costantino Mortati*, n 1. 223.

[43] Above, n 3, 2680.

[44] Above, n 7, 1803.

[45] M Galizia, *Profili*, n 31, 103. For the thesis that fascism was a movement aimed at constructing a totalitarian type of organisation, see E Gentile, *Le origini dell'ideologia fascista*, (Bologna, Il Mulino, 2001).

Schmitt, Mortati had shed light on the inadequacies of the pandectists' paradigm, putting the Germans' attacks to good use whilst championing a realist and 'substantialist' orientation.[46] He nevertheless criticised Smend for failing to guarantee a sufficiently stable legislative framework for social order. As for Schmitt, if Mortati shared his criticism of positivism (even in its most scientifically solid variations, such as Kelsen's), one must nevertheless not neglect the fact that Mortati saw the constitution as the fundamental, intrinsic order for a society and holding a precise legal significance, whereas for the German jurist the constitution was, quite simply, *the* fundamental political decision. Consequently, despite his adherence to a decisionist concept of power, Mortati was not an 'occasionalist'; on the contrary, he constantly reasserted the existence of legal limitations on the exercise of power, including discretionary power, precisely because he paid greater attention to institutions and their juridical dimension.[47] Finally, Mortati's rejection of 'any relationship whatsoever with the same Schmittian elaborations during the Nazi period'[48] was influenced by the Calabrian academic's rejection of the organicistic theories of German origin that anchored public law to the people or nation, while Mortati paid attention to the processes of differentiation and specialisation within society,[49] recognising their juridical importance.

If, then, the autonomy of Mortati's juridical thinking in comparison with Schmitt lies in his different conception of the constitution and the connected attempt to see the juridical reconstruction of the political and social order through to the end, the further question that needs to be answered is not so much how Mortati was able to maintain his constitutional theory during the transition from Fascism to the Republic as why legal science (with some exceptions, such as Temistocle Martines) has paid such scarce attention to the political system, political parties and trades unions. The hypothesis that has been put forward is that this occurred precisely as a result of the Fascist period's 'legacy' that, rather than residing in the 'contamination' of legal science, is to be found in an accentuation of its reluctance to study the forces that act within society, contenting itself with the (more orthodox) study of jurisprudence.

[46] Above, n 7, 1803. On this point, see F Lanchester, 'Carl Schmitt: un giurista scomodo' in (1973) *Quaderni fiorentini per la storia del pensiero giuridico*, 511.

[47] Above, n 9, 55; 'Brevi note sul rapporto fra costituzione e politica nel pensiero di Carl Schmitt', in (1973) *Quaderni fiorentini per la storia del pensiero giuridico*, 511.

[48] Above, n 42, 217. See also, by the same author, *La dottrina giuspubblicistica e la costruzione dello Sato democratico: una comparazione con il caso tedesco*, in F Lanchester and I Staff (eds), *Lo Stato di diritto democratico dopo il fascismo e il nazionalismo*, (Milan, Giuffrè, 1999), 291.

[49] M Fioravanti, *Dottrina dello Stato*, n 7, 158.

18

FROM REPUBLICANISM TO FASCIST IDEOLOGY UNDER THE EARLY *FRANQUISMO*

*Agustín José Menéndez**

When legality is enough to save society, legality; when it is not enough, dictatorship[1]

Our mission was not to challenge the new ways of thinking, as they were the only ones up to the task of protecting humankind from the communist menace, but to treat them carefully and sympathetically, and reorient them to the traditional and Christian ways[2]

1 Introduction

On 14 April 1931, the Spanish people took the streets. Local elections had been transformed into a plebiscite against the monarchy. The candidates of the Republican-Socialist coalition had obtained a landslide victory in the large cities. The King fled the country as a liberal and democratic Republic was proclaimed. As the mild spring day came to an end, the strains of the traditional Spanish Republican anthem (the *Himno de Riego*) and those of the *Marseillaise* mingled in the sunset.[3] At a time when Europe was becoming a dark valley of dictatorships and authoritarian governments, this rather unexpected event raised the hopes of European democrats. Only two years before, Spain was an early prey of the dictatorial malaise that shook the old continent. General Primo de Rivera had seized power after a relatively easy *golpe* in 1923. Quickly, he had embarked upon the institutionalisation of a new authoritarian (and corporatist) regime. However, the world economic crisis revealed the weakness of the so-called *dictablanda* ('the soft dictatorship') and precipitated its fall and that of the parliamentary monarch.

* Senior Researcher, Arena, Universitetet i Oslo. Many thanks to all participants in the *Perceptions of Europe* workshop, and especially to Julio Baquero and Massimo La Torre.

[1] J Donoso Cortés, *Sobre la Dictadura*, in *Obras Completas*, (Madrid, Biblioteca de Autores Cristianos, 1946), I: 644.

[2] E Montero, *Los Estados modernos y la nueva España*, quoted by E Díaz, *Notas para una historia del pensamiento español actual*, (Madrid, Tecnos, 1983), 30.

[3] G Jackson, *The Spanish Republic and the Civil War* (Princeton, Princeton University Press, 1965), 25.

By early 1936, hope had given way to tension. The enthusiastic espousal of the Republic had vanished. The hope elicited by the first Republican-Socialist cabinets was not enough to bring forth broad social support to the 1931 Constitution. Moreover, the limited social reforms of the *bienio reformador* ('the two years of reform') were almost completely reversed from late 1933 by a series of conservative executives. The access to government of some representatives of an openly corporatist right-wing party in October 1934 was interpreted as a first step towards a Dolfuss' style involution. It unleashed a massive protest. The working-class region of Asturias underwent a full-scale revolution. The army, led by a young official called Franco, quickly crushed the workers. The revolution was defeated, but also the hopes of the more conservative forces of an easy transformation of the Republic. When a broad centre-left coalition obtained a short but decisive victory in the elections of February 1936, the more reactionary elements of the right saw their nightmares come true and ran into the arms of the army and the emergent fascist militias. It was not long before a *golpe de estado* shattered the Republican order.

In this decisive and turbulent interlude of five years, intellectual life had been much enriched in the country. The coming of the Republic was also the time of a new blossoming of Spanish cultural life.[4] The Republican-Socialist coalition had promoted the arts and letters and had set education as a policy priority. Quite unsurprisingly, most of the intellectuals, whether university professors or modest teachers, were or became committed Republicans.

It was in such a context that a new generation of legal scholars came through. They were truly European-minded jurists. They had been able to study abroad and inject into Spanish academia 'European' themes and debates. One could expect that they would tend to stand in support of the Republican order. But as the war started, some chose to become active ideologues of the new regime. The price was to shift their legal dogmatics from constitutional republicanism to semi-fascist revolutionary propaganda. The reward was a chance to shape the rather vague and undefined political and legal philosophy of the victorious rebels.

The purpose of this paper is to explore three basic points. Firstly, it is questioned whether we can seriously speak of a Spanish *fascist* legal theory. It is here argued that legal scholarship was in the process of being *fascistised* between 1936 and 1945 [section 2]. This process was only halted by the outcome of the Second World War. Secondly, who were the most articulated 'legal philosophers' of the regime? (Or, who were the Fascists?). Paradoxically but quite predictably, a good deal of the official intellectuals of the new regime happened to be former liberal *Republicans* who turned into radical *Franquistas* at short notice [section 3]. The two authors that are considered

---

[4] See M Tuñón de Lara, *Medio siglo de cultura española* (Madrid, Tecnos, 1970) and JC Mainer, *La Edad de Plata*, (Barcelona, Libros de la Frontera, 1975).

in some detail, Conde and Legaz, had endorsed the liberal constitution of 1931, but were quite ready to become the *intelligentsia* of the new regime. Thirdly, which were the materials used in constructing a legal and state theory for the new regime? It is argued that they were rather heterogeneous. But one might claim that a key reference is the work of the Spanish counter-revolutionary Juan Donoso Cortés [section 4]. His work, occasionally quoted, but not much read, was rediscovered by Carl Schmitt in the 1920s. Through him, Donoso became a central reference point, quoted alongside Schmitt himself.

2 Destination Fascism

2.1 An Authoritarian or a Fascist Regime?

If political commentators and intellectuals seemed to agree on something during the turbulent and divisive years of the Republic, it was on the improbability of Spain turning Fascist. Committed Republicans feared a reactionary involution on an authoritarian pattern; a new *dictablanda* of the style of Primo de Rivera's regime. Right-wing political forces rallied around the 'accidentalists', conservative groupings that gave tepid support to the 1931 Constitution and favoured a transition to corporativism, but through legal means (a sort of improved version of the Primo dictatorship). As late as October 1937, Manuel Azaña reaffirmed his belief in the nature of the regime that would come out of an eventual rebel victory:

> There are or might be many Fascists in Spain. But there would never be a Fascist regime. If the rebel movement against the Republic won, we would see the establishment of a military and ecclesiastic dictatorship of the traditional kind.[5]

However, things turned out to be rather different. Azaña might have proved right if the *golpe* had led to quick success, if traditional conservative parties would have kept on being major players and if the Fascist and Nazi support to rebels had been less decisive. But these three factors led to a rather different outcome.

The *golpe* resulted neither in the seizure of power by the rebels nor in their defeat at the hands of the legitimate Republican government. The shape of the new regime was, in a way, determined as the war was being fought.

The sheer length of the war reinforced the power basis of the more radical elements.[6] The anti-Republican coalition was rather heterogeneous, but participants in the *golpe* had agreed to set aside the question of the shape of the

---

[5] M Azaña, *Memorias Políticas y de guerra* (Barcelona, Grijalbo, 1978), 313.

[6] See E Moradiellos, *La España de Franco (1939–1975). Política y sociedad* (Madrid, Editoral Síntesis, 2000), ch 2.

ensuing regime until their actual coming to power.[7] The need of fighting a long war increased the weight that the army carried in the coalition. This ensured a radicalisation of the goals of the rebels. On the one hand, the leading army officials tended to project to the civil war their previous experiences of colonial war in Morocco. It might not be exaggerated to argue that a good deal of the terrible repression can be explained by the characterisation of Republicans as the *aboriginal* people to be conquered and then exploited or suppressed.[8] On the other hand, some sectors of the military were receptive to German and Italian fascist ideologies. The crucial material assistance offered by Mussolini and Hitler, and the logistical support to be expected from Salazar's Portugal, only increased the predisposition to consider such regimes as role models.[9]

The rapid expansion of Falange, and its increasingly secure hold on power up to 1942, is to be partially explained by the external setting, in particular the crucial aid of Germany and Italy during the war, and their victories in the early years of the Second World War. However, it is also to be accounted for by the fact that it constituted a safe harbour for those who were shifting sides. This is to be traced back to the superficiality of the Falange's baroque doctrine, its original willingness to become a broad-based movement, to overcome the class-based and elitist character of monarchical groups.[10]

Moreover, Franco's eventual leadership was determinant, although rather coincidental. It was only the death of more likely candidates that eased his way to power. General Sanjurjo, who had already attempted a putsch in 1932, happened to die when flying from exile to take the lead in the rebellion. José Antonio Primo de Rivera, the leader of Falange, was arrested by the Republicans and subsequently executed. Franco seized the opportunity and managed to get proclaimed Head of State by the military junta at the end of September 1936. From then onwards, he consolidated his position by gathering all military and political power in his hands. On 1 April 1937 the *unification decree* merged the main political factions of the rebel camp into a single party.

---

[7] The confused character of the early forces supporting the coup is exemplified by the fact that for some months after the *golpe*, the rebel troops still used Republican symbols. Actually, not all rebels favoured the reestablishment of the Monarchy. Mola, for example, was in favour of an authoritarian Republic that would get rid of the 'leftist' concessions in the 1931 Constitution.

[8] M Richards, *A time of silence: civil war and the culture of repression in Franco's Spain, 1936–1945*, (Cambridge, Cambridge University Press, 1998). Further analysis in M Richards, 'Morality and Biology in the Spanish Civil War', (2001) 10 *Contemporary European History*, 395–421.

[9] See S Balfour and P Preston (eds), *Spain and the Great Powers in the Twentieth Century* (London, Routledge, 1999) and E Moradiellos, *El reñidero de Europa*, (Barcelona, Península, 2001) on the attitudes of the main world powers towards the Spanish war. Salazar's Portugal offered considerable logistic support. Franco partisans also regarded the *corporatist dictatorship* as a source of inspiration. See the extensive study of A Pena Rodríguez, *El gran aliado de Franco : Portugal y la guerra civil española : prensa, radio, cine y propaganda* (Sada, Ediciós do Castro, 1999).

[10] JL Rodríguez Jiménez, *La extrema derecha española en el siglo XX* (Madrid, Alianza, 1997), 208–9.

This strengthened Franco's position and signalled the clean break of the new regime with the liberal, parliamentarian model. The ensuing military success in the Northern Front was followed by an initial set of institutional decisions apparently inspired by the Italian Fascist State. In January 1938, Franco formed his first regular Cabinet. The army and the more *fascistised* members of Falange were allocated the most relevant posts.

The war had radicalised the stakes. Whether this is sufficient to classify the resulting regime as fascist or totalitarian is still an open question. Indeed, historians, political scientists and other scholars have devoted considerable time and effort to provide answers to such question.[11] In my view, such characterisation is rather tricky. The right answer depends on the purpose of the question and on the period on which we focus. When assessed in a comparative setting (that is, on the background of a family definition of fascism), the early *franquismo* qualifies as fascist.

Firstly, the authoritarian characterisation of *franquismo* tends to be based on an excessively narrow definition of fascism. A comparative study of the phenomenon favours a more encompassing 'family' definition. This should be narrow enough to allow us to make distinctions, but sufficiently wide as to encompass the different political regimes that presented a sufficient degree of resemblance.[12] Such an approach allows us to cut through the rhetorical claim to *national originality* which is characteristic of all pro-fascist regimes.

Secondly, any proper answer needs to be based on the distinction of several periods of Franco's regime. The sheer length and transformation of the internal and external circumstances makes it necessary to differentiate between several periods and inclinations of the dictatorship.[13] In that respect, it seems beyond doubt that the *early* or *first franquismo*, which might be said to have

[11] JA Schumpeter, *Capitalism, Socialism and Democracy* (New York, Harper and Brothers, 1950), 380, note 1 seems to have characterised the Franco regime as a mere military dictatorship. The usual authority of the *authoritarian* characterisation is JJ Linz, *Una teoría del régimen autoritario. El caso de España*, in M Fraga, J Velarde and S del Campo (eds), *La España de los años 70, volumen III, El Estado y la Política* (Madrid, Moneda y Crédito, 1970), 1468–1531. From the standpoint of *legal or moral responsibility* for the violations of human rights that took place under the regime, the category into which the regime might fit is rather irrelevant. One might argue that the key question is not whether such crimes were committed in the name of this or that ideology, but the concrete evidence and individual responsibility for the facts. To those at the wrong end of arms, so to say, it was quite irrelevant whether fascists or authoritarians were violating their rights. An overall assessment is in E Moradiellos, n 6.

[12] One such definition is provided by SG Payne, *A History of Fascism, 1941–5* (London, University College, 1995), 14: '[Fascism was] a form of revolutionary ultranationalism for national rebirth that [was] based on a primarily vitalist philosophy, [was] structured on extreme elitism, mass mobilisation and the *Führerprinzip*, positively [valued] violence as end as well as means and [tended] to normatize the war and/or the military values'.

[13] J Fontana, 'Reflexiones sobre la naturaleza y las consecuencias del franquismo'. In J Fontana (ed.), *España bajo el franquismo*, (Barcelona, Crítica, 1996), 1–26; J Pradera, 'La dictadura de Franco: amnesia y recuerdo', 100 *Claves* (2000), 52–61 and E Moradiellos, n 6.

extended from 1936 to 1945, shared a considerable number of the substantive goals, political phobias and symbols of fascist regimes.[14] If one considers the shape of its institutions, the *brutality of the repression*, and the intense control over economic activities, one might find sufficient resemblance between Franco's Spain and Mussolini's Italy or Hitler's Germany. Franco retained an almost absolute power, which was limited only by the will of the *Caudillo* himself. From May 1937, *Falange* (renamed 'Falange Española Tradicionalista y de las JONS') became the sole-party and sole-trade union. Moreover, the brutal repression that characterised the actions of the rebels from the very beginning of the war continued after March 1939. The actual number of victims would never be determined, as the regime was quite active in suppressing a good deal of incriminatory evidence.[15] However, the figure has been recently estimated as high as at four hundred thousand victims, either executed or imprisoned under inhumane circumstances, which condemned prisoners to death.[16] One should keep in mind that a considerable number of Republicans had already died in the war or left for exile. Moreover, and despite the rhetorical endorsement of private property, the *autarchic* economic policy and the transformation of labour relations under the fascist model (the *sindicato vertical)* gave government an enormous capacity to influence the economy. This was actually used to favour partisans and punish enemies. Finally, the jurisdiction of ordinary courts was severely curtailed by 'exceptional jurisdictions' for the purpose of 'purging' the administration and punishing political enemies, in physical and material terms.[17]

2.2 Fascist Legal Dogmatics?

Scepticism towards a fascist involution in Spain was partially grounded on the almost complete lack of a Fascist intelligentsia before the war. Indeed, fascism did not have a warm reception in Spain. This might be explained by reference to the socio-economic circumstances of the country or its political history. However, one should also add that the well-established pedigree of Spanish reactionary thinking might have 'crowded out' fascist ideas. A look at the intellectual panorama of the early 1930s does not reveal the presence of many Fascists. Liberal Republicans and traditional conservatives dominated the scene.

---

[14] M Richards, note 8, E Moradiellos, note 6 and A Cazorla, *Las políticas de la victoria* (Madrid, Marcial Pons, 2000).

[15] P Preston, 'An awareness of guilt', *Times Literary Supplement*, 29 June 2001, stresses this point.

[16] M Richards, n 8.

[17] M Lanero Táboas, *Una Milicia de la Justicia. La Política Judicial del Franquismo* (Madrid, Centro de Estudios Constitucionales, 1996). See F Bastida, *Jueces y Franquismo: El pensamiento político del Tribunal Supremo en la dictadura*, (Barcelona, Ariel, 1986) for an assessment of the role of the Supreme Court, with special emphasis on the late franquismo.

On the one hand, Liberal Republican thinking blossomed during the late 1920s and 1930s. The foundations of this second golden age of Spanish culture were laid by the Krausist authors of the late nineteenth century. Later on, the opening of Spanish scholars to foreign ideas, through personal stays in foreign Universities and the lecturing of international figures in Spain, had the beneficial effect of *europeanising* Spanish academia. The *Junta de Ampliación de Estudios* played a major role by means of financing the stays abroad of a good number of scholars.[18] This explains the reception and engagement with Continental legal philosophy and scholarship, especially with the German tradition.

On the other hand, the representatives of conservative and reactionary thinking were too attached to neo-scholastic thinking as to provide a good reception to more modern reactionary thinking. Reactionary thinking had an established pedigree in Spain. The liberal flavour of the majority of the first *Assemblée Constituant*, las Cortes de Cádiz (1808–1814), was counterbalanced by an emergent reactionary, anti-Liberal thought.[19] Partially influenced by the main European figures (eg De Maistre or De Bonald) and somewhat inspired by a rather fictive 'Spanish' philosophical tradition, these authors rejected Liberalism and advocated a return to a mythic, pre-modern and religious past. From the 1830s, this philosophy was identified with the *carlismo*, a sketchy set of political dogmas contingently associated with the dynastic dispute over the Spanish crown. The *carlismo* managed to elicit sufficient support to provoke three civil wars in the course of the nineteenth century, and to remain a major political force in certain parts of Spain up to the 1936 civil war.[20]

Among the philosophers of reaction, one can argue that José Donoso Cortés offered the more systematic and modern work.[21] However, his writings had only

---

[18] See F Laporta, 'La Junta para Ampliación de Estudios: primeras fatigas', 14 *BILE* (1992), 39–51 and F Laporta, A Ruiz, V Zapatero, J Solana and T Rodríguez, 'La Junta para ampliación de estudios', 499 *Arbor* (1989).

[19] J Varela, *La Teoría del Estado en los orígenes del constitucionalismo hispánico: Las Cortes de Cádiz* (Madrid, Centro de Estudios Constitucionales, 1983).

[20] For a recent overview, see J Canal, *El carlismo* (Madrid, Alianza Editorial, 2000).

[21] Donoso started his career as a moderate or *doctrinarian* liberal politician, close adviser of the Spanish Queen Elisabeth II and of Pope Pius XIII. As such, he was a staunch advocate of a limited parliamentary monarchy, with full protection of classic or negative rights (life and limb), but quite fearful of more full-blooded variants of democracy. As one of the fathers of the 1845 Constitution, he is said to have authored a report that later became the preface to the fundamental law. The text is a short outline of his relatively moderate early thought. See J Donoso Cortés, *Obras Completas,* (Madrid, Biblioteca de Autores Cristianos, 1970), II, 74–87, but compare with the overt authoritarian overtones of J Donoso Cortés, *Lecciones de Derecho Político* (Madrid, Centro de Estudios Constitucionales, 1984) and J Donoso Cortés, Juan *Obras Completas*, note 1, I, 644 (containing a melancholic eulogy of social, political and religious unity even at the peak of his liberal years). See also the introduction of J Álvarez Junco to *Lecciones de Derecho Político*, quoted in this same note. His liberal overtones replaced by frankly authoritarian ones. In his role as ambassador in Berlin and Paris he played the game of political conspiracy at a European scale. Among other

an indirect influence on Spanish reactionaries. His ideas were popularised by French Catholic propagandists and later on by German philosophers. As we will see, Carl Schmitt's reconstruction of his thought proved determinant of the renewed interest on this author in Spain.[22] The intellectual discourse of reactionary forces was probably more directly influenced by authors such as Balmes,[23] Vázquez de Mella[24] or Ramiro de Maeztu.[25] Quite paradoxically, a major reference of Primo's dictatorship was Joaquín Costa,[26] who was also cheered by Liberals.

It is only the increasing tension which led to the war and the later 'fascistisation' of the regime that explains the rapid transformation of the intellectual panorama. This is reflected in the origins of the *intellectuals of franquismo*, who were of two main types.[27] On the one hand, were the conservative philosophers, who aimed at shaping and characterising the new regime in the mould of the traditional reactionary and authoritarian model (such as Victor Pradera).[28] On the other hand, were those who endorsed the task of shaping something new, either out of their pre-existing Fascist beliefs (such as Sánchez Mazas or Giménez Caballero), or out of a sudden radicalisation (such as Legaz and Conde). As we will see (section III), it was thus not surprising that the newcomers were more prone to a process of rapid induction into fascism.

This radical turn was fostered from above. On the one hand, academia was among the professions where the impact of *purges* was highest. The few Republicans who did not leave for exile[29] were silenced and

---

performances, he was a major player in the *Louis Philippe* coup in 1851. See JT Graham, *Donoso Cortés. Utopian Romanticism and Political Realist* (Columbia, University of Missouri Press, 1974). His increasing theological turn made him one of the close advisors of Pius IX, and a driving source of inspiration for the later (in)famous *Syllabus of Errors*. By 1848 he became the major speaker of reaction and dictatorship in Europe. His fame was forged by a set of three speeches, *On Dictatorship* (1849), *On the general state of affairs in Europe* (1850) and *On the general state of affairs in Spain* (1950). However, his most articulated work was the lengthy *Essays on Catholicism, Liberalism and Socialism* (1851).

[22] M Blinkhorn, *Carlism and Crisis in Spain* (Cambridge, Cambridge University Press, 1975).

[23] See J Balmes, *Política y Constitución* (Madrid, Centro de Estudios Constitucionales, 1988).

[24] *Hacia la Dictadura*, in his *Complete Works*, volume XIII, 341, quoted from JL Rodríguez Jiménez, n 10, 82

[25] JL Villacañas, *Ramiro de Maeztu y el ideal de la burguesía en España*, (Madrid, Espasa-Calpe, 1999).

[26] See his speech *Quiénes deben gobernar después de la catástrofe* at J Costa, *Oligarquía y Caciquismo. Colectivismo Agrario y otros escritos*, (Madrid, Alianza Editorial, 1984), 218–33. This speech was much quoted and probably not very read. Costa flirts with the idea of 'revolution from above', but the text can be read more as a plea for getting rid of an asphyxiated political system by means of civil society control than a plea for an iron surgeon.

[27] See JA Biescas and M Tuñón de Lara, *España bajo el franquismo* (Barcelona, Labor, 1980), 436.

[28] See V Pradera, *El Estado Nuevo* (Burgos, Editorial Española, 1937).

[29] JL Abellán, 'Filosofía y Pensamiento: Su Función en el exilio', in JL Abellán (ed), *El Exilio Español de 1939: III. Revistas, Pensamiento, Educación* (Madrid, Taurus, 1976), 151–208.

repressed.[30] On the other hand, the new regime gave preferential attention to the development of its legal and political theory. In September 1939, a centre of political studies, the *Instituto de Estudios Políticos,* was founded in the vacant premises of the monarchical Senate.[31] This institution was conceived as a sort of think tank of Falange. In its first five years, under the direction of Alfonso García Valdecasas,[32] its scholars articulated the most sustained attempt at producing a legal scholarship imbued by the new principles of the regime. Valdecasas wrote in the first issue of the *Revista de Estudios Políticos* (the main organ of the *Instituto*) that the aim of the new publication was the 'development of a scientific method based on the *radical truth* of the single party'.[33]

The scholars of the *Instituto* were active on several fronts. On the one hand, they played a major advisory role in the drafting of several of the 'fundamental laws' of the regime. Their influence was considerable in the *Ley de Cortes*[34] (1942), but they also had a say in the *Fuero de los Españoles* (1945)[35] and the *Ley de Principios del Movimiento* (1956).[36] Its affiliated professors were also behind the basic administrative and commercial laws in the 1940s. On the other hand, the *Revista de Estudios Políticos* published a good number of articles on the *radical* transformation of Spanish law[37] and also essays on totalitarian legal scholarship.[38] Moreover, two of the best-read and articulated philosophers of

---

[30] S Giner de San Julián, 'Libertad y Poder Político en la Universidad Española: el Movimiento Democrático bajo el franquismo' in P Preston (ed), *España en Crisis,* (México, Fondo de Cultura Económica, 1977), 303–55; A Reig Tapia, 'La depuración intelectual del nuevo Estado franquista' 88 (second series) *Revista de Estudios Políticos* (1995), 175–98.

[31] Decree of 9 September 1939. The Institute was aimed at 'researching with political criterion and scientific rigour the problems and developments of the administrative, economic, social and international life of the *patria*'. The decree also sets as missions of the *Instituto* the education of the high-rank officials of the regime and its consulting role.

[32] Alfonso García Valdecasas, professor of Civil Law at the University of Madrid, was one of the three original leaders of Falange, next to Primo de Rivera.

[33] See A García Valdecasas, 'Introducción' 1 *Revista de Estudios Políticos* (1941), 1–5.

[34] The basic law regulating the functioning of a sort of scarcely representative Parliament. See JM Thomàs i Andreu, 'La Configuración del Franquismo. El partido y las instituciones' 33 *Ayer* (1999), 41–63.

[35] A catalogue of the alleged rights and duties of Spaniards.

[36] A baroque piece updating the basic principles of the single party.

[37] See, among others, J Garrigues, 'La Reforma de la Sociedad Anónima' 1 *Revista de Estudios Políticos* (1941), 205–37 and 'Hacia un nuevo derecho mercantil' 6 *Revista de Estudios Políticos* (1942), 197–226, on company law, L Díaz del Corral, 'La Ley Sindical' 1 *Revista de Estudios Políticos* (1941), 239–67 and J Martínez de Bedoya, 'El sentido de la libertad en la doctrina falangista' in 10 *Revista de Estudios Políticos* (1943), 313–34, on labour law.

[38] See JW Hedemann, 'Los Trabajos Preparatorios del Código del Pueblo Alemán' 2 *Revista de Estudios Políticos* (1941), 259–82 and E García del Moral, 'Normas Fundamentales del Proyectado Código del Pueblo Alemán' 11 *Revista de Estudios Políticos* (1943), 137–46, on the Code of the German People, J González, 'Política inmobiliaria. El sistema hipotecario danés' 2 *Revista de Estudios Políticos* (1941), 461–86, on Danish mortgage law or G Mazzoni, 'Los principios de la Carta del lavoro en la nueva codificación italiana' 6 *Revista de Estudios Políticos* (1942), 227–50, on Italian labour law.

the regime, Francisco Javier Conde (*Espejo del Caudillaje*, 1941 and *Representación política y régimen español*, 1945) and Luis Legaz y Lacambra (*Introducción al Estado Nacional-Sindicalista*, 1939 and *Cuatro Estudios sobre Sindicalismo Vertical*, 1939), were related to the works of the Instituto and eventually became its directors.[39]

As the more pro-fascist elements of Falange saw their influence diminished, the *Instituto* also lost ground. In 1942, Serrano Súñer, for a period Minister of Foreign Affairs and openly pro-Nazi, fell in disgrace. This suspended the Instituto's influence until the end of the decade, when Conde came to its directorship. This change in fortune might have been reflected in the creation of a competitor for the *Instituto*, the new Faculty of Political Science at the University of Madrid in 1943.

This process of 'fascistisation' was slowed down and eventually halted as the likely outcome of the Second World War fell into doubt. Defascistisation was slow and painful,[40] requiring a search for alternative theoretical foundations for the new regime. The theoretical pedigree, once based in its affinities with Nazi Germany and Fascist Italy,) would be now established by reference to corporatist and anti-Communist doctrine.[41] The committed Catholicism of Franco's regime would be affirmed, with a view of avoiding any association with the worst war crimes of the Nazis and Fascists. The *revival* of corporatism was reflected in the *Fuero de los Españoles*, a charter containing the rights and duties of Spaniards, not by chance carried into law in 1945.

3 Who were the Fascists? The Radicalisation of Modernisers

In the previous section, we singled out Legaz y Lacambra and Conde as two of the most articulated and well-read thinkers of the franquista intelligentsia. It is rather interesting to observe that neither of them were arch conservatives—on the contrary, they were among the most promising members of the young Republican academia. Although both had a Catholic background, they seem to have firmly endorsed the Constitution of 1931.[42] They can both be said to have

[39] Juan Beneyto Pérez, another major ideologue of franquismo and author of *El Nuevo Estado Español* (1939), collaborated with the *Revista* quite frequently.

[40] The quarterly chronicles of international and national affairs to be found in the *Revista de Estudios Políticos* are quite revealing in that respect. The one published in the second issue of 1944 still hopes a Nazi Germany would put an end to the war. In the next issue, published only three months later, the same author becomes more cautious on what regards the outcome of the war. Moreover, he manages to shift his position towards a more neutral one.

[41] See J Corts Grau, 'Sentimiento español de democracia' 25–6 *Revista de Estudios Políticos* (1946), 1–41 and 'La Otra democracia' 95 *Revista de Estudios Políticos* (1956), 7–13.

[42] See L Legaz y Lacambra, 'El Estado de Derecho en la Actualidad' *Revista de Legislación y Jurisprudencia* (1933), 722–97, especially ch VIII. It must be granted that other paragraphs offered a somehow reluctant endorsement of the Republic. See 757 (criticism of partitocracy), 767 (the

developed a *constitutional patriotism*, reflected in Legaz's seminal *El Estado de Derecho en la actualidad* and Conde's socialist militancy. Both had been able to enjoy the benefits of the Republican cosmopolitan approach, through stays in Germany financed by the *Junta de Ampliación de Estudios*. However, in the period between 1933 and the beginning of the war, their ideas shifted dramatically, and they led the elaboration of a legal and political theory of *franquismo*—the so-called *nacional-sindicalismo*.

Luis Legaz y Lacambra[43] came from an Aragonese Catholic milieu. He took his law degree at the University of Zaragoza. A prolific writer, he had time to complete several essays on 'progressive' Catholic journals whilst still an undergraduate. He moved to Madrid in order to complete his Ph.D. He shifted to more liberal and secular positions as a result of his prolonged stays in Germany, where he made the acquaintance of notables such as Hans Kelsen or Hermann Heller. With the coming of the Republic, he became quite politically active through his membership of right wing but openly Republican parties and groupings, which took positions different from that of the CEDA. In 1933 he published a lengthy article (*El Estado de Derecho en la Actualidad, The Rechsstaat now*),[44] which synthesised his outspoken position in favour of a Liberal Republic and his fierce criticism of Bolshevism and Fascism. In November 1933, he stood as a candidate in the general elections for *Derecha Liberal Republicana* (Liberal Republican Right, led by President Alcalá-Zamora and Miguel Maura), but was defeated, as the moderate right-wing party was sidelined by the CEDA.[45] Thereafter he seems to have focused on his academic career, and by 1935 he became professor at La Laguna. He stayed there only briefly, as one year later he obtained a position at Santiago de Compostela. When the war started, he appears to have been in that city.

Legaz sided with the rebels almost immediately.[46] His was the zeal of a convert.[47] He reported late in his life that he had become a local leader of

---

exceptional measures of defence of the republic) and 787 (truth as the ultimate basis of politics). However, he clearly criticised those praising a parenthesis of legality (769) and also argued in favour of a combination of liberalism and 'proletarian' rights (751).

[43] For biographical details, see JP Rodríguez, *Filosofía política de Luis Legaz y Lacambra* (Madrid, Marcial Pons, 1997) and E Galán, 'Luis Legaz y Lacambra', in *Enciclopedia Filosofica Sansoni* (Firenze, Sansoni and Centro di Studi di Filosofia di Gallarate, 1967), volume III.

[44] L Legaz y Lacambra, n 42.

[45] I have found no reference to his acquaintance with Ramón Serrano Súñer, a major leader of the CEDA in Zaragoza and later on the second man of the Franco regime, or with Franco himself, who was director of the Military Academy of Zaragoza until its closing down under the Azaña government, but it is plausible that he had met them in Zaragoza in the late twenties.

[46] In his speech at the occasion of leaving the presidency of the *Instituto de Estudios Políticos*, Legaz granted that he had been a local leader of Falange in the early days of the war. See Instituto de Estudios Políticos, *Refundación* (Madrid, Instituto de Estudios Políticos, 1974).

[47] JP Rodríguez, n 44 seems to have oral evidence of the fact that Legaz was one of the 'leftist' that rebels aimed at 'arresting' (an euphemistic term which could mean summary execution) in the early hours of the coup.

Falange in the first days of the war. Later on, he was transferred to Santander, a stronghold of the rebels, where he took a prominent position in the Ministry of Labour. Before the end of the war, he had completed a new version of his *El Estado de Derecho en la actualidad*, in which he repudiated the first, 'Republican' edition.[48] He published it together with other essays that aimed at providing the groundwork of *franquista* legal and political theory.[49]

Legaz was a rather more complex figure. On the one hand, he was highly honoured by the regime. He became the rector of the Universidad de Santiago de Compostela in 1942, a position he enjoyed until he obtained a chair in Madrid in 1960. He was member of the *Cortes* and eventually became director of the *Instituto de Estudios Políticos* between 1970 and 1974. On the other hand, he acquired a certain reputation as a relatively open professor amidst the Franquista academia. He even cultivated his friendship with the Spanish exilees (and also with Hans Kelsen). Among his wide publications, his *Filosofía del Derecho* was well received—and quickly translated into German, a rare achievement for a Spanish monograph.[50] When Franco died, Legaz provided new evidence of his convoluted character. At the same time that he reaffirmed his loyalty to the memory of the dictator, he confided to close friends that his past prevented him from adopting any different position.[51]

Francisco Javier Conde took his law degree and doctorate at the University of Madrid. He seems to have then moved to the University of Seville,[52] where he was assistant professor of Political Law, a discipline at the crossroads between law and political science.[53] He benefited from scholarships from the *Junta de Ampliación de Estudios*, which allowed him to spend time in Paris and Berlin. In the latter city he laid the ground for his thesis on Bodin,[54] and made the acquaintance of Carl Schmitt. Conde seems to have originally been a

---

[48] L Legaz y Lacambra, *Introducción a la Teoría del Estado NacionalSindicalista*, (Barcelona, Bosch, 1940), 6.

[49] Having said that, it must be acknowledged that the text contains certain errors that might betray a codified meaning. It is difficult to believe that his reference to the Republic as the 'Third Spanish Republic' (when actually it was the Second) is not either an intentional mistake or a revealing unconscious impulse.

[50] See L Legaz y Lacambra, *Filosofía del Derecho* (Barcelona, Bosch, 1953). *Rechtsphilosophie*, (Newied am Rhein, Luchterhand, 1965); B Rivaya, *La Filosofía del derecho en el franquismo* (Madrid, Centro de Estudios Constitucionales, 1998) points to the need of disentangling his work as Franquista intellectual and his *scientific* production.

[51] JP Rodríguez, n 43.

[52] A Reig Tapia, 'Aproximación a la teoría del caudillaje de Francisco Javier Conde' in 69 (second series) *Revista de Estudios Políticos* (1990), 61–81.

[53] For a historical analysis of political law, see JM Vallés, *Political Science in Contemporary Spain: An Overview*, Working Paper 1/90 (Institut de Ciències Polítiques i Socials, 1990).

[54] FJ Conde, *El pensamiento político de Bodino* (Madrid, Tip. de Archivos, 1935).

socialist sympathiser.[55] Like many other upcoming legal theorists, he followed Heller's lectures in Madrid in 1933.

When the war broke out, Conde was a guest lecturer at the University of Berlin, something that must have been rendered possible by Schmitt. Like Legaz, Conde left behind his Republican past and joined the rebel side.[56] He was part and parcel of the pro-Nazi intelligentsia that gathered in the Frascatti, a coffee bar in Madrid apparently named after an Italian chef.[57] He even courted Pilar Primo de Rivera, sister of the Falangist leader and a prominent figure in the *Sección Femenina*, the extremely conservative female branch of the Falange.[58] Quite soon he became an active author, offering a theory of the *caudillaje*, an adaptation of the *Führerprinzip*.[59] The pinnacle of his career as the 'intellectual-in-residence' of the regime came with his nomination as director of the *Instituto de Estudios Políticos* in 1948. He aimed at both turning the theoretical basis of the regime towards a totalitarian path and recruiting a number of intellectuals who were not necessarily well regarded by the regime, as was the case with García Pelayo[60] or with Linz, who had a brief stay at the Instituto before starting his academic career in Columbia and Yale.[61] However, the political tension that cumulated in 1956 resulted in his being ousted from the *Instituto*, thereby frustrating his participation in the drafting of the *Ley de Principios del Movimiento*. In a move typical of the regime, Conde was offered a golden exile as diplomat. After being assigned to embassies in Manila, Montevideo and Ottawa, he managed to become ambassador to the Federal Republic of Germany, where he died in 1974.

[55] ML Marín Castán, *Critical review of Estado y Derecho en el franquismo. El Nacional-Sindicalismo: FJ. Conde y L. Legaz y Lacambra*. Available at http://www.cepc.es/recensiones1.htm, A Reig Tapia, n 52 and the hagiographic J Molina Cano, 'Javier Conde y el realismo político', 100 *Razón Española* (2000).

[56] As a matter of factual evidence, García Pelayo, who became the first president of the Spanish Constitutional Court in 1979, was also in Berlin at the time and returned to join the Republican Army, in which he reached the rank of captain. García Pelayo gives an account of how he was invited by Schmitt to dinner before returning to Spain in August 1936. See M García Pelayo, 'Epílogo'. In C Schmitt, *Teoría de la Constitución* (Madrid, Alianza Editorial, 1982), 373–7, at 377.

[57] R Morodo, *Atando Cabos: Memorias de un conspirador moderado*, (Madrid, Taurus, 2001), 231.

[58] P Preston, *Comrades. Portraits from the Spanish Civil War* (London, Harper Collins, 1999), 136.

[59] FJ Conde, *Escritos y Fragmentos Políticos* (Madrid, Instituto de Estudios Políticos, 1974), I 365–94 (*Espejo del caudillaje*). This work had been published as a serial in the *falangista* daily Arriba in February 1942. See G Morán, *El Maestro en el Erial*, (Tusquets, Barcelona, 1998), 117.

[60] M García Pelayo, *Obras completas* (Madrid, Centro de Estudios Constitucionales, 1991), I, 10.

[61] On Linz's biography and contribution to Spanish political science, see A De Miguel, 'The Lynx and the Stork' in R Gunther (ed), *Politics, society, and democracy, the case of Spain. Essays in honour of Juan J. Linz*. (Boulder, Westview Press, 1993), 3–10.

Leaving aside normative assessments, this relatively sudden and abrupt conversion can be partially explained by the fact that the traditional reactionary scholars were not well equipped to produce a radically new legal and political theory. As the regime directed its energies towards fascistisation, only those well read in Fascist and Nazi theories could push forward the half-baked ideas of Spanish reactionary thought into a more coherent and post-modern canon. Both Legaz and Conde knew not only the works of Kelsen and Heller, but also those of Schmitt and the Fascist legal theory. After all, they had spent more time abroad than at home during the troubled years of the Second Republic.[62] At the same time, the sudden and abrupt conversion explains the partial reversal of their stands. Once the international climate changed, and the fascistisation process was halted and subsequently reversed, they were able to reinterpret their arguments into a more traditional authoritarian framework.[63]

4 The Genealogy of *franquista* Legal Theory: the *Schmittian* Donoso

The basic elements of the political philosophy of the *early franquismo* are to be traced back to the main philosopher of antiliberalism in Spain, José Donoso Cortés. The work of the latter had had an *indirect* influence on Spanish reactionary thinking, mainly through French Catholic writers and, later on, through Carl Schmitt.[64] The most novel aspects of the theory of Conde and Legaz were taken from the interpretation of Cortés offered by Carl Schmitt (from the *Schmittian Donoso*, one might say). The German constitutional theorist knew Donoso's work quite well. His close knowledge of Spain, his frequent lectures in Madrid and his friendship with many of the upcoming legal philosophers made of him one of the scholastic authorities of the 1930s and

---

[62] If one considers the early version of his *El Estado de Derecho en la actualidad*, one could see quite clearly that Legaz interprets or constructs Spanish reality having in mind the developments in Austria and Germany (although the work seems to have been written before the actual coming to power of Hitler). The same goes for Conde, who, as was argued, had become visiting professor in Berlin at the time the war erupted.

[63] For example, neither Recasens nor Eustaquio Galan (himself a legal scholar in Franco's Spain, see B Rivaya, 'Eustaquio Galán y Gutiérrez' 9 *Dereito* (2000) 1, 143–77) referred to Legaz's *militant* writings in their accounts of his work. See L Recasens Siches, *Panorama del pensamiento jurídico en el siglo XX* (México, Porrua, 1963) and E Galán, n 43.

[64] The Spanish National Library includes 65 references to books or pamphlets by or on Donoso published in Spain. Out of these, 8 items were published between 1831 and 1860, 5 between 1860 and 1915, and the rest (52) after 1915, most of them after the Civil War. The first monograph on Schmitt was the translation of a German title in 1935, an initiative cherished by Schmitt. See his *Donoso Cortés interpretato in una prospettiva paneuropea* (Milano, Adelphi, 1996). After the war, *regime intellectuals* such as Legaz, Elías de Tejada and Tovar wrote books on Donoso. Ernesto Giménez Caballero went as far as recreating his character in the novel *The Visionary* in 1939. The first edition of his works was published as late as 1892 a fully edited version only appeared in 1946.

1940s.[65] This dual *Donoso-connection* explains the ambivalent character of their thinking—that they were simultaneously anchored in traditional authoritarian thought but also open to more radical conceptualisations.

In order to show the actual influence of the *Schmittian* Donoso on Legaz and Conde, I will focus on three main issues of their political and legal theory: (1) the justification of the *coup d'état* as the way to power, (2) the legitimacy of the new regime and the nature of law and (3) the concept of the nation.

4.1 The politics of coup d'état: negative and positive legitimacy of force

Triumph in the civil war was portrayed as evidence of the *rightness* of Franco and his followers. For months, the ritual of victory parades was repeated and widely reproduced in the press. However, an insufficiency of what has been termed as 'legitimacy of origin' was early felt among the rank and file of the regime.[66] The association of *nacional-sindicalismo* with order was in stark contradiction with its origins in the coup d'état, where it aimed at subverting the legitimately established Republican order. Moreover, its religious credentials could be contested on the basis of the brutality of repression.

In December 1938[67] a Commission was established with the clear objective of 'proving' the illegitimacy of the Republican government. Unsurprisingly, the commission came to the conclusion that 'extensive fraud' had voided the outcome of the February 1936 elections.[68] More than the actual works of this Commission, what was relevant was the perceived need to add something to 'martial' legitimacy.[69]

Legaz and Conde were among the main players in the establishment of the legitimacy credentials of *franquismo*. Their argument was two-fold. On the one hand, they attacked the legitimacy of the Republican constitutional order,

---

[65] Schmitt spoke and read Spanish fluently. He lectured several times in Spain, more frequently in the early 1940s. He was closely associated to the German Iberoamerican Institute. He cultivated friendship with several of the upcoming Spanish legal philosophers. Several of his works were translated before the Spanish Civil War, including the *Theory of the Constitution* and *On Dictatorship*. Anima Schmitt, daughter of Carl, married a second-rank Spanish Fascist, Alfonso Otero. See R Morodo, n 57, 76.

[66] P Aguilar Fernández, *Memoria y olvido de la guerra civil española*, (Madrid, Alianza Editorial, 1996).

[67] Boletín Oficial del Estado (*Official Journal*), 22 December 1938.

[68] In the immediate aftermath of the elections, Gil Robles pressed President Alcalá Zamora to declare the results void and deny to the Republican-socialist coalition victory. The incoming Congress spent some time in a thorough investigation of the alleged electoral irregularities. See P Preston, *La destrucción de la República en España* (Barcelona, Grijalbo, 2001).

[69] The same argument was clearly made by Conde when he argued that 'Truth is not the product of the fight, it comes before it. Fighting we find our way, not to establish truth, but to rescue it'. See FJ Conde, *Representación Política y Régimen Español* (Madrid, Ediciones de la Subsecretaría de Educación Popular, 1945), 81.

characterising it as an instance of the Liberal Rechsstaat. On the other hand, they argued that the new regime re-established the substantive Spanish constitutional order. The *golpe* and the *war* should be reinterpreted as democratic means of restoring the constitutional order, which had been subverted and undermined by the Republic.

4.1.1 The Critique of Parliamentary Democracy

Legaz raised three main arguments against parliamentary democracy. Firstly, he argued that the days of the democratic *Rechtsstaat* were gone to the extent that societies did not longer accept the basic preconditions of liberalism. A system based on discussion could not work when participants did not hold any common set of values. The atomistic character of liberal regimes, their acceptance of factions in the form of political parties, would have depleted the social capital needed for the unity of the fatherland, and would have turned deliberation into economic bargaining.[70] Secondly, liberal democracies were not able to mobilise society, to move people to economic sacrifice, and this was becoming essential in order to face the new economic conditions.[71] Finally, Legaz argued that the *Rechtsstaat* had become a mere façade, and that liberal states were already becoming totalitarian. If that was true, then, the question was not to decide whether we preferred a democratic or a non-democratic state, but rather which totalitarian state was better.[72]

Conde added a fourth theme, namely, the sterility or incapacity to take decisions of liberal democracies. The formalism characteristic of the *Rechsstaat* would lead to an 'impersonal nomocracy' that would quickly degenerate into anarchy. The late days of the Spanish Second Republic would provide evidence to this point.[73] This line of reasoning is clearly inspired by the *Schmittian Donoso*.

Donoso Cortés had become a renegade of political reason in the 1840s. He developed a thorough critique of parliamentary democracy. Human reason was said to be keen on deceiving human beings—its sinful claim to liberate us from faith led into error.[74] This was so for three main reasons, which anticipate Legaz's and Conde's argument. Firstly, the liberal commitment to discussion leads to self-dissolving ethical relativism. It puzzles not only our insight that something must be right and wrong, but also undermines any common set of

---

[70] L Legaz y Lacambra, n 48, 64. The parallelism with Schmitt and Hayek is to be noticed. See W Scheuermann, 'The unholy alliance of Carl Schmitt and Friedrich A. Hayek', 4 *Constellations* (1997), 172–88.

[71] L Legaz y Lacambra, n 48, 147. Industrial technology required that 'a very complicated mechanism be kept ready permanently'. The argument was that the counterpart of new production technologies should be a totalitarian political form.

[72] L Legaz y Lacambra, n 48, 98 and 123.

[73] FJ Conde, n 59, I, 376.

[74] J Donoso Cortés, n 1 (1946), II, 379.

values.[75] Secondly, parliamentary democracy is sterile and self-defeating. A system based on discussion is unable to take and implement decisions, that is, to act; where action is necessary for the survival of the political community.[76] Thirdly, the right answer to practical questions could not come from discussion, because what leads to truth is not the procedure, but the moral rightness of the participants.[77] On such a basis, concluded Cortés, 'discussion is the name under which death travels when it does not want to be recognised and works *de incognito*'.[78]

The apocalyptic language[79] of Donoso seems to have captivated Schmitt. The characterisation of parliamentary democracy as the regime of the *burguesía discutidora* (*the deliberative bourgeoisie*) constitutes one of the essential insights of *The Crisis of Parliamentary Democracy*, and also underlies his *Theory of the Constitution*.[80] Schmitt provided a more modern and radical interpretation of Donoso,[81] which opened vistas to a radical and thorough rejection of electoral democracy.

4.1.2 The Legitimacy of the Material Constitution

The act of force of the *golpe* of 1936 was then to be regarded as an attempt at showing the emptiness of parliamentary democracy. However, this was not sufficient to establish the legitimacy credentials of the new regime. If liberalism was doomed, not only fascism, but also other political systems (e.g. communism) could be considered as alternatives. A positive theory of the legitimacy of *nacionalsindicalismo* was thus needed.

The key argument of Legaz and Conde was that the new regime was the true political regime of Spain.[82] Against the atomistic tendencies of liberal democracies and the atheistic impulses of socialism, it affirmed unity around the true

---

[75] Above, II, 446.

[76] Above, II, 446.

[77] Above, II, 366.

[78] Above, II, 447.

[79] Donoso furiously attacked Liberalism. However, he did not deem it as the main target of his speeches. That condition was reserved to socialism. Even if he defined the latter as a philosophy for 'easy-talking persons and clowns', it considered it as the most powerful political theory because it was not relativistic, but a full-blown alternative theology (a sort of anti-theology) in which Proudhon would play the role of Anti-Christ (above, II, 504). Socialists were bold enough to say in the open what liberals implicitly assumed, namely, that reason should completely put faith aside.

[80] C Schmitt, note 64, 34 and C Schmitt, n 56, 52 ff. See G Balakrishnan, *The Enemy. An Intellectual Portrait of Carl Schmitt* (London, Verso, 2000), 76. Schmitt was also clearly sympathetic with the claim that deliberation was a way of avoiding decisions, assuming responsibilities. See Schmitt, n 64, 38.

[81] C Schmitt, *The Crisis of Parliamentary Democracy* (Cambridge, MA, The MIT Press, 1985), 70 and Schmitt, n 64, 38 and 43.

[82] Quite intentionally, L Legaz y Lacambra, n 48, 13 considers the issue of state legitimacy as the secular equivalent of the mystery of the Trinity.

religious form (Catholicism) and fatherland (the imperial Spain) as the only basis for Spain as a political community.[83] These were the 'very essences of the national community', the 'essential legal norms' (*juridicidad esencial*).[84]

Under such a premise, it was possible to interpret the intervention of Franco, sword in hand, as aimed at postulating a new *grundnorm* of the Spanish legal system. The Caudillo was the guardian of the Constitution, which could not be understood in a formalistic, self-referential way. Order power and not legal power was at the foundation of the Spanish legal system.[85]

Their argument led to a deproceduralisation and rematerialisation of the constitution, so to say. The substance was provided by a 'humanitarian totalitarianism',[86] which turned every political and social truth into a theological one.[87] The scope for state action was almost limitless to the extent that the state was now in charge of the 'salvation of the souls of citizens'.[88] Freedom was also transformed. It no longer had to do with Kantian autonomy, but was equated with the opportunity to save one's soul. This is based on the neat distinction of body and soul. As with heretics, political enemies need to be disciplined so that they can be saved. They must be enlisted in the militia of salvation.[89] Killing them is permitted if done in order to save their soul.[90] It becomes an almost altruistic act, and therefore, the executor obtains a mark of distinction.[91] In such a way, the Civil War can be depicted as a magnificent event, which led to the establishment of peace[92] and the salvation of men.[93]

The positive theory of legitimacy of the *franquista* legal and political theory is also clearly indebted to Donoso and Schmitt.

The works of Donoso do not provide a clear political blueprint-Schmitt regretted his incapacity to see clear alternatives aside from an unqualified frontal reaction to mass politics.[94] The Spanish reactionary philosopher seems to have been blocked by his anthropological pessimism.[95] However, we can trace

---

[83]   Above, 120: 'No collective life is possible if not founded on absolute truths' and FJ Conde, n 69, 136: 'What matters is, above all, truth'. See above, 92.

[84]   L Legaz y Lacambra, n 48, 92.

[85]   Above, 86. A similar idea is conveyed by FJ Conde, n 69, 136 and n 59, I, 381 through reference to *superlegality*.

[86]   Above, 227.

[87]   Above, 100. Cf also FJ Conde, n 69, 91.

[88]   L Legaz y Lacambra, n 48, 137.

[89]   Above, 257.

[90]   Above, 139 and 170.

[91]   FJ Conde, n 59, I, 394.

[92]   L Legaz y Lacambra, n 48, 90.

[93]   Above, 83.

[94]   On this, see Schmitt, n 64, ch 1 and Balakrishnan, n 80, 131.

[95]   Let us disentangle some of his arguments. First, there is a certain 'vicious circle' between sin and moral transgression and the genetic lot of the individual. He affirms that repeated sinning will lead to a transformation of the genes of the sinner, so that he will transmit that drives and impulses to his/her descendants. See J Donoso Cortés, n 1, II, 473. This possibility of transmitting 'sin' is

back to Donoso the identification of Western civilisation with Catholic dogma. He put forward a thick conception of politics, according to which living together was based on the suppression of difference,[96] on the representation of unity. This was coupled with the sociological hypothesis that social life is only possible under a single authority.[97] He anticipated the attribution to the state of the task of saving individual souls and the redefinition of freedom as a matter of salvation, which compels us to comply[98] with what is defined as the good.[99]

Schmitt provided Legaz and Conde with a more refined version of Donoso's argument. On the one hand, the German scholar put forward a constitutional theory which presented the defence of the substantive or essential constitution against the formal one as a matter of postulation of a new grundnorm. This was implicit in Schmitt's characterisation of the constitution as the actual expression of a will and the *dictatorial* powers attributed to the *pouvoir constituant*.[100] As we will see, his *organic* conception of democracy severed the link between the democratically elected institutions and the people. On the other hand, Schmitt had made a major effort to offer a political reading of the Catholic form.[101] This provided the basic materials with which Legaz and Conde could elaborate their *theological* conception of politics and their *political* conception of Catholicism.

4.2 Law and Power: Decisionism and Caudillaje

For *franquista* legal and political theory, law should cease to be a formalistic and impersonal social phenomenon and be rematerialised and contextualised. One could say that law should stop being regarded as a special case of general practical reason and rather become a matter of political decision. The liberal theory of law was thus to be replaced by a theory about how law is to be decided.

---

necessary in order to give a modern explanation of the doctrine of the *original sin*, but it also supports pseudo-Lombrosian affirmations of the kind that there is a harmony between moral and physical diseases (above, II, 426), and that a drive to sin leads to a vicious and dissipated existence (above, II, 485). In more political terms, it lays the foundation of the vicarious liability of a whole people for the acts committed by certain individuals belonging to it, something which explains why God punishes whole peoples (above, II, 517). Secondly, the way out of this vicious circle is physical suffering. Redemption becomes possible through painful fight (above, II, 411), and the final salvation of the soul might require the elimination of the physical body.

[96] Above, II, 538.

[97] Above, II, 359 and 198. Both Donoso and the latter formulated the law of the direct relationship between religious faith and room for political freedom. See also J Balmes, 'Faith and Liberty' in B Menczer (ed), *Catholic Political Thought*, (London, Burns Oates, 1952), 185–91, at 186.

[98] J Donoso Cortés, n 1, II, 398.

[99] This constitutes the justification of the death penalty (above, II, 521), and one might add, of war as such.

[100] C Schmitt, n 56, 99. On the dictatorial character of its power, see above, 78–9.

[101] See C Schmitt, n 64.

The Spanish version of such a theory was the *teoría del caudillaje* (closely resembling the *Führerprinzip*, as already hinted). The selected wise are to make decisions.[102] The last word is reserved to the *Caudillo*. He becomes the holder of sovereignty, and as such, his personal will becomes the wellspring of all laws.[103] The two personalities of the body politic in the liberal tradition were projected over the Caudillo himself, who was both the *pouvoir constituant* and the *pouvoir constitué*. This got rid of any potential limit to his power.[104]

Even if the conception of sovereignty of the theory of *caudillaje* was openly decisionistic, it could not rule out the establishment of some more formal legal system, if only for *pragmatic* reasons. In ordinary times, the Caudillo would rule by law. His legal system would translate the Christian idea of justice into a set of precise and singular statements.[105] This is the core idea of the characterisation of the state as the Church-State (*la Iglesia-Estado*). The key insight is that of a dual state, in which the law could be determined either by the legal or the moral code. This intellectual construct not only reiterated the theological connotations of the new regime, but also allowed justifying unbound discretion while retaining the form of law. The Caudillo retained an ultimate power to interpret both the moral and the legal code, in his standing as a secular and religious authority.[106]

One could claim that the role model for Legaz's and Conde's Caudillo was the Pope.[107] It is not a mere coincidence that Donoso had managed to shape the modern account of the doctrine of the infallibility of the Pope.[108] He transferred to politics[109] his conception of Papal power as a matter of exceptional or emergency powers, as a matter of taking decisions and not making general

---

[102] L Legaz y Lacambra, n 49, 149.

[103] Above, 60. The way in which both Legaz and Conde referred to Franco was extremely reverential. Franco was the saviour of the Spanish tradition, sword in hand, assisted by God, 'a charismatic power who announces, reveals, creates and orders a new set of values and commandments, who forces a radical spiritual and behavioural change'. See FJ Conde, n 59, I, 377, 381.

[104] L Legaz y Lacambra, n 48, 60.

[105] Above, 121.

[106] Above, 137: 'The Church should be subject to the instrumental needs of the state in what concerns mundane interests (. . .) and the State should protect the Church of deviation from its high spiritual mission'.

[107] Above, 177.

[108] See B Tierney, *Origins of papal infallibility, 1150–1350: a study on the concepts of infallibility, sovereignty and tradition in the Middle Ages* (Leiden, EJ Brill, 1972) for a historical study of the doctrine. The First Vatican Council transformed infallibility into dogma. It must be noticed that the driving force was Pius IX, who we have already said was heavily influenced by the late Donoso. It must also be noticed that this is one of the issues in which Donoso changed track after 1848. Before that date, and in order to justify the sale of Church properties conducted by some liberal Spanish governments, he had argued that the Pope is only due obedience in religious terms. See J Donoso Cortés, n 21 (1970), II, 115.

[109] As a matter of fact, it must be said that the Pope had only recently lost his *earthly* powers, something that Donoso commented upon and regretted. See J Donoso Cortés, n 1, II:370.

rules.[110] Thus, in his speech *On Dictatorship*, he modelled political emergency powers on God's miracles.[111] Dictatorship is consequently characterised as the means of last resort to achieve order and avoid anarchy. Donoso attributed this power to the 'wise'. The right form of dictatorship is the one that comes from above: from the sword—the aristocracy—and not from the dagger—the populace.[112] This reflects his hierarchical conception of society, half way between feudalism and class discrimination.

Schmitt provided a 'legalistic' complement to Donoso. He reinterpreted the works of the latter as a forerunner to his recharacterisation of politics as the domain of the exceptional, but connected it more clearly with legal theory. In his early work as legal theorist, Schmitt had focused on the context of the adjudication of norms.[113] He had attacked Kelsenian formalism by stressing the 'decisionistic' jump involved in the process of adjudication. His 'theological turn' in *Political Theology* led to his exaltation of the moment of decision as the essence of politics.[114] As we will see in the next section, this will be combined with a radical criticism of the liberal theory of representation and with an opening towards an organic form of representation of the popular will. The theory of *caudillaje* was openly inspired by Schmitt, but it retained the less modern flavour of Donoso's decisionism.

4.3 The Organic Community: the Nation

The exaltation of the nation, its sacred unity and its 'mission' was a characteristic theme of Spanish philosophy, of a reactionary bent and otherwise.[115] This reflected the 'incompleteness' of the Spanish nation-state.

It is thus not surprising that Legaz depicted the nation as the second person of the secular Trinity (the first was the Caudillo and the third the single party, *Falange*).[116] The organic character of reactionary conceptualisations of the nation was further developed. Legaz defined the nation as a

---

[110] See C Schmitt, n 64, 43.

[111] J Donoso Cortés, n 1, II, 190.

[112] Above, II, 203.

[113] In his *Law and Judgement*, published in 1912.

[114] The book starts with the (in)famous definition of the sovereign as 'who decides on the exception'. C Schmitt, *Political Theology* (Cambridge, The MIT Press, 1985), 5.

[115] See SG Payne, *Fascism in Spain*, 1923–1977 (Madison, The University of Wisconsin Press, 1999); Villacañas, n 25; and S Ellwood, *Prietas las filas*, (Barcelona, Crítica, 1984). See G Jensen, 'Military nationalism and the state: the case of fin-de-siècle Spain' 6 *Nations and Nationalism* (2000), 257–74 for the breed of nationalism cultivated by the army. See X Bastida Freixedo, Xacobe, 'La Búsqueda del Grial. La teoría de la Nación en Ortega' 96 (second series) *Revista de Estudios Políticos* (1997), 433–76 and *La Nación Española y el nacionalismo constitucional* (Barcrlona, Ariel, 1998) for a critical analysis of the concept of the nation in the most influential Spanish philosopher of this century, Ortega y Gasset.

[116] As a matter of curiosity, it might be added that the role model for *Falange* was the *Compañía de Jesús*. See L Legaz y Lacambra, n 48, 40.

'corpus mysticum' mobilised in pursuit of the 'human destiny in the universal',[117] a characteristically empty phrase taken from the original rhetoric of Falange. The nation aspired to become 'an ideal Christian Community founded on love',[118] something which required its 'identification' with the *Caudillo* in arms.[119]

The nation as an organic community was easily combined with forms of organic representation. Conde praised this alternative to the liberal, vulgar reduction of representation to the *counting* of private interests. In a Catholic vein, representation should be about rendering visible what is invisible.[120] It should not be a matter of transmission of will, but of its actual conformation.[121]

National unity was one of the political realities that could be enjoyed under an organic mode of representation. This was to be grounded in the fact that the national community constitutes and defines citizens and not the reverse,[122] so that citizenship could be plainly denied to those who were *different*, who were constituted in a different way.[123] This organic conception of the nation is at the basis of the substantive conception of the constitution and, as I argued, provides the standpoint from which to attack the 'treacherous' belief in democratic majorities. The enemy, turned into a radical other, must be eliminated to bring life back into the nation.[124] Afterwards, the masses should be *re-educated* into the national spirit.[125]

This organic and transcendental conception of the nation is clearly inspired by the 'essential' definition of the nation to be found in Donoso. Against the allegedly liberal tendency to place economic interest at the foundations of political community, Cortés affirmed his conviction that blood was the ultimate basis of politics.[126] From this conception, as was indicated, follows a transcendental, atemporal definition of membership and citizenship and the affirmation of an organic conception of representation.

Schmitt's influence is easy to discern as regards the definition of representation. The German constitutional theorist had actually established the case for seeing the Catholic Church as the ultimate *reservoir* of an anti-economic, anti-technological conception of representation.[127] He had also established the

---

[117] FJ Conde, n 69, 145.

[118] FJ Conde, n 59, I, 95

[119] Above, I, 374. This is an intriguing phrase that probably intends to paraphrase the British formula of 'The King in Parliament'.

[120] Above, I, 436. Cf also S Lissarrague Novoa, *La Ley Creadora de las Cortes* (Madrid, Ediciones de la Revista del Trabajo, 1942), 8.

[121] FJ Conde, n 69, 446.

[122] FJ Conde, n 59, I, 350.

[123] L Legaz y Lacambra, n 48, 249 and Lissarrague Novoa, n 120, 34.

[124] L Legaz y Lacambra, n 48, 200 and FJ Conde, n 59, I, 360.

[125] L Legaz y Lacambra, n 48, 245 and FJ Conde, n 69, 83.

[126] Donoso Cortés, n 1, II, 491.

[127] C Schmitt, *Cattolicesimo romano e forma politica* (Milano, Giuffrè, 1986), 36ff.

groundwork for a concept of *organic* democracy. Public opinion and rule by acclamation were presented in a favourable light,[128] and *habilitated* as alternatives against procedural democracy. Finally, his concept of the political was clearly influential upon Legaz and Conde.[129]

5 Conclusions

This paper has dealt with the legal and political theory of *franquismo*. At the end of the Spanish Civil War, a great number of scholars either left for exile or were silenced. However, some law professors exchanged constitutional patriotism for ideological propaganda and became ideologues of Franco's regime. There are good reasons to consider that for a period, this new political system was moving towards fascism, and that the companion *franquista* political and legal theory aimed at being the outlook of a fascist regime. It is also argued that the most outstanding members of its *intelligentsia* were liberal republicans who adopted fascism at relatively short notice, among them Francisco Javier Conde and Luis Legaz y Lacambra. This is not that surprising once we take into account that they were better read in Fascist and Nazi doctrine than the *traditional* philosophers of reaction. Without opening the difficult chapter of personal responsibilities, it is observed that this *sudden and relatively brief fascistisation* opened the possibility of a later reconstruction of their work into a more classic and convenient pattern. Their personally 'tolerant' attitude and their occasional double meanings helped this. At any rate, it is pointed that a good deal of the sources of the legal theory of franquismo can be traced back to Juan Donoso Cortés, the arch-philosopher of reaction in Spain. However, his influence was mediated by Carl Schmitt. It was the German philosopher who *rediscovered* Donoso, and also who influenced the *reading* and *interpretation* of his works.

Beyond these set of facts, hypothesis and conjectures, it seems to me that the study of the legal theory of *franquismo* adds evidence to the need of a contextualised analysis of legal dogmatics. On the one hand, *memory* of the past is a precondition of proper understanding of the present. The works of Elías Díaz,[130]

---

[128] C Shmitt, n 56, 100: 'It would be a mistake—by the way, an *anti-democratic mistake*—to consider that the political methods of the XIXth century [parliamentary democracy] as the ultimate and definitive manifestation of democracy'. See also 107. Even more clearly 238: 'Only the truly assembled people is *the people*, and only the truly assembled people can do what corresponds specifically to the people: to acclaim, that is, to shout their consent or dissent, to shout long life or die, to commemorate a leader, to applaud the king or somebody else, or to refuse to acclaim through silence'.

[129] See C Schmitt, n 114, 26.

[130] E Díaz, *Notas para una historia del pensamiento español actual (1939–1974)* (Madrid, Cuadernos para el diálogo, 1974).

Juan Antonio García Amado,[131] Benjamín Rivaya,[132] Ricardo García Manrique,[133] José Antonio López García[134] or Mónica Lanero Taboas[135] have contributed to the map of the legal production of the late 1930s and early 1940s in Spain. But their audience seems not to have been sufficiently wide. It is not improbable to read rather bland and depoliticised accounts of the period, or to simply get accounts of the works of the authors in which their role as ideologues of *franquismo* goes unnoticed.[136] On the other hand, there is a need of pushing further the historical, comparative and multidisciplinary assessment of the period. The forgetful character of the Spanish transition to democracy has rendered Spanish citizens, but also Spanish scholars, insensitive to the mostly unintended, but rather sinister, continuities with the past. In that sense, learning from the Spanish past, but in a comparative perspective, seems the unavoidable next step.

---

[131] JA García Amado, 'Cómo se escribe la historia de la filosofía del Derecho del nazismo. Paralelismos y diferencias con la historiografía de la filosofía del derecho bajo el franquismo', in F Puy, M C Rovira and M Otero (eds), *Problemática actual de la historia de la filosofía del derecho española* (Santiago de Compostela, Servicio de Publicacións e Intercambio Científico da Universidade, 1994), 19–44.

[132] B Rivaya, 'La Filosofía Jurídica en los comienzos del Nuevo Estado Español' 131 *Sistema* (1996), 87–103; B Rivaya, n 50; B Rivaya, '¿Fascismo en España? (La Recepción del Pensamiento Jurídico Fascista)' 7 *Derechos y Libertades* (1998), 377–407.

[133] R García Manrique, Ricardo, *La Filosofía de los Derechos Humanos durante el franquismo* (Madrid, Centro de Estudios Constitucionales, 1996) and 'El Franquismo y los Derechos Humanos: Uso y abuso de una idea', 154 *Sistema* (1999), 73–91.

[134] JA López García, *Estado y Derecho en el Franquismo. El Nacionalsindicalismo: F.J. Conde y Luis Legaz y Lacambra* (Madrid, Centro de Estudios Constitucionales, 1996) and 'La Presencia de Carl Schmitt en España' 91 (second series) *Revista de Estudios Políticos* (1996), 139–168.

[135] M Lanero Táboas, n 17.

[136] See PF Gago Guerrero, 'Legaz y El Estado', 90 *Revista de la Facultad de Derecho de la Universidad Complutense* (1998), 89–134; M Figueras Pàmies, *Apuntes iusfilosóficos en la Cataluña franquista* (Lleida, Edicions de la Universitat de Lleida, 2000).

19

AUTHORITARIAN CONSTITUTIONALISM: AUSTRIAN CONSTITUTIONAL DOCTRINE 1933 TO 1938 AND ITS LEGACY

*Alexander Somek**

A No-Name Period

The story begins with a myth and ends with a folk tale. The myth is that of the so-called 'self-elimination' (*Selbstausschaltung*) of the Austrian Parliament on 4 April 1933.[1] Retrospectively, this event marked the end of Austria's first experiment *qua* democratic republic. The folk tale emerges in post-World War II Austria: with the *Anschluss* in 1938 Austria became the first 'victim' of the Third Reich.

In the period between the supposed self-elimination of Parliament and the annexation by Germany—the period from 1934 to 1938—Austria was ruled by an authoritarian regime. Finding a suitable name for the regime is not an easy task.[2] Notably, its characterisation has become a much debated issue among post-war historians.[3] Whereas some historians, in particular those sympathetic to the then defeated Social Democrats, refer to the regime as 'Austro-fascist'[4] or even 'Clerico-fascist', others are more cautious.[5] They avoid characterisations going beyond that of 'authoritarian'[6] or assume that

* Professor of Law, University of Vienna. For helpful comments on earlier drafts of this article I would like to thank Stanley L Paulson, Viktor Mayer-Schönberger, Sabine Somek and Neil Walker. The usual disclaimer applies.

[1] For a brief account, see W Brauneder & F Lachmayer, *Österreichische Verfassungsgeschichte* (Vienna, Manz, 1992) at 232.

[2] See W Wippermann, *Europäischer Faschismus im Vergleich 1922–1982* (Frankfurt/Main, Suhrkamp, 1983) at 90.

[3] For an overview of the debate and a very balanced statement, see E Hanisch, *Der lange Schatten des Staates. Österreichische Gesellschaftsgeschichte im 20. Jahrhundert* (Vienna, Ueberreuter, 1994) at 310–15.

[4] It should be noted, however, that the name 'Austro-Fascism' was introduced by the *Heimwehr* leader Ernst Rüdiger von Starhemberg to designate the programme of this quasi-military organisation. See Hanisch, n 3, at 290. On the *Heimwehr* see below n 26.

[5] For a very balanced account, see Hanisch, n 3, 317.

[6] See Wippermann, n 2, at 90–91.

the regime essentially amounted to a perplexing recurrence of nineteenth century 'neo-absolutism'.[7]

The question of a suitable characterisation is not, however, my interest. Rather, what I would like to draw attention to here are responses by Austrian constitutional scholars to a government that was undoubtedly authoritarian and that wanted the public to know that its programme of national reconstruction was animated by Catholic social philosophy. These responses are worthy of our attention, in particular, where attempts have been made to locate the developments in Austria in a broader European context. In these attempts a mode of discourse comes to the fore which I would like to refer as 'authoritarian constitutionalism', an ideal type, not a position or a movement that has left a salient imprint in the history of constitutional ideals.

The Notion

Authoritarian constitutionalism accepts structures of governance that contain most of the features of constitutional democracy with the noteworthy exception of (parliamentary) democracy itself. Thus, the type of constitutional law to which authoritarian doctrine favourably responds may well include the rule of law, the protection of basic rights and traces of the separation of powers, but nonetheless exclude the election of, and control by, popular assemblies. Agreement with such a system of governance is not the only defining characteristic of authoritarian constitutionalism. It is distinctive in that it defends the absence of democracy by pointing to a goal—the goal of social integration—that it assumes can only be achieved by authoritarian government and that its attainment would be seriously undermined if co-operation were sought with Parliament or civil society. The lack of democratic representation and of democratic accountability is accepted for the sake of a project of social integration or social reconstruction.

Lest I raise high expectations I should add, at the very outset, that I shall not consider the works of those who may be regarded, rightly or not, as the ideological mentors of the authoritarian government in Austria, in particular the two pronounced champions of a corporatist society, the theologian Johannes Messner[8] and the economist Othmar Spann.[9] A discussion of their theory of

---

[7] See Hanisch, n 3, at 314–15.

[8] Messner served, indeed, as an advisor of chancellors Dollfuß and Schuschnigg. On his career, see A Pytlik, *Berufsständische Ordnung— Entwicklung der Idee bei Johannes Messner* (Doctoral Thesis, University of Vienna, Faculty of Catholic Theology, 1993).

[9] See, for example, O Spann, *Der wahre Staat. Vorlesungen über Abbruch und Neubau der Gesellschaft* (Graz, Akademische Druck und Verlaganstalt, 1972). On Othmar Spann, see the monograph by one of his faithful students: W Becher, *Der Blick auf das Ganze. Das Weltbild Othmar Spanns* (Munich, Universitas, 1985).

corporate society or its relation to the social vision that was expressed by Pope Pius XI. in his Encyclical *Quadragesimo Anno*[10] is beyond the purview of this paper. It cannot be denied, though, that a sober discussion of the political theology of inter-war Catholicism would be of great intellectual merit.

Self-Elimination

Before turning to a discussion of how some legal scholars in Austria responded to the turn of events in 1933 and 1934, I should like to review these events briefly.

The First Republic of Austria, from its very inception, was permanently threatened by divisive political forces. Even though there existed a number of smaller parties, such as Communists, Liberals or National Socialists, the existing class-division was mirrored in the cleavage between two grand parties, the Social Democrats on the one hand and the Christian-Social party on the other. At least from the point of view of the latter, this division could not be overcome.[11] A Christian, as the slogan had it, can never be a Socialist.[12] Against this background, the events following 4 April 1933 can be recast as though they followed a fatal script. They brought an end to wary and tired compromises. Austria's first experiment with democracy ended in February 1934 in a civil war. In April 1934, the authoritarian government adopted a new constitution for the 'Austrian Federal State'.

It all began with the aforementioned 'self-elimination' of Parliament . When in a turbulent session a vote had to be taken on pardoning the leaders of a recent railroad strike, the chairman and the two remaining vice-chairmen of the Austrian Parliament—more precisely, its first chamber, the 'National Council'[13]— resigned. It appeared as if the Assembly had been left without an official head.[14] Led by the Christian-Social chancellor Dollfuß, the government

---

[10] See the Encyclical of Pope Pius XI, 'On Reconstruction of the Social Order', May 15 1931, http://www.vatican.va/holy_father/pius_xi/encyclicals/documents/hf_p-xi_enc_19310515_quadragesimo-anno_en.html.

[11] On the divisive relationship and attempts at rapprochement, see E Hanisch, *Die Ideologie des politischen Katholizismus in Österreich* (Vienna & Salzburg, Geyer-Edition, 1977) at 19–23.

[12] This slogan reappeared in the papal encyclical *Quadragesimo Anno*. See Hanisch, *Die Ideologie des Politischen Katholizismus*, n 11, at 18.

[13] In the following, I will simplify the matter by speaking of 'Parliament' even though the purported 'self-elimination' affected only the house of representatives, that is, the so called 'National Council' and not the second chamber, the 'Federal Council'. Indeed, members of the second chamber assembled and vehemently demanded a new meeting of the National Council. However, the Federal Council was not able to exercise any legislative powers without the National Council. See the joint remonstrance of Social Democrats and National Socialist in the Federal Council in K Berchtold, *Verfassungsgeschichte der Republik Österreich*, vol. 1: 1918–1933 (Vienna & New York, Springer, 1998) at 739–40.

[14] See Berchtold, n 13, at 702–5.

seized this opportunity to proclaim that Parliament had dissolved itself and had thus cleared the path to authoritarian government, that is to say, a government without Parliament.[15] As the Members of Parliament reassembled eleven days after this memorable session, the police threatened to disperse the 'illegal gathering' with force.[16] After a short speech by the second vice-chairmen, in which he claimed that his resignation was null and void, the Members of Parliament dispersed.[17]

The Emergency Law of 1917

The authoritarian government then began issuing regulations on the basis of an Emergency Law that dated back to the late Habsburg monarchy. Enacted in 1917,[18] it had conferred power on the government to pass regulations necessary to re-establish and promote economic life, to avert economic harm, and to provide for the subsistence of the population under the 'extraordinary economic circumstances' caused by the war.[19]

In 1920, with the adoption of the Constitution of the Republic of Austria, this Emergency Law was incorporated into the constitutional law of the Republic.[20] The incorporating constitutional statute added a clause, however, to the effect that the government would lose its power of emergency legislation only if Parliament passed a bill declaring that the 'extraordinary economic circumstances' caused by the war had come to an end. Such a law was never adopted by Parliament . With almost Marshallian grandeur, therefore, the government continued to issue regulations by claiming legality for its measures, suggesting that almost any measure, perhaps even a constitutional amendment, could conceivably be rationally related to the aims of re-establishing and promoting economic life in a post-war situation.[21]

---

[15] See Berchtold, n 13, at 712. According to Berchtold (n 13, 708) the position of the government was not completely implausible. Under normal circumstances the parties could have reached an agreement on how to handle this unusual situation.

[16] Berchtold n 13, at 731–32.

[17] Of course, the President of the Republic could have recalled Parliament on the basis of emergency legislation, however, his power to do so depended on a proposal by the government, which, understandably, refused to submit. President Miklas deplored this impasse. See Berchtold, n 13, at 729–30.

[18] *Kriegswirtschaftliches Ermächtigungsgesetz*, Juli 24 1917, RGBl. Nr. 307.

[19] § 1 above.

[20] See § 17 2 of the *Verfassungsübergangsgesetz* 1920.

[21] See the excellent analysis by E Voegelin, *Der autoritäre Staat. Ein Versuch über das österreichische Staatsproblem* (Vienna & New York, Springer, 1997) at 166.

Self-Elimination, Part II

In a sense, therefore, the government was in the position to claim what it had really wanted to claim from the beginning, namely, the legality of its authoritarian measures. Of course, there were good reasons to suspect that the regulations exceeded the scope of powers conferred by the Emergency Law of 1917. Nevertheless, the government went to great pains to uphold the appearance of legality, never mind that this required recourse to highly questionable and even paradoxical moves.

When the city of Vienna challenged several measures that had been issued on the basis of the Emergency Law before the Constitutional Court, the government 'persuaded' some members of the Court to resign.[22] Not unlike the legislature, the Court was seen as having 'eliminated itself'.[23] Still, notwithstanding the loss of three of its members and four of its deputy members, the Court was still capable of assembling and handing down decisions. The government, to be on the safe side, therefore issued a further emergency regulation. Those members of the Court who had been appointed by means of a proposal from Parliament were excluded from sessions of the Court unless all members appointed by that body held their respective offices. Since the latter was no longer the case in the wake of the resignation of three members on their own motion, the Constitutional Court had fewer judges than were necessary to reach a decision.[24]

The Patriotic Front

It comes as no surprise that the politics of the government was met with fierce resistance from the opposition. It culminated in a short civil war at the end of which the Social Democrats, who had their own military forces, the *Republikanische Schutzbund,* were defeated. In February 1934, the Social Democratic party was declared illegal. Already in 1933, the Communists and the National Socialists had been dissolved. The representatives of these parties lost their seats in the legislative assemblies at the state and local levels. In addition, the Christian-Social party was merged with the fascist[25] *Heimwehr*— a Catholic paramilitary association composed of loyalists, former World War I

---

[22] See above n 13, Berchtold, at 751.

[23] See above n 1, Brauneder & Lachmayer, at 233.

[24] See above n 13, Berchtold, at 752–53.

[25] In the so-called 'Korneuburger oath', which was officially promulgated on 18 May 1930, the members of the *Heimwehr* professed adherence to principles closely resembling those of Italian Fascism, such as the deification of the state and the outspoken rejection of parliamentary democracy. See Hanisch, n 3, at 290. See also Wippermann, n 2, at 87.

soldiers, farmers, students and even members of the learned professions[26]— and other associations into the so-called *Vaterländische Front*.

The Patriotic Front was meant to be a political bulwark against 'Marxists and the brown Socialists'.[27] It had been founded by Chancellor Dollfuß in 1933, with the aim of uniting all people who were 'self-consciously and professedly Austrian-minded'.[28] Accordingly, it should support the 'right and the duty of Austria to exist— this for the fulfilment of its mission in the heart of Europe for the greater good of everything German *(zum Wohl des gesamten Deutschtums)*.'[29] At this point an idea comes to the fore that would become part of the ideological baggage of the authoritarian regime, namely, the self-image of the Austrians as 'the better Germans'. In 1934, the Front—even then far from resembling a fascist mass movement—was transformed into the official state party.[30] Later, in 1936, it was declared to be the only expression of the people's will in Austria.[31]

The Constitution of 1934

The next major stage in the transformation of the Austrian political system, taken in 1934, was the adoption of a new constitution, the 'Constitution of 1934'.[32] It represented an instrument of government that was markedly different from a parliamentary democracy. The spirit animating this constitution had been already announced by Chancellor Dollfuß in his so-called *Trabrennplatz* speech in 1933. He pointed out that the time was ripe for a new beginning and called for a 'social, Christian, German state of Austria on a corporate basis and under strong, authoritarian leadership.'[33] As we shall see, both pillars of this new Austrian constitution, the corporate and the authoritarian, resonated in Austrian constitutional doctrine.

On the basis of a draft prepared by the Governor of the Land *Vorarlberg* and Minister for Constitutional affairs, Otto Endler, the Constitution of 1934 was

---

[26] It is difficult to characterise the *Heimwehr* accurately from an ideological perspective, for it covered the whole Catholic spectrum ranging from Christian-Socials to those who had strong affinities to National Socialists. See, for example, Wippermann, n 2, at 85–8. The more conservative and Christian factions of the *Heimwehr* was strongly supported by the peasantry (it was strong in Tirol, for example), whereas the more radical right-wing bloc recruited itself of a potentially violent urban mob. See Hanisch, n 3, at 289. Be that as it may, the *Heimwehr* supported the government during the civil war against the Social Democrats.

[27] Dollfuß quoted in Berchtold, n 13, at 749.

[28] See the call for membership in the *Wiener Zeitung* of May 21 1933, quoted in Berchtold, n 13, at 750.

[29] *Ibid.*, n 28.

[30] BGBl. 4/1934–II.

[31] BGBl. 160/1934.

[32] BGBl. II, Nr. 1/1934, 'Verfassung 1934'.

[33] Quoted in Brauneder & Lachmayer, n 1, at 234.

initially imposed in the form of a government regulation on the basis of the 1917 Emergency Law.[34] Even to those sympathetic to the new authoritarian rule, it was clear that the exercise of governmental powers on this basis was excessive. Government could not introduce a constitution on the basis of a power whose use was restricted to restoring economic prosperity and to alleviating the plight of a suffering populace. Since the authoritarian government wished to maintain the semblance of formal legality and continuity with the Constitution of 1920, it called Parliament for one final meeting, on 30 April 1934. The sole purpose of the meeting was to legalise, at least for the time being, authoritarian rule. Since the Social Democrats had lost all their seats in the meantime, it was the meeting of a rump of the Parliament. The only task on the agenda of this assembly was to adopt another Emergency Law, namely the 'constitutional amendment concerning extraordinary measures in the sphere of constitutional law'.[35] Among other things, this Emergency Law of 1934 conferred on the government the full and unfettered power to enact constitutional law and provided for the dissolution of both chambers of Parliament.[36] Democracy would not be restored in Austria until after World War II.

So much for the course of events leading to authoritarian rule. But how did constitutional doctrine respond to those dramatic developments? In short, Austrian constitutional doctrine accommodated the new developments. I should like to explain why, and I shall distinguish three different modes of accommodation of which only the third will be examined more closely.

Political Catholicism: The Virtue of Accommodation

If the prominent Austrian historian Ernst Hanisch is right, accommodation and the readiness flexibly to adapt to changing political circumstances were perspicuous habits of Political Catholics in Austria.[37] The attitude of accommodation is not without support in Catholic doctrine. Pope Leo XIII had officially blessed the neutrality of the church vis-à-vis competing political regimes. Catholics ought to try to get along with the regime at hand, so long as that regime does not threaten severely to undermine the authority of the church or the Pope.[38] Thus, the fact that the most remarkable constitutional scholars

---

[34] Verordnung der Bundesregierung vom 24. April 1934 über die Verfassung des Bundestaates Österreich, BGBl. I, Nr. 239.

[35] BGBl. I, Nr. 255/1934, 'Ermächtigungsgesetz 1934'

[36] Or, more precisely, the dissolution of the first and second chamber of parliament.

[37] See Hanisch, *Ideologie des Politischen Katholizismus*, n 11, at 2–3. In the eyes of Carl Schmitt, adaptability has always been a defining and admirable feature of Roman Catholicism. See his *Römischer Katholizismus und politische Form* (Stuttgart, Klett-Cotta, 1984) at 2–4.

[38] See P Mikat, *Kirche und Staat* In *Staatslexikon der Görres-Gesellschaft*, vol. 3 (Freiburg, Herder, 1987) 475–78. This view found extreme expression in the writings of Adolf J Merkl, see 'Die Staatsbürgerpflichten nach katholischer Staatsauffassung' (1937) 17 *Zeitschrift für öffentliches*

publishing in that period were Political Catholics and, hence, acted in an accommodating way, should not surprise us. After all, the authoritarian state heralded a Christian mission and presented itself as the vanguard of the church in Europe.[39] Some scholars appeared in fact to agree with the regime, which is not implausible when one considers that *any* regime, even a dictatorial one, was to be preferred by the typical Political Catholic to socialism or communism.[40] It was taken for granted that a regime is good so long as it prevents socialist revolution.

It should not be forgotten, however, that accommodation is not just an attitude stemming from religious beliefs. It was also the attitude of those who feared they might become the victims of political persecution.[41] The *venia legendi* of some professors was revoked, notably that of Max Layer, a professor of constitutional law who had published powerful criticisms of the abuse of the Emergency Law of 1917.[42] Similarly, the German nationalist Karl Gottfried Hugelmann was forced to retire (*Zwangspensionierung*). At the same time, there were instances of ordinary opportunism and low profile accommodation. People continued teaching or even took a new position in the faculty without any professed support of the government. Ludwig Adamovich, who earlier had served on the Constitutional Court, became the successor of the dismissed Layer.[43] In his writings Adamovich appears as a totally 'apolitical' figure. Publishing a treaties on Austrian constitutional law in 1935,[44] he avoided meddling with political issues and attempted to offer an account of the constitutional situation in value-neutral terms. One might suspect, however, that to assume the detached attitude of the positivist legal thinker vis-à-vis an authoritarian government is little short of posturing. It may well have been the case, therefore, that demonstrations of humility and sobriety worked to Adamovich's personal advantage. After all, he held important political offices towards the

---

Recht 1–36, reprinted in *Gesammelte Schriften*, ed. D. Mayer-Maly et al, vol. I/2 (Berlin, Duncker & Humblot, 1995), 277–317.

[39] See Hanisch, n 3, at 315.

[40] I assume that this is true for the most flexible and accommodating of right-wing Catholics, Alfred Verdroß. On Verdroß, see A Carty, 'Alfred Verdross and Othmar Spann: German Romantic Nationalism, National Socialism and International Law' (1995) 6 *European Journal of International Law*, http://www.ejil.org/journal/Vol6/No1/art6.html.

[41] On the following, see G Winkler, *Die Rechtswissenschaft als empirische Sozialwissenschaft. Biographische und methodologische Anmerkungen zur Staatsrechtslehre* (Vienna & New York, Springer, 1999) xvi–xvii.

[42] See M Layer, 'Ermächtigungsbereich des kriegswirtschaftlichen Ermächtigungsgesetzes' (1933) 38 *Verwaltungsarchiv*, 203–18.

[43] See Winkler, n 41, xix–xxv. See also O Rathkolb, 'Die Rechts- und Staatswissenschaftliche Fakultät der Universität Wien zwischen Antisemitismus, Deutschnationalismus und Nationalsozialismus 1938, davor und danach' in G Heiss et al. (eds), *Willfährige Wissenschaft. Die Universität Wien 1938–1945* (Vienna, Verlag für Gesellschaftskritik, 1989), 197–232, at 208.

[44] L Adamovich, *Grundriss des österreichischen Staatsrechts (Verfassungs- und Verwaltungsrechts)* (Vienna, Springer, 1935).

end of the regime. Even though he never published anything that would have been supportive or critical of *any* regime, he was dismissed by the Nazis in 1938. In 1945 he was appointed first President of the University of Vienna.[45]

Accommodation and its Modes: The Emergence of Authoritarian Constitutionalism

Among the modes of accommodation, which are indeed reflected in juridico-political writings, at least three different responses to the new constitutional situation emerge. They are intriguing for they reflect different stages in the affirmation of what was taken to be the essence of the new constitutional situation.

The *first response* is formulated from within the perspective of Austrian positivist legal science. I shall consider it only briefly. The second and the third response are more noteworthy. Since the new constitution was seen to be corporate and authoritarian in its nature,[46] each of these aspects invited further elaboration. Accordingly, the *second response* highlighted, in some respects even critically, the vanguard role that the Austrian government purported to play in the realisation of the Catholic ideal of a corporate society. By contrast, the *third response* was sanguine enough to have grasped the authoritarian nature of Austrian government, drawing out its claim to legitimacy.

Upon closer inspection, it turns out that the three responses can be arranged in an interesting sequence. In moving through this sequence, authoritarian constitutionalism works itself pure. What adherence to rightful authority means according to positivist doctrine, which is in the foreground of the first response, is spelt out in terms of the second response's obsession with faithful submission to temporal authority.[47] Blind submission to those who have authority, however, is a principle that cannot be defended on its own terms.[48] The reasons claimed in support of faithful submission turn up differently in the second and the third responses. What they have in common, however, is that they grant government ample powers to bring about social integration where integration is perceived to be seriously threatened by parliamentary democracy. Thus understood, authoritarian constitutionalism is different from Hobbesian authoritarianism, owing, above all, to its historical specificity. It presupposes experience with the

---

[45] From all that, it may safely be concluded that those scholars who ostensibly supported the regime were also the least prudent.

[46] See AJ Merkl, *Die ständisch-autoritäre Verfassung Österreichs. Ein kritisch-systematischer Grundriss* (Vienna, Julius Springer,1935) at 15.

[47] See Merkl, 'Staatsbürgerpflichten', n 38, at 309–10; 'Die Enzyklika gegen den Kommunismus', *Wiener Neueste Nachrichten* of 23 March 1937, 4–5, reprinted in *Gesammelte Schriften*, n 38, 269–75.

[48] See J Raz, *The Morality of Freedom* (Oxford, Clarendon Press, 1986).

messiness of *modern* parliamentary democracy and offers an alternative. In this respect, authoritarian constitutionalism is also different from Madisonian republicanism, which is also concerned with disruptive energies of factious forces that may be unleashed in a representative democracy without, however, abandoning the latter.[49]

The authoritarian alternative claimed to pave the way to a brighter future. The authority of government was taken to provide the key, but it was not mistakenly seen as an end in itself. Authoritarian constitutionalism, nonetheless, rejected parliamentary democracy as a means to the end of integration.

The European Dimension

When it comes to articulating the reasons for submission to authoritarian government, both the second and the third response purport to discover a *European dimension* in Austrian problems. They thus bespeak a strong desire to locate the development, in particular the breach of constitutional continuity, in a broader European context. In the second response, Catholic antiliberalism matters a great deal, whereas in the third, implications are drawn out as to what is presented as 'the' European constitutional tradition. The first offers some arguments in support of the *Ständestaat* and thereby intends to underpin indirectly the authoritarian regime's claim to legitimacy. The second borrows from French constitutional language and attempts in this more tangled way to present what has happened in Austria as an 'ordinary development' by European standards.

For another reason, however, these responses have a European dimension, which is worth pondering. The political language of authoritarian constitutionalism has a *descriptive* import, which is frequently neglected. In the second half of the twentieth century, scholars have become highly suspicious of the diagnostic potential of anti-liberal or authoritarian doctrine. Descriptive notions are inextricably linked to an underlying normative agenda. One should take heed of that and not fall victim to a seductive idiom. To a considerable extent this fear is not ungrounded. Prudent reactionary doctrine couches authoritarian pretences in normalising language. The caution that is required when reading the texts of Carl Schmitt is a case in point. Carl Schmitt's *Verfassungslehre* represents a conceptual scheme designed to insulate the *rechtsstaatliche* element of a constitution from its democratic component.[50] Clearly, the whole venture runs foul of the Atlantic constitutional tradition. It adheres faithfully, however, to the agenda of releasing political leadership from

---

[49] See in particular, *The Federalist Papers*, (Baltimore & London, Johns Hopkins University Press, 1981), no 10, 16–23.

[50] See C Schmitt, *Verfassungslehre* (Berlin, Duncker & Humblot, 1989).

narrow legal restraints.[51] One should be aware of the likelihood to encounter constantly such tricks in the genre of authoritarian constitutional doctrine. Thus guarded, however, its study may be of use. Concepts that have more or less disappeared after the Second World War may turn out to be valuable when it comes to elucidating our present situation. This may hold true, in particular, in respect of the anti-democratic emphasis of authoritarian doctrine and practice.

The First Response and its Catch

I shall consider the first response only briefly. It is manifest in the doctrinal analyses of Adolf J Merkl. In these analyses Merkl emerges clearly as a disciple and former colleague of Hans Kelsen. Merkl was quite outspoken about the limits set to government in relying on the Emergency Law of 1917 for purposes of amending or altering the constitution.[52] With positivistic rigor, Merkl rejects the idea that the new constitution can be traced back, inasmuch as its legal pedigree is concerned, to the Constitution of 1920.[53] If anything, the Constitution of 1934 is a revolutionary departure from existing constitutional law.

Viennese Positivism, that is, the positivism associated with Kelsen's *Pure Theory of Law* has a catch, though. It can easily accommodate breaches of existing constitutional law by describing them *as* new constitutional law once political developments indicate that a new regime with its own built-in standards of legality has been established. On the ground of the distinction between the intra-systemic transfer of validity and the external effectiveness of a normative order,[54] the Constitution of 1934 can be cast, in positivist terms, as constitutional law provided that it is bolstered by a new authority. Lest we forget, the conditional of Kelsen's *Grundnorm*—ie the hypothetical norm required for describing an existing coercive system as the law of the land—presupposes the effectiveness of such a system. There is no legal validity without effectiveness. An order of constitutional law, hence, loses its validity if it is no longer effective.[55]

---

[51] See, for example, C Schmitt, *Der Hüter der Verfassung* (Berlin, Duncker & Humblot, 1985) at 156–9; *idem*, *Legalität und Legitimität* (Berlin, Duncker & Humblot, 1980) at 70–4.

[52] The reasoning was elegant. Merkl explained that the emergency powers of government cannot exceed those of the president of the Republic. See AJ Merkl, 'Die Verfassungskrise im Lichte der Verfassung' (1933) *Der österreichische Volkswirt*.

[53] See Merkl, *Verfassung Österreichs*, n 46, at 10, 14.

[54] This distinction is the Achilles heel of the Pure Theory. See H Kelsen, *Die Reine Rechtslehre* (2nd edn., Vienna, Deuticke, 1960) at 212–14.

[55] Above 214–15.

At a certain stage, however, Merkl may have realised that it would have been inopportune to tackle the revolutionary legal nature of the regime explicitly.[56] After all, the government claimed that the new constitution was derivative of, and continuous with, the former. For that reason, I surmise, Merkl's writings exhibit reluctance to state clearly where he perceived discontinuity.[57] In perspicuous moves he throws the positivist *Grundnorm* over board and turns to what he takes to be Catholic natural law.[58] He is very outspoken about the consequences this engenders for the description of legal systems. Legal validity, thus understood, is entirely derivative of religious norms. 'The religious approbation of the secular sphere of norms', he writes, can be understood as 'the most grandiose historical case of the reception of one normative order by the other'.[59] This religious approbation extends to any normative order, regardless of whether a regime is democratic or not, for—within copious limits— Catholicism is indifferent among various forms of state authority and the substance of its laws.[60] The objections that may be levelled against the continuity of the new constitution from the standpoint of legal science do not extend, therefore, to the allegiance that it may legitimately command. The very fact of its existence entails the duty to obey.[61] As Merkl puts it, Catholic natural law does not see the legality of state authority as something hinging on the legitimacy of its origin.[62]

The Second Response: Papal Positivism

This brings us to the second response, which is even more accommodating than the first.[63] It is also most clearly reflected in Merkl's writings, more precisely, in

---

[56] Voegelin, to be sure, was quite outspoken about the inability of the Pure Theory to identify revolutionary change. All that can be done according to that theory is to identify two different legal systems, however, there can never be a breach since this presupposes a prior normative relationship between them. See Voegelin, n 21, at 150–51.

[57] The catch of Viennese positivism goes even deeper. For if a certain act can be described as valid only on the ground of a re-interpretation of the norms conferring the powers for its creation then the whole constitution has changed once the act becomes effective. Voegelin, in following the interpretations of continuity proffered by government, followed exactly that track. See Voegelin, n 21, at 168–69.

[58] See Merkl, *Verfassung Österreichs*, n 46, at 10–12.

[59] A J Merkl, 'Staatsbürgerpflichten', n 38, at 285.

[60] See above at 285, 306.

[61] See above at 289.

[62] Quoted in Winkler, n 41, xviii.

[63] I hope that my few comments on Viennese positivism (*ie*, the Pure Theory) suffice to explain why, taken on its own terms, it is a toothless instrument against the subversion of a constitutional order. Every act that may appear to be unconstitutional can be defended, in principle, by pointing out that it institutes, owing to its very effectiveness, a new order of law. Kelsenian sobriety can thus be put to very accommodating uses.

those of the period from 1934 to 1938. They offer a substantive defence of the new constitution by highlighting its contrast to parliamentary democracy. In Merkl's view, the new constitution avoids the chief ill of parliamentary democracy, which lies in the constant subversion of the rule of the people by partisan struggle.[64] Under conditions of a polarised party system and the absence of a democratic tradition, parliamentarism merely sets the stage on which political parties pursue and mutually check their 'dictatorial' interest in usurpation.[65] In marked contrast, a system of corporate representation may allow for a more genuine representation of the will of the people[66] by eradicating class conflict at its root. At this point, Merkl is in fundamental agreement not just with Pope Pius XI but also with the former chancellor and Christian-Social politician Ignaz Seipel.[67]

Of the many things that Merkl had to say about the Catholic background of the authoritarian-corporate constitution, I would like to sketch briefly what I take to be his claim to Austrian exceptionalism. In this context, Merkl's Political Catholicism exhibits its strongest assertive dimension.

Austrian Exceptionalism

Above all, Merkl underscores that, in contrast to Germany and Italy, Austria is not a totalitarian state. The authoritarian state does not permeate the whole life of its subjects[68] (the desire to fare better than the Italians and the Germans has never ceased to be a constituent element of Austrian national identity). Moreover, in comparison with Germany and even with Italy (despite its mitigating duality of the *Duce* and the King) Austria is not a *Führerstaat*.[69] The Austrian constitution is merely authoritarian, not totalitarian. This is not just

---

[64] This is a favourite topic of conservative constitutional right-wing writers of that period. See Schmitt, *Hüter der Verfassung*, n 51, at 84–85; E Forsthoff, *Der totale Staat* (Hamburg, Hanseatische Verlagsanstalt, 1933) 26. Merkl was a devout Catholic who agreed with the Pope that of all conceivable political ideologies communism is by far the worst (See 'Enzyklika gegen den Kommunismus', n 47, at 270).

[65] See Merkl, *Verfassung Österreichs*, n 46, at 2, 5.

[66] Above 8.

[67] See I Seipel, *Der Kampf um die österreichische Verfassung* (Vienna, Braumüller, 1930) 203–04.

[68] In Merkl's conceptual scheme, anti-totalitarianism concerns substantial limits to state action. Even an authoritarian state may decide to adopt such limits for itself. Hence, an authoritarian state is not tantamount to a totalitarian one. In Merkl's eyes, social democracy with its zeal to regulate every aspect of human life, was totalitarian but not authoritarian. See Merkl, 'Die individuelle Freiheit im autoritären und ständischen Staat', (1936) 65 *Juristische Blätter*, 265–73, reprinted in *Gesammelte Schriften*, n 38, 201–25, at 207.

[69] See Merkl, 'Der autoritäre und der totale Staat', *Neue Freie Presse*, 29 August 1937, 1–3; reprinted in *Gesammelte Schriften*, note 38, 245–50, at 247; idem, 'Die Führerstellung des Bundeskanzlers', (1936) 65 *Juristische Blätter* 177–83.

owing to the inclusion of a Bill of Rights (which never became effective, though) and the principle of legality in the constitution,[70] it is also observable in that professional corporations, in marked difference to fascist Italy, are granted a semi-autonomous status.[71] The authoritarian nature of the state is thereby not denied. It is counterbalanced by a corporate element, which is to become effective whenever government deems it appropriate.[72]

In a *Berufsständestaat*, which is an instance of a constitutional system, professions, trades and other groups performing a social function (*soziale Leistungsträger*) have political rights and participate in political decision-making.[73] Even though Merkl grants that in *Quadragesimo Anno* the Pope spoke of a corporate organisation of society, and not of a *Ständestaat*,[74] he praises the Constitution of 1934 as an unprecedented experiment in transposing the teachings of the Pope to the organisation of the polity. This makes Austria exceptional on a world-historical scale[75] and, indeed, sets an example with which other conflict-ridden European countries also ought to comport.[76] For a corporate ordering of society does not map individuals according to their position in the labour market, rather, they are aligned according to social functions.[77] Class-conflict between individuals can be prevented within the corporate sphere where conflict among estates is to be resolved on the level of the state.[78] Put in modern language, 'partnership' is the core idea of a corporate constitution.[79]

---

[70] See Merkl, 'Der autoritäre und der total Staat', note 69, at 250; idem 'Individuelle Freiheit', n 69, at 223–24.

[71] See Merkl, 'Individuelle Freiheit', n 69, at 210. Merkl gleefully reports that the Italian system has been criticised by the Pope himself in *Quadragesimo Anno*. See his 'Staatsbürgerpflichten', n 38, at 297.

[72] It should be noted that the corporate part of the constitution will never become fully effective, in particular, the corporate representatives will never be elected but appointed by the President of the Republic. See Brauneder & Lachmayer, n 1, at 235.

[73] See 'Individuelle Freiheit', n 69, at 206.

[74] Above at 206. See *Quadragesimo Anno*, n 10, at para 82.

[75] See Merkl, 'Staatsbürgerpflichten', n 38, at 297. See also AJ Merkl, 'Geschichtlicher und autoritärer Ständestaat' *Wiener Neueste Nachrichten* of 20 March 1934, 1–2, reprinted in *Gesammelte Schriften*, n 38, at 127–8.

[76] See AJ Merkl, 'Geschichtlicher und autoritärer Ständestaat', n 75, 123–8.

[77] See already, *Quadragesimo Anno*, n 10, para 83. Compulsory membership to a *Stand* is the mirror image of the fact that the persons belong to the same community of fate. See AJ Merkl, 'Die Enzyklika 'Quadragesimo Anno' und die Verfassungsfrage', *Wiener Neueste Nachrichten* of 14 March 1934, 1–2, reprinted in *Gesammelte Schriften*, n 38, 115–21, at 117.

[78] Even though Merkl admits of the liberty to change one's profession, he is more or less convinced that professional estate determines one's social position. Liberty is always part of a greater organic whole.

[79] It should not be overlooked that the 'partnership' would have been based on unequal terms. For example, Merkl speculated that employers, even though less in number, should have relatively more seats in the corporate representation than employees. See AJ Merkl, *Probleme der ständischen Neuordnung Österreichs* (Vienna, Steinemann, 1938), reprinted in *Gesammelte Schriften*, n 38, 319–55, at 338–39.

The interpretative principle of charity may require us to view Merkl's favourable treatment of the authoritarian constitution in the light of his high hopes. I think he believed that the corporate element would in the future out-live the authoritarian structure, which has given birth to it. Whether the corporate idea is defensible is another matter. I think it is not, for it lures the powerless into coalitions with the wealthy and privileged classes in which they are likely to be given a raw deal.[80] The latter, at any rate, is confirmed by historical fact. Social inequality increased during the period of the authoritarian regime considerably.[81]

Even though the corporate organisation of society, at least on the level of the *Realverfassung,* stays with us until today, one should take heed of conflating post-Second World War 'corporatism'[82] with its pre-Second World War counterpart. The new corporatism takes class-division for granted and seeks conciliation through government-brokered deals. Authentic corporatism, by contrast, subsumed the working-class under a social function for the greater benefit of ruling elites.

The Third Response: Authority and Statehood

What is an 'authoritarian state'? The notion gained some currency in Germany with the advent of the Papen government in 1932, and it was clear to commentators that an 'authoritarian government' wishes to cut itself loose from the constraints set by a parliamentary majority.[83] The 'authoritarian' style of government is thus opposed to its majoritarian counterpart.[84] This is not to say that an authoritarian state could do without popular approval. In the memorable concluding remarks of his *Legalität und Legitimität,* Carl Schmitt left no doubt that even an authoritarian government needs to tap the resource of consent by the governed, at least in the course of intermittent plebiscites.[85] Even though such a government is in the position to pull out of negotiations with different groups and political parties, it can only survive in the long run by turning

---

[80] Hermann Heller had noted that a corporate state is the ideological fig leaf for the dictatorship of the privileged and powerful classes of society. See his 'Rechtsstaat oder Diktatur?' (1929) in his *Gesammelte Schriften,* vol. 2 (Leiden, A.W. Sijthoff, 1971) 443–64, at 458.

[81] See Hanisch, n 3, at 316.

[82] For an excellent analysis, see C Offe, 'Korporatismus als System nichtstaatlicher Makrosteuerung? Notizen über seine Voraussetzungen und demokratischen Gehalte' (1984) 10 *Geschichte und Gesellschaft* 134–56.

[83] For a contemporary discussion of the relevant ideas, see O Kirchheimer, 'Verfassungsreaktion 1932' (1932) reprinted in *idem, Funktionen des Staats und der Verfassung* (Frankfurt/Main, Suhrkamp, 1972) 62–78.

[84] See H Heller, 'Autoritärer Liberalismus?' (1933), reprinted in *Gesammelte Schriften,* vol 2. (Leiden, A.W. Sijthoff, 1971), 643–53, at 643.

[85] See C Schmitt, *Legalität und Legitimität,* note 51, at 93–94; for a critique, see O Kirchheimer, n 83, at 103–4.

on mass-mobilisation as the source of democratic legitimacy. It has to resort to popular support by asking the right questions at the right time.

In Erich Voegelin's treatment of the authoritarian state, which I would like to consider next, the notion of the authoritarian state emerges differently. His monograph *The Authoritarian State. An Essay on the Austrian State-Problem* appeared in 1936.[86] At that time he held the position of an Associate Professor of Political Science and Sociology *(Staatslehre* and *Gesellschaftslehre)* in the Vienna Faculty of Law. The book evidences Voegelin's conversion from a scholar sympathising with social democracy into a conservative of sorts.[87] It cannot be denied that it offers a masterful account of the first Austrian republic's most fundamental predicament: founded in 1920, the democratic republic was a state that no political party had really wanted. In addition, the book contains learned conceptual analyses from which one might even benefit today.

Voegelin commences by saying that the authoritarian state, understood as a political ideal, is not something peculiarly Austrian. It is a European idea whose inception can be traced back to the very origin of statehood in Europe.[88] Evidently, Voegelin wishes to suggest that the authoritarian state is the state in its most original and primary form. Since the origin of the modern state lies in France, Voegelin explains that French constitutional doctrine provides the key to understanding the state as the modern type of human association.[89] Paradoxically, Voegelin does not vindicate what he takes to be an internal relation between authority and the emergence of statehood with reference to Bodin and the *politiqués;*[90] rather, he draws on the writings of the turn of the century jurist Maurice Hauriou,[91] for according to Voegelin it was him who had recently restored the notion of European statehood and thus rescued it from sinking into oblivion.[92]

Before giving a brief account of how this relation is explained in *The Authoritarian State,* I should like to introduce one of Voegelin's guiding ideas by looking at how his thought had developed twenty years after the publication of this book. I surmise that this will make access to Voegelin's conception easier.

---

[86] E Voegelin, *Der autoritäre Staat. Ein Versuch über das österreichische Staatsproblem* (Vienna & New York, Springer, 1997).

[87] See Winkler, n 41, at 144. On Voegelin's early years in Austria, see also TV MacAllister, *Revolt Against Modernity. Leo Strauss, Eric Voegelin, and the Search for a Postliberal Order* (Lawrence, University of Kansas Press, 1996) at 17–20.

[88] See Voegelin, n 21, at 6–7.

[89] See Voegelin, n 21, at 4, 51.

[90] See M Kriele, *Einführung in die Staatslehre. Die geschichtlichen Legitimationsgrundlagen des demokratischen Verfassungsstaates* (4th edn., Opladen, Westdeutscher, 1994) at 50–51; R Schnur, *Die französischen Juristen im konfessionellen Bürgerkrieg* (Berlin, Duncker & Humblot, 1962).

[91] I have only had access to a German translation of Hauriou's works. See M Hauriou, *Die Theorie der Institution und zwei andere Aufsätze,* ed. R. Schnur (Berlin, Duncker & Humblot, 1965).

[92] Voegelin notes that the author responded to what he perceived to be the weakness of the Third French Republic. See Voegelin, n 21, at 42–43, 51.

Representation: The August Notion of Authority

In an important chapter of Voegelin's well-known and widely acclaimed study *The New Science of Politics*[93] the reference to Hauriou recurs.[94] This time it appears in the more general context of a political theory of representation. In an existential sense, Voegelin notes, representation presupposes the 'articulation' of society, that is, the very process in virtue of which human beings form themselves into a society.[95] As Voegelin explains: 'In order to come into existence, a society must articulate itself by producing a representative that will act for her.'[96] The reference to Hauriou is made at the juncture at which Voegelin points out that through the action of a representative, a society is salvaged from disintegration. Twenty years earlier the same was said by Voegelin—with almost identical references to Hauriou—of an authoritarian ruler.

According to Hauriou, as read by Voegelin, a ruler or a regime is legitimate if it acts on behalf of an institution.[97] In our case, the institution in question is the state. A state, in turn, is a national community whose existence materialises in the 'political people'.[98] Acts of a state are expressive of the will of the people to exist over time and to control their own destiny.[99] In the process of the institutionalisation of a state, one decisive step has to be taken by a ruler or a regime. It consists in 'the creation of a politically unified nation by transforming the pre-existent, unorganised manifold into a body organised for action.'[100] From that follows that national unity would be impossible to achieve if it were not for leadership exercised by authority.

The task of a leader *qua* representative, which is not restricted to avoiding disintegration, would be substantially empty, though, if it were not geared to the realisation of an idea. The exercise of leadership is directed by an idea, Hauriou's *idée directrice* of political leadership,[101] by virtue of

---

[93] (Chicago & London, Chicago UP, 1972).

[94] See above at 48–50.

[95] See above at 37.

[96] See above at 41. It goes without saying that this pragmatic conception of representation is closer to Hobbes 'notion than to Schmitt's fanciful idea that 'representation' presupposes something 'higher' which is made present despite its absence in the process of representation. See his *Römischer Katholizismus*, n 37, at 26–36; *Verfassungslehre*, n 50, at 210.

[97] According to Hauriou, n 91, at 34, 46, an institution is the idea of a work or a project that is realised and legally manifest in a certain social milieu. In particular, the conception of the institution as creative achievement animates Hauriou's notion of the institution.

[98] See Voegelin, n 21, at 4. It goes without saying that in this respect Voegelin is borrowing from Carl Schmitt. On the state as a people which is in the state of political unity, see *Verfassungslehre*, n 50, at 205.

[99] See above.

[100] Voegelin, *New Science*, n 93, at 48, and *Der autoritäre Staat*, n 21, at 48.

[101] See Hauriou, n 91, at 37.

which, irrespective of its specific content,[102] action is poised to augment and to increase the power of the institution of the state. The institutionalisation of the state as an institution is complete when, first, the ruler or regime becomes subordinated to the idea and, second, the members of society respect the norms of the institution with the attitude of habitual obedience. *Consentement coutumier*, consent to the institution as such,[103] is indispensable for the institution to persist over time. The representative has and exercises authority 'insofar as he is able to make his factual power representative of the idea.'[104]

In the *Authoritarian State* Voegelin concludes that if the state is understood as an idea which materialises in a community of human beings on a certain territory then the achievements of founding, preserving and augmenting are specifically authoritarian in that they are indicative of the authorship and creative energy of a ruler or a ruling elite.[105] This is the core of Voegelin's recurring formula with which he explains what I would like to call his *august* notion of authority: authority means an authorial achievement in the founding and preservation of the state.[106]

Two Other Notions of Authority, Or: What Makes the August Notion Distinctive

In a manner echoing Carl Schmitt, Voegelin notes that the authorial power giving birth to an institution precedes 'existentially' the allocation and regulation of legal powers through positive law.[107] Moreover, this power does not disappear once it has been channelled in the streams of jurisdiction. Normativism, that is, the doctrine according to which the meaning of a constitution is the same as the meaning of a set of norms, cannot account for the fact that following the rules laid down in the constitution is only one way among others of preserving the institution over time.[108] At certain times even a breach of consti-

---

[102] According to Hauriou the *idée directrice* is indeterminate and rendered determinate through the exercise of leadership. Owing to this dialectical relation it must not be conflated with the 'purpose' of an organisation. See Hauriou, n 91, at 37–9.

[103] See Voegelin, n 21, at 50.

[104] Voegelin, *New Science*, n 93, at 49, and *Der autoritäre Staat*, n 21, at 48.

[105] See Voegelin, n 21, at 49.

[106] See above at 49, 211. The origin of law, Voegelin notes, 'cannot be found in legal regulations but must be sought in the decision which replaces a litigious situation by ordered power.' See *New Science*, n 93, at 48–9.

[107] See Voegelin, *New Science*, n 93, 49. See also Schmitt, *Verfassungslehre*, n 50, at 9. Likewise, according to Hauriou the leadership exercised on behalf of the *idée directrice* cannot be constrained by rules of competence allocation. Institutions grow from the inside out. See Hauriou, n 91, at 37.

[108] See Voegelin, n 21, at 49, 158.

tutional rules may be necessary to bring about that effect. Reducing legitimacy to legality rests on a misunderstanding of institutional causality.[109] To the continuous existence of a state, the 'true' representative matters, and not the positive constitutional procedures of representation:

> [I]f a government is nothing but representative in the constitutional sense, a representative ruler in the existential sense will sooner or later make an end to it; and quite possibly the new existential ruler will not be too representative in the constitutional sense.[110]

Besides this august notion of authority as an original achievement of founding and preserving, at least two other notions of authority are present in Voegelin's analysis. The second notion is the one which is also used by Merkl. Authoritarian is any government whose position does not depend on approval by the electorate and which is not accountable to a representative body. In this understanding, Voegelin contends, 'authoritarian' may do its service in the formal language of modern constitutional law, however, it implicates that dictatorship, absolute monarchy or even a plebiscitarian monarchy may equally go under the name of an authoritarian government.[111] In this sense, the notion of authoritarianism is not specific enough, rather, it is tantamount to sovereignty.

The *third* variant in which 'authoritarian' is used by Voegelin appears in his discussion of the English Reform Bill of 1831. He quotes approvingly from the writings of Earl Grey. According to this notion, authority is held by the elite that runs the country. The government is in a position to rule 'authoritatively' if the members of Parliament and the members of the government are recruited from the same leading families and belong to the same class which is distinguished through its hereditary wealth. Moreover, the authority of government is also secured through its influence in the composition of the representative body. In such a situation, it can resort to Parliament as the voice of 'public opinion' without reservations and without having to fear that it might encounter powerful resistance. If such resistance is never to be expected, government need not strike deals with and among interest groups or political parties and faces only minor constraints in the pursuit of the common good.[112] This notion of authority as the social power of those who 'run the country' does not conflict with Voegelin's more august notion. For his analytical purposes, however, it is not technical enough.

In marked contrast, the *august* notion of authority—despite a partial overlap with the concept of sovereignty in that authority is regularly conjoined with the former—denotes *also* a distinct source of legitimacy. In this sense, a state is authoritarian if and only if the legitimacy of the supreme executive body is

---

[109] See also Schmitt, *Verfassungslehre*, n 50, at 107–8.
[110] Voegelin, *New Science*, n 93, at 49.
[111] See Voegelin, n 21, at 182.
[112] See above at 216–21.

owing to an *authorial achievement* in respect of the founding, preservation and augmentation of the state. In particular, legitimacy does not flow from some other source, such as democratic self-rule or the sacredness of the king.[113] The very point of authoritarian rule is, more precisely, to advance founding, preservation and augmentation in the absence of a political people.[114] An authoritarian state is, thus understood, the only alternative there is to the disintegration of society.[115] As an authoritarian constitutionalist, Voegelin endorses this as a justification of authoritarian rule.[116]

The Core Problem of Austrian Constitutional Law

The analysis provided by Voegelin of Austrian constitutional history builds upon this understanding of the authoritarian state. I need not give a summary here and instead turn to his conclusion regarding the legitimacy of authoritarian rule in Austria.

According to Voegelin, since the turn of events in 1934 Austria represents the model case of an (almost purely) authoritarian government.[117] The particular problem of Austrian statehood is that, historically, there has never been a people that would have provided the basis for an Austrian state.[118] Against the background of this 'no-demos-thesis' Voegelin claims that the authoritarian state upholds the unqualified good of the state[119] on an *anonymous basis* since it cannot derive its authority from the people's *pouvoir constituant*.[120] No objection can be made to authoritarian statehood in Austria, for even during the First Republic, parliamentarism notwithstanding, Austria had not been a true democracy. Even though Voegelin grants that democracy provides a higher source of legitimacy than authoritarian leadership,[121] the formal scaffolding of

---

[113] See above at 182, 211, 261. According to C Schmitt, *Legalität und Legitimität*, n 51, at 93, 94, this is next to impossible for there is no way of getting around plebiscitarian legitimacy.

[114] According to Voegelin, Dollfuß's *Trabrennplatzrede* gave expression to Hauriou's idea. Not that he assumes that Dollfuß studied Hauriou. He takes it as a manifestation of an arche-scene of European Statehood. See Voegelin, n 21, at 50–2.

[115] See Voegelin, n 21, at 182.

[116] I note, in passing, that an authoritarian state in this sense differs from the types of dictatorship which were identified by Carl Schmitt. Whereas the 'commissarial dictatorship' depends on a certain commission, a task that has to be executed by the dictatorial body, and ends once the task has been completed, 'sovereign dictatorship' is authorised by the *pouvoir constituant*, which is perspicuous by its absence in the case of Voegelin's authoritarian state. See C Schmitt, *Die Diktatur. Von den Anfängen des modernen Souveränitätsgedankens bis zum proletarischen Klassenkampf* (Berlin, Duncker & Humblot, 1978), at 146.

[117] See Voegelin, n 21, at 182.

[118] See above at 182.

[119] See above at 87.

[120] See above at 185.

[121] See above at 86–87.

parliamentary proceedings and recurring elections did not suffice to generate democracy in Austria. Democracy presupposes the existence of a people. In his view, the formal democracy of the First Republic concealed the fact that a political people had never existed in Austria and that, therefore, Austria had never been a true democracy.[122] It remained in an uneasy post-imperial mode of existence.[123] Rightly understood, the written constitution of the republic amounted to a lie.[124] Parliament provided the turf play-ground on which political parties tried to hold each other in check by playing bad normative tricks on one another. Only with the turn to authoritarianism in 1933, Austria has taken the decisive step towards statehood.[125]

Even if Voegelin had been completely right concerning the Austrian no-demos problem, ironically, he was simply wrong in identifying the authoritarian state as the cure. Voegelin's support of the authoritarian turn is self-defeating, for the authoritarian government, which to a considerable extent turned on the support of the former nobility, the clergy, professionals and bureaucrats, enlisted the very same old elites who had been running the former Austrian empire. This makes Voegelin's stern commitment to authoritarian rule so paradoxical. While he rejected the Austrian post-imperial state of existence, he completely overlooked the fact that the actual authoritarian state amounted to nothing short of its prolongation. Why should the old elites now have the energy to create a people after they have failed to do so for more than a century? Schmitt, it seems, was right at this point. An authoritarian state whose authority is merely nourished by the prudence of bureaucrats and backed up by military threat is doomed to be haunted incessantly by an irremediable deficit of democratic legitimacy.[126]

The Authoritarian Test

I conclude my discussion of contemporary Austrian doctrine here. In my remaining remarks I will attempt to draw out an important consequence that the study of authoritarian constitutionalism might have with regard to the present situation in Europe. My conjecture is that the discourse of authoritarian constitutionalism—as exemplified by adherents such as Voegelin and Carl

---

[122] See above at 84, 93, 69, 100–1.

[123] From an empire that was permanently threatened by ethnic strife Austria developed into a formal democracy that was deeply divided along the lines of partisan struggle. See Voegelin, n 21, at 93–94, 101.

[124] See Voegelin, n 21, at 177, 252.

[125] See above at 6.

[126] See Schmitt, *Legalität und Legitimität*, n 51, at 94.

Schmitt[127] or, more importantly, by critics such as Hermann Heller[128]—offers a conspicuous intellectual advantage provided, however, that its use is restricted to a specific purpose.[129] This purpose lies in submitting existing practices and ideas to a test. The test requires simply to determine, first, how practices and ideals would look from within the perspective of authoritarian constitutionalism and, secondly, whether or not they would be endorsed by its adherents on the ground of a description. Evidently, the point of the test is to translate what is presently cast in the technocratic language of political science and legal expertise into the political vernacular of our European tradition. If the result of the second part of the test is positive we should have reason to suspect that pertinent practices or ideas are of questionable value—at least from the vantage point of constitutional democracy. In other words, such a test allows to tease out and render normatively intelligible what may otherwise be rendered obscure owing to the present currency of complacent language in both law and political science.

Ignoring the critical potential of such an 'authoritarian test' may exact a high price when it comes to charting the structure and distribution authority in present-day Europe. It cannot be overlooked that snobbish references to 'non-majoritarian institutions' and the major role played by technological or economic 'experts'[130] put a neutral face on thorny political issues. From the vantage point of authoritarian (and even classic) constitutional theory it emerges clearly enough that the claim to legitimacy of such institutions is in

---

[127] See his treatment of the 'authoritarian state' in *Legalität und Legitimität*, n 51, at 93. See also his endorsement of the 'qualitative' and strong totalitarian state, which has the power to de-politicise certain sectors of the economy, as opposed to a 'quantitative' and weak totalitarian state whose agents cannot escape the demands of interest-group pressure, at, 96 and his 'Starker Staat und gesunde Wirtschaft' (1932), reprinted in *idem, Staat, Großraum, Nomos. Arbeiten aus den Jahren 1916–1969*, (ed) G. Maschke (Berlin, Duncker & Humblot, 1995), 71–85, at 74, 81, and 'Weiterentwicklung des totalen Staats in Deutschland', in *Positionen und Begriffe im Kampf mit Weimar—Genf—Versailles 1923–1939* (Hamburg, Hanseatische Verlagsanstalt, 1940) 185–90, at 186–87. As always, however, Schmitt flirts with fascism in noting that the military and the bureaucracy are major institutions upon which the authority of the strong state rests and that a strong state can neither accept the existence of political opposition nor leave the technological means of propaganda and control in the hands of its opponents. A strong state, in other words, cannot be liberal in the political sphere. Finally, it should not be overlooked that Voegelin, note 21, at 15, refused to incorporate Schmitt's concept of the 'total state' into his analysis, for in his opinion the concept was too deeply ingrained in political controversy to be susceptible to 'scientific' clarification.

[128] See Heller, 'Autoritärer Liberalismus', n 84, at 651–53.

[129] It goes without saying that the cautionary remarks from pp 370–71 apply here with equal force. One always ought to take heed of the pernicious moves performed by proponents of authoritarian constitutional law.

[130] See, for that matter, G Majone, 'Europe's 'Democratic Deficit': The Question of Standards', 4 *European Law Journal* (1998) 5–28, at 15.

essence aristocratic or, even worse, oligarchic.[131] Proponents of authoritarian constitutionalism turned on our traditional European political vernacular, even if not with the best intentions.[132] Why should we not follow their example and shift our terms of debate by speaking of an 'authoritarian network of national and European bureaucrats' rather than 'deliberative supranationalism'[133], in particular in light of Voegelin's (third) use of 'authoritarian' in the sense of the group that 'runs the country'? Would it not be more accurate to claim that bureaucratic elites make their normative choices 'authoritatively' rather than 'deliberatively', in particular, with an eye to the excluded public?[134]

In the following , I should like to point to instances in which the application of the authoritarian test may indeed yield—or has already yielded—illuminating results. They concern different 'layers' of the contemporary multi-levelled system of governance in Europe. I begin with a perspective on the European Community and end with a comment on the retrenchment policies, which are presently pursued by 'strong' neo-liberal governments in the Member States.

Applying the Authoritarian Test

Form the perspective of authoritarian constitutionalism, the talk of the European Union's 'democracy deficit' is misleading. It suggests that there is a temporary insufficiency which may be cured in the future. If, however, the European Union is an institution that for its successful operation depends *vitally* on the reproduction of such a deficit, then it might be more accurate to characterise it as the mode in which the authoritarian component of constitutional law has re-asserted itself in Europe after the Second World War. This, at any rate, appears to be the message underlying Puntscher Riekmann's magisterial study of European integration in which she claims that the incremental growth of the Community and Union is not at all unprecedented but another instance of state-building by overcoming the resistance of local elites through

---

[131] See N MacCormick, *Questioning Sovereignty. Law, State, and Nation in the European Commonwealth* (Oxford, Oxford UP, 1999), at 146–48.

[132] Even Merkl knew this with respect to the Austrian government. Carl Schmitt knew it with respect to parliament, however, this was Schmitt's peculiar way of knowing things.

[133] See C Joerges & J Neyer, 'From Intergovernmental Bargaining to Deliberative Political Processes: The Constitutionalisation of Comitology' 3 *European Law Journal* (1997) 273–99; C Joerges, 'Transnationale deliberative Demokratie oder deliberativer Supranationalismus? Anmerkungen zur Konzeptualisierung legitimen Regierens jenseits des Nationalstaats bei Rainer Schmalz-Bruns' 7 *Zeitschrift für internationale Beziehungen* (2000) 145–61.

[134] See, in principle, JS Drysek, *Deliberative Democracy and Beyond: Liberals, Critics, Contestations* (Oxford University Press, 2000) 31–56.

the aid of 'governance by commission'.[135] Even though Puntscher Riekmann's emphasis on the 'dispositive' that was used for the purpose of European integration is much more nuanced and specific than Voegelin's theory of the authoritarian state, her account of the integration process has it that the flexible use of authoritarian Commission rule by the Member States (*qua* 'principals') is a major reason for its success.[136] Understanding governance in Europe requires a sober perspective of what can be accomplished by the executive branch once Member State governments decide to co-operate.[137] Moreover, as a political scientist Puntscher Riekmann has little reservation to count the judiciary among the camp of an authoritarian ruling elite—rightly so, for the attributes 'authoritarian' or 'authoritative' need not be restricted to the state acting through the government. As is well known, but barely acknowledged, there is also authoritarian common law, that is, the judicial pronouncement of new law with the purport that such law is in line with the internal reason and justice of already existing law.[138] It cannot be denied that where judicial review has been institutionalised the seat of constitutional authority has shifted from the legislature to the Constitutional Courts.[139] This is all the more plausible given that the normative underpinnings of judicial law-making are most often only

---

[135] See S Puntscher Riekmann, *Die kommissarische Neuordnung Europas. Das Dispositiv der Integration* (Vienna & New York, Springer, 1998); 'Die Meister und ihr Instrument. Institutionenkonflikte und Legitimitätsprobleme in der Europäischen Union', in M Bach (ed), *Die Europäisierung nationaler Gesellschaften* (Opladen, Westdeutscher, 2001).

[136] It is striking to see that Puntscher Riekmann, in a manner reminiscent of Voegelin, claims that there is no subject of the pouvoir constituant in Europe and that thus the place of the sovereign is 'empty' (*Kommissarische Neuordnung*, n 135, 195). For a dismal perspective on technocratic rule which eclipses sovereign authority, see E Forsthoff, *Der Staat der Industriegesellschaft. Dargestellt am Beispiel der Bundesrepublik Deutschland* (Munich, C.H. Beck, 1971) 44–46, 72. There is no room to enter into a detailed critique of Puntscher Riekmann's narrative, however, I might merely mention that the account is beset by two perplexing dis-analogies with regard to the classical practice of commissarial administration. First, in the case of European integration the principal granting the commissioner ample power to homogenise and dismantle existing political and economic structures was not a monarch who wished to expand his power and influence but nation-states, which are at the same time the winners and losers of that process. Secondly, the legal process underlying the integration process, which gives rise to a constitution of anti-discrimination, is not adequately accounted for.

[137] Pursuing the matter even further, it may be asked to which extent the regulation of Europe and its underlying logic of national blame avoidance can be recast as authoritarianism in a new key. For doesn't it fit comfortably with the notion that the agents who have the authority because they 'run the country' institutionalise a new set of rules in order to escape the grip of democratic responsibility?

[138] We owe Thomas Hobbes the debt of gratitude that he was the first to have taken issue with the conceit of judicial authority. See Thomas Hobbes, *A Dialogue Between a Philosopher and a Student of the Common Laws of England* (1681), (ed) J. Cropsey (Chicago & London, University of Chicago Press, 1971).

[139] For a related observation in the context of German constitutional law, see E Forsthoff, 'Das politische Problem der Autorität' In *Rechtsstaat im Wandel. Verfassungsrechtliche Abhandlungen 1950–1964* (Stuttgart, Kohlhammer, 1964), 99–110, at 109.

insufficiently explained in major decisions while it is fairly obvious that the majority of a judicial body pursues a certain agenda. It comes as no surprise that the revolt against the authoritarian deliverance of constitutional law by judges has occurred in that country which has had the longest exposure to the constitutional authority of judges, namely, the United States.[140] Yet, it is not merely authoritarian constitutional common law what we get from the Courts. They also pledge, authoritatively, their support to a Common Market agenda and advance it in decisions, which come to be revered as 'landmark' cases, such as *Cassis, Francovich, Centros, Angonese* etc.

Secondly, in light of the foregoing we may well do better to refer to institutions in charge of regulating the Common Market straightforwardly as 'authoritarian' in the critical sense employed by Heller in his characterisation of 'authoritarian liberalism'.[141] After all, their claim to legitimacy rests on the idea that certain economic objectives may be better achieved, first, by deregulating markets and, second, by withdrawing re-regulation from the democratic ballot and entrusting it to the judgment of expert bodies.[142] Weiler, I might add, almost identifies what accounts for the authoritarian quality of this economic liberalism when he refers to the political class inhabiting the world (or 'netherworld') of EU committees as 'a group of persons who share common worldviews and a common vocabulary and where, as a result, moral premises are presumed and not discussed.'[143] Regrettably, he returns to appeasing jargon by describing the core of European politics, that is, policy-making in the first pillar, in terms of a 'Weberian or Schumpeterian competitive elites model of democracy'.[144] What he has in mind, though, is something different, namely 'legitimation through accomplishment rather than through the messy process of democracy' as the defining feature of 'the internal Commission culture'.[145] Would it not be more accurate to characterise legitimation through accomplishment as something typically 'authoritarian'?[146] Is not legitimation through action regardless of its democratic authorisation the hallmark of any authoritarian regime?

---

[140] See, for example, P Brest, 'Constitutional Citizenship', 43 *Cleveland State Law Review* (1986) 1–43; RL West, 'The Authoritarian Impulse in Constitutional Law', 42 *University of Miami Law Review* (1988), 531–52; RD Parker, *'Here, the People Rule'. A Constitutional Populist Manifesto* (Cambridge, Mass, Harvard UP, 1994), 110–11; MV Tushnet, *Taking the Constitution Away from the Courts* (Princeton, Princeton UP, 1999).

[141] See Heller, 'Autoritärer Liberalismus', n 84, at 650.

[142] For a sophisticated defence of this idea, see Majone, n 130.

[143] JHH Weiler, 'Prologue: Amsterdam and the Quest for Constitutional Democracy' in D O'Keeffe & P. Twomey (eds), *Legal Issues of the Amsterdam Treaty*, (Oxford & Portland, Hart, 1999), 1–19, at 19.

[144] See JHH Weiler, *The Constitution of Europe. 'Do the New Clothes Have an Emperor' and Other Essays on European Integration* (Cambridge, Cambridge UP, 1999) at 283.

[145] See Weiler, n 143, at 8.

[146] Carl Schmitt was quite outspoken about this in claiming that authoritarian rule presupposes accomplishments on the part of the ruler. See his 'Starker Staat, gesunde Wirtschaft', n 127, at 84–85.

Thirdly, the notion of authoritarianism may come to new fruition with regard to political developments in the Member States too, in particular, inasmuch as such developments unfold in response to the European standard of budgetary discipline.[147] What I have in mind here is that authoritarianism— understood as the state practice exemplified by Voegelin with reference to parliamentary oligarchy—may have returned in the last few years. Given the tangled nature of modern constitutional law, authoritarian governments are difficult to make out. But that does not mean that they resist identification. It merely presupposes to recognise that modern Western constitutional democracies are composed of at least two constitutions: a constitution of liberty on the one hand, which is laid down in what is referred to customarily as constitutional law, and a constitution of inclusion on the other. The latter concerns, roughly speaking, social policy and allows for the participation of several political actors in the arena of public policy making, although their standing is usually not officially recognised by the laws of the constitution of liberty.[148] Governments, as is presently the case in Austria, pull out of a long-standing scheme of co-operation with social partners and impose reforms—retrenchment programmes, mostly—for the professed sake of preserving the financial integrity of the state. They do so with the aid of Parliament alone and by stretching domestic constitutional constraints to their utmost limits. Linking up the traces to authoritarian constitutionalism may be particularly rewarding here. It may be argued that, as the pursuit of neo-liberal reform programs does not affect the standing of elected representatives but nonetheless disrupts those modes of democratic participation which are closely associated with the constitution of inclusion (interest group bargaining), this practice has a certain 'neo-authoritarian' dimension. In this context, thinkers as diverse as John Gray and Roberto Mangabeira Unger have rightly observed that economic liberalism is *deeply* at odds with a functioning democracy.[149] As Carl Schmitt stressed[150]

---

[147] There is a great deal of blame avoidance in the way in which the requirement to meet convergence standards is communicated to the public by Member State governments. See P Pierson, 'Social Policy and European Integration' in A Moravcsik (ed), *Centralisation or Fragmentation? Europe Facing the Challenges of Deepening, Diversity, and Democracy* (Council of Foreign Relations, 1999), 124–58, at 151, 155. For a human-rights problem that may be involved here, see P Alston & JHH Weiler, 'An 'Ever Closer Union' in Need of a Human Rights Policy: The European Union an Human Rights' in P Alston (ed), *The EU and Human Rights* (Oxford, Oxford University Press, 1999) 3–68, at 16.

[148] See A Somek, 'A Constitution for Antidiscrimination. Exploring the Vanguard Moment of Community Law', 5 *European Law Journal* (1999) 243–71.

[149] See J Gray, *False Dawn. The Delusions of Global Capitalism* (New York, New Press, 1998) at 8; RM Unger, *Democracy Realised. The Progressive Alternative* (London, Verso, 1998) at 70. What if economic authoritarianism with the tiresome battle cry for 'leadership' and its attendant oligarchic aesthetics were presently about to spill over into the sphere of politics? For an analysis, see PE Gottfried, *After Liberalism. Mass Democracy in the Managerial State* (Princeton, Princeton University Press, 2000).

[150] See Schmitt, 'Starker Staat, gesunde Wirtschaft', n 127, at 77.

and his critic Hermann Heller grudgingly admitted in a daunted comment,[151] the de-politicisation of the economy—namely, the shrinking of the state to its 'regulatory'[152] function and the removal of redistribution and macro-economic policy from the agenda of politics—presupposes a 'very strong' state which is powerful enough to keep those at bay to whom the purportedly natural working of the market presents itself as a deeply political matter.

Conclusion: The Contest of Languages

My observations may prompt the objection that prodigious institutional mutants, such as the EC and the EU, merit description in fresh political language. Why tinker with concepts that were crucial for authoritarian constitutionalism and whose initial sphere of application may have been the ancient city-states or the empires of princes? By comparison with the standards of modern political and legal science, terms such as 'sovereign authority', 'representation' or 'demos' appear unfit to compete with more fancy designators, such as 'multi-level governance',[153] 'policy networks',[154] 'markets as polities'[155] or even 'meta-constitutionalism'.[156]

Dismissing the old notions, however, may be premature, even from the vantage point of those who are concerned with constructing a fresh constitutional language[157] in an age which, no doubt, has given birth to new spheres of authority.[158] Although the major legal building blocks of the Westphalian world, constitutional law and public international law, are presently pushed to their limits,[159] the champions of 'late sovereignty' are aware that the baby must not be thrown out with the bathwater. Walker suggests that the emerging pluralism of different 'sites' of constitutional authority suggest 'fundamental continuity'[160] with the conceptual apparatus that we inherit from the age of the

---

[151] See above, n 84, Heller at 653.

[152] See G Majone, 'Understanding Regulatory Growth in the EC' in (eds) D Hine & H Kassim *Beyond the Market. The EU and National Social Policy*, (Routledge, 1998), 14–35

[153] For references, see P Craig, 'The Nature of the Community: Integration, Democracy, Legitimacy' in P Craig & G de Búrca (eds), *The Evolution of EC Law* (Oxford, Oxford UP, 1999) 1–54, at 17.

[154] See K-H Ladeur, 'Towards a Legal Theory of Supranationality. The Viability of the Network Concept' 3 *European Law Journal* (1997) 33–54.

[155] See Joerges, n 133.

[156] For the latter, see N Walker, 'Flexibility within a Metaconstitutional Frame: Reflections on the Future of Legal Authority in Europe' In G. de Búrca & J. Scott (eds), *Constitutional Change in the EU. From Uniformity to Flexibility?* (Oxford, Oxford UP, 2000), 9–30.

[157] Above, n 156, Walker at 10.

[158] See JN Rosenau, *Along the Domestic-Foreign Frontiers. Exploring Governance in a Turbulent World* (Cambridge, Cambridge UP, 1997).

[159] See above, n 156, Walker at 21–2.

[160] N Walker, 'Constitutional Pluralism and Late Sovereignty in the European Union', *European Forum Paper, Robert Schuman Centre*, Florence, February 2001, at 5–6.

sovereign state. All that is presently required, in their conceit, is a shift in attention from territorial to functional and partially overlapping spheres or 'sites' of constitutional authority.[161] The new vocabulary, it seems, could therefore readily accommodate linguistic conventions associated with the authoritarian test.

In any event, viewing matters in a more 'traditional' way promises to escape the spell of novelty which has dumbfounded European Community scholarship in the last decades.

---

[161] Above 6, 8–9.

EPILOGUE

Europe's Dark Legacy
Reclaiming Nationalism and Patriotism

JHH Weiler[*]

I

Shoah fatigue is a widespread and understandable condition. Like the 'flu, it comes in many variants. There is the narcissistic, self-pitying (and self-promoting) Walser strain—fairly repulsive even if innocuous. There is the far more virulent Nolte strain: angry, accusatory and sanctimonious. There are the pathological cases of Holocaust Deniers. And then, like the common cold, there is the Garden Variety: on a Saturday evening, all things told, I would rather see *The Hours* than *The Pianist*. Put the latter off, as another burdensome task, like this essay, for another day.

So now, in a field, European Union studies, that seemed not to have a history, we have the Dark Legacy and *Europe*! No less. Is there no escape?

'Why,' very appropriately ask the Editors in the opening passage of this volume, in the first of two questions, 'explore the era of National Socialism and Fascism while Europe undertakes such efforts to get ahead with its integration project?'[1] Indeed, as enlargement brings to a real and symbolic end the last vestiges of World War II and as we find ourselves in a new century can we not finally put that past where it belongs, in the past?

And to what extent, they add with extraordinary caution, might one 'insinuate [that is the precise word they use] that there are European dimensions to these dark pages of Germany's history . . .?' After all, '[t]he project of European integration is an *answer* to Germany's aggressive nationalism, which must not be suspected to have inherited elements of that past.'[2]

To the first question their answer is as simple as it is powerful:[3]

---

[*] University Professor and Jean Monnet Chair, New York University School of Law.

[1] Preface at *ix*.

[2] *Id*.

[3] A third, somewhat unexpected, truly Socratic, answer is given in the stunning Prologue to this Volume by Michael Stolleis with his inimitable calm and modest voice: when it comes to law and jurisprudence, so little accomplished, so much more to be done. Unexpected as we run out of shelf

We have to face our past in order to understand our present and we do so in the interests of our future.

This answer is partly cognitive—to understand who we are. They cite, appropriately, Jürgen Habermas' contribution to the *Historikerstreit* on the uniqueness of Auschwitz: 'Our form of life is connected with that of our parents and grandparents through a web of familial, local, political, and intellectual traditions that is difficult to disentangle—that is, through a historical milieu that made us what and who we are today.'[4]

It is partly instrumental—to learn lessons for the future so as, presumably, not to repeat the past.

These are powerful reasons but maybe incomplete. Habermas was writing within a quintessentially German context. '*Our* form of life' is of course somewhat problematic if with no more we would extend it from the murderers and their accomplices to those, like, say, the British, who fought them. And the instrumental reason loses much of its bite as new generations come into social ascendancy.

One should, therefore, add perhaps another reason which is neither cognitive nor instrumental but, I think, no less compelling.

To articulate this reason we need to digress into the often annoying *arcana* of the Jews' laws and customs. Despite thin scriptural authority, Jewish law and custom prescribe elaborate rites for mourning the dead. Normally the full rigor of these duties falls on a certain class of relatives, principally sons and daughters, and their immediate surrounding community. These norms and practices set out decreasing degrees of separation between mourner and community by establishing specific regimes for the first seven days (the *Shiva*), thirty days (the *Shloshim*) and eleven months of mourning, followed by a life long commitment of remembrance on specific days each year. Typically their *raison d'être* is thought to be an astute psychological way of dealing with the pain of losing a beloved relative and at the same time of achieving closure and returning to normalcy.

But, as Moshe Halbertal explains, that cannot be the only, nor even the deepest meaning of such laws and practices. Such is the normative (as distinct from psychological) importance of mourning that should someone die without relatives, thus leaving no one in need of psychological healing, the Talmud indicates that the Community must appoint surrogate mourners who themselves must assume the duties of survivorship and who are treated by the community as if they had actually suffered loss. Nobody is in psychological need, and yet we go through the communal motions of mourning.

This extreme measure is predicated on the abhorrence of allowing someone to die without due notice. To do so would diminish life itself, and indicate a

---

space (and reading time) for the ever increasing volume of Holocaust studies. Socratic, since only the pre-eminent authority in this field can define what it is that we do not yet know or understand.

[4] Preface, at *ix*.

profound failing of the community. It is about the human dignity resulting from being born in His image—the dignity of the dead but also of the living.

To explore and actively remember—the two are inextricably linked[5]—is thus, not only, as Habermas teaches, about *understanding* who we are—creatures of an '. . . historical milieu that made us what and who we are today.'[6] It is *constitutive* of who we are. It helps make us who we would want to be.

Even if you are not among those who experience the '. . . new collective sense of shock when contemplating the Holocaust' of which Stolleis writes in his prologue, consider yourself an appointed Mourner.[7] Though the generation of tormentors is dying out, there are still survivors aplenty, many prominent jurists known to us all amongst them. 'Closure Now!' is just a bit too premature.

And yet that very laudable imperative with its multiple reasons which underlie this project is not without its problems. 'It is as difficult as it is essential to avoid the instrumentalisation of historical facts, guilt, and shame' write the Editors. Can there be a non-instrumental approach to this subject? Is it desirable? We do not want, after all, to remove the Holocaust from normative and political discourse or so historicise it through some form of 'sanctification' so that every use other than the purely ritualistic would be considered 'sacrilege.'[8] The very reasons the editors give for remembering—'the interest of our future'—is instrumental. What they meant, surely, was an exhortation to avoid abusive instrumentalisation: abusive in employing the memory of the Holocaust for ulterior inappropriate purposes or in the manner in which the memory is used—notably in the field of Art.

The lines are difficult to draw but examples of such abuse abound. For example, as many Israeli social critics have argued, successive governments of the State of Israel have from time to time made crass and manipulative use of the Holocaust for both domestic and international purposes.[9] And, as Stolleis

---

[5] The Editors switch, appropriately, between exploration and remembrance in their Preface: 'It seemed simply obvious to us, that National Socialism and Fascism must be remembered, if and because they form such an essential part of our contemporary history.' *Id.*

[6] J Habermas, 'On the Public Use of History', in *The New Conservatism* (Cambridge, MA, MIT Press, 1990), 233.

[7] It is hard to imagine anyone who would not experience that sense of shock in reading Part V of Goldhagen's *Hitler's Willing Executioners* (New York, Knopf, 1996)—dealing with the Death Marches at the closing years of the War.

[8] The biblical word holocaust—signifying one of the daily prescribed sacrifices—is an inadvertent and unfortunate slip in that direction. In what sense were the Jews, Gypsies and their fellow racial victims 'sacrificed?' They were not 'sacrificed' nor did they 'die' or 'perish' or other such cleansing euphemisms. They were murdered after, as Goldhagen in one of the non-controversial theses in his otherwise problematic book amply demonstrates, gratuitous and shocking torment and torture.

[9] See eg T Segev, *The Seventh Million* (New York, Hill & Wang, 1993); I Zertal, *From Catastrophe to Power* (Berkeley, California University Press, 1998).

himself softly mentions there are not insignificant commercial interests in the so-call 'Shoah business.'[10]

In politics, calling one's opponent a 'Fascist' became so common as to denature that word. Comparisons to Hitler of, say, Saddam Hussein, Arafat, or, more recently by a German Minister, George Bush, have suffered the same inflationary consequences. And in academia a sure way to occupy the high moral ground and, simultaneously, to boast a critical mind is to stick scare quotes around that ubiquitous whipping boy, 'liberalism,' proclaimed or otherwise, and to show a Fascist, Racist, or, *quelle frisson*, Nazi association. Thankfully, *that* trend seems to have run its course. But the admonishment of the Editors shines through: it is indeed difficult to avoid the perils of instrumentalisation.

The difficulties are present in this very volume. Lustgarten rightly refuses to remove the dark legacy from our present day politics. He is also aware of the risks:

> More controversial is the search for parallels between Nazi thought and policy and that found in liberal societies today. Dr Mahlmann declares that 'it is plainly a question of responsibility for the future to understand clearly what went wrong in the past.'[11] So it is; and there is if anything an even graver responsibility to inquire whether at the present time we are in the process of replicating the mistakes of the past. The comparison across time is not for purposes of crude political or philosophical name-calling: 'so-and-so is advocating Nazi policies' as a way of denigrating an opponent. Rather there are two justifiable purposes. The first would enrich historical understanding: if some solution to a purported problem adopted by the Nazis continues to command adherence despite the odour of the association and passage of time, their similarities to the mainstream of Western politics would appear more marked and the thesis that they were a pariah or aberrational movement is correspondingly weakened. Further, the existence of such similarities would tell us hard truths about the dark side of our proclaimed Liberalism, or call into question the depth of our commitment to it. Similarity does not mean identity, but it is in assessing the degree of similarity that the hard and uncomfortable questions have to be faced. The existence of continuum rather than chasm is a frontal challenge to the morality of contemporary politics.[12]

The purpose is noble through and through, though the triple dangers of guilt by association, of trivialising the truly evil by facile analogy and of inadvertently becoming an apologist for that for which no apology is needed are not easy to escape.[13]

---

[10] Denouncing the Shoah business in ever more shrill and indignant tones and basking in the glow that accrues to those who 'dare' slay Holy Cows has in itself become something of an industry with *its* set of rewards. Cf e.g. T Cole, *Selling the Holocaust* (New York, Routledge, 1999); NG Finklestein, *The Holocaust Industry* (London & New York, Verso, 2000).

[11] M Mahlmann 'The European Order in Fascist and Nazi Legal Thought', *EUI Review* Autumn 2000, 14–17, available at http://www.iue.it/PUB/EUIReviewPDF/ERAutumn00.pdf (footnote in the original excerpt from Lustgarten).

[12] This volume at 116.

[13] Most of the examples Lustgarten gives from contemporary British legal discourse are troubling. It is not, however, always made sufficiently clear to my mind whether they are exceptions

II

So why Europe?

Turn first to the sure hand of Stolleis: part of the story is—uncomfortably—an European story and hence European history. In a totally non-inflammatory manner Stolleis reminds us that the Germans had their willing accomplices among many of the nations that came under their occupation, at times shattering long held myths as Tamm's work on Denmark illustrates. The Netherlands is still awaiting its Tamm as do many of the new Member States of East Europe.

One should be hugely careful not to tarnish with too broad a brush as, it would appear to me, has been too often the case with, say, Poland. One must remember, too, that often we are talking of societies which themselves suffered enormously under occupation (even if, simultaneously outdoing their own oppressors) a suffering that has oft not been acknowledged. And one should valorise the admirable selfless courage in saving 'Others' which is, too, part of that history as brought out in works on, say, Italy.[14] After Hochhuth's tendentious 1963 *Der Stellvertreter* an Open Season on the Vatican and the Catholic Church became *à la mode*, slanderously distorting a record which whilst far from unblemished was justly and appropriately acknowledged by survivors and victims in the immediate post war period. This is decidedly not a monochromatic story of German villains and their hapless victims—although it is that too. It is also not only about the Holocaust. The historical canvass is both wider and more complex. It is a European canvass. Fritz Stern, whom no one would suspect of having an apologetic agenda, captures this perfectly:

which prove a general norm of liberalism or are indicative of the anti-liberal ethos which permeated the 'analogous' policies in the 1930s. The different context would and should not excuse bad or evil polices but *response* to policy is an integral part of the comparative matrix and since most if not all examples he gives have been widely commented upon in the past and already been subject to much criticism, the value of the comparison to Nazi rhetoric and policy beyond sensationalism becomes less convincing. For example, the proposals for Dangerous Severe Personality Disorders confinement have worrying and problematic aspects and are justly criticized. But to 'Himmler-ize' them strikes me as tendentious and unhelpful as does the facile comparison between today's psychiatric profession and Nazi Criminal Biology. Employing in this context the Nolte—'could it be said'—technique of saying something whilst pretending not to say it as in 'Could it be said also that in some sense the Nazis had the courage of others' convictions?' belongs in the same category of breathtaking decontextualized comparisons. At the end of the day the added value of Lustgarten's well intentioned piece is not in the unoriginal finger pointing at troubling policies which have been fingered by many others, but in a comparison which fails in my view precisely in what it is supposed to achieve: enriching historical understanding or illuminating the dark sides of our 'proclaimed' liberalism, which thus risks being perceived as precisely the crude political and philosophical name calling Lustgarten admonishes against.

[14] See S Zuccotti, *The Italians and the Holocaust* (New York, Basic Books, 1987).

Can one even try to explain the Holocaust . . . without regard to its historical context? Should one? The Inferno occurred at a given historical moment, at a time of mounting barbarism and moral indifference, which had returned to Europe in unimaginable force during the Great War, barely diminished in the interwar years, and reached an apogee during the second world war. National Socialism, we know was at once Germany's most criminal and most popular regime, Hitler the centruy's most charismatic leader. The terror that he launched in Germany spread to conquered Europe: German troops of various formations extended the terror to Poland, Russia, Greece, everywhere. Thus villages were burned, hostage shot, and men, women, and children hounded, starved, separated, and killed—all that and everywhere. There were thousands of massacres in Poland, and 2.5 million Russian prisoners of war were deliberately starved to death. The links that connect this pervasive brutality to the systematic extermination of European Jewry cannot be found in specific documents or individual decisions, but can those links be doubted? Furthermore, scholars have now established that both Germans and non-Germans knew far more far earlier about the Holocaust and the atrocities in the east than was once assumed. But most of these people worried about their own predicaments and tried to preserve their complacent self-regard, their moral self-esteem, by choosing not to know or believe—a denial that has marked much of the world in our century. In brief the Holocaust took place in the long night of organized bestiality. That is the context.[15]

Against this very European context, enlargement, risks becoming Europe's very own triumphalist 'End of History' as heralded at the 2002 Copenhagen Summit, bringing closure to that which in fact has had very little openness. Of the Austrians it has often been said jokingly that they have somehow convinced the world that Beethoven was Austrian and Hitler German. But playing the victim and shifting all responsibility for the most vile behaviour onto the Germans or 'The Nazis' is not an Austrian speciality.[16] If you care to read some of the darker pages in the World War experience, start with Riga, to pick a random example, that is if you have an iron stomach. One cannot, thus but have much admiration for that segment of German political culture of which this volume is part. It has repeatedly refused the many calls from within for closure and continues to carry the heavy custodial burden of the discomfiting Memory. It is fitting and appropriate that those who had the courage to lift the mirror and unflinchingly gaze at themselves, have now found the courage to lift up a mirror to the European self of which they are part, a European mirror into which other Europeans are reluctant to glance or which they wish to disown.

The 'European Construct' may be of recent post World War II vintage, but, want it or not, the history of its Member States and of its peoples is Europe's history. The memory of a marriage goes back to courting, engagement and subsequent matrimonial life. But the identity of the couple who make up the

---

[15] F Stern, 'The Past Distorted: The Goldhagen Controversy' in *Einstein's German World* (Princeton and Oxford, Princeton University Press, 1999), 272 ff, at 285.

[16] Cf R Cazzola & GE Rusconi, *Il 'Caso Austria'* (Torino, Einaudi, 1988).

marriage will also be determined by the previous pasts and memories of each of the partners. Europe is not only a phenomenon of historical European integration but of an integration of European history.

This is not a trivial semantic point. In the subtle opposition to the very project of Europeanising the dark legacy, the editors report to us the expected knee-jerk reactions: '[t]he project of European integration is an *answer* to Germany's aggressive nationalism, which must not be suspected to have inherited elements of that past.'

This calls for some comment. The issue is not, in the first place, one of inheriting elements of the past but of constructing our self-understanding of the *telos* and *ethos* of European integration. One of the most widespread tales about the European construct is that it started as an economic venture and in more recent times has become a political project. This is a veritable Old-Wives' Tale for anyone who cares to re-read (or perhaps read) the idealised self-understanding as encapsulated in the Schumann Declaration and the Preamble to the Treaty of Paris or in the less starry-eyed historical accounts: Europe began as a political project *par excellence* served by economic instruments.[17]

If, then, Europe is an answer—what is the question? The dark legacy is an intrinsic part of that question; and now, as we write a new 'Constitution', is not the time to forget that. We claim Europe to be a community of values—but which values? The tired old trio which are usually trotted out are democracy, human rights, and the rule of law. This is like saying that the purpose of living is in breathing. Democracy, human rights and the rule of law are foundational, so much so that we have justly come to regard them as means, not ends. Europe is not an answer to the problem of achieving democracy, protecting human rights or establishing the rule of law within our societies. They are not the questions to which European Integration is the answer. Is Norway's democracy, commitment to human rights and the rule of law at risk because she decided to stay out of the European Union? To argue that would be both arrogant and laughable. Europe is, principally, the answer to relational issues in the intercourse among states and peoples. Its originality and deepest value, constitutional tolerance, is neither in the field of democracy,[18] nor human rights[19] but in constructing a different relational matrix which transcends and recasts the boundaries among its Member States and its constitutive peoples.[20] The Dark

---

[17] The primacy of politics over economics in this context is not contradicted by the hard nosed, non-sentimental accounts of, say, the Milward School.

[18] Indeed, ironically Europe continues to suffer from persistent and deep-seated democratic deficiencies in its process of governance.

[19] This is another of Europe's exquisite ironies—its failure to adhere to the European Convention on Human Rights, whilst making such adherence a condition for all candidate Member States.

[20] Cf JHH Weiler, *The Constitution of Europe* (Cambridge, Cambridge University Press, 1998) and Weiler, 'Federalism and Constitutionalism: Europe's Sonderweg' (Jean Monnet Paper 10/2000, www.jeanmonnetprogram.org).

Years is an integral part of this construct. Put yourself to the 'Elementary School Test:' Your 12 year old asks you—*what is European Integration about?* Would the 12 years between 1933 and 1945 not be an integral part of your answer, of any answer?[21]

One can go even further. Margalit, in his important new book, *The Ethics of Memory*[22] rightly distinguishes between the impersonal universal nature of morality, and the collective consciousness which is necessary for the construction of ethical communities. Europe aspires to be an ethical community—not simply a coalition of market interests—such as EFTA—committed to some minimal universal normativity such as the European Convention of Human Rights. Europe claims a specificity, an identity which is to be understood exactly with the vocabulary of the ethical community. Just as Democracy is premised on the existence of *demos* (however defined).[23] Community and identity are premised on the existence of memory. The Dark Years are an important part of our historical legacy, an indispensable element in European memory. Europe is the appropriate custodian of that memory for without it, it makes so much less sense. And Europe most certainly should not be seen as an agent of amnesia.

III

However the tantalizing part of this project lies elsewhere. It is the claim, foreshadowed by Laughland's *The Tainted Source*[24] that the intellectual apparatus that was built around National Socialism (and its less murderous European affiliates) by the likes of *Reichsgruppenwalters Staatsrat* Prof. Dr. Carl Schmitt and others in that Rogues' Gallery[25] of enthusiasts, apologists and sundry

---

[21] Sometimes I think that Britain's unique position in this history—neither occupied, nor accomplice—explains the different ethos which seems to have underlined her self-understanding of Europe.

[22] A Margalit, *The Ethics of Memory* (Cambridge, MA, Harvard University Press, 2002).

[23] The definition of demos is of course varied. To say that democracy is premised on the existence of demos is not to endorse, say, an ethnically based demos.

[24] J Laughland, *The Tainted Source: The Undemocratic Origins of the European Idea* (London, Warner, 1997).

[25] Rogues might be a bit too disrespectful. Still, this is the Schmitt who convenes in 1936 a conference of leading figures in the legal world to discuss *Das Judentum in der Rechtswissenschaft* ('Jewry in Legal Science'). In the concluding address to the Conference, Schmitt begins with the books, 'Säuberung der Bibliotheken' ('Cleansing the Libraries') and then moves to their authors: 'Der Jude hat zu unserer geistigen Arbeit eine parasitäre, eine taktische und eine händlerische Beziehung' ('The Jew's relation to our intellectual work is parasitic, tactical and haggling'). Consequently they are defined as a 'Todfeind' ('deadly enemy'). His concluding words, unchanged, are priceless: 'Was wir suchen und worum wir kämpfen, ist unser unverfälschte eigene Art, die unversehrte Reinheit unseres deutschen Volkes. "Indem ich mich des Juden erwehre" sagt unser Führer Adolf Hitler, "kämpfe ich für das Werk des Herrn"' ('What we search for and what we are striving for is our unadulterated genuine species, the unscathed Purity of our German *volk*. "When fending the Jew", says our *Führer* Adolf Hitler, "I fight for the Work of the Lord."') Thus the

fellow travellers, constitutes its own Dark Legacy extending, apparently, into the very heart of European integration.

The claim is partly sociological and partly conceptual, even if the two cannot be fully separated. Conceptually, the claim is that some key notions in the European construct are somehow tainted by those strands in their intellectual heritage. Sociologically, the Dark Legacy is said to have a human genealogy which extends far beyond the twelve years. Schmitt begat Ipsen and Ipsen begat . . . etc. right into the heart of the (German) European law professoriate. One of the principal issues becomes, thus, the phenomenology of adaptation and adjustment through which this entanglement could take place. This is the approach taken in large measure by Stolleis. The most radical thing in the Prologue is his matter-of-fact shift from, and comparative analysis between, the 'horrible jurists' of the Twelve Years to their disciples, followers and students in the Federal Republic and in the European construct.

Stolleis is so compelling, it is worth taking the sociological detour and attempting to add a few footnotes to his theoretical gain. Let us first set the genealogical scene.

There is, first, Generation M—Berber, Larenz, von Mangoldt, Maunz, Schmitt, Smend and countless others in relation to whom two issues require explanation: their original adaptation to National Socialism and their subsequent smooth and highly successful reinsertion into the post-War legal professoriate. Personally I find Generation M of limited interest and in any event I cannot improve on the analysis offered by Stolleis in his many writings,[26] and by Joerges.[27]

Then there is Generation S, that of the students, then assistants and today's (*circa* 2003) illustrious senior professors who sat at the feet of Generation M, washed their hands (or at least their blackboards), wrote for their *Festschriften*, visited them on their birthdays but rarely if ever questioned them about their past or questioned their past, thus becoming a critical element in the successful reintegration of Generation M back into the professoriate.

They are followed by Generation G, the Nasty Girls, now at the height of their University power (if not intellectual prowess,) who came to academic and intellectual maturity around the '68 period and who were those who for the first

---

'Schlußwort des Reichsgruppenwalters Staatsrat Prof Dr Carl Schmitt', in Vol 1. 'Die deutsche Rechtswissenschaft im Kampf gegen den jüdischen Geist', in *Das Judentum in der Rechtswissenschaft*, (Berlin, Deutscher Rechts-Verlag, 1936). Stolleis usefully reminds us that in 1949 Schmitt publishes 'Amnesty, the power of forgetting.' Amnesty and forgiveness without forgetting is surely more gracious.

[26] Some now also accessible to the non-German reader: Michael Stolleis, *Law under the Swastika* (Chicago, University of Chicago, 1998).

[27] See C Joerges, 'Continuities and Discontinuities in German Legal Thought', paper delivered at 'Tyranny, Justice & the Law: The Nazis and Beyond, The Simon Bond International Wannsee Seminar'. Touro Law School—The Free University Of Berlin—The Institute On The Holocaust & Law, July 7, 2002—July 10, 2002, Berlin.

time (with some interesting earlier swallows) began to raise awkward questions about Generation M, frequently with shrill denunciatory tones.

And, finally, there is Generation GG, the recently-become professors in search of their own holy cows.

Generation S are the focus of Stolleis comparison and rightly so. For it is, after all, they who forged the identity of post War German legal academia. In his conclusions, aimed at theoretical gain, Stolleis seeks some answers to the interesting relationship between Generation M and Generation S.

> The reluctance to glance in the mirror may be morally reprehensible, but in retrospect, there is a certain rationality about it. It served, and still does, as the cement that bonds groups who are threatened or who feel threatened and who seek to climb back up the ladder. Too much retrospective or introspective thinking would appear to be detrimental to an outward assertiveness. And so, as the saying so aptly goes, the skeletons were left in the closet, in the hope that the problematic memories would disappear into thin air all by themselves—that time would take care of them (the so-called biological solution), though participants tended to forget that their own biological solution was nearing and that they would not be able to tell the following generation what to think, let alone to seal their lips.
>
> What I find surprising is not so much what the philosopher Hermann Lübbe called the 'communicative silence'[28], but the fact that it worked so well for so long. However, there is an explanation for that, too. *Small groups, such as the clergy, business managers or academics have a tendency to co-opt younger colleagues. In other words, they push their own disciples through the eye of a needle to make them part of the system. This makes the up and coming generation extremely dependent on the patronage and good will of the older generation. In such a situation, breaking the taboo of mentioning the past can be a risky business. The cartel of silence does not collapse until public pressure on the older generation increases or until the job market expands and diversifies to the extent that the profession can no longer respond homogeneously* (emphasis added).
>
> This can be observed in retrospect at the threshold already mentioned: the period from 1964 to around 1970. Since then, we have seen that it is indeed possible to ask questions about the Nazi past of the legal profession. . . .[29]

The explanation relies much on co-optation, on subtle coercion (*risky business*) and generally on instrumental reasons of career advancement. The image it presents is of a generation who, but for the risk to their careers would have 'outed' Generation M. This, no doubt is an important part of the story.

But there are, I think, other important parts which render the analysis more complex and the moral judgment of Generation S even more delicate. The silence, after all, was not confined to the legal professoriate, not even to the world of employment and public life in general. It was a feature of both public and private life. Members of Generation S were not only the students and

---

[28] H Lübbe, 'Der Nationalsozialismus im deutschen Nachkriegsbewußtsein,' *Historische Zeitschrift* (1983), 579–599 (footnote in the original).

[29] This volume at 16–17.

assistants of Generation M. They were also the sons (few women in Generation S of the legal professoriate) of their own fathers. To ask awkward questions and normatively challenge their professors would inevitably mean also to ask awkward questions and normatively question their own fathers. This is always very difficult. Challenging one's father, especially if loved and admired, or feared, or both is not easy. In, say, Britain and the US 'what did you do in the War' was a banal part of growing up. In Germany it was a risky business. As all those who have studied another communicative silence—that which takes place in families where incest takes place—know, there are certain things that sons (and wives) just do not want to know about their fathers. So strategies develop of averting one's eyes, closing one's ears, and inevitably gagging one's mouth. The communicative silence was, thus, as much part of a general psychological difficulty of that generation of fathers and sons as it was a matter of the sociology of the profession and the calculation of career.

The transition of the late 1960s had, thus, as much to do with the coming of age of Generation G—that of the Grandchildren—as it did with expansion of the job market and the pressure of public opinion.[30]

Stolleis rightly speaks of co-optation. But that word does not perhaps capture the richness of the relationship between the professors of Generation M and their students, assistants and eventual heirs. The *Berbers* and even the *Schmitts* who reintegrated had, after all, purged from their writings and utterances the most offensive. Many truly buried that shameful episode in their past. To their post War students they presented the same persona as they would have to their pre-1933 students. Generation S—the one's worrying now about their own *Festschriften*—were then the hand picked young successors. The relationship they had to their professors of Generation M was often one of admiration, awe and love. In an academic milieu we are acculturated to admire the intellect. Schmitt wrote, said and thought some very evil stuff. In his post War career he betrayed, like Heidegger, a streak of arrogant cowardliness. But he had a mesmerizing intellect which was seductive and evidently transcended any moral qualms. Some of the key figures of German public law fell and remained under his personal spell all his life and continue to be under that spell to this day.

This is true not only for the likes of Schmitt. Even run-of-the-mill and mediocre professors enjoy that hallowed status. The difference in age and in knowledge[31] between professor and aspiring professor is a powerful potion which breeds admiration, awe and, loyalty. It is, thus, not surprising that well after they got their *Rufs*, and became established professors, and really did not have to worry that mentioning the unmentionable would be a risky business,

[30] This generational psychology is very much in evidence in an extreme yet telling context in P Sichrovsky's *Schuldig geboren: Kinder aus Nazifamilien* (Köln, Kiepenheuer & Witsch, 1987).

[31] When you are young, the fact that someone older read a few more books and had more time to think about them, makes a huge impression and can be misinterpreted as signs of a superior intellect. All of us have had the experience of suddenly realising how mediocre judges can be, and how intellectually weak their judgments.

you find Generation S writing lavishly in the *Festschriften* of Generation M, making annual pilgrimages to them after their retirement and eulogizing them at their funerals. This has, in my view, only little to do with ideological commitment—check the *Festschriften*. Most of Generation S would find repulsive the tainted writings of the likes of Maunz or Larenz or even Schmitt during National Socialism. It has to do with the deceptive seduction of the intellect and the nexus of admiration and loyalty—and the replication, especially in the German context, of an almost filial type relationship between professor and assistant.

It seems, thus, that a generational lag is the norm—psychological and sociologically predetermined. That it will normally fall to the grandsons to challenge grandfathers rather than to sons to challenge fathers. This is easily observable (with different normative baggage) in subsequent generations. Generation G was very apt at challenging Generation M, their 'grandparents,' but much less at challenging the communicative silence of their immediate predecessors, Generation S. I have spoken to many of my colleagues in Generation S about their relationship to Generation M, trying to fathom their silence. One datum always struck me as salient. The fact that all those with whom I spoke told me that not once were they challenged or even asked about these issues by their own assistants and students. It is only Generation GG which has finally found the voice to challenge Generation S, especially in forcing the various professional associations still controlled by Generation S to face the past. But then Generation GG has not been noted for challenging the often otiose and questionable judgments of Generation G during the Cold War, and the *Anni di Piombo*, which means that there is much fun still in store.

IV

We may return now to the intellectual genealogy, the one which is not about personalities but about ideas and ideology. There seem to be two theses in play.

The first tries to find in the intellectual architecture of European integration contaminatory traces of the dark past—all kinds of legitimate and illegitimate children to Schmitt's *Großraum* and associated concepts. Let the readers decide how persuasive the evidence is, how tainted the result.

The second thesis, more intriguing, is elegantly found in John P McCormick's contribution to this volume:

> But Schmitt still prompts us to question what *specifically* characterizes Europe's internal commonality and its distinction from the outside world today. He compels us to ponder what are the means by which such a supranational union might be administered. In a resoundingly un-Schmittian move, Jürgen Habermas, for instance, has suggested that the common experience of having happily—albeit with great difficulty—overcome nationalism provides a unifying principle and a cautionary lesson

against future excesses in Europe.[32] He promotes a system of governance by which deliberating publics constituting a European civil society that sustains a continental party and parliamentary system generates law that is rational and responsive to the popular will. But Habermas has not answered what might definitively justify the very demarcation of a European *Großraum* from the rest of the world; and his plan for legal-democratic governance in the EU is hardly operational at the present time. Until these questions and problems are addressed, Schmitt's work and career haunts the study of European integration like a specter (footnote in the original).

These are serious challenges and I cannot here but give some shorthand answers. Elsewhere, for what it is worth, I have suggested that the specificity of Europe may be found in the very special way, unprecedented in time and space, by which it has chosen to define its relationships to each Other.[33] And so long as the boundaries of Europe are determined pragmatically (e.g. limiting the size to make its democracy real) or not artificially (e.g. historical boundaries of Europe) and not racially or religiously (e.g. not excluding Turkey because of the religious faith of its citizens) the demarcation of Europe from the rest of the world does not pose a particularly burdensome normative question.

But embedded in John McCormick's text is a different facet to the Dark Legacy of Schmitt and Co., which presents a challenge all of its own. Note the way in which the claimed defeat of nationalism has been normalised, practically put beyond normative discussion. Indeed, it would seem that at least in the academic and intellectual discourse that is attendant on European integration, the only nationalism that is permitted is Post Nationalism, the only patriotism that is not mocked, Constitutional Patriotism. It is one of the more pernicious aspects of the Dark Legacy that nationalism and patriotism have been left to the likes of Haider and Le Pen and the pens at their service.

A liberal nationalism is possible and it has its virtues as well as its dangers. I have always held the view, the specifics of which I shall not elaborate here, that Supranational Europe was the very setting which could valorise the virtues of a liberal nationalism and contain its dangers and risks.[34] One particular virtue of a liberal nationalism has become especially relevant in the age of multi-culturalism which places so much emphasis on the tribal, cultivates so forcefully the monocultural political persona and leads to a bizarre throwback to the corporatist State idea of political organisation. Nationalism as an expression of a loyalty, responsibility and social solidarity which both tolerates and transcends the political cleavages of multiculturalism is not something which we should exclude from our political discourse and political imagination.

---

[32] See several of the essays contained in J Habermas, C Cronin and P de Greiff (eds) *The Inclusion of the Other: Studies in Political Theory* (Cambridge, MA, MIT Press, 1998) (footnote in the original) and M Pensky (ed) *The Postnational Constellation: Political Essays* (Cambridge, MA, MIT Press, 2001).

[33] JHH Weiler, 'Sonderweg', n 20 above.

[34] JHH Weiler, 'To Be a European Citizen: Eros and Civilization' in J Weiler, *The Constitution of Europe* (Cambridge, Cambridge University Press, 1998).

Patriotism, the love of country and countrymen, is indeed that: an ethos of love. It has, as is often the case with love, its attendant dangers. But it has considerable virtues for it is an ethos of unselfish love and non-instrumental love and it embodies, as is so often not the case with romantic love, commitment, constancy and an ethic of giving, not only taking. Why, then, leave that territory of our public life to the *Le Pens* of the world who invert patriotism into a message of hate? Constitutional Patriotism has, of course, an important role to play in our public ethos. One can have a strong moral commitment, even passion for the values embodied in a constitution. But that kind of commitment attends to different parts of the soul and the very universal values which are constitutional traditions typically militate against that part of our lives.

European Patriotism can also be given a meaning—especially within the current constitutional architecture of Europe, which respects and is premised on the distinct identities of its constituent societies. We should not flinch from using two other terms which have been banished from our political vocabulary because of the pathological usage made of them in the Dark Years: destiny and fate. Europe can think of itself as a Community of fate in the sense that different peoples and different States committed in their internal organization to democracy, human rights and the rule of law have decided to face the challenges of the future together, to share a destiny and hence a responsibility (even redistributive) towards each other, to make one's fate dependent, co-dependent on the fate of Others. There need be no blood and no soil in such a vision; it is a noble way to think of Enlargement—which will demand considerable sacrifice if it is to be successful—European Patriotism is the political expression of a different form of love—Love Thy Neighbour. It is a noble way to think of European Patriotism. These, I would suggest, are challenges no less compelling than those put forward by MacCormick.

Finally, one can abolish another taboo resulting in no small measure from the Dark Legacy by toppling the walls of the last ghetto and reclaiming into the discourse of European Integration the richness which may be found in Europe's Christian heritage, not least in the social and political reflections which have developed since Vatican II. We cannot allow Schmitt's *Roman Catholicism and Political Form*[35] premised on his superficially seductive Friend-Foe worldview, and similar works, to define for us the potential contribution of Christian thinking to the self-understanding of Europe. To reclaim the relevance of Christian thinking into the discourse of European integration is not tantamount to an evangelising mission nor is it to exclude from the European construct non-Christians. But, perhaps, all that can wait for another occasion.[36]

---

[35] (Westport, Greenwood, 1996) (*Römischer Katholizismus und politische Form*, Hellerau, Jakob Hegner, 1923).

[36] JHH Weiler, *A Christian Europe* (forthcoming).

INDEX